GREG HANSEN

Principles of Management and Organizational Behavior

Principles of Management and Organizational Behavior

Justin G. Longenecker
Baylor University

Second Edition

Charles E. Merrill Publishing Co.
A Bell & Howell Company
Columbus, Ohio

To Frances

International Standard Book Number: 0-675-09576-X
Library of Congress Catalog Card Number: 69-12806

Printed in the United States of America

5 6 7 8 9 10 11 12 13 14 15-76 75 74 73 72 71

Preface

This book deals with the work of managers and the behavior of people in organizations. Although present knowledge in these areas is far from complete, the efforts of management researchers and organizational theorists continue to broaden our understanding. *Principles of Management and Organizational Behavior, Second Edition* blends recent developments in management thought with older concepts of classical theory to provide a strong conceptual foundation for successful managerial performance. Such a foundation is important because a manager's understanding of organizational relationships and his conception of management greatly affect the extent to which his organization achieves its fundamental goals.

In recent years, adaptation of systems theory to the study of management has provided a valuable integrating viewpoint. According to this viewpoint, an organization may be visualized as an open, living system. The systems concept is introduced in Chapter 2 of this edition to provide a perspective for subsequent discussion of the management process.

In the management of any organizational system, the manager performs a number of functions. These functions — that is, the planning, organizing, directing, and controlling activities performed by managers at all levels — provide the basic framework for the sections of this book. The treatment of management functions differs from older conventional approaches, however, in a number of ways.

First, the signficance of the organization as a social system is reflected in the analysis of each management function. Traditional viewpoints are re-examined and restated in the light of the behavioral sciences. In addition, Chapters 15-19 are devoted to a more detailed consideration of the social aspects of organizational behavior. The intention has been to maintain a balanced viewpoint that avoids an excessive dependence upon any one particular school of thought. Traditional thinking is not discarded but is modified by current developments. Throughout the book, management theory is treated in terms of the more recently developed systems concept.

As open systems, business organizations constantly interact with their environment. The practical significance of current social and economic problems and other features of the prevailing environment is explicitly recognized. Chapter 3, in particular, focuses attention upon changing environmental factors imposing constraints upon management. The content of other chapters has also been made current by reviewing recent innovations in behavioral science, quantitative methods, comparative administration, and other areas of management thought and practice. Many of the books and articles cited in end-of-chapter reading lists draw attention to these newer developments.

Major corporations of American business — General Motors, Du Pont, General Electric, I. B. M., and many others — are prominently featured in this study of the management process. Practical examples provided by organizational problems and practices of such companies make management theory understandable to the reader. Such references not only give substance and meaning to abstract concepts but add interest to subjects that too often seem painfully dull.

Finally, case problems at the end of the book portray concrete situations confronting administrators in a variety of industries and at various levels of management. Experience with these cases indicates that they help the reader to understand the complexities of managerial decision making.

I am greatly indebted to a number of people whose helpful comments assisted me in completing this second edition. In particular, I have been aided by the cooperation and encouragement of my chairman, H. N. Broom, and by the Dean of the Hankamer School of Business, Emerson O. Henke.

The following people read the entire manuscript for this new edition. Grateful acknowledgment is expressed to them for their help: Professor Arlyn J. Melcher — Kent State University; Thomas R. O'Donovan, Ph.D. — Associate Administrator, Mount Carmel Mercy Hospital; and Professor William Sexton — University of Notre Dame.

Two colleagues, Roderick L. Holmes and Burke A. Parsons, read and made valuable suggestions on portions of the manuscript. I also appreciate the work of Miss Cynthia Burns and Mrs. Linda Goacher in typing the manuscript a number of times. The cooperation and understanding of my wife, Frances, and daughters, Linda, Nancy, and Jane, were also most helpful in making this book a reality.

Justin G. Longenecker

Waco, Texas

Contents

Cases

Introduction to Management

1

The Task of Management in Perspective

Every organization requires managerial leadership in order to accomplish its objectives. Except for very small companies, all business firms have a chief executive and also a group of lower-level managers. Non-business organizations likewise have some type of management hierarchy. It is the purpose of this chapter to investigate the nature of the management task as performed by all levels of management and to develop a perspective with which to view their activities.

Management and Cooperative Activity

The Men Who Manage

A manager provides the dynamic force or direction that combines static resources into a functioning, productive organization. He is *the man in charge*, the one who is expected to get results and to see that things happen as they should. If a small business fails to achieve its objectives, a new proprietor appears, and a sign goes up: "Under New Management." In a large corporation, an organization shakeup occurs, with dismissals, transfers, demotions, promotions, and new appointments.

The manager is not only blamed for failure but also credited with success in reversing downward sales and profit trends and expanding profitable operations. An example is provided by the dramatic improvement in the business fortunes of the Stanley Works of New Britain, Connecticut.[1] This company was described as "one of those technically proficient but crusty old New England companies that was left behind as the nation's heavy industry burgeoned." It was founded in 1843 by Frederick T. Stanley, who made bolts and barn hinges and peddled them on horseback to local farmers. The company became renowned for the quality of its products—and then went to sleep. When the lethargic firm showed new signs of life in the early 1960's, a new manager was credited with the awakening. Over the three-year span of 1963 to 1966, the company increased profits 95 per cent on a sales gain of nearly 70 per cent. Stanley was led to these achievements by Donald W. Davis, who assumed the executive vice presidency in 1962 and who was promoted to president in 1966. Davis was aided in directing Stanley's transition from "sleepy corporation" to "aggressive, market-oriented company" by Garth W. Edwards, who was named vice president for finance in 1960. These managers were described as "chief architects of Stanley's rejuvenation."[2] It is the managers who are expected to get results and who are rewarded for achievement of corporate objectives.

The manager may carry any one of many different titles. At the top, he is known by such titles as *chairman of the board, president, chief executive officer*, or *managing director*. At somewhat lower levels, a manager is called *vice president* (an infinite variety), *division control officer, manager of sales, manager of production planning, general manager of manufacturing, director of engineering, director of industrial relations, controller, treasurer, works manager*, or *chief design engineer*. At lower levels of the organization, such titles as *foreman, supervisor, office manager*, and *unit chief* make their appearance. In each instance, the title is expected to give some indication of the function and level of the manager. Although their positions vary widely, all of them have in common the responsibility of management.

Need for Management in Cooperative Endeavors

The need for some type of management arises as soon as cooperative endeavor is required to accomplish an objective. Of course, one

[1] "Stanley Tries the Faster Track," *Business Week*, No. 1940, November 5, 1966, pp. 84-87.

[2] *Ibid.*, p. 85.

might visualize a very simple operation — hunting or fishing by two or three individuals, for example — in which there is little apparent management. Very soon, however, any project or undertaking that involves the contribution of more than one person necessitates someone's taking the lead. If the operation is quite small and the tasks relatively unspecialized — such as those in a barber shop — the amount of managerial leadership required is at a minimum. In most establishments with as few as a half dozen employees, however, the need for careful organization and direction of individual contributions is quite evident. In a large institution involving a great amount of work specialization, the task of organization and management becomes one of Gargantuan proportions. The General Motors Corporation, for example, must blend the contributions of some 700,000 different employees in producing and selling the corporation's products and achieving profits for its stockholders. These employees perform thousands of different tasks, each making some contribution to the organization and its objective.

It is the task of managers to provide the leadership necessary to secure the individual efforts of organization members and to direct the order and nature of this work. Managers are responsible for synchronization of effort from individuals in such a fashion that it adds up to organizational accomplishment. Without management, a group is capable of little more than mob effort.

Universality of the Management Process

The need for management exists in all types of organizations. In industrial concerns, work activities are grouped into sales, production, finance, and other divisions. In a university, different colleges and departments are assigned areas of specialization, and some university administrator coordinates the activities to assure the requisite teaching and research programs. Hospitals and government establishments likewise employ executives to synchronize specialized activities.

Even such activities as those of a football team require exercise of the leadership function. In fact, a well-executed play on the gridiron requires, for the moment, a degree of organization and management surpassing that displayed in most organizations. Considerable artistry is required as the unique contributions of eleven different team members are so timed and coordinated as to achieve their mutual objective. A touchdown is expected on any offensive play in which each individual flawlessly performs his own task and the individual efforts are properly combined. A great team involves more than the brilliant play of a few individual stars. These great individual efforts must be integrated into a team effort — a process that necessitates management.

Definition of Management

The term *management* is often used as a noun to refer to individuals who exercise leadership in an organization, that is, to the managers. It is important to recognize, however, that management may also be viewed as a *process*. In this sense, it is comprised of the manager's activities in decision making, coordination of group effort, and general leadership. Some have described management, rather tritely, as "getting things done through people." This distinguishes *managerial* from *nonmanagerial* work but tells us very little about the actual process of managing or how it gets results through people.

There is some similarity in the activities of all types of managers. Thus, the duties of a manager of an office or storeroom have something in common with those of the president of the organization. These activities are described as functions and are discussed at greater length in Chapter 2. At this point, it should be clear that management consists of those activities that are necessary to secure the contributions of individuals and to regulate these contributions to achieve the organization's goal.

The work of a manager must be performed at all levels of an organization—from chief executive to first-line supervisor. It would be possible to slice the management structure into any number of vertical levels.[3] In the following tabulation, three levels—top management, middle management, and supervisory management—are recognized. Any of these might, in turn, contain a number of vertical levels. The statement of activities, however, reveals some of the differences in focus and outlook at these different levels.

Top Management:

Develops and reviews comprehensive, long-range plans.
Evaluates overall performance of major departments.
Evaluates leading management personnel preparatory to key executive selection.
Confers with subordinate managers on subjects or problems of general scope.

---

[3] See, for example, John M. Pfiffner and Frank P. Sherwood, *Administrative Organization* (Englewood Cliffs, N.J.: Prentice-Hall, Inc., 1960), pp. 141-149. These authors suggest four levels: (1) corporate management, (2) top production management, (3) middle management, and (4) supervisory management.

Middle Management:

Makes plans of intermediate range and prepares more comprehensive, long-range plans for review by top management.
Analyzes managerial performance to determine capability and readiness for promotion.
Establishes departmental policies.
Reviews daily and weekly reports on production or sales.
Counsels subordinate managers on production, personnel, or other problems.

Supervisory Management:

Makes detailed, short-range operating plans.
Reviews performance of "operatives" and minor supervisors.
Supervises day-to-day operations.
Makes specific task assignments to personnel.
Maintains close contact with operative employees.

Historical Changes in the Task of Management

Having examined the general nature of management and its broad application to organized endeavor, it is desirable to note its historical dimension. The current interest in management, human relations, and organizational behavior tends to create an impression that the practice and problems of management are of recent origin. That this is not strictly true is evident in the history of human organizations.

Ancient Organized Activity

The need for management assumes the existence of an organization having some specific objective or objectives. A moment's reflection shows that neither organization nor management is an innovation of the twentieth century. One of the early examples of organized activity is found in the story of Moses, leader of the nation of Israel (Exodus 18). As this group of people, several hundred thousand in number, began their pilgrimage from Egypt to Canaan, the task of leadership rested heavily upon Moses. As a result, he was busy from early morning until late at night in solving problems brought to him for settlement. In discussing this problem with his father-in-law, Jethro, Moses explained his dilemma, one that is not uncommon among modern corporation executives.

The solution proposed by Jethro involved the organizational concept of decentralization. In effect, the father-in-law suggested that Moses delegate authority in a different way than he had done in the past. Tribal leaders were to be designated, and these leaders were to dispose of most questions without the need of Moses' personal intervention. Only the most serious or difficult issues were to be brought to the personal attention of Moses. The arrangement is remarkably similar to that advocated by twentieth century management theorists.

This illustration shows that the process of management and the existence of organizational problems are as old as the history of cooperative endeavors. Wherever and whenever in the course of human history it has been necessary to utilize the efforts of large numbers of people in some common undertaking, it has been necessary to devise an organizational pattern and to provide for administrative leadership in accomplishing the desired objectives.

Although the management process is as old as history itself, it was not until the last century that systematic analysis of management and the development of a theory of management had their origin. In fact, the major portion of management research has occurred during the last few decades — much of it since World War II.

Increasing Complexity of Management

The problems of leadership and management have increased in complexity during the centuries and particularly in recent decades. A number of factors have contributed to this growth in the difficulty of management. One factor is that of size itself. As organizations became larger, the task of managing them also grew in difficulty. It is more difficult to provide leadership for an organization of 10,000 employees than for a group of 10 employees. Although some examples of large-scale organizations can be cited from centuries ago, the prevailing pattern of organization in earlier centuries was based upon small groups.

Another reason for the increasing difficulty of management is the more extensive specialization of labor and the greater complexity of the work that is involved in the typical modern organization. Consider, as an example, the construction of a highway by use of the physical labor of Chinese coolies. Thousands of workers may carry dirt in buckets in the accomplishment of such a project. The organization is large, and thousands of individuals may contribute labor to the project. The contributions of the different workers, however, are basically simple and essentially similar, and the management problem is primarily that of directing the large numbers of individuals who are involved in the project.

In contrast, the design and assembly of a modern airplane necessitates work that is highly specialized. The design and specifications may require thousands of man-hours and tons of paper. Thousands of different parts become part of the finished plane. Some of these are manufactured within the company, while others are purchased from other concerns. Some must be combined into subassemblies before entering into the final assembly. The mental and physical labor on a project of this kind involves the work of purchasing clerks, inventory and supply clerks, draftsmen, engineers in various fields of specialization, welders, sheet metal workers, instrument mechanics, electricians, foremen, personnel clerks, top management personnel, and hundreds of other types of employees. Successful completion of the project requires the integration of these efforts and the scheduling of these numerous different activities in such a way as to make possible the orderly construction of the airplane.

The problems and challenges of management have also increased as a result of the changed status of employees. A few decades ago, there was no question as to who was boss. The right of the manager — who was frequently the owner — to hire and fire was both recognized and exercised. Open disagreement with management brought swift retribution. Members of present-day organizations are, on the average, much better educated. As citizens, they carry greater political power. In the work place, they are often represented by unions. The net result is a considerably greater independence on the part of subordinates than was faced by managers of an earlier era. This transformation calls for greater finesse on the part of contemporary managers.

In addition, today's managers must be broadly skilled to deal with highly complex and technical operations. Consider, for example, the management of research programs running into the millions of dollars in a modern corporation. A research administrator ideally should be trained in science, be at home in the laboratory, and be familiar with the methods of research. At the same time, he must have some conception of research costs and profit prospects. He is expected to regulate the activities of scientists without stifling their initiative and creativity. To intensify his problem further, there are few factual data to support many of his decisions. Predicting the degree of success and profit in a contemplated research project may be virtually impossible. The management problems faced by a research manager may be as baffling, therefore, as the problems in science itself.

Management in an Age of Innovation

Today's managers must manage in a world of accelerating change. Compared with earlier periods of history, the scientific and technological discoveries and developments of the last half century have been great. Dramatic industrial changes are resulting from the developments in atomic energy, space technology, and electronic computers. Business concerns are likewise affected by shifts in political and military factors. These changes, some of which are discussed in Chapter 3, affect not only individual firms but entire industries and the total economy.

Business corporations are themselves agents of change. Through research they develop new products, and through marketing programs they introduce new products to the consuming public. Firms must also react alertly to changes introduced by others. Strategic moves by competitors, for example, require product improvements and new products or services to meet this competition and to avoid obsolescence. Techniques of production and distribution are constantly changing. Markets expand and change in nature. New materials, new equipment, and new processes are required to remain competitive.

The acceleration in the rate of innovation has altered the requirements for managerial success. Managerial awareness of the nature and significance of change is of primary importance. This requirement runs counter to a somewhat natural human inclination to recognize past change but to assume the present will continue with little change into the future.

The U. S. petrochemical industry, centered on the Texas gulf coast, provides a striking example of the change and ferment within the managerial environment. By 1966, the industry's excess capacity of the early 1960's had disappeared, and a huge expansion of production facilities was under way.[4] Other aspects of the changing industrial situation were the following:

1. Money for expansion was a "worry" to all but a few companies.
2. Construction workers had become scarce.
3. Specific products were suffering from the competition of imports.
4. Minimum efficient plant size had sharply increased — possibly as much as fivefold in six years. (In 1960, a 100

---

[4] "What Puts Zip Into Petrochemicals," *Business Week,* No. 1946, December 17, 1966, pp. 40-43.

million pound plant could make ethylene; in 1966, one firm refused to consider any plant with a capacity less than 500 million pounds.)

5. Market projections predicted increases of 100 to 900 per cent in demand for a number of the industry's end products by 1975.
6. Ammonia producing facilities were inadequate to satisfy the soaring demand for synthetic fertilizers and for explosives for the war in Viet Nam.
7. A geographical shift of production facilities was under way as heavy new construction occurred along the Mississippi River in Louisiana.
8. Change to naphtha as a raw material replacement for liquefied petroleum gas or natural gas was anticipated. This change would alter the entire pattern of production, requiring a company to generate a whole range of intermediate petrochemicals, which in turn would involve construction of many more processing units.
9. A long-term shift of the center of world petrochemical production from the United States to Japan and Europe appeared possible if the United States did not make a radical change in its oil allocations.
10. Slackening in the export market for petrochemicals seemed likely.

In decisions about markets, materials, methods, money, or manpower, a manager in the petrochemicals industry is thus confronted with a shifting, unstable situation. The changes are fundamental in nature and pervasive in scope. In such an atmosphere, a manager can ill afford to emphasize tradition, accept the status quo, or rely upon "experience."

Modern management is ineffective to the extent that it is unable to recognize and deal with innovation. Nor is it sufficient to assume that random product improvement, spasmodic market research, and haphazard improvement in production processes will be adequate. Management must instead deal rationally, imaginatively, and systematically with the innovative forces affecting the organization.

Trends in Management Thought and Practice

As noted in the preceding section, the problems and complexities of management have greatly increased during the centuries of its history. There have also been changes in the theory, practice, and philosophy of management. In fact, this field is one of continuing change. To develop a sense of perspective, attention is directed in this section to a few of the major shifts or trends in management thinking. In later chapters, consideration is given to more specific changes and developments.

Applying Science to Management

Frederick W. Taylor is known as *the father of scientific management.* This title recognizes his pioneering efforts in attacking the traditional approach to management by the substitution of more systematic and analytical methods. Although his work was primarily concerned with shop management, the general approach that he advocated is applicable to all varieties and levels of administration.[5]

Taylor learned the machinist and patternmaker trades in the 1870's in Philadelphia and in 1878 went to work for the Midvale Steel Company. In this plant, he progressed to positions of machinist, gang boss, and higher positions in the management hierarchy. In 1890, Taylor left the Midvale Steel Company to engage in consulting work, and, in 1898, he entered the employment of Bethlehem Steel Company.

During his early years in management positions of the Midvale Steel Company, Taylor applied a fresh and novel approach to the practice of shop management. He was quick to question traditional techniques of management and ready to devise and experiment with different methods. During his years as a consultant, he continued many of the same type of studies, and he later followed the same scientific management approach in his work with the Bethlehem Steel Company.

Taylor's Studies of Pig Iron Handling

It is enlightening to examine some practical examples of Taylor's revolutionary approach to shop management. One of the classic examples associated with Taylor's work is his study of pig iron handling at the Bethlehem Steel Company. According to Taylor, the circulation of this particular illustration was so widespread that some people equated scientific management with handling pig

---

[5]For a collection of Taylor's writings, see Frederick Winslow Taylor, *Scientific Management* (New York: Harper & Row, Publishers, 1947).

iron! The reason Taylor cited this particular example was the fact that pig iron handling represented the simplest kind of human effort. It was his idea that proof of advantages from scientific management of such simple tasks would demonstrate the general advantages that might accrue from scientific management.

The pig iron study occurred at the Bethlehem Steel Company, which had five blast furnaces and a gang of seventy-five men manually handling pig iron. A railroad siding ran into a field with pig iron in piles alongside. A plank was placed against the side of the railroad car, and the worker picked up a pig of iron weighing about ninety-two pounds, walked up the inclined plank, and dropped the pig in the car. In studying pig iron handling, the motions and steps of the workers were analyzed minutely, and attention was given to the proper distribution of work and rest.

Employees were then carefully selected and given detailed instructions in the new method. Management insisted upon exact performance according to prescribed methods. Employees could earn substantially more than their average rate by following the prescribed methods. At the time the experiment began, each worker in this gang was loading an average of about twelve and one-half tons a day. After the study and changes, the output of these men was increased almost four times to forty-seven and one-half tons of pig iron a day!

Taylor's Shoveling Experiments

Another of Taylor's well-known experiments concerned the work of shoveling various types of material in the steel yard. At the time this experiment began at the Bethlehem steel works, each worker furnished his own shovel, the shovels varying according to the whims of the worker. The first step in developing a "science of shoveling," as Taylor called it, was to determine the proper shovel load according to weight. This required study of the size and shape of the shovel and the weight of the material being shoveled. At the time, a shoveler in the yard might go from shoveling rice coal with a shovel load of three and one-half pounds to handling iron ore with a load of thirty-eight pounds to the shovel. As Taylor pointed out, both of these loads could hardly be right. It was the task of scientific management to determine the size of the proper load.

The investigators selected good employees, whom Taylor referred to as "first-class shovelers," and recorded the performance of these employees while using shovels of different sizes. They started, for example, with a thirty-eight pound shovel and recorded the daily output. Then they recorded the output with a thirty-four pound shovel and found that the daily tonnage increased. Their conclusion, based upon numerous studies of this type, was that the shovel should be of the proper size to carry a load of twenty-one and one-half pounds.

In applying this "scientifically-determined" work standard, the company provided shovels in a number of sizes to replace employee-owned shovels. Small shovels were to be used for heavy material and large scoops for light materials. The company then carefully selected employees for learning the new system, instructed them thoroughly, and controlled their performance in detail.

The Essence of Scientific Management

Taylor was careful to differentiate between scientific management and the techniques associated with its early applications. Workmen in the experiments described above were paid on a piecework basis, but Taylor insisted that scientific management was not a scheme of incentive wage payments. Neither was it the use of a stop watch, the study of motions, nor the instruction of workmen in the proper methods of job performance. Viewed more broadly, he saw scientific management as the systematic or scientific investigation of all the facts and elements connected with the work being managed. It was the very opposite of management by tradition and rule of thumb. The following statement by Taylor expresses the viewpoint that he felt management and labor must adopt to utilize scientific management:

> Both sides must recognize as essential the substitution of exact scientific investigation and knowledge for the old individual judgment or opinion, either of the workman or the boss, in all matters relating to the work done in the establishment. And this applies both as to the methods to be employed in doing the work and the time in which each job should be done.[6]

There were many criticisms of the work of Taylor and the scientific management movement. The work of an employee was analyzed as one might analyze the operation of a machine, and the goal was maximization of efficiency of this human "machine." Be-

---

[6]"Taylor's Testimony Before the Special House Committee," reprinted in Frederick Winslow Taylor, *Scientific Management* (New York: Harper & Row, Publishers, 1947), p. 31.

cause of this emphasis upon physiological factors, the work has been called *physiological organization theory*.[7] Over a period of several decades, many came to realize the serious inadequacies of such views concerning labor.

Those using scientific management were accused of speeding up and exploiting labor. Although Taylor's views of personnel were typical of those of his day, he did exhibit in his own writings a real sense of fairness toward employees and a desire to see them properly rewarded for their efforts. As he recognized, some managers adopted certain techniques of scientific management without being truly scientific in the use of these techniques. It was this practice that gave scientific management a rather bad name.

In fact, Taylor's work and the scientific management movement fell into such ill repute that Congress undertook an investigation of it. A Committee of the House of Representatives was formed to investigate Taylor's and other systems of shop management. In January 1912, Taylor appeared before this committee and gave a careful exposition of scientific management as he understood and practiced it. He vigorously defended the basic concepts of scientific management against the attacks of those who felt that they had served to exploit and take advantage of labor. In spite of these criticisms of Taylor's work, it does stand as a pioneer, revolutionary approach to management that makes its creator one of the outstanding figures in management history.[8]

Contemporary Use of the Scientific Method

Although many of the techniques of scientific management are of only incidental importance today, management still clings to the concept of the scientific method in the solution of business problems. This point of view stresses investigation of the facts in the analysis of business problems. It is the antithesis of management by rule-of-thumb methods. The decision-making process discussed in Chapter 7 employs a form of the scientific method.

It is his respect for the scientific method that sharply distinguishes the modern professional manager from his predecessor who was

---

[7]James G. March and Herbert A. Simon, *Organizations* (New York: John Wiley & Sons, Inc., 1958), p. 13.

[8]Taylor was, of course, only one of many contributors to development of a scientific approach to management. Other pioneers included Henry L. Gantt, Frank and Lillian Gilbreth, Harrington Emerson, Wallace Clark, and Henry R. Towne, to name but a few.

inclined to "fly by the seat of his pants." The modern manager may well recognize the limitations on his ability to acquire enough data to solve all problems scientifically. This does not reduce his appreciation of the scientific method, however. He relies upon the factual approach and follows it as far as possible. And he recognizes the dangers involved in any necessary use of hunches or intuition.

During recent years, much attention has been given to refinements in the use of the scientific method, particularly by the utilization of newly developed quantitative techniques. These modern approaches to the scientific analysis of business problems are discussed in Chapters 3 and 7.

Recognition of Human Relationships

Another notable change in management thinking and practice has occurred in the area of human relationships. In this development, the work by Elton Mayo and his research group was unusually significant.[9] Mayo, an Australian, was born in 1880 and trained in psychology. Coming to the United States, he was appointed as head of the Department of Industrial Research at Harvard in 1926, remaining there until his retirement in 1947. Although his academic background was in psychology, his most significant contributions were more closely related to industrial sociology.

According to the general viewpoint prevalent in management circles of the day, management's relationships were with the employees as individuals, and these relationships were thought to be primarily contractual in nature. In fact, Mayo eventually took issue with what he called the *rabble hypothesis* of society. According to the rabble hypothesis, society is made up of unorganized individuals, each of whom acts in a manner designed to serve his self-interest and thinks logically in the pursuit of this purpose. Mayo's attack, then, was directed toward this simplified viewpoint of employees and their motivation.

Research Studies of Employee Behavior

Mayo's most notable research occurred during the 1920's, although the results of some of it were not known until the 1930's. He conducted some early investigations in a textile mill in Philadelphia in an attempt to determine the causes of high labor turnover

---

[9]For a presentation of Mayo's philosophy, see Elton Mayo, *The Human Problems of an Industrial Civilization* (New York: The Macmillan Company, 1933).

among a certain group of workers in that plant. In this investigation, it appeared that Mayo was preoccupied with a viewpoint connected with individual psychology and physical conditions of the job. It was the transition from this viewpoint that was to constitute his most significant contribution.

Mayo's better-known research, occurring in the late 1920's, was conducted at the Hawthorne plant of the Western Electric Company. In this investigation he was assisted by F. J. Roethlisberger of the Harvard Business School and William J. Dickson of the Western Electric Company. The experiments in the Western Electric Company, which are described at greater length in Chapter 15, were originated to discover methods for improving the productivity of employees. They were primarily concerned with the physical environmental aspects of the job, such as the effects of lighting and fatigue upon output. The most notable result of the research was its revelation of the great limitations of the engineering or physical hypotheses that provided the foundation for the studies. In the experimentation, employees refused to behave according to management's image of them as simple biological organisms. The experiments revealed the inadequacy of the traditional viewpoint concerning employees — the type of viewpoint that characterized management thinking in Taylor's day.

The practical impact of the work of the Mayo group was to reveal to management the significance of human relations in organizational behavior. Even though detractors have criticized certain extremes of the human relations movement, it has been impossible since Mayo's day for serious thinkers to shrug off the concepts developed during this period. Employees were discovered to be much more complex in their makeup and motivation than had been generally realized. The human aspects and relationships of industry were found to be of critical importance in the day-to-day functioning of organizations.

The Behavioral Sciences in Modern Management

Some managers and management experts adopted the human relations approach with such enthusiasm that they tended to go overboard in the opposite direction. The naive formula "Be nice to people" was often adopted without concern for its limitations. In concentrating upon human relations, some managers tended to ignore other important factors in the situation. Emphasizing human relations, they forgot that employees also worked for money. Some rather unscrupulous individuals viewed human relations as a clever way to manipulate personnel. The phrase *human engineering*, when used in this context, is descriptive of this general approach.

As a result of these weaknesses or excesses in the human relations movement, numerous well-founded criticisms and reservations have been voiced. As a result, many management viewpoints have of necessity made some adjustments in response to these criticisms. At the same time, general management philosophy has not reverted to the pre-Mayo point of view. Management practitioners and philosophers alike have been reluctant to "throw out the baby with the bath water."

Contemporary management thought, as a result, has become considerably more sophisticated in this area. Behavioral sciences are receiving more attention as managers and scholars seek explanations of the way organizations really work. There is a general recognition that economic factors, while extremely important, are not the only aspect that is important in business administration. Management has turned to sociology, psychology, cultural anthropology, and other social sciences to supplement the technical knowledge concerning business management.

The Role of Management in Modern Society

Separation of Ownership and Management

At one time, our economy was characterized by small-scale enterprise. The operations of these small concerns were primarily local in character, and ownership was generally combined with management of the business. An entrepreneur would launch a new enterprise and operate it during his lifetime—passing it on to his son or selling it to some other *owner-manager*.

Development of national markets and the economics of mass production led to growth in the size of industrial concerns. Capital requirements often exceeded the resources of the individual entrepreneur and his immediate family. Public sale of stock became necessary to finance such business ventures. Some of these corporations have grown to the point that they now have hundreds of thousands of stockholders and invested capital amounting to billions of dollars. With such diffusion of ownership, the concept of the owner-manager became obsolete.

A classic study by Berle and Means investigated the nature of ownership and control of large business corporations in 1929.[10] The

[10] Adolph A. Berle, Jr. and Gardiner C. Means, *The Modern Corporation and Private Property* (New York: The Macmillan Company, 1932).

study revealed a substantial amount of control by management groups having no more than nominal holdings of stock. Berle and Means defined control as the "actual power to select the board of directors (or its majority)."[11] As corporations grow and ownership becomes dispersed, power to select new directors tends to gravitate to the existing management even though stock ownership of the management group is negligible. Forty-four per cent of the largest 200 nonfinancial corporations in 1929 were found to be management-controlled.[12] The General Electric Company and United States Steel Corporation, for example, were classified as management-controlled; the largest stock holding in either company was less than 2 per cent of the total. (Other types of control were "private ownership," "majority ownership," "minority control," and "control through a legal device without majority ownership.") A recent review of the Berle and Means study indicates a continuing trend toward management control of large firms.[13] As of 1963, 84.5 per cent of the 200 largest nonfinancial corporations were found to be management-controlled. The decline of owner control has thus been documented, and this decline undoubtedly extends far beyond the 200 largest corporations.

The increase in the complexity of industrial operations also demanded a type of professional knowledge or competence greater than that possessed by the typical owner-manager. To direct the operations of the large corporation, it became necessary to rely upon some individual whose personal competence qualified him, rather than upon those who could claim the right of management by virtue of investment in or ownership of the business.

Emergence of the Professional Manager

As a result of the developments noted above, a new type of manager, the *professional manager*, appeared. He typically assumed the corporate leadership as a result of a strong background of knowledge and experience in engineering, production, financial administration, or sales. It was his ability to understand and deal with complex problems in these areas and to make intelligent decisions concerning such problems that made him an individual qualified to lead the corporation. This significant transition from the owner-manager

---

[11] *Ibid.*, p. 69.

[12] *Ibid.*, p. 94.

[13] Robert J. Larner, "Ownership and Control in the 200 Largest Nonfinancial Corporations, 1929 and 1963," *The American Economic Review*, Vol. 56, No. 4, September 1966, pp. 777-787.

to the professional manager has been described as a "managerial revolution."[14]

Business firms are constantly making this transition to professional management, usually quietly, with only routine attention in the business press. An owner-president may name a professional manager as vice president. As the president moves up to chairman, the professional manager becomes president. Retirement of the chairman brings the corporation completely under professional management. The Ralston Purina Company, started in 1894 as a St. Louis riverfront feed store, only recently shifted to a completely professional type of management.[15] Two generations of Danforths, the founding family, dominated the company as it became the country's largest marketer of grains and feed supplements for animals. In 1956, the death of a Danforth executive resulted in the appointment of the first nonfamily president, Raymond E. Roland. In 1963, the company promoted Roland to chairman and named R. Hal Dean, a professional manager, as president. For the first time, a Danforth was neither chairman nor president of Ralston Purina.

Although the philosophy of the professional manager is not directly opposed to that of the owner-manager, a different emphasis is apparent in his thinking. His primary concern has come to be the corporation and its health and growth rather than his personal investment in the corporation. He is inclined to view his objectives somewhat differently than did the owner-manager, as will be noted in Chapter 4.

Although the manager may be viewed as a professional manager, it is important to realize this is not the equivalent of a completely *scientific manager*. We would expect him to respect the scientific method, of course. But management deals with issues that exceed the limits of scientific analysis. Science in management is not exact and must be supplemented with managerial art or judgment in contemporary management of business corporations.

The Distinctive Skill of Administration

We have come to recognize that management and the abilities that go to make up the manager are quite separate and distinct from the activities and abilities required of operating personnel. At one

---

[14]James Burnham, *The Managerial Revolution* (New York: The John Day Company, Inc., 1941).

[15]"Ralston Ties on a Bigger Feedbag," *Business Week,* No. 1944, December 3, 1966, pp. 77-82.

time, it was customary to promote the most proficient worker when filling a management vacancy. Although this procedure had much to recommend it, it ignored the fact that ability to direct the work of others is substantially different from that of doing one's own work. Capable employees who had performed in an outstanding manner as craftsmen or office employees proved disappointing when moved into managerial positions. Gradually, it became clear that the manager requires talents or must exercise abilities that are quite different from those of nonmanagerial personnel.

The distinctive nature of managerial ability was further revealed by the discovery that managerial skills were somewhat transferrable from one field of endeavor to another. Thus, managers could move from production to sales and do an effective job in either area. Other managers moved from business to government, and vice versa, with effective management in both areas.[16] Although there is undoubtedly a desirable minimum amount of knowledge necessary concerning the field being managed, it is evident that the skill and ability of the manager is distinct from the technical knowledge associated with the field. Certainly, the manager does not need to be the greatest technical expert in the field in which he is managing.

In 1966, Robert Douglas Armstrong, former president of Chrysler Corporation's leasing operations, became president of Toronto's Rio Algom Mines, a company reputed to hold the world's largest reserves of low-cost uranium.[17] Although Armstrong had no mining experience whatever, he possessed those management skills essential for successful performance in any major business organization. Trained as an accountant, Armstrong previously had worked in such diverse fields as oil exploration, aircraft engines, and railroading before going into marketing at Chrysler.

Responsibility of Modern Management

In the last one hundred years, business management has come to possess immense power. The business corporation occupies a position of key importance in contemporary society. To a great extent,

---

[16]Peter F. Drucker contends that the requirement for economic performance on the part of corporate managers means that their skills and experience cannot automatically be transferred and applied to other types of insitutions such as governmental, religious, or educational institutions. See Peter F. Drucker, *The Practice of Management* (New York: Harper & Row, Publishers, 1954), pp. 8-9.

[17]"Robert Douglas Armstrong: You Don't Have to be a Mining Man," *Forbes,* Vol. 98, No. 10, November 15, 1966, p. 29.

our national welfare is dependent upon its effective performance. Cold war strength can be achieved only by the contribution of industrial concerns. Economic growth is likewise realized through the progress of America's business corporations. These corporations are, in turn, dependent upon the quality of business management.

Management has emerged as a leading group in our industrial society. It is recognized as an essential class, distinct from labor and separate from ownership. The emergence of management has been described by Peter F. Drucker as a "pivotal event in social history." "Rarely, if ever," as Drucker sees it, "has a new basic institution, a new leading group, emerged as fast as has management since the turn of the century."[18]

With power comes responsibility. As a result of this powerful position of the business manager, he can no longer be completely self-centered or capricious in his actions. Society expects a capable, responsible performance and is inclined to tolerate little less. The nineteenth century corporate leader has often been villainized (with some justification, of course). Today business leadership has a much greater degree of public acceptance. This is true despite the lack of sympathy for those who ignore proper standards of business behavior. In fact, the lessening degree of public tolerance of improper behavior reflects the greater measure of acceptance of business management as an institution. Business leadership is recognized as having great importance and is expected to act accordingly.

Content of This Book

This book is devoted to a study of management in the modern business organization. In this chapter, we have looked at the management process broadly in order to gain a perspective for the study. The remaining chapters of this introductory section are concerned with management functions and the changing problems and methods of management.

Later sections of the book devote groups of chapters to management's activities in planning, organizing (and the social aspects of organizing), directing, and controlling. The final chapter considers the role and responsibilities of professional managers in a changing world.

Summary

Managers provide the dynamic force necessary to transform the resources of a business organization into a productive, operating

[18]Drucker, *op. cit.,* p. 3.

concern. They are responsible for directing an organization in the achievement of its objectives. The services of management are necessary in all cooperative endeavors.

The practice of *management* is as old as the history of human cooperation. In the last century, however, managerial problems have increased in complexity. To some extent, this has resulted from growth in the size of organizations. The extreme complexity of modern industry similarly contributes to the difficulty of management, as does the changing status of members of business organizations. An accelerating rate of change in all aspects of business and management likewise complicates the managerial process.

The introduction and adoption of the *scientific method* has been a notable development in the history of management. Another major trend involves the increasing attention to *human relationships* in business organizations. Frederick W. Taylor and Elton Mayo were particularly associated with these two developments.

Growth of business organizations has led to the separation of ownership and management and the rise of the *professional manager*. Business management now constitutes a distinct class in our society, wielding great power and facing great responsibilities.

Discussion Questions

1. According to the best usage, should the word *management* apply to managers or to the process of managing?

2. In what significant ways does the managerial job of the president of General Motors differ from that of Moses?

3. In the late 1950's, a large manufacturer more than a century and a half old was losing momentum. Its reputation for production-line innovation established as late as the 1930's was not being continued. Management was finding difficulty keeping pace with the changing patterns of business in the markets it served. Plant facilities had become outmoded, and overhead costs had soared. This situation occurred in a company having experienced, successful management. What was the apparent problem, and what solution or solutions are called for?

4. What was the major contribution of Frederick W. Taylor to management thought?

5. Of what significance to management theory was the pig iron handling study of Taylor?

6. In what ways does contemporary management's use of the scientific method differ from the scientific management of Frederick W. Taylor?

7. Explain the *rabble hypothesis* and point out its weaknesses.

8. What was the greatest contribution of the Western Electric studies to an understanding of the management process?

9. What factors have encouraged the professionalization of management?

10. One chief executive of a business firm remarked, "Running a business well is like painting well, or playing a violin. If you don't have a feel for it in your antenna, you can't learn it in a book." Comment.

11. Does the modern manager have any greater responsibilities to society than did his predecessor of a century ago?

Supplementary Reading

Dale, Ernest, *Management: Theory and Practice*, Chapters 8-15. New York: McGraw-Hill Book Company, 1965.

Donham, Paul, "Is Management a Profession?" *Harvard Business Review*, Vol. 40, No. 5, September-October 1962, pp. 60-68.

Fox, William McNair, *The Management Process: An Integrated Functional Approach*, Chapter 1. Homewood: Richard D. Irwin, Inc., 1963.

Gordon, Robert Aaron, *Business Leadership in the Large Corporation*. Washington: The Brookings Institution, 1945.

Gross, Bertram M., *The Managing of Organizations*, Volume 1, Part II. New York: The Free Press, 1964.

Hertz, David B., "The Unity of Science and Management," *Management Science*, Vol. 11, No. 6, April 1965, pp. B-89 — B-97.

Hoffman, Frank O., "The All-Purpose Manager—Does He Exist?" *Personnel*, Vol. 40, No. 1, January-February 1963, pp. 8-16.

Irwin, Patrick H. and Frank W. Langham, Jr., "The Change Seekers," *Harvard Business Review*, Vol. 44, No. 1, January-February 1966, pp. 81-92.

McLennan, Kenneth, "The Manager and His Job Skills," *Academy of Management Journal*, Vol. 10, No. 3, September 1967, pp. 235-245.

Mee, John F., *Management Thought in a Dynamic Economy*. New York: New York University Press, 1963.

Merrill, Harwood F., ed., *Classics in Management.* New York: American Management Association, 1960.

Packard, Vance, *The Pyramid Climbers.* New York: McGraw-Hill Book Company, 1962.

Prasad, S. Benjamin, "The Profile of the Managerial Mind," *Academy of Management Journal,* Vol. 8, No. 1, March 1965, pp. 44-47.

Richards, Max D. and Paul S. Greenlaw, *Management Decision Making,* Chapter 1. Homewood: Richard D. Irwin, Inc., 1966.

Sonthoff, Herbert, "What is the Manager?" *Harvard Business Review,* Vol. 42, No. 6, November-December 1964, pp. 24-36ff.

Taylor, Frederick Winslow, *Scientific Management.* New York: Harper & Row Publishers, 1947.

2

Management: System and Process

Two basic concepts of management thought — those of the business organization as a *system* and of management as a *process* — will be introduced in this chapter. The business firm may be visualized as a system within which managers perform various roles. By observing managers in action, we can examine the management process that regulates the system. An analysis of this process makes possible a grouping of managerial activities around a few basic management *functions*. In this chapter, the concept of the business system will be treated first before turning to an examination of the manager's functions.

Systems Concepts and Business Organizations

The Systems Concept

In recent years, a new perspective on the work of managers has been provided by the adaptation of *systems theory* to business organizations and management.[1] The basic idea of a *system* is that

[1]For examples of pertinent literature, see the supplementary reading list at the end of the chapter. Two books of particular significance are Richard A. Johnson, Fremont E. Kast, and James E. Rosenzweig, *The Theory and Management of Systems,* Second Edition (New York: McGraw-Hill Book Company, Inc., 1967); and Stanley Young, *Management: A Systems Analysis* (Glenview: Scott, Foresman & Company, 1966).

of a set of components that are related in the accomplishment of some purpose. A functioning physical organism or a machine is a system. General systems theory and research deal with system problems in such diverse fields as medicine, population, national defense, and industrial organization.

Studies of general community problems such as crime, control of wastes, information flow in government, and transportation illustrate the broad applications of systems analysis and research. In 1965, four areospace companies used the systems approach in conducting preliminary studies in these fields for the state of California.[2] Aerojet-General Corporation, for example, applied its experience in space and military systems to the complex problem of treating waste products to eliminate air and water pollution. North American-Rockwell Aviation attempted to find the synthesis of existing transportation methods with other, newer methods that would provide the answer to moving people, merchandise, and raw materials in the future. In each case, a vast, complex problem was examined as a whole to discover the web of contributing and relevant factors and the interrelationships among those factors.

The systems concept entails the idea of parts or units functioning in combination with other units. Collectively they comprise a system — either conceptual or physical in nature. The economist's *model* is a system, as is the real economy it represents.

> Initially we can define a system broadly and crudely as *any entity, conceptual or physical, which consists of interdependent parts*. Even without further refinement of this definition it is clear that in systems research we are interested only in those systems which can display activity, i.e., *behavioral* systems.[3]

The latter distinction (the behavioral feature) would exclude such systems as number systems or philosophical systems. Furthermore, the primary interest of systems researchers is in the type of system that is subject to manipulation or control—such as economic systems in contrast to systems of astronomy.

It should also be noted that some systems involve people as parts of the system whereas other systems do not. Medical research which

---

[2]For a description of this undertaking, see "What Aerospace Sees on the Ground," *Business Week,* No. 1882, September 25, 1965, pp. 87-90; and "Aerospace Firms Seek to Turn Their Talents to Curing Urban Ills," *The Wall Street Journal,* June 9, 1965, p. 1.

[3]R. L. Ackoff, "Systems, Organizations, and Interdisciplinary Research," in *Systems: Research and Design,* ed. Donald P. Eckman (New York: John Wiley & Sons, Inc., 1961), pp. 27-28.

studies the physical organs as a part of the functioning body system is an example of the latter. In the study of management, our principal concern is the type of system involving people. As a matter of fact, most *people systems* are really *people-equipment systems.*

The Business Firm and the Systems Concept

A business organization, or any organization for that matter, may be viewed as a system of interrelated parts. The elements of such a system, as indicated by the following diagram, are input, process (or operation), and output.

Input ⟶ Process ⟶ Output

In a business organization, employees, physical facilities, money, and the managers themselves are parts of the system. The outputs are the products, services, and satisfactions provided by the organization. Inputs are the materials, information, and energy flowing into the firm. Raw materials which enter the production process of a factory constitute an input. Automobiles and replacement parts are inputs in a repair shop. Other inputs are informational in nature — for example, a customer's order or an outside auditor's report. The physical and mental work of employees may likewise be visualized as an input.

In reality, the business organization involves a series of systems or, perhaps more accurately, a complex system encompassing smaller or more specialized systems. The office typewriter and the milling machine in the factory are, in themselves, systems of component parts. These machines and the personnel who operate them are, in turn, parts of office systems and production systems. These and other business systems are social systems if they involve people; describing them as social systems draws attention to the interpersonal relationships that are involved. They are also physical processing and distribution systems if a physical product is involved.

The process of communications and decision making provide linkages for integrating the separate parts or specialized systems into the comprehensive business system. The following outline was designed to show the *information flow* occurring in a restaurant.[4]

Menu —(Printed Words)⟶ Customer —(Spoken Words)⟶ Waitress —(Written Notes)⟶ —(Spoken Words)⟶ Cook —(Prepared Food)⟶

[4]Elias H. Porter, "The Parable of the Spindle," *Harvard Business Review,* Vol. 40, No. 3, May-June 1962, p. 62.

(Of course, the last item — prepared food — is a physical item and not information.) The existence of a system is evident, and it is apparent that physical activities are controlled by the information flow.

Managerial Work and the Business System

The management team of an enterprise constitutes the decision-making or regulating subsystem of the organizational system. Managers are thus not only parts, but they are special — directing and controlling — parts of the total organizational system. Consequently, the managerial role should be seen in its relationship to the total organization. The manager's activities should, ideally, maximize the output of the total system.

The thread that binds together the seemingly disparate activities of managers is revealed by this view of the managerial task. Individual managers do not work in isolation, and neither is one function or activity performed without reference to another. The planning of Manager A must be harmonized with that of Manager B if organizational goals are to be achieved. Similarly, a manager's control of system outputs may reveal defects that, in turn, call for modification of inputs to the system.

An observer may see either the parts of the system or the system itself. The following comments reveal the change of thinking involved in shifting from a *components* to a *systems* point of view:

> Had I been asked a few years ago to advise on human relations problems in the restaurant industry as a professional psychologist, my approach would have been limited to what I now call a "component" approach. My thinking would have been directed at the components in the system — in this case, the people involved. I would have explored such answers as incentive schemes, human relations training, selection procedures, and possibly some time-and-motion studies. My efforts would have been limited to attempts to *change the components to fit in with the system as designed no matter how poor the design might be.*
>
> But now I would first concern myself with the "information" which must be "processed" by the system. My concern would be centered on the functions which would have to be performed by the system and how they might best be performed.[5]

The value of the systems concept is its stress on the interrelatedness of all parts of the organization. The manager is often tempted

---

[5]*Ibid.,* p. 63.

to see organizational problems and activities in isolation. On the basis of the systems viewpoint, however, the manager may understand that he is operating (or functioning as part of) a complex machine. Manipulation of one control affecting one part inevitably produces repercussions of some magnitude in other parts of the system. In subsequent chapters of this book, we shall return to the systems concept from time to time to note its implications for particular aspects of management.

The Concept of Management as a Process

Managerial Versus Nonmanagerial Duties

An examination of the management process in an organizational system must be concerned with managerial activities — that is, with activities performed by all managers, ranging from president to first-line supervisor. It must also include managers who function in different areas of business — production, sales, finance, research, and so on.

Not all duties of managers can be properly classified as managerial in nature. *Managerial* activities are those concerned with the functioning of the organization as an institution. They are related to the work and accomplishments of subordinate managerial and operative personnel. The distinctive contribution of a manager is his blending of individual work, just as a symphony conductor blends the musical efforts of individual musicians into a performance of harmony and beauty.

Nonmanagerial duties, on the other hand, include those activities that are performed by the manager on an individual basis. Sales calls on customers, for example, constitute the work of selling rather than managing — whether the visit is made by a salesman, a sales manager, or a president. Public relations activities of executives fall into the same category. A company president may cut short a business conference with his executives (managerial) to make a public address in support of an educational fund drive (nonmanagerial). A first-line supervisor, in the office or shop, may personally perform a part of the work — preparing invoices, maintaining accounting records, or operating equipment in the shop. As a non-business example, educational administrators also teach classes and engage in research projects.

Most managerial positions, then, involve a combination of managerial and nonmanagerial activities. And there is nothing necessarily wrong, of course, with a manager's engaging in nonmanagerial work. That is, no principle states that managers should perform managerial work exclusively. It may be mandatory, in fact, for the president to make a sales call on an important customer. There is some danger, it must be recognized, in allowing nonmanagerial activities to encroach unduly on time available for management itself.

The importance of the distinction here is in outlining the area of investigation involved in studying the process of management. Our primary concern is with the managerial activities of management personnel. Any concern with the nonmanagerial functions is purely secondary in that they may have an effect upon the managerial functions.

How a Manager Spends His Time

The pattern of activities for any one manager is often unique, reflecting his individual personality and the particular industrial and administrative situation. On the surface, the approach of one executive to his work may be quite different from that of another. Consider, as an example, the following description of the pattern followed by Wilton Robert (Witt) Stephens, chairman and president of Arkansas Louisiana Gas Company.[6]

> Mr. Stephens, whose Arkla salary is $67,116 a year, picks up many of the ideas for new ventures for his company from the stream of visitors who parade through his unpretentious office on the third floor of the Stephens Building here every morning between eight and noon. Associates say he literally will see anybody about anything. The variety of subjects covered in a typical morning is astonishing. On a recent morning he talked with farmers about cattle, cotton and possible construction of a sorghum mill, with lumbermen about a new process for treating wood, with bankers about loans and economic conditions and with a committee from a small Arkansas community seeking help on an industrial development program.
>
> Between visitors he scans reports from division and department heads and dashes off occasional needling telegrams, such as the following: "Noted in the weekly report you were considerably behind quota on gas dryer sales. Do you need any help? Call on us if we can assist. Witt Stephens, assistant sales manager."

---

[6] "The New Bosses: Stephens Revitalizes a Slow-Moving Utility by Invading New Fields," *The Wall Street Journal,* January 17, 1962, p. 6.

> Though Mr. Stephens gives his executives and local managers considerable authority to act independently, one subordinate says on major decisions he "pretty much flies by the seat of his pants," often going against the advice of associates. Mr. Stephens himself notes he told none of his assistants or executives about the gas light idea "because they probably would have talked me out of it."[7]
>
> At noon on many business days, Mr. Stephens breaks away from his office for four or five hours. With an assistant or two and perhaps a visitor, he heads for his 2,500-acre farm 40 miles south of Little Rock in his Cadillac. Enroute the party eats a picnic lunch prepared by the company kitchen.
>
> Once at the farm, talk of Arkansas Louisiana Gas affairs ends. Mr. Stephens may direct land-clearing operations or oversee the building of a fence; a guest may drive a tractor or help round up cattle.
>
> The group is rolling back to Little Rock by 5 p.m. for the second half of Mr. Stephens' business day. Typically, Mr. Stephens holds a business conference over steaks at the Coachman's Inn, a plush Little Rock motel in which he owns an interest. After dinner he often returns alone to his office to dictate letters to a dictating machine till midnight.

In addition to the activities described above, Mr. Stephens even makes occasional house-to-house calls to sell gas air-conditioning units! Other chief executives no doubt operate in a quite different manner. Even subordinate managers in Mr. Stephens' own company probably function in drastically different ways.

Talking Time and Silent Time

Such variety in the activities of managers makes classification of their activities challenging, to say the least. The first section divided these activities into *managerial* and *nonmanagerial* categories. Managerial activities may, in turn, be grouped in various ways. For example, the time spent by managers on managerial work might be divided into the time spent in talking with others and the time spent alone.

One review of studies of managerial activities discloses that an extremely large proportion of the manager's time is spent in talking.[8]

---

[7]Footnote by author of this book. Mr. Stephens saw two old-fashioned gas lights in a restaurant and felt they would appeal to many people. A subsidiary was put to work producing them, and many were installed by home owners in Arkla territory.

[8]Robert Dubin, "Business Behavior *Behaviorally* Viewed," in *Social Science Approaches to Business Behavior,* ed. George B. Strother (Homewood, Illinois: Richard D. Irwin, Inc., and The Dorsey Press, Inc., 1962), pp. 11-15. Used with permission.

Higher-level executives, in particular, appeared to spend a large percentage of their time in conversation with other personnel. In fact, from 60 to 80 per cent of their working time was apparently used in this way. As Dubin expressed it, "We start, then, with a picture of the executive scarcely able to close his mouth, with an extremely high proportion of his time spent in discourse with others in his environment." In the case of foremen, the proportion of time spent in talking is less than that for top management. Even here, however, studies show that more than 50 per cent of the foreman's time may be spent in such interactions.

Having observed the practice of extensive talking, the next question concerns the nature or purposes of such conversations. Some studies, for example, have classified management contacts according to such purposes as getting information, advising and explaining, making decisions, and giving orders. A popular misconception holds that managers spend most of their time in making decisions and giving orders. One of the interesting features evident in Dubin's review of studies of this kind is that only a relatively small proportion of time is spent on making decisions. An even smaller percentage of time, in most cases, is concerned with order giving.

This review of managerial activities leaves unanswered some questions about the nature of management work. What subjects were they talking about? What kinds of decisions might have been made during discussions or by the manager alone? What did managers do when they were not talking? Even though much has been learned in the study of managerial behavior, additional research can add still further details to the picture of the manager in action.

Three Jobs of Management

Another analysis of the activities of business management, by Peter F. Drucker, sees the manager as simultaneously performing three jobs.[9] These jobs are the following: *managing a business*, *managing managers*, and *managing workers and work*.

The first of these tasks is concerned with the economic performance of the business. The manager is successful only if the business achieves the economic goal of supplying goods and services at a cost less than the price customers are willing to pay. Management is more than a creature of the economy; it must also be a master of economic circumstances.

[9]Peter F. Drucker, *The Practice of Management* (New York: Harper & Row, Publishers, 1954), Chapter 2.

Managing managers, the second job, is necessary to make a productive enterprise out of human and material resources. This job includes the welding of managers and their functions into an effective, productive organization. It also involves the setting of goals for management people and the direction of their activities. Although the emphasis here is upon the management structure, operative employees may be considered partly managerial if they share responsibility for decisions concerning work.

The final function is that of directing employees and their work — the work of unskilled, skilled, and professional employees. This involves organization of the work and organization of employees to perform the work. It implies consideration of the employee both as a resource and as a human being.

Identification of Management Functions

Another approach to analysis of management activity identifies certain basic *management functions.* A manager's discussions with his subordinates, for example, may have any of a number of different purposes. The manager, in some cases, is checking on work progress and comparing it with the anticipated completion time. At other times, he is outlining future work projects and explaining requirements and details to the subordinate. The manager also discusses the type of work assignments to be made to different subordinates and the extent to which particular employees should be allowed to make decisions. Each of these, and others as well, is different in purpose and nature. In the same way, a manager's time that is spent alone in his own office may be directed to the accomplishment of various different purposes. In attempting to identify basic management functions, we are seeking some fundamental categories or classifications that permit a logical grouping of managerial activities according to their purpose and nature.

There is no universally recognized set of management functions. Different theorists have cut the pie in pieces of different size and shape. Such functions as planning, organizing, controlling, leading, staffing, and directing have been identified by different writers. Some suggest as few as three, while others propose a dozen or more. There is actually considerably less disagreement than might be imagined from a superficial examination of the various schemes of classification. A number of basic functions are widely recognized, even though there is some variation in labeling them.

In this book the following four functions will provide the framework for our analysis of management activities:

1. Planning.
2. Organizing.
3. Directing and Motivating.
4. Controlling.

Each of these functions is discussed briefly in this chapter and also serves as the basis for a major section of the book. In practice, these functions are intertwined in the day-to-day performance of a manager.

Planning

Nature of Planning

The general meaning of managerial planning is consistent with the common usage of the term. It involves thought and decision concerning a proposed course of action. The plan may be concerned with not only a decision to take action but also such aspects as "who," "when," and "how." Planning is concerned with the future. It anticipates and precedes action, as contrasted with reflective thinking about past events. How far a plan extends into the future varies, naturally, according to the type of plan.

By providing a factual basis for future action, planning aids or facilitates the action being planned. Otherwise, there would be little value in planning. Subjecting almost any unplanned activity to the process of planning demonstrates the general validity of this proposition. Students can discover the road to improvement in learning through properly planned study. Such planning involves the allocation of time to study versus other pursuits. It also requires thought as to the order of study and the environmental conditions for study.

The importance of planning is easily overlooked, but it is vital to business efficiency and success. Analysis of business firms that have become bankrupt shows frequent deficiencies in planning. Failure to plan leaves one ignorant of trends and developments affecting any business operation. To remain competitive, business managers must be effective and consistent in planning the activities of the organizations that they manage.

Types of Plans

In general, a plan is a program of action. It may be a production schedule for the week, a sales promotion program, a group of design projects and work assignments for a drafting room, or numerous other types of plans. On an individual basis, the activities scheduled for the day or week constitute a work plan for the employee. As the president's secretary schedules his appointments, she is preparing a work program for him.

There are many ways of classifying plans. In terms of time, a distinction is evident between long-range and short-range plans. Some may extend for five or ten years into the future, or even longer, while others are concerned with activities of a day-to-day nature. Some statements and devices formulated by management may be regarded as standing or continuing plans. For example, objectives, policies, and operating procedures may be considered as types of plans. They affect the goals and methods of operation and differ from other plans in terms of their continuity and applicability to projects and programs of different types extending over a period of time.

In terms of scope, a distinction may be made between company-wide plans and departmental plans. Comprehensive plans for the overall organization are typically broken down and supplemented with detailed plans for particular organizational components. Also, some company-wide plans encompass more than one functional area. There may be a production plan or a sales plan that is company-wide in nature. On the other hand, some plans of a company-wide nature — the master budget, for example — touch upon several different functional areas. The most comprehensive planning, then, affects a variety of functional, product, and possibly geographical areas.

Forecasting and Budgeting

Predicting the future is both difficult and hazardous. In business planning, one of the great uncertainties confronting the manager is the direction of business trends. This is true for the business as a whole and also for its individual product lines and territories. The prediction of sales trends for a particular business involves consideration of business trends for the economy as a whole and for the particular industry and locality in which a concern is operating.

Forecasting at its simplest level involves rough estimates by salesmen concerning future business. These sales predictions may be refined in various ways, and they are more and more being supplemented by analyses prepared by professional economists serving in a staff capacity to the company. Business forecasting may also utilize analyses of business trends prepared by outside agencies.

Overall business planning for a company typically culminates in a financial budget. This may be thought of as the most basic business plan for the concern. It applies to a given period of time, typically one year, although it may be of any length. The budget is based upon sales predictions and incorporates the operational plans necessary to meet anticipated sales levels.

The extent to which business forecasting and budgeting are used is one mark of the degree of an organization's sophistication in planning and in general management. Most large corporations, for example, would find it extremely difficult, if not impossible, to operate without comprehensive financial budgets.

ORGANIZING

Nature of Organizing

A road map is of little value without an automobile. Similarly, implementation of a business plan requires an organization. Viewed broadly, organizing includes the provision of physical facilities, capital, and personnel. It is also concerned with the determination of relationships among functions, jobs, and personnel. Each of these is a part of the creation of the organizational machine that is designed to accomplish some objective. The determination of organizational relationships is viewed here as the core of the manager's organizing function.[10] Staffing, which is discussed in Chapter 14, is also considered as a part of this function.[11]

The organization function might be visualized as breaking down an overall objective into the specific functions and assignments necessary for the accomplishment of that objective. Major divisions

[10]The design and provision of physical facilities are basically technical or engineering functions and for this reason are excluded from detailed consideration in a study of general management. Much the same reasoning applies to the provision of capital, which is a part of the specialized field of financial management.

[11]Staffing, which borders on the specialized area of personnel management, is treated by some as a separate management function. See, for example, Harold Koontz and Cyril O'Donnell, *Principles of Management,* Fourth Edition (New York: McGraw-Hill Book Company, 1968), Chapter 3.

or departments represent major functions of the business, and these are further subdivided into individual jobs. The organizing function is also concerned with the relationships among functions and jobs.

Superior-subordinate relationships are of primary importance in organizing. The manager creates a structure of relationships that links each employee, directly or indirectly, to the organization head. The connecting lines running downward from top management to operative employees provide the channels for communication between superiors and subordinates and make possible a transmission of plans, instructions, problems, and progress reports. By organizing, the manager also determines relationships among employees and groups of employees. For example, the relationship of a production control unit to a manufacturing unit and the relationship of a member of a stenographic pool to an engineer using that pool are stipulated by the organization plan.

A sound organization structure is imperative for effective and profitable performance. Without proper organization, there may be duplication of effort, inadequate attention to certain functions, rivalry and friction among personnel, and delays in decision making. There is general recognition of the fact that organization problems are among the most perplexing problems confronting modern management.

Types of Organization Structure

Very small companies typically use a type of organization known as *line* organization. In this type of organization, each person is connected with a single line of responsibility to his superior. He is accountable to, and receives orders from, only one superior. It is a simple form of organization without special service groups or advisors. As organizations grow, however, they develop a need for specialists to furnish advice and service. This leads to a type of organization that is known as *line and staff*. In a line and staff organization, the staff experts and service departments supplement the basic line organization. Most large organizations are line and staff in nature.

Committees are customarily used in large organizations. Sometimes the use of committees is considered to be a distinctive type of organization and is referred to as *committee organization.* It is true that some companies make such extensive use of committees that group management through committees is an outstanding characteristic of their structure. It is simpler, however, to think of committees as organizational arrangements or devices that supplement the basic organization structure. In other words, a line and staff organization is a type of organization that utilizes committees in its operation.

Organization structures may also be distinguished according to the basic patterns that they follow. A customary pattern for business firms is that of business *functions*. There are departments of production, sales, and finance. These departments, in turn, may be divided into more specialized functional areas. As companies grow, other patterns develop and find application. Two patterns which have been used extensively are based upon the *products* sold by a company and the *territories* in which it is located. In other words, some companies establish geographical or territorial divisions which perform the various business functions within their prescribed boundaries. Other companies establish product divisions which are responsible for different functions such as the manufacture and sale of the particular line of products.

Basic Issues in Organization Design

One basic issue in organization design that goes to the heart of the organizing process concerns the extent to which managers can or should organize work. Some hold that detailed organization of work tends to be restrictive and hampers effective performance. Others feel that extensive organization planning is not only possible but necessary for most efficient operation. There is some conflict in thinking, then, between *organization planners* and those who feel that people will manage on their own initiative to work out suitable methods of working together.

Another question confronting the manager as organizer is the extent to which authority and decision making should be delegated downward in the organization. Any manager finds it necessary to make some decisions personally. This is particularly true with respect to the most important decisions confronting his organization. Other decisions may be made personally by the manager or passed to lower levels. In recent years the decentralization of decision making has been a popular movement in American industry. Some companies have climbed on the bandwagon, however, only to discover that too much decentralization may be as bad as too much centralization. In organizing, therefore, a fundamental question concerns the proper extent of authority delegation.

Another subject that has received increasing attention in recent years is the social nature of business organizations. Organizations have come to be viewed as social institutions. Management has discovered the existence of an informal organization supplementing or conflicting with the formal structure. Many questions have been raised as to the discrepancy between the way organizations are supposed to function and the way that they actually function. The relationships between superiors and subordinates are being re-examined to discover the proper conditions for most effective performance.

Directing and Motivating

Nature of Directing and Motivating

The organizational machine must be activated or energized in order to carry out management plans. It is the function of directing that sets the organization in motion. We sometimes speak of a manager giving the "go ahead" or "green light" to a program or plan. This step authorizes subordinates to begin work in accordance with the program and constitutes direction on the part of the manager.

One of the clearest examples of direction is found in a formalized production control system. In a manufacturing plant utilizing such production control, the manufacturing processes are planned, tooling is arranged, and materials are allocated. The order or project is then held until the appropriate time. At the right time, the manufacturing order is released to the production department, and manufacturing begins. The release of the work order constitutes the function of directing, and this function is further carried out by subsequent assignments of work to individual employees.

The term *directing* may carry a connotation of harshness or autocratic management. The military organization, for example, merely passes orders downward through its chain of command. It is not necessary to consider the function of directing as highly authoritarian in nature, however. Any organized effort requires some centralized planning and decision making. The process of communicating these choices to members of the organization may be thought of as the function of directing. Some motivation beyond mere order giving may also be required to get the organization in motion as desired. This is becoming increasingly the case as managers come to realize the strength of positive motivation and also as organizations develop a more democratic atmosphere.

Varying Approaches to Directing and Motivating

One of the principal variables in directing is the degree of autocracy in the manager's directions. Direction can range from quite direct commands to guidance through much less direct means. Subordinates may be permitted and even encouraged to contribute suggestions and ideas for consideration by the manager. In the extreme case, direction may appear to be largely self-direction on the basis of some common understanding of goals and objectives.

Closely related is the extent to which managers manage in detail. Some managers look over the shoulders of their subordinates almost constantly. They insist on personally approving every change. Other managers provide only general supervision, and subordinates enjoy considerable latitude in the discharge of their responsibilities.

Another variation in leadership concerns the principal focus of the manager. Some managers are primarily concerned with work. Reaching or achieving work objectives by scheduled dates is uppermost in their thinking. Although they may be completely fair in dealing with subordinates, it is work rather than people that demands their major attention. In contrast, other managers are strongly oriented toward people. The employee and his problems have greater urgency for such managers. Although these managers may be quite aware of their work responsibilities, it is people who are their first concern.

Controlling

Nature of Controlling

Controlling refers to the regulation of the organization to insure the achievement of organizational objectives and the completion of organizational plans. It corresponds, in a sense, to the steering and braking of an automobile. The organization's performance must be examined and checked to insure that the organization is on the right track. Some organizations have an accounting executive, specialized in this function, who is called the *controller*, but controlling is also a part of the responsibility of every manager in the organization.

As an example of the control function outside the business enterprise, consider the operation of a well-coached college football team. An observer, perhaps an assistant coach, sits in the press box far above the field but maintains telephone communication with the bench. On offensive plays, he watches for missed assignments or other hitches interfering with progress. He is also alert to spot possible weaknesses in the enemy's defenses. A spectator may see a coach or quarterback at the edge of the field pick up the phone and engage in conversation with the press box observer. A few moments later, a substitute trots onto the field. An adjustment is made in the pattern of play, and, if all goes well, a touchdown results.

Comparing Performance with Standards

Perhaps the most obvious feature of controlling is the comparison of organizational or individual performance with standards. As an automobile driver reaches a particular town on a cross-country trip, he checks his location with the road map and his schedule for the day. Occasionally, he may find that he is running behind schedule — or even going in the wrong direction! In the manufacturing plant, inspectors check manufactured products for compliance with product specifications. This is a part of the quality *control* function, and the inspectors may be assigned to the quality *control* department.

The purpose of checking performance is to see that it meets expectations. The anticipated results may be thought of as standards. Such standards may take various forms. The quality specification referred to above is one example. A schedule of output for a specific time period is another type of standard. Time standards, set on the basis of time and motion study, provide work standards for individual employees. The general quality objectives of an organization as a whole also provide a type of objective with which performance may be compared. The financial budget, as a comprehensive financial plan, provides a standard or set of standards that may be used to judge overall performance.

At some points, comparison of performance with standards is accomplished in a simple, direct manner — simply observing the product or performance and noting any deviations from expectations. Often, however, the comparisons are of necessity much less direct in nature. An evaluation of performance by one who is physically removed from the scene of action may be necessary. This leads to a need for reports of performance. The quality and timeliness of such reports have much to do with the effectiveness of the control effort. Current information is most useful from a control standpoint, while reports of past performance are primarily of historical interest.

Corrective Action by the Manager

If deviations from standards are revealed, it is the responsibility of the manager to take corrective action. This means that he must get performance back up to the time schedule, get quality up to par, or make other adjustments necessary to meet the expectations previously established. Knowing of the deviation is futile if no corrective action is taken. It is here that a manager proves his worth as controller — by getting his organization back to standard performance.

The action necessary for correction takes many different forms. In the case of the deviation from quality control standards, for example, there may be a number of explanations for the deviation and, therefore, a number of points at which corrective action may be needed. A machine may require adjustment, or its speed of operation may need to be changed. It is also possible that the operator requires training or, perhaps, that he should be replaced with an operator of greater ability. Another possible solution is the substitution of better material. It might also be that changes are required in the physical environment to eliminate noise or dust that might contaminate the product or interfere with the operator in the performance of his duties.

Management Functions in Contemporary Business Organizations

Management Functions and the Manager's External Relationships

A manager's activities are not confined to relationships with his own subordinates. Much of his work involves outside contacts or public relations of one type or another. He not only represents his company to those completely outside the business, but he also confers with individuals in other departments of the same firm.

As noted earlier, outside contacts may be nonmanagerial in nature and thus merely supplement the performance of the managerial functions. The manager performs nonmanagerial work — for example, when he participates in a United Fund campaign. The demands for such service from business executives are increasing to the point that they often seriously erode the time available for internal management. David Rockefeller, president of New York's Chase Manhattan Bank, has estimated that 40 per cent of his sixty-hour work week is devoted to public service.[12] Less noted executives and even small business entrepreneurs also find such requests both compelling and time consuming. Often the manager attempts to solve the resulting time problem by extending his own work week accordingly.

---

[12] "Good Works, Inc.," *The Wall Street Journal,* September 22, 1965, p. 1.

Other outside contacts of the manager are related to the performance of his managerial functions. For example, a manager must contact individuals in other departments, outside his official jurisdiction, in planning and controlling the flow of work through his own department. Note the following description of his work by a middle manager in a large organization.

> I have a terrible time trying to explain what I do at work when I get home. My wife thinks of a manager in terms of someone who has authority over those people who work for him and who in turn gets his job done for him. You know, she thinks of those nice, neat organization charts, too. She also expects that when I get promoted, I'll have more people working for me.
>
> Now, all of this is unrealistic. Actually, I only have eighteen people directly reporting to me. These are the only ones I can give orders to. But I have to rely directly on the services of seventy-five or eighty other people in this company, if my project is going to get done. They in turn are affected by perhaps several hundred others, and I must sometimes see some of them, too, when my work is being held up.
>
> So I am always seeing these people, trying to get their cooperation, trying to deal with delays, work out compromises on specifications, etc. Again, when I try to explain this to my wife, she thinks that all I do all day is argue and fight with people.[13]

This manager's description of his own activities emphasizes the importance of relationships with dozens of outsiders, many of them involving difficult negotiations.

Management Functions in Various Types of Organizations

The functions of management are basic in that each is applicable, in some degree at least, to the work of all managers. All types of organizations necessitate performance of the management functions. In fact, the very existence of management has been suggested as an essential feature in distinguishing organizations from other groups.

> Organizations are assemblages of interacting human beings and they are the largest assemblages in our society that have anything resembling a central coordinative system. Let us grant that these coordinative systems are not developed nearly to the extent of the central nervous system in higher biological organ-

---

[13]Leonard Sayles, *Managerial Behavior* (New York: McGraw-Hill Book Company, Inc., 1964), p. 43.

> isms—that organizations are more earthworm than ape. Nevertheless, the high specificity of structure and coordination within organizations—as contrasted with the diffuse and variable relations *among* organizations and among unorganized individuals—marks off the individual organization as a sociological unit comparable in significance to the individual organism in biology.[14]

It is management, through the functions described in this chapter, that provides the central coordination.

Among business organizations, the central coordinative activities of management are exercised in such varied institutions as manufacturing firms, insurance companies, public utilities, banks, and marketing institutions. All components of a business organization likewise require the performance of the management process. This includes a diversity of organization types—manufacturing units, sales offices, maintenance shops, drafting rooms, computer centers, research laboratories, and many others. In each, it is necessary to plan, organize, direct, and control the work.

In organizations outside the field of business enterprise, the same management functions are in evidence. The organization and management of leading churches and educational institutions, for example, have been subjected to evalution in much the same way that the management of private business organizations has been appraised. In hospital management, administrators have pioneered in establishing standards and in raising the quality of management toward a high professional level.

All sizes of business institutions are likewise subject to the management process. Dun and Bradstreet has for many years cited poor management as the principal factor contributing to the failure of small business enterprises. Some universities offer professional training in small business management. In large corporations, the management process is generally conceded as being of great importance to the effectiveness of the concern. Indeed, some corporations have established their own management institutes.

Management Functions and Business Functions

In manufacturing companies, the three most basic functions are production, distribution, and finance. These functions are normally

---

[14]James G. March and Herbert A. Simon, *Organizations* (New York: John Wiley & Sons, Inc., 1958), p. 4.

performed by manufacturing, sales, and finance departments. Each of these may grow into an organization of large size — possibly headed by a vice president or other executive of high rank. Assuming growth of this type, each functional area requires a sizable staff — whether composed of machine operators, salesmen, or financial analysts. Effective utilization of personnel in these fields demands performance of the management functions with respect to these specialized activities.

Management Functions at Various Levels of Management

Management at all levels of the organization must perform the same management functions. It is true, of course, that the nature of the functions varies somewhat. Departmental managers plan and control work in terms of broad objectives. Manufacturing foremen, in contrast, plan and control operations on a day-to-day basis.

The emphasis and time spent on the different management functions also vary according to the level in the organization. At lower levels, management personnel spend relatively more time in directing and controlling work. It is not uncommon for them to spend a considerable amount of their work day "on the floor" checking with operators and supervising operations. In contrast, managers at higher levels spend a greater proportion of their time on planning. Planning at higher levels also tends to be longer-range planning. The foreman's day-to-day and hour-to-hour determination of what should or will be done, however, must be recognized as planning just as much as the five-year plan approved by the board.

The different levels of management also vary with respect to their requirements for managerial personnel. At lower levels, managers may be specialists, but at higher levels, it is necessary that they be generalists who can see beyond the boundaries of functional areas. This is a significant distinction and one that acts as a barrier to the upward advancement of many managers.

Summary

The systems concept provides an integrating view of the functions of management. This approach — that of *systems theory* — stresses the *interrelatedness of all parts and functions of a business organization.* The emphasis is upon the system and its overall operations rather than the component elements of the system.

It is important to recognize management as a *process* or group of related and continuing activities. In examining management in this manner, it is possible to identify the following basic management functions: *planning*, *organizing*, *directing and motivating*, and *controlling*.

The planning function involves the determination of future courses of action. This entails not only a determination of what is to be done but also concerns the manner and timing of performance. *Forecasting* and *budgeting* are important elements of the planning process.

Organizing, broadly conceived, includes the provision of physical facilities, capital, and personnel. More specifically, it is concerned with the determination of relationships among people, jobs, and functions. In organizing, the manager chooses some type of organization structure and also resolves such issues as the proper extent of organization planning and authority delegation.

In directing and motivating, the manager sets the organization in motion. His activities in this area include the issuance of orders and instructions, but they also include other types of motivation. The manager may utilize various approaches, differing in their degree of *autocracy* and also in other ways, in securing effective performance.

In the function of controlling, the manager regulates organizational performance to insure achievement of objectives. This entails a comparison of performance with standards and any necessary corrective action.

Management functions must be performed in all types of organizations and at all levels of management. Their performance often entails contacts and relationships outside the manager's immediate organization and even outside the firm. The emphasis placed upon the different functions differs from one situation to another, but each function appears in some form or other in each managerial position.

Discussion Questions

1. Explain the *systems* concept. What seems to be the distinctive feature of this idea?
2. What is the difference between a *conceptual system* and a *physical system*? Illustrate.
3. Give several examples of systems which do not involve people as components.

4. In what way may the business organization be visualized as a system? Is a manager a "cog" in the system or is he a manager of the system? How are the parts of the system hooked together?

5. Of what possible significance is classification of activities as *managerial* and *nonmanagerial*?

6. Is it likely that the extensive amount of "talking time" of executives is a reflection of a gregarious type of personality that is associated with management careers? Explain.

7. What relationships exist between the functions of *planning* and *organizing*? *Planning* and *controlling*?

8. How is a financial *budget* related to the functions of planning and controlling?

9. Distinguish between *business functions* and *managerial functions*.

10. What is meant by the *degree of autocracy* in the performance of the directing function?

11. Why should managers at lower levels spend relatively more time in directing and controlling work than do top-level executives?

Supplementary Reading

Boulding, Kenneth E., "General System Theory — The Skeleton of a Science," *Management Science*, April 1956, pp. 197-208.

Brown, David S., "POSDCORB Revisited and Revised," *Personnel Administration*, Vol. 29, No. 3, May-June 1966, pp. 33-39.

Davis, Ralph Currier, *Industrial Organization and Management*, Chapter 3. New York: Harper & Row, Publishers, 1957.

Drucker, Peter F., "Managing for Business Effectiveness," *Harvard Business Review*, Vol. 41, No. 3, May-June 1963, pp. 53-60.

Ehrle, Raymond A., "Implications of a Systems Approach to Organization and Management," *Personnel Journal*, Vol. 44, No. 2, February 1965, pp. 76-79.

French, Wendell, "Processes Vis-A-Vis Systems: Toward a Model of the Enterprise and Administration," *Journal of the Academy of Management*, Vol. 6, No. 1, March 1963, pp. 46-57.

Harvey, Allan, "Systems Can Too Be Practical," *Business Horizons*, Vol. 7, No. 2, Summer 1964, pp. 59-69.

Horrath, William J., "The Systems Approach to the National Health Problem," *Management Science*, Vol. 12, No. 10, June 1966, pp. B-391 — B-395.

Johnson, Richard A., Fremont E. Kast, and James E. Rosenzweig, "Systems Theory and Management," *Management Science*, Vol. 10, No. 2, January 1964, pp. 367-384.

————, *The Theory and Management of Systems*, Second Edition. New York: McGraw-Hill Book Company, Inc., 1967.

Kast, Fremont E. and James E. Rosenzweig, "Management and Accelerating Technology," *California Management Review*, Vol. 6, No. 2, Winter 1963, pp. 39-48.

Koontz, Harold, "The Management Theory Jungle," *Journal of the Academy of Management*, Vol. 4, No. 3, December 1961, pp. 174-188.

Koontz, Harold and Cyril O'Donnell, *Principles of Management*, Fourth Edition, Chapter 3. New York: McGraw-Hill Book Company, Inc., 1968.

Martin, E. W., Jr., "Ideational Items: The Systems Concept," *Business Horizons*, Vol. 9, No. 1, Spring 1966, pp. 63-64.

Odiorne, George S., "The Management Theory Jungle and the Existential Manager," *Academy of Management Journal*, Vol. 9, No. 2, June 1966, pp. 109-116.

Petit, Thomas A., "A Behavioral Theory of Management," *Academy of Management Journal*, Vol. 10, No. 4, December 1967, pp. 341-350.

Porter, Elias H., "The Parable of the Spindle," *Harvard Business Review*, Vol. 40, No. 3, May-June 1962, pp. 58-66.

Suojanen, Waino W., "Management Theory: Functional and Evolutionary," *Journal of the Academy of Management*, Vol. 6, No. 1, March 1963, pp. 7-17.

Tannenbaum, Robert, Irvin R. Weschler, and Fred Massarik, *Leadership and Organization: A Behavioral Science Approach*, Chapter 15. New York: McGraw-Hill Book Company, Inc., 1961.

Tilles, Seymour, "The Manager's Job: A Systems Approach," *Harvard Business Review*, Vol. 41, No. 1, January-February 1963, pp. 73-81.

Wadia, Maneck S., "A Reappraisal of Management Principles," *Advanced Management Journal*, Vol. 31, No. 2, April 1966, pp. 53-57.

Yanouzas, John N., "The 'Victimized' Middleman of Industry Re-examined," *Personnel Administration*, Vol. 28, No. 6, November-December 1965, pp. 18-24.

Young, Stanley, *Management: A Systems Analysis*. Glenview: Scott, Foresman & Company, 1966.

————, "Organization as a Total System," *California Management Review*, Vol. 10, No. 3, Spring 1968, pp. 21-32.

3

Management in a Changing Environment

Business firms do not operate in a vacuum. As is true of all human organizations, they are properly described as *open systems*. This means that they interact with their environment and are subject to the constraints imposed by that environment. It also means that changes in the environment may affect the life and internal functioning of the firm.

To some extent, each firm's environment is unique, but certain aspects are common to most business organizations. In this chapter, the following major features of the business environment are selected for review:

1. Government and business.
2. International developments.
3. Technological change.

There is no stability in any of these areas. Business management today functions in a different world from that of business in earlier decades. In examining these selected features of the environment, it is important to develop a sense of the direction in which the environment is changing.

Government and Business

The Expanding Role of Government

The great expansion in government size and activities during the past forty years is a matter of common knowledge. As this expansion has occurred, the points of contact between government and business management have also increased. Some view this trend as an unfortunate and unnecessary drift toward socialism. Others favor an even more active role for the government. In considering the growth of government and such conflicting views concerning it, it is well to begin by examining some of the factors contributing to its expansion.

Military defense provides one example. In view of our struggle with the Communistic nations, few would question the need for a strong military posture. This leads not only to a large military establishment but also to a closer relationship between business and government. As a part of this effort, the Defense Department each year spends billions of dollars through contracts for goods and services of American business. Major contracts of this kind tie the contracting companies closely to the government. Some governmental contracts are a source of considerable profit, even launching companies into new fields and developments that later become commercially profitable.

The threat of economic recession and public unwillingness to accept a repeat performance of the depression of the 1930's have likewise contributed to big government. Since World War II, a reasonably satisfactory level of prosperity and employment has been maintained only with substantial expansion of total debt, including the public debt. This has led to federal budget deficits during both Democratic and Republican administrations. As a result of the increase in the national debt, the Treasury and Federal Reserve System necessarily assume a major role in financial decisions affecting the business community.

The increasing interdependence of individuals in society likewise exerts pressure for more governmental services and regulation. To some extent, this interdependence results from the technological considerations leading to large-scale enterprise and concentration of industry in various geographical areas. Population growth and the trend toward urbanization provide further impetus in this direction. From the standpoint of the business firm, its decisions and activities affect many people. As corporations introduce labor-saving machinery or move to new locations, for example, many employees may lose their jobs. If these conditions become widespread, they lead to requests for governmental aid to economically blighted areas, programs for retraining employees for different types of work, and other proposals and activities of this type.

The public attitude toward the proper role of government also changed noticeably during the 1930's. The economic collapse, and perhaps other forces, produced a significant shift in public thinking away from the strong laissez-faire philosophy that had previously prevailed. The willingness to accept "New Deal" measures involving a more powerful role for government was quite evident. In the years since, this greater measure of public acceptance of governmental activity has continued.

In view of the above factors and others that might be noted, the increase in the role of government has some logical justification. The expansion of government represents more than empire building by clever politicians. Of course, the *exact* size of government and the *precise* amount of governmental participation in business is a subject of considerable controversy. Certainly the proper boundary between government and business must be, to some extent, a matter of opinion. In spite of disagreement concerning the precise scope of governmental activity and regulation, however, it is clear that the factors discussed in this section have made considerable growth in government inevitable.

Our system has always been a "mixed system" with some activities performed by business and some by government. This system has emphasized the area of freedom left to the individual and the business firm. Furthermore, most of us attach great value to maintaining a large area of freedom and rather grudgingly accept limitations in the form of bigger government. At the same time, one cannot rationally ignore these trends that justify a substantial expansion of government.

Mutuality of Interest

In considering the relationship of government and business, it is easy to fall into the trap of seeing only a conflict of interest. The situation may appear to involve strife rather than cooperation between government and business. An inherent hostility may appear to exist.

A moment's reflection is sufficient to reveal some degree of error in such reasoning. The achievement of full employment—a primary government objective — for example, is possible only when business prospers. Thus, a mutuality of interest exists on this point between government and business. The same is also true in other areas — space exploration, national defense, highway construction, and so on. Even though the objectives of business and government may not always appear identical, there is more harmony than conflict between them.

One area of direct cooperation between industry and government involves the promotion of fair competition through the development of industry-wide trade practices. Ethical practices — the type of practices that should be in the best interest of private industry — are established through consultation among private firms in the industry. The adopted code, spelling out discriminatory practices or outlining types of advertising considered to be misleading, is then enforced by the Federal Trade Commission. Such cooperative regulation avoids certain difficulties that are present in unilateral action by either business or government. Business self-regulation, for example, entails the hazard of restraining competition and therefore tends toward conflict with the anti-trust laws.

Extensive Influence Over Business Decisions

The influence of government upon managerial decision making extends far beyond the application of a few specific regulations. In many diverse types of decisions, the factor of government lurks in the background. An executive can no longer intelligently decide issues from the narrow viewpoint of the individual firm without regard for public policy. It might be added that this does not imply a particularly public-spirited attitude on the part of management. If it is to be rational, decision making for the best interests of the company and its owners must take into account the factor of government.

Consider the varied types of decisions subject to governmental influence. The question of a business merger constitutes such an issue. Even though management may believe the combination of two firms is necessary for effective competition and survival, the attitude of the Department of Justice cannot be ignored. Is there agreement on the part of the "anti-trusters" that the merger has no tendencies to restrain trade? Is there a possibility that the government may take action to block the move or even to conduct an extensive investigation? Can the company afford an investigation and legal action even if it is convinced that the merger would not harm competition?

Capital outlays and related financial planning are dependent upon depreciation provisions of pertinent tax laws. Note the reflections of an executive as he mulls over the conference he has had with his financial executive, Peterson:

> Pete expects business to continue to increase. If it does, we may need more working capital than we planned on. But Pete says that he really can't estimate how much we should borrow until he knows more about how Washington is going to interpret the new depreciation schedules. Are we going to modify our own equipment expenditure schedule? How many of our customers will modify theirs? If we change or they change, it will influence our need for cash because of the effect on our own cash flow. Also, it'd have a lot to do with earnings over the long term, and might affect dividend policy, too. Pete says any figures he produces will probably have to be changed, because so much depends on what is going on in Washington.[1]

In labor negotiations, government stands in the background or actively intervenes. The executive continues his reflections as he thinks over union relationships at a branch plant:

> Fox tells me he's ready to make a final offer to the union in the Huntington plant. It's a fair offer, too, but the leadership down there is in no mood to talk sense. Actually, we can stand a strike right now a lot better than the union can, and they know it. But suppose the Secretary of Labor sends one of his people down to get into the act? There's no doubt about it; any intervention by the Labor Department will weaken our bargaining position. It's a little late to do anything about it, but it's worth a try.[2]

As a result of these reflections, this executive designated a representative to talk to someone in the Labor Department to make sure they understood the company's competitive position and problems before the labor dispute came to a head.

This list of examples could be greatly expanded. The business manager must be conscious of government as he deals with decisions concerning pricing, financing plans, and tax treatment on stock options. Area redevelopment plans of the government may affect some areas in which the firm operates. Governmental outlays may influence the industry and markets in which the firm competes. Business performed under contract with the government is, of course,

---

[1]Gilbert H. Clee, "The Appointment Book of J. Edward Ellis," *Harvard Business Review,* Vol. 40, No. 6, November-December 1962, p. 80.
[2]*Ibid.,* p. 81.

subject to direct influence by contracting decisions of governmental agencies. As a result of this discussion, it should be clear that there are few important decisions in the large corporate enterprise in which government has neither direct nor indirect influence.

Management Attitude Toward Government

Government's greater involvement in business is a fact of the current business environment. It is true regardless of the feeling or attitude of business management. Wishing it were not so does not alter the realities of the situation. Nor is there any great likelihood that this trend will be reversed. For the foreseeable future, it is unlikely that this nation can avoid the costs of waging a cold war or neglect programs of aid to underdeveloped countries. These considerations plus such factors as technological change and population growth will continue to provide pressure for extensive governmental influence in business management.

In view of these facts, the thoroughly negative attitude occasionally expressed by businessmen — to the effect that all governmental activity and all changes in governmental regulation are unquestionably and completely unwise — appears unrealistic. Whether one is politically conservative or liberal, the constructive and increasingly necessary role of government should not be ignored. In the following statement, the president of the General Electric Company displayed an awareness of complexities of our present world and the need for a constructive relationship between business and government:

> Certainly the government is a major participant in the economy as purchaser, tax collector and—to an increasing degree—regulator. No businessman today can afford to be unconcerned with government economic policy, and neither government nor business can any longer afford old-fashioned attitudes of antagonism toward each other.[3]

The national purpose can be achieved only by the proper collaboration of government and business. This is true in terms of both international responsibilities and the domestic economy. The respective roles of business and government, of course, may need to be better defined. The additional comments of General Electric's president expressed an opinion regarding the emphasis or direction of government's role:

---

[3]Gerald L. Phillippe, "In Defense of Corporations," *Dun's Review and Modern Industry,* Vol. 81, No. 2, February 1963, p. 52.

> Yet it remains true, in my judgment, that the growth of the economy continues to be primarily dependent, as it always has been, on the initiatives and actions of business rather than government. And it follows that public policy for accelerating economic growth should be directed toward the encouragement of private initiative and private investment.[4]

This reasoning suggests a distinction between quantitative and qualitative aspects of growth of government and governmental regulation. Some regulation — such as fiscal and monetary controls — is powerful in effect but indirect in application. Other controls — such as those over prices of specific commodities — are direct in their impact. Business management appears to oppose most violently those activities of government that alter traditional patterns and that impose new direct restrictions on individual freedom.

The steel crisis of 1962 provided a significant example of governmental influence in a type of decision making that had been traditionally conceded to be the province of private industry. The U. S. Steel Corporation, traditional pace-setter in pricing, announced a price increase following a labor settlement that was presumed to be noninflationary in nature. When the price hike was announced, an immediate negative reaction was sounded throughout the federal government. President Kennedy bitterly denounced the action of U. S. Steel as irresponsible. The pressure of public opinion and the threat of governmental intervention became so strong that the company was forced to withdraw its price increase.

This incident resulted in strong and varied reactions from business leaders. Many business executives viewed it as a trend toward a qualitatively different type of control. A survey of executive thinking at the beginning of 1963 indicated greater worry on the part of executives concerning government-business relations than was reflected in a survey conducted four years earlier.[5] The uneasiness voiced by these executives was less concerned with the growth in size of government than it was with the growth in governmental power. Respondents to this survey frequently cited the steel dispute in support of their observations. It appeared that these business leaders were expressing more than simple opposition to the New Frontier.

> . . . feelings run much deeper than simple anti-Administration sentiment. Rather, the reaction to a perceived powerful and

---

[4] *Ibid.*

[5] "Management Problems in 1963," *Harvard Business Review,* Vol. 41, No. 1, January-February 1963, p. 7.

> antagonistic government is part of a more basic attitude that businessmen are beset with an adverse environment with which they are less able to contend effectively than once was the case.[6]

In summary, much of the growth of governmental involvement in business is understood and accepted by industrial leaders. At the same time, this trend is a cause for concern on the part of many business managers. This is particularly true of controls that are perceived by managers to directly restrict management freedom and that are seen to represent a significant departure from customary relationships.

Political Activity

While recognizing some logic in the increase in governmental expenditures and control, management is not committed to the status quo. It is possible to do more than sit back and criticize as government makes the rules and determines the conditions for cooperation. Management thinking can be aggressively applied to altering and shaping the appropriate and desirable relationship between government and business.

This has led to suggestions that business leadership should actively participate in political activities.

> The logical answer is for businessmen to pay more attention to who gets sent to Washington to write our laws. That is, *businessmen must get into politics.*[7]

As a matter of fact, business *has been* and *is* in politics; the statement above is really a plea for *more* political activity.

The attempt to "get into politics" takes different forms. Some companies undertake political education of employees, including top-level executives, encouraging them to accept an active role in political campaigns and other political activity. Others receive campaign contributions for the party of the employee's choice. Advocates of expanded political activity by businessmen often suggest that the activity should be nonpartisan.

> . . . any business program has to be conducted on a genuinely nonpartisan basis in that there can be no company identification with a political party or its candidates. The entire undertaking centers around the individual. The modus operandi for the com-

---

[6]*Ibid.*

[7]Horace E. Sheldon, "Businessmen Must Get Into Politics," *Harvard Business Review,* Vol. 37, No. 2, March-April 1959, p. 37.

> pany essentially is one of exhorting its executives or staff members at lower levels to speak up on public issues and participate in political affairs *for their own good.*[8]

Some go so far as to urge the advancement of a company point of view on political issues. Such programs are not without hazards. The political freedom of the individual member of the corporation must be preserved. If a company position on a partisan political issue is vigorously promoted, there is a possibility of subtly threatening those who will not go along.

> If corporations do not sensibly restrict their political activity, they run one final and most serious risk: partisan electoral activity by corporations will bring forth redoubled effort by labor. The end result might then be what businessmen have long abhorred—a class conflict in American party politics.[9]

It is well to recognize that the interests of the corporation and society are not always identical—that business management is not divinely ordained to serve as guardian for society. Furthermore, the scope of business interests is somewhat restricted—that is, some public issues are important to business, while others are not.

Moreover, practical politics is not the only route to political influence. The practice of lobbying and the presentation of testimony to legislative groups are legitimate techniques for expressing company interests. In practice, the business point of view has not been ignored, even though some business leaders sometimes feel that only labor is heard. The Taft-Hartley Act, for example, is hardly the product of union politicking. The appropriate political role for business management is, therefore, a complex issue requiring careful definition to express forcefully the legitimate interests of the company without infringement on individual freedom.

International Developments and the Multi-National Firm

Expansion of International Business

The international relationships and responsibilities of American business firms are increasing with the growth of international busi-

[8] *Ibid.*, pp. 43-44.

[9] Michael D. Reagan, "The Seven Fallacies of Business in Politics," *Harvard Business Review*, Vol. 38, No. 2, March-April 1960, p. 68.

ness and foreign trade. In recent years, numerous companies have acquired an international dimension that has modified their basically domestic character. Firms are constantly expanding exports or imports, establishing foreign subsidiaries, or creating international departments. The general broadening of the international commitments of American business is indicated by the rise in foreign trade portrayed in Table 1. It is obvious that, within the past decade, there has been a substantial growth both of exports and imports. The objectives, planning, decision making, and direction of American business are consequently coming to reflect the international developments in business activity.

TABLE 1. Indexes of U. S. Exports and Imports (1957-59=100)

	1955	1960	1965
Exports			
Quantity	87	112	144
Value	82	113	152
Imports			
Quantity	81	109	153
Value	82	108	152

Source: *Statistical Abstract of the United States*, 1966, p. 874.

The Competitive World

American industry must compete in world markets with the industrial concerns of other nations. Furthermore, this world-wide competition is constantly growing more severe. In the decade following World War II, the reconstruction of the shattered economies of many nations produced formidable competitors for American concerns. Indeed, American foreign aid programs were committed to this goal of strengthening the economies of other nations.

As a result of the Treaty of Rome in 1957, the European Common Market was formed. This community of nations has developed sufficiently to provide American business with some of its strongest competition. As these six countries have reduced the tariff barriers that divided them, their economies have prospered. In addition, the rebuilding of industrial facilities that was necessary after the war—the new steel mills, for example—gave them a competitive edge over some older American plants.

In many cases, the net effect of this competition has been to place American concerns on the defensive. In pricing, American based world market prices are for the most part a thing of the past. Although world market prices of automobiles, steel, coal, oil, aluminum, and other major products were at one time based upon American prices, this structure began to collapse in 1959.[10]

In spite of stiffening foreign competition, however, the U.S. has succeeded in expanding exports and also in maintaining a favorable balance of trade. Continued success is dependent upon the efficiency of American industry. Manufactured products from the U.S. must be priced competitively, and this type of competition will demand continually rising productivity and declining unit labor costs. Business managers find it difficult to reduce many costs — for example, wage costs established by industry-wide contract. For any company, however, the degree of its internal operating efficiency determines its competitive strength in the market. As an example of proposals for strengthening the position of American firms, one leading consultant suggests concentration upon three or four products or activities rather than offering a full product line.[11]

The Domestic Market

The American business firm has no monopoly on business transacted in the U.S. German steel, Japanese radios, and French automobiles compete with American industry in its own home territory. Furthermore, this foreign competition in U.S. markets has expanded significantly during recent years, particularly in certain product areas. To illustrate the intensifying competition faced by some manufacturers, note the increasing imports evident in Table 2.

TABLE 2. Imports of Selected Commodities, 1958-1965

Commodity	1958 (Millions of Dollars)	1965 (Millions of Dollars)	Per Cent Increase
Electrical apparatus	167	639	283%
Iron and steelmill products	171	1,140	567
Nails, screws, and bolts	41	101	146
Clothing	174	543	212
Machinery	483	1,799	272

Source: *Statistical Abstract of the United States,* 1966, pp. 862-863.

[10]Peter F. Drucker, "This Competitive World," *Harvard Business Review,* Vol. 39, No. 2, March-April 1961, p. 132.

[11]*Ibid.,* p. 135.

The pressure of foreign competition in local markets leads to demands for protective tariffs. Although such tariffs can provide direct protection against low-price imports, the indirect effects are often undesirable. By eliminating "undesirable" imports, we choke off the market for other types of American exports.

The Committee for Economic Development has dealt with this conflict between individual interest and general advantages in liberalizing trade restrictions. The following statement reveals the difficulties involved and the steps suggested for combating the problem:

> A general decision to reduce tariff barriers should be agreed to by the United States and other industrial countries apart from and prior to the decision about tariff rates on particular commodities. U.S. experience has shown that if we start at the other end, and try to build up a package of tariff concessions by including all the specific reductions that seem desirable, and excluding all specific reductions that seem undesirable, we probably would not obtain the tariff concessions from others that we strongly desire. This is because, when we look at each case separately, the interests of the particular producer in not having that tariff reduced is clear but it always seems that the national interest in tariff reduction could be served by reducing something else. If we add together decisions made in such terms for each particular case we find that the general national interest has figured in the decisions little if at all. But if a general agreement to reduce tariffs is made first, adjustments and exceptions to take care of particular cases can be accommodated within it.[12]

Generally speaking, the U.S. has been committed to a program of relatively free trade. As a matter of fact, however, some protective features receive considerable emphasis. There are "peril point" and "escape clause" provisions, for example, in our trade agreements. For some business firms, tariff protection provides an advantage, but for others it constitutes a handicap. From an economic viewpoint, national welfare benefits from an expansion of foreign trade. This is not to deny, of course, the severe problems faced by particular industries and companies in facing foreign competition.

Rise of the Multi-National Corporation

Expansion of international business involves more than an expansion of the volume of foreign trade in the conventional sense. It is

---

[12] *A New Trade Policy for the United States,* Committee for Economic Development, New York, April 1962, p. 15. For another discussion of foreign trade and investment, by a leading corporate executive, see "United States Foreign Trade and Investment in a Changing World," a speech by M. J. Rathbone, President, Standard Oil Company (New Jersey), before The Economic Club of Detroit, April 9, 1962.

true that U. S. corporations are increasing exports to other nations and that foreign business firms are expanding sales in the U. S. market. A more important development during the past decade, however, has been the growth of multi-national corporations — firms that straddle international boundaries.

The domestic corporation engaged in foreign trade carries out its foreign business as a part of its total sales activities. The multinational corporation, on the other hand, may establish production facilities and research centers in two or more countries. It is this type of firm that has accounted for most of the increased involvement of U. S. firms in international business. Nearly 3,000 American firms now have foreign subsidiaries, and their sales are double the volume of United States exports.[13] Many companies, moreover, earn a substantial share of their profits from foreign operations. In 1960, for example, 14 per cent of General Motors' profits, 40 per cent of Pfizer's profits, 60 per cent of National Cash Register's profits, and 80 per cent of Heinz's profits resulted from foreign operations.[14]

The Standard Oil Company of New Jersey provides an excellent example of the multi-national firm.[15] With 48 per cent of its assets and 59 per cent of its profits abroad, Jersey Standard is directly concerned with the economic and political postures of some 100 countries. Its executive vice president, Emilo G. Collado, has a rich background of experience in international monetary and political affairs, having served, for example, as the first U. S. Executive Director of the World Bank. It is not difficult to visualize the need of this company to keep abreast of international developments. Jersey Standard's concern with government policies that would curb U. S. investment overseas illustrates the type of politico-economic issues confronting such a multi-national firm. In fact, Collado appeared before a U. S. Senate international finance subcommittee to discuss the significance of overseas investment as it is related to the U. S. balance-of-payments problem.

The growing emphasis upon international business forces American managers to understand and work with cultural patterns that differ from our own. Chapter 16 examines these cultural variations in some detail and considers their implications for the manager.

---

[13] Martyn Howe, *International Business* (New York: The Free Press, 1964), p. 1.

[14] *Ibid.*, pp. 44-45.

[15] "A Statesman in the Boardroom," *Business Week,* No. 1943, November 26, 1966, pp. 186-190.

International Business and International Relations

Business and its management are not passive bystanders in the global struggle between East and West. Such conflict inevitably involves economic and industrial factors. Some American business firms were expected to contribute supplies to ransom Cuban prisoners. The right of American corporations to trade with Communist nations is restricted. American business is expected to play a leading role in investment in the underdeveloped countries.

The proper role of private business in international development is most complex. The relationships between government and business in underdeveloped areas differ from the patterns in highly industrialized countries. There is general agreement, however, regarding the important contribution that can be made through private foreign investment—either on an exclusive control or joint venture basis.

> The role of foreign private investment, especially direct investment, as one of the great engines of economic growth, has been amply documented in recent years. It can play an especially important part in helping to develop a strong domestic private sector—in fostering local entrepreneurship, local skills, and a local sense of participation in a growing economic system.[16]

To the extent that foreign private business does have such a constructive effect, private business corporations can contribute directly to the achievement of the goals of American foreign policy. On the other hand, irresponsible behavior of U.S. corporations in other parts of the world will only strengthen the image of the "ugly American."

The Impact of Technological Change

Rapid Advancement in Scientific Knowledge

The present age is an exciting one from the standpoint of increasing scientific knowledge. Discoveries in "pure" science have extended man's knowledge of the world in which he lives, and applications of this knowledge have provided the means for a more comfortable (as

---

[16]Lincoln Gordon, "Private Enterprise & International Development," *Harvard Business Review,* Vol. 38, No. 4, July-August 1960, p. 138.

well as an admittedly more dangerous) life. Even within the lifetime of those living now, there have been the invention of the airplane, the discovery of nuclear energy, and the introduction of space flight. Knowledge has not only increased, but it has increased at an accelerated rate. Much greater progress, for example, was made in the last decade than occurred during the first decade of the century.

Such advancement in scientific knowledge affects business organizations in many ways. The very structure of industry itself may be altered. Completely new companies and industries make their appearance. Think of the impact of space technology on various geographical areas and industries. Established companies attempt to get into space technology, and new space-age companies appear. In some industries — chemicals and drugs, for example — new discoveries and developments constitute major elements of competition, and huge research budgets are typical. Greater scientific knowledge also affects the technology of industry. The methods of production do not stand still, but reflect the discoveries of the scientific laboratory.

The same discoveries that make it an exciting world, then, also make it a bewildering world. Scientific advancements provide both threats and opportunities. Indeed, technological change contributes to and is a part of the other environmental features discussed in this chapter. Certainly technological change makes it difficult for managers to relax and maintain the status quo. And the tempo of development is such that the business, its methods, and its personnel may be obsolete before management appreciates the significance of the change.

Increasing Mechanization

Since the beginning of the Industrial Revolution, business firms have increasingly mechanized their operations. Through the years, the investment in tools and equipment per worker has grown larger and larger. The substitution of other forms of power for manpower and the installation and improvement of machinery and equipment have combined to increase output per employee and to raise the standard of living for the country generally. In this country particularly, high labor costs have also encouraged the introduction of labor-saving equipment.

In almost every field of industry, improvements are being made in the way of greater mechanization. In 1966, for example, the

American Machine and Foundry Company installed a highly automated kitchen system in a Minneapolis drive-in — the first of many contemplated installations.[17] The system includes a hamburger machine that cooks single or double patties or cheeseburgers, mating them with toasted buns and wrapping each one in plastic; an entree fryer that drops seafood or other main courses into paper boats; and automated equipment to produce french fries, frankfurters, three flavors of milk shakes, and four types of soft drinks. The system is operated by an employee who enters orders into the keyboard of an electronic control unit. The system can hourly dish out 400 hamburgers, 400 franks, 360 servings of french fries, 175 orders of fried chicken, seafood, or onion rings, plus hundreds of malts and cold drinks.

Warehousing is another area that has seen numerous developments in the handling and storage of material. A recently-constructed Genesco distribution warehouse at Nashville, Tennessee, can receive as many as 50,000 pairs of shoes in one day and ship in one eight-hour shift up to 40,000 pairs to 1,500 dealers.[18] If the system gets an order on the weekend, it can report confirmed shipping information back to the customer on Monday. Management knows at all times just how many shoes are in stock, how many on order, and their exact location in the warehouse. Fewer than sixty employees are required to operate the system. The economy and effectiveness of the system are explained by the automatic conveyors, elevators, on-line computer, and other specialized components of the system.

Every shoe box has stapled to it an IBM identification card. This card is punched when the shoe is ordered, stays with the box until the shoes are sold, and then becomes an automatic re-order form. When shoes are brought by conveyor from the storage area to fill customer orders, a special purpose computer reads the IBM card on each box with a specially built reader. At an incredible speed of more than one box a second, the computer identifies shoe size and style, scans its memory to find an order that needs such an item, assigns the box to one of 170 spur conveyors, shunts the box off onto that conveyor, and prints on the IBM card the customer order number. Each conveyor spur gets one customer's order, and packers move from spur to spur, preparing orders for shipment.

---

[17]"Robot Dons Chef's Hat to Speed Up Burgers," *Business Week,* No. 1912, April 23, 1966, p. 42.

[18]"A Computer Ships the Shoes," *Business Week,* No. 1819, July 11, 1964, pp. 96-102.

Pervasive Effects of Technological Change

It may appear that technological changes are isolated events with little practical significance for the typical company. For many companies, however, changes in facilities occur continuously. The pervasive effects of technology upon a single, large corporation are illustrated by a sampling of Du Pont's major modernization projects on a single day in the fall of 1961:

> At Circleville, Ohio, a coating tower was being replaced; at Old Hickory, Tenn., a coal pulverizer and burner was making way for a newer one; the Seaford, Del., nylon plant was in the process of being rebuilt, practically from the ground up; at the Chambers Works, in Deepwater, N.J., 50 modernization projects were underway; at Orange, Texas, six were in progress.[19]

In illustrating the modernization of facilities, Du Pont Vice President Robert L. Hershey referred to the Belle Works near Charleston, West Virginia, one of the first synthetic ammonia plants in the United States.

> Originally, it used coal as the starting point for the whole process. Today, the technology in the field has moved well beyond coal. Now natural gas is the best raw material and so much more economical than coal that we found that if we didn't convert the Belle Works to the use of gas, the plant literally would have to go out of business.[20]

The Goal of Automation

The ultimate goal of mechanization is the completely automatic plant, and occasionally a particular operation — the manufacture of hamburgers, for example — approaches this degree of automation. The Robertshaw Controls Company now manufactures controls that will completely automate a remote pipeline pressure booster station. With no one within eighty miles to man the compressor station, its job of boosting gas pipeline capacity by some forty million cubic feet a day is managed by the company's pneumatic engine control system. The controls perform all steps needed to stop or start the big gas engines. They monitor everything from cooling to fluid level to vibration. In case of serious malfunctioning, they shut down the

---

[19] "The 'Desperate Race Against Obsolescence,' " *Better Living,* January-February 1962, p. 1.

[20] *Ibid.,* p. 2.

engine and send an "SOS" to faraway headquarters to head off any drop in pipeline service.

As a practical matter, most production processes have not yet come close to that stage of complete automation. Movement toward automation is proceeding at a rapid pace, however. It is certainly a matter of immediate and critical interest in American industry.

Effects of Automation Upon Labor

As a result of technological advancement, employees have earned higher wages, giving them a higher standard of living and providing the dollars to purchase the greater output of more efficient industrial concerns. However, a problem of technological unemployment has also accompanied the mechanization of production processes. As an immediate effect, the introduction of machinery has often eliminated jobs. In some cases, workers have rebelled—even by physically destroying the machines that threatened their jobs. The loss of jobs is very real to workers who are directly involved in the process of mechanization.

At least some of the unemployment of the early 1960's seemed to result from changes in production technology. In 1960, for example, the automobile industry produced 64 per cent more vehicles than in 1947 but employed 5.5 per cent fewer workers.[21] This development in the automobile industry was blamed for at least part of the unemployment problem in the state of Michigan. The problem appeared much less acute, however, when substantially full employment accompanied the national prosperity of the mid 1960's.

It is inevitable that there should be employment changes resulting from technological advances. In the past, the economy has been able to adjust adequately to avoid a severe problem of technological unemployment. Workers thrown out of employment in one industry or company have been absorbed by another. In many cases, the very corporations introducing greater mechanization have managed through transfer and retraining to avoid layoffs. Of course, there have been the inevitable situations of localities and individuals in which immediate re-employment was impossible.

Technological unemployment is regarded by many as a particularly thorny and significant problem. In 1966, the National Com-

[21]"UAW Heats up Automation Issue," *Business Week,* No. 1647, March 25, 1961, p. 45. See also, "Special Report: Automation," *Forbes,* Vol. 91, No. 11, June 1, 1963, pp. 27-30.

mission on Technology, Automation, and Economic Progress—whose distinguished membership included management, labor, academic, and public figures appointed by the President pursuant to Public Law 88-444—reported on the economic and social implications of technological change.[22] In general, this report viewed optimistically the ability of the economy to adjust satisfactorily to current and anticipated technological change. Although the commission recognized that technological change causes unemployment of particular persons in particular occupations, industries, and locations, they found no evidence that there will be in the decade ahead an acceleration in technological change more rapid than the growth of demand can offset, given adequate public policies. The excessive unemployment following the Korean War was attributed to an economic growth rate too slow to offset the combined impact of a productivity increase and a growing labor force.

Development of Information Technology

The traditional approach to solution of business problems has placed considerable reliance upon the judgment of the manager. Possibilities for use of the scientific method have not always been recognized. In fact, many managers have lacked professional training with its stress upon investigation of the facts of the situation. Instead, managers have been inclined to fall back upon intuition and hunch in the solution of problems confronting them. Even when managers desired to use the scientific method, many factors were not subject to quantification. Or the labor required in scientific problem solution made it impractical. As a result, managers often used their judgment even though they recognized the potential advantages of a scientific approach.

Great strides are being made currently in the utilization of electronic computers and the application of mathematical and scientific techniques in the solution of business problems. Developments in this area have been described as *information technology*. The following explanation may provide some understanding of the nature of this new technology:

> The new technology does not yet have a single established name. We shall call it *information technology*. It is composed of several related parts. One includes techniques for processing large

[22]National Commission on Technology, Automation, and Economic Progress, *Technology and the American Economy* (Washington: U. S. Government Printing Office, 1966).

> amounts of information rapidly, and it is epitomized by the high-speed computer. A second part centers around the application of statistical and mathematical methods to decision-making problems; it is represented by techniques like mathematical programming, and by methodologies like operations research.[23]

One of its significant achievements thus far has been the analysis of large amounts of data with sufficient speed to improve and speed up the decision-making process. Rather than waiting weeks for a report, the manager has it available immediately. Information technology emphasizes quantification, requiring assumptions and judgments to be made explicit. The decision process can thus be improved through the use of information technology by allowing more data to be considered, a broader range of alternatives to be explored, greater speed of analysis, and a more comprehensive view of a decision's impact.

Numerous types of business problems are being solved by use of the new techniques. Although some mathematical approaches may be utilized without the electronic computer, the computer is basic and is used in most of the newer methods. The following summary, which appeared in June 1957, shows the diverse types of problems being subjected to computer analysis by leading companies:

> General Foods is using its computer to schedule shipping to minimize transportation costs.
>
> G.E.'s jet-engine plant outside Cincinnati is using a giant computer to simulate, mathematically, the design of planes still on the drawing boards, instead of making expensive and time-consuming models to test.
>
> The Texas Co. uses its computer to determine the optimum way to operate its big refineries. The computer tells managers in fifteen minutes how to get the most profit from the crude runs available that day, relative to demand for hundreds of refinery end products whose prices fluctuate daily.
>
> Lockheed Aircraft uses two big computers to predict labor, material, and parts requirements as far as six months ahead.[24]

The Challenge of Technological Change

Vice President Robert L. Hershey of Du Pont has referred to the "desperate race against obsolescence." His comments convey a

---

[23]Harold J. Leavitt and Thomas L. Whisler, "Management in the 1980's," *Harvard Business Review,* Vol. 36, No. 6, November-December 1958, p. 41.

[24]William B. Harris, "The Astonishing Computers," *Fortune,* Vol. 55, No. 6, June 1957, p. 137. Courtesy of *Fortune.*

feeling of urgency for management attention to technological developments.[25]

> Frankly, from the point of view of turning out our products at the lowest possible cost, management will want to do the same thing in the same way all the time. Set your dials and adjustments and step back, let the goods roll out forever. Change presents problems and disruption, raising unit costs. The best thing is to establish a routine and stick to it.
>
> There's only one thing wrong with this. . . . You'll be driven out of business. The truth is that the best product today can be the most unsatisfactory tomorrow. Improved technology will make your present operations obsolete and your product will not be able to satisfy the market. So you've got to change. Part of the skill in managing industrial production lies in maintaining the delicate balance between doing things in the same way, yet changing to keep up with, and ahead of, competitive technology.
>
> And I see no end to this rapid obsolescence of plant and equipment. The improvements will become more rapid, the costs greater, the changes in plant appearance and in the kinds of people working for Du Pont greater.

No doubt automation will have far-reaching effects on many aspects of management. Some of these effects are only dimly seen at present, while the shape of other changes is becoming more definite. Some feel pessimistic about management's ability to respond to the changing technology. The following statement reflects such an attitude:

> Frankly, I have little hope for many members of the current management generation. A few of them have not learned to use a telephone properly. Many have not learned to use a dictating machine. Practically none has learned to use a computer.[26]

It would appear that each of the management functions will be affected in some way.

In the future, the higher investment in facilities and equipment will place greater stress upon careful planning. Capital outlays must be planned wisely because of the great risk involved in commitments of this magnitude. Production must also be planned carefully to maximize productivity in the use of given facilities. The planning

---

[25]"The 'Desperate Race Against Obsolescence,' " *Better Living,* January-February 1962, pp. 2-3.

[26]Richard C. Raymond, "Betting on the New Technologies," in *Technological Planning on the Corporate Level,* ed. James R. Bright (Boston: Harvard University Graduate School of Business Administration, 1962), p. 21.

process itself should be aided by the greater amounts of information that can be made available through the new information technology.

Numerous changes and modifications in the organization will no doubt result from the process of automation. It appears that the nature of work flow in an automated plant creates pressures for organizational arrangements to facilitate this flow. It is possible that modifications may be required in traditional line and staff organization arrangements. The status of different management levels may also be changed somewhat. There have been predictions to the effect that middle management may decline in importance because of the feasibility of greater centralization of decision making.[27] Changes in management skills and abilities will also be necessary. It seems likely that greater technical knowledge and proficiency will be required of all management personnel.[28] This same requirement will also apply to many nonmanagerial positions.

Changes in personnel will call for different approaches in direction and motivation. Many routine jobs disappear as work is automated, and technical and scientific personnel achieve greater prominence in the organization. Direction of these personnel may require greater skill on the part of the manager. It also seems that direction will emphasize technical instructions and communications to a greater extent.

With regard to changes in the controlling function of management, vast amounts of control data can now be rapidly processed and made available to the manager. This should facilitate and improve the control function. At the same time, the investment in equipment and the nature of the process of automation will place great pressure upon the control system to assure maximum productivity with any particular installation.

In view of the pervasive effects of technological change, the present discussion of its impact on managerial functions must necessarily be merely introductory in nature. Many of the treatments of specific topics in later chapters will reflect this factor of technological change and deal more specifically with its significance in particular areas.[29]

---

[27]For example, see Harold J. Leavitt and Thomas L. Whisler, "Management in the 1980's," *Harvard Business Review,* Vol. 36, No. 6, November-December 1958, pp. 44-45.

[28]Walter Buckingham, *Automation: Its Impact on Business and People* (New York: Harper & Row, Publishers, 1961), pp. 62-63.

[29]For example, the relationship of technology to job design and to job satisfaction is discussed in Chapters 8 and 23, and the relationship of technological change to organizational adaptation is discussed in Chapter 13.

Summary

The assessment of broad and fundamental environmental factors such as those treated in this chapter is a formidable task. Books could be written on each topic. However, business managers function within this environment that imposes various pressures and constraints. Realism demands an awareness of its importance. One significant feature of this environment is the *growing influence of government* upon business. In many phases of managerial decision making, the factor of public policy must, directly or indirectly, be taken into consideration. Changing social and national problems have been at least partially responsible for this expanded role of government. To be realistic, management must recognize the forces leading to the expansion of government and governmental regulation. As a part of determining its response to this feature of its environment, management must define the scope and nature of its own *political role.*

International relations constitute another significant aspect of the changing business environment. American industry is facing strong and growing foreign competition both in domestic and world markets. In addition, privately owned business firms are expected to assist in the achievement of the goals of American foreign policy. International business has been rapidly expanding in recent years, and the multi-national firm with operations and facilities in two or more countries has accounted for most of this growth.

The trend toward *automation* forces corporate management to engage in almost constant change and modernization in order to avoid obsolescence and to remain competitive. One of the particularly difficult problems in this area concerns the *effects of technological change upon labor.* The increasing use of the *electronic computer* is another element of the advance in technology that directly affects the management process.

Discussion Questions

1. What nonpolitical factors might account for growth in the role of government in its relationship to business?

2. Does the existence of nonpolitical factors favoring expansion of governmental activity mean that the expansion will occur at the same rate during Republican and Democratic administrations?

3. Would corporate management be more critical of government control involving regulation of interest rates or of compulsory arbitration of labor disputes? Why?

4. How can a business corporation express itself politically without interfering with the political freedom of its employees?

5. What values for business exist in a free-trade policy? Do these same values hold for labor?

6. What is the relationship between the rate of mechanization and wage rates?

7. How may *information technology* affect management's planning and control functions?

8. Beginning about 1961, the U. S. Commerce Department began opening permanent U. S. trade centers in several major cities of the world such as London, Frankfurt, Milan, Bangkok, and Tokyo. According to Commerce Department plans, trade fairs at these centers will help to increase exports of U. S. products. Does this development constitute "more government in business"? What is likely to be the attitude of business managers toward the program?

9. Does it seem likely that relations between the steel industry and the government will continue to deteriorate as a result of the sharp price conflict in 1962?

Supplementary Reading

Aitken, Thomas, Jr., "Can Business Carry the Flag?" *Business Horizons*, Vol. 5, No. 4, Winter 1962, pp. 101-107.

Bright, James R., ed., *Technological Planning on the Corporate Level.* Boston: Harvard University Graduate School of Business Administration, 1962.

Champion, George, "Creative Competition," *Harvard Business Review*, Vol. 45, No. 3, May-June 1967, pp. 61-67.

Corson, John J., "More Government in Business," *Harvard Business Review*, Vol. 39, No. 3, May-June 1961, pp. 81-88.

Diebold, John, "Automation — Perceiving the Magnitude of the Problem," *Advanced Management Journal,* Vol. 29, No. 2, April 1964, pp. 29-33.

Fowler, Henry H., "National Interests and Multinational Business," *California Management Review,* Vol. 8, No. 1, Fall 1965, pp. 3-12.

Gordon, Lincoln, "Private Enterprise and International Development," *Harvard Business Review,* Vol. 38, No. 4, July-August 1960, pp. 134-138.

Hayden, Spencer, "Problems of Operating Overseas: A Survey of Company Experience," *Personnel,* Vol. 45, No. 1, January-February 1968, pp. 8-21.

"Is There a New Economy?" *Dun's Review and Modern Industry,* Vol. 85, No. 6, June 1965, pp. 38-41, 71-72.

Jacoby, Neil H., "Impacts of Scientific Change Upon Business Management," *California Management Review,* Vol. 4, No. 4, Summer 1962, pp. 31-43.

Jarett, Irwin M., "Electronics and the Management Art," *Advanced Management-Office Executive,* Vol. 1, No. 6, June 1962, pp. 7-10.

Kolde, Endel J., "Business Enterprise in a Global Context," *California Management Review,* Vol. 8, No. 4, Summer 1966, pp. 31-48.

National Commission on Technology, Automation, and Economic Progress, *Technology and the American Economy.* Washington: U. S. Government Printing Office, 1966.

Raymond, Jack, "Growing Threat of Our Military-Industrial Complex," *Harvard Business Review,* Vol. 46, No. 3, May-June 1968, pp. 53-64.

Rezler, Julius, "Managerial Functions in the Era of Automation," *Advanced Management Journal,* Vol. 29, No. 2, April 1964, pp. 57-65.

Seligman, Ben B., *Most Notorious Victory: Man in an Age of Automation.* New York: The Free Press, 1966.

Van Cise, Jerrold G., "Regulation—By Business or Government?" *Harvard Business Review,* Vol. 44, No. 2, March-April 1966, pp. 53-63.

Managerial Planning

4

Determining Objectives

Most human activity is purposeful in nature. Every organization, for example, is created and exists to accomplish some objective or objectives. Individual members of organizations also contribute their services because of their desire to achieve certain objectives. Such objectives may be visualized as targets or goals. These goals — those of the organization and its members — will be examined in this chapter, which opens our consideration of the planning function.

Nature and Purpose of Objectives

Nature of Objectives

Planning should begin with a consideration of the objectives or goals that the organization is attempting to achieve. Operational plans should be formulated and performance of the firm evaluated in accordance with these objectives. Clarity and consistency in objectives are essential for effective operation.

If there is only a vague and confused picture of goals, an organization or individual may stray from the most direct route to success. There is a danger of muddling along without objectives and progress. A high school graduate, for example, needs a strong sense of the importance of a college education and a real determination to acquire it if he is to avoid settling for something less! A business may similarly go along with no clear-cut picture of its future and experience disastrous results.

One major corporation, the American Viscose Corporation, was recently reported to be floundering without a long-range objective.

> "We're really in a bind," admits Chairman Frank Reichel. "There's no great growth potential in our main fields and we have no actual plans about setting a corporate goal."[1]

(The company was primarily a producer of viscose rayon and cellophane.)

Values of Carefully Formulated Objectives

Objectives provide a focus for policy making and for management decisions of other types. The various activities and policies — in production, sales, finance, and so on — should be directed to the achievement of these objectives. As an example, suppose that a chemical manufacturer desires to lead not only in the production of standard chemicals but also in research and the introduction of new products. The company's personnel policies and practices must provide for the recruitment and retention of creative scientists for its research laboratories. The financial planning of such a manufacturer must permit the investment of large amounts in research and facilities over a long period of time before a dollar is ever realized from these investments. Production planning must be sufficiently flexible and imaginative to adapt to new production techniques and to assist in the development of production processes for new products. Marketing personnel must be able to assess and develop markets to permit exploitation of new discoveries originating in the laboratory.

Clearly formulated objectives enable all parts of an organization to work toward the same goal. Production and sales departments need not work at cross purposes with each other if there is a common objective. If production policies call for a product of high quality, advertising will not stress price to the exclusion of quality. Nor will prices be set on the basis of a competitor's inferior line of products.

Clear objectives also encourage a consistency in management, planning, and decision making over a period of time. Long-run goals caution against action that is merely expedient in a short run. If, for example, a sizable company proposes to develop personnel strength

---

[1]"Company in Search of a Goal," *Forbes,* Vol. 88, No. 11, December 1, 1961, p. 12.

in research and general management, it should not vacillate greatly in this effort. A brief downturn in business cannot logically be permitted to eliminate recruitment and development programs that were attractive when business was good. Such short-run expendiencies could play havoc with programs of long-term value. Recognition of the goal thus provides a stabilizing force in month-to-month and year-to-year management decisions.

Objectives often exist in the thinking of management without being made explicit. Every organization obviously has some sort of goals that have brought it into existence and that keep it operating. The managers may never have verbalized these, however. Merely implicit recognition of goals involves the dangers of inconsistency, lack of coordination among departments, and temptation to compromise. If a student is not thoroughly committed to a college education, the attraction of a good job or marriage may easily side-track him.

Types of Objectives

Profit Objective of the Business

A sign on the wall of a neighborhood restaurant reads, "This is a nonprofit organization—although we didn't plan it that way!" A business organization never plans it "that way." The firm is in business to earn a profit. Profit is basic to the philosophy of the free enterprise system. Adam Smith saw profits as the device which transforms the selfishness of mankind into channels of useful service. "It is not from the benevolence of the butcher, the brewer, or the baker that we expect our dinner," wrote Adam Smith, "but from their regard to their self-interest. We address ourselves, not to their humanity, but to their self-love, and never talk to them of our necessities, but of their advantages."

Profits are observed carefully as a measure of the success of a business. They may be reported as a percentage of sales, a percentage of net worth, or in various other ways. If profits are growing, the business is generally regarded as healthy. If they are declining, a question exists as to the trend or future of the firm. Continued inability to earn satisfactory profits often portends a change in management. It is profits that constitute the acid test of management.

Expression of a profit objective does not imply a simple profit maximization rule, however. One must distinguish, for example, between short-run profits and long-run profits. Investments in research and development may increase long-term profits but reduce short-run profits. Moreover, the motivation of managers to maximize profits as well as their ability to do so has been questioned. Some have argued that business firms simply do not maximize profits.[2] Some of the criticisms of a simple profit maximization theory as an explanation of managerial behavior are as follows:

1. Profit maximization is impractical. To maximize profits, the manager must equate marginal revenue with marginal cost. This requires a large amount of information, such as the volume that could be sold at various prices and the marginal cost that would exist at different volume levels. However, the manager seldom if ever possesses the necessary information to accomplish this. In pricing, therefore, he often bases the price upon full cost estimates determined through cost accounting rather than upon marginal cost estimates.
2. Uncertainty as to the future makes it impossible to know which of various alternative courses of action will in fact maximize profits. Therefore, firms maximize profits only by chance even when they try to do so.
3. Business firms provide luxurious company offices and contribute to charitable organizations even though profits are reduced accordingly. If charitable contributions are made because of their indirect effect upon profits, as is often alleged, why do these contributions fall during recessions?
4. Managers often try to maximize sales or to acquire a specified share of the market even if the firm is less profitable by doing so.

These criticisms admit the profit goal but suggest modifications to it. The manager presumably seeks some reasonable or satisfactory rate of profit. It is not realistic, however, to assume that he is able to maximize profits in every situation or that he pursues this goal with complete disregard for all other considerations.

Profit goals are formulated as a guide for decision making. One example of the many measuring devices that may be used is the return on the firm's equity. The general objective is to optimize, in the long run, the average rate of return on equity. This objective

---

[2]A review of this controversy appears in Joseph W. McGuire, *Theories of Business Behavior* (Englewood Cliffs: Prentice-Hall, Inc., 1964), pp. 80-86; and in Richard M. Cyert and James G. March, *A Behavioral Theory of the Firm* (Englewood Cliffs: Prentice-Hall, Inc., 1963), Chapter 2.

provides a measure of top management's performance including its skill in the use of outside financing. Adoption of such an objective permits evaluation of new investment proposals. Such an evaluation would require the rejection of projects that might improve sales but fail to provide the desired return on equity.

Profit goals are typically the most explicitly formulated goals of the enterprise. In more detailed form, they comprise standards of performance for the management of the organization. The overall profit goal provides the basis for performance standards throughout the organization. The result is a hierarchy of objectives, culminating at lower levels in budgets for relatively short periods of time.

Attainment of the profit objective is essential for the health and growth of a business concern. Only a profitable business can expand, modernize, or even replace its capital equipment to continue operation. If the firm cannot show profits on its operations, investors are reluctant to invest additional funds in the enterprise. If the business were to experience financial losses over a period of time, the firm would eventually become bankrupt. An unprofitable firm is also a poor employer.

To achieve the profit goal, a business firm must consider additional subsidiary objectives. Goals with respect to the desired amount and rate of growth for the concern constitute one example. Other such objectives include the company's position in product development —whether it will push innovation or act as a follower. The business firm must also establish objectives for production, marketing, financial, and related programs.

Service Objective of the Business

Emphasis upon the profit objective tends to obscure the existence of other goals of the enterprise. Every business has another objective that it must accomplish, however, in order to make its sales and realize its profits. An electric utility must supply electricity to justify the dollars of the utility customers. A manufacturer produces some physical product of value to other business firms or to ultimate consumers. An insurance company provides protection. Marketing institutions transport and store products and arrange for the transfer of ownership. Each type of business firm thus performs some useful function that is desired by its customers.

This objective appears clear as we think of the business organization from the standpoint of society. Our society permits the existence of organizations that are harmless or that perform some constructive role. It prohibits or outlaws organizations whose functions are considered detrimental to society. The opium den, for example, is not a legitimate business institution in the United States. Business organizations have a claim to existence because of their contribution of goods or services.

The service objective exists not only in this general sense — the goal of providing *some* useful product or service — but is given specific form as a firm chooses the particular combination of goods and services it will produce. These specific choices of a service objective or objectives are often critical in determining success or failure. The Borden Company's record as the most profitable major dairy company in 1962 (although second in sales volume) has been attributed to two specific decisions affecting its service objectives.[3] About 1937, the company decided to diversify geographically and began building plants overseas for its powdered milk. At about the same time, a second decision led to substantial product diversification. Borden at that time made casein, a milk product used for adhesives. But synthetics threatened this market, and Borden needed to decide whether to go into synthetic adhesives or to get out of the adhesives area. It decided to stay in adhesives and branched out into formaldehyde, a basic component of an adhesive for plywood. As a result of these decisions, Borden emerged from World War II with a foothold in two fields having explosive growth potential — foreign markets and chemicals. Its greater profitability in 1962 appeared to result from this choice of objectives.

Careful formulation of overall business strategy is essential for survival and growth and deserves the close attention of top management. Otherwise, changes in the environment and industry may leave the company without a successful business. The problem is complicated by the fact that problems in basic business strategy are often obscured by more pressing current problems. In pursuing operating efficiency, management may fail to observe the decline in its industry or the need to develop new products.

> By contrast, strategic decisions are not self-regenerative; they make no automatic claims on top management attention. Unless actively pursued, they may remain hidden behind the operations problems. Firms are generally very slow in recognizing conditions under which concern with the operating problem must give way to a concern with the strategic.[4]

---

[3]"Borden Beats the Rule of Two," *Forbes,* Vol. 91, No. 5, March 1, 1963, p. 20.

[4]H. Igor Ansoff, *Corporate Strategy* (New York: McGraw-Hill Book Company, 1965), p. 9.

This suggests the need for an aggressive and objective attitude on the part of management in selecting and scrutinizing long-run service objectives.

Of course, decisions concerning the service objective affect not only the nature of the product line but also qualitative aspects of products and services supplied to customers. Business concerns differ in the importance they attach to service objectives. All business firms have at least some awareness of their significance. This does not imply altruism on the part of the business firm but merely reflects the self-interest of the firm. It is necessary for survival. Because of the nature of the business, the weakness of management, or the lack of competition, however, some organizations give only minimum attention to the service role. Others consider it of critical importance and stress it as the key to business success. They often go to extreme lengths in their service for particular customers. Some manufacturers of industrial equipment, for example, make elaborate studies of systems and problems of industrial customers, adapting equipment when necesssary to meet the peculiar needs of individual customers.

Social Objectives of the Business

The service objective discussed above is one type of social objective. There is a much broader sense, however, in which one may think of social objectives. The business corporation may recognize goals with reference to the community or the general public going far beyond the customers of the business. The *social responsibility* of business, as it is often termed, implies a sense of obligation on the part of the business toward the general public. This takes various forms and involves such areas as educational and philanthropic projects, community planning, government service, and general operation in conformity with the public interest.

Social responsibility of business has become a matter of evident concern on the part of many business leaders. Business periodicals carry frequent articles dealing with the concept of the businessman's social responsibility. Some are merely for a cheap type of public relations value, but others seem to indicate a genuine concern on the part of business leaders. There are, no doubt, numerous factors contributing to this apparently growing interest concerning social obligations. The corporation's weakened ties with stockholders and the professionalization of management both contribute to the emphasis on objectives of this type. In many areas, business shutdowns, layoffs, and relocations have significantly affected public thinking regarding the responsibility of business firms. The corporate manager often finds that the expectations of the public and the employees are presented to him as forcefully as are the expectations of stockholders. The pressure or threat of pressure in terms of government regulation and union activity is often in the background.

One example of social responsibility in action is found in the reconstruction of the downtown area of Pittsburgh.

> According to the folklore of the city, this enterprise was actually sparked when General Richard Mellon, back in town after several years' absence during World War II, awoke in his hotel room the first morning and looked out the window. He was appalled by what he saw: a city that was so smoky the lights had to be left burning at midday. "I had forgotten how bad this is," he is reported to have said. "Something is going to have to be done."
>
> So he enlisted Van Buskirk in the effort, and the Allegheny Conference on Community Development was formed. This group, made up primarily of business leaders, was designed to supply the muscle to implement the ideas and technical know-how which already had been developed over some years by the Pittsburgh Regional Planning Association. Without the power plant represented by the Conference, the possibilities in Pittsburgh remained simply sketches on a shelf, ideas in a planner's mind.[5]

"Business responsibility" is a rather glib phrase, but in many cases the relationship between business operations and the public interest is indeed complex. The very size of corporations, for example, is a matter of public concern. If they grow too large to be most effective economically, the public interest is sacrificed. Or they may grow too large to guarantee management practices in accordance with the public interest. This possibility is suggested by the professed innocence of top corporate executives in the Westinghouse-General Electric price-fixing conspiracy. The optimum size of a corporation is difficult to determine, but the public interest does dictate some limit at the point where size leads to restraint of trade or results in inefficiency in management.

---

[5]Edward C. Bursk, "Your Company and Your Community: The Lessons of Pittsburgh," in *Business Responsibility in Action,* ed. D. H. Fenn (New York: McGraw-Hill Book Company, 1960), pp. 31-32.

> Quite a few people who otherwise are clearly "pro business" would even argue that a business better be split up when it gets so big that "what is good for the company is good for the country." This, they would say, is too big for a company's freedom of economic action; and, further, the country's welfare should not depend so much on the fortunes of one private enterprise and on the decisions of one group of executives.
>
> As time erodes the public memory of the GE-Westinghouse affair, the public may also forget its concern with the limits of manageability which the affair pointed out. But big-business executives better remember it — and do their homework on it.[6]

This does not constitute a criticism of bigness *per se*. It simply notes that bigness may, in a given case, involve a threat to the public interest.

Justification for a sense of social responsibility on the part of business is grounded in the freedom accorded to business by society. Not all societies permit private enterprises to function freely, and society may expect, in return for this consideration, a performance consistent with general social goals.

> I think it is important to remember that the American economy does not belong to the stockholders of corporations, nor to any corporation, all corporations, or all property owners in the country. The American economy belongs to the people of the United States. The people who constitute management in the United States hold their jobs in particular companies because the board of directors has selected them to fill those jobs. But they hold their jobs as managers of the American economy because the people of America still trust private management to operate the American economy.[7]

There may be a price in ignoring the existence of social responsibilities. Although businessmen are at times tempted to concentrate upon the profit objective to the exclusion of service and social objectives, this path can lead to difficulty. There is always the threat of government control in the background. To the extent that business management fails to meet the expectations of society, it is possible that these obligations may be forced upon them. In recognizing

[6]Peter F. Drucker, "Big Business and the National Purpose," *Harvard Business Review*, Vol. 40, No. 2, March-April 1962, p. 56.

[7]Alexander R. Heron, "How Responsible Can Management Be?" *Advanced Management*, November 1954, p. 7.

social responsibilities, then, management is not necessarily disregarding the best interests of business owners.

> They are reacting prudently to the collective needs of the enterprise for which they are responsible. Their responsibility to the owners of corporate property is not side-stepped when they recognize duties to others who contribute to the well-being of the enterprise. A prudent regard for *all* the interests that merge in making the business a going concern now and in the future is, in fact, the only way to protect and to augment shareholder equity.[8]

Conflict or Harmony in Business Objectives

In the ideal world of perfect competition, profits could be realized only by meticulous regard for the service and social objectives of a business. Dollars of customers would go to the firms that best met the customers' desires for goods and services. As a matter of fact, however, the economy is not that competitive. Business concerns may occasionally profit at the expense of the customer. Business organizations may also, at least in the short run, disregard the social consequences of their actions. In the absence of specific statutes, they may pollute streams or manipulate employees. They may also neglect community planning and refuse to support educational and charitable endeavors. To some degree, then, business management has a choice regarding objectives. Service and social goals are not achieved automatically on the basis of earning a profit.

To some extent, of course, there is a natural harmony or consistency among the goals of the business enterprise. Flagrant disregard of customer wishes would lose business or lead to the emergence of new competition. A callous disregard of social values might prejudice customers and employees against the firm. Some regard for social objectives, therefore, is simply good business.

It would simplify matters greatly if this consistency of goals were always real and evident. Unfortunately, the world is a bit more complex. It is possible to be successful with any of several different degrees of social conscience. Management is confronted with some range of alternative behavior and must choose the extent to which various, sometimes conflicting, goals will be recognized.

What, then, is the controlling objective? Must profit be regarded as the basic or primary goal and all conflict resolved in favor of the

---

[8]Richard Eells, "Social Responsibility: Can Business Survive the Challenge?" *Business Horizons,* Vol. 2, No. 4, Winter 1959, p. 41.

profit objective? "The governing rule in industry," according to one critic of the social responsibility doctrine, "should be that *something is good only if it pays*."[9] This seems to have a natural appeal, at least in theory, to businessmen who are accustomed to emphasizing the profit objective. Such statements as the following have the appearance of old-fashioned honesty:

> The objective of executive development for the sake of the individual executive is pure balderdash. The real objective of executive development is increasing profitability of the company.

But even some managers who say that profits provide the criterion for decision may be found making administrative decisions on the basis of what appears to be human or social considerations. If questioned, they may rationalize on the basis of profits, but it seems doubtful that profit is always uppermost in the mind.

This raises a question as to whether managers are, or should be, motivated by a single goal, namely profits. Should all social responsibility be evaluated in terms of either short-run or long-run effect on profits? A somewhat different view of multiple objectives has been suggested by Mary Parker Follett. It is her contention that individuals are constantly resolving conflicting objectives, rather than consistently subordinating one objective to another.

> When people talk of substituting the service motive for the profit motive I always want to ask: Why this wish to simplify motive when there is nothing more complex? Take any one of our actions today and examine it. There probably have been several motives for it. It is true that if anyone asked you why you did so and so, you would probably pick out to present to the public the motive which you thought did you the most credit. But the fact of the actual complexity remains. We work for profit, for service, for our own development, for the love of creating something. . . . The professions have not given up the money motive. I do not care how often you see it stated that they have. Professional men are eager enough for large incomes; but they have other motives as well, and they are often willing to sacrifice a good slice of income for the sake of these other things.[10]

Perhaps the dilemma can be resolved by granting the existence of varied corporate goals. Some of these are consistent with each

---

[9]Theodore Levitt, "The Dangers of Social Responsibility," *Harvard Business Review,* Vol. 36, No. 5, September-October 1958, p. 48.

[10]Mary Parker Follett, "When Business Management Becomes a Profession," *Advanced Management,* July 1955, p. 26.

other and reinforcing in nature. Others involve potential conflict. Within each area, however, there is a varying degree of fulfillment which is acceptable.

If the corporation's economic goal is accepted as the starting point, other goals can be visualized as constraining and influencing its formulation. The profit goal is subject to the constraint of corporate citizenship — the social objective. It may be modified to the extent that the social objective is recognized or given priority. Personal goals of individual participants likewise influence the firm's economic objective as will be seen in the following section.

Decisions requiring the reconciliation of goals may well be troublesome. Even if decisions are theoretically made on the basis of profits, the profit effect of various actions in the social sphere is not always clear. If a course of action is to be considered without direct regard for profit implications, the manager's problem is even more perplexing. Suppose a contribution is to be made to higher education. How much should be given? What guides can be used in such decisions? This type of decision is certainly one of the dilemmas confronting modern management.

Personal Objectives

Profit, service, and social objectives might be thought of as goals of the business firm. In addition, individual members of organizations — those contributing capital and services — have objectives that induce them to make their respective contributions. These individuals are "stakeholders" in the firm — that is, individuals whose lives and welfare are affected by the corporation and its activities. Stockholders and employees, including managerial personnel, are obvious stakeholders, but suppliers and customers likewise have a stake in corporate decisions.

Some writers have been so impressed with the significance of individual goals that they see corporate objectives as a composite of individual objectives. Corporate goals are visualized as the "negotiated consensus" of objectives of influential individual participants.

> We have argued that the goals of a business firm are a series of more or less independent constraints imposed on the organization through a process of bargaining among potential coalition members and elaborated over time in response to short-run pressures. Goals arise in such a form because the firm is, in fact, a coalition of participants with disparate demands, chang-

> ing foci of attention, and limited ability to attend to all organizational problems simultaneously.[11]

Most members of business organizations are motivated to some extent by financial rewards. Stockholders expect dividends, and managers work for salaries, bonuses, stock options, and other financial inducements. Not all goals of organization members are financial in nature, however. Each individual has different needs or objectives, some of which may be satisfied through affiliation with a particular organization. Some needs, for example, are social in nature and are satisfied through associations provided in the organization. Other needs, such as the desire for accomplishment or for doing something worthwhile, are individual and may also be satisfied through work. It seems that many executives are motivated more by a drive for achievement than by financial rewards.

The objectives of stakeholders in the organization are diverse to some extent, both among classes of participants and among individuals. The stockholder's concern with earnings and dividends contrasts with the manager's desire for a maximum salary and bonus. Among stockholders, moreover, preferences vary as to stability of earnings, riskiness in corporate investments, and dividend rate. Some managers, youthful and eager to achieve preeminence in business careers, may favor aggressive and venturesome corporate strategy. Other managers, older and nearing retirement, may prefer conservative decisions and policies that will preserve the business without "rocking the boat." Each participant tries to realize his personal goals through the corporation, and, to the extent of his power, attempts to influence corporate decisions accordingly.

The relationship of the firm with its employees and owners, then, entails some integration of business and personal objectives. By contributing to the achievement of organizational goals, the individual is able to realize his own personal objectives. An obvious question concerns the degree of congruence between such personal goals and organizational goals. Is the decision or strategy that satisfies a particular stakeholder's personal objectives also most satisfactory for the total organization? It is clear that perfect integration of personal and business objectives is not always achieved. Social approval in the work group, for example, may require an antagonistic attitude toward the company and curtailment of production. Enthu-

---

[11]Richard M. Cyert and James G. March, *A Behavioral Theory of the Firm*, ©1963, p. 43. By permission of Prentice-Hall, Inc., Englewood Cliffs, New Jersey.

siastic effort, on the other hand, is a mark of successful integration of personal and business objectives. Some organizations attempt to promote this condition by profit sharing or other incentive schemes that link individual financial rewards directly to organization gains.

In large corporations operating under imperfect competition, managers are the most influential participants. Although the minimum demands of all groups must be satisfied, the management group typically has some latitude in resolving the conflicting demands of participants, including their own.

> From this viewpoint, management emerges as the chief member of the coalition; its role as the coordinating and initiating agent as well as its preferred access to information permit it quite naturally to assume this primacy position. Thus, although in certain circumstances it may be necessary to give special attention to shifts in demands made by members of the coalition other than managers, under "normal" conditions it may be entirely appropriate to take the demands of the other members (for wages, profits, product, and so forth) as *given* and leave to the discretion of the management the operation of the firm in some best sense.[12]

In view of management's key role in resolving the welter of interests in the corporation, their own interests become of paramount importance. Can it be assumed that managers operate in the stockholder's interest in some profit-maximizing way? The assumption that firms always maximize profits has been challenged, as indicated in the preceding section. The following comments on managerial motivation further question his profit-maximizing inclinations:

> Our departure from the conventional view of the firm is in the assumption of what is "best." Traditionally, this requires that managers choose to operate the firm in a stewardship sense of attending to the stockholders' best interest by maximizing profits. The behavioral model proposes that managers operate the firm in the only fashion consistent with the assumption of self-interest seeking — in their *own* best interests.[13]

Managers can exercise some discretion in resolving conflicting interests because of the imperfect nature of competition and the existence of *organizational slack*.[14] *Organizational slack* refers to the

---

[12]O. E. Williamson, "A Model of Rational Managerial Behavior," in Cyert and March, *op. cit.*, pp. 240-241.

[13]*Ibid.*, p. 241.

[14]Richard M. Cyert and James G. March, *A Behavioral Theory of the Firm*, © 1963, pp. 36-38. By permission of Prentice-Hall, Inc., Englewood Cliffs, New Jersey.

disparity between the resources available and the payments required to retain the services of organization members. Slack exists when payments to members exceed the amount required to maintain the organization. Stockholders may receive larger dividends than necessary to keep them as stockholders, and executives may enjoy luxuries in excess of those required to retain their services. This means that managers may work out solutions that are reasonably satisfactory to the various participants. As long as the minimum demands of each group are satisfied, management is free to vary the degree of recognition accorded to each group.

In summary, objectives of individual participants are influential in determining corporate objectives. Some integration of these individual goals with corporate goals is essential for effective cooperation, but a perfect harmony of individual and business goals is seldom achieved. In large corporations, top management officials play a key role in resolving these conflicting interests, including their own, and achieving a workable compromise. The manager has some freedom in working out the blend of individual goals, because the possible inducements for all participants typically exceed the minimum inducements required. This slack permits the manager to discover solutions that satisfy minimum expectations of each group.

Ethics in Management

Ethics and Business Activity

Business activity, as a part of life, poses ethical problems for management. And, although these are decisions of the business firm, the ethical problems become personal problems for the administrator. In his decision making, the executive is influenced by his own standards of what is right or wrong.

> *Character,* one of the greatest words in the English language, defies both analysis and definition. Yet no talent for administration, however brilliant, can long endure in a man without it. The fine executive invariably possesses a code of values which he himself has established.[15]

Ethical considerations in the business organization are important to managers as individuals. Personal life and business life cannot be neatly compartmentalized with respect to moral judgments. A

[15]Clarence B. Randall, "The Making of an Administrator," *Dun's Review and Modern Industry*, Vol. 80, No. 3, September 1962, p. 47.

number of factors have been suggested as important in making ethical questions a central concern of administrators.

> (1) For the individual the job is the center of life, and its values must be in harmony with the rest of life if he is to be a whole and healthy personality.
>
> (2) This is an industrial society, and its values tend to become those of the entire culture.
>
> (3) The public is insisting that business leaders are in fact responsible for the general social welfare — that the manager's responsibilities go far beyond those of running the business. They have delegated this responsibility to the business executive whether he wishes to play this role or not.
>
> (4) Even if the administrator insists on a narrow definition of his function as merely the production of goods and services as efficiently as possible, it is nevertheless essential that he take these intangibles into account since they are the real secrets of motivating an organization.
>
> (5) Besides all this the administrator needs a better set of "skyhooks" himself if he is to carry his ever-increasing load of responsibility without cracking up. The fact that so many administrators are taking time to rationalize, defend, and justify the private enterprise system is an outward indication of this need for more significant meanings.[16]

Current Ethical Problems and Management Attitudes

A brief reading of the business news of the day is sufficient to reveal many examples of current ethical problems in the business world. Although the type of ethical problem in the news changes from month to month and year to year, there is always an abundance of such difficulties. Recent or current examples include price fixing, deceptive advertising, padding of expense accounts, conflict of interest cases, "insider" trading in the stock market, and slanted oil wells.

In view of the personal nature of ethical standards, it is not surprising to discover wide differences of opinion regarding ethical issues. What is accepted as ethical behavior by one manager is viewed as unacceptable by another. The nature of the issue, of course, determines the extent of agreement.

---

[16]O. A. Ohmann, "'Skyhooks' With Special Implications for Monday Through Friday," *Harvard Business Review,* Vol. 33, No. 3, May-June 1955, p. 36.

Consider the following question: Is it wrong for a $10,000-a-year executive to pad his expense account for about $500 a year? In a survey of some 1,700 *Harvard Business Review* executive readers, 86 per cent considered this unacceptable regardless of the circumstances.[17] Six per cent felt it was acceptable if other executives did the same thing, while still others approved if the executive's superior knew about it but did nothing.

Another type of situation might involve the inside knowledge of a large corporation board member concerning the impending merger of a smaller company. The stock of the smaller company is selling so low that public news of the merger will almost certainly cause it to rise. Should you, the director, buy some stock for yourself? In the survey cited above, 42 per cent said "yes," and only 56 per cent said they would "do nothing" — that is, not even tell a good friend or a broker.[18] These responses reveal the evident disagreement of business executives concerning the ethical aspects of business behavior. There is no universally accepted set of "ten commandments" applying to many of the practical issues confronting administrators.

Levels of Business Ethics

Numerous examples can be cited of practices involving high standards of ethical conduct. Business firms stand behind their products and services — a practice that differs rather sharply from the standards of an earlier era. There has been considerable elimination of the "let the buyer beware" atmosphere and a revealing of facts concerning products being sold. Numerous companies have adopted fair employment practices and seek to observe high standards in their treatment of employees. The fact that these steps frequently create favorable business results does not detract from their ethical quality.

On the other hand, some observers are still impressed with the fact that there is a rather low level of ethics and morality prevailing throughout the business world. As they see it, there is considerable opportunism and self-seeking rather than the high ethical values that we like to think prevail. One industrial vice president has expressed the following observations of the business scene:

> There is no disemboweling of men or stretching them on a rack. That would be preferable, for then the perpetrators would have

---

[17] Raymond C. Baumhart, "How Ethical Are Businessmen?" *Harvard Business Review*, Vol. 39, No. 4, July-August 1961, p. 16.

[18] *Ibid.*

> to face the concrete evidence of what they were doing. But there is a stifling of ambition where it is found, a denial of participation, a lack of natural love and affection, a thwarting of brotherhood, a suppression of creativity, a general attitude which says, "Do just what you're told; take your pay and go home." Any attempt at a warm and full relationship is stiff-armed away by suspicion, greed, and envy.[19]

Apparently a majority of business executives recognize a considerable degree of unethical behavior as present in the current business world. The survey of 1,700 executive readers cited above included the following questions:

> In every industry, there are some generally accepted business practices. In your industry, are there any such practices which you regard as unethical?[20]

In answering this question, 59 per cent admitted *a few* and 9 per cent admitted *many* such practices existed! Thirteen per cent said they did not know, and only 19 per cent felt no such practices were evident. This appears to constitute rather widespread recognition of "general unethical behavior."

More than half of the respondents pointed out the one practice in their industry they would most like to see eliminated. The following comments provide a sample of these responses:

> INSURANCE EXECUTIVE: "Seeking preferential treatment through lavish entertainment."
>
> MANAGER, CONSUMER SERVICES COMPANY: "Kickback to purchasing department employees."
>
> PERSONNEL DIRECTOR, WESTERN MANUFACTURING FIRM: "The idea that industry should have a few women employees on the payroll for entertainment of prospective customers."
>
> FINANCIAL COUNSEL: "Payoffs to government officials."
>
> SECRETARY, CONSTRUCTION FIRM: "Price rigging between supplier and contractor."
>
> PRESIDENT OF SMALL COMPANY: "Accounts of similar size, purchasing ability, and credit rating are charged prices varying as much as 25% (by our competitors). So far, we have not deviated from our policy of charging the same price to everybody."
>
> PRESIDENT, CONSUMER SERVICES COMPANY: "Occasional exchanges of price information prior to contract bidding."

---

[19]Letter from John Rhodes, Vice President, Interstate Wells, *Harvard Business Review*, Vol. 33, No. 4, July-August 1955, pp. 132 and 134.

[20]Raymond C. Baumhart, *op. cit.*, p. 160.

VICE PRESIDENT, COMPANY MAKING INDUSTRIAL PRODUCTS: "The payment or large gifts to employees of other companies, customers, or competitors for 'favors' or information."

SALES MANAGER, PHARMACEUTICALS: "Misleading ad claims."

TOP EXECUTIVE, MASS COMMUNICATIONS FIRM: "Deliberate distortion of facts."

RESEARCH AND DESIGN EXPERT: "Ambiguous advertising intended to mislead consumers."

YOUNG FINANCIER: "Mutual fixing of rates of interest to be charged a borrower at two or more banks."

VICE PRESIDENT, MANUFACTURING COMPANY: "Underbidding with the intention of substituting inferior workmanship or materials."

PRESIDENT, CONSULTING FIRM: "Selling a 'tremendous bill of goods' of which the buyer knows too little."

MANAGER, MIDWESTERN BANK: "Loaning customer *more* than he needs or more than is prudent for him to borrow."[21]

Determining the exact level of business ethics is not possible. Not only is it impossible to look inside the numerous business activities and decisions to examine their ethical content, but there is no reason to think that ethical standards are consistent from business to business, industry to industry, or locality to locality. Neither is there any great advantage in trying to catalogue the precise level at which ethical standards exist today. Without doubt, there is much behavior that is commendable in nature and representative of high ethical standards. At the same time, there is ample opportunity for vast improvement in the ethical standards and relationships prevailing in the business world. It is a never-ending challenge to meet these ethical problems and to develop solutions that are acceptable in the light of individual and community moral standards.

Thorny Nature of Ethical Questions

There is a great tendency to oversimplify the matter of ethical problems in business organization. Frequently, we visualize decisions as involving simple choices between right and wrong, black and white. As a matter of fact, decisions with ethical overtones are often considerably more complex. The "right" decision from an ethical standpoint may indeed be hazy. Often there are conflicts in

[21] *Ibid.*

values, and the manager perceives different obligations which seem to conflict in their implications. Hammering out a decision that is the right decision is not necessarily an easy matter.

In addition, it is difficult for the manager to free himself from bias and prejudice and to look at issues objectively. In spite of good intentions, the individual becomes involved in the situation and becomes identified with certain positions or points of view. It becomes difficult to step back and to take a detached point of view in examining the issue from an ethical standpoint.

Codes of Ethics

What is legal serves merely as the minimum ethical standard. The question of ethics is often discussed in terms of deviations from the law. Some have urged a shift from a negative to a more positive point of view through the adoption of ethical standards known as *codes of ethics*. Throughout the years, various groups have worked at the task of developing such codes, generally applicable to particular industrial groups. In 1961, Robert W. Austin suggested a simple positive code of conduct for business management generally. It had the following principles:

> The professional manager affirms that he will place the interest of his company before his own private interests.
>
> He will place his duty to society above his duty to his company and above his private interest.
>
> He has a duty to reveal the facts in any situation where his private interests are involved with those of his company, or where the interests of his company are involved with those of society.
>
> He must subscribe wholeheartedly to the belief that when business managers follow this code of conduct, the profit motive is the best incentive of all for the development of a dynamic economy.[22]

How valuable codes of ethics are in lifting the standards of business conduct is a matter of question. They apparently summarize accepted standards at a given time and provide a basis for checking individual performance on the part of individual managers and business concerns. After the famous price-fixing cases in the electrical industry, the national electrical manufacturers association adopted

---

[22]"A Positive Code of Ethics," *Business Week,* No. 1659, June 17, 1961, p. 166.

a statement of principles to guide members in compliance with antitrust laws.[23] The code of ethics was concerned with guarding independence in pricing on the part of the individual companies. It provided that the businesses should gather market information only through legal and proper channels and that businesses should limit their meetings to discussion of problems of a proper nature not including prices, terms, and conditions of sale. It is interesting to note that this particular code of ethics was enacted after, and apparently as a result of, the legal action to force compliance with the law.

Foundation for Business Ethics

Ethical values in the business world reflect the ideals and standards of the society of which it is a part. Each culture has a distinctive system of moral values. It is impossible, therefore, to divorce questions of business ethics from the traditions and standards of the larger culture. It is unlikely that the general level of ethical standards in business conduct will differ in any substantial way from the ethical standards observed in nonbusiness areas of society. In considering business ethics, therefore, we are dealing with only one part of the broader issue of ethical standards in society.

In the U.S., there are generally accepted ethical concepts and traditions that are associated, in their origin at least, with our religious life. They are sometimes described as our *Judeo-Christian heritage*. The dignity and importance of the individual are basic elements of this creed. While some consider religious ideas and theological concepts as the rationalization of accepted practice, it is also possible to see them as the conceptual basis for ethical behavior. In a provocative article, "Can the Businessman Apply Christianity?"[24] Harold L. Johnson has suggested that the historic Christian doctrines can furnish a foundation for business ethics. He holds that these doctrines provide a perspective from which to view modern commercial life and a frame of reference in making decisions.

As an example of Johnson's reasoning, consider the concept of God as a personal, transcendent Being closely associated with human life. The significance of this concept is to place everything human under the rule of God, warning against the idolatry of putting the business firm or career at the center of life. The doctrine of creation

[23] "Electrical Trade Group Adopts Code of Ethics for Member Companies," *The Wall Street Journal,* June 22, 1961.

[24] Harold L. Johnson, "Can the Businessman Apply Christianity?" *Harvard Business Review,* Vol. 35, No. 5, September-October 1957, pp. 68-76.

holds that material things are not evil and provides a concept for stewardship. In fact, Johnson suggests that this doctrine furnishes a part of the religious foundation for the philosophy of the social responsibility of the businessman. The Christian view of the nature of man reveals his weaknesses, serving as a warning to ambitious executives and against an inflated view of their own abilities. It warns managers at all levels that self-interest and pride may be woven into decisions believed to be objective. It also cautions against excessive optimism that human relations and social responsibility can bring the heavenly city here on earth by teaching that all, including ourselves, have the taint of sin.

Although there is no monolithic code of ethics in society, some of the general cultural values condition the viewpoint of most managers. In view of the diversity in this area of our culture, however, there is still a principle of individual responsibility and choice. Because issues are seldom "black and white" in nature, an executive may follow ethical standards that are regarded as either more or less acceptable in terms of generally prevailing beliefs. Although the individual manager cannot be completely indifferent to generally accepted standards, managerial choices must also reflect his personal code.

Summary

Business objectives constitute the *goals* of the business enterprise. They include not only the *profit objective* but also *service and social goals*. While these goals may work in harmony, the manager is often confronted with the practical problem of reconciling conflicts in particular cases and of striking some sort of balance among the values that are involved. The individual members of the business organization also have *personal objectives* that motivate them to make their individual contributions to the enterprise.

Business activities involve numerous questions of an *ethical* nature. These ethical questions are frequently complex, involving more than a simple choice between right and wrong. *Codes of ethics* have been established by some groups in an attempt to provide positive statements to serve as a guide for business behavior. The foundation of ethical action is to be found in the spiritual values of our culture and religious life.

Discussion Questions

1. How can you explain the fact that a major business corporation is seemingly floundering without a long-range *objective* (p. 78)? Who is responsible?
2. In what way does a clearly stated objective enable all parts of an organization to work effectively together?
3. What is the relationship of the *profit objective* of a business concern to its *social responsibilities?*
4. One well-known business executive said (speaking of his corporation), "We feel very strongly that we must support our private colleges and universities and that in so doing we are serving our company's interest." What type of objective is he expressing, and how is it related to other objectives?
5. Why isn't the corporation whose management exhibits the finest sense of social responsibility always the one that earns the highest profits?
6. Could an insurance salesman simultaneously have two *goals* —his own desire for a commission and the customer's security?
7. In your opinion, what would be the most powerful personal objectives of a corporate executive earning $500,000 annually?
8. Why can't business managers agree as to what is *ethical* or *unethical behavior*?
9. Of what value is a *code of ethics*?

Supplementary Reading

Ansoff, H. Igor, *Corporate Strategy*. New York: McGraw-Hill Book Company, 1965.

Baumhart, Raymond C., "How Ethical Are Businessmen?" *Harvard Business Review*, Vol. 39, No. 4, July-August 1961, pp. 6-19, 156-176.

Brooks, Robert C., Jr., "A Neglected Approach to Ethical Business Behavior," *The Journal of Business*, Vol. 37, No. 2, April 1964, pp. 192-194.

Cheit, Earl F., ed., *The Business Establishment.* New York: John Wiley & Sons, Inc., 1964.

Cyert, Richard M. and James G. March, *A Behavioral Theory of the Firm.* Englewood Cliffs: Prentice-Hall, Inc., 1963.

Drucker, Peter F., "Big Business and the National Purpose," *Harvard Business Review,* Vol. 40, No. 2, March-April 1962, pp. 49-57.

England, George W., "Organizational Goals and Expected Behavior of American Mangers," *Academy of Management Journal,* Vol. 10, No. 2, June 1967, pp. 107-117.

Garrett, Thomas M., *Business Ethics.* New York: The Meredith Publishing Co., 1966.

Gilman, Glenn, "The Ethical Dimension in American Management," *California Management Review,* Vol. 7, No. 1, Fall 1964, pp. 45-52.

Granger, Charles H., "The Hierarchy of Objectives," *Harvard Business Review,* Vol. 42, No. 3, May-June 1964, pp. 63-74.

Guth, William D. and Renato Taqiuri, "Personal Values and Corporate Strategy," *Harvard Business Review,* Vol. 43, No. 5, September-October 1965, pp. 123-132.

Levitt, Theodore, "Why Business Always Loses," *Harvard Business Review,* Vol. 46, No. 2, March-April 1968, pp. 81-89.

McGuire, Joseph W., *Business and Society.* New York: McGraw-Hill Book Company, 1963.

————, "The Finalité of Business," *California Management Review,* Vol. 8, No. 4, Summer 1966, pp. 89-94.

Miller, J. Irwin, "A New Partnership: Business, Education, Society," *Business Horizons,* Vol. 10, No. 1, Spring 1967, pp. 21-30.

Newman, William H., "Shaping the Master Strategy of Your Firm," *California Management Review,* Vol. 9, No. 3, Spring 1967, pp. 77-88.

Petit, Thomas A., "Making Socially Responsible Decisions," *Academy of Management Journal,* Vol. 9, No. 4, December 1966, pp. 308-317.

Phillips, Charles F., Jr., "What is Wrong with Profit Maximization?" *Business Horizons,* Vol. 6, No. 4, Winter 1963, pp. 73-80.

Towle, Joseph W., ed., *Ethics and Standards in American Business.* Boston: Houghton Mifflin Company, 1964.

Walton, Clarence C., *Corporate Social Responsibilities.* Belmont: Wadsworth Publishing Co., Inc., 1967.

5

Formulating Policy

The sign on an executive's desk proclaims, "There's no reason for it—it's just our policy!" No doubt the expression accurately summarizes the feelings of many who conform to policies having little apparent justification. The more serious view of business policies, however, sees them as based upon reason. Those policies are selected that will enable the organization to accomplish its objectives most effectively.

Nature and Value of Business Policy

Definition of Policy

A policy may be visualized as a device that establishes certain constraints or boundaries for administrative action. In a 100-yard dash, for example, the lanes are marked, and a sprinter is expected to stay within those limits. He does have a bit of latitude, however, as to his exact position within the lane. No one is greatly concerned about his movement unless he gets outside his own lane.

Policy might be defined as *a basic statement serving as a guide for administrative action.* By saying it is a guide, there is an implication that the policy does not usually specify detailed answers to particular problems. The manager has some degree of freedom.[1] As an example, a policy that says "No discrimination in hiring" does not dictate the employment choice. It simply eliminates one factor as an element in the choice. It would still be desirable to analyze the ability of all candidates. In fact, the effect of the policy would be to extend the scope of recruitment and selection, producing an even greater number of potential candidates.

Some policies are particularly concerned with the "how" of administrative action.[2] By establishing an objective, as explained in the preceding chapter, the organization determines its destination. Many policies are concerned with the route for reaching that destination. In other cases, objectives are given substance as they find expression in policies. Personnel objectives, for example, are abstract statements until they become embodied in concrete policies.

Although it is customary to think of policies as written statements, this is not necessarily the case. Any consistently followed pattern of decisions in dealing with particular problems would indicate the existence of a policy. For example, a firm may simply decline to consider handicapped employees in the selection of new personnel. In effect, this becomes an effective policy even though the organization may never have verbalized its position and accorded formal recognition to the practice.

Types of Policies

Each of the functional areas of a business requires its own policies. In this manner, guidelines are established to control buying and selling, borrowing and credit extension, and various other activities pertinent to business operations. Marketing policies, for example, must deal with all aspect of selling—including pricing, distribution channels, advertising, and numerous other aspects of the marketing program. Figure 1 illustrates the variety of questions that must be treated in a comprehensive set of marketing policies. In the same way, policies are required in production, financial, personnel, and other areas of the business.

Policies differ according to the level of the organization. The broadest and most basic policies apply to the organization as a whole.

---

[1]In contrast, a *rule* — such as "no smoking" — permits no discretion regarding action to be taken.

[2]A policy establishes general guidelines, in contrast to a *procedure,* which specifies the chronological sequence of steps or tasks.

Others apply only to specific components. For example, a national company with a number of production plants usually has some policy variations between plants. Of course, policies of the branches would be expected to conform to general company policy.

Figure 1. *Marketing Policies*
(Some Questions to be Treated in Marketing Policies)

1. *Product Policies*
   (a) Quality level.
   (b) Extent of variety or specialization.
   (c) Color or colors.
   (d) Design features.
2. *Price Policies*
   (a) Uniform or varying selling price.
   (b) Odd prices.
   (c) Price leadership.
   (d) Types and amounts of discounts.
3. *Distribution Policies*
   (a) Exclusive agency arrangements.
   (b) Channels of distribution.
   (c) Nature or extent of relationships with dealers.
4. *Brand Policies*
   (a) Use of brands or trademarks.
   (b) Single or "family" brands.
   (c) Production or sale of brands controlled by others.
5. *Sales Promotion Policies*
   (a) Use of institutional and/or product advertising.
   (b) Type of advertising media.
   (c) Merchandising assistance to dealers.
   (d) Use of advertising agencies.

Values in the Use of Policies

Administrative actions originating from spur-of-the-moment decisions are often less sound than those growing out of carefully established policies. There are a number of reasons accounting for this. Policies can and should be adopted on the basis of a thorough consideration of all pertinent aspects of the situation. By engaging in a policy study, adequate time may be directed to an investigation of this type. Without a policy, time pressures are often such as to prevent sufficient time for analysis of the facts in providing an answer for the question of the moment. Or, a single case may not justify a thorough study. In any specific case, urgencies of the moment often seem to have unusual importance. It is easy to lose a sense of perspective and to forget features that are important.

In the absence of policy, each case is resolved on its own merits. The result, reflecting the unique circumstances of individual cases and a tendency to look at problems differently from week to week, is variation in business decisions over a period of time. In addition, differences in individual judgment contribute to variations among departments, with the result that Department A and Department B are solving the same problem quite differently. On trivial matters, of course, little is lost in such individual variations. On matters of some significance, however, such fluctuation in administrative action appears capricious and possibly unfair. Consistency of action is made possible by the adoption of basic policies providing guidelines applicable to various executives and remaining stable over a period of time.

By adopting policies, a higher-level executive can provide guidance to lower levels of the organization. It is not necessary for subordinate managers to guess what their general position should be in a given situation. Nor is it necessary for the superior to "breathe down the neck" of subordinates. As a result, an executive may view a policy as a tool that facilitates some transfer of decision making to lower levels of the organization.

In the absence of a policy, similar questions must be considered time after time. Lack of a policy means that the organization has established no continuing position. As a result, it is necessary to assess each new situation on the basis of its own merits. Different components of the organization may also go through the same evaluation process simultaneously. Depending upon the nature of the case, such investigation and study may involve the time of a number of individuals. The use of a policy substitutes one period of study — that involved in formulating the policy — for the numerous periods of evaluation that are otherwise necessary.

Business Policies and Competitive Strength

The values of business policies cited above are general advantages available to all concerns. This does not mean, of course, that all companies are equally skillful in their use of policies. Some firms establish a competitive superiority merely by using policies in an industry or market in which others are given to a haphazard type of management. It is also possible to improve the firm's competitive position by selection of policies that are qualitatively superior to those of other firms.

As an example of unique policies that have apparently produced an unusual degree of success in a fiercely competitive market, consider the case of the Magnavox Company.[3] Although the company was incorporated in 1911 and adopted the name "Magnavox" in 1917, it experienced more technical than financial success in its early life—even going into voluntary bankruptcy in 1937. It was during the decade of the 1950's that Magnavox began its fabulous growth. From 1952 sales of $37.4 million, it climbed to $333 million in 1965. During the same period, profits rose from $1.1 million to $23 million. The company's return on investment has been one of the highest among U. S. industrial companies. In 1965, it was 28.4 per cent!

What accounted for the startling achievements of this apparently mediocre company? The individual circumstances in a case of this type are certainly too complex to justify an assertion that it was any *one* factor. It is clear in this case, however, that some Magnavox policies differed sharply from those of competitors. In 1950, Frank Freimann assumed the company presidency and sparked the growth of the next decade. The combination of his dynamic leadership and distinctive policies led to the series of successful achievements that have been noted.

In terms of policy, Magnavox adopted a marketing approach in marked contrast to that of competitors. In the days of mass discount merchandising in the radio, TV, and phonograph field, Magnavox emphasized high-quality products by aggressively promoting higher price, higher profit units. These were distributed directly (rather than through suppliers) to its own carefully selected, franchised dealers who were pledged, and policed, to maintain retail prices. This arrangement made possible a close control over the marketing of its products and apparently provided adequate profit margins for retailers (thus encouraging their loyalty) as well as a higher margin for Magnavox.

Company policy, then, is one of the battlefields in the competitive struggle for survival and success. On any given policy subject, there are likely to be differences of opinion within the firm and within the industry (as was evident in the case of Magnavox). The wisdom dis-

---

[3]"Balancing One-Man Rule with Team Play," *Business Week,* No. 1738, December 22, 1962, pp. 38-40; "Magnavox Set to Tune In Sharply Higher Results," *Barron's* August 22, 1966, p. 20. Reprinted by courtesy of Barron's National Business and Financial Weekly.

played in adopting the right policy is eventually reflected in the company's sales and earnings.

Phases of Policy Making and Policy Use

Policy Formulation

Formulation of business policy includes the background study necessary to consider the wisdom of the policy and to determine its exact nature. If the policy is to be based upon the needs of the situation, appropriate facts must be gathered and analyzed. Various components of the organization may need to be consulted. Tentative drafts of a policy may be prepared and circulated for comment. At the conclusion of such a study, a particular statement is adopted as representing the official position of the organization.

A frequent weakness of policy formulation is the tendency merely to consider the various viewpoints of different managers, adopting one of these viewpoints or a compromise position. These individual proposals are not subjected to careful investigation and analysis. Although this practice has some of the earmarks of a scientific approach, it may fail to delve deeply enough into the facts of a situation.

The effectiveness of some policy decisions may be improved through the utilization and analysis of quantitative data. The story is told of a manufacturer of a low-price consumer product who engaged in an evaluation of quantitative data in developing a policy of stabilized production and employment.[4] This company was confronted with the dual problems of a marked seasonal sales fluctuation and a vigorous union whose demands for wage and fringe benefits had grown to the point that they appeared unreasonable to management and far in excess of those applying to comparable workers in other firms. It was suggested to the company management that its policy of laying off more than one-third of the employees in slack months contributed to employee anger and led to the growing difficulty in negotiating bargaining agreements. Although management regretted the necessity for this practice, it believed that workers could make up for lost work by extensive overtime pay during periods of high sales and high production. Many

---

[4]Melvin Anshen, "Price Tags for Business Policies," *Harvard Business Review,* Vol. 38, No. 1, January-February 1960, p. 75.

employees, however, found the problem of managing an irregular income to be unpleasant.

The company's position in the matter was based upon a belief that costs associated with holding inventories and risks of shifts in consumer demand were such that no alternative course of action was financially feasible. Although the company's product could be stored without physical deterioration, some risk existed because of changing customer tastes. These assumptions had never been quantified, but they were accepted as the basis for the production policy.

A feasibility study was undertaken in an attempt to resolve these problems, and various aspects of the situation were subjected to quantitative estimates. The company discovered, by analyzing sales fluctuations and other consumer demand shifts of the preceding ten years, that a remarkable stability in annual sales existed, with an annual growth factor of from 5 to 8 per cent. The storage costs associated with stable output were defined with precision. A dealer survey indicated that proper discount schedules encouraging off-season purchases could shift as much as 30 per cent of the holding charges to retailers. A reduction of about 15 per cent in labor costs was anticipated by the use of a stable level of production without overtime pay, reflecting both a smaller average work force and retention of skilled workers. Members of management were then asked to make, on the basis of their knowledge, experience, and judgment, quantitative estimates for two factors — the maximum one-year cost associated with changing consumer tastes and the average annual gain resulting from reduction of union demands and the improvement of worker morale. For both costs and gains, high estimates were approximately 50 per cent above the low estimates. Even on the basis of the most unfavorable figures, it was possible to demonstrate a significant advantage in shifting to a policy of stabilized production. In this case, then, the subjection of the policy to careful quantitative analysis led to the discovery of a costly existing policy and to an improvement in the company's production policy.

Policy Communication

Policies often affect many who are not directly involved in their formulation. Managers at lower levels, for example, are expected to apply policies adopted at "headquarters." Employees, including managerial personnel, are also expected to conform to policies regulating personal behavior. This creates a need for communication of policies to all personnel who are concerned with them. Such communication typically requires more than an initial announcement of the policy at the time of adoption. Managers are subsequently appointed without background knowledge concerning the policy, and it is necessary that they understand the existing policies of the business.

Written policies have the advantage of providing a source for future reference. They can be rechecked from time to time without the necessity for relying on memory. In addition, a policy may be communicated in writing without the garbling that often results from verbal transmission. Written policies are particularly useful to new personnel who are expected to understand and apply them. Media for written communication of policies include letters, bulletin board announcements, newspaper accounts, handbooks, and policy manuals. Policy manuals, often maintained on a looseleaf basis, provide an orderly collection of current policies for use by managerial personnel.

One problem in written policy communication that is common to all such communication concerns the use of language. The choice of terminology and style of writing must be understandable to the reader. There is a frequent tendency to express policies in an official language that may be misleading or even incomprehensible to those who are expected to apply or observe them.

Oral communication is also useful in disseminating policies. In the case of important policies, it is better used as a supplement to, rather than a substitute for, written communication. Communication of this type normally uses regular supervisory channels. Significant policy changes may be announced, explained, and justified in this way. In fact, it is ordinarily desirable to have changes announced through regular channels in order to preserve the leadership position of the manager. If a manager discovers a new policy after his subordinates hear about it, he appears unimportant in their eyes.

Many policies are far too complex to permit complete transmission by simple announcement. Training in the nature of such policies is a prerequisite for their effective use. Consequently, supervisory and management training conferences frequently devote sessions to an explanation and discussion of existing policies. In this way, the purposes and underlying reasoning for policies can be made clear by the executives leading the conference. Questions may be raised by conference participants to clarify obscure points that may exist.

Policies that are followed without being explicitly expressed may be communicated in more subtle ways. A general understanding may develop on the basis of some observed consistency in decisions and administrative behavior. The newcomer learns that the organization always follows a given course of action. Of course, some unwritten policies may simply be explained orally. Occasionally, however, policies are unwritten because of features that would make a written policy subject to criticism. Such policies are usually communicated by less direct means.

Policy Application

Application of policies requires the exercise of administrative judgment. The specific situation is always unique. The policy may specify that managerial vacancies are usually to be filled by promotion from within. But the factors in the individual situation govern the way in which the policy is to be applied. The choice of candidates still confronts the executive in applying the policy, and he must decide if the case calls for appointment from outside on the basis of an unusual situation. The manager, then, develops judgment as he continues to apply policies in the decisions that he makes.

Assuming a sound policy, consistency in its application is important. In the policy mentioned above, we would not expect to find half of the vacancies filled by outside appointments. Vacillation indicates uncertainty or weakness and may create unfavorable attitudes on the part of those affected. Fairness demands consistent application of policy. In the case of the promotion policy, qualified members of the organization have a right to expect application of the policy as stated. Otherwise, they may have a justifiable feeling that management is engaging in favoritism.

At the same time, some flexibility is necessary in administration. The policy statement on promotion from within should not be so rigid as to require this type of appointment in all cases. Such rigidity would presumably bind the organization to make promotions even in the absence of well-qualified candidates. A rigid policy would fail to recognize a special need for outside appointments in critical positions in which inbreeding is particularly dangerous. Flexibility and consistency may appear irreconcilable, but careful administration can recognize the unique elements in each situation without eroding the basic policy position. Of course, an administrator cannot be allowed to violate the policy under the guise of flexibility.

Policy Review and Appraisal

In a rapidly changing company, policies easily become obsolete. Production policies adopted in the 1950's or 1960's may be outdated in the 1970's. Changes in technology, products, strategy of competitors, labor contracts, organization, or other factors contribute to their obsolescence. Policies that are entirely appropriate in their day may simply not fit at a later period. Periodic review is essential to avoid retaining outmoded policies.

Such a review calls for initiative on the part of management. If the company is doing well, policy examination does not appear necessary. Only if the profit position is poor does a serious review of company policy seem imperative. There is no guarantee, however, that policies are perfect merely because a business is making money.

Existing policies tend to become hallowed through age, acquiring greater luster with the passage of time. To inquire into the wisdom of existing policies, then, requires a tough, aggressive attitude on the part of management. Management cannot be satisfied with the status quo or accept a policy merely because it was enunciated by the founding fathers and made traditional by succeeding generations of managers.

> Social customs and mores, even business policies, adhered to through the years and not subjected to review, can become intellectually untouchable — the most vicious kind of ritual.[5]

The case has been cited of a research policy that hardened with age. This company adopted a policy of maintaining industry leadership in research and development. The policy was adopted when the company's product line and those of its competitors were small and yielded recognizable benefits.

> Today's research expense claims a considerably larger share of the budget than in earlier years. Furthermore, zealous application of the policy has extended the scope of research, so that efforts to improve products and processes, and to discover new ones, are now under way along the whole front of the firm's operations, including both areas where the company holds a dominant market position and areas where its position is weak, sales low, profits small, and opportunities limited. In fact, some competitors pursue a follow-the-leader strategy with respect to this organization's research discoveries, often with notable success as a result of reduced risk and expense.
>
> A few members of the management group question the research budget and the underlying research policy. They propose (1) measuring the return on the research dollar, and (2) assessing the wisdom of pushing research in all product areas rather than identifying as avenues for exploration those that promise the highest return on the research investment. But they run into a

---

[5] Melvin Anshen, *op. cit.*, p. 72.

> wall of unyielding adherence to established policy. "It was good enough for the founding fathers, and it must be good enough for us."[6]

Some companies, however, are willing to question and, if necessary, to scrap traditional policies. In 1959, for example, Firestone Tire and Rubber Company broke with founder Harvey Firestone's decree that no tire should ever be made without the name "Firestone" emblazoned on the side.[7] This decision to enter the private-brand market—accounting for 40 per cent of replacement-tire sales—enabled Firestone to compete for and, in 1962, to snare Montgomery Ward's $40 million-a-year tire business. This coup, coupled with other moves, apparently propelled Firestone into the No. 1 volume position in tire sales, ahead of its rival and traditional front runner, the Goodyear Tire and Rubber Company.

Some policies are more susceptible to appraisal than others. The sales impact of a revised advertising policy, for example, may be quite evident. Corporate policies regarding charitable contributions, on the other hand, are more difficult to assess. The profit effect of corporate giving is indirect at best and possibly nil. Indeed, the policy may be followed because of a concern about corporate citizenship. In any event, evaluation of such a policy requires a considerable degree of subjective judgment. As a result, existing policies may be continued indefinitely without any clear idea of their usefulness. Some firms are attempting to evaluate performance in such areas, however, in spite of measurement difficulties. An alert management may join those firms in seeking to establish standards and measure performance in non-profit areas.

Satisfaction with the status quo is destructive in nature and leads to rejection of desirable policy changes. Such an attitude reduces the effectiveness of management and eliminates the possibility of such a successful policy change as that by Firestone.

Responsibility for Policy Making

External Forces in Policy Making

Although policy making is a part of the manager's planning function, he does not have a completely free hand in the process. One

---

[6] *Ibid.*, p. 73.

[7] "Firestone's Bid for the Top," *Forbes*, Vol. 91, No. 4, February 15, 1963, pp. 22-25.

of the external factors conditioning his policy decisions is the body of applicable law. In any legitimate business concern, operating policy must conform to pertinent legal standards. As an example, the Federal Trade Commission may institute criminal proceedings in accordance with the Wheeler-Lea Act for false advertising of foods, drugs, and cosmetics. Moreover, concealment of a relevant fact or a statement which, although true, is incomplete may be held to constitute false advertising. The Commission has taken steps to eliminate many types of misleading labeling—for example, requiring companies selling rebuilt tires or typewriters to mark these products plainly as "rebuilt." Marketing policy must avoid features that would lead to violation of such labeling standards as specified according to federal law.

The law provides policy controls not only in marketing but also in matters of finance, personnel, production, and other areas. In each of these cases, the law specifies a minimum standard. Within the broad limits established by law, policy makers have latitude for discretionary judgment. Although the Taft-Hartley Act prohibits discrimination against employees for union activity, the law does not specify a precise degree of required cooperation. Some companies negotiate at "arm's length," barely inside the minimum requirements of law, fighting the union with every legal weapon available. Other firms pursue a policy of active cooperation.

Union pressures themselves represent another external force that must be reckoned with in the establishment of company policy. For plants that are unionized, management is unable to set personnel policy unilaterally. Personnel policies that are subject to negotiation may be incorporated in the labor contract. The following policy extracted from a labor contract illustrates a provision of this nature:

> When it becomes necessary to reduce the working force, layoff of employees within the bargaining unit shall be determined on the basis of ability to perform the required work and to maintain or improve the efficiency of the organization. Where ability to perform the required work and to maintain or improve efficiency is substantially equal, length of service shall be a factor of consideration in selecting employees for layoff.

Strictures on policy making imposed by unions are normally limited to personnel policies. In fact, the same labor contract specifies:

> The determination of the type of products to be manufactured, the location of plants, the methods and schedules of production, and the means of manufacture are solely the responsibility of the company.

This provision has the effect of stipulating managerial prerogatives which are recognized as being beyond the control of the union. As a matter of fact, the field that is subject to unilateral control by management has been one of the narrowing boundaries within recent years.

Employees, even apart from their union relationships, may exert some influence upon policy making. Administrators are often concerned with the probable reaction to policies under consideration. It may be calculated that a given policy would "stir up a hornet's nest." The policy is tailored to fit the policy maker's conception of the expectations of personnel who are affected by the policy. Without asking for formal cooperation by these personnel in setting the policy, their position and views nevertheless function as an external influence in the policy decision.

No doubt other external forces affecting the policy-making process could be cited. For example, the trade association, chamber of commerce, or agencies of this kind may exert significant influence in policy formulation. Even though the firm is a voluntary member, it is often customary to go along with programs advocated by such groups.

Top Management in Policy Making

Policies that are broadest in scope and in nature are adopted by top management of the concern. As a part of its responsibility for overall company direction, top management must have control of key policy decisions. Broad policy decisions are closely related to the determination of company objectives. Normally, higher-level executives are not personally concerned with detailed policies that are not broadly significant from the standpoint of overall operations.

It is possible, of course, for general policies to be suggested by members of management at lower levels. A proposed policy, for example, may be presented to the chief executive or executive committee for consideration. It is top management that exercises final judgment on such matters.

Policy-Making Role of Staff Personnel

The staff role is often one of leadership in formulating and interpreting policy. This arises from staff's specialization in a given functional area. Staff agencies are presumed to be expert in a particular field and well informed on all aspects of the subject. On a particular subject, for example, they should know the applicable law, practices of other companies, and matters of this type. The following descriptions of the activities of specialized staffs in different companies indicate the nature of their policy-making role:[8]

> FORD MOTOR COMPANY: The staff is responsible for formulating or advising on plans and policies.
>
> ARMCO STEEL CORPORATION: The staff gives opinions upon proposed plans and policies.
>
> STANDARD OIL COMPANY OF CALIFORNIA: The staff advises management and recommends policies in its areas for management's approval.
>
> GENERAL FOODS: The staff assists top management in the development of company policies in its specialized areas.

The staff agency may also assume leadership because of the need for getting an outsider to coordinate a variety of viewpoints. If the subject cuts across departmental lines, someone must pull together the thinking and positions of the different interested groups. As an example, the personnel staff is expected to play a key role in formulating overall personnel policy.

Lower Management and Policy Formulation

At each level of management, there is some policy-making function that exists. Policies are seldom made so comprehensive at the top that they require no detailing at lower levels. Each level of management, then, makes such specific policies as are necessary in adapting the broad policies of the company to the particular organizational component. In addition, each part of the organization has a unique situation that may call for special local policies of no concern to other parts of the firm.

There is also the practice, followed in some corporations, of calling upon lower levels of management for assistance in establishing general corporate policy. Such an approach assumes that lower levels have experience or insights that provide a valuable contribution to the policy under consideration. The McCormick Spice Company has used a formal organization of lower-level personnel to suggest improvements and policy changes to the company's Board of

---

[8]Adapted from Louis A. Allen, *Management and Organization* (New York: McGraw-Hill Book Company, 1958), pp. 229-230.

Directors.[9] Topics considered by the Junior Board over the years have included

> . . . the dead stock list, routing magazines through the office, discontinuance of slow sellers, changing the bylaws, sales follow-up on dormant accounts, familiarizing junior executives with manufacturing operations, a survey of correspondence, auditing cash sales and city order sheets, dispatching of merchandise, subscription to the trucking code, standard correspondence pads for salesmen, dental clinic prices, and dittoing export orders.[10]

Clearly, some of the subjects cited above include matters of a policy nature. The policies proposed by the Junior Board in this case are reviewed by the Senior Board of Directors, which may either accept or reject them.

Summary

Policies are basic statements serving as a guide for administrative action. They are developed in various functional areas of the business and also at the different echelons. Among the values realized in the use of formal policies are the careful consideration of alternative courses of action, consistency in administration, facilitation of delegated decision making, and conservation of time. Effective policies may also give one firm an advantage over its competitors.

Policy making and use include a number of phases. Policy *formulation,* for example, involves a determination of what the policy should be and may include extensive analysis of the issue. Policy *communication* involves the dissemination of policy information to appropriate personnel and any necessary training in the use or interpretation of such policy. In the *application* of policy, managerial personnel should recognize the importance of consistency and flexibility. It is also desirable that policies be *reviewed* periodically to avoid the retention of those that have become obsolete.

Policy making entails contributions by top management, middle and lower levels of management, and staff groups. It is performed within a broad framework created by law and is also subject to other external forces.

---

[9]Charles P. McCormick, *The Power of People* (New York: Harper & Row, Publishers, 1949), p. 16.

[10]*Ibid.,* p. 37.

Discussion Questions

1. What is the difference between *objectives* and *policies* in business management?
2. Summarize the advantages resulting from the use of written policies.
3. What reasons are there for avoiding extensive study and analysis in the *formulation* of business policies?
4. Compare the benefits of written versus oral *communication* of policies.
5. If a manager is flexible rather than rigid in applying a policy, does a policy really exist?
6. Why should existing policies become "sacred cows" that are difficult if not impossible to change?
7. What determines whether management has prerogatives (and thus need not consult the union) in certain areas of policy making?
8. What level or type of manager within a large business organization should be responsible for initiating policy changes or suggesting new policies?
9. In 1964, a publishing company vice president resigned following a policy dispute. The company had used uncoated paper for printing a children's magazine but switched, in 1963, to coated paper which was preferred by advertisers. When newsstand sales dropped, company officials blamed the coated paper—children presumably found it more difficult for drawing and parents presumably considered it less substantial. Consequently, the company decided to resume use of uncoated paper, and the vice president walked out. Why should the seemingly prosaic process of formulating policy about quality of paper lead to such drastic action—the departure of a high-ranking executive?
10. In 1966, such color-TV set makers as RCA and Motorola were planning to shift from tubes to transistors and integrated circuits. Zenith Radio Corporation, on the other hand, was reported as sticking with vacuum tubes and wired circuits. Zenith's president was quoted as saying, "These are just pro-

motional moves, and they'll add to costs right now without improving performance." Will Zenith's conservatism in policy making allow it to remain competitive in such a rapidly changing industry?

Supplementary Reading

Anshen, Melvin, "Price Tags for Business Policies," *Harvard Business Review,* Vol. 38, No. 1, January-February 1960, pp. 71-78.

Cullman, W. Arthur, "Policy Reappraisal and Maintenance," *Business Horizons,* Vol. 2, No. 4, Winter 1959, pp. 68-73.

Eells, Richard, *The Government of Corporations,* Chapter 13. New York: The Free Press, 1962.

Flippo, Edwin B., *Management: A Behavioral Approach,* Chapter 4. Boston: Allyn & Bacon, Inc., 1966.

Higginson, M. Valliant, *Management Policies I: Their Development as Corporate Guides,* AMA Research Study 76. New York: American Management Association, Inc., 1966.

__________, *Management Policies II: Sourcebook of Statements,* AMA Research Study 78. New York: American Management Association, Inc., 1966.

Koontz, Harold and Cyril O'Donnell, *Principles of Management,* Fourth Edition, Chapter 9. New York: McGraw-Hill Book Company, 1968.

McFarland, Dalton E., *Management: Principles and Practices,* Second Edition, Chapter 6. New York: The Macmillan Company, 1964.

McMaster, John B., "Essentials of Policy Control," *Office Executive,* Vol. 35, No. 5, May 1960, pp. 23-24, 30.

Odiorne, George S., *Personnel Policy: Issues and Practices,* Chapter 1. Columbus: Charles E. Merrill Publishing Co., 1963.

Wrapp, H. Edward, "Good Managers Don't Make Policy Decisions," *Harvard Business Review,* Vol. 45, No. 5, September-October 1967, pp. 91-99.

Yoder, Dale, "Management Policy and Manager Dissidence," *Personnel Administration,* Vol. 31, No. 2, March-April 1968, pp. 8-18.

6

Making Long-Range and Short-Range Operating Plans

The forward look is characteristic of successful managers. One often hears such expressions as "We don't do as much planning as we should," or "More time should be devoted to planning." Such remarks indicate a concern about the future and a desire for adequate preparation in facing changes. Analysis of business failures, on the other hand, often reveals management personnel who live only in the present (or past) and who appear oblivious to changes occurring in the economy. Having considered the establishment of objectives and policies in the preceding two chapters, the discussion here shifts to the development of operating plans.

Nature and Importance of Planning

Planning for business growth and operations, including long-range planning, has become a function of vital concern to top management. As noted in Chapter 4, selection of a basic strategy of the firm can no longer safely be left to chance. Progressive business corporations are coming to select corporate objectives and to develop supporting plans on the basis of careful study and evaluation. The best available talent in the firm is often assigned the responsibility of peering into the future and charting the most desirable course of action.

Example: An Introduction of Basic Business Planning

A recent example of the introduction of overall business planning is provided by the Standard Oil Company of Ohio.[1] Sohio, as the company is commonly known, was part of the Standard Oil Trust dissolved by the Supreme Court in 1911. The Sohio part of the trust had been designed to market oil in the state of Ohio. Following dissolution, Sohio proceeded to follow the original pattern for many decades, marketing refined oil products throughout the state of Ohio. During the 1950's, the limitations of this operation became apparent. Sohio's sales and profits failed to keep pace with those of the industry.

Under the direction of Charles E. Spahr, after his promotion to president in 1959, the company embarked on an extensive program of change and development. The plan called for rapid diversification through acquisition of other companies and through internal expansion. As part of this program, Sohio expanded in such fields as plastics, petrochemicals, luxury motels, and automatic vending.

Improvements in both sales and profits were soon evident. Although the company increased sales only $82 million (from $300 million to $382 million) between 1953 and 1962, sales jumped almost 40 per cent the following three years. Profits, which had hovered around $25 million between 1953 and 1962, nearly doubled between 1962 and 1965. In 1965, sales exceeded $531 million, and profits reached a new high of $49.7 million, more than 9 per cent of sales.

Comprehensive planning constituted a major innovation of the new administration. Although planning was not new at Sohio — the organization chart had had a box with this label since the mid 1950's — one executive described the change by saying "He [Spahr] made the box function." President Spahr called in an ex-professor and petroleum industry consultant for assistance in planning. After two years of work, a three-hundred page report, laying out the aims and tactics of corporate growth, was issued. The Sohio master plan is kept under close wraps; the two dozen copies are locked in top executive files. Its main lines are evident in company actions, however. The plan is flexible, since it is updated each year, and is due for complete revision every three years. General features of the plan are evident from Sohio's entry into gasoline markets in neighboring

---

[1]"The Plan That Put Fire Into Sohio's Profits," *Business Week,* No. 1902, February 12, 1966, pp. 107-116.

states (under the Boron Oil Company name), diversification into plastics, and developments in petrochemicals.

Sohio's success is largely attributable to the aggressive planning instituted by a new president. By virtue of this planning, a successful but somewhat lackadaisical company was given a direction and momentum that substantially improved its position. It seems evident that the introduction of basic planning constituted a key element in this transformation.

Nature of Planning

As noted in Chapter 2, planning involves thought and decision concerning a proposed course of action. It entails the selection of a given path to the future from the various alternatives open to an organization. It is an intellectual process preceding the activity being planned.

Planning is a continuing activity of management. A manager never reaches a point at which he stops planning. This does not mean, however, that he never completes work on a specific plan. The budget for a given year may be adopted, but the manager who approves it must immediately turn to other planning and must soon begin consideration of the budget for the following year.

Plans require decision making, a topic treated in the following chapter. Selection of a proposed course of action necessitates a decision in favor of this particular course of action and a rejection of other possibilities. Decision making is not synonymous with planning, however, because it is also required in other functions of management.

Plans are directed to the accomplishment of some objective or to the solution of some problem confronting the organization. Overall planning is concerned with broad company objectives. Departmental planning is directed to the achievement of subsidiary goals which contribute to realization of the company's more fundamental objectives. At each level of the organization, some planning occurs, and it is concerned with the specific mission of the particular organizational component.

As noted earlier, a firm's objectives are themselves one type of plan. The same is true of policies, which were described as continuing or standing plans. The operational planning discussed in this chapter must not only achieve objectives but also mesh with the more fundamental planning embodied in business policies. The policy framework stresses values of basic and continuing importance to the firm. Adherence to them in devising operating plans avoids certain dangers of expediency and opportunism.

The Systems Concept in Planning

The systems concept in planning highlights the relationships between the corporate system (that is, the business firm) and its environmental systems. In particular, the relationship of the firm with the social, economic, and industrial systems in which it functions becomes important in developing long-range and short-range plans. The fact that the business firm is part of larger systems calls for careful adjustment of plans and strategy to the evironmental systems. As indicated elsewhere in this chapter, business planners must utilize economic forecasts and evaluate political conditions as a basis for planning. They must also assess the strategy of competitors in order to plan effectively.

A second contribution of the systems concept to planning theory is found in its implications for the integration of planning, both long-range and short-range, carried on within the firm. In practice, much of the planning is carried on by individual departments and specialized staff offices. Systems theory emphasizes the need for tying together the various individual plans into one set of plans. Full adoption of this concept results in a hierarchy of plans. The planning of subsystems (for example, production or research functions) must be woven into overall planning for the company as a whole. Implications of decisions in one area for other areas of the business must be sensed. As a practical example, recall the type of planning involved in an annual budget. The budget prescribes the activities expected of each part of the system. The budget integrates the activities of specific departments into the overall system by relating them to the activities of other departments. Production performance, for example, is conditioned by estimates of the selling part of the system.

The type of comprehensive corporate planning now employed by many modern business corporations, integrating and coordinating departmental plans, utilizes the systems concept. Departmental plans which individually appear logical may, when considered collectively, exceed the resources of the company or entail other inconsistencies. Comprehensive planning produces an internally consistent hierarchy of plans, starting with the broad plans for the total enterprise and including the supporting specific and detailed operational plans. The systems view requires that the planning throughout the corporation or system be integrated into a consistent whole.

The concept of *suboptimization* is directly pertinent to the concept of planning for the entire system. It is possible for a given department to optimize its output by reducing the efficiency of other departments or other functions. Simultaneous optimization of all departments may be impossible. The ideal combination of plans calls for optimization of company-wide operations. This often necessitates suboptimization—that is, operating at less than ideal conditions in particular departments—in order that the overall operations of the entire company might be optimized.

> The common credit-sales controversy is an example of this. One objective of the credit department is to maintain a low ratio of bad debts while the objective of the sales department is to increase sales volume. The sales department therefore tends to deemphasize the credit risk factor whereas the credit department—more cautious, and seeking high credit standards—emphasizes this factor. If the credit department is autonomous, or at least free to determine the organization's credit standards, it may reject many potential customers, thereby reducing the sales volume. The bad debt ratio may be extremely low because of these high standards, but the benefits so derived may be more than offset by losses in sales.[2]

It is easy to visualize other potential conflict situations in which individual departments may be tempted to pursue their own goals and to disregard the corporate consequences. The systems viewpoint insists upon the comprehensive view of the planning process even in a complex system.

Systems planning also includes the use of the newer quantitative techniques. In considering the business in terms of a system, operations research is of particular interest. It is the objective of this tool to analyze operations from an overall or systems point of view. Its analytical approach, in other words, is based upon this same underlying concept that the business firm constitutes a system.

Historical Development of Business Planning

Extensive business planning is a comparatively modern development. Early industrial and marketing organizations concentrated upon production and selling—upon doing rather than planning. This was partially a reflection of the size of industrial concerns.

[2]From *Management: A Systems Analysis* by Stanley Young, p. 150. Copyright © 1966 by Scott, Foresman and Company.

Small-scale operation permitted much planning to be done informally. Business was also less complex. Many factors of great significance today—such as labor and public relations, tax legislation, consumer preferences, and foreign trade—were relatively unimportant in an earlier period.

Various developments have created a need for more extensive business planning. Growth in size made it difficult to operate without formalized planning. In the field of production management, the work of Frederick W. Taylor and the scientific management movement placed great stress upon detailed production planning. Periods of economic recession and the great depression of the 1930's in particular revealed the planning defects of marketers who were caught with shelves of high-priced inventory. The following explanation is based upon a firsthand observation of these conditions:

> In the case of the smaller specialty stores it was the depression of the 1930's that stimulated more detailed plans and procedures. On this point I can offer some personal testimony. No longer than 30 years ago it was the exceptional merchant in the men's wear field who attempted anything resembling merchandise planning. Merchants generally were more interested in selling than in watching their stocks. They paid little attention to turnover; very often the only effective restraints on inventories were those imposed by limited capital. Gross profit margins varied widely according to the over-all cost of doing business. Stocks were frequently unbalanced; price lines were haphazard. I wrote many letters in those days urging retailers to work out seasonal buying plans and operating budgets and to improve their gross profit margins.[3]

Since World War II, there has been a substantial increase in corporate planning of a comprehensive nature. In earlier years, there was a tendency for planning to be performed on a departmental, piecemeal, fragmented basis. Planning was performed unevenly throughout the company, and the result was a collection of plans which controlled the operations of individual segments of the business but lacked overall unity. The experience of the Standard Oil Company of Ohio, cited earlier in the chapter, is merely one example of the transformation in management planning that has occurred in numerous companies. Hundreds of larger corporations

[3]Meyer Kestnbaum, "The Essential Components of Business Planning," in *Planning the Future Strategy of Your Business,* eds. Edward C. Bursk and D. H. Fenn (New York: McGraw-Hill Book Company, 1956), p. 41.

have now adopted the practice of comprehensive corporate planning, regularly preparing formal long-range plans. Corporate planning staffs have also been established in numerous companies to coordinate planning at the top management level.

The constantly accelerating rate of change in the environment, products, markets, and methods of business also forces attention to planning. A company and its management must "run fast" just to stay even with competition. Discoveries and new product introductions by competitors render existing product lines obsolete. Lead time for introducing new products and exploiting new markets is shortened by the rush of competitors to duplicate the success of others. Rather than calmly selecting a future path in a predictable environment, the manager must frantically jump from crisis to crisis as the world of business changes. In this atmosphere of change, planning is necessary for survival. The accelerating rate of change creates frustrations for the planner but at the same time renders the planning function indispensable.

Today the need for planning in business administration is widely recognized. With one voice, corporate executives stress the importance of planning in business. It has become popular not only to plan but to use such sophisticated tools as electronic computers in plotting the desirable course of action for the business. The major question today, thus, is not whether to plan but how to plan most effectively.

Not only has the amount of planning increased, but this planning has become considerably more complex as a result of changes in the business and its environment. Complexities in planning just one function of the modern corporation are illustrated by the following quotation describing new developments in production planning:

> Most publicized, perhaps, have been the growing complexity, specialization, and precision of *production planning*—the result of scientific discoveries, new materials and products, mechanical achievements and higher-speed manufacture, and quality control. It is indeed a far cry from the manufacture of a simple, single-model car to the geographically decentralized assembly of the modern automobile in hundreds of combinations of model, accessories, optional equipment, furnishings, and color; from the oil still to huge, intricate, electronically controlled refineries producing a stream of primary and derivative products in various combinations; from many small machines individually operated to integrated batteries of automated machines and transport equipment performing a succession of operations without human intervention. Entirely new technologies are

being incorporated in productive processes. Nuclear-power generation and heating, radioactive measurement and isotope tracers, ultrasonics, cryogenics, and automatic machine and process control are familiar examples.[4]

Primacy of Planning

What is the relationship of planning to other functions of management? One proposal suggests a *primacy* of planning that gives to it a unique role in the performance of the other managerial functions.[5] Of course, we must recognize that the various functions are interrelated in that no one function can exist without the others. Furthermore, operating experience and data collected in connection with the control function are used extensively in subsequent planning. The idea of a primacy of planning, however, stresses the fact that goal setting and operational planning are necessary before any intelligent consideration can be given to organizational relationships, staffing, direction, or control.

This reasoning suggests the possibility that planning may be relatively more important than the other managerial functions to the successful functioning of the organization. Although defective performance in any area is undesirable, planning errors go to the very heart of the organization. Serious mistakes or omissions in planning can hardly be offset by effective organizing or controlling.

In spite of its primacy, planning is perhaps the most easily neglected of all managerial functions. It is a rare manager who does not find himself too busy. The natural reaction is to devote time to those activities clamoring for attention. March and Simon have suggested a "Gresham's Law" of planning in which daily routine drives out planning.[6] Organizing and directing must go on, but long-range planning, in particular, may always be postponed a bit longer.

The disastrous effects of neglected planning are not always apparent in the short run. In fact, the business may proceed from month to month and year to year with little outward indication of its weakness in planning. Eventually, however, and often disastrously, management deficiencies in planning are revealed.

---

[4]Melville C. Branch, *The Corporate Planning Process* (New York: American Management Association, 1962), p. 29.

[5]Harold Koontz, "A Preliminary Statement of Principles of Planning and Control," *The Journal of the Academy of Management,* Vol. 1, No. 1, April 1958, p. 49.

[6]James G. March and Herbert A. Simon, *Organizations* (New York: John Wiley & Sons, Inc., 1958), p. 185.

Long-Range Planning

In recent years, much interest in industry has centered about the subject of long-range planning. Just what length of time should or can properly be included in such planning is a matter of opinion and, to some extent, dependent upon the nature of the industry.

The lead time required to take a product from realization of need to completion of design and production is one significant factor. In automobile manufacturing, for example, approximately three years are required to develop and introduce a completely new model. Detroit's product planners were undoubtedly planning in early 1968 for the 1971 models. The length of time necessary to recover funds invested in plant and equipment is another factor determining the planning horizon.

In practice, business firms exhibit great variation in their time spans of planning. While three-, five-, and ten-year plans are frequently used, lumber companies have reforestation plans covering a century. Even within the same company, plans of varying lengths are prepared for different segments of the business. For example, the same automobile manufacturer which plans its models three years in advance also studies the future of transportation thirty years in the future.

One of the most widely used planning periods is five years. For many companies, this apparently provides enough time to evaluate the results of current decisions. A longer period, moreover, tends to strain the long-range vision of the planners. The five-year plan is one of only intermediate length in some industries, however. In electric and communication utilities, for example, it is often necessary to develop facilities and plans for service extending twenty or thirty years into the future.

Of course, considerable flexibility is necessary in long-range plans. Because the plans extend so much further into the future, less accuracy can be expected than is true for short-range plans. In fact, the greater uncertainty may discourage management from even attempting such planning. Unless the future is completely unpredictable, however, some long-range projections are superior to none.

In long-range planning, the factors to be included are broad in nature and involve basic objectives of the business. As an example of the content of long-range planning, one company developed the following standard outline for each division's planning:

The industry	Working capital
Our position	Return on investment
Competitors' activities	Location of new facilities
Sales forecasts	Manpower requirements
Present products	Management controls
New products	Pricing policies
Capital investment requirements	Appraisal of strengths and weaknesses

Special problem areas[7]

Long-range planning of a comprehensive nature must be performed or coordinated at a level very close to top management. Only at this level is there the necessary breadth of view and knowledge for the most general type of long-range plans. Top-management interest, if not active participation, in the planning process is likewise essential in providing the motivation required for the success of such projects.

Capital budgeting — that is, the planning of long-term financial commitments, particularly investments in fixed assets — should be an integral part of the firm's long-range planning. It is, of course, dependent upon the projection of economic trends and predictions concerning market developments. Long-range plans must be integrated carefully with the capital budget if best results are to be achieved. Overall strategy of the company and the opportunities in various product and market areas must be considered in the allocation of financial resources.

Variations in Plans

There is a great diversity in business planning. Planning at one organizational level in one functional area appears much different from that in another area at a different level. The plans differ on the basis of various features.[8]

The time factor evident in the discussion of long-range planning is one of the differentiating features of plans. As another example, plans may apply to various functional areas of the business, such

---

[7]H. Edward Wrapp, "Organization for Long-Range Planning," *Harvard Business Review,* Vol. 35, No. 1, January-February 1957, p. 44.

[8]Thirteen different aspects or "dimensions" of plans are suggested in the following: Preston P. LeBreton and Dale A. Henning, *Planning Theory* (Englewood Cliffs: Prentice-Hall, Inc., 1961), p. 23.

as marketing versus production plans. Some plans are also repetitive and basically simple — such as replacement of a standard piece of office equipment. Others are extremely complex — such as introduction of a completely new product or location of a new branch plant. Numerous other points of difference could be cited.

The firm's operational planning normally culminates in a financial budget. This constitutes the most comprehensive plan used by most companies and is a standard element in the planning of most well-managed organizations. Because the budget is also used as a control device, its discussion is included in Chapter 25.

Planning Premises

Nature of Planning Premises

The planner is confronted with numerous uncertainties in the business environment. Some of these are external to the firm and beyond the control of its management. The health of the economy represents one such factor. Planning of necessity involves some consideration of these factors. What would be good planning based upon one premise becomes unwise planning if this premise proves to be wrong. Effective planning, thus, requires an awareness and accurate identification of the planning premises.

Classifying these as premises or assumptions does not indicate that they are accepted blindly or picked out of thin air. Premises involve predictions, and the predictions should be made as scientifically as possible. In some cases, of course, they can be little more than educated guesses.

As planning becomes longer-range in nature, the establishment of sound premises becomes more difficult. In the short run, the facts at hand provide the basis for more discriminating judgment. In the distant future, however, many significant factors are subject to change. Regardless of the difficulty involved, an explicit recognition of assumptions and an attempt to assess the probable range of variation appear superior to planning with "blinders" that shut out the surrounding environment.

Public Policy

One of the primary assumptions required for business planning concerns the role of government and public policy. The general attitude of government is often viewed by corporate management as "friendly" or "unfriendly" to business. An unfriendly administration may act less favorably toward business in any number of ways. It is possible, of course, that popular thinking may exaggerate the magnitude of political differences as far as their practical effect on business is concerned. Assessment of this attitude is made, explicitly or implicitly, by the reflective business planner.

In 1966, the Pittston Company, a diversified company producing both coal and oil, was described as hesitant to expand its coal mining business. The reason for the hesitancy was not the industry's prospects, which looked good at the time, but rather Pittston Chairman Joseph P. Routh's assessment of the political situation.

> Routh says he is uncertain because of "the political climate." He thinks the coal industry needs higher prices, but he's afraid President Lyndon Johnson's attitude toward business may restrict profits growth. "If President Johnson continues punitive action," he complains, "the outlook is bad for all businesses. I call it 'killing the goose that lays the golden egg.' "
>
> As the unquestioned boss of Pittston, 72-year-old Joe Routh clearly has the power to hold back expansion until the political situation is more to his liking. Whether he is *right* to hold back is very much an open question. "We're shifting emphasis from oil to coal," he insists. But, as things now stand, he seems to be referring to a mood, not a deed.[9]

At any given time, furthermore, a specific political and economic institutional arrangement exists, and some assumption is demanded as to its continuation. Long-term financial commitments in steel, for example, require consideration of the degree of freedom from government regulation and control that may be expected. The cold war constitutes one of the current great uncertainties in planning. If international tensions were to increase, the country would move closer to a wartime footing. During a war or mobilization period, price controls, profit controls, rationing, and manpower controls are typically imposed. Indeed, if a major nuclear war were seriously anticipated, much business planning would be virtually meaningless.

Defense expenditures themselves constitute a significant element in the political environment of the planner. Not only do they serve as a prop to the economy as a whole, but they constitute a major part of the market for some companies and industries. In firms directly affected by defense policy, planning demands an assump-

---

[9]"I Was Proved Wrong," *Forbes,* Vol. 97, No. 3, February 1, 1966, p. 25.

tion regarding such policy and related expenditures. If defense policy dictates a greater emphasis on missiles and less emphasis on aircraft, for example, certain aircraft manufacturers are likely to suffer. Their planning, accordingly, may properly call for retrenchment.

Government fiscal policy has a direct impact on the economy and thus on most business concerns. The President is advised by a Council of Economic Advisers who constantly study the economy — its health and rate of growth — recommending appropriate public policy to the President and Congress. If public policy calls for a budget deficit, a stimulation of the economy is provided. Inflation may also be anticipated as a result of government fiscal policy, with an effect on business plans. Public works expenditures, for example, produce a stimulating effect on economic conditions.

Public monetary policy is likewise significant to business planners. The Federal Reserve Board has power through its control of interest rates, regulation of credit, and other measures to stimulate or retard business activity. For most business concerns, the planner's concern with monetary policy arises from its effect on business conditions generally. For certain financial institutions, of course, planning would be affected by the direct impact of changes in monetary policy.

Tax legislation and changes in taxation cannot be disregarded in planning. An expected rate of local property taxation, for example, is often one of the factors considered in choosing a business location. Federal tax policy also influences business prospects in a number of ways. An investment tax credit makes investment in new facilities more attractive to many companies. A general tax reduction causes general stimulation to business. The 1964 tax reduction provided a dramatic illustration of this fact. Even financial planning requires some assumption concerning tax policy. Different methods of financing may be chosen on the basis of their respective tax advantages.

Economic Conditions

Business conditions and the business cycle are of interest to almost every businessman. With an upswing in business activity, most firms tend to prosper. A severe recession, on the other hand, can reduce profits or result in financial losses.

Planning must anticipate probable economic conditions in selecting the best course of action for the future. In fact, the planner's interest is not limited to short-run economic conditions. Long-run business prospects and the rate of economic growth for the economy and for specific industries are important to many decisions. Expansion plans involving major commitments, for example, must be based upon predictions of this type. The tremendous error of Sewell Avery of Montgomery Ward in financial and expansion policy following World War II is now a legend in the history of American business. While its competitor, Sears, Roebuck and Company, expanded, Montgomery Ward guarded its cash and waited for a depression.

Montgomery Ward was not alone in its pessimistic anticipation of a post-war depression. Black and Decker Manufacturing Company, maker of power tools, also looked for a post-war slump and formed a committee to find new markets to help them through the expected depression.[10] The committee reasoned that hard times would drive many people to do-it-yourself projects, and the company introduced a number of home tools. The market for home tools did develop but for a different reason — leisure activity of prosperous wage earners. Because of the incorrect assumption about the depression, however, Black and Decker failed to build new capacity, planning to serve the do-it-yourself market by using facilities idled by the slump. As a result, many orders simply could not be filled. With industrial and home markets booming, Black and Decker prospered but still watched competitors acquire a larger share of the market than would have occurred otherwise.

Prospective economic conditions will affect production and inventory levels. The labor force and production facilities may be expanded if a period of prosperity is anticipated. The business firm attempts to build inventory in expectation of an expanding market. Whenever a downturn is indicated, however, business planning calls for the opposite approach.

Financial planning similarly requires consideration of probable economic conditions. Borrowing may be reduced during a recession. Plans for working-capital loans may be needed when business recovery is imminent. New stock or bond issues must be appropriately timed to obtain a maximum price for the securities.

Business Forecasting

It is the function of business forecasting to predict trends in economic conditions. The need for such assistance in planning has encouraged the employment of economists in industrial concerns. It is not uncommon for a corporate economist to have the ear of

---

[10] "Second Chance," *Forbes,* Vol. 97, No. 8, April 15, 1966, pp. 66-67.

top management. In the Du Pont Company, for example, the Economist's Office reports directly to the company's Executive Committee along with the other major departments of the company.

In its simplest and least dependable form, economic forecasting simply involves a guess by the businessman as to future conditions. He may rely on intuition or hunch. His observations or estimates may be affected by reading trade periodicals and by discussions with other businessmen. Observation of the purchasing patterns and purchasing plans of his own customers provides another checkpoint for the businessman. As forecasting becomes more scientific, less reliance is placed upon intuition, and more attention is devoted to the analysis of economic data.

Certain indicators may be used as barometers or guides in the prediction of business trends. Various of these indicators are often combined to form an index, and movements of the index are reported periodically. To illustrate, *Business Week* presents a weekly report on an index reflecting the movement of such indicators as steel production, automobile production, electric power consumption, car loadings, and industrial power consumption. These items are weighted and combined to provide a general index of business conditions.

The business press regularly presents analyses of business conditions and reviews of current trends. Many banks issue periodic reviews of this type, and both trade and general business periodicals are filled with reports of this nature. The following paragraph is quoted for purpose of illustration from the "Trend of Business" presented monthly by *Dun's Review and Modern Industry*:

> Many economists are a shade more optimistic than they were a few months ago about the trend of business over the rest of this year. Fewer see a downturn — the result of a growing belief that government spending not only will absorb any slack developing from a slowdown in consumer and private spending, but will provide the impetus to push the economy moderately upward.[11]

The methods of statistical analysis used in business forecasting are described in standard textbooks on business statistics. They include trend extrapolation, mathematical models, diffusion indexes, and various other techniques. Effective utilization of such tools requires considerable ability and experience in the methods of quantitative analysis.

---

[11] "Business Trends," *Dun's Review and Modern Industry,* Vol. 89, No. 3, March 1967, p. 11.

Business forecasting is normally extended from the prediction of general economic conditions to forecasting the market for the particular industry and firm. These estimates provide basic data for use in planning sales volume. The sales estimate, in turn, provides the starting point for short-run operational planning. Business forecasting thus affects planning of production schedules, inventory levels, and other basic elements of business operations.

Fashion Trends

Among the many other external factors affecting business planning is that of fashion trends. The seriousness of this factor varies, obviously, from one type of business to another. Its influence often exists, however, in industries that have the appearance of immunity to fashion change. If the product being produced or sold is subject to rapid fashion obsolescence, an error in planning can be critical. The warehouse may quickly be filled with items that are no longer in style.

As an example of fashion influence in business planning, consider the matter of color. The significance of color in women's clothing is well known, but it is also influential in many other industries. Some companies go to great length to determine trends in the use of color. A stylist of auto upholstery fabric, for example, was reported to prowl Paris fashion salons to detect color trends a year or so before they reached the U.S.[12] Trend predictions and attempts to influence trends do not always work out as expected, with unfortunate effects upon plans based upon such premises.

> A few years ago men's wear retailers and manufacturers got stuck with mountains of inventory when their best selling color — pink — suddenly went dead. "We went too far in one direction," ruefully admits a big retailer. "We gave men everything pink — slacks, shirts, coats, ties, socks and sweaters; we made our customers look like uniformed milkmen."[13]

Fashion trends, then, pose a real challenge to the business planner. Though sometimes difficult to fathom, they can hardly be ignored.

> Nobody's crystal ball can show up the fashion future in complete detail. If it could, a lot of brain power would be unemployed; a lot of fun would go out of life. But this much is certain: the fact that an industry invests billions of dollars in

---

[12]"Prosaic Items Sport Such Fashion Hues as Breen, Banana Yellow," *The Wall Street Journal,* August 27, 1962, p. 1.

[13]*Ibid.,* p. 4.

> equipment is no guarantee of a continued market for its products. Fashion is absolutely and callously indifferent to any monumental achievements in manufacturing proficiency. If anything, she takes capricious delight in nullifying man's industry — or pretenses to rationality. All of the fame and bulk of a leading textile, appliance, construction, or automobile company will not save it from fashion's dust bin if she so wills. She, and not the so-called fashion dictator — as Paul Poiret always professed — is the true autocrat; and only in a totalitarian state, where the consumer's taste is legislated by government edict, does she meet her match.[14]

Other External Factors

Various other external conditions or factors are subject to change and demand assumptions of some type as the basis for planning. Competitors' plans and activities constitute one such factor. If a competitor succeeds in introducing an improved or a revolutionary new product, the market for conventional or unimproved items is clearly reduced. Sales promotion campaigns of one competitor may likewise take business away from other firms. By the same token, weaknesses in competition provide opportunities that may be exploited through planning.

Raw materials and labor markets are also significant in business planning. Anticipated price increases or shortages in raw materials, for example, may lead to planned stockpiling. Provisions being written into major labor contracts and general trends in personnel practices affect expectations of personnel in most companies. If wages in other companies are going up on the average of 5 per cent, it may be unrealistic to budget on the basis of stable labor costs.

Population trends and shifts to urban (or suburban) living likewise affect planning by many types of concerns. Textbook manufacturers have planned for the boom in college enrollment occurring in the 1960's and 1970's. Many types of business concerns find their location planning strongly affected by the shifting residential patterns of the population.

No doubt numerous other factors having a significant effect on the planning process could be cited. These are merely suggested as some of the basic elements requiring attention by most concerns. In any particular enterprise, any one factor may have unusual im-

---

[14]Dwight E. Robinson, "Fashion Theory and Product Design," *Harvard Business Review,* Vol. 36, No. 6, November-December 1958, p. 138.

portance because of the nature of the business or because of some unique situation that exists at a particular time.

Organization of the Planning Function

All Management Personnel

Who should do the planning in a business enterprise? Clearly, all management personnel must accept some planning responsibility. As a basic management function, planning is an inherent part of each manager's duties. Although a plan may be prepared by one individual manager, many plans are the joint product of the efforts and influence of a number of individuals. This point will be evident in the following chapter's discussion of decision making.

A distinction may be made, however, as to the relative amounts of planning to be performed by line managers in contrast to that performed by staff offices. By drawing upon the experience of operating management, top management achieves greater practicality in business plans. Operating managers know that at least some proposals will or will not work satisfactorily. Broad management participation is also necessary for genuine acceptance of adopted plans. Otherwise, a line manager is inclined to blame the plan if difficulty is experienced or to ignore it as much as possible. A major problem of operating management in planning is shortage of time. Other responsibilities are constantly demanding attention.

Top-management leadership and involvement in the planning process are also essential if comprehensive corporate planning is to be achieved.

> Probably the single most important problem in corporate planning derives from the belief of some chief operating executives that corporate planning is not a function with which they should be directly concerned. They regard planning as something to be delegated, which subordinates can do without responsible participation by chief executives. They think the end result of effective planning is the compilation of a "Plans" book. Such volumes get distributed to key executives, who scan the contents briefly, file them away, breathe a sigh of relief, and observe, "Thank goodness that is done — now let's get back to work."[15]

---

[15]Myles L. Mace, "The President and Corporate Planning," *Harvard Business Review,* Vol. 43, No. 1, January-February 1965, p. 50.

As an example of broad management participation, Texas Instruments, Inc., has made a systematic attempt to involve general managers in overall company planning.[16] Beginning in 1952, the company instituted a series of formal, annual planning conferences. The first such session, then confined to the manufacturing division, involved a two-day conference in Colorado Springs. It was attended by all six department heads of the manufacturing division, the executive vice president, the president, and the chairman of the board. The result of the conference was a set of objectives, plans for attaining them, and criteria for judging future performance.

In the years following this beginning, many adaptations were made in the scope, length, and general format of the annual planning conference. It has also been supplemented by quarterly review sessions. The central feature of the annual sessions, however, continues to be the establishment of plans for all of TI's divisions and the integration of these into an overall set of plans.

The Planning Staff

A planning staff is sometimes created and assigned a responsibility for developing or guiding the development of certain plans — particularly those of a long-range nature. Use of such a staff has the advantage of making planning the major responsibility of a particular group. For this group, it is not an activity that must be squeezed into an already busy operating schedule. As a result, there is the possibility of more intensive investigation of pertinent facts and more thorough analysis in devising, analyzing, and coordinating plans. A planning staff may confer with the various parts of the organization, securing information from them and directing their preparation of plans. A primary responsibility of a typical central planning staff is the coordination of plans prepared by major components of the company. Such coordination requires scrutiny to assure their proper interrelationships and consonance with long-range objectives. To function effectively, such a planning office must have a close advisory relationship to top management.

In some cases, however, planning projects involve questions somewhat divorced from the direct interest and concern of the firm's regular operating management. On such projects, staff planners can proceed independently in their study.

---

[16]C. J. Thomsen, "The Annual Planning Conference," from *Planning for Growth: Three Company Programs,* General Management Series No. 185 (New York: American Management Association, 1957), pp. 32-41.

A specialized staff office such as engineering or personnel may also be expected to head up planning in its own area, even though other departments share some responsibility for the planning. The employee relations staff, for example, may coordinate personnel planning even though specific personnel plans are prepared by the various operating departments. The controller's office may likewise carry managerial responsibility in budgeting. Each organizational component would typically prepare its own tentative budget, but these would be integrated into an overall budget under the leadership of the controller and, possibly, a budget committee.

Contributions of Subordinates to Planning

Traditionally, we have viewed the manager as the complete planner for his part of the organization. Information was funneled to him, but he did the planning. According to the concepts of delegation and decentralization, however, planning should be pushed downward in the organization. Specific plans should be formulated by the divisions and departments responsible for carrying out the work, within the framework of overall objectives and policies.

It is also clear that managers vary in the degree to which they use subordinates in their own planning. This is true even apart from the manager's delegation of authority whereby he assigns planning of a more limited or detailed nature to subordinate levels. If a manager wishes to draw extensively upon the thinking of his subordinates in planning, he may arrange special ways to encourage such contributions. Subordinates may be asked to submit proposals or suggestions or to criticize tentative plans that have been drafted. They may also be appointed to serve on planning committees that work out plans for the entire organization. Utilization of subordinates in planning has the advantage of getting the practical point of view of those closer to the scene of operations.

Summary

Planning has become a function of vital interest and importance to all levels of management, including the top executive group. Planning consists of the activities involved in choosing courses of action to achieve company objectives. To some degree, the planning function has a position of *primacy* or priority in its relationship to other managerial functions. The systems concept in planning stresses the integration of individual departmental plans into a comprehensive corporate plan and also emphasizes the need for careful analysis of the relationship between the business system and the environmental systems of which it is a part.

In planning, it is necessary for management to adopt certain assumptions or *premises* — particularly with regard to factors of an external nature — that serve as a background for the planning function. One major premise of this type involves *public policy* and the relationship of government to business. Prospective *economic conditions*, which are subject to evaluation through business forecasting, constitute another factor of importance in business planning. Still other factors such as *fashion trends*, *competitive developments*, and *population trends* must be taken into consideration in any attempt at intelligent planning.

Planning is a part of the activities of all management personnel. Some use is made of staff planners, however, who have the advantage of being able to devote their full attention to the analysis of business problems and the preparation of specific plans. Managers differ in the degree to which they utilize the thinking of subordinates in planning for the future of their organizations.

Discussion Questions

1. "A good decision maker is also a good planner." Evaluate this statement.
2. What is the relationship between *objectives*, *policies*, and *operational planning*?
3. What accounts for the increasing importance of planning in business organizations?
4. Explain the concept of the *primacy of planning*.
5. What determines the length of the future time period that should be covered by business planning?
6. In view of the uncertainties confronting most business organizations, how can you justify attempts at *long-range planning?*
7. What is the advantage, if any, of employing a business economist versus utilizing the economic forecasts published by other organizations?
8. Compare the effectiveness of planning performed by a staff office in contrast to planning performed by line managers.

9. In past years, major innovations in various fields occurred every fifteen or twenty years. The intervals are now much shorter — five or ten years — and may shrink even further in the years ahead. What are the planning implications of this change?

Supplementary Reading

Branch, Melville C., "A View of Corporate Planning Today," *California Management Review,* Vol. 7, No. 2, Winter 1964, pp. 89-94.

__________, *Planning: Aspects and Applications.* New York: John Wiley & Sons, Inc., 1966.

__________, *The Corporate Planning Process.* New York: American Management Association, 1962.

Ewing, David W., "Corporate Planning at a Crossroads," *Harvard Business Review,* Vol. 45, No. 4, July-August 1967, pp. 77-86.

__________, ed., *Long-Range Planning for Management,* Revised Edition. New York: Harper & Row, Publishers, 1964.

Greenwood, Frank, "Effective LRP Requires Action," *Academy of Management Journal,* Vol. 7, No. 3, September 1964, pp. 224-228.

Hoopes, Townsend, "The Corporate Planner (New Edition)," *Business Horizons,* Vol. 5, No. 4, Winter 1962, pp. 59-68.

LeBreton, Preston and Dale A. Henning, *Planning Theory.* Englewood Cliffs: Prentice-Hall, Inc., 1961.

Litschert, Robert J., "Some Characteristics of Organization for Long-Range Planning," *Academy of Management Journal,* Vol. 10, No. 3, September 1967, pp. 247-256.

Murdick, R. G., "The Long-Range Planning Matrix," *California Management Review,* Vol. 7, No. 2, Winter 1964, pp. 35-42.

Schaffer, Robert H., "Putting Action Into Planning," *Harvard Business Review,* Vol. 45, No. 6, November-December 1967, pp. 158-166.

Scott, Brian W., *Long-Range Planning in American Industry.* New York: American Management Association, 1965.

Sord, Burnard H. and Glenn A. Welsch, *Managerial Planning and Control.* Austin: Bureau of Business Research, The University of Texas, 1964.

Steiner, George A., "How to Assure Poor Long-Range Planning for Your Company," *California Management Review,* Vol. 7, No. 4, Summer 1965, pp. 93-94.

__________, ed., *Managerial Long-Range Planning.* New York: McGraw-Hill Book Company, 1963.

St. Thomas, Charles E., *Practical Business Planning: A Manager's Guide.* New York: American Management Association, 1965.

Summer, Charles E., Jr., "The Future Role of the Corporate Planner," *California Management Review,* Vol. 3, No. 2, Winter 1961, pp. 17-31.

Thompson, Stewart, *How Companies Plan,* American Management Association Research Study 54. New York: American Management Association, 1962.

7

The Decision-Making Process

Managers must of necessity be decision makers, because the decision-making process is a part of the fabric of management. Some consider decision making the equivalent of management. Decision making is not always easy or pleasant, however. In the executive suite, in fact, there is a tempting tendency to postpone decisions, to wait for further developments, to engage in additional study. Of course, such a procedure is often logical. There comes a time, however, when choice is necessary. Effective managers distinguish themselves by their ability to reach logical decisions at such times. Although a manager may be scholarly and possess great human understanding, he is ineffective as an administrator without the ability to reach timely decisions.

The Nature of Managerial Decision Making

What Is Decision Making?

Managerial decision making involves a *conscious choice* on the part of the manager. By making such a choice, he comes to a conclusion and selects a particular course of action from two or more alternatives that are open to him. Choice, of course, need not always be conscious. A particular behavior pattern may be selected on the basis of habit or rule of thumb. Although some would classify all choices as decision making, our particular concern is with conscious choices made by management. In this chapter, accordingly, the concept of decision making is limited to those decisions in which the manager perceives the alternatives and consciously makes his choice.

In defining decision making, there is a tendency to focus upon the final moment in which the manager selects his course of action. A decision is announced, for example, that a new branch plant will be built in a particular city. Management has obviously made a decision. This concentration upon the final choice, however, tends to obscure the fact that decision making is in reality a process in which the choice of a particular solution is only the final step. Deliberation, evaluation, and thought are involved. The various stages of decision making, which are described in another section of this chapter, include steps of investigation and analysis as well as the final choice of alternatives.

Decisions are often more complex than they appear on the surface. A choice of the type mentioned above—opening a new branch plant—undoubtedly involved extensive analysis by sales, production, and other executives prior to culmination in the final choice. In addition, numerous subsequent decisions would be required in implementing a plan for construction of the new plant.

Decision making is also a much slower process than it seems would be the case. Rather than occurring in a matter of hours or days, decision making often drags on, surprisingly, for weeks, months, and even years! This tendency toward slowness in rendering decisions has been verified through empirical investigations.[1] As one example, a period of almost four years was required for a decision regarding installation of electronic data processing. In another case, the question of replacing overhead cranes with magnetically controlled cranes, for safety reasons, required two years for decision. These involved problems with single issues, not extremely complex in nature. These and other examples reported by researchers seemed to represent standard practice rather than exceptional or unusual cases.

A manager makes decisions because he has been delegated the necessary authority to make choices of this type. He is presumed to have the right to make decisions pertaining to the organization and activities subject to his direction. He thus makes choices affecting

---

[1]Robert Dubin, "Business Behavior *Behaviorally* Viewed," in *Social Science Approaches to Business Behavior,* ed. George B. Strother (Homewood: Richard D. Irwin, Inc., and The Dorsey Press, Inc., 1962), pp. 30-32. Used with permission.

not only his own behavior but also that of subordinates. His decision-making authority is not absolute, however, with respect to his subordinates. His ability to make effective decisions affecting subordinates may be limited by the subordinates themselves—a possibility discussed in Chapter 18.

Discussing decision making as the task of a particular manager may be a bit misleading. Behavioral scientists have stressed the numerous organizational influences at work in reaching a given decision. Many managers and even nonmanagerial personnel often have an effect upon the final choice. Herbert A. Simon refers to the *composite* decision and suggests that almost no decision made in an organization is the task of a single individual.[2]

Figure 2 shows the series of key business decisions involved in the development of "Surlyn" A ionomer resin by the Du Pont Company. It is clear from this figure that a series of decisions was involved in developing this product. It is also apparent that the management levels at which these decisions were made varied with the nature and importance of the decision. Of necessity, any such diagram oversimplifies the actual process of decision making. No doubt some decisions that are portrayed as the responsibility of one individual were in reality composite decisions. And it is obvious that there were numerous additional decisions supplementing the key decisions indicated in the figure.

Types of Decisions

A distinction can be made between decisions concerning *ends* and decisions concerning *means*. The former are concerned with basic goals and involve value judgments as to what the organization's objectives should be. For this reason, decisions establishing goals (except for intermediate goals involved in reaching broader objectives) are not reached through a strictly rational process. Many of the business objectives, as discussed in Chapter 4, are ends rather than means. Some decisions do not fall neatly into either category but involve elements of both.

As a practical matter, many business decisions are concerned with means. Our primary emphasis in this chapter is upon decisions of this type. In such decisions, the profit goal is assumed and the alternative that appears likely to contribute most to profits is chosen.

---

[2]Reprinted by permission of The Macmillan Company from *Administrative Behavior* by Herbert A. Simon. © by Herbert A. Simon 1957.

Figure 2. *Who Decides What: Key Business Decisions in the Development of "Surlyn" A Ionomer Resin*

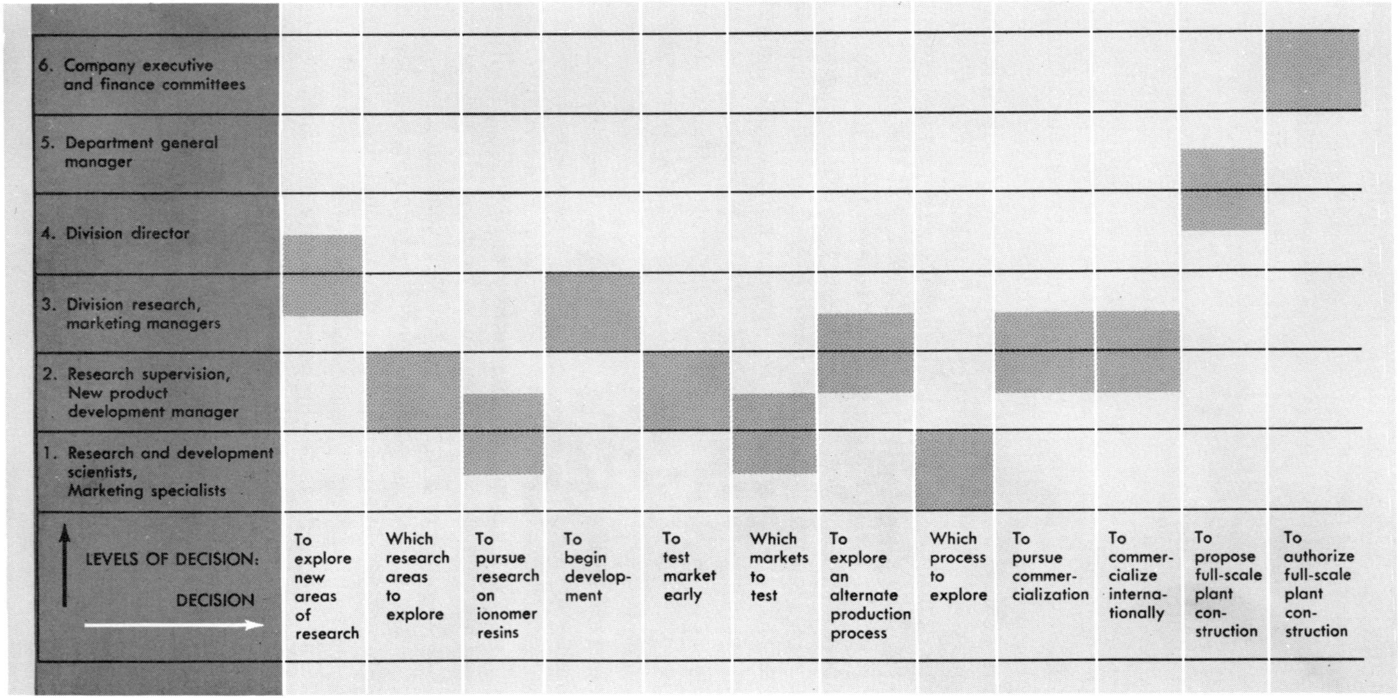

Source: *The D of Research and Development* (Wilmington: E. I. DuPont de Nemours and Company, 1966), pp. 28-29.

As a matter of fact, the goals of the business organization are often much more specific than merely making a profit. Alternatives can thus be selected on the basis of the greatest contribution to the goal. Suppose that the issue for decision is the purchase of an electronic computer. The feasibility study is designed to reveal total costs, savings, and improvements in operating efficiency. While decisions concerning means (as contrasted with ends) do not necessarily exclude value judgments, such decisions are basically *rational* in their nature. Irrationality in decisions regarding means amounts to inefficiency.

> Decisions can always be evaluated in this relative sense—it can be determined whether they are correct, given the objective at which they are aimed—but a change in objective implies a change in evaluation.[3]

The correctness of a "means" decision can be judged, then, in the light of the controlling objective. It is not always possible, however, to prove conclusively that one particular decision is the *best* of all possible decisions.

In addition to the ends-means distinction, decisions may also be classified on the basis of their importance. Those made at top levels are in general the most critical decisions in terms of organization success.[4] Another set of decision categories distinguishes between *strategic*, *administrative*, and *operating* decisions.[5] Strategic decisions pertain to the relationship of a firm with its environment and are concerned with such questions as the firm's product mix and extent of product diversification. Operating decisions are those pricing, marketing, and production decisions that are designed to make operations profitable. Administrative decisions are organizational decisions, including structuring of authority, determining work flows, and locating facilities.

It is also possible to distinguish between *routine* and *nonroutine* decisions. Routine decisions are repetitive in nature and follow

---

[3]Reprinted by permission of The Macmillan Company from *Administrative Behavior* by Herbert A. Simon. © by Herbert A. Simon 1957.

[4]According to William R. Dill, critical decisions do not require particularly different modes of analysis than those used for other decisions. The essential difference concerns the greater time delays and the tendency of noncritical decisions to cause postponement of the most important decisions. William R. Dill, "Administrative Decision-Making," in Sidney Mailick and Edward H. Van Ness, eds., *Concepts and Issues in Administrative Behavior* © 1962, pp. 42-43. Used by permission of Prentice-Hall, Inc., Englewood Cliffs, N. J.

[5]H. Igor Ansoff, *Corporate Strategy* (New York: McGraw-Hill Book Company, 1965), p. 5.

established patterns or procedures. Inspection of completed products to established tolerances illustrates this type of decision, as does planning daily work assignments in a typing pool. Nonroutine decisions present unique problems requiring individual analysis and solution. Suppose the organization is contemplating construction of a new office building. The fact that the company does not build a number of such office buildings one after another means that this project requires special study concerning layout and other details of construction. It is nonroutine decisions that provide the major challenge to decision makers.

How Decisions Are Made

Asking an executive how he makes decisions is somewhat like asking a swimmer how he swims. Effective administrators find it difficult to dissect the mental processes they employ in reaching decisions. Attempts to probe the decision-making process have encountered such reactions as the following:

> I don't think we businessmen know how we make decisions.
>
> I don't know how I do it; I just do it.
>
> There's no formula for effective decision making.
>
> Thinking only causes mistakes.

Such remarks indicate that decision making involves more than a strictly rational analysis of cold facts. Judgment or intuition is apparently used in the process. Behind this, undoubtedly, is the fact that many of the significant elements in decisions are intangible in their nature. Even those considerations that are more tangible may require considerable judgment in assessing their importance. It is not easy to analyze the psychological processes involved in reaching a business decision.

Of course, simple decisions that are repetitive in nature may be made on the basis of habitual approaches and standard operating procedures. These, however, are not the really difficult managerial decisions.

Attention focused on decision making in recent years has been concerned with improving its rationality. Intuition is to some extent being replaced by logical reasoning. This is not to say that all subjective judgments can now be laid aside. But the challenge is to reduce the area in which the intuitive approach is required. Significant factors in decisions are being identified, underlying assumptions are being recognized as such, and more data are being included in analyses. More precise calculations are being substituted for judgment.

The ideal approach is the completely logical or fact based method of decision making. In most decisions at present, this can only be approximated. Attention to the question, however, can serve to improve the process even though certain intangibles and imponderables remain.

Decision Making and Management Functions

Decision making pervades all functions of management, because each function entails choices among alternative courses of action. In organizing, for example, the manager must determine the types of activities assigned to particular departments. In addition, he must decide upon the degree to which authority will be delegated to subordinates.

It seems appropriate to discuss decision making in the context of the planning function, however. It is in this connection that the decision-making process has received its greatest attention and most thorough analysis.

The Systems View of Decision Making

When decision making is examined in the light of systems theory, its complexity becomes apparent. Problems do not exist in isolation. The manager discovers that there are many "angles" or facets involved in individual decisions. An adjustment to one part of the system may throw another part of the system out of adjustment. Following is an illustration by the president of the Ford Motor Company of a problem of this nature that his company subjected to systems analysis:

> Let me cite an example from an experience at Ford as an illustration of how systems analysis can aid decision-making in a complex situation. In response to demand, the industry has sharply increased the range of models and options. As a result, the problem of suppling the customer with the exact type of car he wants—at the time he wants it—has become more and more difficult.
>
> Several years ago we decided to apply the systems approach to this problem. Our first step was to set forth our multiple goals—(1) responding quickly to shifts in demand, (2) keeping

our dealers supplied with proper stocks, (3) controlling inventory costs, and (4) keeping our plants running with schedules as level as feasible.[6]

It is obvious that these objectives are somewhat conflicting in nature. Improving performance in achieving one of the objectives could decrease performance in attaining another objective. Minimizing inventory costs, for example, would call for minimum inventory levels which might, in turn, interfere with speedy response to dealer orders. To reach the best decision, Ford's decision makers considered the implications of proposed solutions in terms of each of the four objectives. Costs and benefits of alternative courses of action were evaluated simultaneously for all of the objectives.

The methodology of operations research, described later in the chapter, incorporates a systems view of problem solving. Through operations research, the manager can attack complex problems in which the interaction among components is particularly significant. By examining and solving problems from an overall point of view, the operations research effort can provide optimal solutions for the organization or system as a whole.

The systems concept is also applicable to the mechanics or procedure of problem solving. It is possible to visualize the management of an organization as its decision-making system (or subsystem). Problems confronting management constitute the inputs to the system, and solutions or decisions are the outputs. Improvement in management decision making occurs as a result of refinements in organizational problem solving procedures. Stanley Young has described the design and installation of an improved decision-making system in a general hospital.[7] Prior to installation of the new system, the hospital followed the traditional bureaucratic pattern, being divided into nursing, housekeeping, pharmacy, and other departments. Decisions were frequently made in individual departments without the knowledge of other departments that might be affected. As a result of policy inconsistencies among departments and interdepartmental conflict, the hospital administrator adopted the new decision-making system. Proposed decisions by individual department heads were submitted in writing as tentative or suggestive

---

[6]Arjay Miller, "The Challenge of Decision Making," *Advanced Management Journal,* Vol. 31, No. 2, April 1966, p. 20.

[7]From *Management: A Systems Analysis* by Stanley Young, Chapter 12, Copyright © 1966 by Scott, Foresman and Company.

solutions, subject to modification through review and evaluation by other department heads.

> Upon the receipt of a suggested solution the department heads would review it in terms of its feasibility: they would determine if there were any technical or medical reasons why the solution would not work in their particaular area. If the proposal violated medical standards, it would be rejected; or if it was medically acceptable but difficult or impossible to execute because of departmental procedures or capabilities, it would also be denied. For example, a suggested pharmaceutical solution was to reduce its service from twenty-four hours to twelve in order to reduce its operating cost (a legitimate objective) and to resolve the difficulty of acquiring and providing qualified personnel during the evening and early morning hours. However, the head of nursing pointed out that physicians sometimes change their patients' prescriptions during these hours and that nurses could not comply with these changes if the pharmacy were closed. The pharmacy remained open.[8]

In summary, modification of the problem solving system improved the quality of decision making by permitting evaluation of the total effect of interdepartmental decisions.

Steps in Decision Making

It is possible to think of decision making as involving a series of steps to reach the solution of a problem. The discussion below will consider the following:

1. Identification of problem.
2. Search for alternatives.
3. Evaluation of alternatives.
4. Choice of alternative.

Identification of Problem

The problem may take various forms: it may, for example, be a condition of inefficiency, a breakdown in operations, or an opportunity to be exploited. The first step consists of problem identification. Problems requiring analysis and decision making are brought to

---

[8]*Ibid.*, p. 303.

the surface in various ways.[9] As a result, one can never be sure that the most important problems are known or recognized at any one time. Some problems come to a manager's attention in routine fashion on a regular schedule. Budgets, for example, must be prepared annually. Others are detected by management semiautomatically through the operation of various check or control devices. Periodic review of sales figures, inventory levels, or personnel turnover data may point to the existence of certain underlying problems.

Problems sometimes explode in the face of management. A foreman resigns, or a government contract is canceled. Some of the most important problems arise out of new objectives that are set by top management. In other cases, great imagination and perception on the part of management are required to detect the problem. In his study or review of the organization and its activities, a manager may sense problems or needs of which others are completely unaware.

> The principle of the Polaroid Land camera resulted from a chance conversation between the inventor, Edwin H. Land, and his daughter, who asked about having some pictures developed which they had just taken. In a flash he saw here an opportunity to revolutionize photography with a process which would yield a finished print within moments after exposure. This set off the train of events which led finally to the picture-in-a-minute camera.[10]

Occasionally, managers waste time developing solutions to the wrong problems. The reason for this is that problems do not always come clearly labeled. In proceeding with the solution of what appears to be a problem, the manager may discover that he is on the wrong track. Superficial disturbances can be misleading and fail to reveal underlying difficulties. What appears to be a problem may not be the problem at all.

> Management may see a clash of personalities; the real problem may well be poor organization structure. Management may see a problem of manufacturing costs and start a cost-reduction

---

[9]Chester I. Barnard has suggested the following origins of occasions for decision: (1) authoritative communications from superiors; (2) cases referred for decision by subordinates; and (3) cases originating in the initiative of the executive concerned. Used with permission of the publishers from Chester I. Barnard, *The Function of the Executive*, Cambridge, Mass.: Harvard University Press, Copyright 1938, by the President and Fellows of Harvard College, 1966, by Grace F. Noera Barnard, p. 190.

[10]Joseph D. Cooper, *The Art of Decision-Making*, p. 16. Copyright © 1961 by Joseph D. Cooper. Reprinted by permission of Doubleday & Company, Inc.

drive; the real problem may well be poor engineering design or poor sales planning.[11]

Management must constantly strive, then, to sift from the superficial difficulties the true problems that require investigation and solution. The desirability of avoiding some decisions has been suggested by Chester I. Barnard.

> *The fine art of executive decision consists in not deciding questions that are not now pertinent, in not deciding prematurely, in not making decisions that cannot be made effective, and in not making decisions that others should make.*[12]

Search for Alternatives

Consideration of the various possible solutions or alternative courses of action constitutes the second stage of decision making. Ordinarily, a business problem may be solved in any number of ways. If there were only one possible solution, of course, management would be powerless to devise alternatives and no decision would be required. If one is to take an objective or scientific approach to problem solving, however, he must consider alternatives rather than jumping to a conclusion concerning a single proposal.

Imagination and creative thinking are often required to devise possible solutions to a given problem. The entire range of alternatives is not immediately apparent. Certain solutions, of course, are fairly obvious and are part of the thinking of all personnel acquainted with a problem. Thorough exercise of one's own mental faculties, however, can produce unusual and often desirable solutions. Investigation of the experience and thinking of others may supplement one's own thinking in devising possible courses of action. There is an unfortunate tendency for the decision maker to focus on extremes and to see the problem solution in terms of an "either-or" situation.

> The old plant of a small plumbing equipment manufacturer had become obsolete and threatened the company with the total loss of market position in a highly competitive and price-conscious industry. Management rightly concluded that it had to move

[11]Peter F. Drucker, *The Practice of Management* (New York: Harper & Row, Publishers, 1954), pp. 353-354.

[12]Reprinted by permission of the publishers from Chester I. Barnard, *The Functions of the Executive,* Cambridge, Mass.: Harvard University Press, Copyright 1938, by the President and Fellows of Harvard College, 1966, by Grace F. Noera Barnard, p. 194.

> out of the plant. But because it did not force itself to develop alternate solutions, it decided that it had to build a new plant. And this decision bankrupted the company. Actually nothing followed from the finding that the old plant had become obsolete but the decision to stop manufacturing there. There were plenty of alternative courses of action: to sub-contract production, for instance, or to become a distributor for another manufacturer not yet represented in the territory. Either one would have been preferable, would indeed have been welcomed by a management that recognized the dangers involved in building a new plant. Yet, management did not think of these alternates until it was too late.[13]

Just what the alternatives might be depends upon the nature of the situation. Various courses of action may suggest themselves as a result of problem analysis. Overt action, furthermore, is not the only possibility. No action at all is frequently a possibility, and the best decision may be to let things stand as they are.

In searching for solutions, the decision maker faces certain constraints that limit his sphere of discretion. These constraints are barriers which preclude certain choices that would otherwise be possible. In devising a solution to his transportation problem, for example, the average college student is unable to purchase a new Cadillac or Rolls Royce. The reason for this is the existence of economic or parental constraints. In a business organization, the manager similarly faces constraints. Improved technology may be needed, but the firm may lack the cash necessary for complete modernization. The following types of constraints have been suggested as establishing limits to managerial discretion:[14]

1. Authoritative constraints.
2. Biological constraints.
3. Physical constraints.
4. Technological constraints.
5. Economic constraints.

Authoritative constraints would be illustrated by the action of a superior in limiting the range of discretion for a salesman in quoting prices. The other constraints are concerned with biological limitations, physical laws and factors, extent of technological develop-

---

[13]Drucker, *op. cit.*, pp. 359-360.

[14]Robert Tannenbaum, Irving R. Weschler, and Fred Massarik, *Leadership and Organization: A Behavioral Science Approach* (New York: McGraw-Hill Book Company, 1961), pp. 277-278.

ment and knowledge, and the existence of economic conditions or limitations.

Evaluation of Alternatives

The scientific approach requires selection of the best solution on the basis of a careful evaluation of alternatives. The probable consequences of each course of action must be determined and these consequences weighed in choosing the solution. Unfortunately, the consequences are not always clear. The future is uncertain, and factual knowledge is never complete. The trick is to select the solution that will maximize the results in terms of existing objectives. The fact that knowledge is less than perfect is the reason that the decision maker has a function to perform. Otherwise, the complete task of choosing a course of action could be turned over to a computer.

Compilation of all pertinent facts is necessary to assure a decision that does more than reflect the bias or feelings of the decision maker. A problem exists as to the extent one should go in gathering such information. Economic and time factors preclude an unlimited search. And, try as one may, there are usually some facts that are elusive and can never be established. As a result, subjective judgment is invariably required.

After factual information is gathered, it must be classified in some meaningful way. It must also be weighed. Both pros and cons must be considered. Some apparently conflicting evidence is often present. The decision maker must distinguish between significant and trivial facts. He must sense factors that are critical or crucial. As for criteria to use in selecting the best solution, Drucker suggests the following:

1. The risk relative to the expected gain.
2. Economy of effort relative to results.
3. Timing that fits the requirements of the situation.
4. Limitations of resources.[15]

Choice of Alternative

The climax of the decision-making process arrives when the manager exercises the final judgment. He may have gone step by step

---

[15]Drucker, *op. cit.*, pp. 362-363.

through an analysis of the problem and the proposed solutions, but the moment arrives when he must "pay his money and take his choice."

Assuming his choice is based upon a thorough analysis, the decisive manager is to be admired. Indecision often indicates an unwillingness to face up to the situation. By choosing, one commits himself to a given position. In some decisions, his reputation is at stake, and he may risk disagreement and misunderstanding. Decision making can thus be an agonizing process to some managers. The "loneliness" of decision making has been noted by Clarence B. Randall, who described the decision maker's feeling of individual responsibility as follows:

> It is human to wish to share the risk of error and to feel the comforting strength of outside support, like the flying buttresses, along the wall of a medieval cathedral. But the strong man, the one who gives free enterprise its vitality, is the man who weighs thoughtfully the entire range of available opinion and then determines policy by relying solely on his own judgment.[16]

Forthright expression of the decision once it is made can help clear the air of uncertainty. Explanations to those affected may be desirable if the reasoning supporting the particular course of action is not clear. This is often necessary to gain the requisite understanding and support.

Quantitative Methods in Decision Making

Managerial Judgment and Quantitative Analysis

In recent years, many studies of decision making have emphasized a quantitative approach involving the use of mathematics and statistics. As a matter of fact, some quantitative analysis has been used for years in the process of business management. Such factors as the rate of inventory turnover, quality control limits, and return on investment all involve quantitative concepts for use in decision making. The modern emphasis upon quantitative methods involves higher-powered mathematics, but the newer techniques do not con-

---

[16]Joseph D. Cooper, *The Art of Decision-Making,* p. 120. Copyright© 1961 by Joseph D. Cooper. Reprinted by permission of Doubleday & Company, Inc.

stitute a shift from completely qualitative to completely quantitative decision making.

Many business decisions involve a combination of quantitative reasoning and subjective judgment. The latter is sometimes described as *intuitive judgment* to distinguish it from the type of conclusion reached through use of a mathematical formula.

As a result of the emphasis on quantitative techniques, the necessity for much nonquantitative judgment has been questioned. Managers are now attempting to establish quantitative values for factors that were once regarded as a matter of judgment. Certain assumptions must also be made explicit to utilize the quantitative techniques. It has not been possible to eliminate all judgment, but it has been possible to extend the use of quantitative reasoning by quantifying estimates and applying the newer mathematical methods.

Use of Quantitative Methods

In the years following World War II, industry adopted an approach to the solution of business problems known as *operations research.* This approach was originally developed in the analysis of military problems. Its primary distinguishing characteristics have been described as the following:

1. A broad view toward the business problem—that is, the viewpoint of the entire company.
2. The team approach—using personnel with differing backgrounds and from different departments of the business.
3. An emphasis upon statistical and quantitative techniques.

The use of quantitative methods has been stimulated by the advent and expanding use of electronic computers. The reason for this is that operations research often entails the solution of complex, time-consuming mathematical problems. Problems that might require weeks, months, or even years for calculation can be disposed of quickly by the computer. Utilization of such mathematical tools in solving complex business problems thus becomes a practical possibility.

The general methodology of operations research involves an analysis of various alternatives for the solution of a business problem. Relationships among factors (for example, the volume of production and the cost of production) must be specified quantitatively. Effects of certain situations or factors (for example, the effect of stockouts on customers) must be estimated by assignment of quantitative values. These factors are then used in mathematical models to discover a practical, preferably the best, solution to the problem. Modern quantitative analysis uses such concepts and tools as probability theory, sampling, game theory, linear programming, and waiting line theory.[17]

Applications of Quantitative Methods

Many different types of business problems have been subjected to analysis by use of the newer quantitative methods. The following list of problems, while not in any sense exhaustive, indicates the diversified nature of problems solved through operations research:

1. Scheduling refinery runs to determine types of products to be produced from crude oil.
2. Establishing size of inventories for different products in different warehouses.
3. Determining number of service personnel required or number of employees needed in a tool crib.
4. Determining number of machines that one employee should operate.
5. Scheduling production operations.
6. Determining number of unloading docks required for trucks or ships.
7. Selecting advertising media and allocating marketing efforts.

In 1957, a survey was conducted of the industrial use of operations research in the United States and, in some cases, in Canada.[18] Of the 631 companies responding, 324 or 51.3 per cent reported that they were using operations research. The nature of their applications of operations research is presented in Table 3.

Linear programming is one of the most important tools of operations research and has been applied successfully to many different types of business problems. It can be used to select the best choice from a number of alternatives through the use of mathematical formulas. Figure 3 presents an illustration of the use of this tool to mini-

---

[17]See H. N. Broom, *Production Management,* Revised Edition (Homewood, Illinois: Richard D. Irwin, Inc., 1967), Chapter 3, "Operations Research," for a thorough discussion of these and other tools.

[18]David Bendel Hertz, *Operations Research Reconsidered,* AMA Management Report No. 10 (New York: American Management Association, 1958), pp. 22-38.

Table 3. What Jobs Is Operations Research Doing?
(Number of Companies Reporting
Operations Research Application in Each Area)

	Number of Companies
PRODUCTION	152
LONG-RANGE PLANNING	145
SALES AND MARKETING	136
INVENTORY	135
TRANSPORTATION AND SHIPPING	95
TOP MANAGEMENT	92
RESEARCH	90
FINANCE	87
ACCOUNTING	72
PURCHASING	50
PERSONNEL	48
ADVERTISING	20

Source: David Bendel Hertz, *Operations Research Reconsidered*, AMA Management Report No. 10 (New York: American Management Association, 1958), p. 35.

mize freight costs in shipping products from different manufacturing plants to different warehouses.

An Application of the Quantitative Approach

To illustrate the application of the quantitative approach in a more detailed way, let us consider a decision as to drilling an oil well.[19] Normally, this would be considered a type of decision involving a great deal of subjective judgment or intuition. The problem might be expressed as follows:

Problem: Whether to drill a wildcat oil well.

The procedure to be followed in solution might be considered as containing the following steps:

1. Identify alternative courses of action.
2. Determine the possible outcomes of each alternative.
3. Assign probabilities to the various outcomes.
4. Calculate the expected value of each alternative.
5. Choose the alternative with the highest expected payoff.

The first step reveals three alternatives: (1) drill; (2) don't drill; or (3) farm out for ⅛ royalty. Step 2 shows three possible outcomes

[19]This illustration is adapted from material prepared by Dr. C. Jackson Grayson, Jr., Dean of the School of Business Administration, Southern Methodist University, and is used with his permission.

Figure 3. *Lower Freight Costs Via Linear Programming*

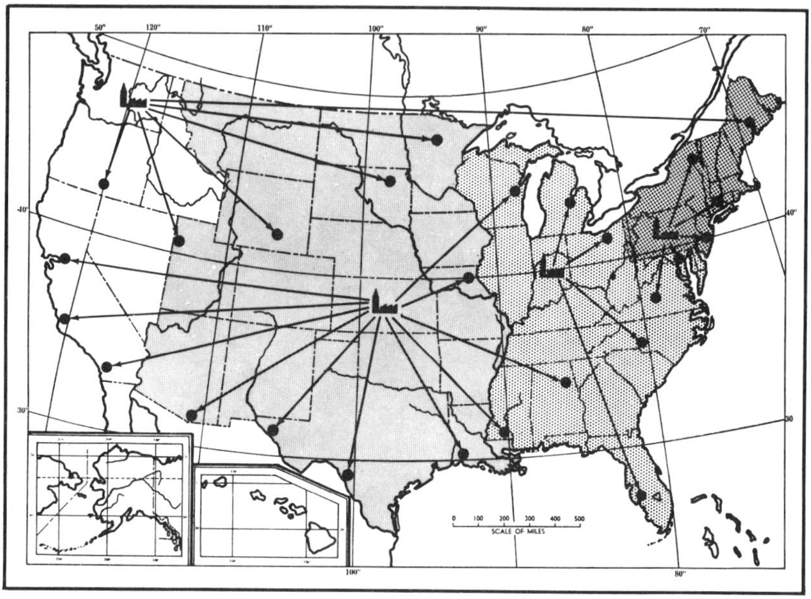

Max Gschwind for *Fortune*

Linear programming is an Operations Research tool with many uses. In the case of one national manufacturing company, it was used to realign plant-to-warehouse shipment of a consumer product so as to minimize total freight costs. The map suggests by colors the company's former regional divisions, each supplied by a regional plant. Quantities are not shown, but both plant capacities and warehouse demands vary. Using mathematical concepts and an I.B.M. electronic computer, O.R. men set up their program. As freight rates or quantities change, adjustments can be made to keep freight costs minimal. Radial lines from plants typify the O.R. solution, which breaks old regional lines, in one case spectacularly: Maine is supplied from the West Coast. Partly because of the Maine anomaly (which is small in volume) the O.R. scheme scandalized old-line traffic men. Mathematics bore out the O.R. conclusions.

Source: Herbert Solow, "Operations Research is in Business," *Fortune*, Vol. 53, No. 2, February 1956, p. 131. Courtesy of *Fortune*.

or consequences of drilling or farming out: (1) dry hole; (2) small well; or (3) big well. The expected gain that would be associated with each outcome may then be estimated on the basis of past experience or the judgment of the oil operator.[20] In step 3, an estimate must also be made, on the basis of past experience or judgment, of the probability of experiencing each of three possible outcomes or consequences (dry hole; small well; big well). The following table summarizes these factors and shows the expected value calculated for each alternative course of action.

It can be seen from the table that the first alternative offers no prospects of gain or loss inasmuch as it is a decision not to drill.

PAYOFF TABLE
(New values after costs)

ALTERNATIVE	OUTCOMES *Dry Hole*	*Small Well*	*Big Well*	EXPECTED VALUE
Don't drill	$ 0	$ 0	$ 0	$ 0
Drill	—50,000	30,000	930,000	72,000
Farm out	0	12,500	125,000	16,250
Probabilities	.6	.3	.1	

The second alternative, drilling, leads to a loss of $50,000 (cost of drilling) if no oil is found. A small well will produce $30,000 over and above drilling and operating costs. A big well will produce $930,000 on the same basis. If the drilling is farmed out (third alternative), a dry hole will avoid the $50,000 loss, but striking oil will produce a smaller return based on a one-eighth return of gross revenues.

The estimated probabilities appear below each outcome. The chances of hitting a dry hole, for example, are thought to be 6 out of 10. The expected value of each alternative is computed by adding the products of the probability and expected gain for each outcome or consequence. Using the estimates described above, then, drilling appears to constitute the most desirable alternative.

The reasoning is presented graphically in the chart on page 160. The alternative of drilling has an expected value of $72,000 in contrast to $16,250 and $0 for the other two alternatives. In this problem, then, the decision maker has reached a conclusion by assigning or assuming specific dollar values for each outcome and precisely estimating the probability of each consequence. The process differs in its nature from one in which the decision maker is somewhat aware

---

[20]In this illustration, the figures for gain in the event of success are really *present value* figures. The cash income from production will not be fully realized for many years, and the figures represent present value equivalents.

of differences but uses his judgment without trying to assign specific values for each variable.

Limitations of Quantitative Analysis

It is apparent that the use of quantitative methods can be no better than the assumptions and estimates employed in reaching the solution. If estimates used in the solution are unrealistic, the results will be undependable. Any formula or model used in the solution of a given problem must accurately reflect existing conditions if misleading results are to be avoided.

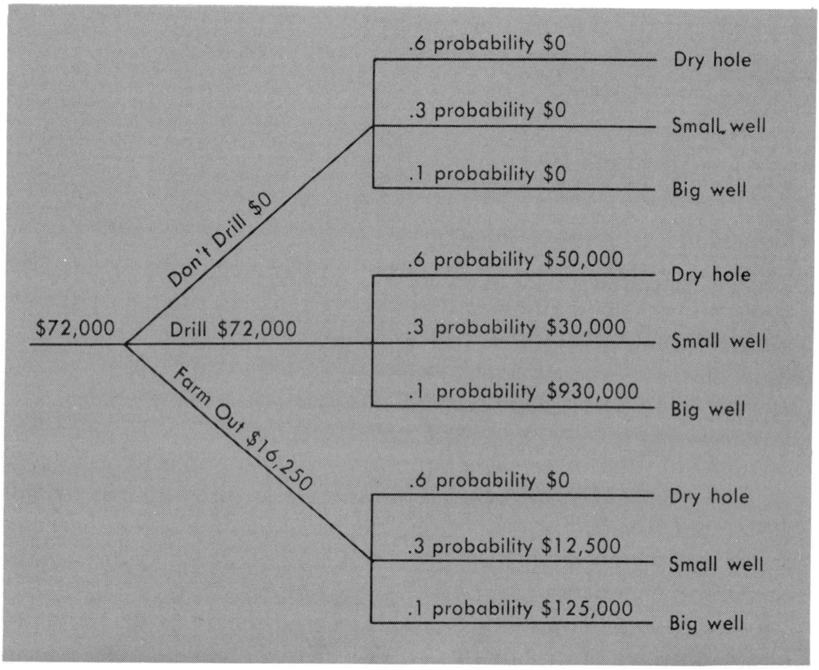

Let us not reject the quantitative approach too hastily, however. Estimates need not be perfect to improve the quality of decision making. Even a fair estimate may be better than a vague feeling in the decision maker's mind. Even so, the ability to devise accurate quantitative data and to determine relationships carefully is a limiting factor in quantitative analysis. Some factors are extremely difficult to quantify. If it cannot be done intelligently, the approach is questionable.

There is also a spurious accuracy that may be associated with quantitative analysis. The use of numbers and equations gives an appearance of scientific accuracy. The resulting willingness to place too much confidence in quantitative methods may be dangerous.

Use of quantitative analysis also demands some knowledge of mathematics and statistical concepts. The experience and training of managerial personnel may be inadequate for this purpose, thus limiting application of these techniques in particular situations.

Furthermore, the more sophisticated forms of quantitative analysis are both elaborate and costly. Large, complex problems can be economically subjected to analysis in this way, but many smaller problems and minor decisions cannot justify such refinements in their solution. Management cannot afford to shoot every sparrow with a cannon.

It should also be noted that the use of quantitative tools is concerned with only one phase of the decision-making process. Quantitative analysis is not ordinarily used to identify the problem or to develop the alternative possibilities that are open. It is only after ground work of this nature has been performed that the adoption of quantitative analysis becomes appropriate. It does not, therefore, constitute a substitute for the entire decision-making process according to traditional methods.

Implications for Management

The possibility of improved decision making through quantitative analysis means that managers must be prepared to use this approach. Although some phases of the solution of problems may be entrusted to specialists, management personnel generally should develop some appreciation of quantitative analysis — its potential and its limitations. If the manager has some conception of the types of problems whose solutions may be approached in this way, he is in a much better position to undertake the scientific analysis of the problems confronting him. It is also desirable that he have some knowledge of quantitative techniques in order that he may communicate intelligently with specialists in the use of such approaches.

It has also been suggested that mathematics can be considered as a language for formulating certain types of problems and that "a person of given intelligence can see certain problems more clearly and solve them more readily with the aid of mathematics."[21] (To

[21]R. K. Gaumnitz and O. H. Brownlee, "Mathematics for Decision Makers," *Harvard Business Review*, Vol. 34, No. 3, May-June 1956, p. 50.

some, this may seem a debatable proposition in view of the confusion that mathematical concepts cause for some individuals.) Furthermore, the outcome of many alternative courses of action is not definitely known. These outcomes may, however, be visualized in terms of some statement of probability. Some acquaintance with probability theory, at least to the extent of permitting use of the concept in simple decision making, is consequently desirable for the individual manager.

LIMITATIONS OF THE DECISION-MAKING PROCESS

Implementation of Decisions

It has been pointed out that decision making is an integral part of each of the functions of management. As a result, it is easy to think of the effective manager as one who can lean back in his chair and think through a difficult problem. There is no doubt that such an ability is an excellent quality of a manager.

The practical administrator, however, spends a great deal of his time in *implementing* decisions — in seeing that they are carried out. This requires an ability to secure the cooperation of others in seeing that plans are followed. Although this entails a type of decision making, the decisions are of a different nature from those contemplated in most of the discussion of this chapter.

In terms of percentage of time, decision making as a part of the planning process may require only a minor portion of the manager's work day. In other words, a manager is an organizer and motivator in addition to being a decision maker. The tasks of organization and motivation are also extremely important tasks. Concentration upon the decision-making activities of the manager, therefore, may produce a distorted view of the manager's functions.

Limited Rationality in Decision Making

As noted earlier in the chapter, some decisions are concerned with ends as contrasted with means. It is not possible to use the same rational approach in reasoning about ends as it is with means. To the extent, then, that the determination of objectives is involved in decision making, to that extent the rational approach cannot be used. Placing other goals ahead of profits, for example, must be recognized as a choice concerning ends.

Studies of decision making have also revealed it to be political in nature, accommodating the dissimilar and sometimes conflicting interests of different individuals and groups.[22] In one case, for example, both the head of a department whose future was in question and executives opposing him used strong direct and indirect pressures in attempting to influence the decision. (The matter of influence in decision making will be treated at greater length in Chapter 18.) Decision making, then, may reflect the influence of departmental and personal interests at the possible expense of organizational efficiency. Such decisions are irrational from the standpoint of the organization. "Empire building," where it exists, is an extreme example of such behavior. This is not meant to condone organizationally irrational behavior, of course, but simply to recognize its existence.

Unfortunately, rationality is also limited by the fact that many business decisions must be made in the absence of complete knowledge. The process of decision making has not yet reached the point that the manager can dispense with subjective judgment. In many situations, he is faced with great uncertainty. The significance of different factors in a complex situation is likewise often difficult to appraise.

Simon has stressed the limited rationality of the decision-making process.[23] Because businessmen never have all the facts and cannot know the consequences of every alternative in every situation, it is impossible for them to maximize. Their minds cannot even conceive of all possible alternatives. Instead of achieving maximum profits in every situation, therefore, managers must settle for satisfactory profits. In other words, they cannot maximize; they must of necessity *satisfice.*

> While economic man maximizes — selects the best alternative from among all those available to him; his cousin, whom we shall call administrative man, satisfices — looks for a course of action that is satisfactory or "good enough." Examples of satisficing criteria that are familiar enough to businessmen, if unfamiliar to most economists, are "share of market," "adequate profit," "fair price."[24]

---

[22]Dubin, *op. cit.*, pp. 33-34. Used with permission.

[23]Reprinted by permission of The Macmillan Company from *Administrative Behavior* by Herbert A. Simon. © by Herbert A. Simon 1957.

[24]Reprinted by permission of The Macmillan Company from *Administrative Behavior* by Herbert A. Simon. © by Herbert A. Simon 1957.

The attention directed at decision making, and particularly the emphasis upon quantitative analysis, tends to reduce the use of intuitive judgment and to make possible greater rationality in solutions to problems. The fact of the matter is, however, that the current state of knowledge is not such as to eliminate extensive use of subjective judgment.

SUMMARY

The decision-making process is an important, integral part of the management process. It involves a *conscious choice* of a particular course of action in the solution of a business problem. The nature of the decision-making process is not completely understood, and managers themselves often admit that they do not know how they make decisions. The attention focused on decision making in recent years has been particularly concerned with increasing its rationality.

The decision-making process begins with the *identification of a problem* and proceeds to a search for possible solutions or *alternative courses of action.* These alternatives have practical limitations in that they must be chosen within the constraints that prescribe the boundaries for the solution. Alternatives must be carefully *evaluated,* and the evaluation should lead logically to the *choice of a particular alternative.*

Although much subjective judgment has been required in decision making, there has been a trend in recent years to emphasize a *quantitative approach* to the solution of business problems. In the years since World War II, *operations research,* with its mathematical and statistical tools, has been developed and applied to numerous types of business problems. Quantitative analysis has definite limitations with respect to the type of problems to which it may be applied, but the possibilities for improved decision making through its use are increasing the need for acquaintance with quantitative methods on the part of managerial personnel.

The manager is an organizer, motivator, and controller as well as a decision maker. It is possible to develop a distorted view of the managerial process by extreme emphasis upon the decision-making function. It is also important to recognize that *nonrational factors* enter into some business decision making and that many decisions must still be made without adequate objective information for completely rational choices.

Discussion Questions

1. What is the difference, if any, between *decision making* and *choosing a course of action*?
2. Why should decision making be such a slow process?
3. What is the relationship between *rationality* in decision making and the type of decisions being made?
4. "Problems, problems—all I have is problems!" These words of one manager indicate a sharp awareness of problems. In what way, then, could *problem identification* be difficult?
5. What are the principal difficulties that hamper the development of *alternatives* in decision making?
6. If the previous steps in decision making are taken, why is the final step of *choosing an alternative* difficult?
7. Why is it difficult to use completely *quantitative methods* in decision making?
8. If a manager is effective as a decision maker, does this indicate that he is a good manager?
9. Explain how the concept of *satisficing* might apply in the decision to purchase an electronic computer for use in a large business corporation.

Supplementary Reading

Alexis, Marcus and Charles Z. Wilson, *Organizational Decision Making.* Englewood Cliffs: Prentice-Hall, Inc., 1967.

Ansoff, H. Igor, *Corporate Strategy.* New York: McGraw-Hill Book Company, 1965.

Archer, Stephen H., "The Structure of Management Decision Theory," *Academy of Management Journal,* Vol. 7, No. 4, December 1964, pp. 269-287.

Argyris, Chris, "Interpersonal Barriers to Decision Making," *Harvard Business Review,* Vol. 44, No. 2, March-April 1966, pp. 84-97.

Clough, Donald J., *Concepts in Management Science.* Englewood Cliffs: Prentice-Hall, Inc., 1963.

Delbecq, Andre L., "The Management of Decision-Making Within the Firm: Three Strategies for Three Types of Decision-Making," *Academy of Management Journal,* Vol. 10, No. 4, December 1967, pp. 329-339.

Dill, William R., "Administrative Decision Making," in *Concepts and Issues in Administrative Behavior,* eds. Sidney Mailick and Edward H. Van Ness, pp. 29-48. Englewood Cliffs: Prentice-Hall, Inc., 1962.

Drucker, Peter F., "The Effective Decision," *Harvard Business Review,* Vol. 45, No. 1, January-February 1967, pp. 92-98.

Gore, William J., *Administrative Decision-Making—A Heuristic Model.* New York: John Wiley & Sons, Inc., 1964.

Hall, Jay, Vincent O'Leary and Martha Williams, "The Decision-Making Grid: A Model of Decision-Making Styles," *California Management Review,* Vol. 8, No. 2, Winter 1964, pp. 43-54.

Hammond, John S., III, "Better Decisions With Preference Theory," *Harvard Business Review,* Vol. 45, No. 6, November-December 1967, pp. 123-141.

Hespos, Richard F. and Paul A. Strassmann, "Stochastic Decision Trees for the Analysis of Investment Decisions," *Management Science,* Vol. 11, No. 10, August 1965, pp. B-244 — B-259.

Hinkle, Charles L. and Alfred A. Kuehn, "Heuristic Models: Mapping the Maze for Management," *California Management Review,* Vol. 10, No. 1, Fall 1967, pp. 59-68.

Kepner, Charles H. and Benjamin B. Tregoe, *The Rational Manager: A Systematic Approach to Problem Solving and Decision Making.* New York: Mc-Graw-Hill Book Company, 1965.

Lundberg, Craig C., "Administrative Decisions: A Scheme for Analysis," *Journal of the Academy of Management,* Vol. 5, No. 2, August 1962, pp. 165-178.

Magee, John F., "Decision Trees for Decision Making," *Harvard Business Review,* Vol. 42, No. 4, July-August 1964, pp. 126-138.

Miller, Arjay, "The Challenge of Decision Making," *Advanced Management Journal,* Vol. 31, No. 2, April 1966, pp. 17-23.

Shuchman, Abe, *Scientific Decision Making in Business.* New York: Holt, Rinehart & Winston, Inc., 1963.

Spencer, Milton H., "The Framework of Management Decision Making," *Business Topics,* Vol. 11, No. 3, Summer 1963 pp. 33-47.

Young, Stanley, *Management: A Systems Analysis.* Glenview: Scott, Foresman & Company, 1966.

Fundamentals of Organization Design

8

Creating the Organization Structure

Business planning is futile unless members of an organization blend their efforts effectively in the implementation of plans. Effective teamwork, in turn, demands proper organization. This chapter is concerned with the first phase of building an effective organization —that of designing individual jobs and grouping these jobs to make possible the coordination of all activities.

Nature and Importance of Organizing

Values in Proper Organization

It is a basic fact that some organization of work is essential for any degree of efficiency. In an extreme case, overlapping of assignments and uncertainty concerning responsibilities could play havoc with business operations. What is not always realized is the extent to which business concerns actually experience and tolerate improper organization. Illogical arrangements often develop and continue in spite of their adverse effects.

Very few managers would contend that their organizations are perfect. The majority, if honest, would probably concede serious flaws. Of course, recognizing weaknesses and correcting those weaknesses are two different matters. Even when weak spots are apparent, corrective action may be difficult. Creating a particularly effective organization structure requires exceptional abilities on the part of a manager.

Occasionally a business firm experiences such problems that the organizational deficiencies cannot be ignored. Drastic action is necessary. What is generally left to evolutionary change must be dealt with quickly and promptly.

Frequent testimonials have been offered concerning the contribution made by good organization. As one example, advantages in launching new business ventures have been cited for the Du Pont Company because of the way it organizes such projects.[1] When the research staff originates a new product having market potential, the company turns its development over to a "venture manager." Resources and personnel are assigned to the venture manager, and this "miniature company" takes the product from the lab bench to the marketplace. As soon as profitability is assured, the project is transferred to an operating department or becomes an operating department on its own. In the eyes of Du Pont management, this organizational arrangement encourages the introduction of new products. It prevents a good idea from dying at birth, because the new operation does not take time and effort away from established products. Using the small "companies" focuses attention upon the new products and maximizes their chances for success. The organizational arrangement, then, appears to have practical importance in bringing research discoveries to fruition.

Difficulties in Organizing

One difficulty of the organizer arises from personnel considerations and limitations in staffing an ideal organization structure. The theoretically proper arrangement may be undesirable, if not impossible, because of such conditions. As an example, managerial personnel with necessary experience and abilities may not be available without a major reshuffling of existing personnel, extended management development programs, or extensive recruitment of experienced personnel from other firms. This question concerning the extent to which the ideal organization plan should be compromised to allow for personnel limitations is discussed at greater length in Chapter 13.

Personal ambitions of employees and managers may also conflict with the concepts of proper organization. Individuals develop vested interests in existing organization structures. A manager's impor-

---

[1]"Venture Manager," *Better Living,* Vol. 20, No. 6, November-December, 1966, pp. 1-5.

tance is partially dependent upon the organization of which he is a part. Changes in organization, thus, pose a threat to the existing status system. Some resistance to organization change, growing out of such personal interests, must be expected by the organizer.

The rapidly changing nature of most business activities presents an additional problem for the organizer. An organization plan that is satisfactory at one time may be obsolete a decade later. This means that organizing is a function of continuing importance to management.

A further potential difficulty in achieving an effective organization is found in the attitudes of organization members. If a firm's personnel very much want it to work effectively, a relatively inefficient structure may work quite well. On the other hand, if members of the organization have a negative attitude toward cooperative endeavor, the best organization may appear to be faulty. In other words, creating a good organization structure does not insure success. The social aspects of organization behavior are most important, and a later section of this book is devoted to issues of this type.

Limitations of Organization Charting

Creation of an organization structure is often considered synonymous with the preparation of organization charts. The chart is a device used to portray the organization, but we must recognize that the chart is only a picture. The chart is no more the organization itself than any symbol is the thing that it represents. The real organization structure is the pattern of human relationships that exists.

An organization chart has limited value, then, in creating an effective organization. It may be used in reasoning about the organization and possibly in communicating the existing or desired organization structure. The chart will not assure action that conforms to the pictured pattern. Existing patterns of behavior may prevail in spite of new charts that are issued. In spite of these weaknesses, however, organization charts do perform a practical, useful function in many companies.

The Systems Approach to Organizing

The Organizing Function

In the light of systems theory, the manager's organizing function may be visualized as a design function — creating the structure or framework of the system. The manager establishes those relationships among component parts that will provide the most effective system. If he is successful, the result is a streamlined, efficient, smoothly functioning mechanism. Otherwise, the result may be a Rube Goldberg contraption that operates with wasted motion and unnecessary delay in accomplishing its mission.

As a part of the organizing function, a manager must design the subsystems of a company — grouping activities into units, departments, and divisions. If he approaches organizing without a systems point of view, however, he may adopt organizational rules of thumb or follow conventional practice with little regard for the unique requirements of the particular system. Apparently, the organizing process often occurs on a components rather than a systems basis.

> When an engineer looks at formal organizational arrangements, he is immediately struck by how seldom such arrangements have been "designed"—in the sense of matching specific groups and structures to the objectives and resources of a particular business. In most companies, the organizational structure is merely the result of a haphazard process of evolution, and, as such, has no particular relationship to the needs, aspirations, or competencies of the people in it — and even less relationship to the company's external strategy.[2]

As we shall see in Chapter 13, some managers question the logic and desirability of organization planning. The organization chart is seen as a series of little black boxes serving to limit or confine the individuals in the organization. The unfortunate consequence, when it actually occurs, results from the lack of a systems approach. Rather than facilitating cooperation — permitting the gears to mesh smoothly — the structure erects barriers that interfere with effective operation.

Organizing from the systems point of view demands that the manager free himself from the components mentality. He must see that he is designing a machine or a system rather than a group of unrelated parts.

Adapting the Structure

Constant change is a fact of life for most business organizations. As changes occur in system objectives and methods, adaptations are

---

[2]Seymour Tilles, "The Manager's Job: A Systems Approach," *Harvard Business Review,* Vol. 41, No. 1, January-February 1963, p. 79.

necessary in the subsystems of the company and in relationships among subsystems. This explains the need for continuing study and modification of organization structures.

As changes are introduced into production and distribution methods, for example, different subsystems are thrown into contact with each other. The need for new cooperative working relationships between staff specialists and line personnel arises. Changes in information technology lead to alterations in the decision-making pattern. The impact of technological changes upon system design is discussed in more detail in Chapter 13.

Designing in Terms of the System's Function

Organizing logically begins with a consideration of the nature of the system — its activity or function or purpose. What is it expected to do and how should it operate? An organizing approach that is eminently sound from a systems viewpoint has been suggested by Peter F. Drucker. To discover the type of structure needed, he proposes three kinds of analysis: activities analysis; decision analysis; and relations analysis.[3] Each of these types of analysis emphasizes the functioning system rather than its parts.

Activities analysis examines the task to be performed. Rather than assuming that a particular firm must have certain traditional functions, the designer takes a fresh look at its essential, basic activities. He does not begin with the assumption that *all* manufacturing plants *must* have separate manufacturing, sales, and engineering departments of precisely the same importance as those of other companies. Instead, he looks at the objectives of the particular company and the nature and relative importance of the activities it must perform. In the women's dress industry, for example, engineering is practically unknown and manufacturing is so simple that it does not deserve equal status with such major functions as design.[4] As another example, a big manufacturer of electric bulbs considers the education of the public in the use of lighting and the development of good lighting practices so important as to require this task to be organized as a separate function.[5]

---

[3]Peter F. Drucker, *The Practice of Management* (New York: Harper & Row, Publishers, 1954), Chapter 16.

[4]*Ibid.,* p. 195.

[5]*Ibid.,* p. 196.

The other forms of analysis proposed by Drucker have the same orientation toward the operating system. *Decision analysis* asks questions about the types of decisions that must be made and the levels at which they can appropriately be made. Questions concerning the extent of decentralization immediately come to mind. Can the system function more effectively by delegating broad decision-making authority to lower levels of management? *Relations analysis* examines the points of contact among activities and personnel. The structure must facilitate cooperative relationships among people whose functions are intertwined. Once again, the focus is upon the functioning relationship of components of the system.

Organizing in terms of activities, decisions, and relations in real life situations often leads to modifications of traditional structures. A striking example is provided by the innovations introduced by Lockheed Aircraft Corporation in carrying out Air Force contracts.[6] One major contract won by Lockheed was the $1.4 billion order for 58 C-5A planes — the world's largest military transport aircraft.

To design and produce the C-5A's, Lockheed adopted an organizational arrangement similar to that used earlier in producing C-141 StarLifter cargo fan jets. Rather than creating a special division or merely using the existing structure, Lockheed set up a "co-organization," or special C-5A organization, within the Lockheed-Georgia Division — the division responsible for C-5A work. Personnel within existing departments — marketing, engineering, finance, quality control, and so on — were designated as C-5A project personnel. Some 11,000 employees are eventually expected to be assigned to the project. Personnel selected for this purpose were not necessarily the top managers in their respective functional areas. The C-5A project organization bypasses the formal chain of command and normal lines of communication. On C-5A matters, project personnel are subject to direction from the C-5A project director. When not needed on the C-5A project, personnel take orders from their regular managers.

This adaptation of the established organization occurred as a result of Lockheed's quest for an efficient pattern to carry out major projects along with the other activities of the corporation. The move thus represents an application of the systems concept by making the organization fit the pattern of activities, decisions, and relationships required in this project.

---

[6]"Lockheed Bets Big on New Controls," *Business Week*, No. 1918, June 4, 1966, pp. 116-120; "New Plane Cuts the Red Tape," *Business Week*, No. 1843, December 26, 1964, pp. 52-53.

The Job as the Basic Building Block

The Drive for Efficiency Through Specialization

The function of organizing consists of the establishment of effective relationships among jobs and people. It is appropriate to begin the discussion of organizing by examining the jobs themselves. The job constitutes the basic building block used in devising an organization structure. The size or shape of the block varies according to the range of duties incorporated in the job, and this requires a fundamental decision by the organizer concerning the scope of particular jobs. We are concerned particularly with the variety of work to be performed by a given individual.

As a small organization grows, some division of duties and specialization of work occurs spontaneously. The efficiency derived from specialization of labor greatly impressed the famous economist Adam Smith as he observed the relatively simple process of manufacturing pins. Following is his well-known description of production in the pin factory:

> One man draws out the wire, another straights it, a third cuts it, a fourth points it, a fifth grinds it at the top for receiving the head; to make the head requires two or three distinct operations; to put it on is a peculiar business; to whiten the pins is another; it is even a trade by itself to put them into the paper. . . . I have seen a small manufactory of this kind where ten men only were employed, and where some of them consequently performed two or three distinct operations. But though they were very poor, and therefore but indifferently accommodated with the necessary machinery, they could, when they exerted themselves, make among them about twelve pounds of pins in a day. There are in a pound upwards of four thousand pins of a middling size. Those ten persons, therefore, could make among them upwards of forty-eight thousand pins in a day. . . . But if they had all wrought separately and independently, . . . they certainly could not each of them have made twenty, perhaps not one pin in a day . . . .[7]

Management theory, as well as economic theory, also came to recognize the value of task specialization. The well-known work of Frederick W. Taylor, leader in the scientific management move-

---

[7]From Adam Smith: *The Wealth of Nations, Representative Selections,* edited by Bruce Mazlish, copyright © 1961 by The Bobbs-Merrill Co., Inc., p. 5. Reprinted by permission of the Liberal Arts Press Division.

ment, was anticipated to some extent by the writing of Charles Babbage, a British mathematical scientist of the early nineteenth century. In a book, *On the Economy of Machinery and Manufactures,* published in 1832, Babbage stressed division of labor as one of the most important principles in the economy of manufacturing.[8] Babbage specifically noted a number of reasons, some of which had also been noted by Adam Smith, for the greater efficiency accruing through specialization. For example, the time required for learning a job and the time spent in changing from one task to another are reduced through specialization of work. In addition, skill is acquired by frequent repetition of the same processes. The division of labor also encourages the development of tools and machinery to facilitate the production process. Furthermore, dividing work into a number of processes requiring different degrees of skill makes it possible for the manufacturer to pay for the precise quantity of labor that he needs at each skill level rather than employing a highly skilled workman to perform a series of tasks involving different skill levels.

In the scientific management movement of the late 1800's and early 1900's, the values involved in specialization of labor were readily accepted. Its leaders were chiefly concerned with the development of the most efficient method for each job. Taylor, in particular, emphasized the importance of eliminating much of the planning phase of the job and making it the responsibility of the foreman.

> The fourth principle is a deliberate division of the work which was formerly done by the workmen into two sections, one of which is handed over to the management. An immense mass of new duties is thrown on the management which formerly belonged to the workmen.[9]

There was also a strong emphasis in the scientific management movement upon work standardization. The employee was expected to perform the task in precisely the same way each time, using the method considered most efficient by a methods analyst. It was thought that the employee would almost invariably follow a less efficient method if he were allowed to introduce innovations of his own.

The continued utilization of the principle of division of labor is a matter of common knowledge. The modern assembly line provides

---

[8]See Charles Babbage, "On the Division of Labour," in *Classics in Management,* ed. Harwood F. Merrill (New York: American Management Association, 1960), pp. 29-44.

[9]Frederick Winslow Taylor, *The Principles of Scientific Management* (Hanover, N.H.: Dartmouth College, 1911), p. 34.

an excellent example. Each employee has only one or a few minor functions in the assembly process to perform. It is this type of specialization in modern industry that has made possible its impressive growth in productivity.

Impact of Specialization on Employees

As work division led to extreme job specialization, jobs were broken down into smaller and smaller pieces. Duties were grouped in such a way as to provide greater homogeneity in the work of each individual. More difficult features were removed from the job and turned over to specialists. A setup man, for example, took over the more demanding duties of the machine operator, while the operator himself became a machine "tender."

While work specialization and standardization greatly increased productivity, as expected by the writers cited earlier, certain negative results were also experienced.[10] From the standpoint of the individual worker, jobs frequently became less attractive. Performing only a very specialized part of a total job gave employees less feeling of accomplishment than they had enjoyed previously. Note, for example, the following explanation of an employee concerning a step toward greater specialization in his work:

> When the plant was running only a few cars through an hour, I used to install the whole front and back seat assemblies. But when the cars speeded up, I was put on the job of installing the rack that the front seat slides back and forth on, and my job was broken up and simplified. I'd like to do a whole fender myself from raw material to the finished job. It would be more interesting.[11]

The repetitive nature of specialized jobs became particularly objectionable to many employees. The same task repeated hour after hour and day after day created a feeling of great monotony. A given job might involve one operation, requiring only a few minutes or possibly just a few seconds, and be repeated over and over and over again. In addition, many such jobs are subject to continuous pacing by the assembly line. The employee is not free to set his own rate

---

[10]For a stimulating discussion of the seriousness of this problem and the extent to which employees *need* involvement in their work, see Robert Dubin, *Human Relations in Administration,* Third Edition (Englewood Cliffs: Prentice-Hall, Inc., 1968), pp. 89-93.

[11]Charles R. Walker and Robert H. Guest, *The Man on the Assembly Line* (Cambridge: Harvard University Press, 1952), p. 58.

of work. The problem is less one of physical fatigue than it is one of boredom and pressure. The following are typical comments of employees critical of the repetitive nature of such jobs in an automobile assembly plant:

> I'd like to do different things on this job. I get bored. It's the same thing all the time. Cars always coming down the line endlessly every time I look up.
>
> I'd like to do more things. That's the trouble with the line. Monotony. You repeat the same thing day in, day out.
>
> I would like to perform different operations, but I do the same thing all the time. I always know what I'm going to do when I come in. There's nothing to look forward to like there was on my old job.
>
> The job gets so sickening — day in and day out plugging in ignition wires. I get through with one motor, turn around, and there's another motor staring me in the face. It's sickening.[12]

Most of the simplified jobs require little skill or training. Removal of skill and craftsmanship naturally affects employee attitudes. It is difficult to take pride or to feel a sense of accomplishment in work that is so extremely simple and that demands so little ability. Sensitivity to the decreased skill requirements is evident from the comments of workers on the assembly line:

> Ten minutes — any junior high school kid could do it — except he wouldn't.
>
> Only took a half hour to pick it up — then it's only a question of speeding up. Some men get it in less than half an hour.[13]

Of course, not all employees experience the same extreme dislike of specialized jobs. Some are apparently capable of adjusting to work that entails little skill and much uniformity. One must be cautious of overgeneralization. The fact of simplification *per se* is often condemned as injurious to worker satisfaction. The assumption seems to be that a job is objectionable just because it entails specialized work. As a matter of fact, some studies show a surprising tolerance on the part of a substantial proportion of employees for specialized work.[14] On the other hand, employees often dislike specialized jobs for reasons that are related to, or grow out of, specialization such as

---

[12]*Ibid.*, pp. 54-55.

[13]*Ibid*, p. 56.

[14]See, for example, Eaton H. Conant and Maurice D. Kilbridge, "An Interdisciplinary Analysis of Job Enlargement: Technology, Costs, and Behavioral Implications," *Industrial and Labor Relations Review*, Vol. 18, No. 3, April 1965, pp. 377-395. Reprinted with permission of the *Industrial and Labor Relations Review*, Copyright © Cornell University 1965. All rights reserved.

the mechanical pacing mentioned above or the absence of a significant opportunity to contribute to product quality. In other words, some employees express satisfaction with specialized duties but dislike the attendant loss of craftsmanship. On balance, it appears that most employees experience some types of dissatisfaction with extremely specialized work.

Job Enlargement

How far can job specialization be profitably carried? Even from an engineering approach, there is a principle of diminishing returns. Continued subdivision of jobs may reach the point beyond which little or no gain can be realized from further subdivision. The basic reasoning of Adam Smith and the scientific managers seems logical enough. We all concede that the Jack-of-all-trades is usually master of none. But how far can the principle be carried? If reducing a job from eight operations to four produces an increase in efficiency, can a comparable increase be expected by reducing the job from four to two operations? Will an employee who installs two bolts be more efficient than an employee who installs four bolts? It is clear that the gains from minute divisions of work are negligible compared with gains from the broader divisions.

Operational inefficiencies may actually result from excessive specialization. As work becomes extremely specialized, for example, it becomes difficult to divide work evenly among all employees. As a result, those with shorter work assignments have some idle time. Quality control responsibility may also be difficult to establish in the case of specialized work.

As an offset to any realized technical gains in work efficiency, we have seen that workers find the monotony and reduction of skill unpleasant. From the standpoint of administration, these are undesirable consequences. In deciding upon the extent to which specialization should be carried, then, the manager must consider the matter from the standpoint of both engineering and human relations. It is possible that a minor gain in technical efficiency may be more than offset by lower morale.

Considerations of this type have led to questions concerning the proper extent of job specialization. The shape or size of the organization building block has been scrutinized. Some organizers have concluded that it is often too small—that some jobs have become overspecialized. This has led to steps in the opposite direction of *despecialization* or what Charles R. Walker has called *job enlargement*. Job enlargement has been defined as "*the expansion of job content to include a variety of tasks, and to increase the worker's self-determination of pace, responsibility for checking quality, and discretion for method.*"[15]

The International Business Machines Corporation is one of the companies that has devoted considerable study to the practicality of job enlargement in various functions and activities. The following account describes the origin and reasoning of the job enlargement in this company:

> Back in 1953, Mr. Thomas J. Watson, the Chairman of our Board—then President—was making one of his frequent visits to our largest plant in Endicott, New York. As he was walking through one of the machining departments, he noticed a girl standing by her machine. He went over to talk with her and found that she was waiting for a set-up man to come by to make and check her setup. She then mentioned that she could make the setup herself, but that it was against the rules. In further conversation, it developed that she had only been in the plant a comparatively short time and she had previously worked in a department store. She went on to say that she could also learn to check the quality of her work.
>
> Briefly, her work involved the placing of a part in the fixture, pushing a lever to start the machine, and taking the part out when the cut had been completed. The machine was set up for operation by a set-up man and the quality of the work was checked by a process inspector.
>
> Mr. Watson went away but there remained in his mind the thought that if this young lady with only a few months experience could set up her machine and check the quality, why couldn't all the other machine operators? He called a meeting of the production executives and gave them his thoughts. He suggested we teach our machine operators to set up their machines and inspect their work. He successfully persuaded the skeptical production people to give the idea a trial.[16]

To the surprise of many, it was discovered that the ideas of Mr. Watson could be applied in many parts of the corporation. Employees

---

[15]Easton H. Conant and Maurice D. Kilbridge, "An Interdisciplinary Analysis of Job Enlargement: Technology, Costs, and Behavioral Implications," *Industrial and Labor Relations Review,* Vol. 18, No. 3, April 1965, p. 380. Reprinted with permission of the *Industrial and Labor Relations Review,* Copyright © Cornell University 1965. All rights reserved.

[16]Dause L. Bibby, "An Enlargement of the Job for the Worker," *Proceedings of Seventeenth Conference, Texas Personnel and Management Association, October 20 and 21, 1955* (Austin: The University of Texas, 1955), pp. 28-29.

learned to set up machines, to inspect their work, and to read blueprints. In the opinion of the company's management, the process of job enlargement led to an improvement in quality, a reduction in idle time, and an increase in the interest and responsibility level of the work of employees.

A well-known midwestern manufacturer of home laundry equipment has pursued a program of removing work from progressive assembly lines and restoring it to single-operator bench stations.[17] As part of this program, complete subassemblies, such as water pumps and control panels for washers or driers, were made the responsibility of one individual. Not only did the company realize significant benefits from this instance of job enlargement, but workers indicated more favorable attitudes toward the enlarged jobs. Table 4 shows how employees who had changed from the assembly line to bench assembly responded to questions about a number of attributes of the specialized and enlarged jobs.

Table 4. Response of Sixty-One Workers to Bench and Assembly Line Attribute Questions

Bench Attribute	Like	Dislike	Line Attribute	Like	Dislike
Bench self-pacing	48	13	Line mechanized pacing	24	37
Bench tie-to-work	55	6	Line tie-to-work	19	42
Bench sub-assembly completion	50	11	Line absence of completion	29	32
Bench quality responsibility	53	8	Line quality anonymity	14	47
Bench quality opportunity	52	9	Line quality opportunity	10	51
Bench amount and variety of tasks	47	14	Line task specialization	32	29

Source: Eaton H. Conant and Maurice D. Kilbridge, "An Interdisciplinary Analysis of Job Enlargement: Technology, Costs, and Behavioral Implications," *Industrial and Labor Relations Review*, Vol. 18, No. 3, April 1965, p. 389. Reprinted with permission of the *Industrial and Labor Relations Review*, Copyright © Cornell University 1965. All rights reserved.

The initial decision of the organizer, then, concerns the scope and nature of the duties assigned to the individual job. This decision must consider the possibility of increased technical efficiency

[17]Conant and Kilbridge, *op. cit.*

through simplifying and standardizing work. But it must also consider the possibility of offsetting disadvantages through a loss of employee morale. Experimentation may be required in particular cases to determine the optimum scope and content of the job.

Patterns of Organization

Choosing a Pattern

Having determined the content of individual jobs, the organizer must next consider the way that jobs and groups of jobs should be related to each other. In grouping activities into organizational components, some integrating pattern or principle is required. The question for the organizer concerns the type of pattern that he should use. It does not help much to say that similar jobs should be combined in the same unit. Jobs are similar in different ways. They may be similar in terms of the nature of the duties, location of the jobs, or in various other ways.

The organizer frequently has a choice of patterns, several of which are widely used and recognized. Perhaps the best known of these is the *functional* pattern in which the type of activity or function serves as the organizing principle. Sales, for example, constitutes one department, while manufacturing activities are grouped in a separate department. In contrast to the functional pattern, a *product* pattern groups both manufacturing and sales activities related to one product into the same department. Other possible patterns are based on the *location* of the activity, the *customer*, and the *process*. Several of these are discussed separately in a later section of this chapter. The list is not exhaustive, however, and various other patterns can be found in addition to these that are rather commonly used.

Different patterns of organization vary in their usefulness for coordinating company activities. The most desirable pattern for any particular situation depends upon the existing work flow and the necessary relationships among people and functions in accomplishing organizational objectives. In other words, the nature of the system determines the best pattern of organization. As industrial firms grow, they often find it desirable to remove production personnel, sales personnel, and research personnel from their functional departments and to place them under product managers. At some point, which may be difficult to identify precisely, work activities are better coordinated by using a product pattern instead of a functional pattern. In other words, the desirable pattern is dependent upon such factors as products, markets, technology, and work flow.

A recent reorganization of the Insurance Company of North America provides a clear example of this point.[18] Prior to the reorganization, this company approached the insurance market with a growing number of separate lines of insurance — automobile, fire, and so on. Each subdivision developed its own support personnel, and communication between subdivisions was almost nonexistent. Customers needing more than one type of insurance dealt with two or more subdivisions of the company. Effective control became difficult, and claims and expenses exceeded premium income in many years. The solution involved a thorough reorganization in which pieces of departments were stripped from the old company structure and fitted into such new divisions as underwriting, administration, sales and agency service, and policyholder's service. The change recognized the new style of insurance merchandising — the package policy that treats a customer's insurance needs as a single entity. In this case, the changing nature of the insurance business dictated changes in the traditional organization pattern.

A Mixture of Patterns

Any large organization utilizes a variety of patterns in grouping its activities. In fact, there is no virtue in striving for a monolithic organization with uniformity of organization patterns.[19] What is appropriate at one point may be quite illogical in another area of the same business. The best pattern must be chosen on the basis of the peculiar nature of the activities and the corresponding managerial requirements.

As a result of these considerations, a mixture of patterns is usual. For example, large corporations with diversified product lines are often divided into major product divisions.[20] These product divisions

---

[18]"INA Ties Itself Into a Package," *Business Week,* No. 1845, January 9, 1965, pp. 52-58.

[19]See Herbert A. Simon, *Administrative Behavior,* Second Edition (New York: The Macmillan Company, 1957), Chapter 2, for an exposition of this point and also a criticism of the ambiguities and overlapping involved in the concept of patterns of organization.

[20]See Harold Stieglitz, *Corporate Organization Structures,* Studies in Personnel Policy, No. 183 (New York: National Industrial Conference Board, Inc., 1961), for examples of organization structures with a mixture of patterns.

may be organized internally along either functional or regional lines. The regional pattern is used in divisions having dispersed operations. At each level and part of the organization, then, it is necessary to select the most logical pattern. The most effective organization demands some blend of patterns.

The Nature of Divisionalization

The large industrial corporation has three patterns available to it as the basis for its overall organization. In the small manufacturing enterprise, the functional pattern is customarily used. At the top level, the functions of sales, manufacturing, and finance serve as the basis for the company's major departments. Large industrial concerns, however, have two other patterns as possibilities. One of these is based upon the product, and the other upon geography (also called *territory* or *location*).

Companies that use either the product or geographical format at the top level have been described as *divisionalized* organizations.[21] Divisionalization frequently goes hand in hand with decentralization of authority. The General Motors Corporation, for example, is divisionalized on the basis of products (Buick Motor Division, Oldsmobile Division, Allison Division, Frigidaire Division, etc.). Each operating division functions autonomously under the broad or general direction of the corporation. Other corporations, of course, are divisionalized on the basis of geographical divisions.

Function as the Pattern

As noted above, small manufacturing enterprises find the functional pattern particularly appropriate. This pattern is not limited to the top level of the organization, however. Within the manufacturing department—a functional department—work may be further subdivided on the basis of function. Organizational components at this level may include drilling, grinding, painting, and so on. Different office units similarly may perform typing, filing, and messenger service.

---

[21]Louis A. Allen, *The Management Profession* (New York: McGraw-Hill Book Company, 1964), pp 190-196. See also Peter F. Drucker, *The Practice of Management* (New York: Harper & Row, Publishers, 1954), p. 205. Drucker's distinction between *federal decentralization* and *functional decentralization* is quite similar to Allen's distinction between divisionalized and nondivisionalized structures.

An example of the functional pattern is found in the organization of National Cash Register Company of Dayton, Ohio, whose structure is shown in Figure 4.

It might be noted that the company's five major product lines—cash registers, accounting machines, adding machines, electronic data-processing systems, and supplies—seem to have a closer kinship than the product lines of the General Motors Corporation.

Efficiency and economy are among the more important advantages of functional organization. This is especially true for relatively small companies. All selling, for example, is concentrated in one department. This permits specialized—and presumably expert—direction of the sales function. Furthermore, only one salesman need call on each customer. He represents the entire line of products. A potential weakness in the functional pattern is its tendency to encourage a narrowness of viewpoint. It is easy for functional executives and personnel to look at problems from the standpoint of selling or manufacturing or some other functional specialty rather than seeing them from the standpoint of the company as a whole.

Growth in a business enterprise may produce strains on the functional organization. Extreme product diversification and widespread territorial expansion, in particular, contribute to the difficulty of successfully operating according to a simple functional pattern. Consequently, growth often requires adaptation of existing patterns of organization.

Product as the Pattern

The possibility of a product pattern exists not only at the top level (divisionalization) but also at lower levels. In a functional sales department, for example, sales personnel may be specialized on the basis of product lines. Or the manufacturing department may include plants specialized in the manufacturing of different products. An example of the product pattern is presented in Figure 5.

The advantages of product divisionalization are particularly significant in the case of a highly diversified product line. The products are quite different from each other. The work and requirements of manufacturing or sales personnel in a consumer products division, for example, are drastically different from those in an atomic power division. Product patterns permit the specialization to be in terms of the product or group of products. Objectives of the various divisions may be established in terms that are significant for the firm as a whole and performance can be judged accordingly.

Figure 4. *The National Cash Register Company*

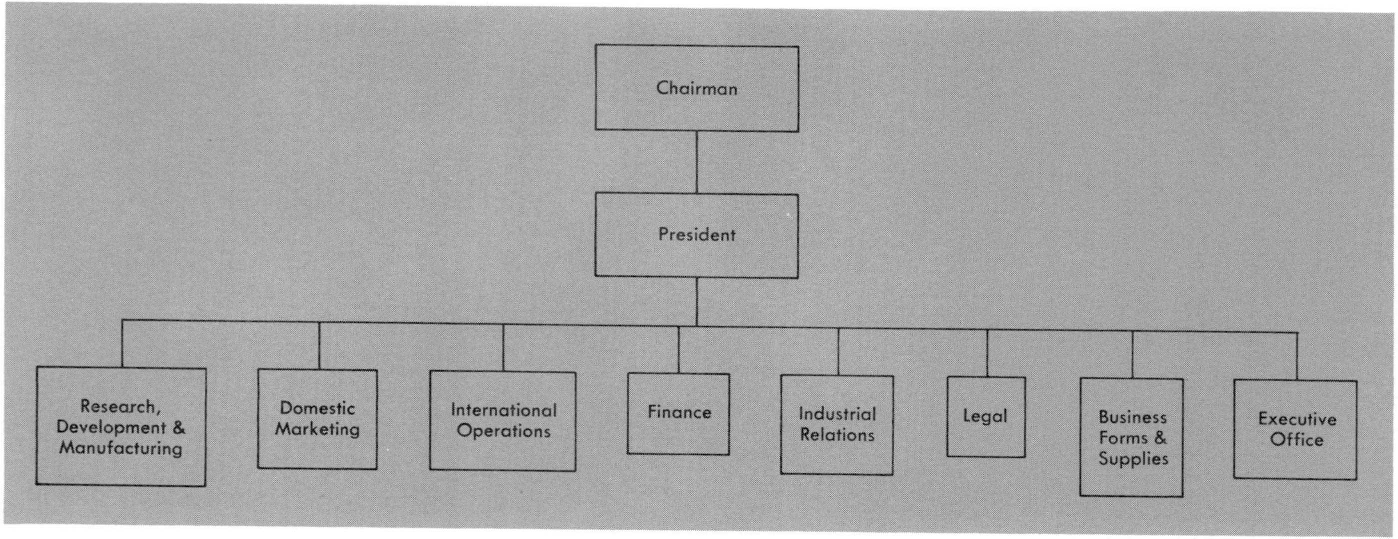

Source: Company Records (1967).

Figure 5. *Westinghouse Electric Corporation Organization**

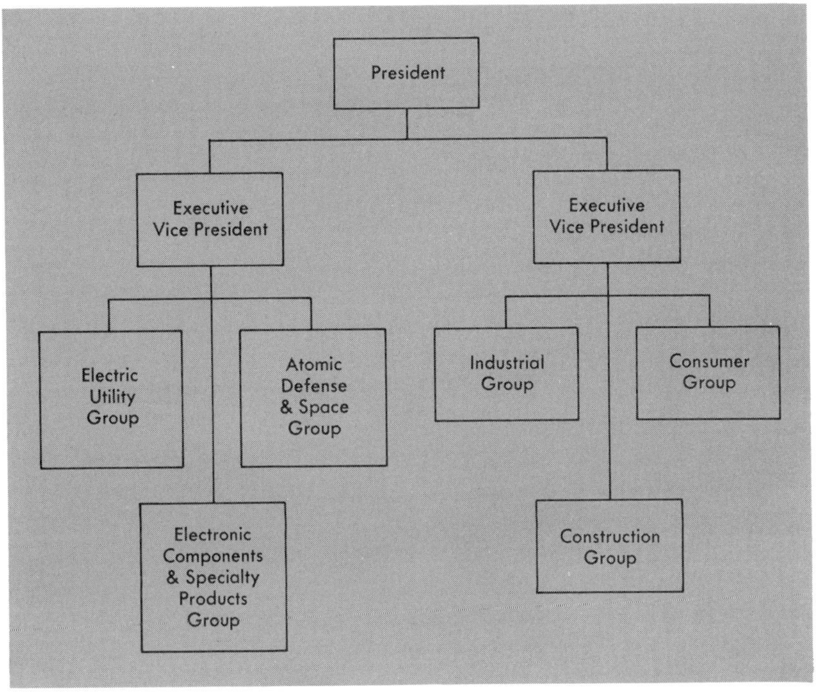

Source: Company Records (1967).
*This simplified chart does not show the various staff offices and associated activities of the corporation.

Executive development may be cited as another attractive feature of product organization. In the functional organization, executives are trained in functional areas and imbued with a functional viewpoint. Only by position rotation or service in different functional areas do they acquire experience outside their own field of specialization. In contrast, the general manager of a product department and his assistant have the responsibility for dealing with problems in various functional areas—including production, sales, and research and development. When an executive committee member or new chief executive is needed, the company has broadly experienced executives from which to choose.

Location as the Pattern

Location of work provides another possible pattern for organization. For the most part, this is a matter of geography—for example, establishing various regional offices—but it may also be necessary to use location in grouping activities in a given plant or office. Maintenance personnel, for example, may be combined into administrative units on the basis of particular buildings or plant areas.

An example of territorial divisionalization is found in the organization structure of the Prudential Insurance Company of America.

Figure 6. *Organization of the Prudential Insurance Company of America*

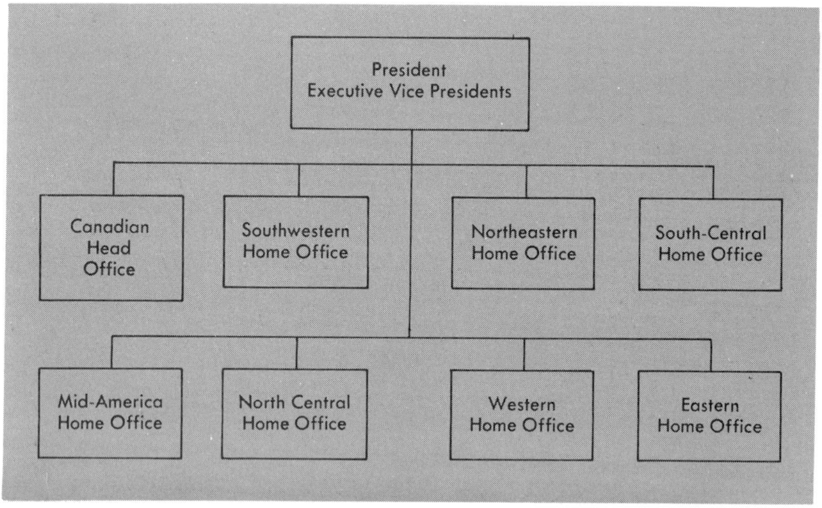

Source: Company Records (1967).

The following explanation reveals the nature of the territorial arrangement and the considerable degree of autonomy permitted to the regional offices:

> Each of Prudential's eight regional offices is headed by a senior vice president accountable to the president for operations in his territory, including the line responsibilities for the selling and servicing of individual and group insurance.
>
> The Actuarial Departments of the regions have freedom to underwrite new business within actuarial standards set by the Corporate Home Office. In special cases, however, rates may be determined by the corporate headquarters.
>
> The regional Investment Departments make mortgage and industrial loans and real estate investments within a total plan set by the corporate department. The responsibility for investment in stocks and bonds is not delegated to the regional home offices.

> All the regional home offices have their own staff and service departments in public relations and advertising, methods, research and personnel administration. A comptroller's organization is attached to each regional home office, but is considered a part of the Corporate Home Office comptroller's department.[22]

It is of interest to note that this company has been one of the most aggressive and rapidly growing large insurance companies.

Organization on the basis of location has certain advantages in common with the product pattern. Breadth of managerial experience is secured in the administration of regional areas. Financial control of operations is also facilitated by permitting separate accounting for the financial results of each territorial unit. In effect, a separate profit and loss statement may be prepared for each territory and a determination made of its contribution to corporate profits.

The locational format is often used in organizing sales activities even though the overall company pattern is that of function or product. Adaptation to local situations and knowledge of customer needs peculiar to a given area are facilitated by the locational pattern.

Customers as the Pattern

In sales organizations, differences in the needs of customers often lead to an organization plan based upon certain customer classifications. Distinctions are often made, for example, in selling to industrial users and in selling to wholesalers or retailers. If customer differences are substantial, an argument for some customer pattern becomes strong.

As an example of the reasoning involved in adopting a customer pattern, consider a change in the organization of the sales force of the International Business Machines Corporation. The Manhattan sales offices of IBM had used the traditional geographical arrangement, but four sales offices were created in 1959 to serve one or more industries that constituted IBM customers.[23] The reasoning was that sales representatives must become specialists in the business of their customers and in the adaptation of IBM equipment to those particular industries. The new offices included a financial office to deal with banks and brokers; an office to sell to insurance companies; an office dealing with textiles, retail trade, and associated business; and an office catering to petroleum, industrial, and transportation

---

[22]Adapted from Stieglitz, *op. cit.*, p. 146.

[23]"IBM Shift in New York Sales Setup May Set Pattern for Wider Change," *Business Week*, No. 1577, November 21, 1959, p. 133.

industries. The new pattern proved effective, and 80 per cent of the IBM sales force was reported to be specialized on an industry basis in 1962.[24]

Changing Patterns of Organization

Growth of a company and changes in the nature of its business may lead to changes in the patterns of organization. A functional pattern that is appropriate for a small company may yield to a product pattern as the firm expands and diversifies. Patterns are not permanently fixed, therefore, at the time of business formation. Along with other aspects of the organization structure, the basic patterns must be re-evaluated from time to time in order to insure the most efficient organization.

An example of the changing organizational patterns is found in the case of the Burroughs Corporation as it changed in 1960 from a product to a functional base.[25] Prior to 1960, the company had utilized product divisions — the Burroughs Division which designed, manufactured, and sold accounting machines and the ElectroData Division which designed, manufactured, and sold electronic computers. The reasoning in support of the change back to a functional organization emphasized the growing tendency of users of the equipment to think in terms of data processing systems rather than isolated pieces of equipment. Placing the accounting machines and electronic computers under the same roof permitted the Burroughs Corporation to deal with the sale of its products on a *systems* basis. An unfortunate feature of the previous product organization was the sales conflict and competition that occasionally developed.

> In one city, ElectroData salesmen might be in one building, Burroughs salesmen in a separate building blocks away — and they both might call on the same bank or utility company. The Burroughs salesmen would offer electromechanical devices for posting and billing; the ElectroData man would come in with a computer and ancillary equipment. The two would do some of the same operations, but neither was a complete data processing system.[26]

Changes in the industry, then, provided pressures leading to this change in the company's organization pattern.

---

[24]"The Switch to Specialized Sales," *Dun's Review and Modern Industry*, Vol. 80, No. 2, August 1962, p. 44.

[25]"Burroughs Puts Sales Under a Single Hat," *Business Week*, No. 1604, May 28, 1960, pp. 62-68.

[26]*Ibid.*, p. 67.

Summary

Creation of a sound organization *structure* is an essential element of effective management. It is important to recognize limitations confronting the manager as he attempts to build an effective organization structure. Because of the social aspects of organizational behavior, an organization may not function in fact as it is theoretically supposed to function. Personnel, with their varying capabilities and attitudes, constitute an important variable to be considered in creating the organization structure.

The systems approach to organizing emphasizes the essential relationships of component parts of the organization. The organizer must begin with a consideration of the nature of the system — its function or purpose. Activities, decisions, and relations must be analyzed in the process of designing the organization structure.

A fundamental organizing decision concerns the *content* of individual *jobs*. In the past, the quest for organizational efficiency has led to extensive specialization and standardization of work. The result of this has often been to reduce the employee's sense of accomplishment and increase monotony of his work. Some organizations have attempted to solve these problems through *job enlargement* which increases the variety of duties in given jobs.

Once job content is determined, it is necessary to group jobs and activities in devising an overall structure. *Patterns* that may be used in grouping include, among others, *function, product, location,* and *customers.* Each of these is a logical and appropriate pattern for particular situations. At the top level of the organization, the choice is commonly made among function, product, and location. Companies using either product or locational patterns for their overall organization are referred to as *divisionalized* organizations. In such companies, this pattern of organization is normally associated with the organizational philosophy of *decentralization.*

Discussion Questions

1. What specific factors might account for the greater effectiveness that results from good organization?
2. How may the personnel of a firm constitute a limiting factor in organizing?
3. In what sense is an organization chart symbolic?
4. How does the systems point of view affect the manager's organizing function?

5. One method of organizing an industrial corporation is to start by breaking the total company business into the basic functions of production, sales, and finance. These are in turn subdivided into more specific functions, and the functions are eventually divided into individual jobs. How does this approach fit into the systems concept of organizing?
6. What explains the historic trend toward narrowing the scope of industrial jobs?
7. How is the thinking of Adam Smith, an economist, related to organizational theory?
8. Evaluate the impact of work specialization upon employees.
9. What is meant by the *pattern* of organization? Why is a mixture of patterns customary?
10. What is the meaning of *divisionalization*?
11. What advantage is found in the *product pattern* of organization that does not exist in the *location* (or *territorial*) *pattern*?

Supplementary Reading

Bucklow, Maxine, "A New Role for the Work Group," *Administrative Science Quarterly,* Vol. 11, No. 1, June 1966, pp. 59-78.

Chandler, Alfred D., Jr., *Strategy and Structure.* Cambridge: The M.I.T. Press, 1962.

Conant, Eaton H. and Maurice D. Kilbridge, "An Interdisciplinary Analysis of Job Enlargement: Technology, Costs, and Behavioral Implications," *Industrial and Labor Relations Review,* Vol. 18, No. 3, April 1965, pp. 377-395.

Evan, William M., "Organizational Lag," *Human Organization,* Vol. 25, No. 1, Spring 1966, pp. 51-53.

Gibson, James L., "Organization Theory and the Nature of Man," *Academy of Management Journal,* Vol. 9, No. 3, September 1966, pp. 233-245.

Hall, Richard H., "The Concept of Bureaucracy: An Empirical Assessment," *American Journal of Sociology,* Vol. 69, No. 1, July 1963, pp. 32-40.

Koontz, Harold and Cyril O'Donnell, *Principles of Management,* Fourth Edition, Chapter 13. New York: McGraw-Hill Book Company, 1968.

Mace, Myles L., "The President and International Operations," *Harvard Business Review,* Vol. 44, No. 6, November-December 1966, pp. 72-84.

Myers, M. Scott, "Every Employee a Manager," *California Management Review,* Vol. 10, No. 3, Spring 1968, pp. 9-20.

Newman, William H., *Administrative Action,* Second Edition, Chapter 9. Englewood Cliffs: Prentice-Hall, Inc., 1963.

Paine, Frank T., "Why Don't They Cooperate?" *Personnel Administration,* Vol. 29, No. 3, May-June 1966, pp. 15-21.

Pelissier, Raymond F., "Successful Experience with Job Design," *Personnel Administration,* Vol. 28, No. 2, March-April 1965, pp. 12-16.

Peterson, Russell W., "New Venture Management in a Large Company," *Harvard Business Review,* Vol. 45, No. 3, May-June 1967, pp. 68-76.

Sorcher, Melvin and Herbert H. Meyer, "Motivating Factory Employees," *Personnel,* Vol. 45, No. 1, January-February 1968, pp. 22-28.

Stieglitz, Harold, *Corporate Organization Structures,* Studies in Personnel Policy No. 183. New York: National Industrial Conference Board, Inc., 1961.

Walker, Charles R., *Technology, Industry, and Man: The Age of Acceleration,* Chapter 5. New York: McGraw-Hill Book Company, 1968.

9

Chain of Command and Span of Control in the Organization

The most fundamental relationship encompassed in organization theory is that between superior and subordinate. Different facets of this relationship are treated in various chapters of this book. In this chapter, our concern is with the structural aspects of the relationship—that is, the nature of the chain of command and the size of the manager's span of control.

The Chain of Command

What Is the Chain of Command?

In its simplest form, a chain of command is the relationship between a superior and subordinate. Starting at the top with the chief executive, we may visualize a series of lines connecting him with his subordinates. These subordinate managers, in turn, are connected with their subordinates. An organization chart diagrams these organizational relationships with lines fanning out from the chief executive and increasing in number at lower levels of the organization. In fact, it has the familiar shape of a pyramid. The total network of relationships constitutes the organization's chain (or, more technically, chains) of command.

Each individual is connected to the chain of command at some point. This means that he reports, either directly or indirectly, to the chief executive and is subject to his command.

Management theorists are fond of calling this series of relationships the *scalar chain*. The different levels in the chain are known as *scalar levels*, and a *scalar principle* stresses the need for this chain of command to include, without haziness or uncertainty, all members of the organization.

Aspects of the Chain of Command

The phrase "chain of command" implies an authoritative relationship, but the chain has at least three distinguishable characteristics —namely, authority, responsibility, and communication.

As an authoritative chain, the manager's status is that of order-giver. The chain is an *official* channel, and the superior's communications are authoritative in nature. Some communications of this type appear as formal orders and directives. In a military organization, for example, orders are often issued in written form. Although some formal orders are found in civilian organizations, much of the authority is exercised through informal discussion and is thought of as working with the superior rather than taking orders from him. In fact, a statement to the effect that the superior is expressing his ideas as an order makes the superior's comments a matter of extreme concern and may cause anxiety because of the implied dissatisfaction with less formal directions. (The nature and limitations of authority are discussed in Chapter 18.)

The chain of command is also a line of responsibility which holds subordinates accountable for their performance. The subordinate is conscious of his superior's surveillance and recognizes his own obligation even though his responsibility may be enforced informally. If satisfactory performance is the rule, there may be little or no mention of the accountability feature of the chain of command. In some cases, however, there are formal performance reviews in which the manager evaluates and discusses quite pointedly the performance of the subordinate.

A system of rewards and penalties is available to the manager to enforce the responsibility of subordinates. These range from commendation and promotion for outstanding service to dismissal for dereliction of duty. It is often said that authority should be commensurate with responsibility. This means that there is a basic unfairness involved in attempting to hold an individual responsible for that which he lacks the necessary authority to accomplish. Unfortunately, there are occasional instances of this type in which higher management fails to see the limitations confronting a subordinate or neglects to confer upon him the necessary authority.

It is the communication between a manager and his subordinates that gives substance to the relationship. In other words, superiors and subordinates experience their relationships through discussion and other contacts with each other. The manager drops in to chat with his subordinate or calls him into the office. Although these communications are official in nature, they are by no means limited to orders or commands. Discussions regularly treat such subjects as the progress of work, problems that are encountered, personal matters, and other information of mutual interest. The nature of the superior-subordinate relationship as a communication link is discussed more thoroughly in Chapter 22.

Figure 7. *Features of the Chain of Command*

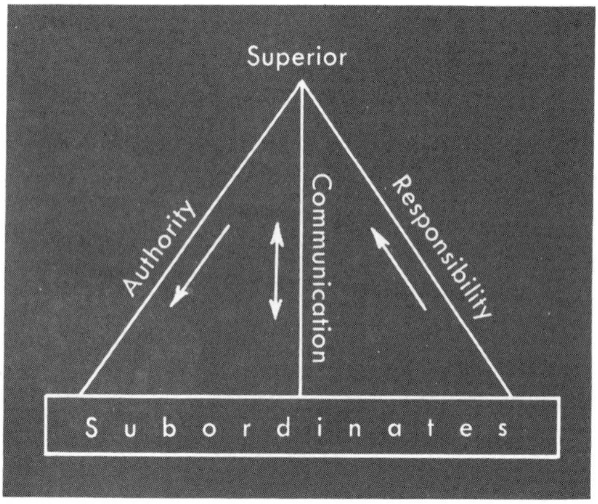

Difficulties in Adhering to the Chain of Command

In practice, adherence to the chain of command can never be complete. The different strata of management cannot be rigidly compartmentalized. A president deals directly with vice presidents, but he also communicates with their subordinates. In all likelihood, these contacts involve not only casual personal conversations but also serious discussions of business matters. Almost any manager is known personally and evaluated by two or three levels of supervision above him. Associations of this type are not confined to *joint con-*

ferences in which several layers of management are present but also include "leapfrogging" that runs counter to the chain of command concept.

Several forces contribute to this flexibility of the chain of command. One of these is the need for speed in communications. Communications through channels necessarily go rather slowly.

Figure 8. *Communication Through the Chain of Command*

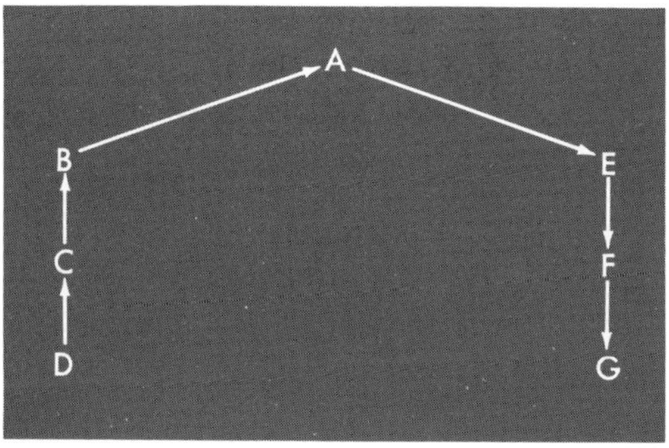

Clearing a communication through several levels of management is time consuming even if the matter is given reasonably prompt treatment. For example, if *D* (in Figure 8) wishes to communicate with *G* through channels, he must go through *C*, *B*, *A*, *E*, and *F*. If one of the managers is out of the office, the communication may be delayed even further.

Need for accuracy in communication also encourages short-circuiting of the official chain of command. Mere transmission of information through a number of individuals tends to introduce inaccuracies and distortions. The president may get, through official channels, reports of progress and problems in plants and departments under his direction. To insure an accurate picture of conditions at any level, however, the president may need to have a look for himself. Of course, he may be accompanied by representatives of intermediate levels of management and thus pay his respects to the chain of command. The point is that the need for complete and accurate information encourages managers to go around intermediate layers in getting closer to the spot where action occurs or knowledge exists.

If the chain of command is followed too carefully, a manager may find himself in the dark regarding managerial talent below the level of his immediate subordinates. Such ignorance, a byproduct of the strict chain of command, may involve both inefficiency and inequity. As Guy Hunter has noted, the intense competition in middle management leads to some amount of jungle warfare between those seeking attention and those fearful of losing it.

> Protocol, a strict observance of chains of command, was largely invented not to prevent but to control this process; it gives rules to the game. To believe that the game can be abolished is surely an illusion.[1]

Yet the rules of the game, if enforced too stringently, can block the superior's understanding of the organization below him and the "bright young men" who are there.

> The tighter the protocol, the more difficult it is to see through the opaque phalanx of immediate subordinates to the younger man below. Many senior managers would laugh at this difficulty: they "'have their ear to the ground," they "know their men." Indeed, they do: but they do so by a large number of minor infringements of the protocol which they officially bless. They stroll round and have a chat; they observe performance of the younger man when his chief is away; they may even invite, however casually, just the comment which the thruster is eager to make.[2]

Some short-circuiting by subordinates is also justified as a protection against unfairness in supervision. Even though managers may be reasonable in considering subordinate needs and fair in discipline most of the time, there are occasional instances of arbitrary and harsh administrative action. In such cases the subordinate has little recourse except to "go over the head" of his superior. In the early days of IBM, Thomas J. Watson encouraged employees to bring their problems, such as unfair managerial treatment, to him personally. An invitation of this type, if taken seriously, could conceivably lead to serious administrative problems by playing one level of the organization against another. But if used with discretion, it can also provide a relief valve in case of unjust managerial decisions. IBM still attempts to preserve a right of appeal to higher levels even though the company has grown tremendously in size.

> The Open Door exists today as it did then. I'm sure that a policy of this kind makes many a traditional manager's blood run cold.

---

[1]Guy Hunter, *Studies in Management* (London: University of London Press Ltd., 1961), p. 31.

[2]*Ibid.*, pp. 31-32.

> He probably sees it as a challenge to his authority or, worse yet, as a sharp sword hanging over his head. But the fact remains that in IBM it has been remarkably effective, primarily because — by its mere existence — it exercises a moderating influence on management. Whenever a manager makes a decision affecting one of his people, he knows that he may be held accountable to higher management for the fairness of that decision.[3]

Some modification of the strict chain of command thus seems a prime necessity to many administrators. Yet, though some relaxation of the chain is necessary, it is not without its hazards, as will be noted in the following section.

Dangers in Short-Circuiting the Chain of Command

Short-circuiting the official chain of command quickly undermines the position of a bypassed manager. The mere practice of bypassing may indicate to the short-circuited manager a lack of confidence on the part of his superior. The natural effect is a weakening of his morale. In contacts between the bypassed manager and his subordinates, the effectiveness of leadership is impaired. His subordinates may well reason, "If his boss does not take him seriously, why should we?"

Dr. Vannevar Bush, who has served as director of a number of nationally known corporations, has noted the existence of this problem at the highest executive level.[4] In considering the relationship between the board and the president, Dr. Bush approved the practice of direct contact between the board and the vice presidents or other key executives subordinate to the president. Such departures from the "hourglass" form of organization, in which internal matters are funneled to and from the president, must be carefully controlled, however, to avoid a challenge to the position of the chief executive. The following statement reveals the thinking of Dr. Bush with respect to this danger:

> But it should always be crystal clear that, except when the president himself desires preliminary board discussion for guidance, nothing goes to the board from the management except

---

[3]Thomas J. Watson, Jr., *A Business and Its Beliefs* (New York: McGraw-Hill Book Company, 1963), p. 20.

[4]Vannevar Bush, "Of What Use is a Board of Directors," in *Problems of General Management,* eds. Edmund P. Learned, C. Roland Christensen, and Kenneth R. Andrews (Homewood: Richard D. Irwin, Inc., 1961), pp. 504-513.

> the considered conclusions and plans of the president, initiated by him or in response to board initiation. If the board is not satisfied with the chief's performance, its members can reason with him privately, and the board can if necessary get a new chief; but it cannot enter into his relations with his staff without creating chaos.[5]

Short-circuiting is often confusing to subordinates of a bypassed manager. In effect, such subordinates are subjected to multiple supervision and to the probable unpleasantness involved in such an arrangement. The immediate supervisor's orders may be countermanded by a higher level of management. General confusion is a distinct possibility.

Short-circuiting is more or less serious depending upon a number of specific circumstances. Emergency situations, for example, lead to greater tolerance of contacts outside the chain of command. No one considers it necessary to shout "Fire" through channels! In the absence of emergencies, the willingness of intermediate management levels to tolerate leapfrogging depends upon such other factors as the importance of subject discussed, the nature of the contact (whether it is confined to discussion or involves decisions), and the extent to which intermediate levels are kept fully informed.

Administrative finesse is required in keeping out-of-channels contacts harmless to the organization structure and positive in their contribution to organizational purposes. There is a fine line, for example, between discussions of an informational nature and discussions in which advice is given or implied. According to Dr. Bush, "The executive who can talk freely with an individual two ranks below him, while keeping it clear that he is issuing no orders, and that he expects the individual to apprise his immediate boss of anything pertinent which occurs, is rare."[6] In view of the potential difficulties in circumventing the chain of command, the practice should be minimized and when the practice is necessary, it should be handled with extreme care.

Unity of Command

The concept of unity of command holds that no individual should be subject to the direct command of more than one superior at any

---

[5]*Ibid.*, p. 509.
[6]*Ibid.*, p. 512.

given time. In practice, this precept is often violated. In some cases, a subordinate reports to two or more superiors of approximately equal status. In other situations, one manager exercises *administrative* control, while another manager provides *technical* control over work. Sometimes organizational relationships are vague, and the subordinate finds that two or more superiors are behaving as though the subordinate reports to each of them. While it may look as though the subordinate should take action in such a case to clear the air, he may be in a weak position to question the company's organization. Any number of situations may thus result in deviation from unity of command.

The reasoning supporting the desirability of unity of command runs to the effect that two or more superiors are unlikely to agree perfectly in their instructions to the same subordinate. The subordinate must then choose the instructions he will follow. The subordinate may also need to assign priorities to projects originating with various supervisors — and of necessity to disappoint one or more of them. Different managers are likewise inclined to have different expectations regarding employee performance.

A number of negative effects, then, result from disunity of command. It becomes difficult, if not impossible, to hold the subordinate accountable. The mere fact of multiple supervision has provided him with a ready made alibi. He may tell Superior X, "I couldn't do it because I was tied up on a project for Superior Y." The subordinate also finds himself in a strategic position to play off one supervisor against another, inasmuch as he is the only individual with complete knowledge of his total assignment.

Business experience has shown that completely unified command is not an absolute requirement for success. Any manager is subjected to influences and pressures from others. Some of these come from staff functions — a relationship discussed in Chapter 10. Even though such outside influence is typically described as "advice," the manager may feel obliged to follow the suggestions. Multiple supervision is also tolerated at times, and organizations have functioned with reasonable effectiveness in spite of such seeming contradictions. A practical view of the unity-of-command concept must recognize the logic of some of these apparent conflicts that occur. It is possible that some duality in command does not necessarily result in conflicting orders. A more flexible view of unity of command holds that a single manager should be responsible for resolving conflicting orders and that sanctions should be employed to enforce obedience to only one superior.[7] Business success, in the case of overt and continued disregard of this type of unified command, constitutes a tribute to the unusual patience and genial nature of individuals subjected to the organizational strains involved in conflict in command.

Limiting the Span of Control

What Is the Span of Control?

The span of control refers to the number of immediate subordinates reporting to a given manager. If the president has only an executive vice president under his personal direction, the president's span of control is one. This is true even though the executive vice president may have a number of subordinate managers who, in turn, direct operations. If the president has six vice presidents reporting to him, however, his span of control is six.

Span of control is the phrase that has been traditionally used in describing this relationship. This phrase itself emphasizes the manager's function of controlling, but the concept is considerably broader. It might also be termed *span of management.*

It is possible to distinguish between the span of control of executives who have subordinate managers reporting to them and the span of control of supervisors who direct operative employees. This is a significant distinction, and the optimum size of these two spans may logically differ. In this chapter, our principal concern is the span of control of the executive who is responsible for the management of other managers.

Relationship to Echelons

The size of the span of control is inversely related to the number of echelons, or layers, in an organization. As the span is broadened, there is a tendency to flatten the structure.

In Figure 9 it can be seen that a span of two would require four echelons to direct eight operative employees, whereas a span of four would require only three echelons.

---

[7]See Herbert A. Simon, *Administrative Behavior,* Second Edition (New York: The Macmillan Company, 1957), pp. 22-26.

Figure 9. *Spans of Different Sizes*

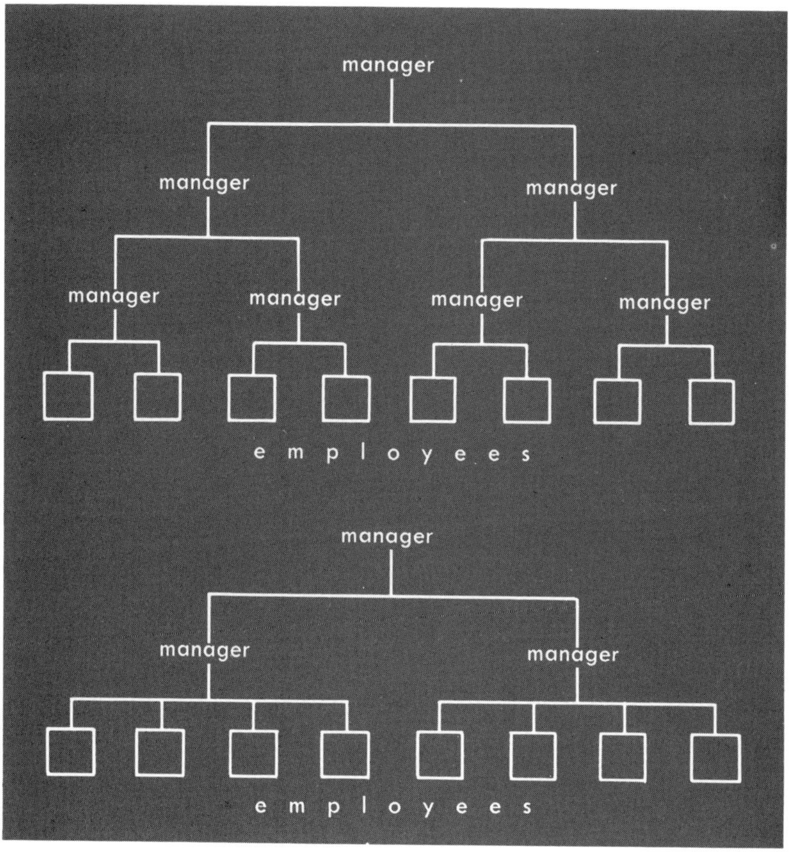

The cure for an excessively large span is the insertion of additional layers. Suppose that a small business grows to the point that eight production workers are employed, in addition to salesmen and other personnel. All of these report to the president. The usual solution is the appointment of a shop supervisor, thereby reducing the president's span of control and creating a third level in the business.

Limiting the Span of Control

The reason for establishing limits on the size of the span of control is plain enough. The strength and time of any manager are limited. One manager, for example, could not personally direct the work of a thousand employees. In an extreme case, then, there can be little argument about the need for reducing the span.

As subordinates are added and organizations grow, the size of managerial spans tends to grow. However, the increasing demands on managers eventually create pressures for reducing the span. An example is found in the recent experience of the Koehring Company, a Milwaukee manufacturer of cranes, mixers, and other construction and industrial equipment.[8] Rapid growth — more than a fivefold sales increase in one decade — led to organizational weaknesses at the top level. Too many divisions reported directly to the chief executive. To facilitate coordination, the twelve domestic divisions and six staff offices were realigned in four operating and three staff groups. This reorganization reduced the top executive span of control from eighteen to seven and provided greater opportunity for top-level corporate planning.

The argument in favor of smaller spans is often extended far beyond the obvious case. If a manager can in some way direct the activities of twelve subordinates, it is reasoned, he should be able to direct eight or six or four even more effectively. The additional time should presumably allow him to decide matters pertaining to his organization more intelligently and more beneficially from the standpoint of the organization. Unfortunately, the case for extending the argument to its logical conclusion is not completely clear. Not only would a span of one be costly, but, as is noted below, there are some who contend that managerial efficiency is not necessarily maximized in such a span.

Quantitative Limits — the Graicunas Approach

In the past, it has been popular to specify rather precise limits to the desirable size of the span of control. One well-known approach of this type is identified with V. A. Graicunas, a French management consultant, who made a mathematical analysis of the span of control.[9] In general, Graicunas suggested that the number of management relationships in a span of control expands at a much faster rate than does the span of control itself. In other words, the addition of one position to the span of control provides a propor-

---

[8]"Koehring Co. Digs Out Its Share," *Business Week,* No. 1892, December 4, 1965, pp. 148-150.

[9]V. A. Graicunas, "Relationship in Organization," in *Papers on the Science of Administration,* eds. Luther Gulick and L. Urwick (New York: Institute of Public Administration, 1937), pp. 181 ff.

tionately greater increase in the number of significant relationships, thereby increasing the complexity of the manager's task.

To understand the Graicunas approach, we must recognize that he was concerned not only with the single, direct relationship between superior and subordinate, but also with other types of relationships within the managerial unit. If Tom supervises Dick and Harry, he can either confer with them individually or speak to them as a pair. Furthermore, as Graicunas saw it, the behavior of Dick or Harry in the presence of the other will differ from his behavior when he is alone with Tom. In addition, Dick's attitude toward Harry and Harry's attitude toward Dick constitute two cross relationships of significance to Tom. These relationships might be summarized as follows:

Direct single relationships	
Tom to Dick and Tom to Harry	2
Direct group relationships	
Tom to Dick with Harry and Tom to Harry with Dick	2
Cross relationships	
Harry with Dick and Dick with Harry	2
Total relationships	6

On the basis of these definitions of significant relationships, Graicunas discovered that, with expansion of the span of control, the number of relationships grew at an astounding rate and quickly reached astronomical proportions. With 4 subordinates, he discovered a total of 44 relationships, but with 8 subordinates, the total number was 1,080. With 12 subordinates, the number of relationships rose to 24,708. On the basis of this reasoning, Graicunas recommended a maximum span of four or five for most management positions. Beyond this point, the management task seemed to become hopelessly complex.

The contribution of Graicunas' reasoning lies in the fact that it draws attention to the increasing complexity of the management process as additional subordinates are added. At the same time, it seems doubtful that the correct size of the management span can be determined with the precision suggested by an analysis of this type. Although Graicunas acknowledged possible exceptions in the case of routine work, his writing suggests a rather rigorous application of the "principle" he developed. It appears that a number of variables discussed later in the chapter deserve greater consideration than they receive in the Graicunas approach. Also, many of the relationships in his analysis are less significant than the mathematical formula would tend to indicate. Some subordinates, for example, have practically no contact with each other, and their cross relationships are thus of little importance to the manager. A manager would need to proceed cautiously, therefore, in applying a span-of-control "principle" to any specific situation.

Variation in Business Practice

A well-known survey of the span of control in industry was conducted by the American Management Association and reported in 1952. According to this study, the number of executives reporting to the president in 100 large companies — that is, those with more than 5,000 employees — ranged from one to twenty-four subordinate executives.[10]

A survey of more than five hundred Ohio manufacturing plants was reported by James H. Healey in 1956.[11] For all executives who reported their spans, the range in the number of immediate subordinates was from one to seventeen. Six subordinates was the number most frequently reported — accounting for 21.5 per cent of the firms. The next most frequent number of subordinates reported was five, with 17.9 per cent of the firms falling in this category. In 93.7 per cent of the main plants, fewer than nine immediate subordinates reported to the chief executive. According to this survey, then, it appears that the typical practice in these manufacturing plants was somewhat greater than the span of control advocated by classical theorists.

A later American Management Association study of the span of control of thirty-nine chief executives revealed much variation in span size.[12] The span ranged from three to twelve, with the exception of four companies in which more than twelve subordinates reported to the chief executive. The four firms with more than twelve individuals reporting to the president were Curtis Publishing Company

---

[10]Ernest Dale, *Planning and Developing the Company Organization Structure* (New York: American Management Association, 1952, Sixth Printing, 1959), p. 77.

[11]James H. Healey, *Executive Coordination and Control* (Columbus, Ohio: Bureau of Business Research, College of Commerce and Administration, The Ohio State University, 1956), p. 65.

[12]K. K. White, *Understanding the Company Organization Chart,* AMA Research Study 56 (New York: American Management Association, 1963), p. 61.

(fifteen), Stauffer Chemical (fifteen), Western Electric (sixteen), and DuPont (twenty-three). Although the practices disclosed by these surveys do not necessarily disprove the logic of a strict span-of-control principle, they do raise a serious question about its general applicability.

Values in Expanding the Span of Control

Effects on Communication

Enlarging the span, as noted earlier, produces a flatter organization by reducing the number of echelons. This facilitates vertical communication by eliminating organizational levels that can become communication bottlenecks. It is true, of course, that a manager with many subordinates has less time, on the average, to spend with each of them. On the other hand, by eliminating intermediate layers he is closer to the scene of action and thus minimizes delays and distortion involved in going through long chains. It seems likely that the communications network as a whole benefits more from the flatter organization with its broader spans of control even though the managers have less time available for communicating with individual subordinates.

Morale Effects

By broadening the span of control, organizations may also experience an increase in morale. As a result of the larger number of subordinates, an executive is forced to use different management methods from those possible with a small span. It is difficult for him to supervise subordinates in detail, to look over their shoulders while they are working. Instead, he must allow his subordinates to operate with greater freedom. The subordinates are, to a greater extent, on their own. There is some evidence that this boosts both morale and productivity, although the evidence is far from conclusive.

A well-known study of this type concerns Sears, Roebuck and Company.[13] In this company, some managers were assigned relatively large numbers of subordinates. These managers were unable to direct and control their subordinates in a detailed manner. Sears'

---

[13]James C. Worthy, "Organizational Structure and Employe Morale," *American Sociological Review,* Vol. 15, No. 2, April 1950, pp. 169-179.

management concluded that the flat organization with a wider span of control resulted in "not only a higher level of accomplishment but, at the same time, a more satisfying type of supervision and a higher level of employe morale." James C. Worthy, in describing this research, went on to say that "flatter, less complex structures, with a maximum of administrative decentralization, tend to create a potential for improved attitudes, more effective supervision, and greater individual responsibility and initiative among employes."[14]

In a more recent study, Porter and Lawler measured the job satisfaction of almost 2,000 managers in companies of various sizes.[15] They found no overall superiority of flat over tall organizations in providing need satisfaction for managers. In smaller companies — those employing fewer than 5,000 employees — however, managerial satisfaction did appear somewhat greater in flat than in tall organizations. The study also showed some variation in satisfaction of different types of psychological needs. A tall type of structure seemed to produce security and social need satisfactions, whereas a flat structure permitted greater self-actualization or self-fulfillment. The nature of these needs is discussed at greater length in Chapter 20.

From these studies, it is evident that the relationship between flatness and morale is not completely clear. The situation is seemingly more complex than it once appeared. Some relationship apparently exists, but additional research is required to determine its nature more precisely.

Reduction in Supervisory Salaries

Another advantage of the larger span of control is the reduction of administrative overhead cost. By having each manager direct a larger number of subordinates, the necessary number of management officials is substantially reduced in any sizable organization. Supervisory salaries may constitute a significant part of the total operating costs. If this reduction can be accomplished without a marked decrease in efficiency, the organization is clearly benefited, from a cost and profit standpoint, by the use of a larger span of control.

The steel industry, for example, became particularly active in an attempt to pare costs as a result of the profit squeeze beginning

---

[14]*Ibid.*, p. 179.

[15]Lyman W. Porter and Edward E. Lawler, III, "The Effects of 'Tall' Versus 'Flat' Organization Structures on Managerial Job Satisfaction," *Personnel Psychology*, Vol. 17, No. 2, Summer 1964, pp. 135-148.

about 1958. One of the major targets in this cost-cutting effort was surplus manpower in the management structure.[16] About 1962, the U.S. Steel Corporation became particularly zealous in trimming supervisory personnel. One division eliminated an entire level in its sales department. The same division also cut back heavily on product supervisors. The overall reduction of management overhead required consolidation of jobs, reduction in the hiring of new managers, and dismissal of some personnel.

Variables Affecting Optimum Size of Span

Nature of Work

It seems clear, in considering the optimum span of control, that the type of work, as well as other variables, has some bearing in determining the appropriate span. The variety of duties, for example, affects the nature of problems coming to the manager's attention. If the work is repetitive in nature and involves few new problems or new situations, the pattern of work becomes well established and requires only minor attention of the manager.

The importance of the work being performed is likewise influential in determining the amount of supervision required. It is natural for managers to be personally concerned and to feel a need for careful consideration of important matters. If subordinates are confined to work of a trivial nature, the manager is less concerned than if these same employees are performing work having a direct and substantial effect upon the company profits. If his subordinates purchase $50,000 items, a manager typically feels a greater need for review and consultation with them than is necessary with subordinates making purchases of $500.

The inherent difficulty of work is another significant consideration. Some work is basically very simple. Few questions are presented by the work itself, in contrast to projects that are complex and that provide baffling problems. As an extreme example, consider the differences in managing a group of research scientists in contrast to the management of a group of file clerks.

The geographical spread of managed activities also tends to limit the efficient size of the span of control. It is more difficult to manage

---

[16]"Big Steel Strives to Thin Its Ranks," *Business Week,* No. 1721, August 25, 1962, pp. 106-108.

a group of employees scattered over a plant of several acres than to direct a number of employees in the same office. Similarly, there are difficulties in directing the work of employees stationed at branch plants or branch offices in various areas of the country or world in contrast to managing a localized group. Improvements in communication and transportation are minimizing this particular limitation. Modern air transportation now makes it possible for an executive to have breakfast in London, lunch in New York, and dinner in California, thereby extending personal supervision over a much larger area than was formerly possible.

The stable or dynamic nature of the industry and business likewise affects the degree of management attention required and the resulting appropriate size of the span of control. Some industries and companies are quite stable in nature. A public utility is often regarded as being in this category. On the other hand, some businesses are in rapidly changing fields, and they expect to develop new products constantly and to find the nature of the business changing every few decades. It seems reasonable that a manager can provide effective supervision over a broader span in the case of stabilized business and industry.

The Executive

In analyzing the optimum span of control, we should not overlook the executive as an individual. All managers do not have the same physical, mental, and emotional characteristics.

Some individuals are tougher physically and more resilient in reacting to the demands of their offices. Some might be described as "easygoing," while others are "ulcer-prone." The mental ability of some individuals also equips them to size up situations and reach decisions more quickly than is possible for others. Such individual differences are recognized among college students in that, to achieve the same grade, some students spend long hours of study while others barely "crack a book."

Other (nonmanagerial) demands on the time of managers reduce the time available for management and thus affect their efficient span of control. A president may spend considerable time representing his company in its public relations contacts. In addition, he may engage in personal selling to important customers of the firm. Time spent in such sales contacts or in making speeches is obviously not available for directing the work of subordinates.

Methods of Management

A number of management practices facilitate direction by the manager and thus contribute to his capacity for adjusting to a larger span of control. One of these is the delegation of authority. If the manager delegates substantial amounts of authority to subordinates and utilizes relatively little detailed supervision, he frees himself from work that can be burdensome and consume a great deal of his time. Effective delegation, thus, permits a larger span of control than would be possible otherwise.

Other managerial techniques affecting the size of the span include the use of budgetary control systems. If the superior has established or approved a course of action in the officially adopted budget, he is relieved of the necessity of evaluating subsequent actions that fall within the scope of that budget. His organization is thus able to function somewhat automatically as long as no exceptions to expected performance occur. Similarly, the superior executive may, through a framework of policies, establish guidelines for lower levels of management. In this way, he is able to rule in advance on general problems and to avoid the need for minute examination of specific issues.

Executives are also able to broaden their span of control by the use of staff assistants. A staff man can provide another set of legs and eyes and ears for the executive whom he represents. It is possible, of course, that the use of staff personnel can result in such blurring of lines of authority that the overall effectiveness of the group is reduced. If this tendency is controlled, however, the superior can entrust to his staff certain problems of investigation and evaluation that otherwise would require additional hours on his own part.

Capacity and Training of Subordinates

The executive who is sufficiently fortunate to have talented, competent subordinates is in a position to minimize his time spent in control of their activities. Competent, well-trained personnel are less prone to make errors, requiring less correction and counseling from their superiors. In addition, the ability of subordinates may manifest itself in the ready identification of problem areas and in devising solutions to these problems. Their creative thinking can also save the time of their superiors.

This difference in the capacity and training of subordinates is significant at any level of the organization. At the higher levels, it involves a great capacity for dealing with broad administrative problems of the organization. It clearly goes hand in hand with the delegation of authority. At the operative levels of the organization, competent workmanship can simplify the task of a first-line supervisor by eliminating errors and minimizing the need for detailed instruction.

Summary

There are significant values realized through adherence to the *chain of command*—notably, the preservation of the status of management officials and the avoidance of confusion to subordinate personnel. Subordinates often find it distressing to receive multiple supervision, whether this results from short-circuiting the chain of command or from conflict with the concept of *unity of command.*

In considering the *span of control,* it appears that the determination of precise, quantitative limits that are generally applicable to many organizations is difficult, if not impossible. There are also difficulties in extending the size of the span of control, but some have found advantages, particularly in terms of communication, productivity, and morale, in the use of a broader span of control that results in a flatter organization. Some of the variables affecting the desirable size of the span of control include the nature of work being performed, the qualities of the manager as an individual, managerial methods and procedures, and the capacity and training of subordinates.

Discussion Questions

1. Explain the three aspects or characteristics of the *chain of command.*
2. What pressures encourage short-circuiting of the chain of command? Do these factors constitute valid reasons or merely excuses for short-circuiting?
3. Suppose a top-level executive feels it is necessary to go outside channels in contacting a manager two or three levels below. How can he minimize any adverse effects?

4. Does the concept of *unity of command* appear to be merely a textbook principle or does it appear to have practical significance in administrative situations?

5. How is the span of control related to the number of echelons in an organization?

6. What weaknesses or limitations exist in the *Graicunas approach* to the establishment of quantitative limits to the span of control?

7. What seems to be the greatest advantage resulting from expanding the span of control?

8. If we assume that the most capable managers occupy top management positions, should they have broader spans of control than managers at lower levels?

Supplementary Reading

Applewhite, Philip B., *Organizational Behavior,* pp. 156-158. Englewood Cliffs: Prentice-Hall, Inc., 1965.

Bell, Gerald D., "Determinants of Span of Control," *The American Journal of Sociology,* Vol. 73, No. 1, July 1967, pp. 100-109.

Blau, Peter M., ""The Hierarchy of Authority in Organizations," *The American Journal of Sociology,* Vol. 73, No. 4, January 1968, pp. 453-467.

Fisch, Gerald G., '"Stretching the Span of Management," *Harvard Business Review,* Vol. 41, No. 5, September-October 1963, pp. 74-85.

Hill, Lawrence S., "The Application of Queuing Theory to the Span of Control," *Journal of the Academy of Management,* Vol. 6, No. 1, March 1963, pp. 58-69.

Jaques, Elliott, "Too Many Management Levels," *California Management Review,* Fall 1965, Vol. 8, No. 1, pp. 13-20.

Nelson, Edward A., "Economic Size of Organizations," *California Management Review,* Vol. 10, No. 3, Spring 1968, pp. 61-72.

Newman, William H., *Administrative Action,* Second Edition, Chapter 15. Englewood Cliffs: Prentice-Hall, Inc., 1963.

Porter, Lyman W. and Edward E. Lawler, III, "The Effects of 'Tall' Versus 'Flat' Organization Structures on Managerial Job Satisfaction," *Personnel Psychology,* Vol. 17, No. 2, Summer 1964, pp. 135-148.

Porter, Lyman W. and Jacob Siegel, "Relationships of Tall and Flat Organization Structures to the Satisfactions of Foreign Managers," *Personnel Psychology,* Vol. 18, No. 4, Winter 1965, pp. 379-392.

Read, William H., "The Decline of the Hierarchy in Industrial Organizations," *Business Horizons,* Vol. 8, No. 3, Fall 1965, pp. 71-75.

Stieglitz, Harold, "Optimizing Span of Control," *Management Record,* Vol. 24, No. 9, September 1962, pp. 25-29.

Thompson, Robert E., "Span of Control— Conceptions and Misconceptions," *Business Horizons,* Vol. 7, No. 2, Summer 1964, pp. 49-58.

Udell, Jon G., "An Empirical Test of Hypotheses Relating to Span of Control," *Administrative Science Quarterly,* Vol. 12, No. 3, December 1967, pp. 420-439.

Urwick, Lyndall F., "The Manager's Span of Control," *Harvard Business Review,* Vol. 34, No. 3, May-June 1956, pp. 39-47.

Worthy, James C., "Organization Structure and Employe Morale," *American Sociological Review,* Vol. 15, No. 2, April 1950, pp. 169-179.

10

Line and Staff Relationships

One of the most troublesome aspects of effective organization is the relationship between *line* and *staff*. It is troublesome to the theorist, who has difficulty in formulating a well-integrated theory about the subject, and to the manager who becomes embroiled in line and staff conflicts and confusion.

THE NATURE OF LINE AND STAFF RELATIONSHIPS

The Need for Teamwork

The basic objective in analyzing formal relationships among individuals and departments is the achievement of teamwork. Harmony is essential if an organization is to achieve its objectives most effectively. The interdependency of individuals and departments in business operations results in numerous opportunities for cooperation or conflict.[1]

In examining the organization structure—and line-staff relationships in particular—the objective of well-coordinated team effort must be emphasized. There is no virtue in proving the superiority

[1]For an analysis of line-staff conflicts in three industrial plants, see Melville Dalton, "Conflicts Between Staff and Line Managerial Officers," *American Sociological Review,* Vol 15, No. 3, June 1950, pp. 342-351.

of some specified definition of "staff" or in arguing that a certain activity is a "line" function unless these distinctions contribute to better teamwork. Regardless of the labels we attach to organization functions, it is important that we understand the factors that build constructive relationships and the practices that generate hostility and conflict.

What Is Line?

A part of the difficulty in understanding and theorizing about line and staff relationships arises from the absence of clear-cut definitions. Discussions of the subject, furthermore, reveal differing ideas concerning the proper basis for any such definitions. Some concepts of line and staff stress the type of business function while others emphasize the type of authority relationships. Some writers have contended that logical distinctions are difficult, if not impossible, and that the traditional concept of line and staff is obsolete. Because of such confusion, they decline to use these particular terms and adopt language of their own. In view of the general disagreement, selection of any basic definition or terminology is necessarily arbitrary. Some definition is essential for further discussion, however, and the definition outlined below places primary emphasis upon the type of business function.

From this *functional* point of view, *line activities are those that contribute directly to accomplishment of the organization's primary objective.* The primary or line functions of a manufacturing concern, for example, include producing and selling of some product. The firm exists to make and sell products, and customers pay for this service. Employees in production and sales, accordingly, are line personnel, and the manufacturing and sales departments are line departments of the enterprise. Inasmuch as most other departments contribute to overall objectives in an indirect manner, they are staff departments. The following comments further clarify this distinction:

> *In terms of work, "line" connotes the work, functions, or organization components that are accountable for fulfilling the economic objectives of the organization.* They are the income-producing components of the organization. This is not to imply that any unit of the company does not contribute to the company's income. But most explicitly, line units are those directly concerned with producing the values in the form of goods and services that the customer will pay for. In terms of basic economics, line units are those that produce "time, place, and form"

> utility. In a manufacturing company, these are generally identified as manufacturing and sales and sometimes engineering when it is an integral part of manufacturing.[2]

One possible objection to this classification is that it does not distinguish between important and unimportant activities. It is possible, for example, to classify finance or accounting as a staff function, but it is dangerous to assume that either is unimportant. In classifying specific functions as line activities, therefore, we must avoid the error of considering staff functions as unimportant.

As noted above, manufacturing and sales departments are generally regarded as line departments. In companies with substantial product research departments, it is possible, with considerable logic, also to include product research as a line function. A strong argument has been advanced against its traditional classification as staff.[3] On the basis of the criterion suggested above (direct contribution to major objective), the function can properly be treated as line. Creation of value for the customer begins "on the drawing board," and the function of product design is as significant to the customer as are the contributions of manufacturing and sales departments. The product must be formed in the designer's mind before it is shaped in the factory. This line of reasoning is particularly true for a company such as Du Pont, in which new product research is a substantial part of the total business and, indeed, supplies the very life blood for future growth and development. The customer pays for a product whose qualities are determined by design as well as by manufacturing. In view of the fact that both contribute directly to the product, a distinction between design and production processes on the basis of mental versus physical contributions appears superficial.

What Is Staff?

Having defined line functions as those contributing directly to accomplishment of major objectives, we have thereby relegated other activities to the category of staff. In a more positive fashion, *staff functions* should be visualized as *supporting functions*. Their performance in some way facilitates the accomplishment of primary

---

[2]Harold Stieglitz, *Corporate Organization Structures,* Studies in Personnel Policy, No. 183 (New York: National Industrial Conference Board, Inc., 1961), p. 7.

[3]Gerald G. Fisch, "Line-Staff is Obsolete," *Harvard Business Review,* Vol. 39, No. 5, September-October 1961, p. 68.

objectives by line departments. A customer has little direct concern with staff functions, because they produce no direct values for him. He would never pay a nickel for staff services, although such services contribute indirectly to the design, production, and sale of the product.

As to the nature of staff work, it is often described as advisory to other departments. In addition, the staff may be used for investigation, fact gathering, and service. In fact, the service contributed by some departments is sufficiently great that some writers make a distinction between service functions and staff functions. There is often a close interrelationship between advice and service, however, and many nonline departments provide a combination of both.

Significance of Line-Staff Distinction

Even with a definition of the type outlined here, it is not easy to classify all activities. There are always borderline functions. Many functions, however, are obviously line or obviously staff.

The significance of the distinction is not classification *per se.* Regardless of what terms are used—and some would prefer to call them *operating* and *auxiliary* departments — the value lies in the emphasis placed upon line functions. These are revealed as the core of the organization. Their failure is equivalent to organization failure, and their success is essential for survival. Understanding the crucial role of line functions enables management to insist that all departments and personnel make a positive contribution to the line functions.

Line Within Staff Departments

All personnel, whether in line or staff departments, are connected by the chain of command to higher management. Assignment to a staff office does not imply that personnel operate without direct supervision or control. The concept of the chain of command as described in the previous chapter applies to staff as well as line functions.

More precisely, a line exists within a staff department. In referring to this *line within a staff,* the focus must be shifted from the organization as a whole to the specific staff department. By narrowing attention to a specific department, its line can be located with the same criterion used above. The basic question is which activities contribute directly to the department's primary objectives. These functions constitute the line within the staff.

The personnel department, for example, is a staff function when the organization or company is viewed as a whole. In looking specifically at the personnel department, however, we can distinguish activities that contribute directly to its objectives. An employee recruitment and selection unit or a job evaluation unit would fall within this category. These units might be called the line within the personnel staff. It is possible to extend this reasoning one additional step and to note that a secondary, or internal, staff may serve the line within the staff department. To illustrate, the personnel department may also contain personnel research, administrative, or records units. These units are of value in supplying information and service to the other parts of the personnel staff.

Types of Staff

Personal Staff

One useful distinction as to types of staff is that of *personal staff* and *specialized staff*.[4] The personal staff is an individual who serves one particular superior. His assignments may be specialized in nature, or he may be a sort of generalized trouble shooter who ranges across a broad subject area in the performance of his duties. The assistant to the president of a firm illustrates this type of staff position.

The personal staff man may perform various types of duties for the superior to whom he reports. Some of these may be described as follows:

1. Review, summarize, and interpret reports for his superior.
2. Represent his superior in answering correspondence, particularly with outsiders, and in making outside contacts, particularly of a public relations nature.
3. Consult with lower levels of management, interpreting and explaining his superior's ideas and objectives.
4. Gather information on the progress of work projects and problems encountered by the organization.

---

[4]Louis A. Allen, *The Management Profession* (New York: McGraw-Hill Book Company, 1964), p. 222.

5. Develop information pertinent to the business future and make forecasts for the benefit of the superior.
6. Analyze problems, making necessary investigations and proposing solutions.

Specialized Staff

In contrast to the service of a personal staff officer, the specialized staff serves an entire organization. It is also recognized as having a special area of competence in which it is expected to be particularly proficient. Such activities as personnel or labor relations, public relations, and legal counsel are examples of specialized staff functions.

The specialized staff furnishes advice and consults with line personnel on the subjects of staff specialization. In the case of a personnel problem, for example, a line official may consult with the personnel department and secure professional advice before reaching a final decision. The sales department, in the preparation of advertising copy, may consult with the legal department to clarify the legal status of the copy and the claims being made.

In addition, the specialized staff often renders service in one form or another to other departments. The personnel department, for example, makes recruiting contacts and performs initial screening of applicants. This involves work that would otherwise need to be performed by departments recruiting additional personnel. It may also operate the company cafeteria and edit a newspaper for employees. The legal department may be asked to prepare and process patent applications to protect new products or processes that have been developed for the company.

The proportion of advice and service furnished by specialized staff varies greatly according to the nature of the function. Some departments are primarily service departments — maintenance departments, for example. Their major contribution is the help, often of a physical nature, that they give to line and to other staff departments.

Authority Relationships

Maintaining Line Authority

Much of the line and staff problem in a typical organization centers about the question of authority between line and staff departments or personnel. Who decides questions of mutual interest to both line and staff departments? In the event of differing opinions, whose opinion is controlling? How far should staff agencies be entitled to go in prescribing standards and procedures applicable to line organizations? In considering this question, it is well to begin by observing the need for maintaining line authority. Subsequently, it will be possible to note desirable or necessary modifications and exceptions.

In using a staff to support the line organization, it is important to avoid the evil of multiple supervision. To preserve unity of command, staff must be denied command authority. Only in this way can line authority be preserved and the line manager be held responsible for results.

> Staffwork is a means to an end, and *not* an end in itself. In the decision-making process, it is a means for putting information in perspective for those who must make and effectuate management decisions. The staff role is thus a role of service to managers.
>
> The staffman's position confers no organization authority upon him. His sole authority is the "authority of ideas."[5]

The staff position often sounds romantic and less demanding in its requirements upon the incumbent. It is a difficult assignment to fill effectively, however, because of the denial of the right to command. The staff official lacks the tool of authority that is built into line positions.

The Basis of Staff Influence

How then can a staff man exert any influence and effectively perform the function for which he is responsible? Lacking authority, he must achieve his objectives in some other way. Since he cannot force his department and its activities or his personal advice "down the throat" of a line department, he must, in effect, sell his staff service. Effective salesmanship in this area demands a good product to sell. At any rate, it is much easier for staff to gain acceptance by the line if the staff has something of high quality to offer. In order to achieve this objective, staff must possess competence and expert knowledge. To provide worthwhile assistance to the line official, the staff must

---

[5]Truman Benedict, "The Staffman in the Decision-Making Process—Scientist or Soothsayer?" *Advanced Management,* Vol. 25, No. 5, May 1960, p. 12.

of necessity know more about the subject, in some of its aspects at least, than the line official.

At the same time, staff is not accepted if it appears unrealistic and "ivory towerish." If staff advice seems impractical, line officials quickly adopt the attitude, "You just don't understand the way we operate." This is the reason that many organizations insist that some staff personnel have previous line operating experience. If a personnel official is proficient regarding personnel questions and if he has previous experience as a line manager, it is difficult for a line official to say or think about him, "You don't know what you are talking about."

In summary, the staff is expected to provide knowledge, service, or advice that is better than what is otherwise available to the line. The quality of this service and advice should be such that staff help and guidance is not only accepted but welcomed. Ideally, staff should be visualized by the line as a part of the same work team, available to make the line a more productive organization.

Staff Infringement on Line Authority

Organizational myopia seems to be an occupational disease of staff personnel. It is difficult for staff officials to see the organization as the chief executive sees it. Rather, the staff sees line problems in terms of a specialized viewpoint.

This natural tendency toward preoccupation with one staff department is a natural result of a number of factors. The staff, particularly the specialized staff, has considerable knowledge regarding a given area. In fact, the knowledge of the staff on a particular type of problem is often superior to that of others in the organization. This situation generates self-confidence in the thinking of staff. For that matter, it is natural for the proponent of any position to feel that his own idea is good.

The staff also lacks a familiarity with other aspects of the line administrator's functions. Staff may have difficulty in grasping or fully comprehending the pressures and frustrations confronting the line and the complex social arrangements that exist. There may be little or no awareness of dangers involved in pressuring for a "good" solution or program.

When the sense of perspective that sees staff as an adjunct of the line is lost, any attitude in the direction of self-effacement and sublimation disappears. The staff official begins to think in terms of group effort in which the contribution of each individual is equally essential. The work of the line and the work of the staff are *jointly* responsible for organizational achievement. The staff official may even decide that he is entitled to a certain degree of cooperation from the line and may expect line officials to feel a duty to facilitate staff progress. Intermediate objectives involved in the completion of staff reports and projects become major, final objectives to the staff. Both line and staff, in the view of staff, should cooperate for the achievement of these staff objectives. As an extreme example, a college owned book store may become so involved in the profitability of the book business that it forgets its educational role. Or, the maintenance department may be so concerned with maintenance costs in the care of buildings that it turns off the heat or air conditioning to save money!

The final stage in this progression is usurpation of line authority. The position of the staff may be such—perhaps a close association with top management—as to carry an implied threat to the line. Bucking the assistant to the president, for example, may seem tantamount to bucking the president himself. Lower line officials or personnel may be unable to distinguish clearly between line orders and staff requests or suggestions originating from headquarters. It is possible that the staff may use its monopolistic control of certain staff services to bring a recalcitrant line department to terms.

Line officials may tolerate a considerable amount of forceful direction of this type. In some cases, it is difficult to know enough about the issue to fight intelligently. If the matter seems too important or if the accumulation becomes too great, some sort of rebellion or opposition may result. Or the line official may simply tolerate staff interference, find it frustrating, and experience greater difficulty in the discharge of his major responsibilities.

Staff Responsibility for Avoiding Infringement

As noted above, it takes courage (if not foolhardiness) for a lowly line supervisor to defy a high-ranking staff officer. Of course, the line manager theoretically has this right, but it is not very realistic to think that he will always exercise it as aggressively as might be desirable. Expecting the defense of line authority to come from the line, then, requires considerable optimism unless the offices are at the same level in the organization structure.

This means that staff must tread softly to avoid threats to line authority. It needs to lean over backwards to avoid making decisions for line managers. The following situation graphically portrays the possible range of behavior open to a staff official as a line manager comes to him for advice:

> To give this the added emphasis that it deserves, how shall the personnel manager respond when the foreman says, "What shall I do about John Doe's seniority?"
>
> To be asked any question for information is, of course, subtly flattering because knowledge is implied. The personnel manager, therefore, is naturally inclined to reply, "Give Doe seniority above Smith." When he does, he will be guilty of encroachment. If he is just a bit wiser than this, he may use the subjunctive mood and say, "I would give Doe seniority above Smith." This carries a connotation of advice, to be sure, but the foreman still will be very likely to return to Doe and say, "The personnel manager says to give you seniority above Smith." This is not much better on the part of the personnel manager and is no better at all for the foreman-Doe relationship.
>
> But now suppose the foreman says to the personnel manager, "What shall I do about John Doe's seniority?" and the personnel manager replies, "What do you think should be done?" This obviously puts the colloquy on an entirely different basis. If the foreman then says, "I'd put him below Smith on the seniority list," the personnel manager can find out why the foreman would so decide and can give his own reasons for a different view. If, in addition, the personnel manager emphasizes that the final decision is the foreman's, an altogether different organization result is achieved. Instead of an order, advice and information have been exchanged.[6]

To be effective, this type of approach by staff must be consistent. As Roy has noted, "Good executives and sound relationships do not result from single incidents but accrue from a multitude of them."[7] And it is staff that must take the leadership in fighting its natural tendency toward domination.

Functional Authority of Staff

The organizational world is not simple. Unfortunately, it is difficult in some cases to observe the proper authority relationships between line and staff. Situations arise in which it appears desirable and more efficient from the standpoint of the organization as a

---

[6]Robert H. Roy, *The Administrative Process* (Baltimore: The Johns Hopkins Press, 1958), pp. 66-67.

[7]*Ibid.,* p. 67.

whole to delegate to staff some degree of decision-making authority. A deliberate decision may place certain issues or decisions in the hands of staff. Such power is often referred to as *functional authority*. This differs from usurpation of line authority in which staff merely moves in and takes over.

One of the most common forms of functional authority is the assignment to specialized staff of controls pertaining to their own areas. Often these are of a routine or procedural nature—"how to do it" rather than "what to do." The accounting office polices accounting procedures, and the personnel department checks certain personnel transactions. In effect, this grants to the staff some measure of authority.

> The difference between functional and staff authority is often hard to distinguish, for in some cases it is more nearly a difference in degree than a difference in kind. Functional authority, as often differentiated, is that degree of authority standing somewhere between the so-called full or command authority of the line officer and the advisory or informational authority of the staff officer. It is frequently called "instructional authority" since the relationship between supervisor and subordinate resembles more nearly that between instructor and pupil than that between master and servant.[8]

Various specific examples of the need for functional authority might be noted. Suppose that industrial production processes involve great hazard to life and property. The need for safety in such a case may be so great as to require line authority for safety inspectors. Although safety is normally regarded as a staff function, it may be desirable to grant the safety inspector authority to shut down an operation in order to insure adequate safety for personnel and equipment.

Another example may be found in the case of a production planning and scheduling function in a manufacturing concern. If production schedules are to be centrally coordinated and established, it is necessary that the schedules be observed. The effect of this is to restrict the freedom of line personnel in manufacturing and to subject them to direct control by a staff office. As a third example, a company engaged in union negotiations may find that its most effective bargainer is the chief of its personnel staff. In such a case, it is quite natural, and indeed necessary, for such a negotiator,

---

[8]E. H. Anderson, "The Functional Concept in Organization," *Advanced Management,* Vol. 25, No. 10, October 1960, p. 18.

regardless of his staff status, to be granted authority to make binding commitments for the company.

It is possible for serious problems to arise in the exercise of functional authority. If the practice becomes widespread, organizational confusion occurs. Line officials experience the frustration of shouldering responsibility while, at the same time, attempting to follow the orders of various staff groups.

To minimize the dangers involved in functional authority, certain precautions must be observed. First of all, there should be a clear specification of the types of questions and the particular staff groups in which functional authority is recognized. The scope of the authority of staff should be carefully prescribed to avoid granting blanket authority over broad areas. If the need for functional authority is not a permanent or continuing need, its time limit should also be clearly stipulated so that the date of expiration may be known.

The Project Manager

The complex activities and relationships required in high-technology industries have required new approaches in coordination and control. One such approach is the use of the project manager position — a type of staff having functional authority.[9] In practice, this position is hybrid rather than pure line or pure staff. Although it has the appearance of a staff office, it often possesses greater authority than is customary in staff functions.

The typical project manager coordinates a development and production project that constitutes a major undertaking for a manufacturer and that involves work in a number of departments. It could be used to manage such undertakings as the introduction of a new consumer product, but to date it has been used primarily in the aerospace industry. A large-scale application of the principle is found in Lockheed's organization of the C-5A military transport aircraft development as described in Chapter 8. When the program reaches its high point, some 18,000 personnel are expected to accept direction from the project director. Most project management programs function on a much smaller scale.

The project manager is responsible for completion of the end product in accordance with performance requirements, budgeted

---

[9]A somewhat similar position is the *product manager* who serves as marketing manager of one product in a multi-product consumer company. See Robert M. Fulmer, "Product Management: Panacea or Pandora's Box?" *California Management Review,* Vol. 7, No. 4, Summer 1965, pp. 63-74.

costs, and projected time schedules. A diagram of his relationships is given in Figure 10. The project manager integrates sales, engineering, manufacturing, and accounting activities by giving directions to personnel in those departments — even though these personnel report on a line basis to their respective functional heads. The project manager does more than offer advice or service. Although there are variations in the amount of authority invested in such positions, he may control expenditures for materials and labor on the project he directs. In this way, he exercises more authority than is traditional for a staff official. However, his authority and responsibility are often unequal in a practical sense. Top management tends to hold the project manager responsible for achieving results that exceed his formal authority. It is clear that serious problems may be involved in an organizational arrangement of this type. Even though the arrangement is not problem free, the device is significant as an innovative response to an operational problem that was not solved by conventional organization theory.

The project management device is, in part, an outgrowth of the recent emphasis on the systems concept. Work which entails a high degree of interdependence among functionally distinct tasks can be brought under unified control in this way. Through the project manager, top management can improve the integration of the various functional activities as they relate to particular projects.

Effective Use of Staff

Clarity in Relationships

The effective use of staff demands relationships that are clearly understood by both line and staff officials. The administrator, in creating a staff office or position, should clearly identify it as such. It may be difficult for subordinates to distinguish easily between line and staff. Anyone from headquarters may be viewed as having authority. A subordinate cannot always examine the line or staff status of the representative. Improper clarification that allows staff personnel to exercise line authority may lead to the problems of confusion and irresponsibility noted earlier or to retaliation by line departments and their refusal to work cooperatively with staff.

Clarification of line-staff relationships necessitates, first of all, a clear identification of duties and responsibilities of particular staff functions and personnel. This means that the relationship of staff

Figure 10. *Project Organization in General Industry*

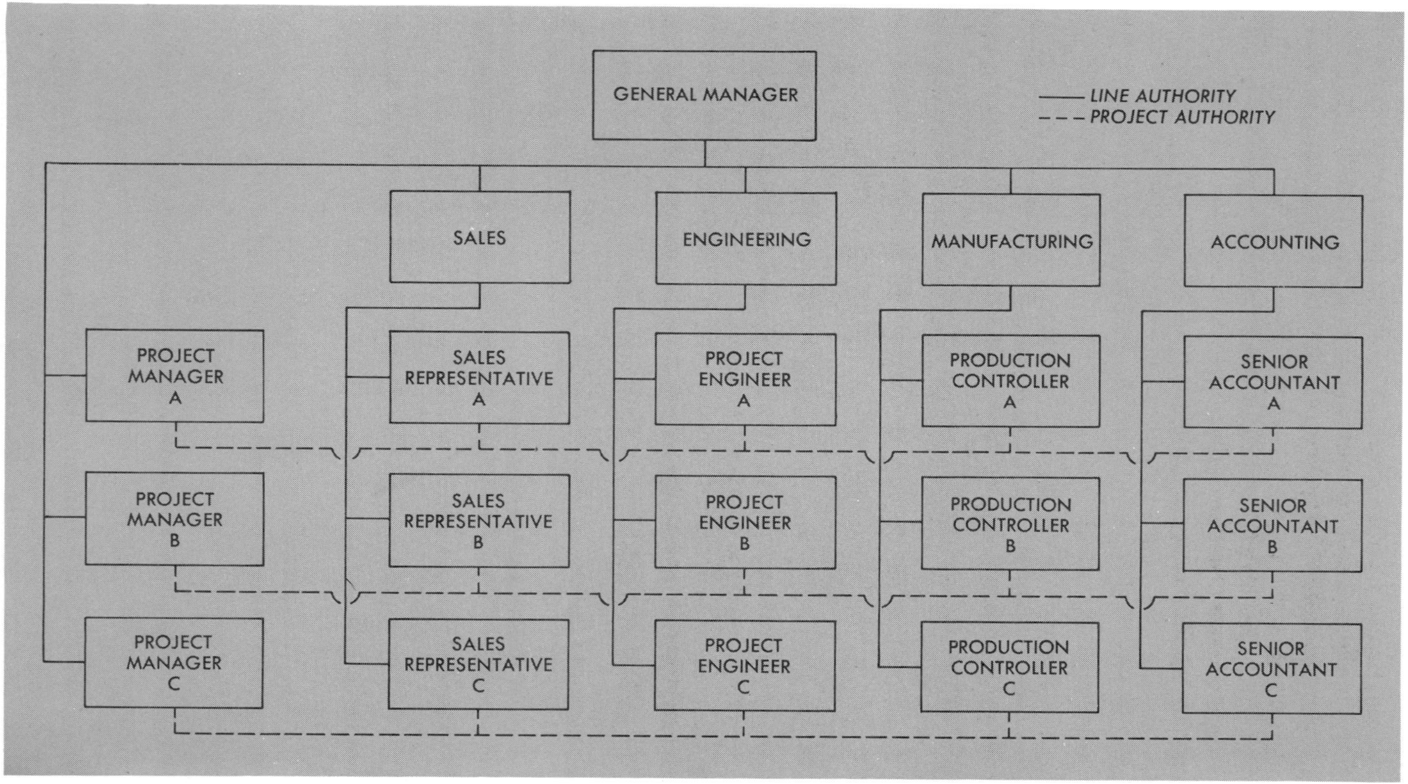

Source: John M. Stewart, "Making Project Management Work," *Business Horizons*, Vol. 8, No. 3, Fall 1965, p. 58.

to line personnel and the limitations on the scope of staff functions should be made clear. In addition, the right—particularly of a personal staff official—to act for a line official in his absence or otherwise should be clearly expressed.

An example of the problems and confusion arising in the case of line-staff relationships can be noted in the following example in which a personal staff assistant was given a nebulous assignment and permitted to spy on subordinates:

> Bill Beaty had had engineering training at college and after graduation had joined a medium-sized food company, working first on the shop floor, then for a number of years as a foreman. Later he became a draftsman and was eventually appointed assistant superintendent. He built up a good production record, attracted the president's attention, and was appointed his assistant.
>
> Neither Beaty nor the president's immediate subordinates were informed of the assistant's duties, relationships, or authority. In fact, the president's subordinates heard about the new position for the first time when they received an "order" from the assistant to change their budget proposals. Beaty was unable to shake loose his past experience of command; in fact, he had not been told he should do so. From then on, the subordinates received one command after another from him.
>
> The president devoted less time to his subordinates than before, and they, in turn, became increasingly resentful. They gave the assistant the minimum cooperation they could get away with, and boycotted him whenever possible. Finally, in desperation, they made one of the vice presidents their spokesman and began to make suggestions aimed at curtailment of the assistant's direct authority.
>
> Some of these suggestions were accepted, and Beaty felt bitter at what he wrongly conceived to be a demotion. He sought vengeance by finding out what was wrong with his chief's subordinates, with their performance and their relationships with each other, and he reported to the president anything adverse he could pick up. In this way he played the "grey eminence behind the throne." Since he could not issue orders directly, he would command through others.
>
> Finally, the embittered subordinates laid a number of well-concealed traps. They withheld information from the assistant, then showed the president that the assistant was not doing his job. Eventually Beaty was fired.[10]

---

[10]Ernest Dale and Lyndall F. Urwick, *Staff in Organization* (New York: McGraw-Hill Book Company, 1960), pp. 172-173.

An Informed Staff

Effective functioning of the organization demands an informed staff. The personnel staff, to perform its mission most effectively, must understand all personnel problems and difficulties confronting the organization. The industrial engineering staff must be aware of the processing problems encountered in the manufacturing operations of the business. The public relations staff must appreciate the points at which the organization has contact with its public and the quality of those contacts. The assistant to the president must understand the president's position and the problems of the business with which the assistant is most directly concerned.

To be informed, staff must be accepted as a vital working partner in the business. The chief executive, for example, must see that vital staff offices are represented in discussions and meetings with which they have a legitimate concern. It may be desirable, for example, to include the personnel staff in overall production planning because of the consequences such activities have in terms of personnel requirements. Line officials should also see the advantage of furnishing full and complete information to staff officers.

To some extent, the staff is responsible for the degree to which it receives information and for the degree to which it is "in on things." Staff must keep in touch with line activities closely enough to be aware of line problems. Staff personnel must also create an atmosphere of confidence that encourages line officials to furnish information freely and generously. Otherwise, staff behavior can cause the line to shut off the flow of information to staff—one of the sharpest defensive tools of the line in any line-staff controversy.

Line Use of Staff Assistance

A competent staff constitutes a valuable resource of any business institution. Full utilization of its service is necessary to maximize organizational effectiveness. It is desirable, then, that the line draw as frequently as necessary upon the resources available from staff agencies.

The use of staff assistance by the line is encouraged by the excellence of the quality of its service and advice. Some have suggested the idea of making staff advice compulsory to the line. This would mean that line officials would be required to consult with staff officials even though the line might reject the proffered advice. The desirability of compulsory consultation is debatable, but certainly full use of a competent staff is essential to obtain maximum benefits from the line and staff organization.

SUMMARY

The objective in outlining line-staff relationships is *teamwork* in the accomplishment of organizational objectives. *Line functions,* those directly concerned with the accomplishment of an organization's primary objectives, are aided by *staff functions* and staff personnel. The staff may be visualized as providing *support* for line activities in the form of service and advice. One classification of staff functions distinguishes between *personal* staff and *specialized* staff.

Staff should generally occupy an *advisory* rather than a command relationship to line. Infringements on line authority can create serious organization problems by causing a deterioration of line morale and making it difficult to hold line officials responsible. As a practical matter, however, the needs of a business organization often require staff to be granted *functional authority* in certain areas. To avoid confusion, this authority must be properly limited.

For maximum effectiveness in the use of staff, it is important that the relationships between line and staff be clearly established and understood. Effective cooperation also requires that the staff be thoroughly informed regarding the line and that the line fully utilize staff service and advice.

Discussion Questions

1. Formulate the best possible definitions of *line* and *staff* in terms of authority relationships. What weaknesses, if any, do you see in these definitions?

2. In view of the confusion and disagreement concerning line and staff terminology, would it appear desirable to drop the terms that have been traditionally used?

3. What limitation or inaccuracy may be involved in viewing staff offices as having merely an *advisory* relationship to line functions?

4. Suppose the chief executive of a growing company employs an attorney and designates him as the "legal department." Is this an example of a *personal* staff or *specialized* staff?

5. If the staff lacks authority, how can it provide any guidance or control? Won't its suggestions be disregarded by line managers? Should it, therefore, be given some degree of authority?

6. What accounts for the tendency of staff officials to become authoritative in their relationships with other parts of the organization?

7. Explain the concept of *functional authority*. What are its weaknesses?

8. A lack of clarity in line-staff relationships is rather common. What are the probable reasons for this condition?

9. Who bears the primary responsibility for keeping the staff informed?

Supplementary Reading

Allen, Louis A., *The Management Profession,* Chapter 19. New York: McGraw-Hill Book Company, 1964.

Bennis, Warren G. and Edgar H. Schein, eds., *Leadership and Motivation: Essays of Douglas McGregor.* Cambridge: The M.I.T. Press, 1966.

Cleland, David I., "Understanding Project Authority," *Business Horizons,* Vol. 10, No. 1, Spring 1967, pp. 63-70.

Dale, Ernest and Lyndall F. Urwick, *Staff in Organization.* New York: McGraw-Hill Book Company, 1960.

Dalton, Melville, "Changing Staff-Line Relationships," *Personnel Administration,* Vol. 29, No. 2, March-April 1966, pp. 3-5.

Efferson, C. A., "In Defense of the Line-Staff Concept," *Personnel,* Vol. 43, No. 4, July-August 1966, pp. 8-15.

Fisch, Gerald G., "Line-Staff is Obsolete," *Harvard Business Review,* Vol. 39, No. 5, September-October 1961, pp. 67-79.

French, Wendell and Dale Henning, "The Authority-Influence Role of the Functional Specialist in Management," *Academy of Management Journal,* Vol. 9, No. 3, September 1966, pp. 187-203.

Fulmer, Robert M., "Product Management: Panacea or Pandora's Box?" *California Management Review,* Vol. 7, No. 4, Summer 1965, pp. 63-74.

Golembiewski, Robert T., "Personality and Organization Structure: Staff Models and Behavioral Patterns," *Academy of Management Journal,* Vol. 9, No. 3, September 1966, pp. 217-232.

Hodgetts, Richard M., "Leadership Techniques in the Project Organization," *Academy of Management Journal,* Vol. 11, No. 2, June 1968, pp. 211-219.

Kubly, Harold E., *The Inspectors and the Foreman.* Madison: The University of Wisconsin, 1966.

Lawrence, Paul R. and Jay W. Lorsch, "New Management Job: The Integrator," *Harvard Business Review,* Vol. 45, No. 6, November-December 1967, pp. 142-151.

Logan, Hall H., "Line and Staff: An Obsolete Concept," *Personnel,* Vol. 43, No. 1, January-February 1966, pp. 26-33.

Middleton, C. J., "How to Set Up a Project Organization," *Harvard Business Review,* Vol. 45, No. 2, March-April 1967, pp. 73-82.

Stewart, John M., "Making Project Management Work," *Business Horizons,* Vol. 8, No. 3, Fall 1965, pp. 54-68.

Toussaint, Maynard N., "Line-Staff Conflict: Its Causes and Cure," *Personnel,* Vol. 39, No. 3, May-June 1962, pp. 8-20.

11

The Use of Committees

Someone has facetiously suggested that a camel is a horse that was put together by a committee. As the tone of the comment suggests, committees have their critics. In spite of their weaknesses, however, the general consensus among administrators is that committees are essential in managing large organizations and often useful in managing smaller groups.

Business Use of Committees

Nature and Importance of Committees

A committee involves a meeting of two or more individuals, but it entails more than a chance meeting and more than an informal discussion of problems. A committee might be defined as a group of individuals who are officially drawn together to consider either specific or general issues pertinent to the organization.

Committees have multiplied as organizations have grown in size and complexity. In large governmental, educational, charitable, and business institutions, committees have become an integral part of the administrative structure. In the business field, they are not limited to large corporations but are also found in relatively small concerns. Nor are they limited to top management levels, but they function at middle and lower levels of the organization as well.

Variation in the Nature of Committees

Committees are almost infinite in their variety. In duration, for example, there are standing committees maintained on a permanent basis, and *ad hoc* (or special purpose) committees appointed to serve only temporarily. In their time requirements, they range from those that meet only occasionally to those that meet regularly on a weekly and, in some cases, even a daily basis.

With respect to purpose, committees may be policy making, administrative, executive, innovative, informational, and so on. The subjects that they consider are as varied as the business enterprise itself, including general management, engineering, product design, research, safety, capital spending, advertising, collective bargaining, public relations, and many others.

Committees may also be distinguished as to their power within the organization. Top echelon committees have greater power or influence than do minor committees existing far down in the same organization. The influence of a committee also differs on the basis of its status as an advisory or decision-making committee.

The highest-level committee within a business enterprise is its board of directors. This group acts as a policy-making committee, working through appointed officers, but it may also overlap the top administrative levels of the concern through the use of an executive committee. That is, the membership of an executive committee may include individuals who serve as both directors and officers of the corporation.

Extent of Use

Different surveys have shown that most companies utilize standing or regular committees of some variety to supplement their line and staff organization. According to a survey conducted by the American Management Association, 110 of the 150 companies surveyed (or 73 per cent) indicated that they had one or more committees meeting regularly.[1] A more recent survey sponsored by the *Harvard Business Review* confirmed this tendency on the part of the majority of concerns to use standing committees. According to their survey results, which are given in greater detail in Figure 11,

---

[1]Ernest Dale, *Planning and Developing the Company Organization Structure* (New York: American Management Association, 1952, Sixth Printing 1959), p. 119.

some 81.5 per cent of the executives responding to the survey reported the presence of standing committees in their firms.[2]

Figure 11. *Extent of Company Use of Regular Committees*

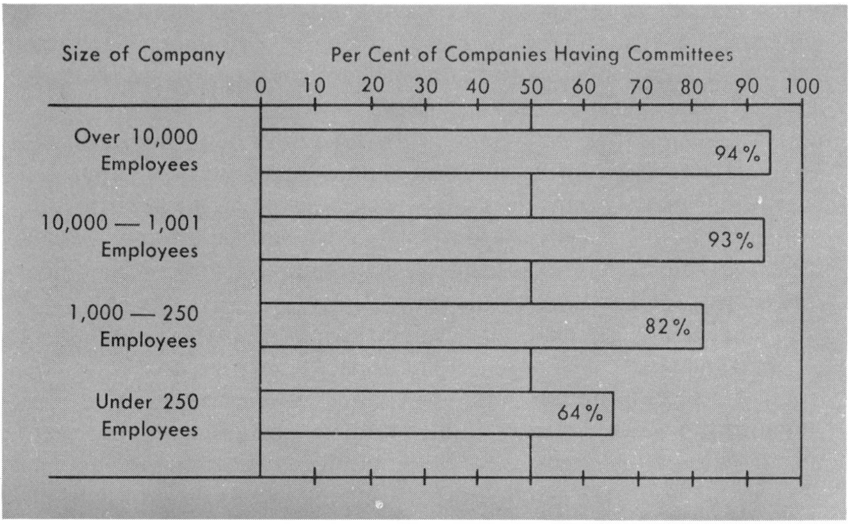

Source: "Problems in Review: Committees on Trial," *Harvard Business Review,* Vol. 38, No. 3, May-June 1960, p. 8.

These results, it should be recalled, pertained only to standing committees and revealed nothing concerning the existence of *ad hoc* committees. It is probable that many companies reporting no regular standing committees use special purpose committees from time to time. It is also likely that companies using and reporting upon standing committees supplement these committees with temporary or special purpose committees.

Some 60 per cent of the executives responding to the *Harvard Business Review* survey reported that they were currently serving on one or more of the regular committees in their organizations.[3] An additional 8 per cent had served on such committees in the past. A higher proportion of executives in top management reported committee assignments than was true of those in lower levels.

On the basis of the surveys reported and on the basis of casual observation of business management in operation, it is not difficult

---

[2]"Problems in Review: Committees on Trial," *Harvard Business Review,* Vol. 38, No. 3, May-June 1960, p. 7.

[3]*Ibid.*

to see that committee management is characteristic of present administrative practice. In fact, it would seem that the trend is in the direction of greater use of committees and that as business organizations grow they become more prone to utilize committees in their organization.

Reasons for Use of Committees

Better Decisions Through Group Deliberation

When confronted with a complex problem or the need for a serious decision, an individual often seeks the counsel of others. Almost intuitively, he turns to a trusted friend or relative to talk it over, trading ideas and getting reactions and possibly advice from the counselor. He does this even though the decision must eventually be his own. Frequently, he feels more confident of the rightness of such a decision that has been checked out with others. The committee system provides an arrangement for systematizing and formalizing group deliberation on organizational problems.

Committee analysis or review of a business problem represents a kind of insurance against a decision based upon faulty reasoning or personal bias. This implies, of course, that the committee is more than a rubber stamp and that members can speak out on issues under consideration. (A cartoon has depicted the chairman putting the question to a vote with "All who object, say 'I resign.' ") It also implies that the executive is sufficiently honest and alert to recognize his own bias or a weakness in his own reasoning when a challenge is voiced in the committee and that he is willing to act accordingly.

The committee can be used to pull together the different abilities and knowledge of its members. No two individuals approach solution of a complex problem in precisely the same way, and the varied analytical abilities of different individuals may, through committee deliberation, be brought to bear upon the same problem. The various departments and functional areas of the organization also involve different points of view which may be discovered and applied to the question at hand.

The extent to which a committee can be genuinely creative is somewhat controversial. Some critics contend that the creative contributions would be fully as great if each individual participant were to concentrate his own thinking on the problem at hand. For example, Ralph J. Cordiner, former chairman of General Electric, has said, "If you can name for me one great discovery or decision that was made by a committee, I will find you the one man in that committee who had the lonely insight—while he was shaving or on his way to work, or maybe while the rest of the committee was chattering away—the lonely insight which solved the problem and was the basis for the decision."[4] An individual is thought to possess a creative force within him. As a result, the committee is viewed as a very weak hope for mobilizing the creative energies of management.

Contrast with the views of Mr. Cordiner the position of Frank Abrams, former chairman of the Standard Oil Company of New Jersey. (Its extensive use of committees has caused it to be dubbed by some as "The Standard Meeting Company.") "It stands to reason," said Abrams, "that if you get five men together and one man is wrong, the mistake is going to be picked up. Or if one man has a good idea, the others will contribute to it and develop it. And if they all have good ideas, what comes out may be better than the separate ideas added together."[5]

Coordination of Work

Extreme specialization of work, both operative and managerial, is one of the distinguishing characteristics of modern large-scale industrial enterprise. The degree to which specialization has been carried makes the problem of synchronization of activities exceedingly difficult. Many of the functions of one department are closely related to and intertwined with those of other departments. As an example, a given decision in the area of research and development may have repercussions affecting sales, production, finance, personnel, public relations, the legal department, and even other activities.

In the organization that has become too large for personal observation by its members, the left hand does not always know what the right hand is doing unless active steps are taken to achieve this objective. The committee provides one way to achieve coordination of effort. In committee meetings, individuals from different departments or different areas of specialization are able to exchange information about their respective areas of specialization, to discover plans and developments in other areas that will be of interest and

---

[4]M. R. Lohmann, *Top Management Committees,* AMA Research Study 48 (New York: American Management Association, 1961), pp. 8-9.

[5]Herrymon Maurer, "Management by Committee," *Fortune,* Vol. 47, No. 4, April 1953, p. 196. Courtesy of *Fortune.*

significance in their own, and generally to discuss matters of mutual concern.

Occasionally, comments are heard to the effect that the use of committees for coordination is carried to excess. One executive, for example, remarked, "We spend so much time hearing about the problems of other departments that we have no time to solve our own." However, experienced committee members rather generally concede the value of committees in coordinating activities.

Securing Cooperation in Execution

In the execution or application of plans and policies, there are certain barriers that interfere with effective administration. Among these are misunderstanding of a given plan or policy and also the feeling that one must follow a policy or plan without an opportunity to express himself about it. The difficulties, then, may occur in terms of both knowledge and desire.

A committee may be used as a means of attacking both problems. For example, discussion in a committee meeting can bring to light mistaken ideas and answer questions concerning the matter under consideration. If a committee member has objections, he may also be given the opportunity to voice them. Even if he disagrees with the final decision of the chairman or group, it is difficult for him to oppose the decision as violently as he might if it were simply handed to him without explanation or opportunity for his comments.

It is possible that a committee may be used as a tactical weapon by an administrator to minimize opposition to his intended action. To the extent that the executive simply uses a committee to approve his preconceived plan with no intention of seriously considering committee reactions, the committee method loses its effectiveness in securing cooperation in execution. Robert H. Roy has described an "Employee-Management Committee" formed by a company president with the hope of improving management-employee relations.[6] The committee meeting observed by Roy lasted about an hour and appeared to have a warm and friendly atmosphere, at least on the surface. The employee representatives, however, did not utter a word until the last few minutes of the meeting but simply listened to management's explanations of inventory problems, the seriousness of current spoilage, and sales and production prospects. How-

[6]Robert H. Roy, *The Administrative Process* (Baltimore: The Johns Hopkins Press, 1958), pp. 162-166.

ever, as Roy noted, "When a committee is formed, expectation is aroused; the employees expect not only to be told but themselves to do a bit of telling."[7] Within a year or two of this meeting, the company was unionized and suffered a six-weeks' strike.

Training of Participants

Development of personnel for all levels of management is one of the important responsibilities of administrators. By being a part of a committee group, a participant is exposed to ideas and knowledge that may lie outside his usual area of responsibility. In addition, the committee member may engage in study and develop himself in the process of preparing for committee participation. This is particularly true if he is given some special responsibilities in connection with committee projects and performance. Perhaps the greatest training value comes from the give-and-take of committee sessions. In this atmosphere, the committee member gains experience in speaking before a group, expressing his own ideas, and defending points of view.

One of the companies that has made extensive use of committees in its managerial structure is McCormick and Company, whose system is referred to as *multiple management*. One of the major advantages visualized by Charles P. McCormick, the originator of this system, was the ability to train employees to study the business and take on responsibility as rapidly as they were able.[8] In explaining the values of committee participation, one young executive of McCormick and Company offered the following explanation of its training value:

> Another thing, the Junior Board helps in more than one way to better prepare you to fill eventually your superior's position and at the same time have a better insight in the business which enables you not only to fill that immediate job but others. Through this channel you receive valuable information regarding the so-called inner facts of the organization that would take years to get otherwise. Because of this added knowledge, you take a greater interest in the business and try to grasp more threads which will help you to become of greater service. By the same token, the older men, realizing that you are striving to go ahead, take an even greater interest in you and materially help you on your way.[9]

---

[7] *Ibid.*, p. 164.

[8] Charles P. McCormick, *The Power of People* (New York: Harper & Row, Publishers, 1949), p. 18.

[9] *Ibid.*, p. 62.

DANGERS AND DIFFICULTIES IN USE OF COMMITTEES

Committees have had their detractors. After Lindbergh's historic solo flight to Europe, Mrs. Charles F. Kettering is reputed to have exclaimed to her husband "Isn't it wonderful! And to think he did it all alone!" "Well," replied Kettering, "it would have been still more wonderful if he had done it with a committee."

Waste of Time and Money

One frequent criticism of committees is that they entail a considerable waste of managerial time and thus of dollars. An analysis by McKinsey and Company, Inc., of committee assignments in an insurance firm disclosed that five vice presidents were each spending 26 hours per month — exclusive of preparation time — in meetings.[10] In an electronics manufacturing concern, vice presidents reported that committee meetings accounted for half their time.

Wasteful committee activities result from a number of factors. Committee action may be wasteful because there are too many committees in existence, because a committee is too large in its membership, because a committee meets too frequently, or because a committee is inefficient in its methods of operation.

Critics have noted that committees fritter away time on subjects of negligible importance or subjects that could be disposed of by one individual without difficulty. C. Northcote Parkinson has formulated what he calls the *law of triviality* which holds that "the time spent on any item of the agenda will be in inverse proportion to the sum involved."[11] His discussion suggests that committees are prone to engage in interminable discussion of items having only passing significance.

A few years ago, the president of Goodyear Tire and Rubber Company attempted to call a meeting on short notice and discovered that all the people he wanted in the meeting were already attending other meetings![12] This led to a study of the use and misuse of committees within the Goodyear organization. Analysts were assigned to investigate committees and committee meetings with the idea of improving them or reducing the waste of time. These analysts dis-

---

[10]J. Alan Ofner, "Are Committees Worth While?" *Commerce Magazine,* Vol. 56, No. 2, March 1959, pp. 64-65.

[11]C. Northcote Parkinson, *Parkinson's Law* (Boston: Houghton Mifflin Company, 1957), p. 24. Used by permission of Houghton Mifflin Company and John Murray (Publishers) Ltd.

[12]"Too Many Other Rump Sessions," *Business Week,* No. 1624, October 15, 1960, pp. 187-190.

covered that more than 20 per cent of the people attending meetings got there late, that about 15 per cent took no active part in the proceedings, and that more than 15 per cent of the participants didn't really need to be there at all. In 15 per cent of the meetings, the chairman did not seem well prepared, and more than 10 per cent of the total meeting time was a complete loss because of tardiness, outside interruptions, and off-the-subject conversations. It is probable that these figures were conservatively stated, because committee participants knew that they were being observed by analysts.

Danger of Compromise

One of the greatest potential weaknesses of committees is their tendency toward compromise decisions. One hears such statements as "All a committee ever comes up with is some middle-of-the-road plan which no one completely opposes but which no one really believes," or "Committee solutions simply represent the lowest common denominator of the thinking of the members on that committee." The general thought is that the group lacks the will or forcefulness to reach the same sound conclusion that might be achieved by one individual operating on his own. The agreement of the group represents a kind of conformity based on the reluctance of members to challenge a popular point of view or to take an extreme position. Not all compromise is undesirable, of course, but there is no guarantee that the middle of the road is always the best part of the road.

One pressure that contributes to a spirit of compromise is the personal work load of committee members. Because these executives typically have full schedules, it is natural for them to attempt to reach a committee decision quickly in order to resume their regular responsibilities. Also, most committee members do not wish to embarrass other members of the same committee. To save face for all participants, the group may accept a conclusion or solution that is not violently opposed by any of the members.

Difficulty in Placing Responsibility

Committee activity may constitute a type of shield behind which an individual manager can take refuge. The fact of committee deliberation may be taken as evidence that the particular executive has been reasonably prudent in exercising his administrative responsibility. A question is implicitly raised as to how a manager can be criticized for a decision on which most people agree. Even though a committee is advisory in its nature, its action provides a stamp of approval for the decision of the individual executive.

Holding an individual manager responsible, then, becomes exceedingly difficult. The higher-level executive seeking to enforce responsibility on his subordinate may appear to be unfair and unreasonable in his expectations. Proceeding against a group of executive personnel is almost impossible. As a result, responsibility may be diffused through committee activity in such a way that it is difficult to say that any one individual assumes full responsibility.

This difficulty in placing responsibility may be alleviated by insisting upon acceptance of full responsibility by individual managers. The advisory nature of committees is forcefully emphasized in the statements and attitude of higher-level management. The understanding is created that each manager who receives committee advice must personally accept or reject any committee recommendation.

Delay and Indecision

Committee action takes time. Individual committee members must assemble, and this requires a reconciliation of time demands of the committee with the various personal schedules and other official responsibilities of the members. Committee activity typically constitutes an extra function for the manager. The more important the committee, of course, the more the other work demands must yield to committee activities. In any case, however, some delay is experienced in getting the members of the committee together and reaching some sort of decision. Even subsequent meetings may be necessary to reach a conclusion.

Early in his career as Secretary of Defense, Robert S. McNamara became perturbed with the slowness of decision making in his department.[13] "The Defense establishment," said McNamara, "could do everything twice as fast as presently." One of two major evils which he felt slowed the decision-making process was the tendency to appoint committees and to "coordinate." Acting upon this evaluation of committees, the Secretary of Defense eliminated 424 committees and scheduled 129 more for deactivation.

Speed of action in a business organization is important, particularly if it is not achieved at the expense of a proper evaluation of

---

[13]"Committees Are of Value Only for Exchanging Ideas," *Armed Forces Management*, Vol. 8, No. 2, November 1961, pp. 22-24.

alternatives. Business opportunities may be lost by failure to act quickly. Smaller concerns are often recognized as having advantages over larger competitors for this very reason. An organization honeycombed with committees moves more slowly than a streamlined organization acting on the basis of individual judgment and decision.

Domination by One Individual

Occasionally, one encounters a committee that operates under the thumb or domination of some one individual. His influence is such as to stifle any vigorous or critical discussion by the group. This individual's reaction provides the key to action by the group. His expression of disapproval, for example, whether verbal or by facial expression, may start the entire group on a negative approach or evaluation. In its most extreme form, such domination results in a committee that constitutes a form of window dressing to approve some pet idea of the dominant individual.

This deterioration of the committee function contrasts sharply with the values that are believed to exist in committees. Committees are presumably characterized by the give-and-take of equals. Committee deliberation represents a pooling of ideas in an atmosphere of mutual respect and tolerance. One member builds upon suggestions of another member. All participants sense a freedom to correct, to question, and to suggest modifications to the ideas and purposes of others.

The dominant individual is ordinarily the chairman of the committee. Frequently, he is also the superior of other members of the committee. The committee may, therefore, be inclined to show deference for this reason alone. If the chairman is a driving, dominant type of leader, it is difficult to change the atmosphere when the scene shifts to a committee room. Even a democratic leader is shown some respect, and there is a natural reluctance to disagree with the boss in the absence of repeated encouragement and reassurance. This is basically a problem of leadership and of the superior-subordinate relationship.

Boards of Directors

Stockholder Control in the Modern Corporation

Many modern corporations have achieved great size by combining the investments of hundreds of thousands of individuals. It is rare, indeed, that one individual can hold a significant percentage of the ownership of any large corporation. As a result, ownership has become greatly diffused, and most stockholders are extremely small in terms of their proportional share of the enterprise's net worth.

Because of the fact that owners are scattered and individually insignificant, stockholder control of the corporation is no longer as close and direct as it was in an earlier era. The legal right of control is, of course, retained in the hands of stockholders, but this right is seldom exercised. It is extremely difficult for any individual stockholder seriously to challenge the corporation's board of directors. To do so requires a strong interest and an almost unlimited bank account.

As a result of the weakened ties between the corporation and its stockholders, the board of directors and top-level corporate management have tended to become self-perpetuating in nature. When a vacancy occurs on the board of directors, for example, it would be quite unrealistic to ask for nominations from stockholders, any one of whom might own no more than a fraction of 1 per cent of the outstanding stock. Instead, the only practical approach seems to be for the existing board to suggest a candidate to fill the board vacancy. The stockholders approve or reject this selection, but stockholder approval is ordinarily a mere formality.

Board Functions

Perhaps the most important function of the board of directors is that of selecting the corporate officers who are responsible for the day-to-day administration of the business. Some have even suggested that the board might be ornamental with respect to other activities and still be a useful and constructive board if it performed this function constructively and intelligently.

As an example of board selection of company officers, consider the search by General Dynamics Corporation for a new chief executive during 1961.[14] The company had suffered losses in the production of commercial jet planes and had appointed an executive committee of the board of directors to correct the situation. For several months, the executive committee examined the corporation's policies and took steps to make changes in the top management. To replace Frank Pace, Jr., previously chief executive officer, this executive

---

[14]"Drama on 40th Floor of Waldorf," *Business Week,* No. 1692, February 3, 1962, pp. 22-23.

committee considered a number of potential candidates. Among these were John McCone (who became head of the Central Intelligence Agency instead); General Lucius D. Clay; and Roger Lewis, executive vice president for administration at Pan American World Airways. The executive committee was composed of Henry Crown (chief stockholder of General Dynamics Corporation) and four other members. The group held discussions with different candidates. Crown reported that "we spent a lot of time with McCone." In describing the committee's first contact with Roger Lewis at New York's Waldorf Astoria Tower, Crown reported that "he sat in a chair in this room and we told him we were considering him as president. We didn't want him to say anything at all. We didn't ask him if he was interested, either. We wanted him to check. And we wanted to check him. At the time, I knew who he was, but had never met him; and we wanted to be sure." Some prolonged negotiations followed. Pan American World Airways discovered the effort to lure Lewis and attempted to retain him. After consideration and further discussion in subsequent meetings, the committee and Lewis were able to reach an agreement including an understanding with respect to salary and other compensation. This, then, is the way in which the directors of one major corporation sought a president from outside.

Another of the functions of the board is that of declaring dividends. In reality, this may be approval of the recommendation of the administrative management of the business. It is, however, the legal right of this group to determine the extent of dividends to be paid or whether the earnings are such as to justify the payment of any dividends whatever. Some corporations consistently reinvest their earnings rather than paying them out as dividends to stockholders. Other corporations maintain a record of consistent dividend payments. Decisions of this kind are a major responsibility of the board of directors.

Another major area of responsibility of the board of directors is its review of management programs and plans. Being somewhat independent of the management of the business, it is expected to examine the activities and programs of administrative management with a somewhat critical, detached point of view. It is expected to judge these management programs and activities but not to formulate or direct them. In other words, the board's review should be accomplished without interfering in a company's administrative management.

A well-known director of several large business corporations and an outstanding public figure, Dr. Vannevar Bush, has suggested that review of administrative management makes the administrator a stronger leader in his own business. "He can lead strongly," said Bush, "and at the same time consult freely with his subordinates if he is being supported by them in presenting his plans before a tough tribunal, not if he is being judged by his own subordinates."[15] Dr. Bush expressed the idea that any executive should be called upon to justify his important plans and programs before some individual body competent to judge them adequately.

Composition of the Board of Directors

In selecting members for its board of directors, a company is interested in obtaining individuals with the necessary competence, time, and interest. This combination of qualities often makes the task of securing a good director difficult. If the company is large, it can provide some prestige to the individual selected as a director. The company may also appeal to an individual's desire for service by offering him an opportunity for rendering a public service. The fees paid to directors may also be viewed as one of the compensations that persuade them to accept the position, but it is unlikely that the fees themselves are adequate inducement for the best directors.

In terms of qualifications, board members should ideally possess a breadth of experience in business. Preferably, they should have some knowledge of the particular concern wishing to appoint them. A few individuals have become so outstanding in the business field as to merit appointment to boards of several leading American corporations. Smaller companies have a more difficult task in selecting qualified individuals inasmuch as they are limited in the prestige that they can offer.

A challenging question regarding composition of the board is the extent to which it should be an *inside* or *outside* board. An inside board is composed of the administrative officers of the company. In other words, these individuals "wear two hats." They are officers and thus have full-time administrative responsibilities. On other occasions, when the board of directors meets, they serve as board

[15]Vannevar Bush, "Of What Use is a Board of Directors," in *Problems of General Management,* eds. Edmund P. Learned, C. Roland Christensen, and Kenneth R. Andrews (Homewood: Richard D. Irwin, Inc., 1961), p. 508.

members, perhaps appointing themselves to positions of administrative leadership. The argument in favor of the inside board runs to the effect that the members of this board are best acquainted with and most fully informed regarding the problems of this particular organization and are thus in a position to exercise the wisest leadership. The Standard Oil Company of New Jersey, well known for its practice of utilizing an inside board of directors, appointed two outside directors in 1966 — Frederick R. Kappel, chairman of American Telephone and Telegraph Company, and J. A. Stratton, chairman of the Ford Foundation. Of course, the board is still dominated by insiders. It has been consistently well managed.

An outside board has the advantage of providing, at least potentially, a detached and critical viewpoint in examining the policies and practices of the administrative management. Some companies compromise by appointing a board including insiders but supplemented with outside representatives. There is a good argument, even in the case of a predominantly outside board, for having the chief executive and perhaps his assistant sitting as members of the board of directors. In this way, it is possible to achieve a mutuality of understanding and purpose between the board and the top executive leadership of the business. This would not mean, however, that the chief executive would necessarily serve as chairman of the board of directors.

Effectiveness of Boards

Many boards are recognized as rubber stamp boards. They meet at specified intervals, usually on a quite infrequent basis, and routinely go through the legal formalities necessary to their role as a board of directors. They perform no active service and carry out no critical review of the corporation's management. Corporations that allow their boards to operate in such a fashion lose many of the potential advantages that may be gained through a strong board of directors.

In order to be effective as a board member, the individual director must have the necessary time to devote to the study of business problems. It is rare that he can perform the job adequately by confining or restricting his attention to the formal business meetings and the presentations of management made during the sessions. This means that, to be effective in his knowledge of pertinent issues, he frequently must dig into some questions between board meetings. To accomplish this, he must have some contact with the administrative management of the organization on an individual basis. In proceeding along this line, it is necessary for him to assume the rather delicate position of having informational contacts but avoiding any personal intrusion into the managerial responsibilities of the operating management. If he permits himself to intrude into the administrative activities of the appointed officers, he will eventually create chaotic conditions and disrupt formal channels of authority. The president and top administrative officials of a company can often supply directors with background information for their study of certain problems confronting the business. In contacts with members of the firm's management, directors develop an acquaintance with particular executives and acquire some background for performing their important function of appointing the executive officers.

It is apparent that directors must have time to devote to the business of the corporation if they are to be effective directors. Competent executive personnel of other businesses are limited, therefore, in the number of committee directorships that they are able to assume. By effective organization of the work and careful briefing of directors, the full-time managers of the corporation are able to minimize time requirements for directors and thus to ease the personal burden on them.

Other Top-Level General Management Committees

The Nature of General Management Committees

Many companies — particularly large corporations — utilize committees at or near the top level of the administrative structure. They report to the board of directors or the chief executive and are responsible for discharging their functions on a corporation-wide basis. Some of these are *restricted* committees that deal with one specific subject area—such as pensions, investments, or purchasing. Other *general management* committees are concerned with a variety of functions and activities affecting the company as a whole. It is the latter type of committee that is of primary interest in this section.

Development of general management committees has been a natural concomitant of the growth of corporations. The difficulties inherent in management of the typical large corporation have led many firms to supplement individual leadership with a *council, management committee, executive committee, executive department, policy committee, advisory board,* or similar group. One of the earliest formal top-management committees in a major corporation was established in 1921 when Irénée du Pont, president of E. I. du Pont de Nemours & Company, Inc., adopted a committee system to deal with the problem of product diversification.[16]

The increasing complexity of management in large-scale enterprise encourages adoption of a team approach in corporate management. In Chapter 3, the growing impact of technology, increasingly international scope of operations, and greater political involvement of business were cited as significant features of the changing managerial environment. These and other forces are combining to make the job of the chief executive of a major corporation more and more difficult. Delegation of decision making to lower levels is one type of solution to this problem. A different type of solution is the formation of a management committee, thereby increasing the capacities of the chief executive office. In view of the trends in business and its environment, it seems likely there may be increasing use of these committees in the future.

While there has been no widespread adoption of the general management committee approach, a number of companies have taken significant steps in this direction.

> In April 1963 the Ford Motor Company set up a three-man Chief Executive Office composed of the chairman, president, and executive vice president, with the company's seven operating groups reporting to the office as a unit.
>
> Six months later the National Biscuit Company announced a "most important change in executive alignment" — the creation of an executive department comprising the president, executive vice president, and four senior vice presidents. The group's collective responsibility is "directing overall planning and policy making" for foreign and domestic operations.
>
> Still another company — beset by the challenge of "going international" — has evolved an arrangement in the last two years whereby five executives share chief-executive responsibilities. In this instance it began with the chairman and president splitting the work load; in time three senior vice presidents were appointed; and now this five-man group collectively exercises the authority of the chief executive.[17]

---

[16] M. R. Lohmann, *op. cit.*, p. 5.

[17] D. Ronald Daniel, "Team at the Top," *Harvard Business Review,* Vol. 43, No. 2, March-April 1965, pp. 75-76.

Extent of Committee Authority

In many cases, these committees function merely to advise the president in his administrative decisions. Other organizations have utilized the top management committee for the purpose of arriving at final decisions regarding administrative problems. The president serves as a member of such a committee, but the decision is that of the committee rather than that of the president himself.

In a survey of top management committees in ninety-three companies, the American Management Association classified general management committees as either *authoritative* or *nonauthoritative.* They discovered, it might be noted, that this distinction was not always crystal clear. In some cases, respondents seemed unsure of the degree of authority, and, in other cases, the status differences of committee members appeared to cause differences between the actual and theoretical powers of a committee. After noting these inconsistencies, the report concluded that

> It is probably more nearly accurate to state that about 25 per cent of the general management committees studied are truly authoritative or executive; approximately 25 per cent are wholly advisory, communicative, or coordinative; and about 50 per cent are mixed, with some authority in some areas.[18]

The authoritative committee seems to offer the most potential for reducing pressures on the chief executive. A five-man management committee, for example, may share speaking engagements and visits to branch plants. Committee members may also possess a breadth of experience and knowledge exceeding that of an individual chief executive. The new executive teams of Ford Motor Company and National Biscuit Company, described in the preceding section, appear to be this type — sharing management responsibilities and directing corporate operations as a unit.

Critical Views of Decision-Making Committees

Many executives profess a strong belief in the need for retaining individual responsibility for business decisions. As a result, they subscribe to the philosophy that individuals should assume final responsibility for action taken and that, under no circumstances, should an executive be able to hide behind a committee.

---

[18]Lohmann, *op cit.,* p. 18.

Among the leading exponents of this point of view is Ralph J. Cordiner, former chairman of the General Electric Company. Mr. Cordiner explained that committees in the General Electric administrative structure never serve as decision-making bodies. He went on to express the following ideas:

> It is my feeling that a committee moves at the speed of its least informed member, and too often is used as a way of sharing irresponsibility. Before decentralization, an official tried to get on a great number of committees. He would lead a very calm, safe, orderly life. Not much would happen, but nothing would ever happen to him.[19]

Mr. Cordiner explained that the General Electric Company did utilize committees as advisory groups and pointed out as an example the executive office of the General Electric Company which met twice monthly as an advisory council for the president. He pointed out, however, that "it must be made abundantly clear that the authority for any particular decision lies with the responsible individual, even if he makes it while sitting with the other Council members."[20]

Successful Utilization of Decision-Making Committees

In spite of both theoretical objections and practical disagreements, companies such as Standard Oil Company of New Jersey, American Can, and Union Carbide utilize powerful decision-making committees. One of the best-known examples of a committee-managed corporation is the Du Pont Company, which is administered by its executive committee.

The executive committee of Du Pont operates under the broad policy guidance of the board of directors and is composed of the president as chairman and the eight vice presidents of the corporation.[21] It is responsible for the day-to-day management and direction of the company's affairs. As individuals, members of the executive committee have no direct supervisory responsibility. Although committee members serve as advisors to the industrial departments, their administrative powers are exercised only on the basis of com-

[19]Ralph J. Cordiner, *New Frontiers for Professional Managers* (New York: McGraw-Hill Book Company, 1956), p. 70.

[20]*Ibid.,* pp. 70-71.

[21]The Du Pont executive committee is described in detail in an article by William H. Mylander, "Management by Executive Committee," *Harvard Business Review,* Vol. 33, No. 3, May-June 1955, pp. 51-58.

mittee decisions. The president and vice presidents personally give orders only to their own secretaries. Committee decisions are made by majority vote, and it is possible that a majority vote may differ from the wishes of the president. The executive committee meets regularly each Wednesday and considers such business as departmental operating reports, sales forecasts, capital expenditures, long-range commitments such as plant construction and new commercial ventures, budgets, and general company policies.

It is the purpose of the Du Pont Company in utilizing a technique like this to provide a breadth of experience and knowledge that is not obtainable from one individual. Typically, members of the committee have had experience in different functional areas — such as production, sales, and research — and different departments of the Du Pont organization. Most of them have been either general managers or assistant general managers of operating departments. The outstanding record of success of this business organization provides some evidence of positive contributions by an executive committee. It would be unwise to say that such a committee would work equally well in all large corporations.

Effective Operating Procedures for Committees

Committee Objectives

In achieving efficiency in committee operation, one of the first and basic steps is to make explicit the objectives and authority of each committee. This is desirable both to provide for the effective functioning of the committee and also to secure the proper cooperation of outsiders in their relationships with the committee. Figure 12 presents a formal statement of committee responsibilities as defined by a machine tool manufacturer.

A periodic review of committees and their objectives is valuable. Committees have a way of starting without extensive study and sometimes without real justification. A critical review both in establishing and continuing committees helps to avoid committees that are vestigial in nature or that are totally unnecessary.

Membership of Committees

Attendance of committee meetings in which an individual has little interest can be a monotonous experience. The objectives estab-

Figure 12. *Objective and Functions of Finance Committee (Machine Tool Manufacturer)*

The purpose of the finance committee is to carry out fiscal policies which will maintain the sound financial condition of the company and provide earnings for the stockholders, commensurate with our contribution to the economy of the country as a whole.
The finance committee has the following responsibilities:

Budget
Approve division and department budgets, and review against actual performance a minimum of once each quarter.
Establish a yearly budget, and review against actual performance a minimum of once each quarter.

Product Price Policies
Establish a flexible price policy which will return to the company all essential costs plus an adequate profit.
Anticipate increasing costs and adjust proposal prices with sufficient lead time to recover increases as they occur.

Expenditures
Establish appropriation procedure setting forth signature requirements for various amounts.
Review over-all appropriation expenditure totals at least once each quarter.
Review all appropriation requests in excess of $5,000, and survey effects on pricing and profit structure. All such appropriations must bear the approval of a quorum of the committee, then follow the regular procedure as set forth in . . . executive standard practice.

Cash Position
Review cash prosition and cash forecasts following each monthly financial report, and make recommendations as to the timing of expenditures in order to avoid any undue strain on the company's credit.
Review provisions for establishment of credit and borrowings against these credits.
Each member of the committee is to be provided with a copy of the minutes of each meeting.

Source: M. R. Lohmann, *Top Management Committees,* AMA Research Study 48 (New York: American Management Association, 1961), p. 37.

lished for a committee help to determine the individuals who should serve on that committee. Membership should be limited to those who are directly involved or who have an important interest in the function of the committee.

In selecting individuals who are to serve, there are a number of points to be considered. For example, the personal knowledge or experience that is useful to the committee and could aid in its functioning is one important factor. The effectiveness of the individual in working with other members of a group constitutes another point in selection. In addition, the need for training of the individual may be given some consideration in his selection for committee assignments.

There is a tendency for committees to grow too large in membership and to become unduly cumbersome in operation. The average size of business committees is about eight individuals, but committee members often express a preference for a smaller number—particularly about five members. Interestingly enough, some cynical committee members suggest a preference for committees with a membership of one!

Agenda for Committee Meetings

A committee agenda is an outline or schedule of subjects to be considered at a committee session. It is normally prepared by the chairman or secretary of the committee and may be circulated in advance of the meeting.

Use of an agenda such as the one shown in Figure 13 has the advantage of assuring consideration of all topics that, in the opinion of the chairman, justify the time and attention of the committee. It has the advantage also of providing a structure for discussion and enables the committee to proceed in a logical fashion to consider one topic after another. Distribution of the agenda in advance of the committee meeting makes the session less of a "surprise party" and enables committee members to come better prepared to take up a particular topic.

The Committee Chairman

The committee chairman is quite likely the most important single factor in determining the efficiency with which a committee operates. Utilization of effective committee techniques are, to a great extent, a reflection of the personal ability and insights of the committee chairman himself.

Figure 13. *Agenda for Wednesday Meeting of Du Pont's Executive Committee*

CHART ROOM

1. Fabrics and Finishes Department regular report for January.
2. Grasselli Chemicals Department regular report for January.
3. Photo Products Department regular report for January.
4. Pigments Department regular report for January.
5. Foreign Relations Department — annual report and operating budget.

COMMITTEE ROOM

Unfinished business

6. Engineering Department — operating budget.
7. Motion picture program based on the Company's programs re: "How Our Business System Operates." Joint report from Advertising, Employee Relations, and Public Relations Departments.

New business

8. Organic Chemicals Department regular report for January.
9. Appropriation project covering partial design, procurement of long delivery equipment, and preparation of construction cost estimate New River Pump House, ash and waste retention facilities, Old Hickory Rayon and Cellophane Plants.
10. Appropriation project — replacement of worn-out pirns, Waynesboro Plant.
11. Credit appropriation — additional power facilities, Spruance Rayon Plant.
12. Appropriation — project for synthesis gas via coal partial combustion — Step #I, Belle Works.
13. Adjustment of permanent investment — QY catalyst facilities, Arlington Works.
14. Supplemental report on accomplishment — second year's operation — continuous polyvinyl alcohol and monomer process, Niagara Falls Plant.
15. History, present status, and future prospects of the "Elvanol" polyvinyl alcohol business. Report from Electrochemicals Department.
16. Miscellaneous items.

Source: William H. Mylander, "Management by Executive Committee," *Harvard Business Review,* Vol. 33, No. 3, May-June 1955, p. 54.

Selection of the committee chairman is, therefore, a most important step in assuring an effective committee. The chairman is sometimes selected on the basis of his position, and, in this case, one can only hope that he is properly qualified for the role. In other instances, the selection may be made from a number of potential chairmen.

In making the selection, knowledge of the subject and experience with the particular problem constitute important considerations with respect to the chairman's qualifications. Mere knowledge of subject matter, however, does not qualify the individual for effective committee leadership. The knowledge and experience background must be supplemented with personal traits that enable the chairman to operate smoothly as a group leader.

The committee chairman does not force his own ideas through the committee without adequate consideration by members of the committee. He must provide the leadership in committee discussion without becoming dictatorial in his manner. This means that he must keep the discussion moving, properly recording and noting progress as it is achieved.

The chairman should have at least minimum human relations skills. Inasmuch as the committee process is a group process involving interpersonal relations, it is desirable that he be particularly adept in seeing that good human relations are maintained in the committee room. It is his task to draw out the reticent individual and to secure from such a person the ideas and contributions that he is able to make regarding proposals under consideration. At the same time, he must manage to hold down the loquacious individual who is inclined to voice any idea without allowing it to mature in his own mind. It is also important that he be able to sense potential disputes, to handle them in such a way that they involve issues rather than personalities, and to direct the discussions so that differences of opinion do not erupt into personal clashes between individual committee members.

The chairman may require or allow the discussion of certain items to be carried primarily by the individual who is most directly involved. When the topic is one requiring a decision, the chairman may conclude the discussion at an appropriate point and may announce his decision at that time. If he chooses to give the committee a more powerful role, he may take a vote or state what he feels to be the general sentiment or consensus of the group. After the meeting, some followup is usually required, and the circulation of the minutes of the committee session can be one phase of the followup activity.

Summary

Committees have become an integral part of the administrative structure of most modern business organizations. They are almost infinite in variety, differing in terms of their permanency, time required for committee work, purpose, subject matter, power, and in other ways.

Advantages resulting from the use of committees include the improvement of decisions through group deliberation, coordination of work, facilitation of cooperation in the execution or application of plans and policies, and training of participants. Among the offsetting dangers and limitations are the waste of time and money, danger of undesirable compromise in decision making, difficulty in placing responsibility for decisions, delays and indecision in administrative action, and domination of the committee by one individual.

The most powerful committee in a business organization is its *board of directors*. In the large business corporation, the board tends to be a self-perpetuating committee. Its major functions include appointment of corporate officers, declaration of dividends, and review of management programs and plans. One significant question, in appointing directors, concerns the extent to which the board should be an *inside* or *outside* board.

Many large corporations utilize general management committees at the top level of the administrative structure. Some of these are merely advisory to the chief executive officer, while others make final decisions regarding administrative problems. The practice of decision making by committees is highly controversial.

Effective committee action requires efficient organization and operating procedures. These include clearly stipulated committee objectives, properly qualified committee members, carefully prepared agendas for committee meetings, and competent committee chairmen.

Discussion Questions

1. Should a decision of a committee be better than the decision of the most capable and thoughtful member of the committee? Why?

2. In what ways does committee activity provide better coordination of specialized departments or activities than that achieved by other administrative techniques?

3. If committee members are selected on the basis of their ability to make an effective contribution rather than their need for training, how can committees serve to develop managerial personnel?

4. Which of the suggested dangers or difficulties in the use of committees appears most serious? What is the basis for your answer?

5. What are the effects upon boards of directors of the weakened stockholder control of large corporations?

6. Explain the relative strength or weakness of an *inside* versus an *outside* board in performing each of the board's major functions.

7. One chief executive said that he found outside directors and a few outside stockholders such a "pain in the neck" and obstacle to imaginative growth that he bought out the latter and threw out the former. Evaluate his point of view.

8. In view of Du Pont's success with a decision-making executive committee, is it probable that the management of companies such as General Electric could be improved in this way?

9. Is it likely that a committee agenda has any practical value if committee members are the usual busy executives?

Supplementary Reading

Anastasi, Thomas E., Jr., "Management Committees — Why and How and Who?" *Advanced Management Journal,* Vol. 29, No. 3, July 1964, pp. 67-73.

Bienvenu, Bernard J., "Boards of Directors Revisited," *Business Horizons,* Vol. 5, No. 3, Fall 1962, pp. 41-50.

Daniel, D. Ronald, "Team at the Top," *Harvard Business Review,* Vol. 43, No. 2, March-April 1965, pp. 74-82.

Drought, Neal E., "The Operations Committee: An Experience in Group Dynamics," *Personnel Psychology,* Vol. 20, No. 2, Summer 1967, pp. 153-163.

Green, Estill I., "The Nature and Use of Committees." *Advanced Management,* Vol. 24, No. 7, July 1959, pp. 24-28.

Kinley, John R., *Corporate Directorship Practices.* New York: National Industrial Conference Board, Inc., and American Society of Corporate Secretaries, Inc., 1962.

Lohmann, M. R., *Top Management Committees,* AMA Research Study 48. New York: American Management Association, 1961.

Newman, William H., *Administrative Action,* Second Edition, Chapter 14. Englewood Cliffs: Prentice-Hall, Inc., 1963.

Nicholson, Scott, "The Mysterious Management Committee," *Dun's Review and Modern Industry,* Vol. 81, No. 5, May 1963, pp. 57-59 ff.

"Problems in Review: Committees on Trial," *Harvard Business Review,* Vol. 38, No. 3, May-June 1960, pp. 6-12 ff.

Solem, Allen R., "Almost Anything I Can Do, We Can Do Better," *Personnel Administration,* Vol. 28, No. 6, November-December 1965, pp. 6-16.

Towl, Andrew R., "Outside Directors Under Attack," *Harvard Business Review,* Vol. 43, No. 5, September-October 1965, pp. 135-147.

Wedgwood, Hensleigh C., "Where Committees Go Wrong," *Personnel,* Vol. 44, No. 4, July-August 1967, pp. 62-67.

12

Delegation and Decentralization

The President of the United States assigns to his Secretary of Agriculture the responsibility for directing, in accordance with the applicable laws, all federal agricultural programs. Similarly, a corporation's board of directors confers upon the company's president the right to administer the company's operating divisions. At a much lower level, an office manager of an industrial concern requires a filing clerk to determine the cabinet or folder in which various reports and letters should be filed. Each of these constitutes an example of individual *delegation of authority*. When authority and decision making are *systematically* delegated or pushed downward *throughout an organization*, the approach or practice is known as *decentralized management.*

The practice of delegation is an indispensable feature of organized activity. Indeed, many progressive, efficient concerns attach great importance to delegation and decentralization. These facts make it imperative to analyze these subjects in some detail.

The Nature of Delegation

Definition of Delegation

Delegation of authority involves an assignment of responsibility and authority by a superior to his subordinate. Through delegation, a manager is given the right to plan the activities of his unit, direct the work of subordinate personnel, and make other decisions pertinent to the operations of the organization. If authority is delegated to an operative employee, the right is that of deciding various details of the work and utilizing property and supplies belonging to the employer.

Granting authority need not involve a "blank check" to be classified as delegation. Even in similar lines of work, managers differ in the degree of freedom extended to subordinates. It is less a matter of *delegation versus nondelegation* than it is a matter of *more or less* delegation. At one end of the scale is the autocrat who clings tenaciously to his power, while at the other end is the leader who places almost the total burden on his subordinates. Most managers operate somewhere between these two extremes.

There is a significant distinction between delegation of authority that is real and that which is nominal. Many managers go through the motions of delegating authority, subscribe to the principle in theory, and are personally confident that they are truly delegating authority to their subordinates. Examination of their behavior, however, reveals the fact that subordinates rarely initiate action and invariably clear all questions with the boss. In discussion, a superior may easily tip off his subordinate as to the superior's point of view. It is possible, therefore, for a subordinate who is presumably operating on his own initiative to receive detailed control from his superior. As a result, the superior may give lip service to delegation and yet retain power, merely going through the motions of delegation. The proportion of the suggestions, recommendations, and opinions initiated by the subordinate provides a clue concerning the extent to which authority is really delegated.

Responsibility of Delegatee

When authority is delegated, an obligation is thereby placed upon the subordinate. If the manager of a sporting goods department in a retail store is granted authority to purchase the goods sold in his department, he is expected to exercise his authority in such a way as to bring profit to the company. He is rewarded for success and penalized for failure in achieving this objective. Delegation of authority, then, carries the consequent imposition of responsibility on the part of the subordinate. One of the "principles" frequently voiced by writers on business organization is that responsibility and authority should be equal.

The point being made here is simply that delegation of authority is a two-sided coin—a fact that is clearly recognized by any management employee. He is well aware of his obligation toward his superior in exercising the authority placed upon him.

Impossibility of Delegating One's Own Responsibility

Although an executive may delegate authority to a subordinate and thereby create an obligation of the subordinate to himself, this executive does not relieve himself of responsibility to higher management. Instead, delegation simply creates an additional relationship of obligation between subordinate and superior. The executive who delegates is still held accountable by his superiors for the overall mission for which he is responsible.

Figure 14. *Authority and Responsibility*

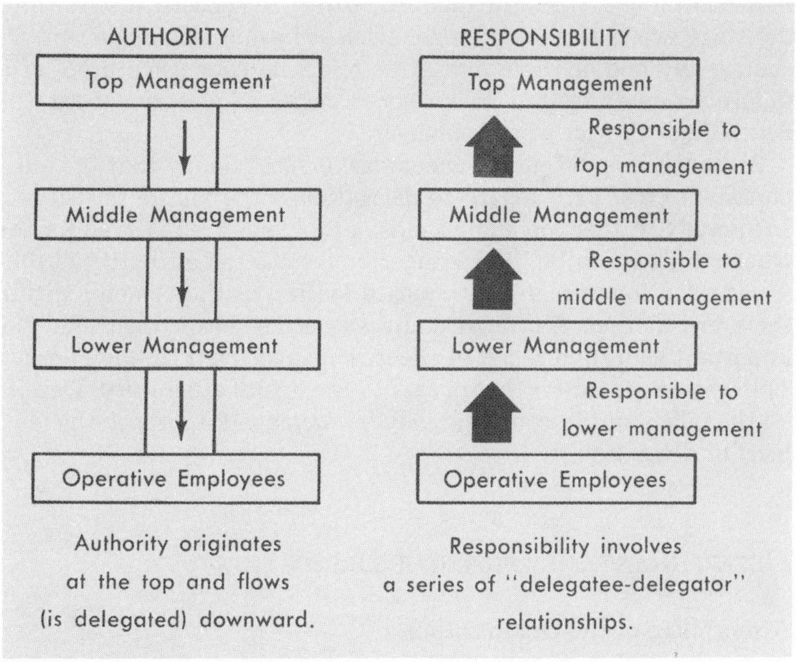

A coach may delegate to his quarterback the right to call a series of plays during a football game. If the quarterback uses particularly good judgment in his choice of plays, the coach can sit back and enjoy the results. If, however, the quarterback comes up with a particularly unfortunate series of calls, the coach must still shoulder his responsibility. Irate fans would hardly be impressed with the coach's explanation that the responsibility was really that of the quarterback and not that of the coach!

Consequences of Inadequate Delegation

Numerous indicators betray the inability or unwillingness of managers to delegate authority. The boss is often extremely busy with current and pressing problems of the business—so much so that he is unable to devote time to forward planning. Subordinates and others who wish to see him must often wait for hours or even days to get his attention, and a waiting line often forms outside his office door.

This manager may also be detected by his attention to trivial details that might well be performed by others lower in the organization. Some presidents who open the mail when the business is small continue to open the mail long after the concern has grown to the stage where this is no longer efficient business management. Of course, any one of these indicators offers no conclusive proof of a failure to delegate, but its presence raises a question about the delegating behavior of the manager.

Although it is difficult to generalize, it seems likely that the most persistent error with regard to delegation is the failure to delegate adequately. Either too many kinds of problems are reserved for the personal attention of the manager or insufficient authority is conferred upon subordinates with regard to the questions coming within their jurisdiction. Although many executives have discovered the important value and secret of effective management through delegation, this group currently appears to constitute a minority. Despite all the talk about it, comparatively few managers approach the ideal level of delegation.

Determinants of Degree of Delegation

Atmosphere of the Organization

The atmosphere or cultural setting of the organization is one factor affecting the extent to which authority is delegated. Some organizations are traditionally democratic in allowing decisions to be made far down in the organization structure. On the other hand, there are organizations in which control and decision making are tightly centralized. For example, educational institutions typically operate in a decentralized manner. It is commonplace for decision-making authority to be passed downward to relatively low levels. Organizations that depend upon the cooperative efforts of many people are likewise inclined to have this sort of organizational pattern. A military organization provides an example in the opposite direction of tightly controlled and centralized management.

Most business institutions are inclined, because of the forces affecting their operation, to fall somewhere between these extremes. Individual companies also differ considerably from one another in their philosophies concerning delegation of authority. During the same years in which Henry Ford I personally directed and controlled the Ford Motor Company, General Motors was developing its noted system of decentralized management.

Nature of Activity Being Managed

Given a particular cultural environment, the degree of delegation is still a variable depending upon a number of individual factors. One of these is the importance of the decision to the organization and to the delegator. Advice is often given to the effect that important decisions should be reserved for the personal attention of the delegator and that less important decisions should be delegated to subordinate personnel.

Of course, this might be carried to the undesirable extreme of suggesting that no important decision should be entrusted to one's subordinate. If only trivial duties are delegated, this is a most superficial type of delegation. It does seem reasonable, however, and consistent with efficient administrative behavior that decisions appearing most vital to the enterprise are those in which the superior is slowest to relinquish the exercise of his personal judgment.

The type of function or work that is being managed also affects the practicality of extensive delegation. A manager may find it utterly impossible to "stay on top" of work performed by his subordinates if the subordinates experience much variation in their required duties. The manager's only recourse may be to allow them greater freedom. One recent study compared the predictability of hospital work—the extent to which unexpected events disturb work routine—with closeness of supervision.[1] A strong, positive correla-

---

[1]Gerald D. Bell, "The Influence of Technological Components of Work Upon Management Control," *Academy of Management Journal,* Vol. 8, No. 2, June 1965, pp. 127-132.

tion was discovered between predictable work and close supervision. Apparently, managers were unable to follow closely those jobs having unexpected variations in their day-to-day content.

The predictability (or unpredictability) concept is particularly pertinent in managing scientists, engineers, and others in professional areas. Professional and even semi-professional work presumably calls for the exercise of professional judgment or knowledge. It seems likely, therefore, that management of professional personnel may necessarily involve looser supervision.

Variations in Managers

A variable peculiar to the individual executive is the degree of his faith or confidence in his subordinates. To some extent, this is a reflection of the ability that has been demonstrated by those in his organization. It also reflects the nature of their training and work experience. In addition, some management personnel are inclined to be more or less distrustful of subordinates, not necessarily because of a lack of confidence in the honesty or integrity of subordinates but because of a fear that subordinates' decisions may be inferior to those of the executive himself.

An additional variable affecting the extent of delegation is the personal management philosophy of the executive. Some managers accept and believe wholeheartedly in the concept of delegation of authority. They believe that this is a sound principle of business organization and that it should be applied, wherever possible, throughout the organization. As a result, they find it convenient and desirable to delegate substantial amounts of authority to those who report to them. In contrast, other executive personnel fail to appreciate the necessity or the substantial values involved in delegating authority.

Control Over Delegated Activity

Delegation vs. Abdication

Delegation cannot be allowed to degenerate into abdication. The reason for this, as explained above, is the inability of the delegator to delegate his own responsibility. This simply means that the executive cannot normally hand over a nonroutine project or assignment to a subordinate and forget about the matter, knowing that the desired results will be satisfactorily achieved. Such a practice would be reasonable only if the superior had a completely trustworthy and dependable subordinate who had demonstrated consistently through past experience that his ability was equal to that of the superior and, furthermore, that the superior could make no significant contribution to the project.

If the matter is of more than trivial importance, then, the superior finds it necessary to exercise some type of surveillance over the delegated activity. He must develop some way to keep in touch with, or keep abreast of, the activities and progress being made on projects under his direction. To do this, he may utilize any of a variety of techniques or devices, or he may employ a combination of these methods. A number of the prominent approaches to controlling delegated activity are suggested in the sections immediately below.[2]

Previewing Direction

One control technique that is frequently used by delegators is an initial discussion with the subordinate or subordinates to reach some understanding concerning the anticipated direction of the project or work. It is possible that the delegator may place the burden for formulating work plans and suggestions upon the subordinate, asking him to present his recommendations, suggestions, and plans for the work at hand. Even so, such a discussion permits the delegator to examine the course of action proposed by the subordinate and to suggest modifications or improvements if such should seem necessary.

It is possible also that the superior may take a more forceful step and indicate the direction that he feels the work or project should follow. In this case, he is probably delegating less authority and reserving more of the decision for his own personal judgment. A considerable amount of skill and restraint is required on the part of the executive during such discussions to avoid directly or indirectly prescribing the details of the operations that are to follow.

Spasmodic Discussion and Questioning

The delegating executive may also keep in touch with progress by spasmodically questioning his subordinate and discussing with him

---

[2]For a stimulating discussion of this subject, see James C. Harrison, Jr., "How to Stay on Top of the Job," *Harvard Business Review,* Vol. 39, No. 6, November-December 1961, pp. 100-108. Some of the approaches discussed in the following sections are similar to some of those suggested by Harrison.

the status of the project. The president of a manufacturing concern may from time to time walk through the shop, questioning the manufacturing managers, or he may visit branch plants on occasion and talk with the managers at the plant level. At various times during the day or week, the office manager may discuss various problems with his immediate subordinates and thus keep himself advised of the nature and progress being made on their work.

Requiring Periodic Reports

Another technique for controlling delegated activity is to require periodic reports of either an oral or written nature. If the report is oral in nature, it differs only from the preceding control tool by the regularity with which it is used and possibly the greater formality of the report. It need not be a highly formalized report, however, to be classified in this manner.

Requiring Final Report

The executive delegating authority to his subordinate may stipulate that the subordinate should "check in" at the conclusion of the project, reporting upon the results either orally or in writing. If this technique is used by itself, it provides a maximum of freedom to the subordinate in the execution of his duties. The requirement for the final report is often accompanied by specification of a deadline date, and the only pressure on the subordinate is to complete the project, using methods of his own choosing, in order to provide a satisfactory report of completion at the specified time.

Use of the deadline-for-final-report technique is accompanied by some danger for the delegator. In effect, it is impossible for the manager using this technique alone to keep abreast of the work or to keep in touch with the progress during the time that the project is under way. If the matter is one of importance, therefore, an executive may have serious reservations about the use of this technique as his sole means of assuring completion of work in accordance with his responsibility.

Impersonal Controls

Management typically supplements personal guidance with a framework of impersonal controls. Business policy, as mentioned earlier, provides guidelines for managers who apply that policy.

Specific rules also serve to limit the independence of subordinates. A rule may prevent a manager from making long distance telephone calls or establish a maximum *per diem* expense allowance for his business trips. While some of the rules which govern managerial behavior are explicit, others are implicit in nature, as indicated by the following:

> Suppose you are the office manager and the Big Boss tells you: "Go ahead, use your discretion in redecorating the office. Anything you say, goes!" Beware! He doesn't really mean that. There are certainly clearly understood rules within which you must work. You must abide by the city building codes and the union contract. You cannot exceed your budget. Further, you must go through the purchasing department, fill out the proper forms, and so forth.
>
> Also, if you are smart, you know that redecorating must play second fiddle to keeping production going. Unless you are on Madison Avenue, the office better wind up looking like an office, not a ladies lounge or a Japanese garden.[3]

The work flow itself may also provide a control mechanism. The worker on a mechanically-paced assembly line has his rate of work determined by the speed of the line.

Another technique that is sometimes adaptable in cases of delegated authority is the arrangement whereby one subordinate automatically checks upon other subordinates. It is this principle, in fact, that provides the *internal check* or *internal control* that is used in the accounting system to protect company assets. The employee receiving money, for example, is checked by another who performs the bookkeeping operation.

It is also possible that the work or project may be arranged by stages so that one unit or department supplies a partially completed project or partially completed work to another department. Any breakdown in the flow of work would thus almost automatically come to the attention of the superior over both of these departments.

Barriers to Delegation

Earlier in the chapter, attention was directed to conditions that may stimulate or retard delegation of authority. In this section,

---

[3]Leonard R. Sayles and George Strauss, *Human Behavior in Organizations* (Englewood Cliffs: Prentice-Hall, Inc., ©1966), p. 160.

several negative factors or barriers are treated at some length for the purpose of better understanding their real nature and minimizing their harmful effects.

Practical Barriers

Any manager contemplating delegation is confronted by an environment which may impose barriers to his delegation of authority. As an example, the manager is limited by the training and ability level of his subordinates. If employees are so inexperienced that their work is subject to frequent error and requires constant checking, it is almost impossible for the manager to delegate extensively. If employees, on the other hand, are well qualified in terms of education and experience, the manager is able to delegate more freely.

There are obviously other practical barriers to delegation that may exist in a specific situation. The time pressure and importance of a particular project may be such as to make it mandatory for the manager personally and continuously to keep in touch with the project and to follow it through to completion. Of course, such a situation would be unusual for most managers and thus constitute an exception to the rule. It is also possible that the "delegating" manager may report to a superior who expects him to keep in touch personally and closely with the progress of the work in his department. Such views of a superior constitute a real barrier to delegation.

Psychological Barriers

Some of the most persistent problems in delegation are those of a psychological nature. There seems to be extreme difficulty on the part of many managers in adopting an approach to management that relies upon delegation of authority. Frequently, the manager has developed a philosophy and approach to supervision that makes little use of delegation and that keeps him in personal contact with all phases of the work. This approach may have been developed over a period of many years and involve a deeply ingrained habit pattern. In some cases, particularly in small firms, the manager has, by reason of ownership and background, a proprietary interest in the organization. This accentuates the tendency to retain rather than to delegate authority downward in his organization. In situations of this kind, the manager may *feel* that he *should* delegate authority and indeed may actually persuade himself that he *is* going to move in this direction. These contrary practices may be deeply established in his own makeup, however, and mere resolution to change may fall short of accomplishing the desired results.

One factor accounting for the existence of a psychological barrier is the feeling of importance attached to the exercise of power. The ego of the manager is involved, and he can sense his own importance as subordinates come to him with questions and refer problems to him for decisions. His importance and significance are less apparent when decision-making power is turned over to others under his direction. Unless he can see the broad picture, delegation may provide a blow to his ego.

It is also possible that a manager's feeling of insecurity may make it difficult for him to be a good delegator. Unfortunately, many managers do find themselves quite insecure in their own positions. Surveys of supervisory and managerial attitudes have shown that a substantial percentage of management personnel, even in well-managed organizations, are quite unsure where they stand with their immediate superiors and the company which employs them. In one of the best-managed companies in the U.S., 18 per cent of its management personnel reported, in response to a survey question, that they did not feel reasonably confident of their standing with respect to job performance.

This feeling of insecurity may affect delegation in different ways. On the one hand, the insecure manager feels it necessary to keep in close touch with work for which he is responsible. He cannot afford to allow things to get out of hand. He is fearful of the consequences if his responsibilities are not carefully discharged. It is difficult for him, with this attitude of mind, to allow a subordinate to take part of the work and perform it without careful scrutiny. Also, the insecure manager may be suspicious of subordinates and think of them as potential or actual rivals for his own position or for higher positions in the same organization. If he sees subordinates as rivals, delegation then appears to constitute aid and assistance to competitors and is hardly consistent with this frame of mind.

It also seems likely that most of us enjoy, to some extent, the exercise of power. It is a little more fun to tell others what to do than to have them tell us. The conditioning influences of society from childhood on are such as to cause individuals to enjoy the exercise of authority. As a result, the supervisor may simply enjoy making decisions and giving directions so much that it is difficult to delegate authority freely to his subordinates.

Overcoming Barriers

Recognizing the existence of a barrier, whether psychological or otherwise, is a long step toward effective delegation. If there is the practical barrier of inadequately trained subordinates, for example, the manager's solution must lie in the acquisition or development of personnel capable of assuming greater authority. In such cases, this may be accomplished to a degree by the process of delegation itself. As long as no authority is delegated downward, the subordinate never learns to make the type of decisions which the superior expects him to make.

In cases involving psychological barriers, the solution is considerably more difficult. One reason for this is the extreme difficulty in recognizing the existence of the barrier. The manager who feels insecure in his position may not recognize his own insecurity or may be hesitant in openly admitting it. The manager who enjoys the exercise of power may not have analyzed his own personality to the extent that he can clearly see this block to effective delegation. If the manager once recognizes the nature of his problem, he can then, with determination, take positive steps in the direction of entrusting greater authority to his subordinates. This may be painful to him, but his recognition of the ultimate objective may well encourage him to follow through and actually to delegate the authority.

Much of the solution to the psychological barriers is dependent upon the type of supervision received by the manager in question. If a general manager understands a department manager's difficulties, he can be of great assistance in guiding the departmental manager toward a practice of more effective delegation. The higher executive, for example, can certainly go a long way in reducing or eliminating tensions and insecurity in his own relationship with the subordinate manager.

Barriers of the Delegatee

Not all of the barriers to delegation are found in the delegator. Frequently, we visualize all subordinates as eagerly looking upward in the organization, wishing to assume greater responsibility and authority and reaching out to grasp any decision-making authority that is proffered them. Unfortunately, the real life situation reveals many subordinates to be somewhat apprehensive about the acceptance of authority. Some employees apparently wish to have decisions made by those above them and find the task of reaching their own decisions uncomfortable. For such individuals, this feeling may serve as a very practical barrier to the delegation process.

The hesitancy of the subordinate, whether he is a manager or an operative employee, in accepting delegated authority is frequently more pronounced at the time a step of delegation is first instituted.

Although the subordinate may learn to exercise this authority very capably in the future, there are a number of uncertainties that may deter him in the initial exercise of the authority.

A constructive supervisory attitude is essential in overcoming the reluctance of a subordinate to assume the authority that is passed on to him by his own superior. Frequently, he comes to the superior with the problem or question that has been presented to him for a decision. Either directly or indirectly, he seeks to obtain guidance and an indication of the superior's judgment. The net effect of this may be to avoid assuming any position on his own part, merely reflecting the implied attitude of his boss.

The behavior of the superior is thus of extreme importance in weaning a subordinate away from reliance upon his superior and enabling him to stand upon his own feet. Probably the most basic condition that must exist is an attitude of mutual confidence between superior and subordinate. The subordinate must understand that, while he must perform satisfactorily, he will not be condemned for every error of judgment in performing his assigned mission. The superior must convey to him the knowledge that he has some leeway, some latitude for making mistakes. Indeed, he may well learn through the process of making some mistakes, and he cannot be condemned on every such occasion. Of course, this cannot be taken as approval of continued inept performance that shows no improvement. There is a difference in refusing to permit unsatisfactory performance and in jumping on one's subordinates for every error in judgment and for every mistake made in the exercise of delegated authority. It is particularly important that any error be used constructively as an educational device rather than as an occasion for destructive criticism of the subordinate. The superior should be alert for every opportunity to give credit where credit is deserved and for encouragement of the subordinate in the exercise of his authority.

Advantages of Delegation

Freeing Higher-Level Executive

A major advantage of delegating authority is that this relieves the delegator of certain time-consuming work. Any manager can be more effective by delegating minor duties. If a manager is constantly immersed in the details of work that could be accomplished by subordinates, he is unable to function effectively with regard to the major responsibilities involved in his own position.

The evidences of inadequate delegation abound. The executive who fails to delegate is burdened with a great amount of detailed work; he works long hours and takes a stuffed briefcase home with him. As a result, he is rushed and feels that he has no time for long-range planning.

Developing Subordinates

One does not learn to play tennis by reading a book. Obviously, it is possible to acquire some knowledge of the rules of the game and certain of the fundamentals in this way. But to develop real skill as a tennis player requires months and years of swinging a racket on a tennis court. In much the same way, one must develop management ability by managing. Books that explain the success of others are of some, but only limited, value in developing the talents necessary to make an organization operate smoothly. In other words, one learns to make decisions by making decisions.

The implications for delegation of authority are clear. By forcing a subordinate to assume responsibility and to make decisions, the superior is insisting upon the subordinate's practicing his management. In this way, the subordinate can take a few practice "swings." If the superior were to make most decisions personally, the subordinate would be deprived of his practice time.

Superficially, the issue seems clear enough. The real difficulty in this type of development is in arranging for the ideal type of delegation to accomplish the objective. The delegation must be real and not imaginary. Delegated tasks and responsibilities must be difficult but not too difficult, and their level of difficulty should increase as the subordinate develops ability. Important responsibilities—those in which there is potential danger in an error—should be entrusted to the subordinate at the proper time. All of this requires considerable finesse on the part of the delegator. It is easy to subscribe to the principle and to acknowledge its worth but much more difficult to follow it consistently and intelligently.

Improving Morale

It is widely believed that personnel respond to delegated authority with favorable attitudes, that they enjoy the greater responsibilities. Obviously, this generalization could not apply to all operative employees or even to all managers. Some individuals—and they can be found in any sizable organization—like the security associated with detailed supervision. They do not enjoy the uncomfortable feeling of making an important decision. For such individuals, delegation of authority is disconcerting and does not improve their satisfaction or their attitudes.

It seems likely that most employees—particularly those in management positions—respond positively toward delegated authority. Even one who is initially reluctant to assume authority often enjoys it once he becomes accustomed to the new role. Without question, delegation does raise the subordinate's position in importance and stature.

Decentralization

Relationship of Decentralization to Delegation

Any manager may delegate authority to his subordinate or subordinates. Delegation may thus be a highly individualized relationship. When delegation is used systematically and extensively throughout an organization, the arrangement may be described as decentralization. In a decentralized organization, authority and decision making have been pushed downward throughout the organization. Decentralization thus necessitates delegation, but delegation, on the other hand, might be used by a particular manager without being part of a decentralization program. Although decentralization is frequently accompanied by geographical dispersal of activities, it is the locus of decision making rather than the physical site of operation that is the essence of decentralization.

From 1934 to 1955, the Safeway food chain was managed by Lingan A. Warren, who was reputed to be an "autocratic president."[4] Mr. Warren dominated the company, and a constant flow of Warren policy directives and Warren operating rules emanated from company headquarters. Each store manager, for example, was ordered to meet competitors' prices, item by item, and division managers were forbidden to communicate with other division managers except through official channels. "We had 25 or 30 manuals that were supposed to contain the answers for everything," one longtime Safeway

[4]"The New Bosses: A Stockbroker Takes Charge of Food Chain, Lifts Profits and Sales," *The Wall Street Journal,* January 2, 1962, pp. 1 and 6.

official recalled. An organization theorist would correctly describe such an organization as highly centralized, even though there may have been instances of substantial delegation here and there in the chain.

In spite of growth, however, the profit record of Safeway was poor. This led to a management change that placed Wall Street stockbroker Robert Anderson Magowan in the presidency. Lacking extensive food chain experience, Magowan proceeded to give executives down the line broad responsibility for their own operations. Division managers were called together—one of the few such meetings that had ever been held—and told by Magowan that they had full authority for operations in their own territories. They were to discover that the delegation of authority was more than an illusion and that they were to wield power over prices, advertising, promotion, purchasing, and development of expansion plans.

By pushing decision-making authority downward to the various divisions and to the 1,800 stores, the Safeway chain was thus decentralized. This change from centralized to decentralized management required not only an act or acts of delegation by the president but also numerous acts of delegation by division managers and other managerial personnel at the lower levels in all sections of the country. It was a type of change that permeated the entire organization.

As is true with delegation, centralization and decentralization are not absolutes. A company is never completely centralized or completely decentralized. In the case of Safeway, the chain moved from a highly centralized management in the direction of greater—indeed, substantial—decentralization.

Divisionalization as a Vehicle for Decentralization

Decentralization of authority and decision making is often centered about product or territorial divisions that receive grants of authority from company headquarters. As noted in Chapter 8, such organization structures are described as *divisionalized.*

It should be clear that decentralization is not synonymous with divisionalization. In a company organized along functional lines, lower-level officials may be granted either substantial or minor authority. Even in a company having product or territorial divisions, there is no guarantee that the divisions are free from close headquarters control—the Safeway chain prior to 1955, for example

—and no certainty that the operating divisions delegate extensively to their components.

Advantages of Decentralization

The advantages cited earlier for delegation of authority apply to decentralization as well. By decentralizing, the company may, for example, develop managerial ability throughout the organization. Autonomous divisions provide "goldfish bowls" in which top management can observe lower level managers in action and in which those managers can develop through the exercise of individual initiative.

Another significant advantage of decentralized management that functions along divisional lines is the *profit-center* principle. The division manager who is given freedom in his management can be held responsible for the profitable operations of the division. Individual operating divisions may be given their own profit-and-loss responsibility. Reports on store sales and profits, for example, are funneled into the Magowan headquarters of Safeway.[5]

Decentralization also facilitates product diversification. It is difficult, if not impossible, for a company having a highly diversified line of products to operate with tightly centralized management. Centralized control over the units of a food chain is much simpler than centralized control of a company producing such diverse equipment as water heaters, electronic equipment and farm implements. Decentralization thus provides an approach to management of the diversified enterprise. In fact, growth by merger often leads to loose or decentralized control of the merged company—particularly when the new addition is dissimilar to the parent company. As an extension of this reasoning, it can be seen that a product emphasis or market area emphasis may be encouraged through decentralization.

It is also a fact that some lower-level decisions are better than higher-level decisions. Headquarters does not always know best. The manager on the "firing line" is close to the problem and often has insights that his superiors lack. In addition, he is in a position to move quickly if he is not required to check constantly with headquarters.

Even Communist countries have become impressed with the advantages of more extensive decentralization. The problems of the

---

[5] *Ibid.*

bureaucratically centralized system of Soviet Russia are described below:

> By the mid-1950's it became increasingly obvious to the Soviet rulers that industrial overcentralization, resulting from the concentration of decision-making powers and initiative in the hands of relatively few high-level administrators, was leading to much inefficiency and waste, as well as to inadequate innovation, in the increasingly complex and expanding Soviet economy. New industries had evolved — chemical, electronics, various consumer goods, new types of machinery, and so on — output was now much more diverse; technology, production processes, and market requirements were all becoming increasingly complex. The problems of efficiently combining factor inputs and securing proper product specifications were becoming more severe. Innovation through local initiative relating to products and processes was now deemed essential in order to raise productivity and satisfy the wants of a population growing restless with shoddy consumer goods. In general, the task of planning, organizing, directing, and controlling national economic activity now required much greater precision. This in turn called for greater managerial initiative and ability at the enterprise level.[6]

A number of steps were subsequently taken in the 1950's and 1960's to increase the authority of plant managers, thereby introducing a form of decentralized management even in a planned economy.

Difficulties in Decentralizing

Centralization of some functions encourages economy of operation. By combining work that would otherwise be scattered among different divisions or individuals, it is possible to achieve more efficient performance. Consider, for example, the college recruitment program of a large corporation having numerous branch plants. If the personnel function were completely decentralized, each branch plant should prepare brochures, contact universities, and arrange to interview prospective graduates. It is entirely possible that different branch plants would have representatives on the same campus at the same time. To avoid duplication and inefficiency, therefore, the corporation may decide in favor of centralized recruitment. Even here, final authority for choice of recruits may be delegated to the

---

[6]Barry M. Richman, *Soviet Management* © 1965, pp. 78-79. Reprinted by permission of Prentice-Hall, Inc., Englewood Cliffs, N. J.

branch plant, but this is less complete decentralization than one in which plants have the entire responsibility for their own recruitment. Similar situations may also arise in production, marketing, or other areas. Economy is, therefore, a factor to be considered in questions of decentralization.

Between 1964 and 1966, the American Can Company moved to improve its profit position by shifting from a loose federation of almost autonomous divisions to centralized management.[7] The earlier decentralized organization had resulted from a series of acquisitions — including Dixie Cup and Marathon Paper — beginning in 1956. Unfortunately, the trend in profits during the expansion was disappointing. Having tried loose control of the major product divisions, the company proceeded to tighten control at headquarters. Headquarters staffs grew much larger, taking over much of the work previously handled by divisional offices in such areas as taxes, law, accounting, and advertising. Centralized purchasing was instituted to provide greater buying efficiencies, with purchase limits of $2,500 set for plant managers. Marketing responsibilities were extracted from the separate divisions and unified under a vice president. Under the previous system, salesmen for various divisions competed for the same customers. Following the reorganization, almost every sector of the company began showing substantially lower operating costs. The profit picture changed dramatically, with per share earnings increasing from $2.70 in 1964 to $3.61 in 1965 and $4.18 in 1966.

A lack of capacity on the part of the lower-level personnel may also limit the ability of top management to decentralize. This may be a vicious circle, however, with the lack of ability an effect as well as a cause of failure to decentralize. If so, it spotlights a serious weakness in higher-level management.

Variables Affecting Decision to Decentralize

In examining the advantages and weaknesses of decentralization, it is clear that the unique nature of a particular situation makes decentralization logical or illogical. Decentralization is not always good, but it has been used successfully in many cases. What are the factors governing the effectiveness with which decentralized management can be used?

---

[7] "The New Package at American Can," *Business Week*, No. 1933, September 17, 1966, pp. 94-100.

Size is certainly one such factor. Relatively smaller firms can be centralized more easily than industrial giants like General Electric and General Motors. Of course, this does not mean that it is necessarily desirable for smaller companies to centralize their management. It simply means that the huge corporation finds extreme centralization unduly cumbersome. The *very* small firm, it might be noted, would automatically avoid decentralization except in unusual situations.

Diversity of product lines is another variable affecting the desirability of decentralization. It was noted earlier that decentralization facilitates diversification. It is easier to maintain centralized control over a dozen divisions each containing the same type of retail store than it is to provide centralized control over a dozen divisions each producing a unique product with different manufacturing and marketing characteristics.

If the business is geographically spread, decentralization becomes more attractive because of the distances involved. It becomes more difficult for headquarters to maintain remote control in a detailed manner. Even an occasional small firm may have branch offices or branch warehouses sufficiently scattered over the state or nation to justify decentralized management.

Some types of functions are also more easily decentralized than others. Manufacturing has traditionally been one of the first to be decentralized, while finance has remained centralized even in many large companies that are otherwise decentralized.

The nature of company growth may also affect the tendency toward centralization. If growth is by merger, the merged business is often retained as an integral unit rather than having its functions amalgamated with those of the acquiring corporation. In the Du Pont Company, for example, the Pigments Department was formed from the Krebs Pigment and Chemical Company, acquired in 1929, and the Electrochemical Department was formed principally from the Roessler & Hasslacher Chemical Company, purchased in 1930.

As noted earlier in the chapter, the importance of particular types of decisions is still another variable affecting the extent of decentralization. Decisions involving major commitments or affecting the future of the business in a substantial way must be brought to top management for decision or approval.

Business Trends Affecting Decentralization

The trend toward diversification of product lines is evident to even the casual observer. Variety store chains open discount houses, an automobile manufacturer gets into space technology, and universities install executive development programs. Because of the close correlation between diversification and decentralization noted earlier, the trend toward diversification is also a trend toward decentralization.

Another pertinent and continuing change in business operations is the revolution in information processing technology. Installation of electronic computers and other data processing equipment permits the analysis of masses of data much more quickly than was previously possible. It appears that this improvement may encourage recentralization by making operating data more manageable. It should be noted, however, that integrated data processing is only one of the factors involved in the decision to centralize or decentralize. The need to develop lower-level management personnel through delegation might lead to a decision in favor of decentralization even though centralized management was technically feasible.

Also, as noted by General Electric's John F. Burlingame, there are two classes of decisions that can be identified.[8] One type of decision defies complete analysis or solution with even the most sophisticated techniques because it involves human beings and intangible, subjective human values. It requires the balancing of social, moral, and economic values and assessment of situations in which information needs cannot be adequately anticipated or adequately filled. The requirement for extensive decision making of this nature makes it appear unlikely that information technology will reverse or even greatly retard the evident trend toward decentralization. Even the automated office cannot yet scuttle its middle and lower management personnel.

Changing technology in manufacturing is another factor which undoubtedly affects the degree of decentralization, although the precise nature of the effect is by no means clear. Closeness of supervision apparently decreases — that is, more delegation of authority occurs — as process technology progresses from a low technology ("craft") to medium technology ("mass production") state.[9] However, changes in extent of supervision are less clear as the technology advances from a medium technology ("mass production") to a high technology ("automation") stage. Further research will be necessary to establish this relationship more clearly.

---

[8]John F. Burlingame, "Information Technology & Decentralization," *Harvard Business Review,* Vol. 39, No. 6, November-December 1961, p. 122.

[9]Elmer H. Burack, "Technology and Some Aspects of Industrial Supervision: A Model Building Approach," *Academy of Management Journal,* Vol. 9, No. 1, March 1966, p. 66.

Summary

Through *delegation,* a subordinate is granted authority to make certain types of decisions and, in turn, assumes responsibility for the proper exercise of this authority. Although a superior delegates *authority,* he cannot delegate his own *responsibility.* The degree of delegation is determined not only by the atmosphere or cultural setting of the organization but also by such individual factors as the importance of the decision, the predictability of the work, the delegator's degree of confidence in subordinates, and his management philosophy.

Delegation differs from *abdication* in that the former involves a continuing sense of responsibility and some control over delegated activity. Among the procedures used to maintain such control are conferences previewing direction of work, spasmodic discussion and questioning, periodic reports, final reports, and various policies, rules, and other types of impersonal controls.

Probably the most serious type of barrier to delegation of authority is the psychological barrier. Failure to delegate authority, when caused by such a barrier, stems from such factors as deeply ingrained habit patterns, sense of individual importance, feeling of insecurity, and enjoyment of exercising power. Overcoming barriers of this type is extremely difficult and normally requires a determined effort on the part of the manager and understanding and cooperation on the part of his superior. Another barrier to delegation takes the form of the subordinate's refusal or reluctance to assume authority that his superior wishes to confer upon him. Among the advantages of delegation are the relief of the delegator from time-consuming work, development of subordinate personnel, and improvement of morale.

Decentralization occurs when delegation is used systematically and extensively throughout an organization. It often goes hand in hand with *divisionalization,* although the two are not synonymous. In addition to the advantages cited for delegation of authority, decentralization aids control through use of the *profit-center* principle, facilitates product diversification, and improves some decisions by permitting them to be made closer to the problem level. Difficulties involved in decentralizing include uneconomical duplication of some operations and limited capability of lower-level personnel. Some of the variables affecting the decision to centralize include size of organization, diversity of product line, geographical spread or concentration, nature of business function, nature of company growth, and importance of the type of decision. The trend toward product diversification encourages the trend toward decentralization, whereas the revolution in information processing technology tends to facilitate centralized control of operations. The effects of recent developments in manufacturing technology are not yet clear.

Discussion Questions

1. Distinguish between *delegation* and *decentralization.*
2. If responsibility and authority are supposed to be equal, as one "principle" of management suggests, why can't a manager delegate his *responsibility* in the same way that he delegates his authority?
3. If the atmosphere or cultural setting of an organization determines the degree of delegation, why did Ford and General Motors differ so markedly in their degree of decentralization for so many years?
4. If control is maintained over the exercise of delegated authority, how can it properly be called delegation?
5. How can a feeling of insecurity act as a barrier to delegation?
6. Discuss the relationship of delegation of authority and morale of employees. Do subordinates really want authority and the responsibility that accompanies it?
7. What advantages do *decentralization* and *divisionalization* have in common?
8. What is the relationship of business size to decentralization?
9. Have you ever worked for a supervisor who delegated very little authority? For one who delegated extensively? Describe as carefully as possible your reactions and the reactions of your fellow employees to either or both types of supervision.

Supplementary Reading

Bell, Gerald D., "Predictability of Work Demands and Professionalization as Determinants of Workers' Discretion," *Academy of Management Journal,* Vol. 9, No. 1, March 1966, pp. 20-28.

———————, "The Influence of Technological Components of Work Upon Management Control," *Academy of Management Journal,* Vol. 8, No. 2, June 1965, pp. 127-132.

Brown, David S., "Why Delegation Works — And Why It Doesn't," *Personnel,* Vol. 44, No. 1, January-February 1967, pp. 44-52.

Brown, Wilfred, "A Critique of Some Current Ideas About Organization," *California Management Review,* Vol. 6, No. 1, Fall 1963, pp. 3-12.

Burack, Elmer H., "Technology and Some Aspects of Industrial Supervision: A Model Building Approach," *Academy of Management Journal,* Vol. 9, No. 1, March 1966, pp. 43-66.

Burlingame, John F., "Information Technology and Decentralization," *Harvard Business Review,* Vol. 39, No. 6, November-December 1961, pp. 121-126.

Cordiner, Ralph J., *New Frontiers for Professional Managers.* New York: McGraw-Hill Book Company, 1956.

Dearden, John, "Computers: No Impact on Divisional Control," *Harvard Business Review,* Vol. 45, No. 1, January-February 1967, pp. 99-104.

Ewing, John S., "Patterns of Delegation," *Harvard Business Review,* Vol. 39, No. 4, July-August 1961, pp. 32-40ff.

Jarman, W. M. and B. H. Willingham, "The Decentralized Organization of a Diversified Manufacturer and Retailer — Genesco," in *Organization Theory in Industrial Practice,* ed. Mason Haire. New York: John Wiley & Sons, Inc., 1962.

Litterer, Joseph A., *The Analysis of Organizations,* Chapter 19. New York: John Wiley & Sons, Inc., 1965.

Morse, Gerry E., "Pendulum of Management Control," *Harvard Business Review,* Vol. 43, No. 3, May-June 1965, pp. 158-164.

Newman, William H., *Administrative Action,* Second Edition, Chapters 11 and 13. Englewood Cliffs: Prentice-Hall, Inc., 1963.

Sayles, Leonard R. and George Strauss, *Human Behavior in Organizations,* Chapter 7. Englewood Cliffs: Prentice-Hall, Inc., 1966.

Zald, Mayer N., "Decentralization — Myth vs. Reality," *Personnel,* Vol. 41, No. 4, July-August 1964, pp. 19-26.

13

Organization Planning and Organization Change

Few businesses retain a static organization for long periods of time. Changes in markets, objectives, and operations lead to modifications of organization structure and relationships. This chapter will examine the nature of organization changes and the methods for introducing them most effectively. It will also deal with the topic of *organization planning*—that is, the analysis and study of organization for the purpose both of improving it and adapting it to changes occurring in the business.

NEED FOR ORGANIZATION STUDY AND ORGANIZATION CHANGE

The Dynamic Nature of Business Organizations

The dynamic nature of business enterprise produces repercussions in organizational relationships. Product diversification, for example, has been noted as an important trend in American business. As a concern adds new and different products, it may be necessary to modify the organization in order to produce and sell the new products efficiently. If the products are drastically different from those in the existing line, completely new departments may be required. Decentralization may similarly be justified by changes of this type.

A business concern often finds it desirable to change the emphasis given certain products, activities, or territories. In an enterprise selling to both foreign and domestic markets, for example, an expansion of foreign business might call for organization changes to cope with the greater volume of foreign trade. If foreign business grew sufficiently large, an international or foreign department might be added to care for that phase of the company's operations.

Personnel changes also lead to organization changes. This is particularly true of replacements at the top-management level. Personal abilities differ among executives, and modifications of organization are made to accommodate the strengths or weaknesses of particular executives. New executives also have their own ideas as to proper organization, and these frequently differ from those of their predecessors.

These paragraphs have suggested that organization structures reflect in some way the functions and purposes of organizations. As the nature of the business changes, its organization structure must likewise change. This assertion that organization structure flows from the nature or strategy of the business has been supported by the scholarly study of American business organizations by Alfred D. Chandler, Jr.[1] Chandler defines strategy as the determination of basic long-term goals and the adoption of courses of action and allocation of resources to carry out these goals. Decisions to diversify or to set up distant plants are examples of strategic decisions. Chandler examined the administrative histories of close to a hundred large industrial enterprises, and he analyzed in detail the organizational development of Du Pont, General Motors, Standard Oil (New Jersey), and Sears Roebuck. His general thesis may be stated as follows:

> Strategic growth resulted from an awareness of the opportunities and needs — created by changing population, income, and technology — to employ existing or expanding resources more profitably. A new strategy required a new or at least refashioned structure if the enlarged enterprise was to be operated efficiently. The failure to develop a new internal structure, like the failure to respond to new external opportunities and needs, was a consequence of overconcentration on operational activities by the executives responsible for the destiny of their enterprises, or from their inability, because of past training and education and present position, to develop an entrepreneurial outlook.

---

[1]Alfred D. Chandler, Jr., *Strategy and Structure* (Cambridge: The M.I.T. Press, 1962).

> One important corollary to this proposition is that growth without structural adjustment can lead only to economic inefficiency. Unless new structures are developed to meet new administrative needs which result from an expansion of a firm's activities into new areas, functions, or product lines, the technological, financial, and personnel economies of growth and size cannot be realized. Nor can the enlarged resources be employed as profitably as they otherwise might be. Without administrative offices and structure, the individual units within the enterprise (the field units, the departments, and the divisions) could undoubtedly operate as efficiently or even more so (in terms of cost per unit and volume of output per worker) as independent units than if they were part of a larger enterprise. Whenever the executives responsible for the firm fail to create the offices and structure necessary to bring together effectively the several administrative offices into a unified whole, they fail to carry out one of their basic economic roles.[2]

The need for continuing attention to the organization structure is thus clear. The accelerating rate of change, as noted in Chapter 3, suggests the likelihood, and even the desirability, of frequent change in structure. In the face of extensive business change, maintenance of an organizational status quo may quickly involve inefficiency in operations.

Organizational Adaptation to Technological Change

Engineers and production managers are constantly seeking to improve efficiency by changing production technology. Such improvements typically affect both equipment and work methods. The movement toward mechanization and automation of production processes is sweeping in nature and widely recognized as a phenomenon of modern industrial operations. Our concern at this point is with the impact of technological change on organizational relationships. Unfortunately, the organizational consequences are not completely clear. Studies of change indicate that changes in organizational relationships occur but do not as yet reveal a distinct pattern of change. It is not always clear which effects are typical and which are unique in the specific case.

One significant study of technology and organization examined modifications of a baking plant organization employing 1,200 employees as it changed from a mill-type plant to a highly automatic

---

[2] *Ibid.*, pp. 15-16.

facility. This study suggested the following areas that will require careful planning in the transition to automation:[3]

1. *Status of Supervisory Job.* The supervisor will regain some discretionary authority. The number of supervisory jobs will shrink, the span of control will be drastically reduced, and the supervisory function will be upgraded from "gang boss" to general overseer, trouble shooter, and coordinator.
2. *Human Relations Effectiveness.* Insecurity and lack of training for the new supervisory job will interfere with improvement in the area of human relations.
3. *Communications.* The gross amount of direct, verbal interaction between workers and supervisor will decline and become more consultative in nature.
4. *Plant Maintenance Functions.* Many companies will suffer prolonged debugging, costly down-time, and reduced morale because of failure to provide an adequate maintenance staff.
5. *Social Structure.* Existing social organization will be disrupted and will tend to become less company-oriented and more personal.
6. *Stand-by Personnel.* Staffing that might be considered by management as excessive will be necessary to care for production irregularities.
7. *Centralization.* Greater centralization of managerial control will accompany automation.

The introduction of the electronic computer constitutes a particularly significant change in terms of its organizational consequences. Soon after computers were introduced for business use in the 1950's, there were predictions that they would virtually wipe out middle management levels in industry. Supervisors would presumably be needed at the work level, but coordination traditionally accomplished by middle managers might be centralized. Experience in use of computers has not supported this prediction, however. But even though results have differed from those anticipated by some, there is no question as to the computer's far reaching effects.

One study of computer installations discovered a number of drastic organization changes.[4] Nine separate sales estimating units

---

[3]Otis Lipstreu and Kenneth A. Reed, "A New Look at the Organizational Implications of Automation," *Academy of Management Journal,* Vol. 8, No. 1, March 1965, pp. 24-31.

[4]Hak Chong Lee, *The Impact of Electronic Data Processing upon the Patterns of Business Organization and Administration* (Albany: School of Business, State University of New York, 1965), pp. 25, 29-30.

in a manufacturing firm were consolidated into three units, each reporting to the general manager of the respective product line. More valuable information was supplied to managers, and they were freed from certain clerical work. The capability of the computer to interrelate functional activities produced a change in the manager's decision-making framework. It became possible to make optimum decisions not merely for departments and divisions but for the company as a whole. In spite of the change in the decision environment, however, there was no evidence of greater centralization of decision making.

Another study utilized empirical data from an investigation of the installation of a computer system in a large utility and from the Bureau of Labor Statistics' studies of installations of computers in twenty offices in a variety of industries. The conclusions from this study were as follows:

(1) The installation of an EDP system reduces office employment in the department in which it is installed;

(2) Whether the need to displace employees will arise or not depends upon such factors as: the growth of the firm's business, the nature of the firm's work force, and the willingness of management and labor to cooperate in planning the system's implementation;

(3) The types of jobs which tend to be eliminated as a result of the installation of an EDP system are generally jobs such as posting, checking records, computing, filing, sorting, and tabulating which are clerical in nature, relatively repetitive, and not related directly to customer contacts;

(4) The new jobs which are created tend to be jobs which are concerned directly with either the computer "hardware" or the transformation of data into a form acceptable to the computer;

(5) Although the nature and magnitude of employee adjustments associated with EDP system installations may vary with the type of work which is being systematized, the following trends are apparent: approximately 20 per cent of the employees in the work unit where the EDP system was installed are assigned to jobs within the same work unit; about 15 per cent of the employees who are transferred to other work units are transferred to the computer group; only a small per cent of the personnel actually are laid off as a result of the system's installation; a large per cent who are recorded as "quits" leave their jobs because of personal reasons;

(6) The employees who form the nucleus of the computer unit may be selected from within the firm. These employees need not be college graduates;

(7) The installation of an EDP system in an office will result in a larger ratio of managerial employees to clerical employees in those areas in which the system is introduced.[5]

Experience of the past few decades with technological changes, including changes in information technology, have demonstrated the powerful impact of these forces upon the organization structure. Space does not permit an extended discussion of the numerous innovations and modifications in organizations that have thus far appeared. Not only do today's organizations reflect the introduction of technological change, but tomorrow's organizations will no doubt be even more different as further technological developments occur. Keeping the organization abreast of such developments constitutes a major challenge to contemporary managers—particularly those in high-technology industries.

Inefficiencies in Existing Organization

Aside from business changes, an organization structure does not always function perfectly even during periods of stability. Problems arise in administration that are perceived by managers as organizational problems. This means that members of management must be concerned with study and analysis of the organization simply to improve its effectiveness.

A few years ago, some common organizational deficiencies were discussed by an American Management Association seminar group under the leadership of a senior partner of McKinsey and Company. Following is a list of weaknesses developed by this seminar group.

1. Slowness in decision-making and in carrying out decisions (too many "channels," too much "paper pushing").
2. Frequent and serious errors in decision-making.
3. Delegation of various decisions to executives who lack knowledge of the phases of the business affected.
4. Inadequate communication.
5. Bottlenecks in production, finance, etc.; failure to meet delivery schedules.

---

[5]Walter A. Hill, "The Impact of EDP Systems on Office Employees: Some Empirical Conclusions," *Academy of Management Journal,* Vol. 9, No. 1, March 1966, pp. 18-19.

6. Decision-making overly decentralized with consequent lack of uniformity in policies; or, at the other extreme, overcentralized decision-making to preserve uniformity of policies.
7. "Below-par" executives—turnover, absenteeism, high sickness incidence, nervous tension, overwork, underutilization, general dissatisfaction.
8. Inadequate long-range planning and research, lack of new ideas.
9. Interdepartmental and personality clashes.
10. Poor balancing and meshing of the different departments.
11. Staff-line conflicts.
12. Excessive span of control.
13. Poor control, lack of knowledge of results, poor compliance.
14. Inefficient committee work.
15. Lack of clear-cut objectives.[6]

Example of Organization Change

It may be helpful at this point to consider a specific example of reorganization and to note the reasons or background for the changes. Such an example is provided by Garlock, Inc., a manufacturer of industrial packings, whose organization has changed substantially in recent years.[7]

The Garlock Company was not driven to reorganization by financial losses. In fact, it had never failed to earn a profit. In spite of profitable operation, however, various difficulties arose, including a delivery problem, a growing proportion of small orders, and a declining share of the market. Behind these symptoms was an outmoded organization structure in which lines of authority were blurred, some people had more than one boss, some managers supervised as many as forty subordinates, and different jobs overlapped.

The changes that made improvement of the organization structure imperative were connected with size and technology. From a small concern, Garlock grew beyond the size permitting it to be directed on the basis of simple observation. It came to employ more than 3,000 persons in eight cities—plus participating in a joint venture in Italy. Technology was affected as its products multiplied in variety

---

[6]Ernest Dale, *Planning and Developing the Company Organization Structure* (New York: American Management Association, 1952, Sixth Printing 1959), pp. 174-175.

[7]"Old Company Makes Itself Over," *Business Week,* No. 1601, May 7, 1960, pp. 79-84.

and became more complex in response to customer demands for special designs, more technical service, and higher quality.

The uncharted organization was replaced with one in which relationships were carefully described by charts, manuals, and job descriptions. Many new jobs were created, including some sixty at the management and professional level. The scope of responsibilities of some managerial positions was also modified. Product managers for each of nine product lines, for example, were given the responsibility for setting prices.

Organization Planning

The Nature of Organization Planning

Organization planning involves the formal analysis and evaluation of organizational relationships. Its objective is the creation of a smoothly functioning and efficient organization structure. It concentrates upon formal organization—that is, the organization as stipulated or as visualized by management. Organization planning is not directly concerned, therefore, with the existence or nature of the informal organization.

The best-known tool of organization planning is the organization chart, an example of which appears in Figure 15. As used by most concerns, the chart provides a graphic representation of relationships as management thinks they exist. Occasionally, a chart presents what are considered to be the ideal relationships with the realization that some deviation from the ideal exists. Normally, however, the chart attempts to present the organization as is. Companies vary greatly in their use of organization charts. Some, including small ones, have carefully drawn organization charts, while others do not use them. Individual firms also differ in the extent to which charts are circulated or maintained as confidential information in the offices of top management.

In companies using extensive organization planning, the charts are supplemented by an organization manual. The manual typically contains not only a complete set of organization charts for the company but also descriptions of the functions assigned to the various organization components and managerial positions within the company. The specification for a managerial position outlines the general functions assigned to that position, the scope of the position and its relationship to other organization components. Responsibilities

Figure 15. *Organization Chart for Employee Relations Department*

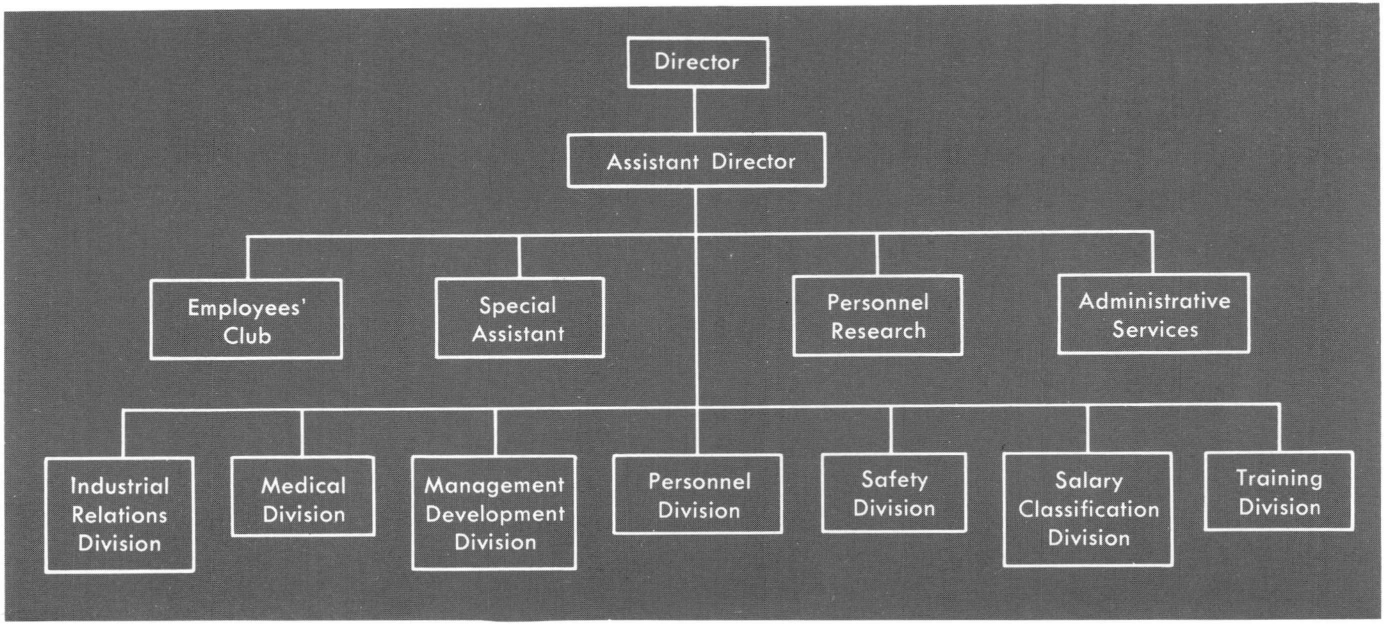

of the incumbent are indicated, and the amount and limitations of his authority are delineated. Organization manuals also contain such items as statements of managerial philosophy, objectives of the enterprise and its major departments, organizational nomenclature, and organizational principles. A sample of a description of the duties of a plant manager in a manufacturing division, as it might appear in an organization manual, is presented in Figure 16.

Figure 16. *Managerial Job Description*
Plant Manager — Burroughs Corporation

PURPOSE: Under the guidance of the Division General Manager, the Plant Manager administers and directs the plant production activities, including the manufacture of all product parts for his plant and some for other plants; the assembly of commercial and defense products; the control of production and quality standards; and the maintenance and improvement of plant facilities.

TYPICAL RESPONSIBILITIES

1. To develop and administer plans and programs to meet manufacturing objectives of the plant in accordance with Division policies, approved marketing forecasts, quality requirements, and budget limitations by establishing operating objectives and determining staffing and facility requirements for the manufacturing activity.
2. To direct the manufacture of product parts and the assembly of commercial and defense products within quality and quantity requirements.
3. To direct the development and control of production schedules for parts and products to (a) meet approved sales forecasts and requirements for inventory and interdivisional transfers and (b) economically utilize facilities and personnel. To direct the requisitioning of raw materials and equipment requirements. To direct supporting activities, including storage, internal and external traffic, packing, and shipping.
4. To direct the control of quality standards to insure that materials received from vendors, in-process parts, and finished products conform to product engineering specifications and also to insure that fabricated parts transferred to other divisions conform to specifications established by the serviced divisions.
5. To direct Industrial Engineering services which provide for the development and improvement of plant manufacturing

tools, equipment, and processes; and for the construction, maintenance, and repair of building facilities and equipment. To direct the establishment and maintenance of production time standards and methods within the manufacturing activity.

6. To review manufacturing activity objectives, budgets, processes, and facilities to determine effectiveness. To initiate studies designed to develop short-term and long-range alternative plans and programs. To evaluate findings and present program recommendations, with supporting estimates of costs and planned savings, to Division management.
7. To collaborate and coordinate with Product Engineering in (a) the formulation of new or modified commercial or defense product proposals by providing cost estimates for manufactured parts, assemblies, tooling, equipment, manpower, and time requirements; and (b) the maintenance or modification of existing products or the effective installation of approved new products by furnishing technical assistance on manufacturing tooling and process requirements during the developmental stages.
8. To utilize supporting staff functions to study and advise in resolving problems and to develop and install programs in areas such as training, budgets, employment, safety, and inventory.
9. To develop and maintain an organization plan for the manufacturing activity by reviewing and appraising staffing and productive effectiveness. To initiate studies or direct changes.
10. To insure the maintenance and development of manufacturing records and statistical data. To discuss status reports with Division management.

Scope and Influence

1. The manufacturing activity of the plant is assigned 750,000 square feet of floor space located in a multifloored structure. The total book value of plant and equipment represents $10 million with an original cost of $28 million. The average book value of assigned inventory is $18 million.
2. As a member of the Division Production Planning Committee, the Plant Manager participates in the review, recommended revisions, and/or Division approval of the preliminary marketing forecast (production schedule). Upon Corporate concurrence in the preliminary schedule, the detailed plant production schedule is formulated by the plant production-control staff and submitted to the

incumbent for evaluation, revisions, and approval before submission to the Division General Manager.

3. Upon corporate approval of the final production schedule, incumbent makes daily operating decisions, including the authorization of capital expenditures within budgeted allocations. However, when scheduled production deviates for reasons including engineering changes, revised sales forecasts, quality problems, equipment or materials shortages, and work stoppages, corrective action may be directed as indicated:
   a. Layoff: More than one day requires General Manager and Industrial Relations Manager concurrence.
   b. Overtime: May be authorized for hourly and non-exempt personnel, but exempt personnel authorization requires General Manager's concurrence.
   c. Hiring: May hire direct labor. Indirect labor hiring requires concurrence of General Manager if the addition exceeds approved manning tables.
   d. Emergency purchase of materials and repairs: Approves requisitions to purchase.
   e. Contracting for outside manufacturing: Approves requisitions for contracting services.
   f. Transfer of production when capacity exists: Generally discussed and agreed upon informally among the Plant Managers.

Source: Gordon H. Evans, *Managerial Job Descriptions in Manufacturing*, AMA Research Study 65 (New York: American Management Association, 1964), pp. 110-113.

Benefits of Organization Planning

The benefits arising from organization planning are those related to what the traditional organization theorist calls *sound organization*. He feels, for example, that charting an organization brings to light and helps eliminate weaknesses, including gaps in responsibility, overlapping of functions, duplication of effort, and working at cross purposes.

In addition, study of organization is felt to be desirable in that it provides the incumbent of a position with a clearer understanding of precisely what is expected of him, thus permitting him to maximize his contribution to the organization. It also stresses unity of command, thus eliminating confusion and making it possible to enforce responsibility upon each individual. The planned organization also specifies the authority assigned to each position, so that the incumbent will be aware of the authority available to him and so that he will not go beyond its limits.

Some Critical Views of Organization Planning

Administrators and scholars do not agree as to the desirability of organization planning. The general argument of its critics holds that some flexibility in organizational relationships and procedures is desirable. They feel that excessive detail in specifying functions and responsibilities tends to be stifling and that firms can operate efficiently without extensive organization planning and without its paraphernalia, including charts and manuals.

One company that has resisted anything resembling formal organization planning is the Ashland Oil and Refining Company.[8] The company's long-time chief executive, Paul G. Blazer, has been described as "allergic to organization charts." Blazer has expressed these reservations:

> You put a job down on paper, and people start getting jealous of their little domain, and when they see people beginning to move in on that domain, they get all upset.[9]

In general, the critics of the carefully planned organization object to rigid chains of command and organization charts that become ends in themselves. In the eyes of such critics, companies may become overorganized. They condone leapfrogging over supervisory echelons if necessary to get to the heart of a problem. Charting relationships and outlining responsibilities are thought to erect barriers to initiative and imagination. Some who stress flexibility in organization even encourage personnel to cross over organization lines, to reach into other departments with ideas, suggestions, and criticisms.

The concept of rationality in organization, which underlies organization planning, has been challenged also by Chris Argyris. Speaking of the assumption of human rationality, he notes:

> The difficulty with these assumptions is not that they are completely false. The difficulty is that as they are stated they are half-truths and incomplete. For example, man may not be able to increase his sense of self-esteem, inner worth, sense of confidence, and commitment to work, all of which are required for

---

[8]"The New Art of Free-Form Management," *Dun's Review and Modern Industry,* Vol. 84, No. 6, December 1964, pp. 30-32, 53-60.

[9]*Ibid.,* p. 31.

> outstanding performance, if he is to know exactly what to do. One might hypothesize that a man will do a good job, and afterward feel like doing another good job, to the extent that he is able to fill in the content of, or have some control over, his job. This does not mean man should not be told anything. Such an extreme would be equally frustrating to the individual as well as damaging to the organization. The point is that most jobs are so narrowly defined in scope and require so few human abilities, that they do not tend to motivate man to perform effectively.[10]

This suggests the possibility of a compromise viewpoint regarding organization planning. This view would admit the desirability of at least some study and specification of organizational relationships. In fact, it is likely that the conflict between organization planners and the "don't-fence-me-in" school appears greater on the surface than it really is in practice. This is not to deny a significant difference in viewpoint but simply to note that organization-planning critics do reach some understanding among executives as to major responsibilities and that planners do admit the need for some flexibility.

Some specification of organizational relationships appears to be desirable. Organization charts, for example, do not seem inherently bad, as some imply. General outline of responsibilities and clarification of the chain of command can have a positive effect in administration. If there is little or no regard for a reasonably systematic approach to organization, the results may be chaotic. Examples abound, as numerous executives can testify, of confusion and inefficiency that might be decreased through proper organization planning. It is possible, furthermore, that strong personal leadership may partially explain the success of companies that function efficiently in spite of poorly defined organization structures.

Planning can be overdone, however. Unused organization charts and musty organization manuals supply evidence that some of the activity in this area is not vital to the functioning of some enterprises. A very detailed prescription of organizational relationships produces a negative reaction in the case of many individuals who are more inclined to take a freewheeling approach. If there is such an excessive preoccupation with specifying organizational relationships, the organization plan may be used as a defensive mechanism rather than as an instrument to facilitate effective administration.

---

[10]Chris Argyris, *Interpersonal Competence and Organizational Effectiveness* (Homewood, Illinois: Richard D. Irwin, Inc. and The Dorsey Press, Inc., 1962), p. 30.

Organizational Status of Organization Planning

In some companies, the organization planning function has been accorded staff status and made the responsibility of a specialized staff department. This is true of the Standard Oil Company of California, Continental Oil Company, Ford Motor Company, and various other organizations. In those companies utilizing such a staff office to conduct organization studies, the function typically appears near the top of the organization, reporting to the chief executive or to one of his immediate subordinates. Its status is clearly that of a staff function, although its recommendations may carry great weight, depending upon the importance attached to the function.

In the majority of organizations, however, responsibility for conducting studies and analyses of organizational arrangements is diffused. It is considered to be a part of the regular management responsibilities of the various departments. At times, committees may be formed to deal with particular issues and questions, but the customary arrangement is for each manager to make such changes as he deems necessary in his own organization.

It might also be noted that outside management consultants are used by some companies for this purpose. This was true in the Garlock Company changes noted earlier in the chapter. The consultant provides a fresh point of view, although he suffers the handicap of a lack of detailed knowledge of the organization and its personalities. He does have the advantage of the outsider's position when it becomes necessary to recommend drastic changes in the organization structure. For this reason, management may occasionally engage a consultant even though it has a reasonably good idea of the changes that should be made.

Steps in Organization Change

Assigning the Responsibility

If a detailed study of a particular organization or organizational problem is to be undertaken, the project can be made definite by assigning the responsibility to a particular individual or committee. This makes it possible for the responsible executive to expect action. Such an assignment also places the necessary authority in the hands of the designated executive or committee to conduct the study and to secure required cooperation from other parts of the organization.

Analysis of Existing Structure

If the evaluation is a generalized analysis of the organization and its weaknesses, a proper point for beginning is the existing organization structure. Even if the study is concerned with some particular question or defect, the study may begin with an examination of the existing situation.

The analysis of an existing structure may be conducted by reference to current organization charts and manuals, if these exist. It will, of necessity, be supplemented by discussion with various interested executives.

Preparation of Ideal Structure

Social scientists are fond of constructing models for use in reasoning about real life situations. The models do not always correspond completely to the situation as it exists in the real world. Even in these situations, however, the model may be valuable as a point of departure for analyzing and reasoning about the situation which differs in some respects from the model itself.

The preparation of an ideal structure involves somewhat this same idea of the perfect model. It represents the theoretically desirable structure for the particular organization. It would be drawn, naturally, in terms of the specific objectives and purposes of the particular organization. As an ideal structure, however, it does not concern itself with the human or other limitations of the particular organization.

The ideal structure serves as a type of objective or standard. It provides a goal toward which the organization is expected to move and also a standard by which an existing structure may be evaluated. Any deviations from the ideal structure can be made with full awareness of the differences between the modified organization and the ideal structure. The ideal structure is sometimes viewed as a kind of long-range plan toward which the company aspires.

Modification of Ideal Structure

Because an organization structure must function in a real world, the organization planner must recognize existing limitations in the creation of that structure. This does not mean that the overall organization plan must be diluted. In specific spots, however, it may be necessary to make concessions based upon financial or human limitations.

There is always a significant question concerning the extent to which compromise is necessary or justified. At one extreme, the organization structure would be molded around particular individuals with little appreciation of the fundamental concepts of organization. At the other extreme, the efficient organization is adopted with little regard for personal consequences. Suppose that the ideal structure calls for an executive who must exercise responsibility exceeding the abilities of the incumbent. Should this executive be replaced, or should the structure be tailored to fit the abilities present in the organization? Clearly, no simple answer exists to a question of this type. If the organization is completely flexible, it may also be a confused and inefficient organization. If the organization rejects all compromise, however, it may be viewed as cold, heartless, and quite possibly impractical.

Modification of an ideal structure may be viewed as a temporary matter. Time often solves organizational problems. Some managers retire, and others develop their abilities with the passage of time. As years pass, then, the organization may be brought more closely into line with the structure that has been devised to function most efficiently.

Putting the Plan Into Effect

In putting the organization plan into effect, the administrator must first consider the magnitude of the change. A minor organization change may be accomplished with relatively little effort, while a major change affects the interest and efficiency of many people. The behavior of many individuals must be altered, and extensive education is often necessary.

The time required for accomplishing the change depends upon the magnitude of the change itself. If organization change involves more than minor adaptations of an existing structure, a gradual change may be desired to provide for an orderly transition to the new plan of operation. In fact, some companies have found that major reorganization—for example, from centralization to decentralization—may require years for achievement. If strong feelings are involved and some individuals are slated to lose jobs, however, it may be desirable to proceed as quickly as possible, thus minimizing the length of time in which active opposition is encountered.

Gaining acceptance of a new organization plan is one of the most difficult assignments for the administrator. Even though he is personally convinced the changed organization is desirable and beneficial for all members, the affected individuals do not always understand or accept changes of this kind without question. Major changes tend to incur considerable opposition on the part of some personnel. If an administrator is to be realistic, he may need to recognize that securing complete acceptance may be an impossibility. In such a case, he must simply proceed on the assumption that he should minimize the objections to his new plan.

In attempting to gain acceptance of the plan, participation by those individuals who are affected is often one rather fruitful approach. Whether this can be useful depends upon the extent to which participative management has been developed and the atmosphere within the organization with regard to relationships of this kind. If a suitable atmosphere does exist, and if the participants have the necessary understanding, participation may provide for useful suggestions and improvements in making an organization change.

Communication with the affected individuals is likewise a desirable way to introduce the new organization plan. Even if participation in changing the organization must be limited, it may be possible to explain the change carefully and to review the reasons for making it. This would fall short of the participative approach but should serve to gain a measure of acceptance for the new plan.

Human Factors in Organization Change

Personal and Organizational Goals

As with other phases of business enterprise, organization planning and change involve values for both the organization and its individual members. These values are not necessarily the same for all parties. What is good for the organization is not necessarily good for the individual.

The purpose here is to examine several goals or values that can be identified and to note the relationship between organizational values and personal values. One of the finest studies of these varied goals is that of Paul R. Lawrence in his analysis of changing organizational patterns.[11] Lawrence discusses the values that are involved in organ-

---

[11]Paul R. Lawrence, *The Changing of Organizational Behavior Patterns: A Case Study of Decentralization* (Boston: Division of Research, Harvard Business School, 1958), Chapter 10.

ization change in terms of three *dimensions*. The change, if it is to be an ideal change, must be beneficial when measured along each of these dimensions:

1. Achievement of organizational purpose.
2. Achievement of self-maintenance and growth.
3. Achievement of social satisfactions.

These concepts will furnish the framework for the discussion below.

Achievement of Organizational Purpose

An organization change is typically introduced because of its presumed benefit for the particular business concern. It is thought that the change will enable the organization to accomplish its objectives more effectively. Formal evaluation of a proposed change is made almost exclusively in terms of this particular value. The desirability of a change depends first of all, then, upon its effect on organizational efficiency. Few changes have a chance for adoption if they cannot be shown to have positive advantages in terms of this dimension. It should be clear that the advantages of a particular move may be subject to dispute at the time the plan is under consideration. Contemplated advantages may be inaccurately estimated or even misrepresented.

Individual Growth and Development

Members of an organization are also concerned with organization change for purely personal reasons. One of the reasons for this concern is the effect that organization change may have on the individual's opportunities for future growth and development. It is customary for the individual—particularly at the executive level—to look forward to a career in which he shows progress, and this value is consequently of vital importance to most people.

Almost any organization change could have quick and profound repercussions in terms of an individual's status and opportunity for growth. Jobs may be eliminated, departments trimmed in size, and the future possibilities for any individual greatly circumscribed or enhanced as a result of the change.

One recent study of motivation stressed the great importance of individual growth and development as a factor in the thinking of employees. "The great frequency with which this need was verbalized," stated the researchers, "indicates that the feeling that personal or professional growth was possible bulked very large in the psychological reactions of the individual to the kinds of situations he described as central to a high [level of morale]."[12]

Social Satisfactions

Employees derive social satisfactions from the work group. They feel themselves a part of a social group and enjoy the contacts and friendships involved in their association with others.

A change of organization may serve to disturb the social group and social relationships of affected employees. It is apparent that the change might be viewed as negative in nature and threatening to existing satisfactory social relationships. Or, the changed situation might be welcomed because of a promised improvement in social relationships.

To illustrate the concept, suppose that production employees worked in small groups with each employee assigned to and a part of a closely integrated team. Suppose also, for technological reasons, that the nature of work arrangements was changed in such a way as to break up the work teams that existed. If these employees were removed from their original groups, scattered as individual members along an assembly line, and denied an opportunity for close social relationships with other employees, one might conceive of the possibility for less satisfaction on the part of these employees. Measured along this dimension, then, organization change prompted by considerations of organizational efficiency might, at the same time, be damaging to the personal social satisfaction of employees.

Some noted studies of the social aspects of work organizations have been conducted by England's Tavistock Institute of Human Relations.[13] In its investigations, the Tavistock group has employed the concept of a production unit as a *socio-technical system.* According to this concept, social and psychological factors are built-in characteristics of work systems rather than supplementary features that are simply classified as "human relations." Work systems entail both a technological organization (equipment and process layout) and a related work organization with social and psychological qualities. The technological organization and work organization are interdependent, but each also has independent values of its own.

---

[12]Frederick Herzberg, Bernard Mausner, and Barbara Bloch Snyderman, *The Motivation to Work* (New York: John Wiley & Sons, Inc., 1959), p. 68.

[13]The studies noted below are described in E. L. Trist, G. W. Higgin, H. Murray, and A. B. Pollock, *Organizational Choice* (London: Tavistock Publications, 1963).

This view proved useful in explaining worker reaction and changes in operational efficiency that occurred as changes were made in coal mining technology. Traditionally, miners functioned as part of small primary work groups, called "marrow groups," in what was known as *single place* mining. A coal face of six to eleven yards in length, called a "place," was worked on any particular shift by one, or possibly two, men. Each miner was a complete miner, performing all necessary tasks at the face — not only removing coal but also setting roof supports, taking up stone in the floor, and so on. The primary work group consisted of the men who worked the same place on the same or different shifts—a maximum of six in a two-man, three-shift group. Individual workers formed their own groups by choosing fellow workmen of similar skill and working capacity. (Earnings were determined by group performance.)

Introduction of belt conveyors led to *longwall mining*—a method that differed greatly from the single place tradition. For example, work roles became specialized and the small marrow groups were replaced by specialized task groups differing from one another in status and attractiveness. This type of work organization led to a number of substandard results—productivity lower than potentially possible, inflated costs, poor management-labor relations, low job satisfaction, and high absenteeism. Subsequent modification of the work organization into a *composite longwall* method, in which there was no rigid division of labor, made possible substantial improvements in these areas. The Tavistock studies thus demonstrate the close relationship between organization and the social satisfactions of work. The social structure of business organizations is examined at greater length in Chapter 15.

Reconciling the Various Goals

It would be desirable, if possible, to create such changes in organization structure, or to create them in such a way, that they would work out satisfactorily in terms of all three goals or dimensions. Unfortunately, this may not always be possible, but Lawrence's tentative conclusion was that the goals are not necessarily irreconcilable.[14]

In reasoning about organization changes and considering the possibility of undertaking organization change, an awareness of the different goals permits careful analysis of alternatives with full con-

---

[14]Lawrence, *op. cit.*, p. 217.

sideration of the different aspects of the case. It may help also in understanding the nature of difficulties or objections that arise in connection with a proposed change in organization.

The Challenge of Parkinson's Law

A few years ago, C. Northcote Parkinson wrote satirically on organization and administration. In his famous "law," he stated that "work expands so as to fill the time available for its completion."[15] Parkinson's suggestion is that organizations do not grow in a logical fashion merely to care for increased work loads. In other words, one can draw no conclusion about the magnitude of the work performed on the basis of the size of the organization. "The rise in the total of those employed," said Parkinson, "is governed by Parkinson's Law and would be much the same whether the volume of the work were to increase, diminish, or even disappear."[16]

If there is a measure of truth in the writing of Parkinson (and as a satirist, of course, Parkinson overstates his case), then it would appear that personal considerations are influential in the determination of organization design. Those in a position to influence decisions regarding organization may act on the basis of "what's best for me" rather than "what's best for the company." The term *empire building* has been applied to situations of this kind, and those thought to be building organizations for the primary purpose of increasing personal prestige have been denounced as *empire builders.*

This idea of Parkinson's goes beyond mere recognition that organization changes affect people either favorably or unfavorably. Far from being mere pawns, the individuals in the organization manipulate the structure to maximize results for themselves as individuals. The extent to which personal considerations may thus directly affect organization planning is unknown. The widespread interest in *Parkinson's Law* on the part of practicing administrators indicates that the possibility may be less remote than sometimes believed. It is probably a subtle influence where it does occur and thus may not be recognized except by those who are unusually perceptive in their observations of administrative behavior. It may also occur in a subconscious way in an executive analysis of a proposed organization plan. Although it is difficult to assess the importance of this danger, Parkinson's Law does serve to alert us to the possibility of an undesirable influence in the design of organizations.

---

[15]C. Northcote Parkinson, *Parkinson's Law* (Boston: Houghton Mifflin Company, 1957), p. 2. Used by permission of Houghton Mifflin Company and John Murray (Publishers) Ltd.

[16]*Ibid.*, p. 4.

Summary

A need for *organization study* and *organization change* arises both from the dynamic nature of business organizations and from inefficiencies in existing organizational arrangements. Technological change, in particular, requires organizational modifications, although the effects of technology's impact on organization structure are only partially understood at present. Administrators and scholars disagree as to the desirability of formal *organization planning* with its emphasis upon organization charts and manuals. Proponents of organization planning believe that it contributes to a smoothly functioning and efficient organization structure. Critics of organization planning contend that detailed specification of responsibilities and functions tends to be stifling and to destroy the initiative of employees.

The steps in organization planning and change include assignment of responsibility for the study, analysis of the existing structure, and implementation of the plan. The last step is often the most troublesome because of the impact of the change upon the interests of individuals who are affected.

Organization planning and change involve *values* and *goals* both for the organization and its individual members. Although personal and organizational goals may conflict, they are not necessarily irreconcilable. Paul R. Lawrence has suggested that organization changes be evaluated in terms of the following three dimensions: (1) achievement of organizational purpose; (2) achievement of self-maintenance and growth; and (3) achievement of social satisfactions. Ideally, a change would produce positive effects along all three dimensions.

According to the argument of *Parkinson's Law*, personal considerations directly affect the design of organizations. Following this reasoning, individual managers *(empire builders)* are believed to manipulate the structure in order to maximize results for themselves.

Discussion Questions

1. Give several examples, including some based upon your own observations, of organization changes caused by the dynamic nature of business enterprise.

2. Examine the list of organizational deficiencies on p. 290-91 compiled by the American Management Association seminar group. Can all of these be corrected by proper attention to the organization structure? Be specific.

3. Explain the nature of organization charts and manuals as used in formal organization planning.

4. Is it true, speaking of formal organization planning, that if you "put a man in a square" you limit him? What would be the nature of this limitation, and how serious would it be?

5. Do you feel that organizations with which you are acquainted would function smoothly if the various members were urged to reach into other departments and to see what improvements might be made?

6. What are the advantages of having a separate staff office charged with responsibility for organization planning?

7. In the study of a proposed change in organization, will participation by the individuals who are involved impede or contribute to the study?

8. Contrast the basic ideas involved in the Lawrence and Parkinson studies of organization change.

Supplementary Reading

Bennis, Warren G., "Organizational Revitalization," *California Management Review,* Vol. 9, No. 1, Fall 1966, pp. 51-60.

Brabb, George J. and Earl B. Hutchins, "Electronic Computers and Management Organization," *California Management Review,* Vol. 6, No. 1, Fall 1963, pp. 33-42.

Daniel, D. Ronald, "Reorganizing for Results," *Harvard Business Review,* Vol. 44, No. 6, November-December 1966, pp. 96-104.

Glueck, William F., "Applied Organization Analysis," *Academy of Management Journal,* Vol. 10, No. 3, September 1967, pp. 223-234.

__________, "Where Organization Planning Stands Today," *Personnel,* Vol. 44, No. 4, July-August 1967, pp. 19-26.

Greiner, Larry E., "Patterns of Organization Change," *Harvard Business Review,* Vol. 45, No. 3, May-June 1967, pp. 119-130.

Hershey, Robert L., "Organizational Planning," *Business Topics,* Vol. 10, No. 1, Winter 1962, pp. 29-40.

Hickson, D. J., "A Convergence in Organization Theory," *Administrative Science Quarterly,* Vol. 11, No. 2, September 1966, pp. 224-237.

Lee, Hak Chong, *The Impact of Electronic Data Processing Upon the Patterns of Business Organization and Administration.* Albany: School of Business, State University of New York, 1965.

Lipstreu, Otis and Kenneth A. Reed, "A New Look at the Organizational Implications of Automation," *Academy of Management Journal,* Vol. 8, No. 1, March 1965, pp. 24-31.

McNulty, James E., "Organizational Change in Growing Enterprises," *Administrative Science Quarterly,* Vol. 7, No. 1, June 1962, pp. 1-21.

Melcher, Robert D., "Roles and Relationships: Clarifying the Manager's Job," *Personnel,* Vol. 44, No. 3, May-June 1967, pp. 33-41.

Read, William H., "The Decline of the Hierarchy in Industrial Organizations," *Business Horizons,* Vol. 8, No. 3, Fall 1965, pp. 71-75.

Shaul, Donald R., "What's Really Ahead for Middle Management?" *Personnel,* Vol. 41, No. 6, November-December 1964, pp. 8-16.

Sherman, Harvey, "Organization Planning: How to Get Results Your People Can Live With," *Management Review,* Vol. 55, No. 10, October 1966, pp. 5-14.

14

Staffing the Organization

A good coach often appears better or worse on the basis of the material at his disposal. Even a mediocre coach occasionally wins a championship if his players are unusually talented. The quality of personnel in a business organization similarly affects the performance of business firms. Acquiring and developing able employees are, for this reason, matters of prime concern to the administrator. Because of the overriding importance of managerial personnel in particular, this phase of staffing has been selected for treatment. Staffing activities include recruitment and development of managers to fill their assigned positions capably and also to advance to higher administrative posts.

The Managerial Job

Quest for Qualified Managerial Personnel

In recent years, we have witnessed vigorous efforts in executive recruitment and development. College recruitment programs have multiplied, with campus visits by industrial organizations becoming commonplace. A few corporations have even established their own management institutes. Others have sent management personnel back to school to participate in some type of executive development program.

Such activities, which at times appear feverish, are based upon a growing awareness of the need for capable management personnel. The success of a business is seen to depend upon its leadership. And, when an organization pauses to examine its managerial potential, glaring deficiencies are often apparent. The need for developing managerial personnel becomes particularly pressing in the case of rapidly changing and expanding organizations.

Increasing Complexity of Management

Demands upon the modern corporate executive exceed those that applied to his predecessor of a half century earlier. The types of ability and performance that were adequate for the earlier period no longer assure business success.

Some of the factors that have contrived to increase the complexity of management are the following:

1. Technological developments.
2. Increasing use of quantitative methods in management.
3. Rising standards of public responsibility for managers.
4. Greater impact of government upon business organizations.
5. International developments affecting business operations.

Because of the increased complexity of management, the problem of staffing has a distinctly qualitative flavor. Business organizations must not only secure the right *number* of managers but also locate and develop enough *qualified* managers. Leaders are needed who can assume the broader responsibilities of the current decade.

The rapid changes in business and in the process of management not only affect recruitment of new managers but also contribute to the obsolescence of those already employed. Unless steps are taken to continue a manager's education and to keep him up to date, he quickly falls behind. As John Mee, Mead Johnson professor of management at Indiana University, has so aptly put it, "All managers are in a foot race between retirement and obsolescence; the best they can hope for is a photo-finish." Individual and even company efforts, as discussed in a later section of this chapter, are necessary to maintain managerial competence in the face of this growing complexity in the role of management.

Managerial Specialization

A modern business organization needs both specialists and generalists in its management structure. Specialists are managers whose responsibilities are concerned with one functional area of the business — sales, finance, research, personnel, and so on. Managers in these functional areas develop expert knowledge and abilities in their respective fields of specialization. The typical business organization needs far more functional specialists than it does generalists. In recruiting, therefore, the search is ordinarily for those who can contribute directly in some functional area.

This creates two staffing problems for the organization. First, the specialist is inclined to view business problems from his own position within a functional area. Because of his restricted viewpoint, the production executive sees a problem as a production problem, while a marketing manager most appreciates its marketing aspects. To minimize this weakness, there is a need to develop within each functional manager some conception of the values inherent in the other functional areas and an ability to take an overall point of view in management decisions.

The second problem concerns the need for general managers. At some level, managers must rise above specialized compartments and provide direction for a number of functional areas. The president or executive vice president or manager of a product division must resolve production, sales, and financial differences for the overall benefit of the business. A background within one field of functional specialization does not in itself equip an executive for the general management role. One staffing objective, therefore, is the transformation of specialists into generalists.

Systems Approach to Staffing

Management development is one phase of staffing that can profitably use the systems viewpoint. Following this viewpoint, development of the individual manager can be visualized as the improvement of one component of the system. If the fundamental weakness lies in the system rather than in the individual, however, the process of development may be misdirected. The manager's abilities may be sharpened for use in a system so weak that even sharp abilities are insufficient. Figure 17 presents a graphic portrayal of a systems view of management development.

One company experienced repeated conflicts between various individuals and units in a manufacturing department.[1] Analysis of

---

[1] Reprinted with permission of The Macmillan Company from *The Measure of Management* by Eliot D. Chapple & Leonard R. Sayles. © by The Macmillan Company 1961.

Figure 17. *Management Development: A Systems View*

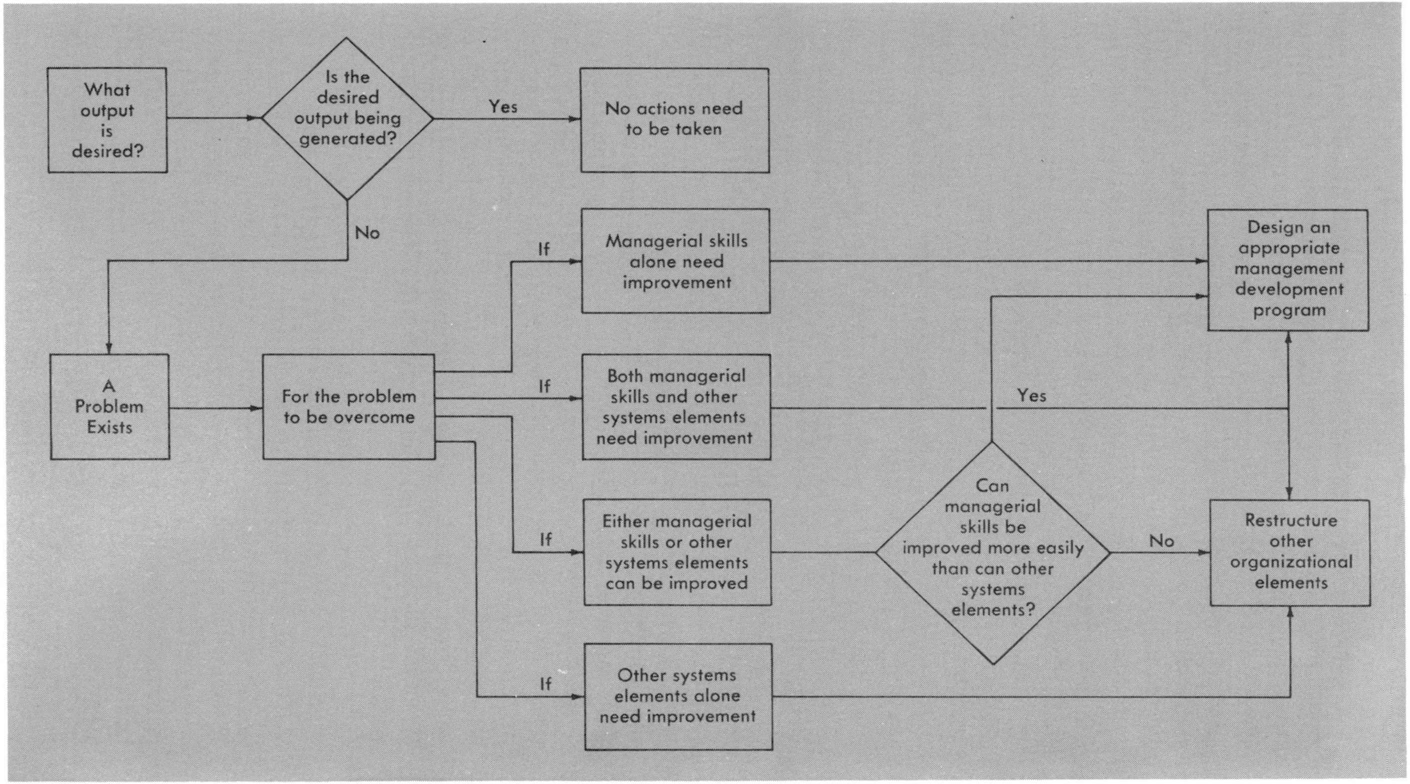

Source: Paul S. Greenlaw, "Management Development: A Systems View," *Personnel Journal,* Vol. 43, No. 4, April 1964, p. 210.

the situation revealed that the friction was an almost inevitable by-product of a faulty organizational arrangement. The work of manufacturing employees who reported to a general superintendent was closely tied to that of inspectors who reported to a chief inspector, material handlers who reported to a production planning chief, and maintenance repairmen who reported to a chief mechanic. Necessary adjustments in materials handling schedules involved a great deal of checking between the manufacturing and materials handling units and their respective supervisors. Arguments went to the vice president of manufacturing for settlement. Higher management might have reasoned that lower-level managers needed human relations courses so that they could learn to cooperate more effectively. Instead, they rearranged the organization structure to eliminate the difficulty—placing material handlers, some repairmen, and even a portion of the inspection function under the direct control of the production superintendent. The perspective provided by a systems viewpoint revealed faulty organization to be the primary cause of the conflict and indicated the inappropriateness of management development as a solution.

The systems concept may also help to explain the inadequacy of much supervisory training. One of the recurring problems is the training of supervisors in better supervisory methods only to find that the system to which they return is not prepared for them and their new methods. The supervisor may be urged to adopt a democratic management style, only to discover that his own superiors do not see it in the same way. Changing the quality of one component in the system is inadequate. The system must in some way be changed as a whole. Training programs that start at the top and work down or that provide for training conferences for vertical or diagonal slices of the organization are attempts to deal with this problem.

Development of personnel data systems for entire organizations represents still another attempt to apply systems management to staffing. A vast amount of information about people may be stored for quick retrieval through use of an electronic computer. If such a personnel information system is fully developed, internal recruitment is simplified. Employees with desired qualifications can be located immediately anywhere within the system. The IBM Corporation has even experimented with the manpower planning technique of simulation.[2] Simulation involves construction of a model of a real

---

[2]John J. Bricker, "The Personnel Systems Concept," in *The Systems Approach to Personnel Management,* Management Bulletin No. 62 (New York: American Management Association, 1965), pp. 16-20.

system so that the researcher can make a change in one part of the model so that the resulting effects on the rest of the model will reflect accurately what would happen with such a change in the real world. The work force simulator of one IBM plant is an example of a computer program model. In evaluating alternative manpower plans involving recruitment, retraining, and so on, management can obtain information from the simulator to assist in making the decision.

Types of Managerial Skills

Qualities of Successful Managers

There have been many attempts to identify the characteristics of effective managers.[3] In analyzing such qualities, the hope is to discover the secrets that will facilitate executive selection and development. Evaluations of executive qualities have attempted to rate such traits as dependability, initiative, fairness, cooperation, and ambition. The primary difficulty in appraisals of this type is that they often distinguish better between good people and bad people than between good managers and bad managers. An effective manager usually has these qualities in some measure, but this has not told us much about his management ability. Crawford H. Greenewalt has expressed this reaction as follows:

> Most recitals of executive virtues sound, as a matter of fact, rather like the McGuffey Readers or those little cards which pop out of penny scales certifying that the customer is loyal, trustworthy, kind, honest, generous, and weighs 198 pounds. The difficulty is that we have seen men who have all of these characteristics, but who would never make good executives. Other men might have a relatively poorer score in certain categories, but would, in their own way, be among the best. People are people and will, I suspect, continue to confound all efforts to classify them in neat little pigeonholes.[4]

Mr. Greenewalt goes on to say that "the basic requirement of executive capacity is the ability to create a harmonious whole out of what the academic world calls dissimilar disciplines."[5] The manager must get teamwork from the members of his organization. The diffi-

---

[3]See, for example, Perrin Stryker, "On the Meaning of Executive Qualities," *Fortune,* Vol. 57, No. 6, June 1958, pp. 116-119, 186-189.

[4]Crawford H. Greenewalt, *The Uncommon Man* (New York: McGraw-Hill Book Company, 1959), p. 61.

[5]*Ibid.,* p. 64.

culty of defining executive abilities should not lead one to the conclusion that there is no such thing. According to Mr. Greenewalt's observation, "while executive ability cannot be catalogued or measured, it can almost invariably be recognized."[6]

Another approach to analysis of executive capacity, as suggested by Robert L. Katz, concentrates upon skills rather than personal characteristics.[7] The three basic skills serving as the basis for successful management are thought to be *technical, human,* and *conceptual.* In the following sections, attention is given to each of these types of abilities.

Technical Skills

Although managerial positions differ in the amount of technical skill required, most necessitate some ability of this nature. A laboratory supervisor, for example, needs to understand the nature of laboratory tests conducted under his supervision. A controller requires a knowledge of accounting. A production manager should have some conception of production technology.

At one time, the best technician was often thought to be the best manager. Managerial personnel were selected, accordingly, on the basis of their technical competence. It was discovered, however, that technical ability and management ability did not always go hand in hand. As a result, a change in management thinking about staffing qualifications became evident. Because technical know-how did not constitute ability to manage, the more obvious requirements — supervisory skill and leadership—were adopted as a substitute. This led to de-emphasis of technical skill as a requirement for management personnel. The search was for managers, not technicians.

The other extreme became just as uncomfortable, however. Polish and effectiveness in group leadership does not completely offset a deficiency in technical competence. It is difficult, if not impossible, to rely exclusively upon the technical knowledge of others.

> It is not contended, of course, that a manager should not make use of experts; in fact, in modern large-scale business it is impossible to operate without them. But the manager who believes he can direct them wisely when he knows nothing about the subject matter is likely to be employing more than his company can

---

[6] *Ibid.,* p. 65.

[7] Robert L. Katz, "Skills of an Effective Administrator," *Harvard Business Review,* Vol. 33, No. 1, January-February 1955, pp. 33-42.

> support and too many whose expertise is actually skill in devising new boondoggles to make themselves appear essential. For example, one company had no less than forty people working full time on organization charts and manuals. Their "full employment" was terminated only after total employment (and profits) had dropped sharply for several years.
>
> Nor is it contended that a manager's work does not require planning, organizing, and the other management skills. But these skills cannot exist in a vacuum, and successful exercise of them depends largely on a knowledge of what is being planned and organized.[8]

A manager need not be the best in a specialized field or have more technical knowledge than anyone else. But he must have sufficient knowledge to lift him above the level of technical illiteracy. The trend toward greater rationality and careful analysis in management decision making makes this a skill of increasing importance.[9]

No doubt the hierarchical level has some bearing on the need for technical knowledge and competence. Near the work level, the appropriate technical skills and knowledge are almost imperative. At higher levels, decision making is concerned with issues of a broader nature. Even here, some technical knowledge may be extremely useful. It is impossible for an executive to be well-informed concerning all detailed areas, however. Many chief executives appear to function effectively with only a superficial knowledge of some functional areas.

Human Relations Skills

Competence in interpersonal relations is an important asset to the administrator. This arises from the fact that a manager accomplishes work through the efforts of other individuals. Managers who are able to develop the confidence and support of others have an advantage over those who rub people the wrong way.

It is clear that executives differ in their ability to secure the cooperation of subordinates and colleagues. Some administrators stand out as a result of their personal leadership, while others find

---

[8]Ernest Dale, "Executives Who Can't Manage," *The Atlantic Monthly,* Vol. 210, No. 1, July 1962, pp. 60-61. Copyright © 1962, by the Atlantic Monthly Company, Boston, Mass. Reprinted with permission.

[9]See Melvin Anshen, "Management and Change," in *Management And Corporations 1985,* eds. Melvin Anshen and George Leland Bach (New York: McGraw-Hill Book Company, 1960), pp. 237-238.

it difficult to win the loyalty, admiration, and cooperation of others. The variation in human relations skills of successful managers indicates there is a range of ability that permits success. Some minimum amount of human relations skill may be required for effective performance, but apparently some managers are effective without exceptional skill in this area.

In choosing individuals for management positions on the basis of human relations abilities, there is a danger of creating conformity while stifling individualism and creative ability. This subject is treated at greater length in Chapter 19.

The human relations movement has placed great stress upon this type of skill as the important element in managerial success. In reaction, some feel that the human relations principle has been blown up beyond its real importance. This is not to say that there is nothing to the idea, but simply that the emphasis has sometimes been too great.

In summary, understanding and skill in human relations constitute important qualities for the administrator. It is possible to overemphasize human relations, however, to the point of obscuring the need for other management talents.

Conceptual Skills

It has often been suggested that an education which teaches one to think is a good education. In business management, the problems are such as to challenge the thinking and mental abilities of the manager. He must be able to discern problems, devise solutions, analyze data, and exercise judgment. These tasks are often difficult and intellectually demanding.

Many business problems, unfortunately, do not lend themselves to easy solutions. Like difficult mathematical problems, it takes both skill and effort to think them through. In production management, in questions of location, in financial administration, and in other areas, the issues may call for the very best thinking of which the manager is capable.

The extent of this requirement varies from position to position within the organization. At lower levels, in which management directs work of a routine nature, it may be possible to perform successfully with minimum conceptual ability. At higher levels and in directing activities of a more complex nature, the demand for conceptual skills increases. The following statement supports the relationship between level and demand for conceptual skills:

> At the top level of an organization, conceptual skill becomes the most important skill of all for successful administration. A chief executive may lack technical or human skills and still be effective if he has subordinates who have strong abilities in these directions. But if his conceptual skill is weak, the success of the whole organization may be jeopardized.[10]

The manager's technical and conceptual skills are combined in the decision-making process. Competency in both areas—that is, both technical and conceptual skills—should lead to excellence in decision making.

Recruitment of Managerial Talent

Planning Managerial Requirements

The staffing process must begin with a determination of executive requirements and the steps necessary to fulfill these requirements. Questions to be answered are both quantitative and qualitative in nature. One question is simply, "How many managers will be required?" A supplementary question concerns the types of duties involved and the qualifications necessary for staffing these positions. While the staffing plan is concerned with managerial requirements for the following year, it may also be a type of long-range planning in which estimates are formulated for managerial requirements for the next five or ten years.

It is possible for an organization to experience a severe staffing problem as a result of the simultaneous retirement of several key executives. In the Whittier-Hawks Manufacturing Corporation (a real company whose name here is fictitious), the age of top-level managers was such that four of the top six executives were due to reach retirement within a four-year period.[11] The diagram on page 320 reveals the nature of this difficulty. The need for planning to minimize problems of this type is clear.

In estimating staff requirements, a number of different factors must be considered. Probable losses from retirements, deaths, resignations, and other losses must be calculated. Estimates of this kind require attention to age distribution of present staff, historical rate

[10]Katz, *op. cit.*, p. 38.

[11]John F. Garde, Jr., "The Insidious Management Cycle," *Dun's Review and Modern Industry*, Vol. 79, No. 4, April 1962, pp. 54-58C.

of attrition, and so on. Any expansion plans of the business similarly affect estimated requirements. This factor necessitates a prediction of business trends as seen by the top policy-making level of the organization. In view of the variety of factors involved in these estimates, it is often difficult to specify an exact number of personnel that will be required at a specified future date. An estimate is usually superior to no estimate at all, however, and the planner may be able to propose a range of requirements containing both conservative and optimistic estimates.

What's Wrong at Whittier-Hawks[12]

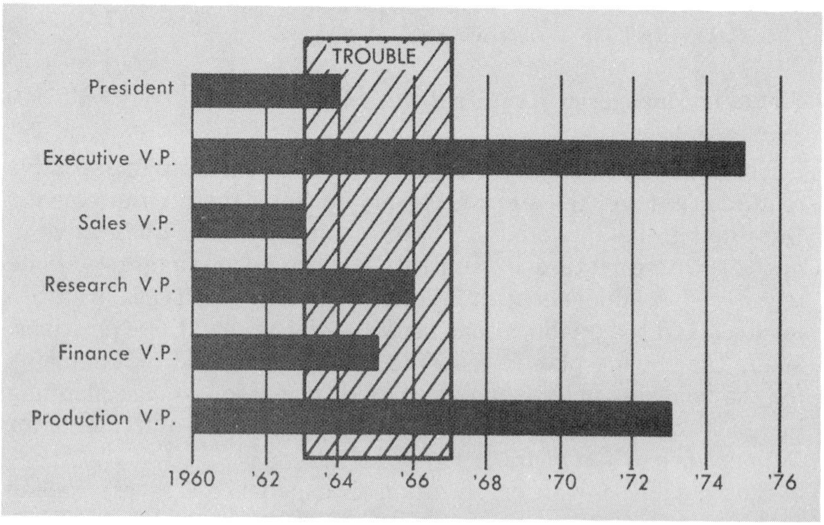

Management sometimes fails to appreciate the importance of careful planning and aggressive recruitment in advance of need. The idea persists that an abundance of applicants exists so that vacancies need cause little concern. As a result of such thinking, the recruitment process proceeds haphazardly. The net effect may be a series of blunders and unfortunate consequences as suggested in the following quotation:

> But why do organizations which openly profess their dependence on the success of professional personnel recruitment make staggering strategic and tactical errors? For instance:

[12]*Ibid.*, p. 54.

- Starting the year with a major program which is abruptly terminated in conjunction with a *layoff* of professionals.
- Trying to hire really exceptional people at salaries so low as to be laughable.
- Hiring people of a given type who leave in droves after a few months because there is no appropriate work for them.

When these flops are studied, it usually turns out that the basic, grass-roots planning was so sketchy that disaster was almost inevitable.[13]

Sources of Management Talent

The story is told of a young advertising executive who, feeling stymied in his job, submitted a detailed application in response to a blind ad calling for a marketing director at a salary of $50,000. He later discovered that the ad had been placed by his own company!

> Summoned by the president, he said: "I expect you want me to leave immediately."
>
> "On the contrary," the president beamed, "we're making you marketing director. We never dreamed you had done so much here until we got your letter."[14]

The moral of this story is that there is a need for evaluation of available sources of management talent and a determination of the extent to which each may be profitably used.

The organization itself constitutes one source of executive personnel. In filling vacancies, many corporations emphasize promotion from within. This has the advantage of rewarding outstanding performance on the part of the existing staff. It also secures executive personnel who have experience with the organization and its methods of operation. As a source of executives, it is limited by the quality of personnel available for promotion. At one time, business organizations employed office boys who eventually became their presidents. This is much less common today, but most organizations have junior executive and professional personnel who may be considered for advancement. A danger in internal recruitment, or at least in extensive reliance upon this source, is the inbreeding that may occur.

---

[13]P. W. Maloney, *Management's Talent Search: Recruiting Professional Personnel* (New York: American Management Association, 1961), p. 9.

[14]"Where are the $50,000 Jobs?" *Dun's Review and Modern Industry,* Vol. 80, No. 2, August 1962, p. 33.

This is particularly serious in positions requiring originality and new ideas.

Other business organizations—often competitors—may also be used to train or supply managerial talent. This leads to the practice of executive recruitment or *piracy*. The practice has both its rewarding and its perilous aspects. College-trained personnel who have been seasoned by experience are superior to college graduates of the same caliber without work experience. A possible weakness is that second-rate ability is most abundant in such markets. If the individual is outstanding, his present employer often has taken steps to discourage wanderlust, thus making it difficult to interest him in outside opportunities. The employing corporations differ in their ability to stand as raid-proof against the enticements of competitors. By using the incentives of attractive salary and challenging opportunity, however, it may be possible to hire executive personnel away from some competitive organizations. Of course, the assumption here is that such recruitment is not based upon the unethical objective of stealing secrets or customers from one's competitors.

There are mixed feelings on the part of management concerning the ethics or desirability of recruitment from other companies. It is an increasingly common practice, however, and is not limited to the lower levels of the organization. For example, the National Semiconductor Corporation announced in 1967 that it had lured from its competitors a new team of eight executives, including a new president![15] The new president moved from the No. 2 spot (general manager) at Fairchild Semiconductor, a division of Fairchild Camera and Instrument Corporation. Other members of the new team also came from Fairchild Semiconductor as well as from Texas Instruments, Inc., Perkin-Elmer Corporation, and the Hewlett-Packard Company. The new executives were administrators, and the new employer received, through this acquisition of managerial personnel, what was described as a "massive injection of management skill."

The practice of job switching (from one company to another) by managers has grown substantially in recent years. A 1965 estimate suggested that about five times as many middle managers were switching jobs annually as was the case five years earlier.[16] Some factors contributing to job switching are the strong demand relative

---

[15]"Fast Footwork in an Industry Talent Hunt," *Business Week,* No. 1958, March 11, 1967, pp. 132-136.

[16]"Increased Job Hopping By Junior Executives Vexes Personnel Men," *The Wall Street Journal,* January 21, 1965, p. 1.

to the available supply of managers, the trend toward professional management (with an emphasis on administrative ability and loyalty to the profession as well as the employer), and the emergence of specialized executive recruiting firms.

Colleges and universities offer still another source for recruitment of executive personnel. This source is discussed separately below.

College Recruitment

In recent years, more and more corporate recruiters have made their way to college placement offices. This trend is apparently based on a widespread recognition that the noncollege executive is rapidly becoming a rare bird. To provide a supply of management potential, a new crop of college graduates is brought into the business each year. This permits the company to obtain college graduates at a salary that is initially lower than that required for direct recruitment from other employers. In addition, the employer has access to the most capable applicants before they have made commitments to other concerns.

This increased attention to college recruiting has led to bidding up salary levels for college graduates — particularly in areas of shortest supply. College placement offices have been established, and recruiting routines have been developed. Business concerns carefully select representatives who will most effectively represent them on the campus. Young, successful operating managers are often assigned recruitment responsibilities.

The type of graduate to be selected is a continuing question. One key controversy concerns the extent to which the graduate should have a liberal education versus specialized training. Business spokesmen sometimes stress the need for broadly educated individuals who can assume general management responsibilities. This type of educational background appears particularly appropriate for top-management levels. Very few college graduates are able to start as presidents, however, and they must consequently be able to function as accountants, engineers, salesmen, or in other positions requiring some special education. Ideally, the applicant should have both a liberal education and specialized training that will make him immediately useful, but it is difficult to obtain a mixture of this type within the limitations of a customary college career.

Another problem in college recruitment concerns the type of young person who may be attracted to a managerial career. Can business organizations obtain a reasonable share of the ambitious, able, educated young people? Or must business content itself with those less-qualified students who fail to respond to the opportunities in college teaching, scientific research, public service, and other non-business positions? Many gifted college students today feel that business careers offer insufficient challenge, that such careers are appropriate for only the practical "plodders" who lack a capacity for the challenging life of the true professional or intellectual. In short, many able students have concluded that business is "for the birds." This type of thinking is sufficiently prevalent that some see it as a significant business problem.[17]

Industry's tendency to withhold responsibility from youthful newcomers too long has been widely criticized for its contribution to this problem. Many training programs are unnecessarily long and serve merely to postpone the day that the young person can hold a responsible position. To improve the image of business in the minds of gifted young people, business must provide career opportunities that permit them to move quickly into positions that challenge their abilities and that provide the satisfaction of performing worthwhile work.

Selecting the Individual with Potential

A stream can rise no higher than its source. In management development, there is likewise a limit established by the quality of the applicant who is employed. A recruit with only middle-management potential does not make an outstanding chief executive.

The big problem is in distinguishing between "winners" and "also-rans." In campus recruitment, particularly, a crystal ball seems essential in confidently picking a winner. If the company waits until an applicant has demonstrated his success elsewhere, the problem is less acute. This is expensive, however, and most firms must employ applicants on the basis of their *potential* for growth and development.

Scientific selection is still more a matter of hope than realization. Tests are often used to assist in selection, but the validity of such selection devices often leaves much to be desired. Of course, the most

---

[17]For discussion of this problem, see Peter Drucker, "Is Business Letting Young People Down?" *Harvard Business Review,* Vol. 43, No. 6, November-December 1965, pp. 49-55; Roger M. Blough, "Business Can Satisfy the Young Intellectual," *Harvard Business Review,* Vol. 44, No. 1, January-February 1966, pp. 49-57; John S. Fielden, "The Right Young People for Business," *Harvard Business Review,* Vol. 44, No. 2, March-April 1966, pp. 76-83.

objective methods possible should be used. At present, however, we can make no claim to any sensational achievements in predicting success for executive personnel.

Development of Managerial Personnel

Basic Elements of Management Development

The effective manager is one who is properly developed in terms of basic intellectual abilities, specialized job skills, and human relations abilities. The first is concerned with the general qualities of the mind, regardless of their area of application. The individual who is properly developed in this area has learned to think and to respect the scientific method with its emphasis on objective, factual information. He is aware of the role of emotion to the point that he can take a basically rational approach to the problems confronting him. He is also able to examine issues and problems in perspective, not allowing significant features to be obliterated by trivial details. The ideas and thinking of others are accepted and given appropriate consideration even though they differ from the personal viewpoint of such an individual.

Much of this basic intellectual development necessarily occurs prior to employment. Indeed, the aims of college education are directly concerned with these attributes. It is not a type of development that can or should be limited to the classroom, however. Private reading, for example, may contribute to the intellectual development of executives whose schooling occurred years earlier as well as to those who have never had the opportunities of extensive education. Many, perhaps most, company training activities contain at least some features of this nature. This is not ordinarily the core of such training efforts, however. Most training programs are specifically job related. Some companies, however, are experimenting with development programs devoted to this type of general intellectual conditioning. A number of leading corporations, including the American Telephone and Telegraph Company and the International Business Machines Corporation now send selected managers to special university courses—from a few weeks to eight or ten months in length — emphasizing such subjects as history, literature, art, economics, philosophy, and logic.[18]

---

[18]"Specialists Try a Wider Track," *Business Week,* No. 1874, July 31, 1965, pp. 56-57.

Though basic intellectual skills provide an excellent foundation for management, they are insufficient in themselves. Specialized job skills must be added. A sales manager, for example, must know a great deal about marketing and managerial approaches that may be used in selling. He must have some knowledge of the products, advertising, motivation of salesmen, and consumer motivation. In a formal college education, some of this knowledge can be acquired. Accountants study accounting theory, and marketing trainees learn something about marketing functions and methods. Probably the greatest part of specialized job skills, however, must be developed following employment. Certainly, any managerial position has some unique features that make such specialized job training indispensable.

Human relations abilities are some of the most difficult to develop. Work experience of the individual is particularly significant in acquiring ability in human relations. In training programs, management often attempts to sharpen the manager's sensitivity and judgment in human relations problems.

Management Development Methods

The Principle of Self-Development. Although an organization can provide opportunities for managerial development, it cannot actually develop the managers. In the final analysis, it is the manager himself who must accomplish his own development. This viewpoint assumes that the process of education or development is not passive. Sending a manager to a training conference, for example, is no guarantee that he will gain the educational value and be a better manager as a result of the experience. If any real development is to occur, the manager must assume some responsibility for his own progress. The extent of his ambition and interest in preparation for effective performance and advancement influences his rate of growth and development. Of course, the organization can create the proper atmosphere, provide opportunities for development, and encourage interest in activities of this kind.

Job-Centered Training. Perhaps the most basic or fundamental approach to management development is that of managerial experience. The manager learns to manage by managing. Every manager owes some debt to his own opportunities for experience as a manager.

Such experience may be more or less productive depending upon the type of direction and guidance provided by higher management. Extensive delegation of authority, for example, seeks to maximize development through managerial experience. The manager who has no opportunity to make significant decisions has little opportunity to develop decision-making ability. If a departmental manager takes no personal interest in the development of his subordinate managers, their learning falls below that which is potentially possible.

Management Responsibility for Executive Development. The philosophy of some companies holds that no planned executive development is necessary. Even some who believe in recruiting people with potential feel that the cream will come to the top by itself. According to such thinking, merely selecting individuals with the requisite ability will result in an adequate supply of capable executive personnel at the appropriate time. Executive development in such firms operates on a haphazard, catch-as-catch-can basis.

There is another point of view which holds that management must assume a responsibility for actively planning the executive development program. Haphazard methods are thought to produce unpredictable and unsatisfactory results. Although some departments may develop managerial personnel satisfactorily without planning, other areas are less fortunate in seeing executives develop the right types of managerial abilities. Some of the skepticism regarding formally planned development is attributable to unfortunate experiences in management development programs that emphasized techniques of training rather than content.

As an example of managerial responsibility for executive development, Henry Ford II insists upon acceptance of this responsibility by all managerial personnel. It is their task to supervise the development of managers reporting to them.

> With him it is not an occasional interest. "If you just do this with your left hand when it is free," he says, "you get absolutely nothing."
>
> He insists that all his executives work as hard at it as he does. Earlier this year, he told them their performance in training management would be a consideration in determining their bonuses.[19]

Job Rotation. One method of improving upon direct job experience in management development is to broaden that experience through a system of rotation. Such a job rotation plan seeks to maximize the individual's experience by shifting him periodically from one job to another. Individuals selected for such programs are moved at the end of some stipulated period—say one year—and the par-

[19]How Henry Ford II Reshaped His Company," *Business Week,* No. 1674, September 30, 1961, p. 61.

ticular positions they hold at any given time are viewed as training positions.

A less formalized variation of job rotation is also used by many organizations. In promotion and transfer decisions, an attempt is made to move individuals in such a way as to facilitate their development. This system does not operate on a calendar basis, however, and there is no planned series of steps or transfers. A manager, for example, may fill a position in engineering for two or three years. If a vacancy occurs in sales or production management at the end of that time, consideration is given to shifting the engineering manager into such a position. Many such moves involve promotions as well as reassignments to other types of work.

Supervisory Coaching. The supervisory manager is normally expected to provide guidance to his subordinates. In some cases, this is formalized to the point of prescribing periodic interviews for the purpose of analyzing the work of subordinates and their training needs. If coaching can be conducted in the right atmosphere, it provides an excellent type of developmental experience. It has the practical advantage of being centered in the "real world"—the manager's work activities—and provides guidance from the one best able to evaluate his performance and to supply help—his superior. The requirement poses a problem for the superior, however, in that his appraisal and coaching may easily be viewed as critical and destructive rather than as helpful and motivating to the subordinate.

Training Conferences. Managerial personnel are often brought together for company or departmental training conferences. The purpose of such conferences is to impart knowledge or to improve skills of participants. It may also be possible through such conferences to effect some change in attitudes by providing for an exchange of thinking on the part of those involved in the conference.

Conferences of this type are particularly appropriate in cases in which a number of managers have somewhat similar training needs. It may be discovered, for example, that certain basic policies can profitably be discussed with an entire group. Or a chief executive may wish to review with subordinate management personnel problems of an overall nature or the outlook for the business as a whole.

Outside Developmental Activities. Some companies find that outside activities or schools are useful in supplementing development provided by the organization or providing a type of training that is not available within the firm. Of particular interest are the management development programs that have been established by many university schools of business. These programs typically range from one to six or eight weeks in length and deal with general aspects of administration. Many of them make extensive use of the case method of instruction. One of the best-known of these programs, the Sloan program for executive development at the Massachusetts Institute of Technology (with a twenty-five year history), brings its executive trainees into contact with top government officials in Washington and with prominent corporate leaders in New York, London, Paris, Rome, and other West European capitals.[20] Among more than 460 alumni of the course are 27 presidents or directors, 30 general managers, and 9 directors of research.

Professional associations likewise provide for training experiences on the part of professional and management personnel. Some of these are limited to such technical fields as engineering or accounting, whereas others are concerned with general problems of management. Participation in activities of such groups exposes a manager to current thinking in the area and also gives him contact with personnel from other organizations whose problems may be similar to his own.

Summary

The management of many firms has become concerned with the need for *recruitment* and *development* of a competent managerial staff. In part, this concern is based upon a realization of managerial limitations in the face of the growing complexity of management and the tendency toward managerial specialization. Systems concepts may be applied to many staffing activities including management development. Staffing functions are designed to produce managers with the necessary *conceptual* skills, *technical* skills, and *human relations* skills.

Recruitment of managerial personnel should be preceded by definite planning for the process. One factor to be considered concerns the sources of management talent. A company has available to it not only internal sources, through promotion from within, but also other business organizations and universities.

Development of managerial personnel is the other phase of staffing, occurring after the staff has been assembled. The basic elements of management development include both a basic intellectual preparation and the development of specialized job skills.

A great number of management development methods are available to produce such skills and abilities. Regardless of what training opportunities may be provided by management, the development

---

[20]"Executive Training by Meeting the Best," *Business Week*, No. 1753, April 6, 1963, p. 46.

must ultimately be *self-development*. The individual must assume a personal responsibility for his own training. The most fundamental type of development is that which occurs in the actual performance of managerial duties. This process may be varied or modified through job rotation which moves the manager through a series of positions in which he is expected to learn and to develop his skills. Also, supervisory coaching may be used to appraise his performance and evaluate training needs. Off-the-job conferences include both those held within the company or department and those in professional associations and schools outside the business organization.

Discussion Questions

1. A number of factors that tend to increase the complexity of management were cited in this chapter. Does it appear likely that the increased complexity will have a greater effect upon staff management or general line management? Can a general manager solve the problem by proper reliance upon staff assistants?

2. In view of the proportional numbers of specialists and generalists in management, what policy would you recommend in recruitment of management trainees?

3. What is the relative importance of *technical* skills, *human relations* skills, and *conceptual* skills at the top-management level versus the first-line supervisory level?

4. Is it possible to overemphasize human relations ability as an essential element of effective managerial importance?

5. Compare the advantages and difficulties in recruiting managerial personnel from competitive organizations.

6. What factors should be considered in choosing the specific colleges or universities to be used in recruitment of management trainees?

7. Evaluate the placement service provided by your college or university. What benefits do employers receive from such service?

8. Explain the reasoning underlying the concept or principle of *self-development* in managerial growth.

9. Describe the ideal conditions for effective on-the-job management development.

Supplementary Reading

Alfred, Theodore M., "Checkers or Choice in Manpower Management," *Harvard Business Review,* Vol. 45, No. 1, January-February 1967, pp. 157-169.

Dale, Ernest, "Executives Who Can't Manage," *The Atlantic Monthly,* Vol. 210, No. 1, July 1962, pp. 58-62.

Drucker, Peter F., "Is Business Letting Young People Down?" *Harvard Business Review,* Vol. 43, No. 6, November-December 1965, pp. 49-55.

Ferguson, Lawrence L., "Better Management of Managers' Careers," *Harvard Business Review,* Vol. 44, No. 2, March-April 1966, pp. 139-152.

Fielden, John S., "The Right Young People for Business," *Harvard Business Review,* Vol. 44, No. 2, March-April 1966, pp. 76-83.

Greenlaw, Paul S., "Management Development: A Systems View," *Personnel Journal,* Vol. 43, No. 4, April 1964, pp. 205-211.

Hekimian, James S. and Curtis H. Jones, "Put *People* on Your Balance Sheet," *Harvard Business Review,* Vol. 45, No. 1, January-February 1967, pp. 105-113.

Hinrichs, John R., *High-Talent Personnel.* New York: American Management Association, 1966.

House, Robert J., "A Commitment Approach to Management Development," *California Management Review,* Vol. 7, No. 3, Spring 1965, pp. 15-28.

————, "Leadership Training: Some Dysfunctional Consequences," *Administrative Science Quarterly,* Vol. 12, No. 4, March 1968, pp. 556-571.

Kirchner, Wayne K., "Needed: A Return to Reality in Management Selection and Development," *Personnel Journal,* Vol. 42, No. 7, July-August 1963, pp. 341-345.

Lundberg, Craig C., "Management Development Refocused," *Personnel Administration,* Vol. 29, No. 1, January-February 1966, pp. 39-44.

Mahler, Walter R., "Every Company's Problem: Managerial Obsolescence," *Personnel,* Vol. 42, No. 4, July-August 1965, pp. 8-16.

McFarland, Dalton E., *Management: Principles and Practices,* Second Edition, Chapters 20 and 21. New York: The Macmillan Company, 1964.

Porter, Elias H., *Manpower Development.* New York: Harper & Row, Publishers, Inc., 1964.

Stolz, Robert K., "Executive Development — New Perspective," *Harvard Business Review,* Vol. 44, No. 3, May-June 1966, pp. 133-143.

Social Aspects of Organizing

15

The Organization as a Social System

From an operational point of view, a business organization consists of a series of work operations that are integrated by means of the organization structure. In concentrating upon this view of the *mission*, or the work to be done, one gains little awareness of the nature of human relationships that are involved. Such a notion of organized behavior furnished the basis for the philosophy of Frederick W. Taylor and is still followed by many contemporary managers. In contrast to this view, a more recent and quite different emphasis has been suggested by students of organizational behavior. According to this newer approach, human relationships provide the core of any organization. The organization itself is visualized as a social system.

The Social Structure of Industry

The Human Side of Organization

A business firm requires a group of people—a human organization—to direct its operations and to provide the mental and physical services necessary in accomplishing its objectives. The official responsibilities and relationships of these people may be indicated in a general way by an organization chart. The lines on such a chart represent *interpersonal* relationships, and these relationships provide the skeleton for the social structure. A subordinate reports to a superior, one person to another. When we say that a laboratory supervisor reports to a department manager, this means more than one box on a chart reporting to another box. It means that Jones, the laboratory supervisor, reports to Wolfe, the department manager. It further means that Wolfe directs Jones in his duties and evaluates his performance. Jones must satisfy Wolfe if he is to progress in the organization.

The social structure of an organization encompasses more than the formal superior-subordinate relationships. Any member of the organization normally has contact with other members of the same organization. Two employees work side by side in a shop or share adjoining desks in an office. Employees also eat lunch together in the cafeteria or ride in the same car pool. All of these relationships, if they are continuing in nature, are a part of the social structure of the organization.

An organization, therefore, is more than a collection of individuals. To understand its nature, we must recognize the social relationships that exist and understand their significance. An organization member is more than an isolated individual. Instead, he is located at some point in a web of relationships. The studies described below were noteworthy in drawing the attention of managers and students of management to the nature and importance of these relationships.

Western Electric Illumination Experiments[1]

In 1924, the Western Electric Company, manufacturer of telephone equipment, initiated a series of illumination experiments that were later to become famous. The studies were conducted in the company's Hawthorne plant in Chicago in cooperation with the National Academy of Sciences. Their purpose was to discover the relationship between lighting in the work place and productivity of employees. Implicit in the study was a conception of employees that emphasized their physiological makeup. Specifically, the experiments were intended to determine the level of illumination at which employees would be most productive.

[1]Descriptions of the Western Electric experiments, including both the illumination and other phases, may be found in F. J. Roethlisberger and William J. Dickson, *Management and the Worker* (Cambridge: Harvard University Press, 1946); F. J. Roethlisberger, *Management and Morale* (Cambridge: Harvard University Press, 1941), Chapter 2; and Stuart Chase, *Men at Work* (New York: Harcourt, Brace, & World, Inc., 1945), Chapter 2.

In one phase of the experiments, workers were divided into two groups — a test group and a control group. Lighting affecting the test group was increased from 24 to 46 to 70 foot-candles, while control group lighting was held constant. It was assumed that output of the test group would show some increase in contrast to that of the control group. Results were surprising, however, because production of both groups increased in roughly the same proportion!

In another experiment, lighting of a test group was reduced from 10 to 3 foot-candles, while lighting of the control group was held constant. Rather than declining, however, test group output increased—as did that of the control group! At a later stage, illumination was reduced until it reached the level of moonlight, but not until then did output drop appreciably.

It is evident that some uncontrolled variables were at work. These factors were canceling out any effects resulting from physical changes. As far as the original hypothesis was concerned, the results were inconclusive. The understanding of researchers was deepening, however, as they sought explanations for this behavior. It should be noted that the employees involved in the experiment were aware of the study and were apparently reacting to it in some way. The experiment disclosed that the human element in production was more significant than had been previously realized.

Relay Assembly Test Room Experiments

Following the illumination experiments, the researchers forged ahead with a new series of experiments. This time, they attempted to measure the effect of fatigue or rest upon output. In conducting the study, a group of six girls assembling telephone relays was brought into a special test room. An observer was stationed in the same room to record results and counsel with the girls, but he did not function in the customary manner of a line supervisor.

The general plan of attack was to measure output in different periods of several weeks each. In the early periods, the rate of output was established under "normal" conditions. In subsequent periods, rest pauses of various lengths were introduced. In Period IV, for example, two rest periods of five minutes each were introduced — one in the morning and one in the afternoon. In Period V, rest pauses were increased to ten minutes each.

During the experimentation, which continued for more than a year, output increased as working conditions were improved. Professor Roethlisberger has summarized the results of these experiments as follows:

> During the first year and a half of the experiment, everybody was happy, both the investigators and the operators. The investigators were happy because as conditions of work improved the output rate rose steadily. Here, it appeared, was strong evidence in favor of their preconceived hypothesis that fatigue was the major factor limiting output. The operators were happy because their conditions of work were being improved, they were earning more money, and they were objects of considerable attention from top management. But then one investigator — one of those tough-minded fellows — suggested that they restore the original conditions of work, that is, go back to a full forty-eight-hour week without rests, lunches and what not. This was Period XII. Then the happy state of affairs, when everything was going along as it theoretically should, went sour. Output, instead of taking the expected nose dive, maintained its high level.[2]

Attitudes of the girls toward their work, management, and work group were apparently affecting their work efficiency. According to William Foote Whyte, Period XII provided the birthplace for industrial sociology.[3] Realization of the importance of human relationships in industry increased rapidly from the date of this experiment.

Bank Wiring Observation Room

Another phase of the Western Electric experimentation — that of the bank wiring observation room — also merits consideration. This study involved careful observation of a group of fourteen workmen engaged in wiring certain types of telephone equipment. The group included wirers, solderers, and inspectors.

It was discovered that this group operated as a team rather than as a group of individuals. The group recognized its own informal leaders and also shared various sentiments. For example, a member was expected to avoid turning out too much, thus becoming a "rate buster." Members of the group were expected to conform to these group standards, and life could be made miserable for those choosing to violate the norms.

---

[2]F. J. Roethlisberger, *Management and Morale* (Cambridge: Harvard University Press, 1941), p. 13.

[3]William Foote Whyte, *Men at Work* (Homewood, Ill.: Richard D. Irwin, Inc., and The Dorsey Press, 1961), p. 8. Used with permission.

Subsequent Studies of Work Groups

The Western Electric studies of the social organization of production groups have been treated in some detail because of their historic significance as well as the insights they provide. These studies were only the beginning, however. In Chapter 13, the famous Tavistock studies of organization in British coal mining were cited. Of the many other studies and experiments in this area, two have been selected for discussion.

One experiment in organizing the painting operation of a toy manufacturer failed because it succeeded too well![4] In this operation, eight girls who did the painting sat in a line, with a chain of hooks moving in front of them into a long, horizontal oven. Engineers had calculated the rate at which the hooks moved so that each girl, when fully trained, could hang a painted toy on each hook before it passed beyond her reach. Trouble developed during the training period. The girls learned more slowly than expected and complained that the hooks were going by too rapidly.

In a general discussion of working conditions, the girls requested that they be permitted to adjust the speed of the belt depending on the way they felt. Despite the misgivings of the engineers, it was agreed to try out the girls' idea. A control was installed to permit the group leader to adjust the speed to "low," "medium," or "fast." The girls spent many lunch hours discussing how the speed should be varied throughout the day. Within a week, a pattern developed calling for medium speed the first half hour, high speed the next two and one-half hours, low speed the half hour before lunch and half hour after lunch, and high speed the rest of the afternoon except for medium speed for the last forty-five minutes.

The girls reported satisfaction, worked at an average speed above that specified by the engineers, and maintained quality. Within three weeks, the girls were operating at 30 to 50 per cent above the expected level and earning more than many skilled workers in other parts of the plant. The inequity in compensation led to demands for relief and a growing irritation among members of management and the engineers. The situation came to a head when the superintendent arbitrarily revoked the learning bonus and returned the painting operation to its original status — the belt moving at the time-studied

---

[4]This story is given in George Strauss, "Group Dynamics and Intergroup Relations," in William Foote Whyte, *et al., Money and Motivation* (New York: Harper & Row, Publishers, 1955), Chapter 10.

designated speed. Within one month, six of the eight girls quit, and the foreman also left after a few months. In this case, then, management failed to receive the benefits of a dynamic work group because of complications caused in other parts of the system.

In the early 1960's, Non-Linear Systems, Inc., a California company developing and selling precision electronic instruments, adopted some unorthodox approaches in its management.[5] One change involved the discontinuance of assembly lines, replacing them with a number of seven-man teams. Under the leadership of a competent technician, each group built complete instruments. By mutual agreement, team members decided who would do what and in what sequence. They also set their own pace. Under this arrangement, productivity steadily improved and reached an all-time high. Within the groups, individual employees attained status by virtue of their abilities in various areas. The practice of group members' helping one another by teaching some special technique or skill was evident to observers. In this firm, then, formation of the semi-autonomous work groups led to excellent results in both quantity and quality of output.

The Business Organization as a Social System

The effect of the Western Electric experiments was to turn a spotlight on the social structure of industry and its significance in business operation. In developing theory to incorporate these findings, researchers adopted the concept of the business organization as a *social system*. According to this view, the social system of a factory, store, or office has as its component parts the employees of those organizations. The social system involves more than a group of individuals, however. The component parts — that is, the people — function or work together through patterns of interaction that develop among the members. One part of a company — say the drafting room or typing pool — is a social system, and the entire company is also a social system. In other words, there are systems within systems.

The following explanation by Whyte emphasizes the interrelationships revealed by this view of organizations:

> This is what I mean by a systems approach to organization. My system involves the interactions, activities, and sentiments of

---

[5]Arthur H. Kuriloff, "An Experiment in Management — Putting Theory Y to the Test," *Personnel,* Vol. 40, No. 6, November-December 1963, pp. 8-17.

> the members in relation to the social, economic, and technological environment. I assume a state of *mutual dependence* among the elements of the social system, which means that a change introduced into interactions will be accompanied by change in activities and sentiments; a change introduced into activities will be accompanied by changes in interactions and sentiments, and so on. I also assume a state of mutual dependence between the environment and the social system, which means that a change introduced into the environment will have its effects upon the social system, and changes that occur within the social system may have their effects upon the environment.[6]

A formal organization structure, if it were sufficiently detailed to include all employees, would show all component parts of the social system — that is, all personnel. It would also indicate the approximate formal relationships of these parts to each other. A manual or job description might detail all activities expected from a particular position and describe the intended relationships and methods of working with others.

Functioning of the system is only partially prescribed by the statement of formal organization, however. Employees devise arrangements and procedures that supplement or conflict with the formally prescribed structure. In the bank wiring observation room, the informal set of relationships did not appear on the organization chart or receive formal recognition. (The nature of informal organization will be discussed in more detail in the following section.)

In carrying out its mission of producing goods and services, a business organization functions through its social system to create social satisfactions for members of the group, each of whom has individual needs and sentiments. If the organization provides adequate social satisfactions, the firm is recognized as having good employee relations. The Western Electric experiments showed that social satisfactions were intimately related to accomplishment of economic objectives.

Relationships and interactions among employees are not highly standardized. Indeed, they are often very complex.

> Some relationships fall into routine patterns, such as the relationship between superior and subordinate or between office worker and shop worker. Individuals conscious of their membership in certain groups are reacting in certain accepted ways to other individuals representing other groups. Behavior varies according to the stereotyped conceptions of relationship. The

---

[6]William Foote Whyte, *Men at Work* (Homewood, Ill.: Richard D. Irwin, Inc., and The Dorsey Press, 1961), p. 569. Reprinted with permission.

> worker, for example, behaves toward his foreman in one way, toward his first-line supervisor in another way, and toward his fellow worker in still another. People holding the rank of inspector expect a certain kind of behavior from the operators — the operators from the inspectors. Now these relationships, as is well known from everyday experiences, are finely shaded and sometimes become complicated. When a person is in the presence of his supervisor alone he usually acts differently from the way he acts when his supervisor's supervisor is also present.[7]

Certain factors tend to strengthen the social system, to give it unity and cohesion. These might be illustrated by the rewards provided for working cooperatively in the enterprise. Other factors tend to be disruptive in nature. Among the latter are conditions discouraging cooperation among workers, such as sharp differences in age or race.

Within a social system, evaluations are made that rank one position against another. Not all parts of the system are recognized as being of equal importance. A bookkeeper or a typist is regarded as less important than a president. These distinctions are referred to as *status differences* and exist in every social group. (The subject of status is treated in Chapter 17.)

The degree of intimacy in the relationships among members of an organization varies inversely with *social distance*. The distance between the chief executive and a factory worker, for example, is much greater than that between a supervisor and his immediate subordinate. In any superior-subordinate relationship, the superior's behavior regulates, to a considerable degree, the social distance between the levels. Supervisors taking a democratic approach tend to minimize social distance between themselves and their subordinates.

The patterns of behavior and belief that develop in any social organization are referred to as its *culture*. Industrial organizations often develop special modifications of, or additions to, the general culture. (This aspect of the social system is discussed in Chapter 16.)

Work Groups and Informal Organization

Management creates work groups by specifying interrelated job assignments and by locating employees in proximity to each other.

---

[7] F. J. Roethlisberger and William J. Dickson, *Management and the Worker* (Cambridge: Harvard University Press, 1939), p. 555.

The life and activities of such groups typically extend far beyond the minimum relationships stipulated by the formal organization. Formal work associations are supplemented by friendships that develop among members of work groups. Through luncheon groups, shared coffee breaks, general conversation about nonbusiness subjects, and in numerous other ways the life of formal groups is elaborated. In many cases, strong personal relationships develop along organization lines — that is, within immediate work groups. In other cases, individuals from different work groups are drawn together by some common interest.[8]

Nature and Ubiquity of Informal Organization

Informal organization refers to those relationships, associations, and patterns of working together that develop spontaneously in a business organization. The nature and practices of the informal organization are not stipulated by management. Indeed, this is the contrast between formal and informal organization. Both managerial and nonmanagerial employees are members of such informal groups.

Every organization has some type of informal organization. The only way to avoid informal organization completely would be to eliminate all personal association among members of an organization. Because it is impossible to stipulate all relationships and procedures in detail and because employees are social beings, they naturally supplement formal relationships and adapt procedures that are formulated by management.

Employees in a primary work group, for example, characteristically develop relations among themselves involving unofficial mutual assistance. Also, as one becomes acquainted with the organization, he may discover that the way to get results is to "see Joe." "Joe" does not always appear on the organization chart. Other informal organizations are primarily social in their interests and activities. In one industrial plant, for example, a group of eight factory employees developed an active social life together outside the plant. On weekends, they often went fishing or boating together. One of the members owned a cabin on a lake, and this served as a frequent rendezvous for the group. The socializing after hours had no direct connection with work activities, although most of the group also worked together in the plant. These activities affected in-plant

---

[8]The small face-to-face work groups and social groups discussed in this section are customarily referred to by sociologists as *primary groups*.

relationships, of course, but the principal bond was the social associations outside the plant.

Factors Contributing to Formation and Cohesion

Location stands out as a primary factor in regulating the formation and cohesion of informal groups. Although there are exceptions, individuals must be located sufficiently close to each other to permit the personal interaction necessary for development of group relationships. Groups of engineers, draftsmen, or other types of employees may have common interests but work in different parts of the plant. The absence of regular contacts makes it difficult for them to develop strong informal relationships. It is for this reason that the immediate face-to-face work group often constitutes one of the most important informal groups. Isolation of a particular group from other employees and other groups can similarly serve to encourage the development of an informal organization on the part of the isolated group.

Professional or occupational differences are likewise significant in determining the nature of informal groupings. There is a tendency for those in the same occupation or "job family" to find a common bond in this fact. This is particularly true if there are status differences among the occupations. It is uncommon for engineers or accountants to develop strong informal ties with cooks or electricians.

The homogeneity of work groups likewise affects the degree of cohesion. If a group is composed primarily of Irish, old-timers, young girls, or some other homogeneous group, it is easy for a strong informal group relationship to develop. Within any general work group, it is also natural for smaller informal groupings to form on the basis of such common features as age, race, or outside interests that provide a focal point for organization.

Pressure or threat of danger can likewise encourage the formation of informal groups. Supervisory behavior that is regarded as threatening by a group of employees has a tendency to bind employees together.

Informal Leaders

Informal leaders differ markedly from those appointed by management. In contrast to formally designated leaders, informal leaders are merely recognized or accepted by members of the group in which they exert leadership. They have no formal authority, so their leadership must be based upon other characteristics. In any particular group, there may be one or more individuals occupying positions of leadership. These individuals are not always apparent to an outside observer. Neither can they be detected in all cases by the amount of talking that they do. They may be distinguished as leaders when their recommendations or point of view is taken seriously and followed by other members of the group.

It is difficult to specify the qualities that enable an individual to assume a position of leadership in the informal group. His degree of skill, his age, and his personality characteristics, for example, may all have a bearing on his acceptance. Following is a suggestion of two general characteristics that all informal leaders are thought to possess:

> *a) Ability to communicate*—the informal leader is both a transmitter and receiver of information. He is a sort of clearing house of information for the informal organization. He is "in on the know." And, probably more important, he is willing to transmit all information to his followers in the informal organization.
>
> *b) Ability to embody the values of the primary group*—this characteristic is somewhat more elusive than the first. The informal leader is a kind of living representation of the things the group stands for. He is able to perceive the values of the group, crystallize them into a coherent ideology, and verbalize them to others outside the group. Perhaps this is what is meant when the informal leader is referred to as the spokesman of the group.[9]

The informal leader assists in working out problems among members of the group and in resolving their difficulties with outsiders. The following functions have been suggested for the informal leader:

1. He initiates action.
2. He facilitates a consensus.
3. He provides a link or liaison with the outside world: managers, other work groups, the union.[10]

Orientation Toward the Formal Organization

Informal organization differs from one situation to another in its orientation toward the formal organization. In some cases, it accepts the organization's objectives and supports management in achieving

---

[9]William G. Scott, *Human Relations in Management: A Behavioral Science Approach* (Homewood, Illinois: Richard D. Irwin, Inc., 1962), p. 133. Reprinted with permission.

[10]George Strauss and Leonard R. Sayles, *Personnel: the Human Problems of Management,* Second Edition (Englewood Cliffs: Prentice-Hall, Inc., ©.1967), p. 83.

them. On the other hand, some informal organizations owe their existence to conflict — real or imaginary — with company management or company policy. At any given time, each informal organization might be located at some point on a scale, such as that in Figure 18, on the basis of its relationship to the formal organization.

Figure 18. *Range of Possible Orientations Toward Formal Organization*

Hostile toward management	Indifferent	Cooperative with management

On the basis of a study of 300 work groups in thirty industrial plants, Leonard R. Sayles has proposed a classification of these groups showing their orientation toward the formal organization.[11] The explanations of the following categories show the general nature of each:

Apathetic Groups — Consistently indifferent to management decisions; little group cohesion.
Erratic Groups — Vacillation between cooperative and antagonistic behavior; often highly centralized leadership in the group.
Strategic Groups — Continuous pressure against management; high degree of internal unity.
Conservative Groups — Mostly cooperative; moderate internal unity.

As an example of the strategic work group, Sayles found that the welders in most plants were constantly seeking to improve their own position and to detect the slightest flaws in management behavior. The following comments were made by welders during interviews with researchers:

> WELDER A: We would never permit any of our jobs to be restudied. We wouldn't take none of that bull from the time-study department. They pull that stuff with some of the groups, but they never pull it off with the welders. We would walk out on them.

[11]Leonard R. Sayles, *Behavior of Industrial Work Groups* (New York: John Wiley & Sons, Inc., 1958), Chapter 2.

WELDER B: You bet the welders built up the union. If the others want to take that sort of thing (from management) it's up to them. One thing is clear and that is the welders can get things done. For example, when other workers get base rate on a job, we get average hourly earnings. The company knows we can tie up the whole plant in a day or two and they better not play around with us.

WELDER C: We've stuck together as a group whenever we wanted anything and we've fought for it. A number of times on walkouts and sitdowns we've left the rest of the plant at work. Why are we so united? Maybe it's because whatever sort of work we're doing, if it's welding, it's almost identical, while men on most machines differ by a little bit. We always have every job down pat and know just what we can do on it. We learned when we were on individual piece rates; every man makes sure he knows what he is earning, how fast he should do the job, etc. With the other groups, it's different; most of them leave it up to the gang leader.

WELDER D: We're almost a union by ourselves. If anything goes wrong, we tell the company if they don't come down and settle this by such and such a time, we're not going to do any more of this work. The other groups just aren't as united.[12]

Technology appeared to be most important in shaping the activity of these groups. Characteristics of jobs, interdependence of workers, similarity of jobs at one location, and factors of this type seemed to explain many of the behavioral differences that were observed.[13]

Functions of the Informal Organization

The informal organization provides satisfaction for the social needs of members of the organization. Man is a social being and desires the recognition and friendship of other people. He appreciates acceptance by other individuals and has a desire to belong. The social interaction and friendship provided by an informal group can thus make a significant contribution to the individual. Opportunity for social interaction and satisfaction can make a job or organization bearable even though it may also have undesirable features. Membership in cohesive work groups not only provides opportunities for enjoyable social interaction but also contributes to the emotional well-being of employees. Individual employees are aided in maintain-

---

[12]*Ibid.*, p. 26.
[13]*Ibid.*, p. 93.

ing their emotional equilibrium, particularly in times of crisis or difficulty, by the support they receive from fellow workers.

A second function of the informal organization is that of communication. In this context, the informal organization is called the *grapevine,* and it supplies information to supplement that passed through formal channels. (This aspect of informal organization is discussed at greater length in Chapter 22.)

Standards of conduct are also established and maintained by the informal organization. We are particularly interested in those standards directly connected with organizational objectives. These group standards may be either favorable or unfavorable from the standpoint of management thinking. As an example, the group may support a standard of punctuality in reporting for work and regularity in attendance.

Lupton has described the informal pressures applied in one English factory to enforce the group norm that "You should work hard when work is available."[14] About twenty minutes before finishing time, for example, an employee received a new batch of materials. He was reluctant to make a start on these materials so near quitting time, however. Consequently, he relaxed a bit until a remark from another member of the work group abruptly changed his intentions. With the eyes of the entire work team upon him, he felt uncomfortable and started reaching for materials to begin work.

On the other hand, a group may establish a limit on output and insist that no member of the group exceed that production quota. The primary method of control involves social disapproval of the offending member. He is ridiculed or ostracized in some manner. It takes a strong individualist to withstand such tactics.[15]

Still another function of the informal organization is its direct contribution to work accomplishment. Through the informal organization, individual members are able to share job knowledge and to give one another a hand in the accomplishment of work. One member of the organization may assist in training or supplying job tips to a newer member of the same informal group. If the group accepts management objectives, its control supports the supervisor's position and lightens his work. It has also been suggested that the informal group provides an atmosphere that stimulates creativity and new ideas.

---

[14]T. Lupton, *On the Shop Floor: Two Studies of Workshop Organization and Output* (London: Pergamon Press, 1963), pp. 40-41.

[15]For the story of a crane operator whose fellow workmen refused to speak to him for 367 days as punishment for working during a one-day strike, see George A. Lundberg, Clarence C. Schrag, and Otto N. Larsen, *Sociology,* Third Edition (New York: Harper & Row, Publishers, 1963), p. 70.

> The approval of fellow-workers becomes important in supporting innovation and original ideas, while their disapproval may be sufficient to squelch new ideas. The informal group is the breeding ground in which the individual can experiment with unique ideas without having to "sell the boss" before trying them.[16]

We may summarize, then, the functions of informal organization as follows: (1) provision of social satisfactions for organization members; (2) communication; (3) establishment and maintenance of standards of conduct; and (4) contribution to work accomplishment.

Working with the Informal Organization

The question now confronts us as to how management should relate itself to the informal organization. A constructive approach in dealing with these groups must begin with a recognition of their potentially useful functions. The administrator must realize that activities of informal organizations are not necessarily opposed or hostile to management. Indeed, it is possible that they may support the achievement of management objectives. At the same time, he must be aware of the sharp differences that exist among informal groups and strive to understand the real nature of the groups with which he deals.

While a manager may recognize existence of the informal organization, he may choose to avoid any substantial contact or cooperation with it. Acceptance of the informal organization may be based upon a realization that it is necessary and impossible to eradicate. The manager may, accordingly, attempt to avoid conduct that appears threatening to such informal groups, but still deal with employees on an individual basis.

Another, sometimes more fruitful, approach involves an attempt to work directly and constructively with the informal organization. This begins, of course, with a full appreciation of the positive values of informal organization. The administrator learns the identity of informal leaders and establishes close liaison with these leaders. If he can maintain the confidence and understanding of such individuals, he can expect a greater measure of support on the part of his entire organization. In part, he may use informal leadership as one channel of communication with his organization. This is not to suggest, of course, that he should use the informal organization in

---

[16] Robert Dubin, *Human Relations in Administration, with Readings,* Third Edition, © 1968, p. 106. Reprinted by permission of Prentice-Hall, Inc., Englewood Cliffs, New Jersey.

lieu of the formal structure or that he should attempt to manipulate employees, but rather that he should attempt to improve the general understanding among members of this group and the formal leadership. Extension of this approach to include group participation in problem solving is discussed in Chapter 21.

Summary

The Western Electric experiments served to reveal and increase understanding of the social nature of business organizations. These experiments demonstrated that business organizations are more than collections of individuals. Rather, they are *social systems* in which the relationships among people are of extreme significance in determining organizational behavior.

As a social system, the business organization includes not only the *formal* organization but also *informal* groupings and relationships that supplement the formally prescribed structure. This social system contains elements of a *cultural* nature, including *status gradations.*

One of the most important aspects of the social system concerns work groups and the *informal organization* or relationships that develop. Informal groups and interactions develop spontaneously among employees of an organization. In such groups, certain informal leaders come to be recognized and to exert influence over other members. The informal organization performs various functions for the individual and also for the formal organization. Informal groups may operate constructively with respect to the formal organization, or they may adopt goals conflicting with those of the formal organization. Management sometimes attempts to work constructively with informal organizations and to utilize these relationships in achieving organization objectives.

Discussion Questions

1. The Western Electric experiments were designed to show the relationship between lighting and productivity. What were the results? Explain.

2. Why might the Western Electric Hawthorne plant be called the "birthplace of industrial sociology"?

3. Explain the concept of the business organization as a *social system.*

4. What is meant by *social distance*? How do you think this might affect communication?

5. Identify a number of factors affecting the formation of *informal* groups and explain the significance of each.

6. What accounts for differences in the cooperation or hostility of different informal groups in their relationships to the formal organization?

7. Is the informal organization useful to management? What constructive role, if any, does it have?

8. What should a manager do about the informal organizations in which his subordinates are involved?

9. Is it better for a supervisor to deal with his subordinates as individuals or to encourage development of a cohesive work group? Explain.

10. What action should be taken by a manager whose subordinates have established an unreasonably low ceiling on work output?

Supplementary Reading

Applewhite, Philip B., *Organizational Behavior,* Chapter 3. Englewood Cliffs: Prentice-Hall, Inc., 1965.

Bensman, Joseph and Israel Gerver, "Crime and Punishment in the Factory: The Function of Deviancy in Maintaining the Social System," *American Sociological Review,* Vol. 28, No. 4, August 1963, pp. 588-598.

Bowers, David G. and Stanley E. Seashore, "Peer Leadership Within Work Groups," *Personnel Administration,* Vol. 30, No. 5, September-October 1967, pp. 45-50.

Bucklow, Maxine, "A New Role for the Work Group," *Administrative Science Quarterly,* Vol. 11, No. 1, June 1966, pp. 59-78.

Carzo, Rocco, Jr. and John N. Yanouzas, *Formal Organization: A Systems Approach,* Chapters 5-6. Homewood: Richard D. Irwin, Inc., and The Dorsey Press, 1967.

Cleland, David I. and Wallace Munsey, "Who Works With Whom?" *Harvard Business Review,* Vol. 45, No. 5, September-October 1967, pp. 84-90.

Dalton, Melville, *Men Who Manage.* New York: John Wiley & Sons, Inc., 1959.

Davis, Keith, *Human Relations at Work,* Third Edition, Chapter 13. New York: McGraw-Hill Book Company, 1967.

Etzioni, Amitai, *Modern Organizations,* Chapter 4. Englewood Cliffs: Prentice-Hall, Inc., 1964.

Flippo, Edwin B., *Management: A Behavioral Approach,* Chapter 10. Boston: Allyn & Bacon, Inc., 1966.

Fox, William M., "When Human Relations May Succeed and the Company Fail," *California Management Review,* Vol. 8, No. 3, Spring, 1966, pp. 19-24.

Katz, Fred E., "Explaining Informal Work Groups in Complex Organization: The Case for Autonomy in Structure," *Administrative Science Quarterly,* Vol. 10, No. 2, September 1965, pp. 204-223.

Litterer, Joseph A., *The Analysis of Organizations,* Chapters 5 and 6. New York: John Wiley & Sons, Inc., 1965.

Lupton, T., *On the Shop Floor: Two Studies of Workshop Organization and Output.* London: Pergamon Press, 1963.

Miner, John B., *Introduction to Industrial Clinical Psychology,* Chapter 7. New York: McGraw-Hill Book Company, 1966.

Scott, William G., *Organization Theory: A Behavioral Analysis for Management,* Part II. Homewood: Richard D. Irwin, Inc., 1967.

Seiler, John A., *Systems Analysis in Organizational Behavior.* Homewood: Richard D. Irwin, Inc. and the Dorsey Press, 1967.

Strauss, George and Leonard R. Sayles, *Personnel: The Human Problems of Management,* Second Edition, Chapter 4. Englewood Cliffs: Prentice-Hall, Inc., 1967.

Tannenbaum, Arnold S., *Social Psychology of the Work Organization.* Belmont: Wadsworth Publishing Company, Inc., 1966.

Whyte, William Foote, "A Field in Search of a Focus," *Industrial and Labor Relations Review,* Vol. 18, No. 3, April 1965, pp. 305-322.

16

Cultural Background of Organization

There is a common conception of culture that equates it with fine arts and good manners. According to this point of view, a cultured person is one who reads great books, visits art galleries, and engages in discussion of abstract subjects on a high intellectual plane. For the purpose of our analysis of the relationship of culture to management, this definition is entirely too narrow. In this chapter, we shall be concerned with a much broader view of culture — one that sees it as broadly affecting the way that people live and think both in and outside the places of their employment.

Culture and the Business Organization

What Is Culture?

Culture consists of the behavior patterns and values of a social group. These are patterns of belief and behavior that have been learned from other members of society. They are, as the cultural anthropologist would say, *socially transmitted*. They include the practices that we have learned and that we share. Culture is often described as *custom*, and it includes not only actions but also ideas and manmade objects that are called *artifacts*. Eating lunch at noonday, or eating three meals a day for that matter, is an example of culturally determined behavior. Most of us do it as a matter of course. We consider it the normal method of receiving nourishment, and, in America, we use forks and knives (artifacts) instead of chopsticks. In America, such ideals as individual liberty are also widely accepted and constitute a part of our culture. The religious beliefs of any people likewise are a part of the total culture.

One writer has defined culture as follows:

> Culture in its broadest sense is cultivated behavior, that is, the totality of man's learned, accumulated experience which is socially transmitted, or more briefly, behavior acquired through social learning.[1]

Variations in Culture

We are often unaware of the cultural patterns and values that characterize our own society. We tend to take our own practices and beliefs for granted rather than looking at them objectively. We learn the accepted way and assume that almost everyone behaves or believes in the same way. Whether these practices involve educational ceremonies, religious rituals, living patterns, or employment practices, we seldom think of them as aspects of culture.

Different patterns of culture characterize different societies. Over a period of time, for example, the culture of any society changes. It is also possible to recognize cultural differences when moving from one country to another. Features of this kind become immediately apparent to one traveling in a foreign country. According to one story, a European businessman in New York, with his customary courtesy, held the door open for a New Yorker hurrying behind him. The New Yorker, with some bewilderment, exclaimed, "What are you — a wise guy?" Even within our own country, there are marked differences in culture. This is true even though all of them are a part of the American culture. Some of the differences, indeed, are extreme. The Amish in Pennsylvania, for example, still drive horses and buggies rather than using automobiles. There are other noticeable differences, even though less extreme, between the culture of, say, a small town in Georgia and a large city in California. Even within a given community, there are distinctive individual patterns that characterize certain segments of the community. The internal variations within a general cultural system are referred to as *subcultures*.

---

[1]Felix M. Keesing, *Cultural Anthropology: The Science of Custom* (New York: Holt, Rinehart, & Winston, Inc., 1958), p. 18.

The extent to which a given cultural pattern is accepted and followed is, of course, a matter of degree. Some cultural patterns are followed quite rigidly by everyone, while others have only a general degree of acceptance. Naturally, there must be some consistency in a practice or some uniformity of belief for it to be classified as culture.

Business Firms Within the Larger Cultural System

A business firm, branch plant, or any other institution for that matter functions within the cultural system of the society in which it is located. A firm in Dallas must function within the American culture, including modifications or "wrinkles" peculiar to the state of Texas and the city of Dallas. Similarly, a company located in London must operate within the general British culture and that of London in particular.

The fact that a firm must function within the larger cultural system means that some agreement between the practices of the firm and the culture is necessary. The expectations of the surrounding community with regard to the establishments located within it are based upon the community's cultural traditions. Employees also bring into the firm the cultural values they have assimilated from the community. Both the community and the employees are inclined to expect, therefore, some conformity to prevailing cultural values. As a general example, the American worker has been exposed to a political philosophy that emphasizes the importance of the individual. If the work place provides conditions degrading to his personality and self-respect, as occasionally happens, a serious conflict with the broader cultural background is evident. The disparity may contribute to high personnel turnover, poor public relations, or unionization.

Background Cultures of Other Countries

As noted above, not all cultural patterns are the same. It is easy to underestimate the substantial differences that exist and the implications that these cultural differences have for administration. To understand the nature of the cultural settings for business and to appreciate better the culture with which we are most familiar, it may be helpful to note briefly some features of different cultures of the world. Our particular concern is with illustrative features of significance in business administration.

In many Latin American cultures, for example, class distinctions are much more pronounced and controlling than those in our own society.[2] Class differences are emphasized, and the upper class manages and controls the work performed by the lower class. There is a distinct absence of the democratic atmosphere characterizing the American economy. Such class distinctions tend to inhibit free communication between labor and management and make it difficult to engage in frank discussion even between two levels of management. The subordinate, because of his conditioning in this culture, is inclined to show consistent deference to his superiors, at least on the surface. He is less inclined than is the American worker to speak up to the boss and to say what is troubling him.

In addition, the Latin American attitude toward work is somewhat different from our own. In many Latin American countries, it is not unusual for the "really important" people to shun work as somewhat beneath their status — such important people do not get their hands dirty. Work may be necessary, but it is not the most honorable activity for a person who has achieved success. This contrasts rather sharply with an attitude toward work in the American society that makes it almost mandatory for individuals to work even though they are financially successful and able to support themselves otherwise.

Many cultural practices find their way into the country's laws.[3] In Latin America, the annual bonus has become popular, and many countries now require it, with Venezuela setting two months' pay as a minimum. Holland establishes wage levels, and many European countries require employers to foot much of the bill for family bonus systems. Brazil taxes employers to pay for education of children of employees and also levies a tax on illiterates who are employed, unless the employer undertakes the educational job himself. Laws making it difficult to dismiss employees result in unusual consequences. In one famous case in Brazil, a gold mine could not afford to go out of business even though it had mined its last nugget of gold! And, in another case, the Brazilian Supreme Court ruled that a company had moved too fast in firing an employee who appeared to be sleeping on the job.[4] In the opinion of the court, the company had failed to

---

[2]See William Foote Whyte, *Man and Organization* (Homewood: Richard D. Irwin, Inc., 1959), pp. 8-11, for a penetrating discussion of this and other cultural features applicable to different economic systems.

[3]See "Labor: The 'X' Factor Abroad," *Dun's Review and Modern Industry*, Vol. 79, No. 5, May 1962, pp. 52-55 and 98-100, for a comprehensive review of this and other cultural features among the various nations.

[4]"Praying, Not Sleeping — So Employee Keeps Job," *Business Week*, No. 1733, November 17, 1962, p. 60.

disprove the employee's contention that — as a member of the Esoteric Center of Communion of Thought — he was actually deep in prayer.

The attitude toward time varies greatly from one part of the world to another. Punctuality is a virtue in America, but in some countries the custom is to keep people waiting for an hour or two before seeing them. The workday itself varies widely around the world. The midday siesta is standard practice in Latin America. In Greece, the normal work day is scheduled from 8:00 a.m. to 2:00 p.m., six days each week.

In Japan, other cultural differences distinguish the society and affect the institutions functioning within it. In contrast to the American emphasis upon merit and individual achievement, the Japanese culture places greater emphasis upon longevity and seniority in determining the worth of individuals. It is rare that an employee is dismissed, and it is also rare for an employee to quit a company to accept employment elsewhere. In his study of the Japanese factory, Abegglen cited an equipment manufacturing firm with about 4,350 employees, of whom only five or six were fired each year.[5] These discharges were for such extreme causes as prolonged absence following previous absenteeism or habitual and substantial thievery of company property. The annual labor departure rate for men, for reasons other than discharge, was between 2 and 3 per cent. Most of these left because of retirement, ill health, or the necessity of returning to the family farm after death of a father or brother. Decision making in Japanese business firms is often a group process, and the individual is thus able to avoid the loss of face which is so embarrassing in that society and which might result from individual responsibility for decisions.

It is possible to note distinctive cultural features affecting the cultural climate for business firms in still other countries. Furthermore, with adequate knowledge of local differences, one could further refine this picture of the larger culture by noting variations occurring from locality to locality.

American Culture as Background for Business Organizations

As noted earlier, America also has its cultural patterns.[6] An awareness of these is developed as contrasting cultures are studied. The

---

[5]James G. Abegglen, *The Japanese Factory: Aspects of its Social Organization* (New York: The Free Press, 1958), p. 12.

[6]For a delightful description of certain aspects of American culture, see Horace Miner, "Body Ritual Among the Nacirema," *American Anthropologist*, Vol. 58, No. 3, June 1956, pp. 503-507.

patterns and values of American communities affect the business institutions operating within them in the same way that the Japanese or Latin American cultures affect business institutions operating in those areas.

As an example, American communities differ greatly with respect to their attitudes toward minority groups and their rights in society. These community attitudes constitute cultural values of obvious importance for company management. In some states, the law prescribes "fair employment" as binding in employment practices of the company. In other cases, the application of the same employment practices would seriously conflict with local cultural traditions.

One national company, for example, with a national union, promoted a Negro employee to a higher, nonsupervisory position in its shop organization. This was consistent with company policy and in harmony with the constitution of the national union. The job had never previously been filled by a Negro, however, and other workers were extremely conscious of the nature of the precedent. Because of the conflict between this act and the cultural values of most employees, they engaged in a wildcat strike that lasted for several days. It took considerable effort on the part of both the company and the union to persuade the employees to return to their jobs and to tolerate the conflict with the prevailing cultural pattern.

Other cultural variations between locations are more subtle and difficult to explain. One study of employee attitudes discovered striking differences between employees in "town" and employees in "city" settings.[7] Town workers expressed high satisfaction when on more complex or demanding tasks, whereas city workers were more satisfied when on less complex tasks. There were obvious differences between the two groups in their expectations concerning work. Religious variations between the two settings may have accounted in part for the contrasting attitudes. Unfortunately, the causative factors could not be pinpointed easily.

Subcultures of the Organization

Within any community, one finds certain groups with cultural patterns somewhat distinct from those of the general community.

---

[7]See Arthur N. Turner and Paul R. Lawrence, *Industrial Jobs and the Worker: An Investigation of Response to Task Attributes* (Boston: Harvard University Graduate School of Business Administration, 1965), Chapters 4 and 5. This study was concerned primarily with technological determinants of attitudes and unexpectedly uncovered the variation reported here. Further discussion of this investigation appears in Chapter 23.

For the most part, these are supplementary to the general culture. They are occasioned by the unique activities, interests, or beliefs of the particular group. Any business firm, as a social institution, develops such unique subcultures within its own organization.

The following explanation describes the general content of the subculture of a business organization—a factory in this case:

> The culture of the factory is its customary and traditional way of thinking and of doing things, which is shared to a greater or lesser degree by all its members, and which new members must learn, and at least partially accept, in order to be accepted into service in the firm. Culture in this sense covers a wide range of behaviour: the methods of production; job skills and technical knowledge; attitudes towards discipline and punishment; the customs and habits of managerial behaviour; the objectives of the concern; its way of doing business; the methods of payment; the values placed on different types of work; beliefs in democratic living and joint consultation; and the less conscious conventions and taboos. Culture is part of second nature to those who have been with the firm for some time. Ignorance of culture marks out the newcomers, while maladjusted members are recognized as those who reject or are otherwise unable to use the culture of the firm.[8]

It is possible to classify these subcultures as being either *institutional subcultures* or *professional subcultures.* An institutional subculture is one encompassing the behavior patterns and beliefs of the company as a whole, a department within the company, or a particular work group. Some companies, for example, place a tremendous emphasis upon safety and accident prevention. This value may be stressed to the point that it becomes a part of the thinking of each employee and is accepted with an almost religious fervor. Personnel in such organizations would not think of operating equipment without appropriate safety glasses or driving a company car without a safety belt. The safety message is emphasized and promulgated through various types of activities, some of which become traditional with the organization. Safety conferences are held, contests are conducted, and safety performance is recorded conspicuously for all to see. The value attached to safety and the activities designed to implement this value become a part of the firm's subculture.

A given department within a company may likewise develop its own unique culture. The sales department and engineering department do not necessarily hold to all of the company traditions in pre-

---

[8]Elliott Jaques, *The Changing Culture of a Factory* (London: Tavistock Publications, Ltd., 1951), p. 251.

cisely the same manner. This is true even though both of them may accept the emphasis upon safety that identifies the company as a whole. Similarly, the eastern division and the western division may have their own unique patterns of behavior and belief.

The professional subculture comprises those customs associated with a particular professional or occupational group within the company. Indeed, it is possible for certain values of a professional subculture to cross company lines and to characterize all members of the profession. These cultural differences are focused or centered on the work and the nature of the work. Some professional groups have developed codes of ethics applicable to their professions. Accountants, as an example, recognize principles that are supposed to be observed by accountants without deviation, irrespective of the consequences to the particular firm.

Occasionally the professional culture presents perplexing administrative problems for business managers. Direction of research scientists is a case in point. The orientation of researchers toward freedom of inquiry may conflict with budgetary controls and other administrative constraints. In supervising professionally trained personnel of this type, it is often necessary to adapt customary procedures. The following statement of a laboratory section leader illustrates his recognition of the professional culture:

> In supervising research it is most important to maintain the enthusiasm of the individuals involved. This is a delicate problem when it involves shifting an individual from one type of research to another. It has to be done at length with a great deal of diplomacy. In the case of some individuals, I would not dare to shift them, or direct them, or supervise them. These are people who are very good. They know what they are doing. They know how to do it. I leave them completely on their own. They budget their own time, and are continually publishing. I read their monthly reports.[9]

Other practices that constitute a type of professional subculture are not of a professional nature in and of themselves. A group of laboratory workers, for example, develops a practice of wearing white coats and drinking coffee from laboratory beakers. These practices may have definite values attached to them. Other members of the organization are not granted indiscriminate access to the coffee

---

[9]Simon Marcson, *The Scientist in American Industry* (New York: Harper & Row, Publishers, 1960), p. 133.

beakers. The beakers and coats serve as a kind of badge to distinguish laboratory workers and to set them apart as a separate group.

Value of Cultural Awareness

Reasoning by analogy, we may observe that the facts of technology are clearly significant to a manufacturing enterprise. To remain competitive, a firm must utilize the best, up-to-date equipment and methods that are economically and technically feasible for firms in the industry. Refusal or inability to remain in the vanguard technologically may lead to failure. The point is that the technology of a plant is a matter of fact. A manufacturer has equipment that is either obsolete or up-to-date. The manufacturer would be foolish to ignore the body of technological knowledge. It affects his business and the profits that he earns.

The existing culture is also a matter of fact. The general society of the country and community have certain customs and beliefs. The business itself has created certain traditions. Within the organization, furthermore, there are professional and occupational groups that have adopted values and behavior patterns of their own. These all constitute facts for a manager. To ignore them is dangerous in the same way that it is dangerous to fall asleep technologically. The facts of culture exist whether they are recognized or not, and they affect the business firm and its way of operation. Some negative attitudes toward American business abroad have been attributed to management's callous disregard for local customs.[10] The manager also finds his personal relationships with other managers conditioned by company traditions. Note the following description of beliefs about managerial associations in one factory:

> One of the strongest conventions in the Divisional Managers Meeting was that divisional managers should not criticize each other in front of the General Manager. When a difference occurred between divisional managers, the accepted convention was that the matter should first be taken up privately between the two. Failing a satisfactory solution, it would then be referred to the General Manager, the colleague having first been informed.[11]

---

[10]John W. Houser, "The Delicate Job of American Management Abroad," *Advanced Management-Office Executive,* Vol. 1, No. 1, January 1962, p. 20.

[11]Elliott Jaques, *The Changing Culture of a Factory* (London: Tavistock Publications, Ltd., 1951), p. 281.

It is evident that violation of such a tradition would incur the displeasure and probably the hostility of colleagues.

Components of Culture

Material Culture

The things that man produces—the artifacts mentioned earlier—constitute a part of his culture. These manmade objects are created by technology and are often referred to as the *material culture.* Various types of artifacts are recognized—for example, food, clothing, housing, tools, and transportation devices. The material objects and material culture are not completely separate from the nonmaterial culture. As an example, food may be used for ceremonial purposes, and religious rules regulate its use.

In an industrial organization, one finds artifacts similar to those of society generally. There are often minor variations, of course, as would be found in the variety of clothing evident in any organization. In a hospital, nurses and orderlies are dressed in white uniforms. On a police force, the officers are attired in an identifying uniform. A few years ago, one business firm even considered a distinctive blazer that would identify the "top brass" in the executive ranks!

Perhaps the most significant part of the material culture as far as business organizations are concerned is the tooling or equipment that is used. This aspect of our culture distinguishes it from other cultures preceding it and from many cultures existing elsewhere in the world today. The extensive use of tooling—machinery, power, and automated equipment—has resulted in an industrial culture.

The tooling and equipment and the technology associated with it also affect the nonmaterial culture of industrial organizations. The man on the assembly line adopts practices and beliefs reflecting the technology and material culture to which he is subject. Some assembly lines, for example, are paced mechanically and are not subject to the control of the worker. This pacing of work may result in any number of behavior patterns and beliefs. As one example, a feeling of being driven by a "mechanical monster" can lead to resentment, resistance, and organization of unions.

Ecology and Culture

Previously it was noted that the material culture and technology affect the nonmaterial culture in an organization. Viewed more broadly, they may be considered as part of the *habitat*. In this section, attention is directed to this physical environment as a whole and to its cultural significance. In referring to factors of this type, a distinction may be made between *ecology* and *technology*. Technology was described earlier as including the method of manufacturing. Technology is often intertwined with ecology in a way that makes it difficult to differentiate sharply between them for analytical purposes.

Ecology refers to space and physical layout. The significance of this factor is its possible influence upon the cultural patterns. A general note pertaining to factors of the physical environment is appropriate. Although they are far from completely deterministic of culture, they do constitute a class of factors having some influence. The geographical distances and physical barriers existing among the continents and countries of this world account, in part at least, for distinctive cultures that develop. A group that is effectively isolated from other civilized groups often has a culture that is extremely different from that of others.

The same influence, on a more modest scale, may be noted in the ecology of industrial organizations. To illustrate, one company located its personnel department in a frame building out of the way and behind the main administrative building. In this case, the location and type of construction together seemed to create an impression in the minds of both managers and employees concerning the personnel values of the company's top management. Those who saw the location of the building were inclined to feel that personnel activities in this company were simply regarded as a necessary evil.

It is also interesting to observe parts of an organization that become segregated by some type of physical or geographical barrier. A warehouse may be separated from the main store, or a branch office may be located some distance from headquarters and other branches. It often happens that the segregated group builds up a distinctive pattern of attitudes and behavior, distinguishing it from the cultural practices of the remainder of the organization.

Nonmaterial Culture

There are many facets or aspects of nonmaterial culture which may be noted. The very fact of social organization is one of these factors. As one feature of social organization, consider the status distinctions that exist among people in any social group. The status distinctions (discussed at length in the following chapter) are culturally determined and comprise a part of the total cultural pattern of the society.

Another feature of culture that may be noted is the use of *rituals*. Although these are often associated in our thinking with religious ceremonies, they are not limited to activities of this kind. Many practices that are followed in our society and in business institutions in particular have a ritualistic character to them. Consider, for example, the graduation ceremonies used by school systems. These involve elaborate ceremonies and an unusual (and somewhat uncomfortable) type of clothing that is specially designed for the occasion.

In the business organization, some ceremonies have a definite ritualistic flavor to them. A practice is made, for example, of awarding pins or gifts to employees who have faithfully served the organization for twenty or thirty years. Such presentations are often made at dinners or in ceremonies involving considerable fanfare. At the time of retirement of employees, farewell banquets or parties of some type are held in honor of the occasion. Executives develop techniques for greeting visitors in which they come from behind the desk or out of the office to greet a caller and then engage in small talk for awhile before getting down to serious business. Even business meetings may have a ritualistic, in addition to a practical, value. (In educational institutions, faculty members are often convinced that the *only* substantial value of many such meetings is the ritualistic value.)

Another feature of culture is known as a *taboo*. The nature of taboos, which are activities that are frowned upon or regarded as undesirable or immoral, depends upon the organization and its particular background and personnel who are in it. In some organizations, for example, no one calls the president by his first name. Or it may be considered wrong to accept gifts from suppliers. As another example of a business taboo, consider the practice of some employee groups in establishing maximum output rates. It is expected by members of the group that no employee will exceed the established maximum rate. In fact, the group has methods of punishing its members for acts of noncompliance. In other groups there are standards of dress that must be observed to avoid conflict with the group's taboos. In some offices, it is expected that all members of the group will be attired in dress shirts and ties. One company insists that every sales representative of the corporation wear a hat when calling upon customers.

Another cultural feature may be found in the language variations developed by the particular social group. There develops a special language associated with the group that is referred to as *jargon.* Teenagers, for example, develop a type of slang that is virtually incomprehensible to many adults. Occupational and industrial groups likewise develop somewhat similar terminology so far as its understanding by outsiders is concerned. The jargon identifies the group, and it also identifies those qualified to be recognized as participants and members of the particular group.

Implications of Culture in Management

Importance Of Cultural Values to Individuals

The significance of cultural patterns to management is dependent upon the extent to which they are of primary value to employees. If a particular practice is followed more from habit than from a strong attachment to it, it seems likely that management need have little apprehension about necessary changes in it. If, on the other hand, employees are vitally concerned with such matters, management's ignorance of them may be perilous.

Throughout their lives, members of a society are trained to follow the cultural patterns prevailing in society. One learns to take off his hat in the house and to eat three meals a day. Within the business organization, a continuing process of training serves to adapt the individual to the prevailing subculture. The result of this conditioning is that the culture (or subculture) becomes deeply imbedded in the makeup of the individual and appears completely natural to him. In fact, effort is required to make changes in customary cultural patterns.

The extent to which a custom exerts control over the organization and its members depends upon several considerations. Some customs are strongly developed and carefully observed by the majority of employees. Other practices may be accepted by the majority, but rejected by a substantial minority. In addition, attitudes toward the custom depend upon the nature of the cultural practice itself. Some cultural practices are basically habitual in nature with little pressure toward conformity to the particular practice. We may think someone a little odd who does not eat three meals a day, but no one worries greatly about it. In the case of other behavior patterns, however, there appears a definite feeling that one should or ought to follow the customary pattern. It seems wrong for the individual to deviate from the accepted practice or belief. In the extreme case, conflict with a code or pattern appears repugnant to most members of the organization and leads to the imposition of some type of sanction. Such views often find expression in formal rules or law.

To the individual, then, the existing culture is a matter of considerable significance. First of all, customs tend to be followed on a somewhat habitual basis. Furthermore, because many of them represent accepted views of what is proper, the individual usually accepts in his own thinking the desirability of existing culture. In other words, he not only follows or accepts many cultural practices as a matter of course, but he also attaches values to some of these practices and beliefs.

Introducing Changes Having Cultural Overtones

From time to time, management finds it desirable or necessary to introduce changes that affect established cultural patterns. If the cultural pattern is deeply established, it is important first to question the wisdom of a direct challenge to it. If the custom is one that has been established over a long period of time and seems thoroughly practical and important to those in the organization, difficulty may be encountered in the administrative change. In fact, one may well expect that opposition will develop. In view of the probable opposition, the manager may well hestitate and consider from every angle the importance and necessity for the change. Opposition or conflict that may be engendered by administrative action may take a number of forms. Members of the organization may occasionally engage in open conflict. On the other hand, the opposition or sabotage may be subtle in nature, or members of the organization may simply leave because of their dissatisfaction.

Of course, not all traditions can be regarded as inherently bad or unproductive. Some may contribute to progress or be used to encourage economic development. As Hoselitz has pointed out, even the Hindu's concept of the sacredness of cattle may be used by the government of India to induce peasants to take better care of cattle, to improve cattle strains, and, in this way, to contribute to economic development.[12] Also, the "extended family" kinship system of India facilitates the financing of small artisans' shops.

---

[12]Bert F. Hoselitz, "Tradition and Economic Growth," in *Tradition, Values, and Socio-Economic Development,* eds. Ralph Braibanti and Joseph J. Spengler (Durham, N. C.: Duke University Press, 1961), pp. 110-112.

It is often necessary to make changes, however, and the fact that certain patterns have been established is no guarantee that they are good. In fact, progress is possible only at the expense of some changes. Existing culture represents a status quo that may be less than perfect. The desirable course is to proceed with good judgment in making the really important changes. As one noted industrialist has expressed it,

> Certainly, by innovating, we do stand to lose some traditions that have had value in the past. But right here is one of the tests of leadership: to know the differences between a tradition that is still good, one that needs to be modified, and one that should be abandoned altogether. Those who are to lead adequately in these times not only need to know the differences, but they need the fortitude to act on what they know, painful as this sometimes is.[13]

If the need to change is urgent, the manager must recognize the problem but get ahead with the process of accomplishing the necessary change. His hope is in getting members of the organization to see the management position with regard to the need for such change. "We've always done it this way" is a good argument until one sees there is some reason we can't just go on doing it this way. As explained in Chapters 21 and 22, some types of leadership and communication facilitate change of the type discussed here. In brief, explanation of the why and an arrangement permitting the individual some voice in the change may secure a measure of cooperation in modifying prevailing cultural patterns.

The Multi-National Firm and Other Cultures

The growth of international trade and the emergence of multinational business firms were discussed in Chapter 3. These developments bring American business firms into potential conflict with the differing values and behavior patterns of other countries. Some of these were noted earlier in the chapter. The sharp contrast in values held by employees and managers in other countries and values held by American overseas managers creates perplexing problems. The goal of efficiency, for example, is often viewed differently.

> Not infrequently the overseas manager . . . assumes employees who are members of the indigenous culture pattern share his

---

[13]Frederick R. Kappel, *Vitality in a Business Enterprise* (New York: McGraw-Hill Book Company, 1960), pp. 13-14.

> understanding of, and concern for, the common goal of efficiency. He expects them to adopt Western concepts of accountability for costs and goal direction. He assumes they will exercise self-appraisal and self-discipline and will contribute as best they can to the total effort to achieve the suprapersonal goals of the enterprise. He assumes local employees will respond in much the same way as Western employees if it becomes necessary to exert authority to force a change in their behavior. This type of overseas manager is doomed to disappointment. His assumptions regarding the commitment of local employees to the industrial way of life are invalid.[14]

Successful operation abroad demands effective cultural adaptation of products, business practices, institutional arrangements, employment policies, and personal attitudes. Consider, for example, the modification of American products to foreign markets. Products like Coca Cola may be sold without change, but other products require adaptation to meet local requirements — for example, matching electrical appliances to prevailing electrical systems. Failures occur even in changes of this type.

> An American firm making offset duplicating machines introduced its equipment, with altered electric power specifications, to a developing country which was very proud of its own paper manufacturing facilities. Unfortunately, the widely varying dimensions of the local paper required greater adjustment than the machines could make. It would have been a blow to the country's national pride to use precious foreign exchange to import paper because its own was inferior. Consequently, many of these machines already purchased with foreign exchange are still idle.[15]

Major changes in products or creation of new products to meet unique foreign demands occurs less frequently. Indeed, American business managers experience practical difficulty in thinking seriously in terms of such products. Familiarity with the American culture apparently inhibits a manager's understanding of a radically different culture. For example, American manufacturers have not produced small, low-priced, durable cars for non-Western cultures. American manufacturers fail to grasp the opportunities in foreign cultures just as buggy manufacturers failed to understand and to

---

[14]Ted R. Brannen and Frank X. Hodgson, *Overseas Management* (New York: McGraw-Hill Book Company, 1965), p. 20.

[15]James A. Lee, "Cultural Analysis in Overseas Operations," *Harvard Business Review,* Vol. 44, No. 2, March-April 1966, p. 107.

exploit the opportunities in automobile manufacturing. The unconscious reference to one's own cultural values — the *self-reference criterion* as it has been called—has been suggested as the root cause of most international business problems overseas.[16]

The overseas manager's personal relationships with customers, suppliers, and employees also involve potentially embarrassing cultural conflicts. In Japan, for example, he must understand the ritualistic, snails-pace type of business negotiations. He may wait for hours several days in a row to see a Japanese executive. After extensive discussion, he may then discover this executive is not the one who will make the decision. In the negotiation stage, even more patience is required. The Japanese rarely get right to the point, so considerable small talk is required. The lengthy conversations often entail pauses as well as talk. Conditioned by his own culture, the American manager is naturally inclined—because of the self-reference criterion—to hurry the pace, to get to the point, and to speak up during the seemingly interminable periods of silence. One resident manager was quoted as saying, "I saw a man give away $250,000 of company secrets, just because he couldn't keep his mouth shut at the right time."[17]

To make his management effective, the overseas manager must not only recognize cultural differences but also adapt his own practices accordingly. Following is a suggested approach to dealing with the widespread practice of lateness for appointments:

> Our analysis thus far would indicate that under the circumstances a certain looseness in the other culture's time system is both desirable and functional. How can the American adapt to this system? One solution, of course, would be for him to begin to plan on lateness in others as a rule. He can often arrange to be busy with other work until the foreigner arrives. He should also try to take comfort in the knowledge that his foreign visitor, when he *does* finally arrive, will be patient until the American's substituted activity can be broken off. This is because the foreigner has developed a patience to fit the necessary looseness of his own culture's time system. Conversely, if the appoinment is at the foreigner's office, the American should take his briefcase so he can be busy with other work until the foreigner can see him.[18]

---

[16] *Ibid.*, p. 106.

[17] "The U. S. Executive in Japan," *Business Week,* No. 1815, June 13, 1964, p. 144.

[18] Lee, *op. cit.,* p. 113.

All areas of business—product development, employment practices, personnel policies, decision-making processes, and so on—deserve the same alert consideration to avoid the errors from the self-reference criterion. Of course, some modification of traditional practices may be possible and necessary in the interest of improving productivity. The approach to change, however, should be based upon a careful assessment of the significance of prevailing values and patterns of behavior.

Success stories are available to show that changes can be achieved even in the face of local customs. British Esso Petroleum Company, a subsidiary of Standard Oil Company of New Jersey, was able to report gains in productivity by persuading employees to change work practices that were centuries old.[19] Esso was able to convince eight unions to agree to elimination of overtime, reduction of morning and afternoon tea breaks from a half hour to shorter periods, and elimination of an outdated "mate" or helper system.

Minimizing Conflict Between Administrative Action and Cultural Values

To minimize conflict between administrative action and the culture, the business organization must accept as far as possible the cultural practices prevalent in the community in which it is located. This demands an awareness of the cultural values that characterize the community.

Within the plant, it is also important to recognize the existing culture with which the management may come in conflict. In checking out changes, even of a technical or engineering nature, it is possible to consider pertinent customs that may be involved. Technological changes have backfired in some cases because of management's lack of understanding of the existing culture.

A final caution in preventing conflict is the avoidance of culture-threatening action in the absence of a real need for the change. In other words, change for the sake of change will be unfortunate if there is any threat to customs that have significance for members of the organization.

Summary

Culture refers to patterns of belief and behavior that have been learned from other members of society. The operation and admin-

---

[19]"Labor: the 'X' Factor Abroad," *Dun's Review and Modern Industry,* Vol. 79, No. 5, May 1962, p. 100.

istration of business firms are affected by the cultural system of the country and locality in which they are situated. Each country has a unique culture, and even different localities within the same country show some cultural variations.

Within an organization, two types of subcultures may be recognized. These are *institutional subcultures* which are vertical in nature and *professional subcultures* which are horizontal in nature.

Material culture, technology, and *ecology* are related to the *nonmaterial culture.* The nonmaterial culture includes the *social organization, status system, rituals,* and so on.

Cultural practices have significance to individual members of organizations. They tend to be habitual in nature, and many of them have certain values associated with them. Foreign cultures, in particular, present major problems of adaptation to overseas managers of multi-national firms. These managers must rise above the natural narrowness of viewpoint that is based upon their own cultural values (the *self-reference criterion*) in order to function successfully. In introducing changes having cultural overtones, it is important to recognize the possible conflict with established cultural patterns. If change is necessary, every effort should be made to minimize the conflict with established practices and values.

Discussion Questions

1. Explain carefully the concept of *culture.*
2. Should management accept the larger cultural system as providing the basic rules for managing a particular plant, or should management risk conflict with the general culture if it seems necessary for efficient operation?
3. In what ways do the background cultures of other countries appear to differ from U.S. culture? If you have traveled abroad, suggest an example from your own experience.
4. Explain the meaning of *subculture* and distinguish between *institutional subculture* and *professional subculture.*
5. In the context of the business organization, what is the nature of *material culture*?
6. Explain the relationship of *ecology* to the culture of business organizations.
7. From your own experience, preferably in a business organization, give an example of a *ritual.*

8. Suppose a particular element of the subculture of one department is objectionable to management. What should management do about it?

9. "A lot of trouble has come from technical people trying to operate a company by scientific methods rather than by management methods." Discuss the cultural implications of this statement.

10. The Defense Department recently issued an edict barring employees from accepting any favor or entertainment from contractors. Defense employees were not even to dine at a contractor's plant as his guests except on an infrequent basis and then only when the conduct of official business would be facilitated and payment for meals could not conveniently be made. How is this ruling related to culture?

Supplementary Reading

Aitken, Hugh G. J., ed., *Explorations in Enterprise,* Part III. Cambridge: Harvard University Press, 1965.

Bonaparte, Tony H., "Management in the Cultural Setting," *Advanced Management Journal,* Vol. 31, No. 4, October 1966, pp. 38-44.

Brannen, Ted R. and Frank X. Hodgson, *Overseas Management.* New York: McGraw-Hill Book Company, 1965.

Davis, James W., Jr., "Rules, Hierarchy and Organizational Climate," *Personnel Administration,* Vol. 31, No. 3, May-June 1968, pp. 50-55.

Davis, Keith and Robert L. Blomstrom, *Business and Its Environment,* Chapter 16. New York: McGraw-Hill Book Company, 1966.

England, George W., "Personal Value Systems of American Managers," *Academy of Management Journal,* Vol. 10, No. 1, March 1967, pp. 53-68.

Hoselitz, Bert F., "Unity and Diversity in Economic Structure," in *Economics and the Idea of Mankind,* ed. Bert F. Hoselitz, pp. 63-96. New York: Columbia University Press, 1965.

Lee, James A., "Cultural Analysis in Overseas Operations," *Harvard Business Review,* Vol. 44, No. 2, March-April 1966, pp. 106-114.

Lowe, Howard D., "Doing Business in the Developing Countries," *Business Horizons,* Vol. 8, No. 3, Fall 1965, pp. 25-33 .

Megginson, Leon C., "Lessons from Europe for American Business," *The Southwestern Social Science Quarterly,* Vol. 44, No. 1, June 1963, pp. 3-13.

————, *Personnel: A Behavioral Approach to Administration,* Chapter 28. Homewood: Richard D. Irwin, Inc., 1967.

Oberg, Winston, "Cross-Cultural Perspectives on Management Principles," *Journal of the Academy of Management,* Vol. 6, No. 2, June 1963, pp. 129-143.

Richman, Barry M., "Significance of Cultural Variables," *Academy of Management Journal,* Vol. 8, No. 4, December 1965, pp. 292-308.

Rosenzweig, James E., "Managers and Management Scientists (*Two Cultures*)," *Business Horizons,* Vol. 10, No. 3, Fall 1967, pp. 79-86.

Tagiuri, Renato, "Value Orientations and the Relationship of Managers and Scientists," *Administrative Science Quarterly,* Vol. 10, No. 1, June 1965, pp. 39-51.

Walker, Charles R., *Modern Technology and Civilization,* Part 3. New York: McGraw-Hill Book Company, 1962.

17

Status Systems

Although our democratic philosophy accepts all citizens as politically equal, many types of inequalities among people are clearly evident. These distinctions, moreover, are generally recognized. In industrial groups, such differences—many of them quite subtle in nature—are also understood by employees who assign, in their own thinking, different individuals to different rungs on the corporate ladder. This chapter is concerned with these differences in the status of people in organizations and the implications for management action.

THE NATURE OF STATUS

What Is Status?

Status is concerned with a person's prestige or standing within a group. Different individuals are evaluated in terms of some common yardstick and are assigned positions of relative importance. These judgments about the relative prestige of individuals are based upon consideration of the rights, duties, obligations, restrictions, and limitations applying to them.

Every organization has some type of *status system*. In a status system, all positions are assigned a standing relative to one another. This results in the classification of individuals as equals, superiors, and subordinates. There is no such thing as status apart from other individuals. Status suggests that one is better or more important than another. It is a relative matter. One who has higher status in an organization "carries more weight" than those with lesser status. Deference is generally shown to the individual with higher status.

Different individuals naturally use different weights or values in their individual judgments regarding status. Technically, therefore, there are as many different status systems as there are individuals making judgments of this variety. We often simplify this process, however, by making generalizations about the status of positions. These generalizations are thought to express rather widely accepted attitudes or a general consensus regarding the status of particular individuals, positions, occupations, or groups.

It might be noted that both individuals and groups have their positions in the status system or status hierarchy. An entire group may be regarded as superior to another group, while individual members of that group are then evaluated in terms of individual prestige within the limits of the general standing of the group.

Status Differences in Organization

Any observation of organizational relationships and behavior quickly reveals the existence of prestige preferences. Although there is rarely complete agreement on the part of organization members as to the precise ranking of all individuals, few would argue that a status system does not exist. The most egotistical janitor would hardly suggest that his status is superior to that of the president. A secretary would be conscious of her own superiority over the janitor but, at the same time, would look up to the professional engineers a few doors down the hall. Each individual has some impression of his own status as well as that of other personnel with whom he has sufficient contact to provide a basis for judgment.

Two kinds of status systems have been suggested by Chester I. Barnard.[1] The first of these, *functional* status, is based upon the type of work or activity performed. The professional, whether an engineer, attorney, or otherwise, enjoys greater prestige than nonprofessional members of the organization. The craftsman has a higher status than the unskilled employee. An accountant is a notch above

---

[1]Used by permission of the publishers from Chester I. Barnard *Organization and Management,* Cambridge, Mass.: Harvard University Press, Copyright, 1948, by the President and Fellows of Harvard College, pp. 209-210.

a mechanic. In fact, a white-collar worker generally is viewed as superior to a blue-collar worker unless there are marked differences in income.

Scalar status, on the other hand, is concerned with the level in the organization's hierarchy or chain of command. In a position that is high in the organizational pyramid, the incumbent is considered an important executive or a "wheel." The top of the company is populated with very important people, while the bottom echelons contain the less important people.

In any functioning organization, these two status systems operate simultaneously and complement each other. Figure 19 presents a diagram in which the prestige or status of the position is indicated by its vertical level. In this diagram, one can see the influence of both functional and scalar status. It appears that the public relations function, for example, has less prestige than the other functions appearing near the top of this chart. This is true even though the function is headed by a vice president who reports directly to the chief executive. In fact, because of the nature of this function, the production manager is even a step above the public relations vice president. In the production organization, however, the production manager's status is below that of the production vice president as a result of his scalar position. Yet, because of his function, he does enjoy prestige greater than that of the other managers reporting to the same production vice president.

The two types of status suggested by Barnard—functional status and scalar status—are both descriptive of the position, regardless of the incumbent. These types of status are supplemented by a third variety that might be designated as *personal* status. Although formal position, by virtue of its scalar and functional qualities, goes a long way in determining an individual's status, this status may be augmented or reduced by the individual's personal characteristics. When a brilliant or distinguished individual replaces a lackluster incumbent, the replacement enjoys higher status even though the position may be unchanged. In a business organization this would be true whether the position is that of executive, supervisor, craftsman, scientist, or engineer. In a university, the same would be true of a new president, dean, department chairman, professor, or coach.

The status levels in an organization provide a framework for informal relationships. The lab workers develop informal contacts and associations among themselves. The same is true of the office force. An individual feels comfortable in the presence of his peers, and the informal relationships are thus able to develop naturally in such an atmosphere. Occasionally, a vice president may hobnob with an operator far down the line, but this is a rare situation. As an individual moves up the ladder, consequently, he moves to status levels involving different informal contacts and relationships. The need for changing these informal relationships is one of the painful features of moving up the management ladder.

Business executives need an appreciation of the ubiquity and significance of status systems within their organizations. It is required, first of all, in order to understand the attitudes of those who work in the organization. This applies both to managerial and operative personnel. In addition, executives are constantly making decisions which affect status in various ways. They need, therefore, an awareness of the status dimensions of management action.

Figure 19. *Status Levels of Key Individuals in a Business Organization*

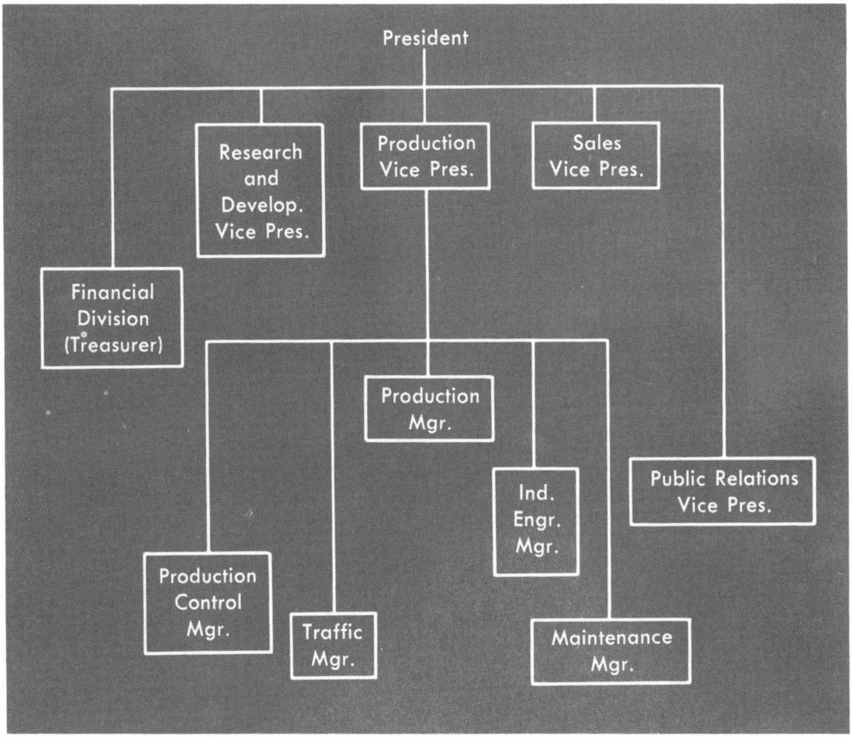

An Example of Status in a Business Organization

One of the most penetrating studies of status in industry was that conducted by William Foote Whyte in his investigation of human relations in the restaurant industry.[2] In Whyte's analysis of the social structure in restaurants, he discovered very marked distinctions in the status levels of the various positions. In the kitchen, for example, he found that the work stations were socially ranked. At the top status level was the range station, where the cooking took place. At that station, the positions were most highly paid and involved the highest degree of skill. It served as a focal point, with other work in the kitchen revolving around it. Below the status level of the range station was the salad station, which involved products of high prestige value. Women vegetable cooks were respectful in their references to work at the salad station and indicated a willingness to work there if they were not already holding positions at the range. Below these two stations, in order, were the chicken preparation and meat preparation stations, the chicken cooking and vegetable preparation stations, and the fish station. The fish station was considered to have the lowest status of all kitchen stations.

The ranking of the kitchen stations was observable in the behavior of workers toward each other. More intensive examination showed that the kitchen stations contained even finer distinctions, each with a ranking system of its own. Following is Whyte's description of the status levels and distinctions involved in the eight positions at the vegetable preparation station:

> There were eight women on vegetable preparation, and, so as to avoid confusion, I will refer to them by number. 1 and 2, the vegetable cooks, organized the work of the station and then concentrated their attention upon the range. 3 divided her time between cooking and preparing. 4 was in charge of the preparation station, under the supervision of 1, and occasionally had some connection with cooking. 5, 6, 7, and 8 did no cooking. The most obvious social distinction fell between those who cooked and those who did not.
>
> These employees all had their regular positions at the preparation table. 3 always worked on the west side toward the range. 4 divided her time between the west and south sides. 5 worked regularly at the south side and 6 at the east side. 7 and 8 always sat at the north side with their backs toward the dishwashing department.

---

[2]William Foote Whyte, *Human Relations in the Restaurant Industry* (New York: McGraw-Hill Book Company, 1948).

Aside from the cooking-noncooking distinction, the influence of status was observed in the distribution of vegetables and in the flow of work. We found that vegetables varied widely in social standing. At the top were the luxury or decorative items such as parsley, chives, and celery. At the top of the regular vegetables were green beans. Next came spinach and carrots. Next to the bottom were sweet and white potatoes, and onions were considered the most undesirable of all vegetables. We did not observe the preparation of other vegetables often enough to be sure of their rank.

Comments of the workers showed that they valued lack of odor, crispness, and cleanness of handling most highly in vegetables, whereas the vegetable that had an odor and that stained the hands or was sloppy to handle was held in low esteem. The low standing of potato peeling is too well-known to require comment, but here at least the workers said they preferred potatoes to onions because they did not smell or stain the hands. (Here potatoes were boiled in their skins and then peeled.) Perhaps spinach might have ranked with potatoes or below except that it did not reach the preparation table until it had been thoroughly cleaned of soil and sand at another station.

4, who was in charge of preparation under the chief vegetable cook, was the only one we ever observed working on parsley and chives. 4 and 5 were the only ones to work on celery. Everyone got a chance to work on green beans, and sometimes they were all at work cutting the ends, but always it was 4 or 5 who moved on to the next step, cutting up the beans for cooking, while 6, 7, and 8 were still cutting ends. There was no division of labor on spinach, since only one operation, cutting off the stems, was performed at the station, but 4 and 5 were sometimes observed working on green beans while 6, 7, and 8 were still on spinach. There were two operations performed on carrots, scraping and dicing. Generally 6, 7, and 8 scraped while 4 diced. At times everybody worked on peeling potatoes, but 4 would soon move on to another vegetable, and 5 would shift over to slicing the potatoes. Occasionally everyone was observed peeling onions, but when a small pile was on hand, 4 and 5 would take to cutting them up or would abandon them in favor of another vegetable.[3]

Determinants of Status

Status levels in any organization are determined by a combination of factors. Some of these factors are regulated or specified by the management of the organization, while others are connected with

[3] *Ibid.*, pp. 35-37.

the individual. As an example of the former, consider the importance of the work as one significant feature in determining the prestige of the worker. It was clear, in the previous discussion of the restaurant kitchen, that cooking was considered a more important type of work than some other types of food preparation. The work of a doctor is considered more important than that of a ditch digger, and the work of a vice president more consequential than that of a mechanic.

Other organizational features affecting status include differences in the ability or skill level required to perform the work, the inherent difficulty in performing various types of work, the physical working conditions and cleanliness of the work place, the rate of pay, and the opportunity for promotion. In addition, great importance attaches to the possession of power and authority. If an individual is able to make important decisions and to exert great influence without detailed supervision, he is typically conceded to have high status in the organization. To some extent, this particular feature may be considered as overlapping the factor of work importance discussed above.

The employee's particular status position is not completely determined by the type of factors noted above. In addition, personal qualities influence or modify status evaluations formed on the basis of these organizational factors. Some of the important features of a personal nature include sex, race, and family connections. Certain racial groups have superior status in the community, and this carries over into the work place. In industry, women are often regarded as being inferior to men. In some cases this is reflected in different rates of pay. Other personal characteristics include those of a personality nature—one may be considered a "good guy"—and intelligence level. In addition, past achievements and present possessions may be significant in determining evaluation and placement on the status ladder.

Relationship of Industrial Status Systems to Those of Society

There is a reasonably close relationship between general social status as established in the community and the particular status inside a specific formal organization. An occupation with low social standing in the eyes of society is unlikely to have much prestige in the work place, and vice versa. Society, for example, does not attach great importance to janitorial work or day labor. In the work place, it is unusual to find personnel in these fields enjoying great prestige and outranking those whom society regards as higher status people. The status of various kinds of craftsmen varies from group to group and culture to culture, however. Among some of the Polynesians, for example, anthropologists found that fishing was considered a more humble occupation than agriculture, whereas the opposite was true in other groups.

Examples of high-status occupations in the United States are the following:

Physician	Architect
Scientist	Minister
College professor	Civil engineer
Lawyer	Airline pilot

There are differences in prestige among these occupations, of course, even though they are all near the upper end of the status scale. At the other end of the scale, the following occupations are widely regarded as having low status:

Taxi driver	Soda fountain clerk
Farm hand	Garbage collector
Janitor	Street sweeper
Bartender	Shoe shiner

Functions of the Status System

Status systems often appear undemocratic in their nature and undesirable in their effects. What is sometimes overlooked is the constructive role of status in our society and in business organizations in particular. In this section, attention is given to the necessary and useful functions of status gradations.

Maintaining Effective and Authoritative Communication

The existence of a status system makes possible effective and authoritative communication. This is essential if any group is to function as an organization rather than as a rabble. Someone must be in a position to provide direction and coordination to the various members associated in the undertaking. The status system permits understanding concerning who is to lead and who is to follow. From the standpoint of the subordinate, this appears completely natural. Members of organizations expect to receive instructions and directions regarding their own activities. In fact, they would consider it a most inefficient organization and quite likely suffer some loss of morale if they detected a substantial lack of status differentiations.

This need for a status system to provide authority in communications is particularly acute in emergency situations demanding quick, unquestioned decisions. The battlefield is no place for uncertainty in leadership. Military forces, as a result, employ a well-defined and widely recognized status system.

In business organizations, the practical application of this concept simply means that the president is the acknowledged leader in reconciling such differences as those between production and sales functions. It does not mean that the president must refuse to consider the thinking of sales or production personnel. In fact, he may adopt proposals emanating from either or both. He is in a position, however, to enforce an integration of viewpoints and to avoid the impasse that could occur in the absence of a status system. Similarly, the chief production executive has the recognized right to make decisions affecting the various activities under his direction. At the bottom of the ladder, the operative employee is directed by his immediate supervisor with respect to daily work assignments.

A similar need for authoritative communication exists in the case of the staff specialists who have functional status. The business economist should be able to provide a more scientific analysis of business conditions than is possible for the nonprofessional. It is true that an individual may be less capable than his status position would indicate. An engineer may be a poor engineer, or a doctor may be a quack. But it is helpful to have some guidelines that indicate probable competence. It is generally more productive to consult a doctor regarding illness than to confer with a mechanic. And the engineer should know more about design than does a salesman.

Providing Incentives for Advancement

The status systems and symbols of status that pervade our society provide strong motivation. Few individuals are content with the status quo, and their aspirations are often linked with conceptions of status as much as they are with hopes of purely material advancement. It appears important to most people that they should live in the "right" section of the city and drive a type of car befitting their positions. One automobile manufacturer recently advertised to the effect that "you have earned the right to drive our type of car." In other words, the customer was told that he had moved upward on the status ladder to the point that he was now on the rung identified with this car.

The status striving of our population is implied by the title of a best-seller of a few years ago, *The Status Seekers*.[4] In his discussion of houses and furnishings and their symbolic importance to people, Vance Packard provided a number of pointed illustrations. Developers in their attempts to sell homes try to help buyers feel that purchasing a home in a higher priced development means that they have "arrived." A consultant advised builders to have their salesmen stress such factors as "upper-brackets," "exclusive neighborhood," and "executive-type buyers." Foremen do not wish to buy homes in the same development with workmen but wish instead to locate in other developments known as offering homes at higher prices. Advertising reflects the same status considerations. A split-level house on Long Island became a "Georgian split with a bi-level brunch bar in a maitre d' kitchen." In the furnishings of a home, status is similarly indicated. A suburbanite wishing to move up into the lower-upper class may buy antiques as symbols of old social position. In the early days of television, the aerials began appearing in clusters rather than at random. Apparently, when one family erected an aerial for all to see, the neighbors quickly emulated the pioneer.

In the business world, executives make great sacrifices in reaching or moving toward the top. These sacrifices are made in terms of effort, time, and even, in some situations, in terms of their own families. Their lives and activities cannot be explained adequately in terms of economic motivation. They seem to have an inner drive, no matter how explicitly recognized, to achieve a certain status level in the corporation.

In recent years, blue-collar workers have also demonstrated a concern with their status in industry. Even when the pay of blue-collar personnel exceeds that of white-collar employees, they are still considered by many as lower-class employees. Their reaction seems to be, "Why shouldn't we have the same dignity and recognition as office personnel?" The United Automobile Workers' bargaining objective of a salary to replace the hourly wage illustrates the direction of this effort. In general, the blue-collar group is

[4]Vance Packard, *The Status Seekers* (New York: David McKay Company, Inc., 1959).

seeking the prestige of a middle-class occupation to replace their traditional working-class label. Even within the blue-collar group, there are status distinctions and status pressures. There is an evident restlessness today, for example, among skilled craftsmen in various industries. Bargaining agreements in the past have tended to compress the wage differences between skilled and unskilled groups, thereby reducing the relative status of craftsmen. Their current demands for more than an average wage increase and their efforts to secure separate union representation indicate a dissatisfaction with their declining status.

The power or strength of status as a motivational force no doubt varies from one individual to another. In fact, most of us are probably unaware of the precise importance that it has in our own lives. It is quite likely that most of us underestimate its significance to ourselves. It seems likely that we should acknowledge status as being tremendously important in our society. The rise in the standard of living that our society has enjoyed may have changed the nature of the status symbols, but it has hardly eliminated the fact of status distinctions.

No matter how much we may disparage status differences, it is important to recognize their powerful influence as a motivational force. Achievement in our society results from such motivation. In criticisms of status factors, therefore, it is well to consider the alternatives in terms of motivational power.

Developing Sense of Responsibility

As a motivational device, status also operates in a negative manner to create and enforce a sense of responsibility. Regardless of one's desire regarding advancement, he usually wishes to maintain his existing position. This means that he must avoid conduct or performance that would result in a reversion to lower status. The individual enjoys a certain prestige based upon past behavior. He would normally hesitate to act in a way that would jeopardize this image. As a result, the status system serves to systematize his behavior.

The desire to avoid a reduction in status appears to be an exceedingly strong feeling in most individuals. In fact, it is probably much stronger than the urge for advancement in status. The phrase "lose face" has been applied to this reduction in status, and most individuals find such a thought repugnant. Imagine the embarrassment of the "expert" who is revealed as a complete phony. This accounts for the search for face-saving devices.

In view of the seriousness of status reductions, employers are typically reluctant to utilize demotions as a personnel tool. A demotion involves a reduction in pay, but it also involves a great deal more than this financial loss. The loss in status that accompanies the demotion is the critical factor in the thinking of the employee involved and in the minds of those who are in a position to observe the demotion. This explains the strong emotional disturbance created by new job evaluation plans. Analysis of jobs to determine the proper level carries the implication that some existing distinctions may be unjustified and thus threatens the status of some individuals.

> Workers find little comfort in the assurance that no incumbent's rate will be reduced, even though a lower ranking may be assigned to the job as a result of the analysis. The fact remains that a worker's job may be relegated to a lower plane, and you cannot depreciate what he *does* without depreciating *him* in the process.[5]

This factor also contributes to the hesitancy of some individuals to move up to higher-level positions, including managerial posts. It is better, they may reason, to forego the higher status than to gain and then lose it. The loss of status would be a humiliating experience.

Protecting Personal Integrity

There is a natural desire on the part of organization members to have orders originate from those of higher status. Accepting orders from a superior appears much better than accepting orders from a nobody. This would be bad, because the low status of the nobody would rub off on the individual accepting the orders. This status differentiation, then, in terms of order giving, serves to protect the personality of the individual. He feels more comfortable about himself as a result of the status system.

Differences in level of ability among individuals also lead to a need for status distinctions. As Barnard has noted,

> The necessity for differentiation from the standpoint of those of inferior ability is that without it they are constantly in a position of disadvantage, under pressure to exceed their capacities, perpetually losing in a race in which no handicaps are recognized, never able to attain expected goals so long as they are treated as the equals of those who are in fact superior; therefore they are always in a position of never securing respect for what they do contribute, of always incurring disrespect for what they cannot do. Men cannot stand this kind of inferiority and its frustra-

[5]James C. Worthy, *Big Business and Free Men* (New York: Harper & Row, Publishers, 1959), p. 120.

> tions. The inferiors will group themselves and command respect by various means if they are not protected by being assigned a formal status, which, though inferior, recognizes their position as being more or less indispensable and participating, even though individually less important.[6]

More capable individuals similarly need the distinctions of the status system. Otherwise, the individual with higher ability is conscious of the fact that his superior ability is not adequately recognized and inevitably has some sense of the unfairness of the system. The status system is thus helpful both to the inferior and superior individual in maintaining a sense of personal integrity.

Symbols of Status

Nature and Function of Status Symbols

Status levels are indicated by various external trappings or indicators closely connected with the individual. These *symbols* permit an observer to understand the prestige level of the individual in question.

As an example, the military services indicate rank by insignia worn by military officers. An officer with an eagle on his shoulder is outranked by an officer wearing a star. By the same token, the one-star general is outranked by those wearing two or three stars. This symbol is very open in that it allows any observer to detect the status of the individual immediately even though he knows very little about the individual wearing the insignia.

In most organizations, the symbols are more subtle than those of the military service. But the symbols are nonetheless real and widely recognized as indicating different levels of importance.

One of the widely recognized symbols in our society is the type of automobile that is driven. "Important" people drive Cadillacs or Lincolns, while those of lower status drive Oldsmobiles or Buicks. Those at the lower end of the social ladder drive old-model Fords, Plymouths, or Chevrolets.

Types of Status Symbols in Industry

Status symbols in industrial organizations vary considerably in nature. They exist at all levels, however, from the level of vice president to the operative employee.

---

[6]Barnard, *op. cit.,* p. 222.

One of the most obvious symbols is the title applying to the position. The title of president indicates that the individual is extremely important in that particular organization. The vice president is obviously less important. A project engineer is above a junior engineer, and a junior engineer probably outranks a draftsman. To a considerable extent, this symbol is determined by the management of the organization. It is possible, however, that employees may use informal titles which connote status. In Whyte's study of the restaurant industry, for example, one employee objected violently to being referred to as the "fish lady."[7] She insisted that her work place was a "sea-food station," and not a "fish station."

Reference was made earlier to insignia worn by an officer. Although civilian organizations do not normally reveal rank in quite this way, there are various material factors that show relative position on the prestige scale. The size of the office, for example, is one indicator of this type. Vice presidents usually have larger offices than those occupied by lower officials. Numerous other features of the office itself reveal its status level. In fact, the very fact that an office is private indicates greater prestige than that of a desk in a larger office. The other furnishings in the office similarly reveal status distinctions. At some level, the offices are carpeted, and metal desks give way to wooden desks. Even wooden desks have their rank, with walnut and mahogany outranking oak. Draperies at the window and paintings on the wall are also symbolic of prestige. Potted plants, lounge chairs, private washrooms, intercom boxes, and adjoining private conference rooms are all suggestive of the prestige of the individual occupying the office.

In addition to material trappings, there are privileges that indicate the status level of the incumbent. Some employees are required to punch a time clock, while higher-level employees are not required to do so. Higher management officials often report at a later hour than other employees, and no one checks closely regarding the precise time of their arrival. (Of course, these same officials may also work later than other personnel.) The executive lunchroom is another noted indicator of status, and some companies even have a series of executive lunch rooms graded on a prestige level. For the company that uses an executive lunch room, therefore, the right to eat in that lunch room is a definite status symbol.

Numerous other types of status symbols could be cited. Each type of position carries its own, and these symbols are extremely meaningful to those close enough to understand their significance. The white collar, the reserved parking place, the private company-

---

[7]Whyte, *op. cit.,* p. 43.

furnished car, the right to make long-distance telephone calls, the privilege of eating lunch with top management — all of these and many others are significant in revealing the status levels of various positions.[8]

Functional Value of Status Symbols

Status symbols communicate the facts regarding status to members of the organization. Without knowledge of status differences, the status system is unable to perform its customary function. By communicating the facts regarding status, therefore, status symbols contribute to the values inherent in the status system itself. They confirm and help maintain this status system.

For example, certain minimum status symbols are useful in providing a type of credentials to members of the organization. Members know that they can listen to a certain individual who speaks regarding certain situations because of that person's status. His title or other indicators of position establish him as one who can speak authoritatively. The status symbol, then, might be viewed as a type of necessary tool for the purpose of accomplishing work more effectively. The manager may, therefore, need some status symbols in order to get a prompt hearing and reasonable acceptance of his position.

This requirement for status symbols does not demand their proliferation. A small number may well serve with sufficient forcefulness to establish and maintain the status system of the organization.

Problems of Status

Increase in Distance Between Organization Levels

Although status performs constructive functions as noted above, it also has its disadvantages. Indeed, some are so conscious of its weaknesses that they refer to the *pathology* of status. One important negative feature concerns the *social distance* between organization levels. It is true, as discussed earlier in the chapter, that authoritative communication is desirable. However, organization levels must

---

[8]For a fictional treatment of this subject, see "Portrait of a Striver," (a condensation of pertinent passages from *Point of No Return,* by John P. Marquand) in *Readings in Sociology,* Second Edition, eds. Edgar A. Schuler, *et al.* (New York: Thomas Y. Crowell Company, 1960), pp. 317-324.

also work together in achieving the objectives of the organization. It is possible, consequently, that status distinctions may become so great or be emphasized to the point that active cooperation is reduced. The subordinate may follow orders but find it difficult to work closely with higher levels.

Chapter 22 considers the difficulties inherent in communication between two organization levels. The fact is clear that the emphasis on the levels may hamper the free flow of communication between them. In other words, as great emphasis is placed upon status distinctions, it becomes more difficult to collaborate smoothly. To illustrate, a machine operator would probably be so ill at ease in a conference with the president of the company that he would find it most difficult to make positive contributions to the conference. It is a fact that some organizations have the status levels so sharply defined that a real cooperative spirit is missing. It is quite likely true, in fact, that the majority of organizations have some difficulties with the problem of distance between the various levels of the organization. One president of a large corporation has deliberately avoided the excessive use of status symbols. He refuses a reserved parking spot, eats in the same cafeteria with rank and file employees, and occupies an office similar in size to those of other executives.

Excessive Preoccupation with Status Symbols

The importance of status symbols has been recognized. Because they reveal the fact of an individual's standing or prestige, they are prized by these individuals. The problem is that the individual may become so preoccupied with these symbols that the entire system is run into the ground. Getting a private office or a staff assistant or an electronic computer becomes important in and of itself, and little regard may be paid to the intrinsic need for these symbolic trappings. Instead, they are conceived as being important merely for the purpose of proving one's value to one's associates.

In distinguishing between a legitimate concern with status symbols and an excessive preoccupation with them, it might be helpful to think of the extent to which there is a rational basis for the symbol. In some cases, there are entirely logical reasons, in terms of practical considerations, for the arrangement or device that comes to have symbolic value. It is possible, in other words, that a higher-level manager may actually need an office of larger size than that of subordinates because of the type of conferences conducted in his office. If this logical justification is apparent, the symbol appears to be understandable and logical in its use. No doubt some minimum use of symbols is justified even aside from such purely technical or practical considerations. Proliferation of symbols and an undue concern for them, however, may properly be regarded as pathological.

In terms of negative effects, the excessive preoccupation with status symbols may be expensive. The salary of an unneeded staff assistant or the rental expense for an electronic computer is a costly method of establishing the standing of particular executives or departments. In addition, executive time and effort may be wasted in an unnecessary struggle to obtain or maintain status symbols. If the symbols come to have such great importance, any irregularities in the arrangement of symbols or changes in them lead to dissatisfaction and unhappiness on the part of members of the organization so affected.

Creation of Friction in Assignment and Work Relationships of Personnel

At any given time, the status system of an organization has assigned values to all positions. Any change is liable to upset this status quo. Some actions by management may improve the standing of positions, and others may threaten the existing status. The working relationships and arrangements of an organization are certainly affected by status considerations.

In the transfer of personnel, for example, individuals react oftentimes on the basis of status considerations. The shop worker is typically happy to take an office job. He lays aside his work clothes, dons a white shirt and tie, occasionally takes a reduction in pay, and still regards the change as a promotion. But attempts to transfer an office employee into the shop area often lead to objections and difficulties of various types. Stories are told of employees so transferred who go to great lengths to use lunch facilities and rest rooms of office employees after being transferred to a shop area rather than using the completely adequate facilities available near their new work place.

In the work place, the woman's position is often reversed from what it is in society. She often is regarded as having lower status than the male worker. As a result, her presence in a job affects the status of that job. Jobs typically filled by women become regarded as women's jobs. Apparently the feeling becomes, "If a woman can do it, anyone can do it." How many young, strong male employees, for example, will seriously consider nursing or secretarial work as life vocations? This may also interfere with the promotion of women to supervisory posts. There is some evidence that the frequent objections to women as supervisors are based, at least partially, upon status considerations. The subordinate may feel that the lower status of the woman supervisor reflects upon the subordinate.

Transfer or assignment of women to jobs traditionally occupied by men may result in a sharp reduction in the status of those jobs. When the first female draftsman was assigned to an all-male drafting room, there were immediate, noticeable reactions on the part of veteran employees. Although the male draftsmen did not voice their objections in terms of status as we have interpreted it here, it seemed apparent that these status considerations lay behind the questions that they raised.

Ignoring Individual Competency by Stressing Position

Status distinctions do not always correspond perfectly to the competence of the individuals who are involved. A doctor may be a quack, and an engineer may be only a poor mechanic. The vice president may be the owner's son-in-law but lack administrative knowledge. The general may have more seniority than he has skill in military strategy.

Normally, some adjustments are made in our thinking about the status of such individuals. For example, the vice president's son may not be taken too seriously. We do not always accept a symbolic title at face value. It may be, however, that the incompetent individual has sufficient power that his position of status is real even though he lacks capacity. The status accorded to the position may tend to obscure the competency or weakness of the individual.

The fault is not so much with the basic idea of the status system as it is with errors in assignment of status. Status is recognized in some cases where it should not be — that is, in individuals who lack the basic competency or ability expected in such positions. Or, an individual is placed in a position carrying considerable status but with requirements beyond his capacity to fulfill.

Through poor policies of appointment and promotion, managers may permit the staffing of a status system to become unsatisfactory or the organization to be filled with incompetent personnel. Management must, therefore, assume responsibility in keeping high status positions filled with people of commensurate ability. Only alert management can minimize the glaring inconsistencies between status and ability.

In removing or dealing with incompetence in positions of high status, once it exists, the executive is confronted with a peculiar problem. There is the fact of incompetence, and there is also the fact of status. It becomes more difficult to deal with the incompetence simply because of the status considerations. As one writer has pointed out, the decision to confer higher status is not readily reversed.

> The difficulty increases when high status personnel, such as presidents, vice-presidents, generals, and admirals, are involved. When a person is removed from a position, the integrity of the appointing officials is at stake. For that reason, an executive is often "protected" even when it seems evident to others in the organization that an error in judgment was made in the appointment.[9]

This leads to such practices as placing high-salaried executives in harmless staff positions, early retirements, and resignations in lieu of dismissals.

Status Anxiety

Members of an organization may experience feelings of anxiety as a result of status considerations. One's status position may appear undesirable, and he may feel powerless to change it. At the same time, he may feel that he is entitled to a higher status position and has the necessary ability for the higher position. For some reason, however, there is a block to realization of his status aspirations. It may be that he perceives his own capacity incorrectly — that is, that he thinks that he is better than he actually is. On the other hand, it may be that some feature or defect of organization exists and contributes to the failure to recognize a real ability on his part. For example, there may be simply too many qualified competitors for a higher position, making it impossible for all capable people to be advanced. Whatever the reason, the inability to improve one's status may produce a sense of frustration within that individual.

Status inconsistency may also lead to anxiety. This means that the various symbols of status are not in harmony. Some of the status symbols may be present and indicate a position of appropriate importance, but some may be missing. The title of the position may be

---

[9]Henry H. Albers, *Principles of Organization and Management,* Second Edition (New York: John Wiley & Sons, Inc., 1966), p. 546.

right, for example, but the incumbent may lack a private office that seems appropriate for the particular level. Status may be recognized by physical facilities but the member may never be invited into the inner circle. Status inconsistency may thus lead to unhappiness as the individual is aware of the deficiencies and inconsistencies.

It is possible that status situations of the type described here have adverse physical effects — literally producing ulcers. Probably more frequently, status problems simply create attitudes that produce individual unhappiness and reduce organizational efficiency.

Summary

Status refers to gradations in standing or rank that exist in any group. These distinctions are evident in society generally and likewise occur within business organizations. Status is *scalar, functional,* and *personal* in nature, and it is determined by a combination of organizational and personal factors.

The status system performs useful functions in administration and in society generally. Among its values are the contribution that it makes to authoritative and effective communication, the incentive that it provides for advancement, the sense of responsibility that it develops, and the protection of personal integrity that it provides. Status is communicated by means of *symbols,* which include not only official titles but also such privileges and physical trappings as private offices, lunch room privileges, and office furnishings that surround the job and identify its status. The primary value of status symbols is their communication of the fact of status itself.

Although status performs useful functions, there are also a number of problems connected with it. It may increase the *social distance* between organization levels, thus making it difficult to achieve completely effective cooperation. In addition, members of an organization may become so preoccupied with status symbols that the system gets somewhat out of hand. Conditions of *anxiety* may also be created within the individual. Difficulties in assignment and friction among employees may likewise result from causes related to the status system. Status sometimes attaches importance to the individual without adequate regard for his competence. This leads to difficulties in following incompetent leadership or in administratively dealing with inconsistencies that occur.

Discussion Questions

1. When the president, in a well-known novel, told a younger executive to call him "Tony," the young man went home in great excitement. Both he and his wife considered it a cause for celebration. How would you interpret this incident in the light of this chapter?

2. Probably few of us would agree on the prestige ranking of the various individuals in an organization of any size. What, then, is the *status system*?

3. What is the basic distinction between *functional* status and *scalar* status? In what way can these concepts be applied to the eight vegetable preparation positions in the restaurant studied by Whyte?

4. Consider a recent change of personnel in a public or private position with which you are acquainted. Was any change of status involved? If so, what caused this change?

5. How is the status system of a business organization related to that of society?

6. Explain the effects of a status system upon vertical communication.

7. Do you believe that the average American works more for money (and the goods and services that money will buy) or for status and the symbols that signify status?

Supplementary Reading

Albers, Henry H., *Principles of Organization and Management,* Second Edition, Chapters 11 and 22. New York: John Wiley & Sons, Inc., 1966.

Anderson, B., J. Berger, B. P. Cohen, and M. Zelditch, Jr., "Status Classes in Organizations," *Administrative Science Quarterly,* Vol. 11, No. 2, September 1966, pp. 264-283.

Davis, Keith, *Human Relations at Work,* Third Edition, Chapter 3. New York: McGraw-Hill Book Company, 1967.

Ditz, Gerhard W., "Status Problems of the Salesman," *MSU Business Topics,* Vol. 15, No. 1, Winter 1967, pp. 68-80.

Dubin, Robert, *Human Relations in Administration,* Third Edition, Chapter 13. Englewood Cliffs: Prentice-Hall, Inc., 1968.

Flippo, Edwin B., *Management: A Behavioral Approach,* Chapter 11. Boston: Allyn & Bacon, Inc., 1966.

Hodge, Robert W., Paul M. Siegel, and Peter H. Rossi, "Occupational Prestige in the United States, 1925-63," *The American Journal of Sociology,* Vol. 70, No. 3, November 1964, pp. 286-302.

Litterer, Joseph A., *The Analysis of Organizations,* Chapter 4. New York: John Wiley & Sons, Inc., 1965.

Mortensen, Vivika, "Are Status Symbols Inevitable?" *Personnel Administration,* Vol. 26, No. 3, May-June 1963, pp. 31-34.

Packard, Vance, *The Status Seekers.* New York: David McKay Company, Inc., 1959.

Pfiffner, John M. and Frank P. Sherwood, *Administrative Organization,* Chapter 15. Englewood Cliffs: Prentice-Hall, Inc., 1960.

Scott, William G., *Organization Theory: A Behavioral Analysis for Management,* Chapter 8. Homewood: Richard D. Irwin, Inc., 1967.

Strauss, George and Leonard R. Sayles, *Personnel: The Human Problems of Management,* Second Edition, Chapter 4. Englewood Cliffs: Prentice-Hall, Inc., 1967.

Whyte, William Foote, *Human Relations in the Restaurant Industry,* Chapters 2, 4, and 23. New York: McGraw-Hill Book Company, 1948.

18

Authority, Power, and Politics

In an earlier era, the word of a chief executive was accepted as law. Compliance, not defiance, was the order of the day. But today questions about managerial authority are being raised. What is the nature of executive authority? What are the limitations on the executive role of commanding or order giving? Can a manager successfully impose his will on subordinates? How do you account for the organization "politician"? Issues of this nature must be examined in our attempt to understand the facts of organizational behavior.

The Nature and Use of Authority

What Is Authority?

Authority may be defined as a superior's capacity, on the basis of his formal position, to make decisions affecting the behavior of subordinates. Authority is evident in the various areas of society. In the family, the parent makes decisions for minor children. At a busy intersection, motorists must respond to commands of a police officer. In football, the quarterback is expected to call plays. In the business world, the manager's authority makes him the decision maker on issues affecting the business. When authority is recognized, the subordinate relinquishes his own right of decision and accepts that of some superior.

Members of organizations recognize the right of command as an inherent part of certain managerial positions. Employees may, in fact, resent officiousness or attempts by fellow workers to act authoritatively when they do not hold positions of real authority. In other words, there is also a recognition that authority does *not* reside in certain positions.

The concept of authority employed here incorporates the idea of power or ability to secure compliance with a superior's orders. Authority might be called *institutionalized power* to emphasize its connection with the formal organization and to distinguish it from other types of power. Members of organizations recognize the power of managers because of their acceptance of the formal organization and its managerial positions. This does not imply that it is absolute power, having no limitations, but the position taken here is that authority must have some degree of effectiveness to be recognized as authority. Otherwise, it is a hollow, meaningless, "paper" right of command.

Authority may be contrasted with *influence* in which persuasion, suggestions, or other discussion is used to affect behavior. Influence does not rely upon formal position or sanctions in getting agreement. In the case of influence, the individual being influenced has the power of choice with freedom to accept or reject. If he is subject to authority, however, he accepts the superior's decision without question. In the words of Herbert A. Simon, "He holds in abeyance his own critical faculties for choosing between alternatives and uses the formal criterion of the receipt of a command or signal as his basis for choice."[1]

In contrast to the concept of authority, *power* requires no formal position to be recognized as power. It refers to capacity or ability to make things happen, to get results. Only a part of the total power is institutionalized. This means that others besides managers have power. In the informal organization, for example, output quotas may be established and enforced. A subordinate also has the option of working cooperatively or refusing cooperation (through uninspired work or quitting). We sometimes speak of an employee's *bargaining power*, particularly if he has an offer of another job.

Only a part of all power is recognized as legitimate. If power is legitimate, those subject to the power must recognize that it is right or proper. The victim of a holdup is subject to power that is contrary

---

[1]Reprinted with permission of The Macmillan Company from *Administrative Behavior* by Herbert A. Simon. © by Herbert A. Simon 1957.

to law, but the power is nonetheless real. In most administrative decisions, the institutionalized power that exists is accepted as legitimate. Even though a subordinate may question the wisdom of managerial decisions, he generally acknowledges the legitimacy of—that is, the manager's right to make—decisions affecting the subordinate. Not all legitimate power is institutionalized or embodied in official positions, however. Members of organizations may also accept the norms or standards of informal groups as proper and right. In other words, they recognize the informal rules as legitimate.

Because of authority, subordinates accept decisions of superiors rather than making their own decisions. Subordinates also accept superiors' decisions that conflict with, or are opposed to, the subordinates' own preferences. They accept such decisions even though they do not agree with them. The latter has been described by Herbert A. Simon as the "right to the last word." The disagreement in thinking between the superior and subordinate is settled by recourse to the superior's authority. Although the "last word" requires authority, the use of authority is not confined to situations involving controversy.

> Too often . . . the element of disagreement in obedience is overemphasized at the expense of the other elements of the situation. The term "authority" would be too narrowly employed if it were restricted to such instances of disagreement.[2]

Determinants of Acceptance of Authority

The behavior of subordinates shows that they accept the claims of authority by superiors. This suggests a question as to the reason or reasons that account for their doing so. Why is it that they subordinate themselves in this way? The answer seems simple at first glance but becomes more perplexing as one reflects upon it. The process by which authority is validated and accepted as the basis for action by individuals may be called *legitimation.*[3] It appears that a number of factors are involved in this process of establishing the authority of the formal organization.

One validating factor is our culture and its embodiment of the roles of order giving and order receiving. Throughout their lives,

---

[2]Reprinted with permission of The Macmillan Company from *Administrative Behavior* by Herbert A. Simon. © by Herbert A. Simon 1957.

[3]See Robert V. Presthus, "Authority in Organizations," in Sidney Mailick and Edward H. Van Ness, *Concepts and Issues in Administrative Behavior* © 1962, p. 127. Used by permission of Prentice-Hall, Inc., Englewood Cliffs, N. J.

members of organizations have been conditioned to accept authority. They have learned a measure of obedience to superiors. Therefore, some tendency to accept orders comes naturally or as a matter of course for most people. In addition, employees have some understanding of and belief in the institution of private property and the free enterprise system.

As a result, employees are culturally conditioned to accept direction from managers. In fact, an individual openly defiant of general managerial authority would encounter disapproval from most members of an organization. According to Simon, "Insubordination can be as embarrassing, under these circumstances, as failure to wear a necktie to church."[4]

Rewards and penalties available to the superior also foster the acceptance of authority. Employee *A* or Manager *A* may be fired if his challenge to official policy becomes too outspoken. Similarly, he may expect the rewards of advancement and other benefits to accompany his cooperation with the programs of his superiors. The motivational strength of these rewards and penalties varies from time to time and from person to person. It has been argued, for example, that these influences are more effective in motivating white-collar workers than hourly-wage employees.[5]

Belief in, or identification with, the purpose of the organization is another reason for the individual to subject himself to authority. This is particularly evident in the case of cooperative organizations. Members accept authority as a part of getting the job done. It is a principle that is not entirely missing from business organizations, however.

Further explanation of subordinate acceptance of authority is found in the superior knowledge, technical competence, or expertise of the superior. "An interesting philosophical basis for this legitimation," according to Robert V. Presthus, "is the ideal of equality of opportunity which in its attempts to overcome ethnic and religious discrimination has enthroned the standard of personal competence as the only moral basis for selection."[6] The element of technical skill or professional competence is particularly important in managing personnel who attach great importance to such qualities —

---

[4]Reprinted with permission of The Macmillan Company from *Administrative Behavior* by Herbert A. Simon. © by Herbert A. Simon 1957.

[5]George Strauss and Leonard R. Sayles, *Personnel: The Human Problems of Management,* Second Edition (Englewood Cliffs: Prentice-Hall, Inc., © 1967), p. 129.

[6]Presthus, *op. cit.,* p. 127.

for example, in managing skilled craftsmen, scientists, or college professors. In some cases, then, the technical or professional qualifications of the superior make him an authority in the eyes of the subordinates. In other situations, the superior's understanding of the "big picture," as a result of his strategic position in the organization structure, makes him a different type of expert.

The factor of personal leadership also affects the acceptance of authority. Some subordinates respond to the orders of superiors because of the subordinates' admiration for their superiors as individual leaders. The subordinates' evaluation of a superior as a leader is based upon the superior's style of leadership and the extent to which it conforms to the expectations of those subject to his command. In any administrative situation, subordinates have some conception as to what is proper leadership behavior. There is an acceptable way for the manager to give orders, a reasonable volume of work that he may require under normal conditions, and a proper social distance for him to observe. Managers who perform in reasonable conformity with such expectations come to be viewed as legitimate leaders whose authority is accorded recognition.

Another validating factor is the desire of some individuals to avoid responsibility. It seems easier for them to accept directions than to make their own decisions. This is particularly true if the task is not particularly unpleasant or if the decision in question lies outside the experience and competence of the subordinate.[7]

In any particular instance, authority may be recognized (achieve legitimation) because of a combination of these factors. There is no need, however, for *all* bases to be present in establishing authority. In a given case, just one factor (such as disciplinary sanctions) may be of primary importance in making the executive position a powerful one.

Limits to the Exercise of Formal Authority

Citizens of a country do not always obey its statutes even though the statutes are recognized as the law of the land. If violation is sufficiently serious, we classify an offender as a criminal. Frequently, however, the offense is viewed less seriously. Motorists, for example, often ignore traffic ordinances. Even good citizens are thus in a position of conflict with established civil authority.

---

[7]Reprinted with permission of The Macmillan Company from *Administrative Behavior* by Herbert A. Simon. © by Herbert A. Simon 1957.

Disobedience to a superior's orders is also an alternative open to every subordinate. He may choose to resist rather than to submit to the rule of higher management. But can he — the subordinate — successfully buck higher echelons of management? Isn't this the same as resigning from the organization? Questions as to the subordinate's ability to resist have been of interest to many writers.

In a notable challenge to traditional views, Chester I. Barnard drew attention to the possibility of a subordinate's rejection of direction by higher authority. In fact, Barnard felt that disobedience of subordinates was commonplace. "It is surprising," said Barnard, "how much that in theory is authoritative, in the best of organizations in practice lacks authority—or, in plain language, how generally orders are disobeyed."[8] Acceptance of the order, then, becomes an important step or part of making the authority of the order giver effective. Following is a more explicit statement of Barnard's position:

> If a directive communication is accepted by one to whom it is addressed, its authority for him is confirmed or established. It is admitted as the basis of action. Disobedience of such a communication is a denial of its authority for him.[9]

This reasoning does not mean that subordinates automatically resent and resist all authority or that they are characterized by a generally rebellious attitude. Many directions are accepted without question. In fact, Barnard suggests the existence of a *zone of indifference* that determines which orders will be accepted.

> The phrase "zone of indifference" may be explained as follows: If all the orders for actions reasonably practicable be arranged in the order of their acceptability to the person affected, it may be conceived that there are a number which are clearly unacceptable, that is, which certainly will not be obeyed; there is another group somewhat more or less on the neutral line, that is, either barely acceptable or barely unacceptable; and a third group unquestionably acceptable. This last group lies within the "zone of indifference." The person affected will accept orders lying within this zone and is relatively indifferent as to what the order is so far as the question of authority is concerned.[10]

---

[8]Reprinted by permission of the publishers from Chester I. Barnard *The Functions of the Executive,* Cambridge, Mass.: Harvard University Press, Copyright, 1938, by the President and Fellows of Harvard College, 1966, by Grace F. Noera Barnard, p. 162.

[9]*Ibid.*, p. 163.

[10]*Ibid.*, pp. 168-169.

The point of this reasoning is that the authority (or institutionalized power) represented by a superior's order is seldom so absolute, unequivocal, or inescapable that the subordinate has no choice whatever. As Herbert A. Simon has expressed it, "the leader, or the superior, is merely a bus driver whose passengers will leave him unless he takes them in the direction they wish to go."[11]

Forms of Resistance to Authority

On rare occasions, subordinates openly defy official orders, and a condition of mutiny exists. Such insubordination represents an urgent problem of serious proportions to an administrator. Either management must back down—often difficult to do gracefully—or disciplinary action must be taken. In other words, an open, direct challenge by a subordinate forces an immediate showdown.

In other cases, employees are represented by a union and, to some extent, voice their opposition to management in the form of grievances and union demands. One of the important functions of the union, indeed, is to supply a legitimate channel of opposition. Historically, many unions replaced employee representation plans that had been devised by management for this purpose. Union spokesmen may be quite vocal in expressing labor's dislike of certain management proposals and policies. Labor weapons, including the strike, may be employed in any particular conflict.

If resistance of subordinates were limited to cases of this type, the problem would be greatly simplified. As a matter of fact, resistance is usually less direct or formal, typically occurring in some subtle form. Subordinates manage to resist without forcing a showdown. They may go through the motions of compliance but fail to follow through with the behavior desired by the superior. It is this type of challenge to authority that is often most baffling and troublesome for administrators.

When a demand comes from a superior, for example, there is a possibility the superior may have expressed it on the spur of the moment and that he will later forget about it. Therefore, the subordinate may also proceed to "forget" about the request and await results. If the superior does not follow up, the subordinate is "home free." If the superior checks again, another type of strategy is called for. It may be necessary for the subordinate in this case to enlist the

---

[11]Reprinted with permission of The Macmillan Company from *Administrative Behavior* by Herbert A. Simon. © by Herbert A. Simon 1957.

support of colleagues, report numerous unfavorable consequences after initiating the requested action, or carry out the request in a half-hearted manner.

In one case that illustrates this point, plant management gave such strong support to a safety program that lower management took steps to conceal accidents.[12] The rank of each department, based on its safety performance, appeared on plant bulletin boards, and supervisors were advised that their futures depended upon departmental safety performance. To protect themselves, lower-level managers worked to keep accidents off the record. In one case in which a worker broke several toes, the foreman drove him to a private physician rather than to the plant hospital. He was treated regularly by the private physician and allowed to take it easy during the period of recuperation. In another case, a production manager secured treatment from a plant physician for a worker's mashed toe but succeeded in having the incident kept off the record.

Rules that presumably control subordinates are also a potential weapon in the hands of subordinates. An overly zealous observance of rules may actually be dysfunctional. The following incident illustrates the limitation that rule keeping may impose upon management power:

> Train crews in a marshaling yard were handling 150 trains a day. Through short cuts (often violating safety rules) they were able to finish their work in six hours. The rest of the time they could sleep or read.
>
> • • • • • • • • • •
>
> Then management decided that since the men had so much free time they could handle 200 trains. Immediately the men began to follow all the rules. They would never move a train even a few feet without having someone to go to the rear and wave a red flag. As a result, the men put in a full day's work, but productivity fell to 50 trains a day. Soon management gave up its demands for 200.[13]

The ability of subordinates to thwart executive authority varies greatly with the social context. In most military organizations, for example, compliance with official orders is more nearly automatic than is customary with business organizations. Business organizations differ among themselves as to the amount of power residing in

---

[12]Melville Dalton, *Men Who Manage* (New York: John Wiley & Sons, Inc., 1959), pp. 80-85.

[13]Strauss and Sayles, *op. cit.*, p. 189.

the official structure. Most business firms, in turn, possess greater authority than organizations of a voluntary nature. The scope of managerial authority also changes over a period of time. Henry Ford I undoubtedly held greater authority than does his grandson Henry Ford II.

The Manager's Use of Authority

In the preceding discussion, we have noted that various methods exist for influencing behavior, one of which is the exercise of authority. Within the zone of indifference, which was discussed above, subordinates willingly subject themselves to the command of their superiors. A fundamental question facing each administrator is the extent to which he should use his authority in his relationships with subordinates. To the extent that authority is dependent upon the coercive power of a manager, its effectiveness depends upon the unique administrative and social situation. If jobs are scarce, for example, the penalties available to a manager may provide sufficient motivation to achieve a high level of performance.

Even within the limits of his potential authority, the manager must decide how much to use in a specific situation. It may be unwise for him to use all the authority that is legally available to him and that will be accepted by his subordinates. The manager needs a philosophical basis for determining the proper limits on his authority—for deciding which situations call for authoritative decisions. As he exercises authority, he must develop some type of balance between his authority as the manager (in the interest of efficiency) and the freedom of his subordinates. An emphasis upon freedom of the individual in the industrial organization is consistent with the values held more broadly in our society.

Two principles that help the manager to rationalize his use of authority are the concepts of *substitutional authority* and *essential authority*.[14] According to the former, a manager's authority is necessary because of weaknesses or deficiencies in the subordinate. As a parent must decide issues which the child is incapable of deciding for himself, so the superior must decide for the subordinate when the superior's greater knowledge or capacity makes this logical. Guidance of a newly-appointed employee provides an example of the application of this principle. Substitutional authority tends to be

---

[14]Robert Albanese, "Substitutional and Essential Authority," *Academy of Management Journal,* Vol. 9, No. 2, June 1966, pp. 136-144.

self-destructive. As the employee develops a capacity for independent action and adopts appropriate attitudes and goals, the manager's authority becomes less necessary. Because of the unique knowledge arising from the position of the superior, however, his substantial authority may never completely disappear.

The second principle, that of *essential authority*, involves the common-sense notion that someone must make choices in work procedures and relationships even among knowledgeable people. There is typically more than one way to proceed in a given situation. Because of this plurality of means, efficiency demands an effective choice that will apply to all. To illustrate the application of essential authority, note its use within a production organization:

> The members of a quality control department pursue their particular jobs and it is up to the quality control manager to unite the various jobs. The quality control manager, in turn, rightly pursues his job as if quality control were the main function of the business (slight exaggeration) and it is up to the production manager to balance the quality control job with the other areas of production. The production manager, in turn, vigorously pursues his job as if all else were secondary and it is the president's job to balance production with marketing and finance. This is admittedly an overstatement to emphasize the essential function of authority.[15]

Even though these two principles do not prescribe an answer for each specific situation, they give the manager a general basis for choosing the amount of authority he will use. Use of more than that required for the above purposes constitutes an unnecessary and unjustified infringement upon the subordinate's freedom. It is in the interest of both the organization and the subordinate, however, to use the full authority necessary for both of these reasons.

The superior is not confined to the use of authority in his relationships with subordinates. Another approach to influencing behavior involves the use of suggestions, persuasion, and discussion.

> Even where a behavior can be secured by the exercise of authority, a superior often and perhaps usually prefers to employ suggestions or persuasion . . . the mere fact that two persons accept the roles of superior and subordinate does not imply that all, or even most, of their behaviors will be instances of the exercise of authority.[16]

---

[15]*Ibid.*, p. 143.

[16]Reprinted with permission of The Macmillan Company from *Administrative Behavior* by Herbert A. Simon. © by Herbert A. Simon 1957.

This approach recognizes the individual member of the organization as capable of making a choice. In the authoritative relationship, the subordinate presumably withholds his own discretion and agrees to accept the judgment of the superior. As an object of persuasion, however, it is assumed that he may decide the matter for himself.

Managers clearly have some discretion in the way they exercise authority. Disciplinary penalties may be fair or unfair, corrective or punitive in nature. Subordinates constantly appraise the fairness or unfairness of superiors in their use of authority. As noted above, managers may also develop strong personal relationships that utilize suggestions and persuasion as authority substitutes. They may also encourage subordinates to ask questions rather than to wait for orders, thus reducing the need for authoritative decisions. Leadership styles thus vary in their motivational approaches and in the emphasis placed upon the use of authority. The subject of leadership and its methods is discussed in Chapter 21.

Power and Politics

The concept of authority as institutionalized power has explained the formal power attached to official positions in the chain of command. Any empirical investigation of organizations in action, however, reveals behavior that is only partially explained in terms of formal authority. Some power is institutionalized, but other power is political in nature.

Political Techniques of Influencing Behavior

Administrative direction by the head of an organization is often supplemented by the influence of other individuals. The direction or control of business operations does not precisely follow the formal chain of command in every case. Decisions may be influenced by the judgment of individuals whose names do not even appear on the organization chart. There may be a power behind the throne. Staff advisors, by virtue of close association with the chief, may express opinions that are accepted with the force of commands (even though they technically may be called suggestions).

Observers of organizational behavior have come to recognize the fact of *political activity* in administrative situations. Unfortunately, the word "politics" has a connotation of unstatesmanlike conduct. As used here, however, political activity is concerned with the manner in which positions of power are established and influence is exerted in the administrative process. There is nothing to indicate the use of power for undesirable ends. The following definition may be helpful in understanding the nature of this concept:

> Thus power and influence are in a sense static. They reside in someone or some office. Therefore we need to have another term to describe the network of interactions by which power is acquired, transferred, and exercised upon others. We call this process *politics*.[17]

Through politics, an executive may first of all build and exert influence over the members of his own department. Activities of this nature include any unofficial efforts to "take care" of his men with an expectation of their loyalty in return.

A manager's political activities, however, are not limited to influencing subordinates. The primary connotation of administrative politics, indeed, is concerned with the manager's relationships outside his own department. Through political activities, an executive may exert some degree of control over colleagues and even his own superiors. Other managers at approximately the same level constitute potential competitors or allies, and the executive typically seeks to exert as much influence as possible in matters of mutual interest. The following quotation describes the political approach toward other executives and toward superiors:

> Frequently indistinguishable from the business politician's competitors by any but apparently accidental circumstances are those who go a step beyond cooperation and become his actual or potential allies. Unlike the professional, the business politician rarely seeks to be a lone wolf — rather he attempts, by much the same devices legislators use, to build up a system of alliances. (Perhaps "attempts" is the wrong word; the only certainty is that alliances, cliques, and relationships of joint support do happen.)
>
> Those higher up in the organization are always regarded by the business politician as superior officers — who must be cajoled, placated, pleased, analyzed — and not as actual or potential friends to be treated informally.[18]

---

[17]John M. Pfiffner and Frank P. Sherwood, *Administrative Organization* © 1960, p. 311. Reprinted by permission of Prentice-Hall, Inc., Englewood Cliffs, N. J.

[18]Stephen B. Miles, Jr., "The Management Politician," *Harvard Business Review,* Vol. 39, No. 1, January-February 1961, p. 102.

While some political activities are inevitable and even contribute to the accomplishment of organizational objectives, company politics may also be destructive. The company politician is often far more concerned with the advancement of his own interests than those of the organization. To prevent such situations from getting out of hand to the extent that political activities dominate rather than supplement normal management processes and personal ambition supplants organizational goals, top management must sense and prevent extreme or self-seeking forms of political action. A program and practice of objective evaluation of subordinates is one essential safeguard against the destructive company politician. Political intrigue that would subordinate organizational goals to narrow personal objectives must be rejected. The climate must be of a nature that prevents an abuse of political power. This is difficult to accomplish, of course, because political action is often carefully camouflaged and rationalized.

The Power Structure

The previous discussion of power has shown it to be the ability to get one's way or to influence the behavior of others. In particular, the importance of political activity as a supplement to formal authority has been stressed as essential to a complete explanation of administrative action. The combination of formal authority and political action creates centers of power or influence in an organization. The framework incorporating these centers of influence might be called the *power structure.*

The power structure differs from the formal organization structure only to the extent that the influence of particular individuals does not correspond perfectly to their positions in the formal structure. In view of the nature of political action, some such discrepancy between formal position and power is to be expected. It would be a rare situation indeed if six vice presidents each had precisely the same influence over company policy.

> In most large corporations it is possible to rank the vice presidents in terms of (1) their influence on general policy, (2) their importance in running the enterprise, (3) their general status or prestige level, and (4) their economic power. The relative rank of top managers in each of these four categories is not stationary, and much of their time and energy is devoted to moving up these ladders. . . .

> All kinds of political devices are used by the top managers to gain influence, prestige, and money. Two or three of them may form a clique to help each other against other cliques. Since the financial and production chiefs have natural "ins" with the president, cliques tend to form about them.[19]

A Case Study of Power and Politics

Melville Dalton has presented a penetrating picture of political activities and the power structure in the Milo Fractionating Center, a fictitiously-named industrial organization having a work force of 8,000 employees.[20] Dalton's charts of the formal organization and unofficial influence in the management of this plant are presented in Figures 20 and 21.

In Figure 21, Dalton has ranked the individuals to show their relative influence in the organization. As an example, the assistant plant manager (Hardy) is shown at the same level as the plant manager (Stevens), thus indicating that their influence in the organization is roughly equivalent. Following is Dalton's explanation of the Hardy-Stevens relationship:

> In executive meetings, Stevens clearly was less forceful than Hardy. Appearing nervous and worried, Stevens usually opened meetings with a few remarks and then silently gave way to Hardy who dominated thereafter. During the meeting most questions were directed to Hardy. While courteous, Hardy's statements usually were made without request for confirmation from Stevens. Hardy and Stevens and other high officers daily lunched together. There, too, Hardy dominated the conversations and was usually the target of questions. This was not just an indication that he carried the greater burden of *minor* duties often assigned to assistants in some firms, for he had a hand in most issues, including major ones. Other items useful in appraising Hardy and Stevens were their relative (*a*) voice in promotions, (*b*) leadership in challenging staff projects, (*c*) force in emergencies, (*d*) escape as a butt of jokes and name-calling, (*e*) knowledge of subordinates, (*f*) position in the firm's social and community activities.[21]

Another position of unusual influence was occupied by Rees, who functioned officially as head of Industrial Relations and was pre-

---

[19]Delbert C. Miller and William H. Form, *Industrial Sociology* (New York: Harper & Row, Publishers, 1951), p. 192.

[20]See Dalton, *op. cit.*

[21]*Ibid.*, p. 23.

Figure 20. *Milo Formal Chart Simplified*

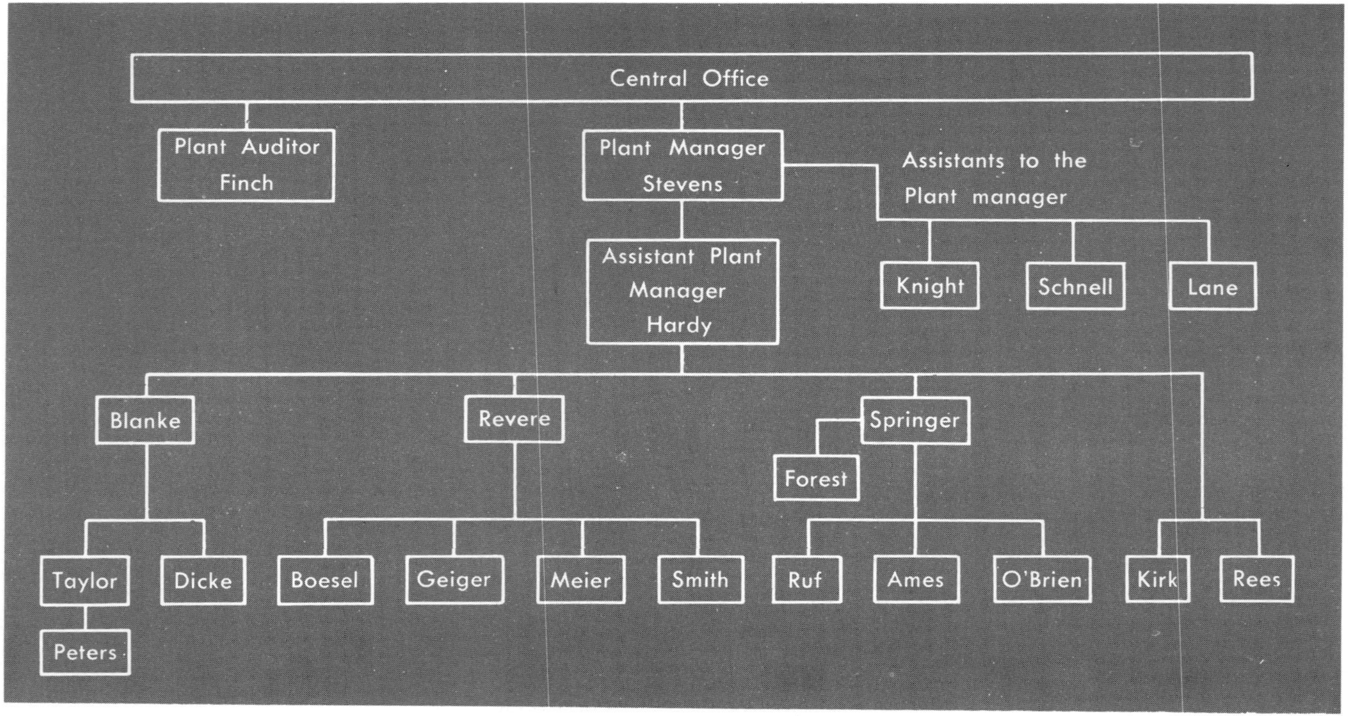

Source: Melville Dalton, *Men Who Manage* (New York: John Wiley & Sons, Inc., 1959), p. 21.

Figure 21. *Milo Chart of Unofficial Influence*

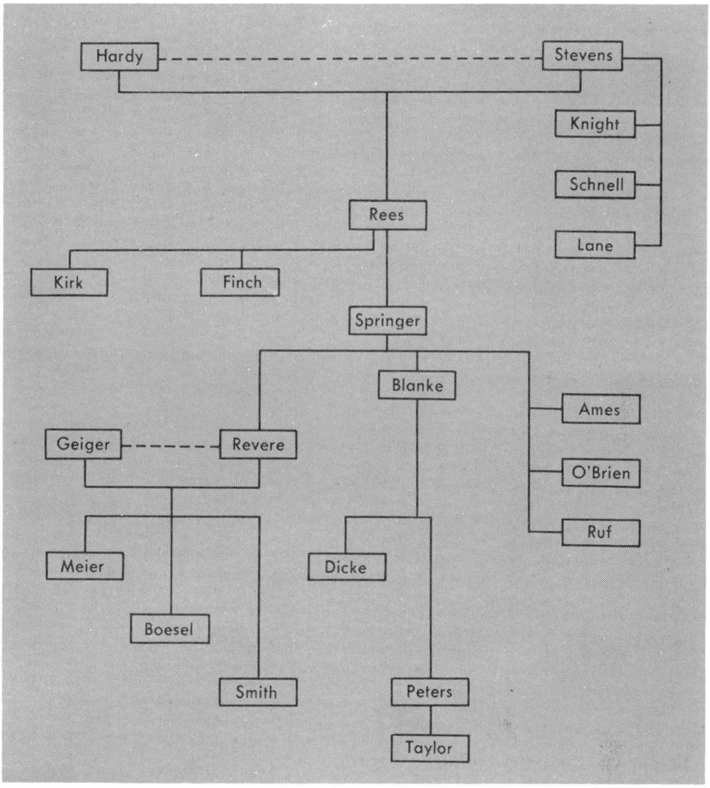

Source: Melville Dalton, *Men Who Manage* (New York: John Wiley & Sons, Inc., 1959), p. 22.

sumably limited to advising on these matters. In spite of this, Rees seemed to carry more weight and inspire more concern than the other managers subordinate to Hardy and Stevens. His influence was partly attributable to the fact that he had been sent from headquarters to strengthen the department. He had replaced a weak manager, Lane, who was made assistant to Stevens. The following incident, as described by Dalton, provides a remarkable insight into the influence of this staff manager:

> For some time the most widespread struggle in Milo had been between line factions favoring and opposing the use of maintenance incentives. Otis Blanke, head of Division A, opposed the

> incentives and persuaded Hardy that dropping them would benefit Milo. At a meeting to deal with the problem Hardy stated his position and concluded, "We should stop using maintenance incentives. They cause us too much trouble and cost too much."
>
> Then as only a staff head, and one without vested interest in this issue or the formal authority to warrant threats or decisive statements, Rees arose and said:
>
> > I agree that maintenance incentives have caused a lot of trouble. But I don't think it's because they're not useful. It's because there are too many people not willing to toe the mark and give them a try. The [Office] put that system in here and . . . we're going to make it work, not just tolerate it!
>
> The surprise at these remarks broke the meeting up in embarrassment for everyone but Rees. His statement quickly spread to all of supervision. Since Industrial Engineering had set up the incentives, one of its supervisors asked the Maintenance Department to aid the pay plan by having its foremen, in addition to the inspectors, count the number of pieces done on various orders in their shops. The appeal was made with the thought that report of nonexistent pieces might be a factor in making the plan "too costly." Rees learned of the request and described the idea as one that "would cause more trouble than it would be worth." This remark was similarly flashed through the plant. Early the following day all line executives who had been approached by the staff supervisor telephoned apologies for their inability to aid him, and they asked him to please consider their position in view of Rees' stand. These and other less overt incidents led Milo executives to see Rees as an unofficial spokesman for the Office. Because he had spent three years there as staff representative of Industrial Relations, local managers assumed he had been selected as "a bright young boy" and "groomed" for the Milo post. His predecessor, Lane, was regarded as "a grand old guy," but was removed to a "safe spot" for a few years until his retirement because he was "not sharp enough to deal over and under the table at the same time." Several of the executives explicitly stated their belief that Rees had powerful sponsors in the Office and that to provoke him would "just be suicide."[22]

Dalton's depth study of the Milo plant reveals conditions of influencing organizational behavior that, to some extent, exist in every organization. The positions of power are not always evident on the

---

[22] *Ibid.*, pp. 24-25.

surface and cannot be read with assurance from the organization chart. Only careful observation of the functioning of the organization reveals the true power centers and the extent to which they differ from the formal organization structure.

Sources of Power

It may be helpful to consider some of the sources from which managers derive their influence. There are, no doubt, many ways in which such power sources could be classified, and this discussion seeks merely to identify some of the commonly recognized sources. The manager's position of authority, for example, certainly constitutes one basis for his influence. In discussing the exercise of formal authority above, we noted that subordinates are normally inclined to follow official orders. This is buttressed by the sanctions, leadership, and other factors that serve to establish authority. Thus, the manager almost automatically has, or is able to exert, this type of influence.

The ability to reward and penalize is not confined to positions of formal authority, however. A staff manager — the personnel chief, for example — may be in a position to help or to hinder a line manager. It may be the politic thing to follow his lead as a means of insuring satisfactory service to one's own department. In considering the position of the secretary to the chief executive, her potential antagonism may be a fearful thing to contemplate even though she lacks formal authority.

No doubt the personal qualities of an executive also contribute to the degree of his influence in the organization. Some individuals have such winsome and attractive personalities that cooperation with them comes naturally. In other words, the human relations skills involved in securing the cooperation of colleagues and superiors vary widely among managers.

Specialized knowledge provides still another basis for power in decision making. This is particularly true in the case of staff experts. It is difficult to challenge the expert who has a detailed familiarity with his subject. It is possible, in fact, that a staff specialist can extend his influence beyond the area in which he has specialized knowledge by creating the impression that he is an expert in all aspects of a given subject. This basis of influence — specialized knowledge — would apply to a line manager as well as to a staff specialist. To the extent that members of an organization recognize the expert knowledge of some official, they are inclined to follow his leadership.

Summary

Authority is defined as the capacity to make decisions affecting the behavior of subordinates. It may also be described as *institutionalized power*, and it differs from *influence*, in which the recipient exercises his own critical faculties in determining his behavior. In the business organization, authority is established by a number of different factors. The general culture, for example, conditions organization members to accept authority. In addition, authority is accepted because of rewards and penalties, belief in the organization's purpose, expertise, personal leadership, and the desire of some to avoid responsibility.

Limitations exist in the extent to which formal authority is accepted by subordinate members of an organization. Chester I. Barnard has suggested the concept of a *zone of indifference*. Within this zone of indifference, employees are willing to accept the orders of those holding formal authority. Forms of resistance include not only open defiance but also subtle disobedience in which there is an appearance of compliance.

The concepts of *substitutional authority* and *essential authority* provide a basis for rationalizing or determining proper limits to the use of authority. In addition to using authority, managers also direct subordinates by means of suggestions, advice, and other types of influence.

In influencing behavior in organizations, the use of *political activity* supplements the manager's formal authority. The relationships and techniques employed in acquiring and exerting influence outside official channels are described as political in nature. This does not indicate that they are necessarily underhanded or shady but simply that they involve alliances, relationships, and approaches that differ from those of the formal organization.

The *power structure* of an organization may be similar to the formal organization, but differences exist in the case of those who hold more or less power than the formal structure confers upon them. In the example of the Milo plant, it was discovered that subordinate managers sometimes held as much real power or influence as their superiors. Power of the manager is derived not only from his formal position of authority, but also from his political relationships and activities. Specialized knowledge, personal attractiveness, and an ability to reward and penalize are also sources of organizational power.

Discussion Questions

1. How does the concept of *authority* differ from that of *power*? From that of *influence*?
2. What is meant by the "right to the last word"?
3. Explain the concept of *legitimation* of authority. In what way is our culture associated with this?
4. What is the *zone of indifference* suggested by Barnard, and how is this related to a superior's authority?
5. If subordinates are inclined to resist authority, what forms may their resistance take?
6. Describe an "organization politician." What practices does he typically follow?
7. What is the *power structure*, and why may this differ from an accurately drawn organization chart?
8. What are the sources of managerial power?

Supplementary Reading

Albanese, Robert, "Substitutional and Essential Authority," *Academy of Management Journal,* Vol. 9, No. 2, June 1966, pp. 136-144.

Barnard, Chester I., *The Functions of the Executive,* Chapter 12. Cambridge: Harvard University Press, 1946.

Batten, J. D. and James L. Swab, "How to Crack Down on Company Politics," *Personnel,* Vol. 42, No. 1, January-February 1965, pp. 8-16.

Burns, Tom, "Micropolitics: Mechanisms of Institutional Change," *Administrative Science Quarterly,* Vol. 6, No. 3, December 1961, pp. 257-281.

Dalton, Melville, *Men Who Manage.* New York: John Wiley & Sons, Inc., 1959.

Davis, Keith, "Attitudes Toward the Legitimacy of Management Efforts to Influence Employees," *Academy of Management Journal,* Vol. 11, No. 2, June 1968, pp. 153-162.

Golembiewski, Robert T., "Authority as a Problem in Overlays: A Concept for Action and Analysis," *Administrative Science Quarterly,* Vol. 9, No. 1, June 1964, pp. 23-49.

Hegarty, Edward J., *How to Succeed in Company Politics.* New York: McGraw-Hill Book Company, 1964.

Katz, Daniel and Robert L. Kahn, *The Social Psychology of Organizations,* Chapter 8. New York: John Wiley & Sons, Inc., 1966.

Mandeville, Merten J., "Organizational Authority," in *Current Issues and Emerging Concepts in Management,* ed. Paul M. Dauten, Jr., pp. 199-207. Boston: Houghton Mifflin Company, 1962.

Miles, Stephen B., Jr., "The Management Politician," *Harvard Business Review,* Vol. 39, No. 1, January-February 1961, pp. 99-104.

Peabody, Robert L., "Perceptions of Organizational Authority: A Comparative Analysis," *Administrative Science Quarterly,* Vol. 6, No. 4, March 1962, pp. 463-482.

Rabe, W. F., "Managerial Power," *California Management Review,* Vol. 4, No. 3, Spring 1962, pp. 31-39.

Scott, W. Richard, Sanford M. Dornbusch, Bruce C. Busching, and James D. Laing, "Organizational Evaluation and Authority," "*Administrative Science Quarterly,* Vol. 12, No. 1, June 1967, pp. 93-117.

Simon, Herbert A., *Administrative Behavior,* Second Edition, Chapter 7. New York: The Macmillan Company, 1957.

Strauss, George, "Work-Flow Frictions, Interfunctional Rivalry, and Professionalism: A Case Study of Purchasing Agents," *Human Organization,* Vol. 23, No. 2, Summer 1964, pp. 137-149.

Strauss, George and Leonard R. Sayles, *Personnel: The Human Problems of Management,* Second Edition, Chapter 8. Englewood Cliffs: Prentice-Hall, Inc., 1967.

Votaw, Dow, "What Do We Believe About Power?" *California Management Review,* Vol. 8, No. 4, Summer 1966, pp. 71-88.

19

Organization and the Individual

Members of an organization are more than contributors to its activities. They are also affected by the organization with its systems and methods of operation. To some extent, the individual is expected to adapt to the organization. But how far can or should the organization go in prescribing individual behavior patterns and in demanding personal loyalty? This chapter considers the impact of the organization upon its individual members—a subject with moral as well as economic dimensions.

The General Social Issue

The Protestant Ethic

For many centuries, various philosophies have embodied a concept of individualism. Perhaps the best known expression of an individualistic ethic is known as the *Protestant ethic*, as formulated by Max Weber, a German social scientist who lived from 1864 to 1920.[1] In his work, *The Protestant Ethic and the Spirit of Capitalism*,[2] he

---

[1]For a description of Weber's work, see Reinhard Bendix, *Max Weber: An Intellectual Portrait* (Garden City, New York: Doubleday & Company, Inc., 1960).

[2]Max Weber, *The Protestant Ethic and the Spirit of Capitalism*, trans. Talcott Parsons (London: George Allen & Unwin, Ltd., 1930).

attempted to show the contribution of the Protestant Reformation to the individualistic philosophy of capitalism.

The spirit of capitalism, as Weber observed it, incorporated the idea of hard work as a duty that carried its own reward. Work was virtuous and satisfying to the worker. Theological doctrines of the reformers were thought by Weber to contribute to this spirit of capitalism. Wasting time, for example, was regarded as sinful, and tireless labor was regarded as a part of God's will.

The Protestant ethic, then, emphasizes the importance of the individual and individualism. It is the individual who stands at the center of society with the responsibility for his own destiny. This philosophy further emphasizes personal freedom and the desirability of individual action. Hard work, self-reliance, ambition, and thrift are all virtues of this system of thought. The individual, in contrast to the group, is central to the Protestant ethic. Relevance of these ideas to organization theory is immediately apparent.

The Social Ethic

In contrast to the Protestant ethic, the *social ethic* emphasizes collective or group action and relationships. Cooperation with others and harmony in association with them are regarded as being virtuous. Conflict among individuals and among groups is deplored and should be minimized. The social ethic, then, shifts the emphasis from the individual to the group.

Man, according to many expressions of social ethic, should belong to some group or groups. In fact, only through participation in group relationships and activities can he find real satisfaction. Indeed, he may be a little sick if he does not properly relate himself to the group. In some versions of the doctrine, the creativity of the group is stressed. The group is thought to bring out the best in everyone, making the group's output greater than the combined output of its members working individually.

Decline of Individualism

In America, the last century has witnessed a relative decline of the Protestant ethic and ascendance of the social ethic. Some indeed, as will be noted below, have found this change profoundly disturbing. Evidences of the change are all about us. The human relations emphasis in industry, as an example, epitomizes the social ethic.

Various factors have contributed to the increasing popularity of the social ethic. One writer has labeled two significant forces in this transition as the *expansion factor* and the *collision effect.*[3] The former of these is concerned with the geographical frontier which existed in this country until about 1900. The frontier represented opportunity for enterprising individuals and offered rewards to those who were sufficiently ambitious, resourceful, and daring. These possibilities placed a premium on individualism in popular thinking. Anything seemed possible for the individual if he worked hard enough for it. Disappearance of this geographical frontier removed one natural support for the ethic of individualism.

The collision effect results from conditions bringing people into close contact—often involving a dependent relationship—with each other. In this country, closing of the frontier and increasing urbanization have brought people into closer contact in a geographical sense. In addition, development of industrial, governmental, and other institutions using large numbers of employees has resulted in further close contact in the world of work. The greater need for working and living in proximity to others led to the development of a philosophy that modified the strongly competitive aspects of the Protestant ethic. We recognize the emerging concept as the social ethic.

Trend Toward Conformity

A trend toward conformity and uniformity of behavior is part of the new life whose theology is the social ethic. In his best seller of a few years ago, *The Lonely Crowd,*[4] David Riesman distinguished between *inner-directed* people and *other-directed* people. The rugged individualists of an earlier day were the inner-directed people. They possessed an internal "psychological gyroscope" which kept them on course. In contrast, the other-directed people are more sensitive to the expectations of their associates. Riesman's analysis suggested that America had experienced a shift in the direction of the social ethic.

> My major thesis in these opening chapters is that the conformity of earlier generations of Americans of the type I term "inner-

---

[3]William G. Scott, *The Social Ethic in Management Literature,* Bulletin Number 4 (Atlanta: Bureau of Business and Economic Research, Georgia State College, 1959), pp. 8-9.

[4]David Riesman, *The Lonely Crowd* (New Haven: Yale University Press, 1950).

> directed" was mainly assured by their internalization of adult authority. The middle-class urban American of today, the "other-directed," is, by contrast, in a characterological sense more the product of his peers — that is, in sociological terms, his "peer-groups," the other kids at school or in the block. In adult life he continues to respond to these peers, not only with overt conformity, as do people in all times and places, but also in a deeper sense, in the very quality of his feeling.[5]

With respect to the trend, Riesman went on to suggest that "since the other-directed types are to be found among the young, in the larger cities, and among the upper income groups, we may assume that, unless present trends are reversed, the hegemony of other-direction lies not far off."[6]

The Individual and the Business Organization

The Psychological Contract

The relationship of the individual to the organization is encompassed in the concept of the *psychological contract.*[7] According to this concept, the member of the organization has various expectations concerning the organization. He expects from the employer a pay check of some specified size, an acceptable working environment, and a reasonable type of treatment and supervision. What will be regarded as acceptable or reasonable in terms of any of these factors depends upon prevailing economic conditions and cultural values. Historically, we can recognize the rising expectations of individuals. For example, the highly autocratic direction once traditional in American industry is no longer acceptable to the majority of employees.

The employer likewise has a set of expectations concerning those on the payroll. Some degree of conformity to organizational requirements is accepted as necessary and proper. Employees are expected to contribute adequate effort, skill, or knowledge to the employing

---

[5] *Ibid.*, p. v.

[6] *Ibid.*, p. 21.

[7] For discussions of the psychological contract, see Chris Argyris, *Understanding Organizational Behavior* (Homewood: The Dorsey Press, Inc., 1960), p. 96; Harry Levinson, *et al.*, *Men, Management, and Mental Health* (Cambridge: Harvard University Press, 1962), Chapter 3; and Edgar H. Schein, *Organizational Psychology* (Englewood Cliffs: Prentice-Hall, Inc., 1965), Chapter 2.

organization. They are expected to be in attendance with some degree of regularity and to respond appropriately to reasonable orders or directions from management. Management may also expect the employee to avoid disparaging remarks about the employer or disclosure of confidential information. As with employee expectations, the employer's expectations are modified by conditions of the labor market, competition within the industry, provisions of the law, and so on.

A conflict may exist between employer expectations (based on organizational efficiency) and employee expectations (based on personal values). Employee behavior that is optimal from the standpoint of the employer may be less than optimal in the eyes of the employee. For example, an employer may specialize jobs in the interest of production efficiency, but these routine, monotonous jobs may cause frustration, conflict, dependence, and submissiveness for the employees in those jobs. Argyris has stressed the likelihood of conflict between individual needs and organizational demands.[8] In many jobs, it is difficult if not impossible to maximize these relationships by optimally satisfying both organizational and employee requirements. Some compromise is typically necessary.

A stable relationship between the organization and its members requires some balance between these sets of expectations. Otherwise, there is pressure to change, and this may be evidenced by excessive turnover, lethargic performance, "get-tough" management, or in other ways.

In deciding what type of behavior may reasonably be expected, the employer must consider the degree of conformity that is proper and the degree of independence that must be allowed. A requirement of strong loyalty to the organization and an insistence upon minutely specified types of behavior may conflict with the member's expectations of freedom. This issue of independence versus conformity is discussed at greater length in the following pages.

Organization Man and the Pressure for Conformity

Business organizations have embraced the social ethic in keeping with the general trend noted earlier. Philosophies of cooperation were developed to harmonize conflicting viewpoints and interests of different groups in industrial organizations. The human relations

---

[8]Chris Argyris, *Integrating the Individual and the Organization* (New York: John Wiley & Sons, Inc., 1964), Chapters 1-5.

movement, in particular, stressed the significance and value of human relationships. Extensive use of participation, democratic supervision, and committee management reflected the social ethic in management action.

In his bestselling work, *The Organization Man,*[9] William H. Whyte, Jr., drew attention to the nation's drift toward the social ethic. He voiced provocative questions about the nature and extent of this trend and in general expressed a critical point of view concerning it. Although Whyte's study was not limited to the business organization, the business manager was one of the prime examples of the organization man he described.

A thorough application of the social ethic in a business organization is thought to produce the type of executive known as the *organization man.* This individual inoffensively shares the values of the group. He is a "yes-man," gets along well with others, and has a special knack for finding a path of compromise and harmony. He is not a trouble maker or a rabble rouser. In short, he is often described as a *conformist,* one who accepts the values of the organization as his own.

> What kind of society is to be engineered? Some critics of social engineering are sure that what is being cooked up for us is a socialistic paradise, a radically new, if not brave, world, alien to every tradition of man. This is wrong. Lump together the social engineers' prescriptions for the new society and you find they are anything but radical. Boiled down, what they ask for is an environment in which everyone is tightly knit into a belongingness with one another; one in which there is no restless wandering but rather the deep emotional security that comes from total integration with the group.[10]

One can hardly fail to note the contrast between such an organization man and some of the famous and colorful characters of business history. Individualists like Ford and Steinmetz differed drastically from the model organization man.

Although the social ethic has permeated modern business organizations, there is no certainty that this is an irreversible trend. Management may in the future adopt a more relaxed or tolerant attitude toward independence of subordinates. In fact, some of the forces presently operating in business tend to destroy the excessive con-

---

[9]William H. Whyte, Jr., *The Organization Man* (New York: Simon and Schuster, Inc., 1956).

[10]*Ibid.,* p. 32.

formity often regarded as typical. Strauss has argued that three current organizational trends — *functionalization, decentralization,* and *computerization* — tend to reduce the organization-man, conformity pressures in business organization.[11] Functionalization, for example, refers to the growth of specialized staff or functional groups such as accounting, personnel, quality control, research and development, engineering, and purchasing. Individuals within these functions tend to adopt individual points of view, to develop functional loyalties, and to advance their own specialties to a professional level. These conditions conflict with the usual picture of the organization man who is blindly loyal to the company and who never thinks for himself.

Selecting and Developing the Organization Man

As the importance of harmony and cooperation is stressed, it becomes incumbent upon administrators to select and develop personnel who will perpetuate that harmony. "Rocking the boat" is viewed as offensive, and it is a fact that some individuals are natural-born "boat rockers." In fact, one might classify them as trouble makers because they constantly threaten the status quo. In hiring or promoting managers, it is natural for the executive imbued with the social ethic and taken up with the idea of good human relations to prefer the smooth and personable applicant. Human relations skills become a prime quality of the candidate.

It may seem that the importance of such values is being exaggerated and that executives would not in fact go to these lengths in developing organization men. In this connection, it may be helpful to examine a recent study of executive attitudes toward management personnel. In 1961, *Harvard Business Review* surveyed a broad sample of its readers on this subject. The following statement summarizes some conclusions drawn from this study:

> *Analysis in depth of executives' preferences between pairs of traits or qualities reveals two general patterns. One pattern is characteristic of executives who are more likely than others to accept qualities such as "dull," "apathetic," and "retiring" in preference to "argumentative," "intolerant," and "egotistical." The second pattern is characteristic of executives who more*

---

[11]George Strauss, "Organization Man: Prospect for the Future." Reprinted from *California Management Review,* Vol. 6, No. 3, Spring 1964, pp. 5-16. Copyright 1964 by the Regents of the University of California.

often favor "accurate," "careful," "precise" subordinates in preference to those who are "courageous," "tolerant," and "capable."[12]

The special preferences of top management in choosing subordinates, in contrast to preferences of managers at lower levels, is of special interest.

Members of top management differ from executives at other levels mainly in their avoidance of the subordinate who falls in the trouble-maker pattern and their willingness to accept in his place a "dull," "apathetic," and "retiring" subordinate.[13]

Techniques for selecting organization men are being developed. One tool that has been enthusiastically adopted by some organizations is the personality test. There is a fundamental difference between tests designed to measure aptitudes or intelligence and tests that attempt to assess personality characteristics. The former are particularly concerned with qualities directly connected with work performance. Personality tests, however, deal with the type of characteristics that distinguish individualists from organization men. Although personality tests may be indirectly related to organizational efficiency, they are quite specifically concerned with the way the individual relates to other people. A user would hope to predict how an individual taking the test would get along as a member of the group.

Executive development and supervisory training programs tend to further develop attitudes of conformity. Many such programs emphasize the use of human relations skills and attempt to develop a sensitivity to attitudes of others. Some courses seek to indoctrinate personnel with the company point of view and to build loyalty to the organization. Much of the training that provides opportunities for participation is designed to develop the ability to work well in a group.

Less formal development methods, such as job rotation, may likewise stress conformity much more than problem-solving skills.

Rotation, as practiced in many companies, is like a game of musical chairs. The trick is not to get left out. As long as you do adequately, you stay on into the next round. You avoid taking risks, because an outstanding performance won't help

---

[12]Lewis B. Ward, "Do You Want a Weak Subordinate?" *Harvard Business Review,* Vol. 39, No. 5, September-October 1961, p. 7.

[13]*Ibid.,* pp. 7-8.

> you very much, while a mistake can knock you out of the running for good. Thus rotation encourages men to play it safe.[14]

Even performance evaluation may reward conformity and penalize individualism. Subordinates are sometimes rated on the basis of personality traits such as cooperation, leadership, and dependability. To earn a high rating, the employee must conform closely to the organization's accepted patterns of behavior.

Dangers of the Social Ethic

Some swing from the Protestant ethic to the social ethic was inevitable. As our society became more complex, it became mandatory that a greater degree of cooperation be developed. Otherwise, the law of the jungle would prevail in a setting for which it was unsuited. But a demand for collaboration need not wipe out the Protestant ethic and the individualistic spirit it represents. In other words, one might approve a shift toward the social ethic without embracing it in its most extreme form. The question raised by the specter of organization man is the extent to which our society, and business in particular, has shifted or should shift toward the social ethic. Does the business organization insist too much upon conformity on the part of its members? Is too much emphasis placed upon the group and insufficient attention devoted to the individual?

One primary danger to be recognized is that of stifling the creative spirit. Many brilliantly creative people, those with great achievements, have been real nonconformists. Some great leaders, indeed, have appeared odd when measured against the average. Not all of them won "most popular student" awards in their school days! If the organization insists upon conformity and adjustment to the group, it may force out such individualists with their potential for creative achievement. There is no assurance that brilliant leadership is always correlated with a pleasing personality. And, further, there is no guarantee that a polished personality is indispensable to success in corporate management.

An interesting example of the creative individualist is found in the case of an affluent inventor, Richard Rhodes Walton.[15] In 1962, Walton saw four of his inventions coming into commercial, royalty producing use. His annual income, it was estimated, would soar to well over $100,000 in 1963. But Walton is an individual inventor

---

[14]Strauss, *op. cit.*, p. 11.

[15]"Affluent Inventor," *The Wall Street Journal*, August 31, 1962, p. 1.

working in the basement of his own Boston home and shunning the corporate laboratory. Mr. Walton became an "independent" after a career which took him into research work with several large companies.

> "I didn't fit into the mass invention technique," he says. He complains that industry often stifles creative persons by forcing them to spend too much time justifying their work to supervisors or trying to look busy. Moreover, he contends that corporate researchers often play it safe and try for small improvements in their company's existing products.[16]

Another objection to the trend toward the social ethic concerns the extent to which the organization should be allowed to invade the privacy of the individual. Must the individual sell himself body and soul to the corporation, or should he be permitted to retain his personal life with his own choices and his own convictions? Some companies, in promoting the "good life," have developed such elaborate personnel programs that the individual has difficulty in enjoying a private social and recreational life. The social activities of some business corporations are reminiscent of the regimentation fostered by military organizations in which it is virtually a capital offense to refuse to join the officers' club. Some organizations go so far as to insist upon interviewing and checking out the wife before employing a new managerial trainee. Apparently the manager cannot even be trusted to select his own family!

Perhaps the question of the individual's privacy can best be framed in terms of the personality test, although this is only one specific instance of the invasion of his privacy. Does the corporation have any right to pry this deeply into the individual's makeup? In view of the type of questions that are involved in measuring personality characteristics, the use of such devices as a condition of employment has been a most disturbing development. Whyte has rather forcefully expressed his objection to this testing of the personality:

> But there is a line. How much more must a man testify against himself? The Bill of Rights should not stop at organization's edge. In return for the salary that The Organization gives the individual, it can ask for superlative work from him, but it should not ask for his psyche as well. If it does, he must withhold. Sensibly — the bureaucratic way is too much with most of

[16] *Ibid.*

us that he can flatly refuse to take tests without hurt to himself. But he can cheat. He must. Let him respect himself.[17]

Individual freedom of thought and action is likewise threatened by an insistence upon a conformity to acceptable patterns of thought and behavior. Following the assassination of President Kennedy, a Dallas executive, American Petrofina Company Senior Vice President Jack Shea, wrote for a national publication an article critical of Dallas and its conservative element. When this article appeared, a storm of criticism erupted in Dallas. The company was faced with a major public relations problem. Eventually Shea resigned rather than accede to company insistence upon prior approval of future public comments.

About a month after the article, and hours after the *Dallas Morning News* took me to its editorial–page woodshed a second time, I was suddenly confronted with a company demand: I must agree never to comment publicly without formally clearing each word in advance and in writing. The issue was not *what* I said, but whether I could say anything at all. It would have been interesting to know if any furor would have developed had the article been just a puff for Dallas. I doubt somehow that the business establishment here would have put pressure on Petrofina. Be that as it may, the company demand made it simple for me. I suggested we might as well discuss my resignation.

Why? It would have been easy enough to keep busy, as I had for seven years, in a good job. . . .

Still, you don't sign away your citizenship for pay. The company policy reached beyond business into personal belief. I would have been promising never to exercise the right and responsibility of a citizen.[18]

The contention that business organizations, along with other areas of society, have increased their emphasis upon conformity and the social ethic seems justified. Whether this shift on a national basis has been such as to justify alarm, however, is debatable. In contrast to the disturbing note evident in the comments of Riesman and Whyte cited earlier, the following observation indicates less concern with the negative effects to date:

---

[17]Whyte, *op. cit.,* p. 201.

[18]T. George Harris, "Memo About a Dallas Citizen." From the August 11, 1964 issue of *Look* Magazine. Copyright 1964 by Cowles Communications, Inc. By permission of the editors.

> Has the modern bureaucratic business organization, applying its pressures with a touch of velvet to force its members to conform to expected roles at all levels, so inhibited the behavior of its personnel as to make them impotent as individuals and important only as cogs in the system? I, for one, doubt that this is the case. One of the factors which convinces me that this picture is not correct is my knowledge of business executives of large firms. From what I have observed of these individuals (and I believe I can call them by that term), perhaps their most important characteristics are their decision-making and risk-taking abilities. These are still the outstanding ingredients for business success and are hardly consonant with the neurotic, bureaucratic images presented by some observers of the modern business scene.[19]

There is considerable accuracy in the observation that individualism is not dead. At the same time, the trend toward conformity justifies some concern. In specific situations, moreover, the deadening effects of conformity may be fully realized to the detriment of the individual, the company, and society.

Executive Attitudes Toward the Problem of Conformity

No doubt business executives hold quite different views concerning the problem of organizational conformity. All shades of opinion are to be expected. Some managers may be unaware that any fundamental issue is involved. Those who appreciate the problem differ in their analyses and prescriptions for dealing with it. It may be informative, however, to note the attitudes expressed by two leading executives.

Consider, for example, the reasoning advanced by Frederick R. Kappel, chairman of American Telephone and Telegraph Company. In his judgment, it is impossible to avoid all conformity.

> But whenever two people come together to do something, there must be some conformity. To some extent they must think and act alike. Otherwise any organized society would be impossible. There is a lot of conformity in every group effort — government, business, education, religion. To be against all conformity is to be against order and for chaos.[20]

---

[19]Joseph W. McGuire, *Business and Society* (New York: McGraw-Hill Book Company, 1963), p. 173.

[20]Frederick R. Kappel, *Vitality in a Business Enterprise* (New York: McGraw-Hill Book Company, 1960), p. 75.

Note that Kappel suggests the need for *some* conformity. He implies some minimum amount is necessary for existence as an organization. But he also recognizes that the member of an organization can make his best contribution only if he is "his own unique self." A conflict exists between the need for conformity and the personal needs of individuals. "Our concern," said Kappel, "is not with conformity as such. Our concern is how to build individual vitality in those situations where some conformity is also required."[21]

The solution proposed by Kappel is that of personal responsibility. If conformity is to be avoided, the individual member of the organization must look to himself in maintaining his individuality.

> Every man who elects to join a business must accept the challenge. He can't leave it to his company to find ways to keep him whole. He must work at it himself.[22]

This prescription places the responsibility squarely upon the individual rather than upon corporate management.

Board Chairman Thomas J. Watson, Jr., of IBM, contends that large organizations today do not stamp out individualism. Even though some are security-minded, he feels that corporate people in general are no less independent than are those in non-business fields.

> I suspect we have our fair quota of security-minded men who are careful never to rock the boat. At the same time I suspect there are some college professors who are absent-minded, some scientists who are eccentric, and some military men who are martinets. But just as these stereotypes do not apply to the general run of people in those occupations, the stereotype of the "organization man" does not apply to all forms of corporate life.[23]

Watson furthermore stresses the importance of maintaining independence in the business organization — the need for "wild ducks" and the danger of "taming" them. The goal of independence is one shared by the corporation and many employees.

> IBM has more than 125,000 employees. A substantial number of them, many of whom I could pick out by name, are highly individualistic men and women. They value their social and intellectual freedom, and I question whether they would sur-

---

[21]*Ibid.,* p. 76.

[22]*Ibid.,* p. 77.

[23]Thomas J. Watson, Jr., *A Business and Its Beliefs* (New York: McGraw-Hill Book Company, 1963), p. 25.

render it at any price. Admittedly, they may like their jobs and the security and salaries that go along with them. But I know of few who would not put on their hats and slam the door if they felt the organization had intruded so heavily on them that they no longer owned themselves. Business may have its share of hypocrites, but I am sure that big business has no more than any other group.[24]

According to Du Pont's Crawford H. Greenewalt, there is a distinction between "voluntary conformity of behavior which we call good manners and the enforced conformity of thought which represents an invasion of personal rights and a brake upon our capacity to follow our own destinies."[25] The more serious type of conformity, in the opinion of Greenewalt, is a conformity in thinking. "In the realm of thought and of ideas, however, we rightfully resist any effort to submerge our personal characteristics into a dull and lifeless composite."[26] Greenewalt goes on to say "Conformity in behavior is a human necessity; conformity in patterns of thought a human danger."[27] This analysis, then, considers adaptation of individual thinking to the official company line as the greater danger. This lowers the self-esteem of the individual and produces a unanimous opinion lacking any inside mechanism for detecting its own errors.

Of course, any system permits some degree of nonconformity. The degree permitted depends upon the nature of the situation, the status and reputation of the person involved, and the behavior itself. This suggests that those in the upper ranks of a company like DuPont may be permitted greater freedom in the type of behavior noted by Greenewalt than those lower in the same organization. The role of the top executives, however, is more demanding and all-encompassing in other ways. Whatever standards of proper behavior do exist for such individuals may apply to them for twenty-four hours a day, seven days a week.

Combating the Problem of Organization Man

The subtle nature of pressures toward conformity in organization complicates the task of avoiding an organization-man philosophy.

---

[24]*Ibid.*, pp. 25-26.

[25]Crawford H. Greenewalt, *The Uncommon Man* (New York: McGraw-Hill Book Company, 1959), p. 50.

[26]*Ibid.*, p. 50.

[27]*Ibid.*

Insistence upon conformity is not so much a matter of deliberate design as it is an unfortunate and perhaps unexpected result of organizational life. Sincere administrators with the best of intentions may develop conformists without knowing it.

In combating conformity, organization members as well as administrators must recognize the problem and the danger that it represents. As administrator Kappel suggested, this is not solely a problem of the organization. Each member has some responsibility for maintaining his own individuality. All too often he is eager to embrace the organization and its values without any question whatever. Perhaps his attitude should be one of criticism — somewhere between the unbridled delight of organization man and the cynical rebellion of the iconoclast. With such a viewpoint, he may establish boundaries on his own life and resist the intrusion of the organization into those areas. The corporation may insist upon less conformity than he imagines. At the same time, he need not make himself a malcontent by despising every aspect of organization life. Some give and take is required in business life as it is in the family, church, and every other social institution.

From the standpoint of the organization, a greater degree of tolerance of nonconformity may be developed. Some types of nonconformity are anathema to any organization. Beyond that point, however, organizations differ sharply in the degree of uniformity expected. Unless its objective is to develop organization men, the organization may consciously attempt to stretch its tolerance to the maximum.

Personality tests were cited above as one example of the organization-man administration. A few years ago, the personnel director of Chance Vought Aircraft is reputed to have withdrawn an offer to an experienced executive who appeared highly qualified.[28] The reason for withdrawal of the offer was the fact that a personality test had revealed the applicant to be "emotionally unstable and insecure." As a result of a change in management thinking, the results of such tests were later burned. (The "emotionally unstable and insecure" executive was employed and rose to the ranks of top management.) This represents a change in corporate thinking and demonstrates a practical step that can be taken by a corporation.

> "We just decided it was time to stop trying to fit everybody into a mold," explains Gifford K. Johnson, blunt-speaking president

---

[28]"Maverick Managers," *The Wall Street Journal,* November 22, 1961, p. 1.

> of Ling-Temco-Vought. "There's plenty of room in our company for the bold, brash individual who's willing to be set apart from the herd.[29]

Although this is only one example, it indicates the direction in which corporate management may go. In administration, greater emphasis can be placed upon individualism. Rather than enshrining the status quo, executives may be asked to study and to criticize the system itself.

Maintaining and Stimulating Creativity

Nature of Creativity and the Creative Individual

In administering the business concern, there is a need for better understanding the nature and importance of the creative process. Creativity involves new ideas, new approaches, and new combinations of existing knowledge. It stands in sharp contrast to memorization of facts and learning of detail devised by others. Business and organizational problems may be solved by the process of creative thinking. In doing so, the individual directs his mind to an understanding of the problem and applies his imagination to the search for a practical solution. Rather than taking an obvious explanation, the creative individual is always questioning, probing for a deeper understanding, and seeking a better way.

It is obvious that the capacity for creative thinking is not uniformly distributed. It is likely, however, that most individuals have greater potential for original and imaginative thinking than is ever exploited. Development and use of the creative talent of ordinary individuals is necessary to avoid the scandalous waste of this resource.

Some individuals have demonstrated great inventiveness and an unusual ability to develop ideas that had never occurred to others. Their combination of an able mind and diligent work has resulted in notable and praiseworthy achievements. We look at such outstanding characters with admiration and a little awe, often failing to realize there is a little of that potential within each of us, and also unaware of the hard work behind many of their achievements. By observing them — Kettering, Steinmetz, Le Tourneau, Salk, and the like — we derive not only inspiration but also some idea of the nature of creative activity.

---

[29] *Ibid.*

Stages in Creative Thinking

Some who have studied the process of creative thinking have suggested the existence of steps or stages in the development of a new idea. The "flash of genius" may be preceded by other stages that are less obvious to an observer. Although these stages may be described in various ways, the following will suggest their general nature:

1. Problem discovery.
2. Investigation.
3. Incubation.
4. Insight.
5. Verification.

In *problem discovery*, the individual becomes aware of some particular difficulty or need. Although it might seem that all should share this ability in common — that of sensing or detecting problems — some are more sensitive to the existence of problems than are others. The possibility for product improvement, as an example, may be visualized as a problem by the unusually perceptive individual. Another may be totally unaware of such a problem. This realization of need for a solution or improvement launches the creative thinker. His mind becomes absorbed with the problem at hand. A production manager, for example, may become concerned with the need for improving some part of the production process.

In the second stage, the individual turns to an *investigation* of the facts. This may merely entail a mental re-examination of what he already knows about the subject. It may also involve a more systematic search of literature, past experience, and various other sources. This is the fact-gathering part of the process.

In the *incubation* stage, the mind reflects upon the problem and related material. The problem solver must turn the matter over in his mind. It is at this point that it is difficult to hurry a solution. If a solution is not immediately apparent, he may leave the problem and return to it later. Often, he considers the matter only in a subconscious way. While busy at other pursuits, his mind may return with some new question or thought about the problem at hand.

If the creative process is completed, a moment of illumination occurs. The pieces may suddenly fit together. This stage of "seeing the light" or acquiring *insight* often occurs quickly. The individual may awaken in the middle of the night with a clear understanding of some problem that has been baffling him. Sometimes it is difficult to record with sufficient speed the ideas coming with this insight into the problem and its solution.

It is necessary to check out or *verify* the ideas that have occurred in the preceding stage. Merely devising a solution does not guarantee that it will be a good one in all respects. If the plan or idea appears basically sound, it is "debugged" and modified as necessary for effective use. Additional cycles of creative thinking may be required in adapting and applying the original idea. If this stage of verification is neglected, the result may be a fascinating but impractical idea.

Stimulating Creativity

As noted above, pressure toward conformity has the effect of stifling the creative spirit. In that discussion, we recognized the importance of minimizing such a stultifying influence on the part of the organization. In this section, we are concerned with the positive approaches that may be used in stimulating creativity. It is important that a fresh, creative spirit prevail throughout the organization. It may be that certain functions of the business — research and selling, for example — may have a more critical requirement for creative thinking than other functions. There is hardly any area, however, in which the creative spirit is unnecessary. Particularly in management, as contrasted with operative positions, there is need for stimulating the imagination and thinking of personnel.

Recruitment of personnel who have an unusually creative turn of mind is the first step in developing this quality in an organization. The employer is interested in the spark that distinguishes the imaginative from the routine employee. Identification of the particularly creative individual is a difficult task, and recruiters must look for something more than educational degrees and years of experience.

> They search, I suspect, for evidence of *curiosity,* of *self-discipline,* and of an *unquenchable desire for accomplishment.* These are intangible qualities; but if the manager knows what he is looking for, the prospect of his finding creative people is the greater.[30]

If an organization is to maximize the creative abilities of its members, it must also grant to them a considerable degree of freedom. This clearly rules out an insistence upon more than minimum con-

---

[30]John J. Corson, "Innovation Challenges Conformity," *Harvard Business Review,* Vol. 40, No. 3, May-June 1962, p. 72.

formity. The employee cannot be limited to following a set of rules and prescribed procedures. Rather, he may be encouraged to think about the work that is his to perform. Through delegation, he may be given considerable freedom and responsibility in devising his own work methods.

It is also possible to grant creative individuals assistance in detailed and routine work. A professor may be given assistance in grading tests and thereby be permitted to engage in research. An engineer may be given assistance in drafting, filing, and typing. The problem is not so much the humble nature of routine work as it is the encroachment of detail upon time that should be devoted to achievement on a higher level.

Stimulation of creative effort may also be attempted through continued recognition of achievement. This recognition includes financial rewards, but it is not limited to them. In fact, the symbolic significance of a financial reward may constitute its greatest value. It is recognition that the contribution itself is important, and this may require some financial reward. The promotional practices of the organization should likewise reflect the understanding and appreciation of management for the creative activities of particular individuals. Whether recognition occurs by financial reward, job title, citation, or in other ways, the important thing is that there actually be recognition. If the individual knows that management is aware of the significance of his contribution, he then has much of his reward.

An openness to criticism and tolerance of uncomfortable questions also contribute to an innovative atmosphere. A willingness to modify traditional organization structures and to change customary procedures is a part of this requirement. Although these characteristics are easy to specify, they are difficult to achieve. The status quo becomes accepted to the point that change is well nigh impossible.

> I would lay it down as a basic principle of human organization that the individuals who hold the reins of power in any enterprise cannot trust themselves to be adequately self-critical. For those in power the danger of self-deception is very great, the danger of failing to see the problems or refusing to see them is ever-present. And the only protection is to create an atmosphere in which anyone can speak up.[31]

---

[31]John W. Gardner, "How To Prevent Organizational Dry Rot," *Harper's Magazine*, Vol. 231, No. 1385, October 1965, p. 20. Copyright © 1965, by Harper's Magazine, Inc. Reprinted by permission of the author.

This may account for the fact that young organizations often (though not necessarily) display greater flexibility than those which are older. But older, well-established organizations can, with effort, take deliberate steps to encourage critical analysis on the part of their own members. This will serve to combat the deadening atmosphere of conformity, organization man, and the status quo.

The role of supervisory management is critical in developing a proper atmosphere for creativity. A supervisor can get into a rut, plodding along with little regard for new ideas. He may know exactly why a new idea *won't* work but care little about developing one that will. It is imperative to have vitality at this level. If a superior's encouragement is evident, the subordinate is much more inclined to devote himself to thought and activities of a creative nature.

> Therefore, what the supervisor does or does not do in fostering innovation is crucial. He can crush it, stifle it, condemn it, or he can cultivate and encourage it. But all too often, he resists any creative effort by a subordinate because for him change is disturbing. It may require more work on his part. Or his subordinate may be viewed as a threat to him.[32]

The manager should continually attempt to understand the ideas of subordinates regarding problems that concern them. Questioning may prod an individual to continue his thinking and investigation. Such an approach provides a type of encouragement that the subordinate understands.

Summary

In America, we have seen a shift from the *Protestant ethic*, the ethic of individualism, toward the *social ethic*. In the words of David Riesman, our people have become less *inner-directed* and more *other-directed.*

The relationship of the individual to the organization is encompassed by the concept of the *psychological contract*. A trend toward the social ethic in business organizations has been evident. Adoption of the social ethic has created the problem of the *organization man*, with an emphasis upon conformity. Its dangers are those of stifling

---

[32]William Brady, "The Management of Innovation," *MSU Business Topics*, Vol. 9, No. 2, Spring 1961, p. 12. Reprinted by permission of the publisher, the Bureau of Business and Economic Research, Division of Research, Graduate School of Business Administration, Michigan State University.

the creative spirit, intruding into the private lives of employees, and destroying their personal freedom.

Business executives have pointed out differences in the nature of *conformity*. One type is simply described as good manners. Another type of conformity, a more dangerous variety, involves a uniformity in thinking. Some organizations have taken steps to reduce required conformity and to stimulate individual effort in their organizations. One particular example of such action is the discontinuance of personality tests as a device for selecting executives.

Creative ability represents a talent that needs to be nurtured and utilized in the business organization. The creative process involves a number of stages, including *problem discovery*, *investigation*, *incubation*, *insight*, and *verification*. Business organizations may stimulate creativity by recruiting particularly creative individuals, maximizing their freedom, providing assistance in detailed work, granting recognition for their achievements, and providing the proper supervisory atmosphere.

Discussion Questions

1. Contrast the *Protestant ethic* and the *social ethic*. What evidences of each do you see in modern organizational life?

2. What has been the trend in our society with respect to the Protestant ethic or the social ethic? Is this an alarming trend?

3. Explain the *expansion factor* and the *collision effect*.

4. How may the *inner-directed* and *other-directed* people described by Riesman be related to the social ethic and the Protestant ethic? To Whyte's *organization man*?

5. What is the nature of the problem of *conformity* in modern organizations? What causes the problem to exist?

6. Evaluate the nature and seriousness of the dangers of the social ethic.

7. Summarize the viewpoints of Frederick R. Kappel and Crawford H. Greenewalt toward conformity as outlined in this chapter.

8. How can managers minimize the problem and dangers of conformity?

9. Identify and explain each of the stages in *creative thinking.*

10. Some employers use lie detectors in selecting new employees and in periodically checking those who are employed. Justify or criticize these practices on the basis of the ideas treated in this chapter.

11. Was the American Petrofina Company justified in bringing pressure upon a vice president who created a public relations problem by expressing politically unpopular ideas?

Supplementary Reading

Andrews, Frank M. and George F. Farris, "Supervisory Practices and Innovation in Scientific Teams," *Personnel Psychology,* Vol. 20, No. 4, Winter 1967, pp. 497-515.

Argyris, Chris, *Integrating the Individual and the Organization.* New York: John Wiley & Sons, Inc., 1964.

————, *Organization and Innovation.* Homewood: Richard D. Irwin, Inc., and The Dorsey Press, 1965.

Cummings, Larry, "Organizational Climates for Creativity," *Academy of Management Journal,* Vol. 8, No. 3, September 1965, pp. 220-227.

Cummings, Larry L. and Gary William Mize, "Risk-Taking and Organizational Creativity," *Personnel Administration,* Vol. 31, No. 1, January-February 1968, pp. 38-47.

Davis, Keith and Robert L. Blomstrom, *Business and Its Environment,* Chapter 7. New York: McGraw-Hill Book Company, 1966.

Etzioni, Amitai, *Modern Organizations,* Chapter 6. Englewood Cliffs: Prentice-Hall, Inc., 1964.

Gardner, John W., "How To Prevent Organizational Dry Rot," *Harper's Magazine,* Vol. 231, No. 1385, October 1965, pp. 20-26.

Golembiewski, Robert T., "Innovation and Organization Structure," *Personnel Administration,* Vol. 27, No. 5, September-October 1964, pp. 3-4, 17-21.

Kallen, David J., "Inner Direction, Other Direction, and Social Integration Setting," *Human Relations,* Vol. 16, No. 1, February 1963, pp. 75-87.

Maier, Norman R. F., "Maximizing Personal Creativity Through Better Problem Solving," *Personnel Administration,* Vol. 27, No. 1, January-February 1964, pp. 14-18.

Marks, Melvin R., "Managerial Innovation: You Get What You Ask For," *Personnel,* Vol. 43, No. 6, November-December 1966, pp. 33-42.

Maslow, A. H., "The Need for Creative People," *Personnel Administration,* Vol. 28, No. 3, May-June 1965, pp. 3-5, 21-22.

McGuire, Joseph W., *Business and Society,* Chapter 8. New York: McGraw-Hill Book Company, 1963.

Schein, Edgar H., *Organizational Psychology,* Chapters 2 and 4. Englewood Cliffs: Prentice-Hall, Inc., 1965.

Scott, William E., "The Creative Individual," *Academy of Management Journal,* Vol. 8, No. 3, September 1965, pp. 211-219.

Stanton, Erwin S., "The Individual and the Corporation: Are They Really in Conflict?" *Personnel,* Vol. 45, No. 1, January-February 1968, pp. 33-37.

Strauss, George, "Organization Man — Prospect for the Future," *California Management Review,* Vol. 6, No. 3, Spring 1964, pp. 5-16.

Thompson, Victor A., "Bureaucracy and Innovation," *Administrative Science Quarterly,* Vol. 10, No. 1, June 1965, pp. 1-20.

Ward, John William, "The Idea of Individualism and the Reality of Organization," in *The Business Establishment,* ed. Earl F. Cheit. New York: John Wiley & Sons, Inc., 1964.

Willis, Richard H., "The Yes Man, the No Man, and the Thinking Man," *Personnel Administration,* Vol. 27, No. 6, November-December 1964, pp. 6-12.

Direction of the Organization

20

Understanding the Employee as a Person

The management process, and particularly the managerial function of directing, presupposes people to be managed and directed. In this chapter, attention is focused upon the individual who is the object of supervision and management. The concepts to be discussed are applicable to both managerial and non-managerial personnel. Even though the discussion at times emphasizes one or the other group, it is well to recall the general nature of these ideas. Blue collar workers, office personnel, supervisors, foremen, middle managers, and executives are all human beings with distinctive needs, abilities, tensions, and problems of adjustment.

The Employee and His Background

Individual Differences in Employees

The fact of differences among individual members of organizations is a matter of common knowledge. The extent of such differences, however, is less clearly recognized. Individual variations exist, moreover, in a number of areas — aptitudes, abilities, attitudes, interests, ambitions, and so on.

In ability and performance, individual variations are often substantial. Even among experienced workers, it is not uncommon for the best performer to produce twice as much as the least efficient employee. Managers likewise show a broad range of capacity and aptitude for managerial work.

People also vary in their motivation to work. Some work primarily for a paycheck, while others are more directly concerned with social satisfactions or advancement. The significance of particular motivational factors also changes over a period of time. Motivation is based upon needs which seem to differ in importance from individual to individual.

Supervision of employees should begin with an awareness of individual differences. In terms of ability, for example, a particular employee may be classified as average, but others are above average and below average. These differences, where they exist, must be accepted as facts. Such an understanding avoids unreasonable expectations concerning below-average employees and provides a basis for understanding the behavior of exceptional employees. It is also necessary for properly matching individuals and jobs. An employee of outstanding ability (the genius or merely the really "sharp" individual) is unsuited for many routine jobs.

The Perceptual World of Employees

Our eyes often play tricks on us. In the following figure, most of us find that Line *A* looks shorter than Line *B*. In reality, of course,

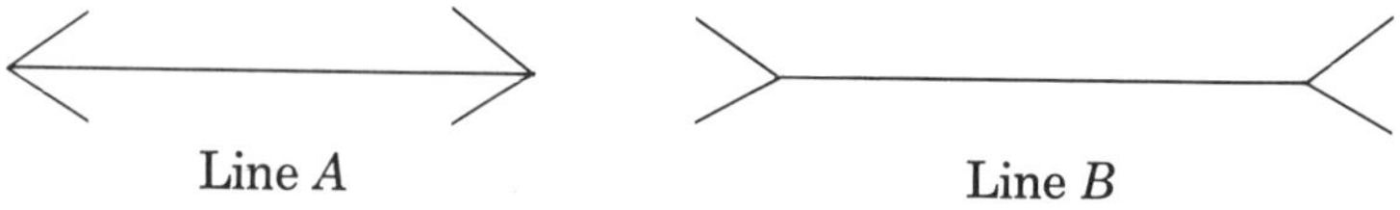

they are the same length, and this can be verified by measuring them. In spite of the fact of the matter, our initial reaction is to see them differently. In other words, our perception of the fact and the fact itself are different.

In the same way, an individual's perception of the facts in an administrative situation may be different from the facts. Suppose that a promising young executive is passed over in a promotion to fill an existing vacancy. In reality, his superiors declined to promote him even though they were convinced of his potential and expected him to move up in the organization. It just happened that the particular vacancy was not the right one for this young executive at this time. But how will he perceive the situation? Will he interpret it in the same way that his superiors interpret it?

The employee's attitude and behavior are governed by his perception of the facts rather than the facts themselves. So far as the individual is concerned, the perceived fact *is* a fact. In his eyes, it *is* reality, and he feels that he is acting rationally when he proceeds on the basis of those facts. If the young executive feels that his superiors lack an appreciation of his talent, this is simply the truth *as he sees it.* If he resigns and looks for a real "opportunity," he is operating consistently with the facts *as he sees them.*

In dealing with subordinates and associates, it is imperative for the executive to be conscious of their perceptual worlds. Rather than regarding them as hardheaded or stubborn, it may be more helpful to see that they sometimes interpret the facts differently. It may be that their interpretation is wrong in differing from the real facts. In this case, achievement of understanding depends upon reconciling the individual's perceptual world with the real world.

There is also a warning for managers to examine the basis of their own thinking. The world as any manager views it always seems to him to be the real world and to be based on the facts. Being the boss often makes the likelihood of error appear even more remote. But the moral of this reasoning is that a manager must realize that one's perception of the facts *is* a perception. There is always the possibility of error, particularly in interpreting the behavior of others. It is well for any manager, therefore, to develop a consciousness of the limitations of his own perceptual world.

Employees — Rational or Emotional?

At the turn of the century, management considered employees to be highly rational in their relationships with the employer. Much of the scientific management movement, in fact, involved assumptions concerning the logical behavior of individuals in organizations. For example, the financial incentive plans proposed by Frederick W. Taylor and others assumed that employees would increase output to earn greater pay. Managers were also thought to be quite rational in deciding issues on the basis of profit maximization. In other words, the individual — employee or manager — was thought to behave logically in terms of self-interest.

More extensive observation of employee behavior, however, indicated that they did not behave in the consistently logical fashion that was thought to characterize them. On occasion, the emotions of employees led them to decisions that were seemingly irrational. They sometimes evidenced unexpected hostility or resistance. Scientific observation of employee behavior served to emphasize the importance of nonrational elements. In the Western Electric experiments described earlier, workers responded in many different ways from those predictable on the basis of management logic. Employees subject to paternalistic management also displayed resentment and even went so far as to strike against their benevolent employers. Managers also acted inconsistently at times in seeking personal prestige at the expense of company profits.

In a subsequent preoccupation with human relations, some managers showed an inclination to go overboard in the opposite direction, assuming employees were emotional *rather* than rational. In view of the discoveries about employee behavior, good human relations seemed to offer the major key. The paycheck, the nature of the organization structure, the content of the job — these were part of the "rational" approach and seemingly were less important than keeping people happy.

The truth of the matter seems to be that organization members are both thinking and feeling individuals. They are capable of logical thought in the solution of problems and in choices concerning their own work and careers. Most employees do seek paths that will increase the size of their paychecks. Managers do follow a logical pattern — for example, utilizing research to determine the most effective marketing methods. Their behavior as individuals and as members of the organization is not completely emotional and irrational. On the other hand, they are not limited to computer-like actions, devoid of feeling or emotional content.

An effective manager, then, must take into account the emotional or irrational behavior as well as the logical or rational behavior of others.

> This perceptiveness to the other person's emotions is necessary as a guide to our relations with them. When "the boss is in a sour mood" we may not ask for that raise we hope to get. When we see that employees are sullen about a change in hours we may not take that particular time to be jovial and clubby with them. When they are pleased and happy about a recent decision, that may be the appropriate time to request their cooperation in tightening up on some laxity which has come to light.[1]

Needs of Employees

The Nature of Employee Needs

Individuals at all levels of the organization strive to satisfy various human needs. As one need is satisfied or partially satisfied, another

---

[1]George S. Odiorne, *Personnel Policy: Issues and Practices* (Columbus: Charles E. Merrill Publishing Co., 1963), p. 92.

takes its place, and effort must be exerted to satisfy it. The needs of individuals that can be satisfied through employment in business organizations may be classified in different ways. The following discussion considers them as falling into three categories — *physiological* needs, *social* needs, and *egoistic* needs.

Physiological needs are those inherited drives directly connected with the physical body. They are perhaps the most obvious of all human needs. The need for food is one example. Through employment, the individual attempts to secure sufficient income to satisfy the physical needs of himself and his family. If denied, physical needs become powerful in motivation of behavior. In America, satisfaction of these needs is more nearly adequate than in many other nations of the world. To some extent, job security is also pertinent to the satisfaction of physical needs. The individual is not content with present fulfillment of the needs; he wants to be sure they will continue to be satisfied in the future. (Of course, physiological needs do not provide a complete explanation of the quest for job security.)

As a social being, man has a need that depends upon others for its satisfaction. In contrast to physiological needs, social needs are acquired and thus vary somewhat from culture to culture. The individual's social need involves a desire to enjoy the association and friendship of others, to feel that he belongs. If fellow employees deprive a typical individual of the opportunity to satisfy this need — turning their backs or refusing to speak — it makes work almost intolerable. Most employees, as is true of people in general, want companionship and shun loneliness. The chatter and banter in an office or shop often make work enjoyable and help to eliminate boredom. In some organizations, groups develop a sense of teamwork that is particularly satisfying to members of the team. Helping others and being helped by them seem particularly rewarding to most individuals.

Egoistic needs are concerned with the individual's view of himself. In addition to a social need for companionship, he develops a desire to amount to something. The individual likes to feel that what he does has significance and is worth while. Even the man who digs ditches becomes perturbed if he is required simply to dig them and then fill them again. The pointlessness of unnecessary work becomes distressing. Among executive and professional personnel, the egoistic need is particularly strong.

The need for accomplishment is an important aspect or element of the egoistic need. Work requiring skill and involving a product of obvious importance helps satisfy one's need for accomplishment.

A desire for some degree of autonomy in work is also a part of one's egoistic needs. If every movement of an employee is prescribed in detail, it is difficult for him to see himself as much more than a machine.

> You know, it's a funny thing. I work all day at the plant and then I come home and what do I do? I work some more — I mean in the shop in the basement. I love to do things with my hands. Funny, that's what I do at work — only it's different.
>
> You see at work I don't have any freedom. That's the difference. The company tells me when to start working, when I get time to go to the john, when I get my lunch and how long (I get .7 hours — that's 42 minutes for anyone who isn't an engineer). They tell me how fast to work and exactly what motions to make. About the only thing I'm free to do is to think how . . . lousy the job is.
>
> Now, at home I'm my own boss — and believe me, that's a wonderful feeling.
>
> — *Autoworker*[2]

Hierarchy of Needs

Some psychologists have suggested a hierarchy of needs on the basis of their importance. At any given time, different types of needs hold different priorities in an individual's thinking. Probably the best-known exposition of this point of view is that of A. H. Maslow in which he outlined five levels of human needs.[3] The stairstep diagram at the top of page 449 ranks five categories of needs in accordance with the reasoning of Maslow.

If needs are viewed in this way, it is the physiological needs that must be satisfied first. In other words, they have first priority. The hungry man seeks food rather than companionship in work. As Maslow has said, man lives by bread alone when there is no bread. It is only after the hunger and other basic needs are satisfied, or at least partially satisfied, that he can think about social needs. Only after belongingness and esteem needs are satisfied can attention be shifted to self-fulfillment needs. Of course, this represents an oversimplification, because the needs are not mutually exclusive. All of them may be present in some degree even though there is a difference in emphasis.

---

[2]George Strauss and Leonard R. Sayles, *Personnel: The Human Problems of Management,* Second Edition (Englewood Cliffs: Prentice-Hall, Inc., © 1967), p. 15.

[3]A. H. Maslow, "A Theory of Human Motivation," *The Psychological Review,* Vol. 50, No. 4, July 1943, pp. 370-396.

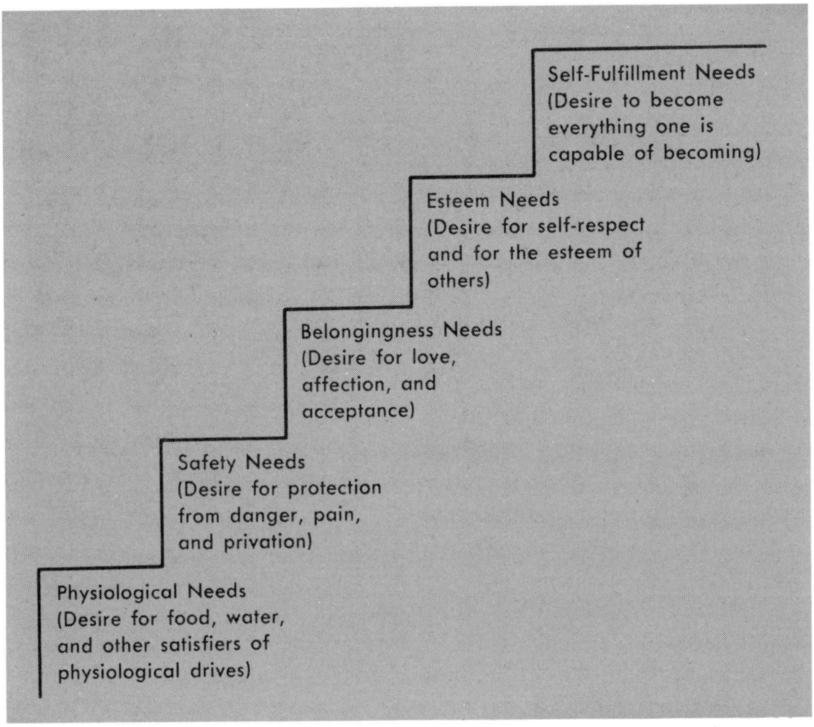

It is the unsatisfied need that assumes first place in one's thinking at a particular time. If a need is satisfied, we take it for granted, and it does not act as a motivator of behavior.

> Consider your own need for air. Except as you are deprived of it, it has no appreciable motivating effect upon your behavior.
>
> When the physiological needs are reasonably satisfied, needs at the next higher level begin to dominate man's behavior — to motivate him.[4]

Contemporary business organizations provide satisfaction of these needs in varying degrees. The physiological needs of employees that can be satisfied in employment present few problems in American industry. It is likely, however, that serious gaps exist in the fulfillment of some of the higher types of needs for millions of employees. Many individuals find it difficult to realize genuine satisfaction of the need for self-fulfillment in their work.

---

[4]Douglas McGregor, *The Human Side of Enterprise* (New York: McGraw-Hill Book Company, 1960), pp. 36-37.

Frustration in Need Fulfillment

An individual may strive to achieve a particular goal without much success. If a serious barrier makes it impossible to satisfy an important need, he may experience a strong emotional reaction known as *frustration*. Reactions to frustration may take different forms. The individual may decide that the blame rests with someone outside himself and proceed to attack the block or barrier in some way. On the other hand, he may blame himself and experience a sense of failure and possibly insecurity. Of course, it is possible that he may consider the problem rationally in seeking an alternative means to satisfy the need. If the goal or need is extremely important to him, however, it is difficult for him to be completely rational concerning it.

The nature of work in much of industry makes it difficult for employees to achieve satisfaction of egoistic needs. Work is often highly routine, involving little skill and allowing little freedom for the employee. The shape of the executive pyramid also means that promotional opportunities for managers thin out as they reach toward the top. At each level, fewer can satisfy their ambitions by moving up. Different individuals attach varying degrees of importance to their goals. Some are able to accept limitation with less discomfort than are others.

The problem of frustration is minimized if the individual's expectations growing out of his needs are reasonably related to his abilities and circumstances. For example, an employee may feel a need for attainments exceeding his ability. Parents sometimes set unreasonable educational goals for their children, having little regard for their natural abilities and interests. In the business world, the son may feel it necessary to attain the same rung on the ladder as his father. One cannot deny the importance of ambition in stretching one's ability to the limit. If the goal is far beyond reasonable expectations, however, frustration is likely to result.

The natural reaction of a self-confident individual to frustration may be to "let off steam" rather than to blame himself. The manager who "blows his top," however, finds the emotional flareup unacceptable to his superiors. He knows that his superiors have higher regard for the individual who shows emotional self-control.

> Thus it is possible for the secure optimist to avoid part of this problem — he can *feel* like blowing up but then stifle his cor-

> responding actions so that what the boss sees is a controlled and rational façade. In fact, many executives in industry probably do just that, thereby perhaps contributing to the psychosomatic illnesses industrial executives are said to develop. For chronic failure to express intense emotion and through that expression to utilize the physiological products of emotion can lead to chronic physiological disturbance.[5]

Conflict in Needs

The needs of individuals are not always perfectly integrated. Instead, there is a possibility of need conflict within the individual. Need *A* can be satisfied only by denying Need *B*. *A* person may be hungry and sleepy at the same time. Or, he may wish to meet the mutually inconsistent expectations of others. In the discussion of frustration above, we found that the block to need satisfaction was outside the individual. In the case of *conflict*, the warfare is within the individual and arises from the competition between different needs.

In the business world, various situations may cause a conflict of needs for the individual. For example, managers must constantly deal with ambiguous situations. Often, there is no one solution to an administrative problem that will satisfy everyone and be consistent with the manager's own values. Likewise, an egoistic need calling for a measure of independence may conflict with an employee's need for security — a need that requires subordination, particularly if he has an overbearing supervisor. Personal ethical standards may conflict with those of the organization. A salesman may be asked to entertain a customer in a manner he considers improper or to stretch a point of truth in making a sale. An executive may ask a conscientious secretary to tell a visitor he is out of the office when he simply does not wish to be bothered.

> Other uses of conflict as devices for controlling behavior can get more serious. Suppose, instead of the threat of discipline, we choose to try to develop "positive" feelings of loyalty and duty to the company — suppose we try to build a "company conscience" into our employees as we do into our children. If we succeed, we are setting up *internal* conflicts this time. Now it is not the boss that the employee must worry about, but his own

[5]Harold J. Leavitt, *Managerial Psychology* (Chicago: The University of Chicago Press, 1958), p. 43.

> feelings of guilt. People who thus begin to feel honor-bound can get themselves into a tense emotional tizzy.[6]

Conflict may result in unfortunate psychological consequences. If the conflict is intense and involves important needs, it may result in neurosis, psychosis, repression, or psychosomatic illness. Serious conflicts do cause serious psychological problems. Finding a practical solution to need conflicts may involve considerable difficulty. In spite of the difficulty, however, the individual and the organization should attempt to find a reasonable solution for such conflicts.

> A conflict exists for a person because to him certain needs seem mutually exclusive. His conflict would be resolved if (1) he could find some new, previously unknown means to satisfy both needs fully, (2) he could change his mind about one of the needs so that he was no longer interested in it, or (3) he could reorganize, in one of a number of other ways, his view of the world so as to set the conflict in a new and less significant perspective.[7]

It is evident that resolution of conflict may be achieved by the action of the individual, the organization, or both. In some cases, effective corrective action may be taken by management. In other situations, major responsibility must be assumed by the individual.

Facilitating Emotional Adjustment

Emotional Adjustment and Emotional Disturbance

Ideally, the organization should have emotionally well-adjusted personnel — individuals who have good mental health. This condition of proper adjustment is sometimes referred to as *equilibrium.* The characteristics of such individuals have been described as follows: (1) they feel comfortable about themselves; (2) they feel right about other people; and (3) they are able to meet the demands of life. Figure 22 describes in greater detail the characteristics of such individuals.

Proper adjustment of the individual is not equivalent to conformity. Outward conformity may appear to entail adjustment while in reality involving great inner conflict. Also, as noted in Chapter 19, conformity constitutes a goal of questionable quality. The goal of a

[6] *Ibid.,* p. 55.
[7] *Ibid.,* p. 62.

reasonably happy, stable, well-adjusted individual, however, is not subject to this same criticism.

Probably every individual is subject to minor fluctuations of an emotional nature. We have our ups and downs. Indeed, minor tensions and anxieties are natural self-protective devices that enable us to meet threats to our safety, happiness, or self-esteem. Occasionally, we worry a little about some problem or fret because of some difficulty that confronts us. Usually, we bounce back quickly and recognize the problem as purely transitory. If the emotional upset involves prolonged or excessive anxiety, however, it becomes a more serious matter. Even so, the emotional disturbance may involve a relatively mild emotional illness — something akin to the common cold. As with physical illness, the disturbance can become serious and result in severe agitation, panic, or inability to exert reasonable self-control. For administrators, the most typical problems of this nature involve relatively minor emotional disturbances.

The Constructive Role of Anxiety

In organizational life, members often experience apprehension or anxiety concerning possible unpleasant events. Such inward tension is typically more of a vague concern about the future than it is the fear of a specific danger. Anxiety of any type is often regarded as an unmixed evil, lacking any redeeming virtues and having no constructive role to perform. When applied to the more extreme forms of anxiety, this assessment of its destructive influence upon the individual and the organization is completely warranted. Milder anxiety, however, may provide desirable motivation. For example, an operative employee who is promoted to a supervisory position initially senses some insecurity or anxiety in his new position. As a result, he will try hard to be successful in the new position. Of course, if his anxiety becomes too extreme, the effect is destructive and damaging to his chances for success.

One study of successful executives in American business firms discovered that they harbored a feeling of apprehension that they might not succeed in meeting organizational standards.[8] Their anxiety might be viewed as "normal" anxiety. For these men, anxiety apparently motivates accomplishment and causes them to work diligently in the hope of assuring success.

---

[8]William E. Henry, "The Business Executive: The Psychodynamics of a Social Role," *American Journal of Sociology,* Vol. 54, No. 4, January 1949, p. 289.

Figure 22. *These Are Some of the Characteristics of People with Good Mental Health*

1 *They feel comfortable about themselves.*

They are not bowled over by their own emotions — by their fears, anger, love, jealousy, guilt or worries.

They can take life's disappointments in their stride.

They have a tolerant, easy-going attitude towards themselves as well as others; they can laugh at themselves.

They neither under-estimate nor over-estimate their abilities.

They can accept their own shortcomings.

They have self-respect.

They feel able to deal with most situations that come their way.

They get satisfaction from the simple, every-day pleasures.

2 *They feel right about other people.*

They are able to give love and to consider the interests of others.

They have personal relationships that are satisfying and lasting.

They expect to like and trust others, and take it for granted that others will like and trust them.

They respect the many differences they find in people.

They do not push people around, nor do they allow themselves to be pushed around.

They can feel they are part of a group.

They feel a sense of responsibility to their neighbors and fellow men.

3 *They are able to meet the demands of life.*

They do something about their problems as they arise.

They accept their responsibilities.

They shape their environment whenever possible; they adjust to it whenever necessary.

They plan ahead but do not fear the future.

They welcome new experiences and new ideas.

They make use of their natural capacities.

They set realistic goals for themselves.

They are able to think for themselves and make their own decisions.

They put their best effort into what they do, and get satisfaction out of doing it.

Source: *Mental Health Is 1, 2, 3.* Produced by the National Association for Mental Health, 10 Columbus Circle, New York 19, New York

In dealing with anxiety among subordinates, managers should distinguish between those who are concerned primarily with attaining success and those who are more concerned with avoiding failure. The latter group may be described as high-anxiety individuals. High-anxiety people require a more supportive type of supervision, and the manager may properly assume greater responsibility himself and focus attention on the task rather than upon the employee. In dealing with a low-anxiety subordinate, the manager may need to present him with a strong challenge.

> The administrator can improve performance by creating some anxiety for the low anxiety, high need achievement person, to keep his level of aspirations and subsequent performance high. He must minimize anxiety-producing demands for the high anxiety, failure avoiding person, to encourage him to work toward suitably high performance levels.[9]

David W. Ewing has also pointed out that the manager must allow for individual differences in tolerance for tension.[10] The degree of healthy tension which stimulates one man may overwhelm another. Tension, therefore, is useful up to a point, and the desirable extent varies with the personality, the circumstances, the time, and other factors.

The Manager and the Emotionally Disturbed Employee

Managers must frequently assume responsibility for dealing with emotionally disturbed employees — usually subordinates but occasionally colleagues. The manager may observe evidence of this difficulty in the work, personal conduct, or interpersonal relationships of the disturbed individual. Levinson has identified the following three signs of emotional distresses:

> 1. The person's usual manner may be overemphasized. A quiet person may become even more withdrawn. A well-ordered person may become overconcerned with details. The hail-fellow-well-met salesman may increase his pace until he is described as "jet-propelled." These people are racing their motors, trying to cope with stresses.

---

[9]Timothy W. Costello and Sheldon S. Zalkind, *Psychology in Administration: A Research Orientation* (Englewood Cliffs: Prentice-Hall, Inc., 1963), p. 156.

[10]David W. Ewing, "Tension Can Be An Asset," *Harvard Business Review*, Vol. 42, No. 5, September-October 1964, p. 77.

> 2. When increased use of the customary personality devices does not work effectively, more obvious signs of distress begin to appear. A person may be restless or agitated. He may be unable to concentrate. He may become tense and jittery, perspire freely, feel panicky, and have other symptoms . . . These symptoms will be evident even to the nonprofessional eye.
>
> 3. Radical change in behavior indicates extremely severe stress. The orderly, controlled person may become alcoholic. The quiet person may become noisy and aggressive. Thoughts and ideas that are irrational may appear.[11]

In other cases, the troubled individual may bring his problem directly to the manager—sometimes overtly expressed and sometimes disguised as a different type of problem.

Having encountered a disturbed employee, what can or should the manager do about it? The answer depends upon the seriousness of the problem. If the disturbance is a relatively minor one, the manager may be able to apply what has been described as *emotional first aid*.[12] For the most part, this involves sympathetic listening—a practice that may provide relief in the case of minor disturbances. The fact that managers lack professional training in psychiatry, however, makes extensive counseling unwise and possibly dangerous. Fortunately, some problems can be talked out in one or two discussions between the manager and the disturbed individual. Often, the troubled employee can make a decision that relieves his anxiety. Unfortunately, however, the seriousness of an apparently minor emotional disturbance is not always evident.[13] As soon as the manager realizes that the disturbance is beyond correction through "first-aid" treatment, he has little recourse but to discontinue his own efforts in this direction. It may be possible in some cases to refer the individual to a professional psychiatrist.

An excessive degree of tolerance with respect to work requirements of disturbed employees appeals to the manager's sympathetic instincts but may be more harmful than a realistic establishment of job requirements and a specification of limits that cannot be exceeded by the sick individual. It may be helpful to a disturbed employee to be advised of the deterioration of performance and the seriousness of its continuation. Even dismissal may be constructive

---

[11]Harry Levinson, *Emotional Health in the World of Work* (New York: Harper & Row, Publishers, 1964), p. 222.

[12]*Ibid.*, Chapter 15.

[13]Robert N. McMurry, "Mental Illness in Industry," *Harvard Business Review*, Vol. 37, No. 2, March-April 1959, p. 80.

and possibly motivate the individual to seek professional help. One consultant's recommendation is as follows:

> Although this will come as a shock to many gentle idealists, I recommend that if, after reasonable effort has been made to help the problem employee, he shows little or no improvement or even retrogresses slightly, the fairest and kindest step management can take is to release him.[14]

Contributions to Disturbance

Certainly, all emotional or psychological problems of employees cannot be laid at the door of management. Many of them involve personal difficulties unrelated to the business. Our attention here, however, is directed to organizational conditions that may in some way create or contribute to employee disturbance. In general, conditions that prevent adequate need satisfaction interfere with the achievement of good mental health or equilibrium. Inability to satisfy needs results in frustration and its attendant unhappiness. For example, selection or placement of employees in such a way as to prevent pleasant social relationships on the job denies satisfaction of a social need. Assignment to work having little apparent significance and requiring no skill thwarts the individual's egoistic needs. Any obstacle placed in the way of employee advancement similarly serves as a disturbing factor.

In addition, conditions in the organization tending to create conflict have a similar effect. Paternalistic attitudes, for example, create a conflict between the needs for loyalty and independence. Situations of any type that place the individual in a spot forcing choice between two important needs would have the same effect.

Overlapping responsibility or insufficient authority may also place an executive in a difficult spot. He is expected to get results, but he lacks control over the situation. Staff departments may seriously interfere with the exercise of his authority. The result may be frustration for the executive.

Several types of management action that create adjustment problems have been examined by Levinson. Based on an analysis of 287 cases, he has suggested six common problem-creating actions that lead to troublesome behavior among subordinates.[15] The errors he identifies are as follows:

---

[14]*Ibid.*, pp. 85-86.

[15]Harry Levinson, "Who Is to Blame for Maladaptive Managers?" *Harvard Business Review,* Vol. 43, No. 6, November-December 1965, pp. 143-158.

1. *Encouragement of Power Seeking.* By rewarding a manager who demonstrates an ability to organize, to drive, and to get results, his superiors may inadvertently encourage a wide-ranging pursuit of personal power. Such individuals may come to adopt an authoritarian approach, over-dominate their subordinates, and experience difficulty in working with others.
2. *Failure to Exercise Control.* Senior managers occasionally condone behavior which is beyond the bounds of common courtesy. Subordinates are permitted to be unnecessarily critical or rude and to spew their anger at colleagues, subordinates, and superiors. The superior may feel afraid of the subordinate's hostility or experience guilt feelings because of his own anger toward the subordinate. At any rate, behavior of this nature is sometimes allowed to continue indefinitely.
3. *Stimulation of Rivalry.* Hostility among subordinates may be stimulated by fostering rivalry among them. For example, the chairman of the board may select an executive vice president to prod the president. Or, a supervisor may be angry with one subordinate and use another subordinate as a weapon to displace his own hostility.
4. *Failure to Anticipate the Inevitable.* Such painful experiences as failing to obtain a promotion, having one's judgment rejected, or having some of one's responsibilities given to another may be described as *psychological injuries.* Failure to anticipate or prepare for such problems tends to create a feeling of shock, manipulation, or exploitation. An opportunity to know about a change and to express feelings about it without fear or embarrassment indicates acceptance of and respect for the individual.
5. *Pressuring Men of Limited Ability.* Some managers, for example, are dependent in nature and try as much as possible to control the situations confronting them and to protect themselves. Attempts to develop the independence of such individuals or to increase their participation may be threatening rather than helpful.
6. *Misplacement.* Management may err by placing individuals in positions with requirements exceeding their abilities or by adding duties and responsibilities to the point that incumbents cannot keep up with job demands. Such an individual

may be left to flounder and to contend with feelings of incompetency.

Contributions to Adjustment

The type of supervision existing in an organization is undoubtedly one of the most important factors contributing to employee adjustment. A given manager can by his own behavior make a job rewarding and enjoyable. Fairness and objectivity in measuring performance contribute to the employee's sense of well-being. Some managers are also much more sensitive to the needs and feelings of their employees than are others. The following chapter considers the subject of leadership in greater detail.

Full and timely communication can make a positive contribution to the psychological health of employees. Many of the difficulties experienced by employees are partially imaginary or based upon incomplete information. If an employee understands the "why," a problem may be avoided or eliminated.

An example of management action to reduce employee anxiety during an initial training period was reported by Texas Instruments, Inc., in 1966.[16] Texas Instruments had found that new assemblers experienced anxiety during the first three months on the job — the period required to attain a level of competence — and that this anxiety interfered with their training in a number of ways. For example, new operators were reluctant to discuss problems with their supervisors, and unnecessary turnover of newly hired employees was caused by anxiety. It also seemed obvious that anxiety dropped as competence was achieved.

An experiment was devised whereby one group of new employees was given an entire day of orientation — rather than the customary two hours — a type of orientation that was specifically designed to reduce their anxiety concerning the training situation. During the day, the likelihood of their success was repeatedly stressed to the experimental group, and the nature of hazing they might expect from fellow employees was explained. They were urged to take the initiative in communication with their supervisors — whose personalities were described as accurately and carefully as possible. An employee

[16]Earl R. Gomersall and M. Scott Myers, "Breakthrough in On-the-Job Training," *Harvard Business Review*, Vol. 44, No. 4, July-August 1966, pp. 62-72.

might be told that his prospective supervisor was strict but friendly, that he tended to be shy, but that he really liked to talk with subordinates who desired to do so. The control groups received the customary type of training, and the differences in orientation between the experimental and control groups were not known by the employees who were involved. The gains were little short of sensational.

- Training time was shortened by one half.
- Training costs were lowered to one third of their previous levels.
- Absenteeism and tardiness dropped to one half of the previous normal.
- Waste and rejects were reduced to one fifth of their previous levels.
- Costs were cut as much as 15% to 30%![17]

The problem of anxiety was not limited to assemblers but also hampered new supervisors and middle managers. As a result of anxiety, new supervisors felt inadequate in dealing with seasoned, competent subordinates, and they cut off downward communication in order to conceal their own ignorance. The management of Texas Instruments attempted to combat anxiety at this level as well as at the operative level. To help eliminate the problem, they developed a plan whereby operators helped train the supervisor. This taught supervisors to rely on subordinates for assistance in solving problems and also gave operators an interest in the success of the supervisor.

Organizational practices discussed earlier in the book may likewise facilitate employee adjustment. Delegation of authority, for example, increases the autonomy of the individual, thereby contributing to satisfaction of his egoistic need. Job enlargement may restore skill and meaning to the job.

Personnel policies also have a bearing upon the maintenance of employee equilibrium. Selection of personnel who are qualified, but not overqualified, to fill existing positions avoids a waste of talent that is depressing to employees. If advancement opportunities do not exist, there is little point in employing people with greater potential than can be used.

Summary

It is the individual employee — managerial or operative — who is the object of the managerial function of directing. Skillful direction

---

[17] *Ibid.*, p. 62.

recognizes the fact of *individual differences,* not only in terms of ability but also in attitudes, interests, ambitions, and other ways.

The individual in the business organization sees the facts from his point of view. His viewpoint constitutes a *perceptual world* that may differ from the *real world.* To the individual, however, his perceptual world seems to be the real world. In their behavior, employees appear to be partly rational and partly emotional; their conduct cannot be explained on the basis of either of these features alone.

Three major categories of individual needs are recognized—*physiological* needs, *social* needs, and *egoistic* needs. It seems likely that some *hierarchy of needs* exists, with physiological needs having a higher priority (or being more basic) until satisfied than social needs and egoistic needs. It is unsatisfied needs that serve as motivators of behavior. If obstacles arise to the satisfaction of important needs, the condition of *frustration* results. Unfortunate psychological consequences may also result from a *conflict* between important needs.

The organization and its management can make various positive contributions to the psychological well-being or *equilibrium* of its employees. The goal is not conformity but a stable employee who feels comfortable about himself, right about other people, and able to meet the demands of life. Although extreme forms of anxiety are destructive and undesirable, milder forms of anxiety are sufficiently general as to be considered "normal." Mild anxiety, moreover, serves a useful function in motivating personnel. Emotional upsets frequently exceed the limits of minor disturbances, however, causing problems for both the employees and their managers. In dealing with emotionally disturbed employees, the manager may provide some relief through *emotional first aid,* but he lacks the training to deal personally with serious problems of this type. Supervision and organization that facilitate satisfaction of needs and minimize frustration and conflict provide a practical basis for achievement of good mental health for employees.

Discussion Questions

1. Of what significance to the manager is the *perceptual world* of his subordinate or colleague?
2. Are employees primarily rational or emotional in their relationships with their employer?
3. What distinction do you see between *social needs* and *egoistic needs* of the individual?

4. Explain carefully the concept of a *hierarchy of needs.* What is the significance of this concept in terms of motivation?

5. What is the nature of *frustration*? What causes it, and what are its consequences?

6. What is the difference between *need frustration* and *need conflict*?

7. What attitude should a manager adopt toward an emotionally disturbed employee? How far should he go in trying to help such an individual?

8. Describe the type of managerial practices that contribute most to proper emotional adjustment.

Supplementary Reading

Bruce, Grady D. and Richard F. Dutton, "The Neurotic Executive," *Personnel Administration,* Vol. 30, No. 5, September-October 1967, pp. 25-31.

Ewing, David W., "Tension Can Be an Asset," *Harvard Business Review,* Vol. 42, No. 5, September-October 1964, pp. 71-78.

Fiedler, Fred E., "The Effect of Inter-Group Competition on Group Member Adjustment," *Personnel Psychology,* Vol. 20, No. 1, Spring 1967, pp. 33-44.

Gomersall, Earl R. and M. Scott Myers, "Breakthrough in On-the-Job Training," *Harvard Business Review,* Vol. 44, No. 4, July-August 1966, pp. 62-72.

Haire, Mason, *Psychology in Management,* Second Edition, Chapter 2. New York: McGraw-Hill Book Company, 1964.

Huddle, Donald D., "How to Live with Stress on the Job," *Personnel,* Vol. 44, No. 2, March-April 1967, pp. 31-37.

Levinson, Harry, *Emotional Health in the World of Work.* New York: Harper & Row, Publishers, 1964.

McKeon, Richard M., "Attention to Tension in Industry," *Personnel Journal,* Vol. 42, No. 6, June 1963, pp. 281-283.

Miles, Raymond E., "The Affluent Organization," *Harvard Business Review,* Vol. 44, No. 3, May-June 1966, pp. 106-114.

Miner, John B., *Introduction to Industrial Clinical Psychology.* New York: McGraw-Hill Book Company, 1966.

Odiorne, George S., *Personnel Policy: Issues and Practices,* Chapter 4. Columbus: Charles E. Merrill Publishing Co., 1963.

Ross, David W., "How to Be a More Effective Counselor," *Personnel,* Vol. 40, No. 3, May-June 1963, pp. 8-14.

Slesinger, Jonathan A. and Ernest Harburg, "Organizational Stress: A Force Requiring Management Control," *Personnel Administration,* Vol. 27, No. 3, May-June 1964, pp. 3-5, 35-39.

Stagner, Ross and Hjalmar Rosen, *Psychology of Union-Management Relations,* Chapter 4. Belmont: Wadsworth Publishing Company, Inc., 1965.

Tannenbaum, Arnold S., *Social Psychology of the Work Organization,* Chapter 3. Belmont: Wadsworth Publishing Company, Inc., 1966.

Webber, Ross A., "The Roots of Organizational Stress," *Personnel,* Vol. 43, No. 5, September-October 1966, pp. 32-39.

Weinstock, Irwin and Arthur A. Thompson, "Administrative Sensitivity to Economic Needs of Employees: Some Distorting Mechanisms," *Academy of Management Journal,* Vol. 10, No. 1, March 1967, pp. 17-25.

Zaleznik, Abraham, "Management of Disappointment," *Harvard Business Review,* Vol. 45, No. 6, November-December 1967, pp. 59-70.

21

Leadership and Motivation

There are striking differences in personal characteristics and methods of leadership among American business executives. Over time and in different types of administrative situations, successful managers have displayed quite different varieties of leadership. Even members of the same family presiding over the same corporation may be as different as night and day. The leadership of Henry Ford I and Henry Ford II is a case in point. This chapter examines the nature of the leadership function and the motivational approaches used by business leaders.

The Leadership Function

Nature and Importance of Leadership

Through leadership, a manager secures the cooperation of members of his organization. The office manager, production foreman, laboratory supervisor, and company president each has a leadership role to perform. Through leadership, the manager accomplishes an objective by mobilization and utilization of people.

Not all that an executive does represents leadership. Personal inventiveness, for example, may constitute the great strength of a manager. But this ingenuity, as applied to product design, for example, is not leadership. In other words, some outstanding "leaders" are outstanding by virtue of their brilliance in such activities as product design or corporate planning and not as a result of leadership. Leadership activities are directed to getting effective work from team members. The unique ability of the leader is a social talent — that of getting the best effort of the organization's members.

Organizational performance is closely related to quality of leadership. Although competent leadership is not the only important ingredient for successful operation, it is an essential one. A bungling leader can wreck morale and destroy efficiency. Strong leadership, on the other hand, can transform a lackluster group into a strong, aggressive, successful organization.

The term *leadership* is sometimes used with the connotation of *positive* leadership — *leading* versus *commanding*. As used here, however, the term includes all aspects of leadership. Any approach, positive or negative, that elicits the efforts of one's subordinates, and even one's colleagues, represents an exercise of the leadership function. An industrial leader may get results by inspiring his followers to give their all for the company or by threatening to fire them. One appeal may be superior to the other, but the use of either constitutes leadership.

Patterns of Leadership

Leadership may be classified in various ways. One common distinction centers on the element of authority in the relationship between superior and subordinate. According to this classification, leaders may be *autocratic*, *democratic*, or *laissez-faire*.

Autocratic leadership emphasizes commanding and order giving. Such a leader makes most important decisions, entrusting relatively little authority to subordinates. In terms of status, he stands out clearly as the boss, and there is little difficulty in identifying him as such. Subordinates may "quake in their boots" in response to his summons. His supervision utilizes negative sanctions and develops a sense of fear in subordinates.

The industrialist of the past may be cited as an extreme example even though the authoritarian leader is not extinct in the present generation. The colorful John H. Patterson, founder of the National Cash Register Company, was an autocratic leader who coupled a flair for the dramatic with his use of authority.[1] In a somewhat

[1]The incident from Patterson's career is taken from the following account prepared by Stanley C. Allyn, a subsequent NCR board chairman: Stanley C. Allyn, "Fiery Furnace Claims Erring Department," *NCR Factory News*, November 1961, pp. 4-6.

bizarre episode, he once abolished a cost accounting system that he considered inefficient. The erring department produced reams of statistics, but the data were too late to be of value. After fretting over the matter for some time, Patterson reached the boiling point one day, jumped up from his desk, and headed for the cost accounting department. He gave the accountants little time for reflection, walking from desk to desk and asking each employee to pick up his accounting books and to follow him. The procession, carrying armloads of accounting records, headed straight for the power house, where they met the engineer in charge.

> "Will these furnaces burn anything except coal?" he asked.
> "Well, sir," said the engineer, "we've never tried anything else."
> Mr. Patterson then threw one of the accounting books into the fire.
> "That burns," he said.
> And with that he ordered the others to do the same with their books. In a little while all of the books had gone up in smoke while the clerks stood speechless. Finally, Mr. Patterson pulled out his watch and said:
> "Gentlemen, it has taken us just ten minutes to get rid of the Cost Department."

Of course, Mr. Patterson did not mean to operate without some cost data. But, as is evident from this account, he devoted little time to sampling employee thinking about changing the existing cost accounting system.

In contrast to an autocratic leader, the democratic leader shows greater deference for his subordinates. Rather than constantly telling them, he is frequently asking them. Their ideas and suggestions are valued, and consultation with them may be used to secure their contributions. Some democratic leaders treat administrative problems as problems of the group and view a solution by the group as the desirable way to solve these problems. Such an approach is often characterized by the use of meetings and committees.

In democratic leadership, the leader plays an active role in stimulating group thinking and developing a solution or reaching a decision. The laissez-faire or free-rein leader, on the other hand, goes a step farther and turns an entire problem or project over to subordinates. Subordinates may be asked to set their own objectives and to develop plans for achieving them. In one sense, this approach is characterized by the absence of any active leadership by the formally designated leader. The formal leader may come close to complete abdication of his leadership responsibilities. Although laissez-faire leadership may be effective in occasional situations in which the group is capable of a constructive response, chaos may also result from this type of leadership.

Other Classifications of Leadership

The leadership categories cited above are only one of various schemes of classification that may be used. One provocative analysis of leadership, for example, suggests a broad range of possible leadership behavior.[2] Rather than forcing all leadership into two or three sharply defined classes, this study suggests that the variety in leadership approaches may be viewed as a continuum. As shown in Figure 23, leadership behavior may involve any of various combinations of authority of the manager and freedom for subordinates. It should be observed that neither extreme constitutes an absolute. The leader always has a minimum of authority, and subordinates never surrender all discretion.

Another pattern of leadership classification has been used extensively in the research studies of the Institute for Social Research of the University of Michigan. This pattern distinguishes between *job-centered* supervision and *employee-centered* supervision.[3] The former type of supervision devotes primary attention to the work to be performed, whereas the latter places the primary emphasis upon development of effective work groups. The same research often distinguishes between managers who supervise closely versus those who supervise generally.

Elements of Effective Leadership

Leadership in a Systems Context

Managers function as parts of complex organizational systems. This interdependence of the manager and the system is not always clearly understood, however. It is often assumed, for example, that a supervisor may change his style of leadership without regard for other parts of the organization. According to the systems concept,

---

[2]Robert Tannenbaum and Warren H. Schmidt, "How to Choose a Leadership Pattern," *Harvard Business Review,* Vol. 36, No. 2, March-April 1958, pp. 95-101.

[3]See Rensis Likert, *New Patterns of Management* (New York: McGraw-Hill Book Company, 1961), Chapter 2.

Figure 23. *Continuum of Leadership Behavior*

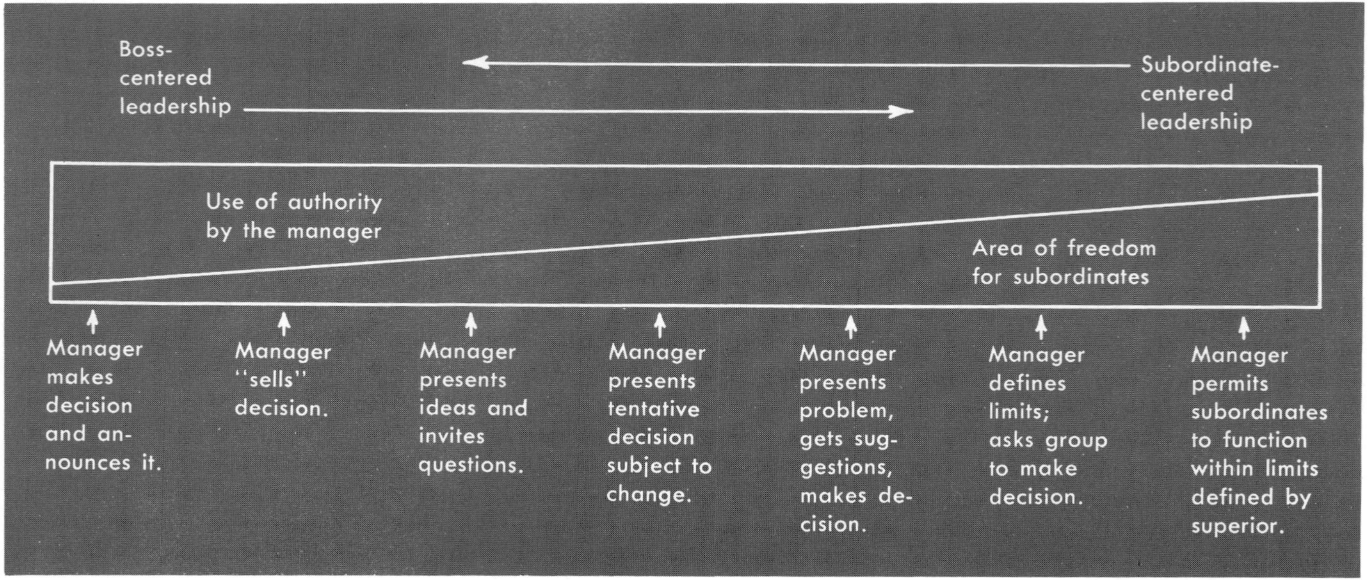
Boss-centered leadership
Subordinate-centered leadership
Use of authority by the manager
Area of freedom for subordinates
Manager makes decision and announces it.
Manager "sells" decision.
Manager presents ideas and invites questions.
Manager presents tentative decision subject to change.
Manager presents problem, gets suggestions, makes decision.
Manager defines limits; asks group to make decision.
Manager permits subordinates to function within limits defined by superior.

Source: Robert Tannenbaum and Warren H. Schmidt, "How to Choose a Leadership Pattern," *Harvard Business Review,* Vol. 36, No. 2, March-April 1958, p. 96.

however, the manager constitutes a part of the decision-making subsystem of the organizational system. As such, he is related in his decision making and other managerial activities to other levels of management, and he functions in relationship to them.

This viewpoint suggests that a supervisor's leadership style is affected by the treatment that he in turn receives from his own boss. The fact of such systems' constraints upon leadership style has been established by a number of research studies. One investigation, reported by Fleishman, evaluated a leadership training course for foremen in the International Harvester Company.[4] Leadership attitudes of foremen were found to vary with the type of manager under whom the foremen served. Foremen who worked under considerate supervisors tended to express more considerate attitudes toward their own subordinates. The training course improved leadership attitudes during the training session but failed to produce permanent changes in either the attitudes or behavior of the foremen when they returned to their regular jobs. Apparently the training was inadequate to counteract the influences coming from higher organization levels.

> An implication of these results seems to be that if the old way of doing things in the plant situation is still the shortest path to approval by the boss, then this is what the foreman really learns. Existing behavior patterns are part of, and are moulded by, the culture of the work situation.[5]

This study indicates that the organizational climate, particularly the type of leadership exercised from above, is an important variable affecting leadership style and behavior of any particular supervisor.

A subsequent investigation confirming the relationship between supervisory styles and influences from higher organizational levels has been reported by Bowers.[6] Rewards in the form of promotions and expressions of approval by higher-level managers were found to affect leadership style. Commendation of a foreman who pressures and drives his subordinates encourages the foreman to adopt the "approved" style of supervision. In other words, the foreman performs in accordance with his perception of the superior's expectation

---

[4]Edwin A. Fleishman, "Leadership Climate, Human Relations Training, and Supervisory Behavior," *Personnel Psychology,* Vol. 6, No. 2, Summer 1953, pp. 205-222.

[5]*Ibid.*, p. 215.

[6]David G. Bowers, "Self-Esteem and the Diffusion of Leadership Style," *Journal of Applied Psychology*, Vol. 47, No. 2, April 1963, pp. 135-140.

concerning him and his leadership style. His place in the hierarchical system, therefore, partially determines the way he acts as a leader.

The chain of command in which a manager functions prescribes only a part of the system constraints affecting leadership behavior. The "leadership situation" described in the following section provides a broader view of the total system in which he functions.

The Leadership Situation

An analysis of the manager's role in the context of the organizational system reveals the *situational* nature of leadership. In other words, different kinds of organizational circumstances call for different kinds of leadership. Any of a variety of supervisory styles may be effective under appropriate conditions. Leadership is always exercised in a specific situation involving real people and a given physical environment. There is some specific leader, and he has individual followers. The most appropriate type of leadership and the traits of the successful leader are dependent, to some extent, upon the particular situation.

As one factor in the leadership situation, consider the type of subordinates. If the work is of a professional nature, the organization's members may be college trained and possibly hold graduate degrees. This could be true, for example, in a research laboratory. Another organization's personnel, in contrast, may lack even a high school education. In a building maintenance department, for example, such a situation would not be unusual. The extreme contrast between the two groups presents the respective leaders with quite different challenges.

Various other factors also distinguish the leadership situation. The traditions of a given organization may be such as to discourage certain types of leadership. Autocratic management may be traditional and have general acceptance by the membership. The stable or dynamic nature of an organization, the possibility of emergency situations, the capability of the leader himself, and numerous other factors could also be cited.

One research study which verified the situational nature of leadership examined leadership differences at various hierarchical levels of a hospital.[7] Variations in the supervisor's "skill mix"—that is, the combination of technical skill, human relations skill, and admin-

[7]From *Leadership and Productivity* by Robert Dubin, *et al.*, published by Chandler Publishing Company, San Francisco. Copyright © 1965 by Chandler Publishing Company. Reprinted by permission.

istrative skill—were analyzed. At lower levels, technical and human relations skills were most highly related to subordinates' satisfaction with the supervisor. At higher organizational levels, however, the supervisor's administrative skills were more closely related to satisfaction of subordinates, with human relations skills only a poor second.

Over the last half century, the typical leadership situation in American industry has changed. As one factor in the change, the average educational level of the labor force has risen from an elementary school level, or lower, to an average level involving some college work. In the past, autocratic management was characteristic. It may be that changes in the situation have prompted the movement toward democratic leadership.

Selecting a Leadership Pattern

A manager is faced with the practical problem of selecting a leadership pattern to use in dealing with his particular subordinates. In doing so, he is limited by the situational factors noted above. But he usually has some freedom of choice in leadership style, particularly in the long run. In making his choice, he attempts to utilize the kind of leadership that will best achieve organizational goals, create good morale, and stimulate individual development.

In recent years, studies of supervision have reported a generally greater effectiveness of leadership emphasizing a somewhat democratic approach. More effective supervisors have been found to be those with a strong personal interest in the people working for them. It is desirable to examine some of these studies in greater detail.

Beginning in 1947, the Institute for Social Research of the University of Michigan began a large-scale program of research into organization structure and methods of leadership and management.[8] In general, this research sought to discover the significant differences in management of the best units as contrasted with the poorest units of organizations. The research is particularly notable for its broad scope, including coverage of many different industries and various skill and professional levels.

A typical study of this series, portrayed in Figure 24, shows that six of seven high-producing sections in one organization were directed by employee-centered supervisors.

In contrast, ten low-producing sections were supervised by seven job-centered supervisors and only three employee-centered super-

[8]See Likert, *op. cit.*

Figure 24. *Productivity of "Employee-Centered" and "Job-Centered" Supervisors*

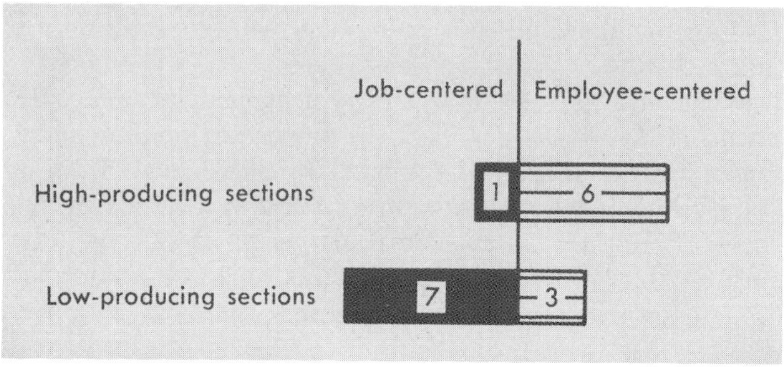

Source: Rensis Likert, *New Patterns of Management* (New York: McGraw-Hill Book Company, 1961), p. 7.

visors. This pattern of results was found in different kinds of work such as clerical, sales, and manufacturing. The different viewpoints of the two types of supervisors are reflected by the following quotations:

Job-Centered Assistant Manager of Low-Production Department:

> This interest-in-people approach is all right, but it's a luxury. I've got to keep pressure on for production, and when I get production up, then I can afford to take time to show an interest in my employees and their problems.[9]

Employee-Centered Manager of High-Producing Division:

> One way in which we accomplish a high level of production is by letting people do the job the way they want to so long as they accomplish the objectives. I believe in letting them take time out from the monotony. Make them feel that they are something special, not just the run of the mill. As a matter of fact, I tell them if you feel that job is getting you down get away from it for a few minutes.[10]

The studies also analyzed the results of general supervision versus close supervision. It was discovered that general supervision was

[9] *Ibid.*, p. 7.
[10] *Ibid.*

correlated with a higher level of productivity. Figure 25 presents the results of a study of differences in productivity between those supervisors who worked under close direction by their own superiors and other supervisors who worked under general supervision.

Figure 25. *Productivity and Closeness of Supervision*

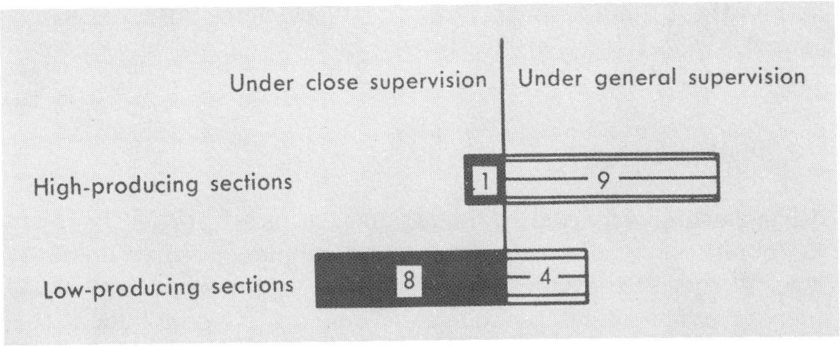

Source: Rensis Likert, *New Patterns of Management* (New York: McGraw-Hill Book Company, 1961), p. 9.

It appears, on the basis of these studies, that the more successful managers typically allow greater freedom to their subordinates. As examples of this freedom, subordinates are often permitted to determine their own work pace and to make certain choices concerning work methods.

The superiority of employee-centered, general supervision seems to be demonstrated by these studies. It should be noted, however, that there is no proof that an autocratic manager may not be highly effective in a particular situation. An understanding of the situational nature of leadership would caution against sweeping generalizations about the effectiveness of leadership styles. One writer has pointed out the following three factors that influence the productivity effects of employee-centered supervision:[11]

1. *Extent to which the job requires teamwork.* When employees are highly interdependent and their work must mesh smoothly, employee-centered supervision seems to pay off.

[11]Saul W. Gellerman, *The Management of Human Relations* (New York: Holt, Rinehart & Winston, Inc., 1966), pp. 34-38.

2. *Consistency of supervisor's behavior.* Supervisors who try to follow an employee-centered style but who lapse into their "natural" styles confuse and worry subordinates.
3. *Personality of the workers.* Employees with *independent* personalities who feel able to decide things for themselves respond to employee-centered supervision more than do those with *dependent* personalities.

Despite these qualifications, however, the evidence furnishes strong general support for the effectiveness of a democratically-oriented style of supervision.

The Managerial Grid

The research reported by Likert and discussed previously treats the qualities of job-centeredness and employee-centeredness as opposite ends of the same scale. It is possible, however, to visualize them as independent variables. The *managerial grid* adopts this approach as indicated in Figure 26.[12] The horizontal axis of the grid indicates concern for production, and the vertical axis indicates concern for people. It is evident that a leader's attitudes may involve any of many possible combinations of these attitudes. The idea, of course, is to move toward the 9,9 position on the managerial grid.

Fleishman has commented upon research involving two qualities of supervision labeled "consideration" and "initiating structure."[13] "Consideration" includes behavior indicating mutual trust and respect between the supervisor and the group. "Initiating structure" includes behavior in which the supervisor organizes and defines the role of each member, plans ahead, and pushes for production. These concepts are closely related to the job-centeredness and employee-centeredness factors portrayed on the grid. He comments as follows:

> Our evidence to date on these patterns suggests that supervisors who emphasize one pattern at the expense of the other are apt to be less effective, but that some balance between them is needed to satisfy organizational as well as individual needs. Supervisors who are low in both patterns are not even seen as

[12]For an extensive treatment of the managerial grid concept, see Robert R. Blake and Jane S. Mouton, *The Managerial Grid* (Houston: Gulf Publishing Co., Book Div., 1964).

[13]Edwin A. Fleishman, *Studies in Personnel and Industrial Psychology* (Homewood, Ill.: The Dorsey Press, 1961), pp. 311-314. Used with permission.

"leaders" by their groups — they are frequently bypassed by their own work groups.[14]

It appears, then, that the two dimensions are not necessarily correlated in either a positive or negative manner. A supervisor might be considerate and lack an orientation toward efficient organization of the work. On the other hand, the supervisor might combine a concern for people and concern for production.

Figure 26. *The Managerial Grid*

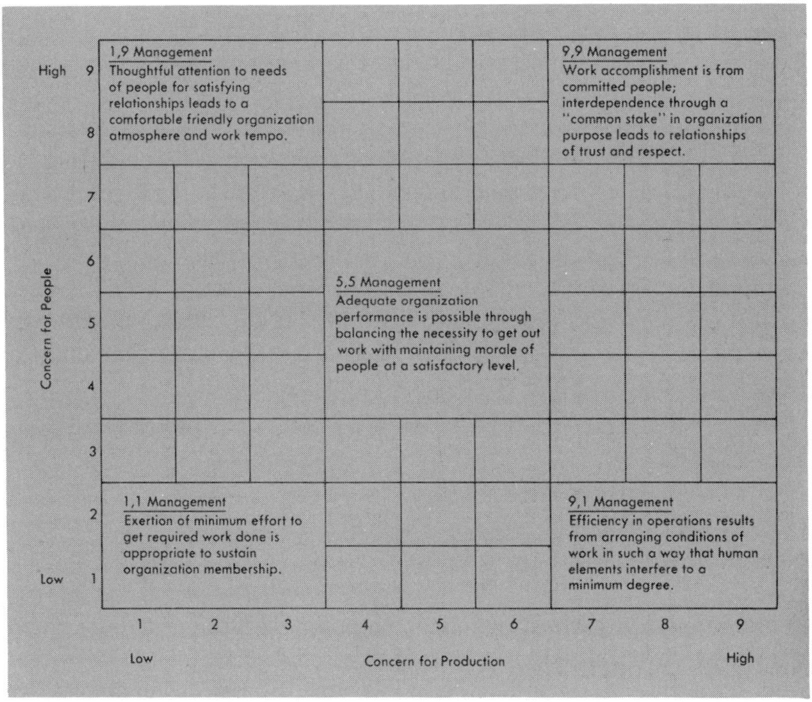

Source: Robert R. Blake and Jane S. Mouton, *The Managerial Grid* (Houston: Gulf Publishing Co., Book Div., 1964), p. 10.

How Democratic Can Management Be?

Some authority is essential in organizational life. Indeed, this is one element distinguishing organized from unorganized activity. As leadership moves toward democratic methods, the formal authority

[14] *Ibid.*, p. 313.

of managers is limited. An inherent conflict exists, at the extremes, between organizational authority and democratic decision making. Some modification of the traditional organization structure and concepts of authority is necessary to allow extensive democracy in administration.[15]

Highly democratic procedures are not yet widely accepted in industry. Steps are being made in that direction, but "bottom-up" or highly participative management is still the exception to the rule. In questioning the popular acceptance (in theory at least) of the democratic approach, one critic contended that it is currently practiced in only a small minority of companies.[16] A research study of executive attitudes recently detected serious doubts about the capacity for initiative and leadership ability of subordinates.[17] This was true, paradoxically, even though the executives felt that subordinates should be informed and brought into decision making.

As a matter of fact, much so-called democratic management is democratic in a relative sense. It is less autocratic than other types of leadership. Complete authority, without provision for review or ultimate approval or control by the superior, cannot be delegated to subordinates. Otherwise, the organization has ceased to perform its expected role. Even those leaders who are classed as democratic maintain a measure of formal control.

Motivation of Personnel

Need for Motivation

Members of organizations must be persuaded to contribute their efforts toward the achievement of organizational goals. Often the work that they perform has little inherent interest or challenge. In fact, much work is either unpleasant or monotonous. In spite of unpleasant features, however, work must be accomplished, and this necessitates motivation of the worker.

Furthermore, motivation entails more than stimulation of minimum work performance. An employee's duties may be performed

---

[15]See Chris Argyris, "Organizational Leadership and Participative Management," *The Journal of Business,* Vol. 28, No. 1, January 1955, pp. 1-7.

[16]Robert N. McMurry, "The Case for Benevolent Autocracy," *Harvard Business Review,* Vol. 36, No. 1, January-February 1958, p. 82.

[17]"How Bosses Really Feel," *Business Week,* No. 1748, March 2, 1963, p. 58.

poorly or well. Efficient performance is necessary for economic operation on a competitive basis. The goal of motivation, thus, is superb performance by all members of the organization.

The task of motivation is to supply a personal incentive for the individual member of the organization. This requires an integration of objectives, merging the individual's goals with those of the organization. The individual should consider it to his personal advantage to perform his assigned responsibilities in the best possible manner.

Approaching motivation in this way may appear to complicate unduly an essentially simple proposition. For many years, motivation was viewed as simply a matter of offering a financial reward for work performance. Modern management has gradually come to realize, however, that motivation is considerably more complex. We have discovered that people work for many different reasons and that the same employee may recognize a variety of goals.

To motivate personnel, a manager has a number of tools available to him. Several of these motivational approaches will be considered in the following sections.

Authority

As noted in Chapter 18, the manager's authority is one factor in motivation of subordinates. The boss may be followed simply because he is the boss. Some degree of authority as a motivational device exists in almost any administrative situation. An emphasis on the use of authority, however, carries with it the threat of penalty — "Do your work or you'll be fired."

It seems clear that authority provides strong motivation in certain cases. If one has a great respect for higher authority, he may respond almost automatically to the orders of a superior. Furthermore, the threat of being fired may stimulate one to supreme effort if the job seems extremely important. If one's family is dependent upon the job and no other jobs are available, the danger of job loss is a serious matter. On the other hand, the effectiveness of authority as a motivating factor is diminished by the existence of a strong union or conditions of labor scarcity and numerous job opportunities.

In addition, there is a question as to the degree of effort that can be obtained by use of the authoritative approach. A minimum performance might be secured in this way. At the same time, any really outstanding performance may be lacking. In other words, the individual may perform sufficiently well to avoid dismissal but lack the incentive to do an outstanding job.

It seems clear that the effectiveness of the authoritative approach has decreased in much of American industry. With satisfaction of physiological needs, the satisfaction of other needs has become important in motivating behavior. The authoritative approach deals primarily with physiological needs by threatening to eliminate the employee's salary. For employees having other job opportunities, therefore, this approach has serious limitations. Many workers have also gained protection through unionization.

Authority involves the application of pressure. When the pressure becomes too strong, employees may react against it and fight back. Such reactions, furthermore, may occur in ways that are difficult to detect or combat. It may be possible, in other words, for subordinates to get away with behavior that is undesirable from management's point of view. It is also possible that too much pressure may produce undesirable nervous or psychological effects. Psychosomatic illness, for example, may result.

> Once we observed a group of working supervisors who had been strongly pressured to increase production under difficult circumstances with no backing from management. There were nine men regularly assigned to the day shift. One had a nervous breakdown, another had a fatal heart attack that was generally attributed to overwork and fatigue. Of the remaining seven, five had serious illnesses and in most cases no organic cause could be determined. All this happened during a period of twelve months. Meanwhile, the men on the night shift, where pressure was much less, had an almost perfect health record.[18]

The long-run effects of strongly authoritarian leadership, then, may be destructive. Even though the immediate response is satisfactory, the stresses may lead to deterioration of the organization.

Financial Incentives

In one sense, the use of authority entails an application of the financial incentive. Loss of a job means loss of income associated with that job. But money may also be used as a positive motivator. Financial rewards may be stressed and employees may be offered higher pay if they increase output or perform well.

---

[18]George Strauss and Leonard R. Sayles, *Personnel: The Human Problems of Management,* Second Edition (Englewood Cliffs: Prentice-Hall, Inc., © 1967), p. 131.

The numerous financial incentive plans prevalent in industry constitute an application of this idea. Frederick W. Taylor and the other pioneers in the scientific management movement popularized a variety of individual piecework incentive plans. In recent years, there has been considerable interest in group incentive plans, one of the best known being the Scanlon Plan.[19] Profit sharing has also been introduced by many employers, one of its well-known applications being in the Lincoln Electric Company of Cleveland, Ohio.[20] In recent years, profit sharing has even been introduced as a collective bargaining issue and incorporated in at least one major contract.

At the executive level, a variety of stock option and bonus plans are in use, many of them offering substantial financial rewards. In some cases, managers earn bonuses much larger than their base salaries. During recent years, General Motors Corporation's bonus payments to salaried personnel have averaged well over $100 million annually. Payments of this magnitude indicate the importance attached to financial incentives by business corporations.

No doubt most employees find some motivation in financial rewards. The important question concerns the effectiveness or extent of such appeals. In devising their incentive plans, the scientific managers assumed a worker who acted rationally to maximize his economic gains. Such an extreme concept of the *economic man* has, of course, been discredited. Even though the theory has been generally rejected, however, management often acts as if it were still true.

> The engineer begins by rejecting economic man but ends by embracing him. He recognizes that money is not all-important and points to certain other factors that may operate on the worker. But then he immediately dismisses these other factors by assuming that they either cancel each other out or cannot be measured anyway.[21]

The hierarchy of needs (discussed in Chapter 20) includes some which cannot be entirely satisfied by money. Financial rewards are closely related to lower level needs — those of a physiological and security nature. To some extent, of course, money also facilitates satisfaction of higher level needs. The pay check, for example, may

---

[19]For a discussion of the Scanlon plan, see William Foote Whyte, *et al.*, *Money and Motivation* (New York: Harper & Row, Publishers, 1955) Chapter 14.

[20]See James F. Lincoln, *Lincoln's Incentive System* (New York: McGraw-Hill Book Company, 1946).

[21]Whyte, *et al.*, *op. cit.*, p. 6.

be a symbol of status as well as a means for obtaining goods and services. However, social and self-fulfillment needs can, at best, be only partially satisfied with monetary rewards. (The ability of financial rewards to satisfy employee needs is discussed further in Chapter 23.)

Studies of the effectiveness of financial incentives have revealed many shortcomings. Although occasional examples of outstanding results have been discovered, they are by no means universal. In fact, the more customary experience seems to involve unsatisfactory, or only partially satisfactory, results. Unofficial work quotas are often recognized by employees, with no production above a "normal day's work." The following explanation by an employee of a production plant reveals a typical pattern of quota restriction:

> From my first day to my last day at the plant I was subject to warnings and predictions concerning price cuts. Pressure was the heaviest from Joe Mucha, day man on my machine, who shared my job repertoire and kept a close eye on my production. On November 14, the day after my first attained quota, Joe Mucha advised:
>
> > "Don't let it go over $1.25 an hour, or the time-study man will be right down here! And don't waste time, either! They watch the records like a hawk! I got ahead, so I took it easy for a couple of hours."
>
> Joe told me that I had made $10.01 yesterday and warned me not to go over $1.25 an hour. He told me to figure the setups and the time on each operation very carefully so that I would not total over $10.25 in any one day.[22]

Establishment of piece rates frequently becomes a matter of matching wits between employees and the management's industrial engineers. Conflict and hostility often seem characteristic of such systems.

Such experience with incentive plans and the improved understanding of the social structure of industry have served to reveal the limitations of financial motivation. Money is one, but only one, of the factors of importance to the worker. The major error in utilizing such an approach is the attachment of undue importance to it. It is wrong to see financial incentives as the only goal of the employee. In many cases, it may not even be the primary motivating factor.

---

[22] *Ibid.*, p. 23.

Competition

Closely related to the use of financial incentives is motivation by competition. Advancement to higher positions and higher pay scales is based upon individual performance. By using a *merit* principle, the employee is stimulated to excel in order to earn a promotion. He must show himself to be superior to his associates.

Various difficulties are involved in motivation through competition. In some areas, particularly in unionized plants, seniority has largely replaced merit as the basis for advancement. The most effective use of competition also requires accurate measurement of performance — a process that is notoriously difficult. Furthermore, excessive competition can be disruptive to the group, particularly in situations in which teamwork is required.

Paternalism

Another approach to motivation is that of paternalism. The paternalistic attitude is expressed by being "good" to employees and providing benefits for them. In return for such gifts, the employee is expected to respond with loyalty and enthusiastic performance. In the early 1900's, many concerns followed this philosophy of paternalism in employee relations. Among the paternalists were such outstanding industrialists as William Hershey and Henry Ford I. Paternalism may characterize an entire company, but it may also be used by individual managers.

The paternalist expects a favorable response from employees and experiences bitter disappointment if they appear ungrateful. Unfortunately, the paternalistic approach does not consistently produce the expected results. Indeed, some paternalism seems to operate in reverse, creating resentment rather than loyalty. Violent strikes have occurred in the plants of employers who prided themselves in their good treatment of employees.

There are a number of weaknesses in the paternalistic approach. First of all, the philosophy assumes that the employer is superior to the employee and that he knows what is best for the employee. This attitude of superiority is offensive to most employees and runs counter to their desire for independence.

Also, benefits lose some of their appeal over a period of time. The Christmas bonus, for example, comes to be expected after it is repeated for a few years.

Implicit Bargaining

One form of motivation that may be practiced by a supervisor has been described as *implicit bargaining*.[23] It differs from explicit bargaining in which management formally bargains with a union. In implicit bargaining, an informal understanding develops between the manager and his subordinates. It is not explicitly stated but simply arises on the basis of behavioral patterns worked out or tolerated by the superior and his subordinates.

Implicit bargaining involves a live-and-let-live attitude. The supervisor permits certain conduct or a certain standard of performance on the part of his employees. In return, the employees perform in a manner reasonably acceptable to the supervisor. For example, the superior may be rather liberal in interpreting plant rules — accepting employee excuses for tardiness or absences or looking the other way when minor offenses occur. Employees, in turn, support the supervisor with at least average production, rather than giving him a bad time or constantly raising grievances.

The nature of the bargain from the worker's point of view is indicated by the following comments of an employee:

> Our policy is to live and let live. We give the foreman reasonable production. He protects us from the time-study man who tries to jack up the output rate and looks the other way if we take a smoke. We look out for each other.[24]

One of the weaknesses of such a motivational approach is its failure to stimulate more than a minimum or average performance.

Need Satisfaction Through Work

The motivational approaches mentioned above have in common a view of work as unpleasant and unrewarding in itself. The employee must be paid in some way for the unpleasantness involved. A different view of work is involved in an approach that attempts to satisfy the worker's needs through his job.[25] Rather than considering work as drudgery, it views work as potentially satisfying and rewarding.

---

[23]For an excellent discussion of implicit bargaining, see Strauss and Sayles, *op. cit.*, pp. 137-139.

[24]*Ibid.*, p. 138.

[25]This motivational approach is carefully analyzed in Strauss and Sayles, *op. cit.*, pp. 142-143.

In this approach to motivation, consideration is given to all the employee's needs. This includes not only his need for money but also his social and egoistic needs. An attempt is made to create an atmosphere in which satisfaction of all such needs is achieved. The nature of industrial technology admittedly makes this difficult or even impossible in some types of work.

In providing satisfaction of egoistic needs, an emphasis is placed upon the significance of the job. Even if a job requires little skill, it may be an important part of an overall operation. In addition, some jobs may be improved through job enlargement or other changes that make them more interesting. The style of leadership is also important in this connection. Social satisfactions are realized more easily in situations involving democratic supervision. Friendships and teamwork may occur more readily in such an atmosphere.

Undoubtedly, this motivational approach calls for understanding and skill on the part of the manager using it. It cannot be applied so easily as some of the other approaches. It has the potential advantage, however, of stimulating better-than-average performance. It also has the potential advantage of contributing to the happiness and satisfaction of employees apart from any contribution to organizational efficiency.

Participative Management

Nature and Benefits of Participation

One method of democratic leadership that has received much attention in recent years is known as *employee participation.* In general, a program of participation attempts to involve subordinates — sometimes managerial subordinates and sometimes the rank and file — more directly in the operation of the business. Subordinates are allowed and encouraged to participate in some aspects of their superior's decision making — an activity that would not be expected, or even tolerated, in many organizations. As one illustration of a participative approach, a unit supervisor may ask subordinates for suggestions or ideas in tackling some problem confronting the unit.[26]

[26] In contrast to delegation of decision-making authority to a subordinate, the concept of participation is primarily concerned with a sharing of the decision-making process between a superior and his subordinate or subordinates.

Much work, even in some supervisory positions, seems monotonous and uninspiring. An opportunity for participation provides a contrast to such unchallenging assignments and is welcomed by many employees. From a psychological point of view, there is a vast difference between *activity* and *participation.* Participation may add meaning to work and permit the employee to become *identified* with it. In contrast to a system in which all important thinking is limited to the superior, participative management places the subordinate on an entirely different footing. Soliciting the subordinate's assistance assumes he has something valuable to offer and that his opinions have significance. This adds dignity to the job and to the incumbent.

An employee's egoistic need, it may be recalled, may be satisfied by a sense of accomplishment. The possible contribution of participation to one's sense of accomplishment is substantial. Employing the individual's mind as well as his hands in the life and operation of the organization makes him a more vital part of it. His contribution assumes greater significance, and he realizes that he is more than a human machine.

Benefits of participation are not limited to the employees. In tapping the thinking of employees, management gets the benefit of their contributions as well as their enthusiastic work. Increased output and product quality improvement have been experienced in some uses of participative management. Also, in introducing changes, participation can help to minimize employee resistance. In fact, some changes occur in direct response to employee participation.

From the standpoint of both morale and organizational efficiency, therefore, participative management has much to recommend it. Subject to the limitations noted later, a manager can increase his effectiveness by the use of a participative approach.

> Perhaps the most persistent and thoroughly demonstrated difference between successful and unsuccessful leadership at all three levels has to do with the distribution or sharing of the leadership function. . . . By and large, those organizations in which influential acts are widely shared are most effective. The reasons for this are in part motivational, having to do with implementation of decisions, and in part nonmotivational, having to do with the excellence of decisions.[27]

It is possible, of course, that a participative approach may be adopted insincerely. A manager may know what he intends to do but

---

[27]Daniel Katz and Robert L. Kahn, *The Social Psychology of Organizations* (New York: John Wiley & Sons, Inc., 1966), pp. 331-332.

ask his employees so they will think it is their idea. Such an attempt is doomed to failure. The employee does not need a Ph.D. to detect insincerity.

Types and Degrees of Participation

Participative management may take many different forms. In some organizations, a gesture is made in this direction through use of a suggestion system. Employees are rewarded financially for submitting usable suggestions. Success of these systems has been spotty. Some systems have garnered valuable ideas from a large number of employees, whereas others have been disappointing in their results. Competent administration of the suggestion system is essential. At best, a suggestion system alone gets the participation of only a minority of the employees. Also, the participation is usually limited to an occasional, specific suggestion.

Multiple management, as treated in Chapter 11, constitutes another form of participation. Members of junior boards participate in problem solving that goes far beyond the normal scope of their customary assignments. A variation of this system takes the form of production committees, composed of employee and management representatives, which devote study to improvement of production efficiency.

Perhaps the more usual form of participation is the type of supervision that might be labeled as *consultative management*. The manager simply uses participation in the day-to-day administration of his organization. Rather than deciding matters unilaterally and passing the decisions on to subordinates, he brings subordinates into the supervisory process. He seeks their thinking and comments on various matters confronting the group.

Managers differ greatly in the degree to which they use participation. The amount of participation is normally greater at upper levels of the organization. At any level, a relatively autocratic manager may check an occasional issue with his subordinates. A distinction may also be made between issues directly affecting the employees—such as scheduling vacation periods—and general problems of management. Managers who make the most extensive use of participation consult with employees frequently on all types of issues.

Managers also differ in the degree to which subordinates are permitted to influence the decision. It is customary to bring subordinates into the discussion of alternatives but to reserve the final choice for the superior. It is not unknown, however, for certain problems or questions to be turned over to subordinates for decision under the general surveillance of the appropriate manager.

Prerequisites for Participation

It seems likely that participation may function more successfully in some settings than in others. The type of subordinates, for example, is one significant variable. Participation assumes the subordinate *can* contribute something worthwhile. This depends, however, upon his ability and background. If the subordinate lacks the proper educational background or if the problem at hand is beyond him, little can be achieved through participation. Participation in such circumstances may represent a complete waste of time. This does not mean, of course, that participation of those with limited ability on some types of issues is never desirable.

Effective participation also requires a set of necessary psychological conditions.[28] The subordinate must be capable of becoming psychologically involved, possess some minimum amount of intelligence, and be in touch with reality. He must favor participation and not feel that the boss always knows best. He must also see the relevance of the problem to his own life and be able to express himself satisfactorily.

The atmosphere of the organization must also be conducive to participation. If a highly autocratic management prevails throughout an organization, a particular manager may have difficulty in adopting a participative approach. The subordinate, accustomed to taking orders, may interpret consultation as a sign of weakness. Over a period of time, of course, the atmosphere may be changed, but a prevailing negative attitude would limit its use at least initially. Strongly centralized organizations also tend to discourage participation.

The existence of a labor union may affect the nature and extent of possible participation. If the union feels that management's attempts to stimulate employee participation threaten the workers' loyalty to the union, opposition can be expected. Responsible, mature thinking on the part of both management and the union is required for effective participation in such situations.

There are still other prerequisites for effective participation, such as the availability of time. Emergency conditions may not permit

[28]These conditions are discussed in Robert Tannenbaum, Irving R. Weschler, and Fred Massarik, *Leadership and Organization: A Behavioral Science Approach* (New York: McGraw-Hill Book Company, 1961), pp. 94-98.

consultation. The financial cost of participation may also exceed its potential values. The various prerequisites serve as limitations, then, in managerial use of the participative approach.

Summary

Through the function of leadership, a manager secures the effort and teamwork of members of an organization. Different types of leadership are noted—particularly the extent to which leadership is *autocratic* or *democratic*. Democratic leadership tends to be *employee-centered* and typically permits greater freedom to subordinates.

Selection of a leadership pattern is somewhat dependent upon the *leadership situation*. In fact, leadership behavior can be properly understood only by observing the systems nature of managerial positions and particularly the relationship of a manager to those above him in the hierarchy.

On the basis of extensive studies of supervision, it appears that employee-centered, general supervision typically produces superior results. Even so, highly democratic leadership appears to be more the exception than the rule.

In securing the cooperation of members of an organization, the leader may employ any of a number of *motivational techniques*. *Authority*, for example, is used to some extent in almost every organization. Although its primary emphasis is negative in nature, it can be effective, particularly in certain situations, in securing at least adequate performance. The use of *financial incentives* is another important motivating influence but one that has often been overemphasized. A *paternalistic approach* expects employee cooperation and effective work performance in response to the good deeds of the employer. In using *implicit bargaining*, the supervisor is motivating through a live-and-let-live approach. Another quite different approach to motivation is one that attempts to provide need satisfaction through the work itself.

Democratic leadership is often expressed through *participative management*. In this approach, management attempts to secure the thinking and suggestions of subordinates in the decision-making process. It is a type of management that can enhance the position of the subordinate and add dignity to his position. Although participation may occur in many different forms, one of the most common varieties is the informal consultation by a supervisor with his subordinates. The prerequisites for effective participation include the necessary minimum ability and psychological conditions on the part of the participants, a permissive atmosphere, adequate available time, reasonable cost requirements, and satisfactory union relationships.

Discussion Questions

1. With what type of subordinates would each of the three patterns of leadership — *autocratic*, *democratic*, and *laissez-faire* — be most effective?

2. Evaluate the leadership approach of John H. Patterson as described in this chapter. Do you think it may have been effective then? Would it be effective now?

3. Distinguish between a *job-centered* supervisor and an *employee-centered* supervisor. On the basis of your own experience, describe the leadership approach of one manager (or teacher) in each category.

4. What is the significance of the *leadership situation* in choosing a pattern of leadership?

5. The study cited in Figure 24 provides evidence of the superiority of employee-centered supervision. What might explain the fact that three employee-centered supervisors had low-producing sections and that one job-centered supervisor had a high-producing section?

6. What are some of the difficulties involved in using a wage incentive plan as a tool for *motivation*?

7. Explain the concept of *paternalism*.

8. *Implicit bargaining* was suggested as one form of motivation. Can you give an example of implicit bargaining from your own experience or observation?

9. How can a manager allow *participation* by subordinates and still retain his position of leadership?

Supplementary Reading

Applewhite, Philip B., *Organizational Behavior,* Chapters 6 and 7. Englewood Cliffs: Prentice-Hall, Inc., 1965.

Blake, Robert R. and Jane S. Mouton, *The Managerial Grid.* Houston: Gulf Publishing Co., Book Div., 1964.

Bowles, Warren, "The Management of Motivation: A Company-Wide Program," *Personnel,* Vol. 43, No. 4, July-August 1966, pp. 16-26.

Davis, Keith, "Evolving Models of Organizational Behavior," *Academy of Management Journal,* Vol. 11, No. 1, March 1968, pp. 27-38.

Dubin, Robert, *et al., Leadership and Productivity: Some Facts of Industrial Life.* San Francisco: Chandler Publishing Co., 1965.

Gellerman, Saul W., *The Management of Human Relations,* Chapter 3. New York: Holt, Rinehart & Winston, Inc., 1966.

Hunt, J. G., "Breakthrough in Leadership Research," *Personnel Administration,* Vol. 30, No. 5, September-October 1967, pp. 38-44.

Kaczka, Eugene E. and Roy V. Kirk, "Managerial Climate, Work Groups, and Organizational Performance," *Administrative Science Quarterly,* Vol. 12, No. 2, September 1967, pp. 253-272.

Katz, Daniel and Robert L. Kahn, *The Social Psychology of Organizations,* Chapter 11. New York: John Wiley & Sons, Inc., 1966.

Likert, Rensis, *The Human Organization: Its Management and Value.* New York: McGraw-Hill Book Company, 1967.

McClelland, David C., "Achievement Motivation Can Be Developed," *Harvard Business Review,* Vol. 43, No. 6, November-December 1965, pp. 6-24 ff.

Myers, M. Scott, "Conditions for Manager Motivation," *Harvard Business Review,* Vol. 44, No. 1, January-February 1966, pp. 58-71.

Newport, M. Gene, "Participative Management: Some Cautions," *Personnel Journal,* Vol. 45, No. 9, October 1966, pp. 532-536.

Ready, R. K., "Leadership in the 1960's," *California Management Review,* Vol. 6, No. 3, Spring 1964, pp. 37-46.

Rodney, Thomas C., "Can Money Motivate Better Job Performance?" *Personnel Administration,* Vol. 30, No. 2, March-April 1967, pp. 23-29.

Sales, Stephen M., "Supervisory Style and Productivity: Review and Theory," *Personnel Psychology,* Vol. 19, No. 3, Autumn 1966, pp. 275-286.

Tannenbaum, Arnold S., *Social Psychology of the Work Organization,* Chapters 6 and 7. Belmont: Wadsworth Publishing Co., Inc., 1966.

Walton, Richard E., "Contrasting Designs for Participative Systems," *Personnel Administration,* Vol. 30, No. 6, November-December 1967, pp. 35-41.

22

The Process of Communication

Effectiveness of leadership is partially determined by the adequacy and clarity of communication. In fact, the manager exercises his leadership through communication with members of the organization. Many of the human relations problems experienced by management — though not all of them by any means — are basically communication problems.

Nature of Communication

Communication and the Management Process

Any type of organized activity demands communication. There is no other way to direct the work of the individual members and work groups of the firm. In laying out work assignments, changing the direction of work or projects that are under way, instructing subordinates, and coordinating the different activities of the organization, the manager must communicate in some way. Subordinates are also communicating with their superiors as they bring questions and reports on work progress to their attention.

The manager's world, therefore, is a *world of words*. Much, perhaps most, of his time is spent in communicating with those about him. According to Chester I. Barnard, the first executive function is to develop and maintain a system of communication.[1] With reference to such communication systems, the positions of managers may be described as *communication centers*, receiving information from various sources and passing it on to other points. The manager is not entirely passive in communication, however, because he also performs his decision-making role through use of the communication system.

It should be evident, on the basis of these comments, that communication in the business organization may be upward, downward, or horizontal in nature. The need for downward communication — giving orders, instructions, and so on — is easily recognized. Downward communication is often incomplete, however. Although instructions and directions are given, there is often failure to communicate the rationale or "why." In addition, downward communication that informs the subordinate of management's appraisal of his performance is often neglected or handled poorly.

Upward communication is even more troublesome and often greatly neglected. The results of such defective upward communication may be far-reaching and damaging in their consequences. In writing about the professed ignorance of top officials of General Electric and Westinghouse concerning unlawful pricing practices in their organizations, Peter F. Drucker offered the following perceptive comments regarding upward communication:

> . . . people familiar with large organizations—executives, administrators, consultants—have known all along that keeping top management informed is the most elusive administrative problem of the big organization (and not of the business enterprise alone). To be usable at the top, information has to be so formalized and abstracted as to lose substantive meaning.[2]

In particular, it appears that reports, surveys, audits, and other formalized techniques designed to inform top management are inadequate. Top management, according to Drucker, needs to get the "feel" as well as the "facts."[3]

Horizontal communication is particularly important among positions or components involving extensive coordination or teamwork.

---

[1]Used with permission of the publishers from Chester I. Barnard *The Functions of the Executive,* Cambridge, Mass.: Harvard University Press, Copyright, 1938, by the President and Fellows of Harvard College, 1966, by Grace F. Noera Barnard, p. 226.

[2]Peter F. Drucker, "Big Business and the National Purpose," *Harvard Business Review,* Vol. 40, No. 2, March-April 1962, p. 55.

[3]*Ibid.,* p. 56.

In some administrative situations, the volume of necessary horizontal communication is as great as the volume of vertical communication. As an example of such a position, consider a production department which depends upon another department for incoming work, which supplies the input of a third department, and which receives special services from a myriad of staff and service organizations.

One barrier to horizontal communication is the threat it poses to the power of an authoritarian manager. As subordinates develop a communication network among themselves and increase their knowledge of the overall operation, the likelihood of authoritarian leadership declines.

Definition of Communication

The general nature of communication requires little explanation. It is obvious that the manager's contacts with subordinates involve communication. To understand better the strengths and weaknesses of communication in the administrative process, however, it may be helpful to note certain underlying concepts.

First of all, communication implies both *transmission* and *reception* of a message. The communication process is not complete unless reception occurs. A sportsman alone in a forest, for example, may speak or shout, but he cannot communicate. All of this seems clear enough. In the administrative situation, however, there is danger in assuming that reception occurs whenever there are listeners. In reality, this does not always happen. Management may issue an announcement, but employees may fail to "hear" it. This may be true even though the announcement is placed on all bulletin boards or broadcast over a public address system. The message may not be received even though it may be physically read or heard. In such a case, no communication has occurred.

It is also important to note *what* is transmitted through communication. Factual information, of course, is exchanged. The manager explains the nature of an assignment to his subordinate, and the subordinate reports work progress to the superior. But communication involves more than the intellect. Feelings and attitudes are also expressed in the process of communication. An employee may come to know quite well how his supervisor feels about him and his work—"To him I'm just a machine." Or, "He really appreciates a good effort on our part." Opinions, predictions, suggestions, ideas—all of these are involved in communication. To understand communication, therefore, we must see that it includes a great deal more than mere facts.

Communication and the Systems Viewpoint

The business organization has been pictured as a system of interrelated parts functioning together to accomplish certain objectives. Such organizations are not only energic systems in which physical materials are changed by the application of human and other energy but also informational systems. In fact, communication provides the means for directing and blending all system and subsystem activities. The critical role of communication is evidenced by the fact that information flow becomes more and more significant as one moves from the area of physical processing to areas emphasizing managerial decision making.

The process of communication may be visualized as the functioning of an organizational subsystem. The formal communications system or network is a decision-making system in that it brings problems and related information to managers who must make decisions in solving those problems. The communication system also takes overall system plans and objectives, as formulated by top management, and carries them downward through the various echelons to the operative level. It is also expected to carry information upward and to provide for a horizontal exchange of information to facilitate operations. In fact, the organization structure constitutes an elaborate system for gathering, evaluating, and disseminating information.

The total communications system is not limited to the formal network, however. The informal organization, or grapevine, is a part of the system even though it is less susceptible to control. Design of the formal organization structure provides a set of officially established and approved communication channels. The mere fact of creating an organization structure and thereby designating these channels sharply reduces the large number of potential channels that could exist otherwise. However, an officially designated communication network is always supplemented to some degree by informal channels.

There are many imperfections in the typical communications system. Various barriers block or distort the flow of information, as will be noted in a later section of this chapter. The systems viewpoint stresses the critical role of communication in the functioning of the total system and the importance of a free flow of information throughout the firm.

Methods of Communication

We all know that language—written and spoken—provides tools for communication. What we sometimes overlook is that language may be supplemented by other less obvious forms of communication. Consider the physical expression of a speaker, for example. What can the listener detect from this? If a supervisor scowls, the subordinate discovers his unhappiness or displeasure. This may lead to various conclusions about the real meaning of the scowl, such as "He's hot under the collar and will forget all about this when he cools off." Or, "He's unhappy about my performance, and my future is clouded." Or, "He really means business, and I'd better get to work immediately." If the supervisor wears a smile, the same message may carry quite a different meaning. Almost instinctively, a subordinate picks up and interprets such signals. By looking at the boss, he knows whether the time is ripe to ask for a raise or to request a day off.

Not only physical expressions and gestures but also voice inflections may tell the listener more than the words themselves reveal. The tone of voice can transform words of praise into sarcasm. No wonder mistakes occur in oral communication.

Even silence, the absence of language, can communicate! Occasionally, someone communicates contempt for another by refusing to speak to him. In management, the same effect may be achieved by silence. If an employee performs exceptionally well or completes a project in an outstanding manner, he might logically expect some word of commendation. Silence, however, communicates indifference or disrespect, whether intended or not.

Perhaps the most forceful method of communication is not language at all. There is an old saying to the effect that "Actions speak louder than words." We observe an individual's behavior and infer something about the person himself. If he is constantly late in meeting appointments, for example, we may conclude that he has little regard for punctuality or little respect for the other party. If he is not well-groomed, we may decide that personal appearance does not seem important to him.

In the administrative situation, subordinates watch the behavior of higher management. If management promotes on the basis of favoritism or family connection, for example, what do subordinates assume? If a supervisor reflects indifference about his own responsibilities, what is the effect on subordinates? From the standpoint of employees, such actions provide the most eloquent expression of management policy and values.

If there is a discrepancy between management's words and actions, a conflict in communication results. The listener is asked to believe a written or oral communication in the face of behavior that suggests it is not so. Almost without exception, the observer takes the actual behavior as representing the truth and assumes that contrary talk is so much "hogwash." A single act may cancel the effects of considerable talking. Managers need to be unusually careful, therefore, in insuring that their actions communicate the same message as their words.

Distortion in Communication

Perfect communication would accurately transmit an idea from one mind to another. Unfortunately, transmission is often imperfect. Something goes wrong in the process of verbalizing an idea and then extracting the idea again from the words. The communicator's idea is not perfectly reproduced in the mind of the receiver. A semblance of the message may be transmitted, but distortion may also be present.

Some distortion occurs almost automatically as communications are passed through channels. Errors creep into the original message as it is passed on. At each point in the communication chain, certain details may be unintentionally omitted or changed. The net effect may be substantial change in communications that are repeated a number of times.

Another reason for distortion in communication is based upon semantics. The same words do not always carry the same meaning for both parties. A supervisor, for example, may intend to commend a subordinate by commenting upon his "satisfactory" performance. The subordinate may take offense at such commendation, however, because he knows he is "superior" and not *merely* "satisfactory"!

Some fields of business develop a language of their own that serves to confuse others. To an outsider, the specialist may as well be speaking in a foreign language. Consider the term *market value* and what it means.

> Although there may be only one definition of market value, there are many different understandings of what market value is. Market value is only one of the many species of value. Many

people use the term market value when they really mean another type of value.[4]

A new employee may need some time to pick up and understand the jargon of the workplace. Consider the dilemma of a recently employed production assembler who might receive the following type of instruction from her supervisor:

> Alice, I would like you to take the sixth yellow chair on this assembly line, which is in front of bonding machine #14. On the left side of your machine you will find a wiring diagram indicating where you should bond your units. On the right-hand side of your machine you will find a carrying tray full of 14-lead packages. Pick up the headers, one at a time, using your 3-C tweezers and place them on the hot substrate below the capillary head. Grasp the cam actuator on the right-hand side of the machine and lower the hot capillary over the first bonding pad indicated by the diagram. Ball bond to the pad and, by moving the hot substrate, loop the wire to the pin indicated by the diagram. Stitch bond to this lead, raise the capillary, and check for pigtails. When you have completed all leads, put the unit back in the carrying tray.
>
> Your training operator will be around to help you with other details. Do you have any questions?[5]

When words that carry special meanings or varying connotations are used, it is not surprising that distortion occurs. The language vehicle for carrying meaning is faulty.

Another factor interfering with clear communication is the listener's inclination to hear what he expects to hear. He may have a preconceived idea of what the other person is trying to say. If so, it is difficult for him to hear anything that differs from his preconception. As noted in Chapter 20, the listener's perceptual world may differ from the real world. Regardless of the accuracy of his perceptual world, however, it does affect the interpretation placed upon communications. Suppose the boss commends a subordinate who is convinced the boss has it in for him. The subordinate may think, "He must be trying to pull a fast one."

Emotions also color one's understanding and interpretation of a communication. If an employee is angry, his reaction to a commu-

---

[4]Walstein Smith, Jr., "Is There More Than One Market Value?" *Baylor Business Studies,* Vol. 65, No. 12, September 1962, p. 7.

[5]Earl R. Gomersall and M. Scott Myers, "Breakthrough in On-the-Job Training," *Harvard Business Review,* Vol. 44, No. 4, July-August 1966, p. 66.

cation is different from his reaction when he is happy. A communication may appear threatening or disturbing to a listener who is himself disturbed or insecure. In recognition of this fact, an effective supervisor may emphasize an employee's strong points before attempting to correct a weakness.

The Listening Side of Communication

As noted above, communication involves both transmission and reception. Much of the study of communication has stressed the transmitter and has tended to ignore the receiver. As we have discovered, however, the listener is not completely passive. A good listener hears more than a poor listener. We say that a person is "all ears" to emphasize his attentive listening.

By aggressive listening, then, management may act to improve communication. Such listening requires effort to understand precisely what the other person is saying and removes certain of the barriers that block or distort communication. The sensitive listener, for example, carefully weighs a speaker's words to make sure of their meaning. He also looks for any hidden meaning behind the words themselves. He asks himself: "What does he mean by that statement about his rate of pay? Is it really the pay that is bothering him? Or is he merely using the paycheck as a talking point?" The unusually sensitive listener is quick to detect statements or indications that would be completely missed by a less alert listener.

Feedback in Communication

Feedback is necessary to determine the extent to which a message has been understood, believed, and accepted. In face-to-face conversation, this often occurs through facial expression. A puzzled look on the face of the receiver indicates that the message has not been transmitted as intended. His remarks may also reveal that he understands or does not understand. Compliance with communicated instructions also shows that communication has occurred.

Feedback does not always occur automatically, however. Silence guarantees neither consent nor comprehension. In the absence of feedback, an executive may become isolated from the lower levels of his own organization, not knowing whether his messages are getting through or whether they are properly understood. The sender must therefore arrange for, or be alert to, feedback to determine the effectiveness of either written or oral communication.

In face-to-face verbal communication, one can check the accuracy of communication by asking questions. He may ask the other party, "Would you tell me a little more about that?" or "Do you mean that— ?" or "Is it your feeling that— ?" Responses to probing questions of this type may reveal the listener's initial impression to be completely inaccurate.

Organizational Role and Communication

The Significance of Role in Communication

The roles of organization members affect and even distort communication within the organizational system because each individual tends to interpret information in the context of his own position. The role furnishes the frame of reference, therefore, in classifying and understanding messages received from outside. A production manager and laboratory researcher see things differently, hear things differently, and generally live in two different worlds.

There is a tendency, furthermore, to protect one's organization or way of looking at his environment. When information is received that tends to conflict with an existing point of view, the individual must resolve the difference in some way. In reference to a person strongly committed to an opinion who listens to a communication attacking that opinion, Festinger and Maccoby comment as follows:

> Certainly, such a listener is not passive. He does not sit there listening and absorbing what is said without any counteraction on his part. Indeed, it is most likely that under such circumstances, while he is listening to the persuasive communication, he is very actively, inside his own mind, counterarguing, derogating the points the communicator makes, and derogating the communicator himself. In other words, we can imagine that there is really an argument going on, one side being vocal and the other subvocal.[6]

Studies show that individuals deliberately seek out information to reinforce shaken convictions or to consolidate those recently acquired.[7]

---

[6]Leon Festinger and Nathan Maccoby, "On Resistance to Persuasive Communications," *Journal of Abnormal and Social Psychology,* Vol. 68, No. 4, April 1964, p. 360.

[7]Raymond A. Bauer, "The Obstinate Audience: The Influence Process from the Point of View of Social Communication," *American Psychologist,* Vol. 19, No. 5, May 1964, p. 323.

Functional areas such as production, sales, and finance constitute organizational subsystems with their particular perceptions or viewpoints of organizational reality. This presents a difficulty in communicating across subsystem boundaries. Rather than functioning as cooperative allies, such functional groups tend to act as competitors. As a result, communication among them is poor. Moreover, their communications to higher levels carry the "slant" that reflects the special interest or viewpoints of the functional specialty.

In a middle-management training seminar, twenty-three managers were asked to identify the major problem of the unnamed company described in a long case history.[8] The managers' backgrounds evidently influenced their judgment. Eighty-three per cent of sales managers considered the *sales* problem to be most important. However, eighty per cent of production managers specified the *organization* problem as the most important. (The parts of the case pertaining to manufacturing featured an organization problem.) It is evident that these managers responded to the same communication on the basis of their past experience, task orientation, and organizational frame of reference.

Communications between management and labor are susceptible to this same weakness. Each group tends to receive communications with the coloring of its own viewpoint.

> Far more often than not, the relationship between management and employees is a competitive one. Each side tends to speak of the other as "they," and of themselves as "we." The very form in which the communications problem is commonly stated — *we* need to get *their* commitment — implies this relationship.
>
> The research results described above suggest that to the extent that a competitive relationship exists between management and employees, an attempt by one group to influence the other will tend to increase each side's commitment to its *own* group and intensify its rejection of the other.[9]

Of all the conflicting roles that interfere with the process of communication, few are more troublesome than those of superior and subordinate. Let us now turn our attention to some of the specific features of this relationship and its effect upon communication.

---

[8] DeWitt C. Dearborn and Herbert A. Simon, "Selective Perception: A Note on the Departmental Identifications of Executives," *Sociometry,* Vol. 21, No. 2, June 1958, pp. 140-144.

[9] Paul C. Buchanan, "How Can We Gain Their Commitment?" *Personnel,* Vol. 42, No. 1, January-February 1965, pp. 24-25.

The Sensitive Superior-Subordinate Relationship

The difference in organizational levels makes communication between Supervisor *A* and Subordinate *X* distinctly different from communication between Supervisor *A* and Supervisor *B* or between Subordinate *X* and Subordinate *Y*. The subordinate occupies a position of dependency with respect to his superior, making the relationship much more than a casual one. To a great extent, the subordinate's future depends upon his superior's judgment. If the subordinate is to advance, earn pay increases, or receive choice work assignments, the decision must be that of the superior. If the superior loses confidence in him, the subordinate may be denied the benefits he seeks or even lose his job.

In view of the critical importance of the superior's opinion, it is small wonder that *upward communication* is affected. It is only natural for the subordinate to wish to control all factors serving to influence supervisory judgment. In communication, therefore, the subordinate desires to transmit a message and *also* to influence his superior favorably. He would ideally wish for every message to convey not only the appropriate information but also a favorable impression about himself.

It takes little imagination to see that the subordinate's personal desires may introduce distortion into the communication. Achieving the goal of favorably influencing the supervisor may require some alteration of the communication itself. In its extreme form, this could involve misrepresentation of facts that would be damaging to the subordinate. But, perhaps more likely, this simply involves a subtle, perhaps almost unconscious, adaptation of the subordinate's communication.

It is impossible for most subordinates to report all facts to their respective superiors. Time pressures require the subordinate to be selective in the matters that he brings to the attention of higher management. In the pattern of material that is selected, it is easy for bias to appear. It is human nature to tell someone what he wants to hear. Even in the discussion of facts, a speaker may emphasize either the positive or negative aspects of those facts. Because most superiors react more favorably to favorable reports, the subordinate tends to brighten information as it is transmitted upward. If the communication goes upward through several levels, it may become increasingly rosy and at the same time farther and farther from reality.

Downward communication may also be distorted as a result of this same sensitive, supervisory relationship. In this case, it is the concern and eagerness of the subordinate that gets him into trouble. As an eager student of the boss, he tries to read between the lines and tends to react too strongly to communications from the superior. The subordinate may attach unusual importance to purely casual comments of the superior.

Other Difficulties in Superior-Subordinate Communication

Not all difficulties in superior-subordinate communication can be attributed to the hierarchical relationship. The rush of work, so characteristic of many management positions, also makes communication difficult. In some organizations, it takes considerable effort even to see the boss. Other activities and other individuals are constantly competing for his time. Contacts that are not urgent must frequently be postponed. In discussions that do occur, the relaxed, leisurely atmosphere that is necessary for certain types of communication is missing. It is impossible for a subordinate to convey his personal feelings or even his job ideas very adequately to a busy supervisor who has a telephone in one hand and a stack of red-bordered "rush" orders in the other.

The subordinate may also lack an ability to express himself adequately. The position of supervisor normally requires a great deal more talking than that of the subordinate. Consequently, the superior acquires experience in speaking and may be able to express himself quite readily. Unless the subordinate's work involves considerable communication, however, an ability for self-expression may never develop. Then, too, the superior usually knows more than the subordinate about various aspects of the work. For this reason, the subordinate may sense a risk of embarrassment in speaking up to a better-informed superior.

Furthermore, as human beings, many superiors simply enjoy speaking more than listening. By having control of the conversation, it is easy to do that which is most fun — the talking. Listening, as noted earlier, calls for greater effort and self-discipline.

Extent of Distortion in Superior-Subordinate Communication

Having noted the tendency toward error in superior-subordinate communication, let us examine the extent of any such distortion.

Is there a serious or substantial alteration of the facts? One might suppose that failures in communication are relatively harmless, with the superior generally well-informed and the subordinate quite understanding of his superior's thinking.

One research study analyzed the extent to which superiors and subordinates agreed concerning pertinent job factors.[10] It was reasoned that adequate communication should result in a mutual understanding concerning these matters. Figure 27 shows the extent of agreement between fifty-eight superior-subordinate pairs.[11]

Figure 27. *Comparative Agreement on Job Factors Between 58 Superior-Subordinate Pairs*

	0 Almost No Agreement on Topics	*1 Agreement on Less Than Half the Topics*	*2 Agreement on About Half the Topics*	*3 Agreement on More Than Half the Topics*	*4 Agreement on All Or Almost All Topics*
Job duties	3.4%	11.6%	39.1%	37.8%	8.1%
Job requirements (subordinate's qualifications)	7.0	29.3	40.9	20.5	2.3
Future changes in subordinate's job	35.4	14.3	18.3	16.3	15.7
Obstacles in the way of subordinate's performance	38.4	29.8	23.6	6.4	1.7

Source: Norman R. F. Maier, L. Richard Hoffman, John J. Hooven, and William H. Read, *Superior-Subordinate Communication in Management,* AMA Research Study 52 (New York: American Management Association, 1961), p. 10.

---

[10]Norman R. F. Maier, L. Richard Hoffman, John J. Hooven, and William H. Read, *Superior-Subordinate Communication in Management,* AMA Research Study 52 (New York: American Management Association, 1961).

[11]Patterned depth interviews were used to secure information from respondents in order to avoid the limitations of a structured questionnaire. Fifty-eight men holding high middle-management positions in five companies and representing all major functions of the organization were selected for this study. Each superior, in turn, selected a subordinate with whom he had frequent contact and with whom he had worked long enough to know him fairly well.

It can be seen that agreement is far from perfect. Even in job duties, 15 per cent of the pairs agreed on less than half the topics. In the case of obstacles in the way of subordinate performance, lack of agreement is striking, with 38.4 per cent showing almost no agreement and 68.2 per cent showing agreement on fewer than half of the points.

The general impression conveyed by the study is that of inadequacy in superior-subordinate communication. The following statement from the research report draws attention to this weakness:

> Thus, the findings in general provide empirical evidence that substantial communication problems exist at high management levels in organizations — problems which one can expect to be reflected in poorer organizational efficiency and distortion of organizational goals at lower levels in the hierarchy.[12]

Overcoming Barriers to Superior-Subordinate Communication

To some extent, of course, weaknesses in superior-subordinate communication are little different from those in any other type of communication. Semantics, for example, may constitute a problem here as well as elsewhere. Accordingly, elimination of communication problems includes all steps designed to foster improvement in general communication. Our concern at this point, however, is with those steps that are particularly significant in the context of the superior-subordinate relationship.

As noted in the discussion of status in Chapter 17, an emphasis upon status distinctions widens the gulf between hierarchical levels. In contrast, a de-emphasis of status should facilitate the flow of communication. Creating a private office and establishing a battery of secretaries through which visitors must proceed, for example, makes communication difficult, to say the least. Part of the difficulty is based upon the physical separation. In addition, such features emphasize the distinction between levels and thus decrease ease of communication by increasing social distance. Achievement of a freer flow of communication depends upon minimizing both physical and status barriers.

In the Baltimore headquarters building of the Aerospace Division of Martin Marietta Corporation, an unorthodox physical layout was adopted for the purpose of facilitating communication.[13] In a new

---

[12] Maier, *et al., op. cit.*, p. 30.

[13] "Doing Your Managing in the Open," *Business Week*, No. 1690, January 20, 1962, pp. 72-74.

building, a general office area replaced the private office arrangement characteristically used for top executives. The president of this 40,000-employee organization occupied a desk in the corner of the second floor — a desk just like every other desk. From this position, the president could see the seven vice presidents, their secretaries, and other office personnel down to the lowliest file clerk. To communicate with subordinates, the president needed only to stand up and beckon to them. To communicate with him, the subordinates could merely glance at his desk to see if he was busy and then drop over to speak with him at a convenient time. The concept of an executive office without private offices reflected President William B. Bergen's deep concern over communication problems within management. The following comments illustrate the freedom with which members of the executive group can communicate:

> "Then the other day," says Bergen, "a jurisdictional union dispute broke out at our Titan II missile site at Mountain Home, Idaho, causing a two-hour work stoppage. Our vice-president for industrial relations got a call on it, walked over to my desk, and told me the story. Under our old setup, he would have had to telephone to me. I probably would have been busy, so he would have settled it without my knowledge or would have delayed a decision until he could see me."[14]

In adapting to the new office arrangement, some personnel were less than enthusiastic at the beginning. They had questions as to how the "bullpen" arrangement would affect their prestige. The president felt, however, that most of the doubters had come to accept the logic of the new arrangement.

> "What we are doing here at Martin," he says, "is so interesting that it transcends the need for nourishment by artificial flattery. Everyone who works here at headquarters has an important position, and he doesn't need artificial status symbols."[15]

An atmosphere of informality has been created in the office area. Executives can walk from desk to desk and engage in impromptu shirt-sleeve conferences. Only occasionally do they need to move into private consulting rooms that are provided for necessary private talks. According to one executive, "This informality stimulates all of us to contribute to solution of management problems."

---

[14]*Ibid.*, p. 74.

[15]*Ibid.*, p. 73.

Regardless of the physical barriers—and removal of office walls is no universal solution—much can be done by creating an atmosphere of tolerance. If a superior wants to improve the upward flow of communication, he must be conscious of the restraints that he places upon his subordinates. While a superior cannot tolerate *extreme* disrespect, it is natural for him to react with antagonism or hurt feelings if *any* criticism is implied by his subordinates. If the superior can tolerate a moderate amount of criticism, however, he can develop the necessary condition for encouraging subordinates to speak up. If the superior's behavior is such as to appear threatening, the subordinate can hardly be blamed for his silence. Only by assuring subordinates, by action as well as by words, of his willingness and ability to accept their critical expressions without retaliation can the superior foster a strong upward flow of information. Asking for their comments and opinions, where pertinent, is one of the simplest and most effective approaches in stimulating upward communication of this type.

Informal Channels of Communications

Nature of the Grapevine

The *grapevine* refers to the network of informal relationships used in transmitting information through unofficial channels. Although formal channels presumably carry all official communications, much of what any organization member knows is gathered through other channels. He may hear it from an employee at the next desk, from a member of his car pool, or even from his wife who in turn picked it up from the wife of another employee! In his daily work associations, lunch contacts, coffee breaks, and social activities, he is constantly trading ideas and information about the organization.

Reflection upon the nature of the grapevine shows that it involves a normal, rather than an abnormal, set of relationships. Informal communication occurs naturally wherever individuals are thrown together in work or social contacts. If an employee had no interest in discussing work matters with fellow employees, he would appear peculiar. If he showed no inclination toward social contacts, we might consider the employee maladjusted.

Occasionally, one gets the impression that only false rumors are circulated by the grapevine. It is true that rumors occur and that wild ones may be rapidly transmitted through informal channels.

But other, more substantial information is also conveyed in this fashion. As a matter of fact, the grapevine usually carries some mixture of truth and error. A few details are often distorted in an otherwise correct account. In one study of thirty rumors occurring in six different companies, sixteen of the rumors proved to be groundless.[16] Nine turned out to be accurate, however, and five were partly accurate. These rumors were concerned with such subjects as transfers, procedural changes, promotions, company relocation, and company reorganization. Almost one-half of these rumors, therefore, gave an accurate or partially accurate prediction of things to come. Emphasis upon the errors circulated through the grapevine may have obscured the extensive amount of substantially accurate information that is transmitted in this way. Some organizations could hardly function at all without the grapevine because of the paucity of their formal communications.

The grapevine is often visualized as a long chain, with *A* telling *B* who in turn passes it on so that it eventually reaches *Z*. Such a pattern of transmission would clearly maximize the chances for error. Studies of the grapevine, however, have provided evidence that conflicts somewhat with this concept. The general pattern, as discovered by one researcher, is that of a *cluster chain.*[17] One link in the communication network informs a number of people instead of just one individual. One or two of each cluster of receivers, in turn, pass the communication on to another group.

In view of the verbal nature of most grapevine contacts, personal association forms the basis for the exchange of information. The individual who has extensive contacts with others is, as a result, often a key link in the chain. The secretary to the boss or the payroll clerk, for example, may fulfill such a role.

The speed of the grapevine is too well-known to require extensive comment. Formal communication has difficulty maintaining a similar pace. The problem of keeping secrets from the grapevine is likewise known by experienced managers. Despite precautions, stories have a tendency to leak out at some point and to become general grapevine information.

Dealing with Errors in the Grapevine

Truth is the best antidote for error. If the facts are not available, the imagination is capable of devising "facts." Some plausible

---

[16]Robert Hershey, "The Grapevine — Here to Stay But Not Beyond Control," *Personnel,* Vol. 43, No. 1, January-February 1966, pp. 62-66.

[17]Keith Davis, *Human Relations at Work,* Third Edition (New York: McGraw-Hill Book Company, 1967), p. 225.

explanation or interpretation occurs to an individual, and he passes it on to another. As the idea is passed on, it becomes regarded as fact rather than a tentative interpretation. Providing complete information, where this is possible, is thus a first step in minimizing grapevine errors.

Once a rumor or error has started, some corrective action is called for. Once again, the error is best removed by a statement of the facts. If a manager discovers an unfounded rumor among his subordinates, for example, he may simply call them together and discuss the matter with them. Whether the facts will be accepted as such depends upon management's reputation for accuracy and candor in previous communication.

Some organizations have established special programs to detect rumors, asking employees to bring them to the attention of management. The rumor is then presented along with the facts concerning the matter. The employee newspaper and bulletin boards, among other media, have been used for this purpose.

Constructive Value of the Grapevine

Any attempt to develop a constructive attitude toward the grapevine requires recognition that the grapevine is not entirely bad. Although its errors and distortions may be lamented, its inevitable existence makes complete condemnation irrational. The grapevine exists whether we like it or not—an emotional blast against it accomplishes little, if anything.

It is well to note the constructive values inherent in informal communication. Unless managers wish to multiply their own communication efforts many times, they cannot channel all information through the official chain of command. Informal communications supplement and amplify those emanating from official sources. Much information about work assignments and company policy, for example, is picked up from fellow employees. Official announcements are likewise heard by some employees and passed on to others.

The grapevine transmits useful information and messages that cannot be easily transmitted through formal channels. Orders and proclamations of management may be explained by employees to each other in language that they can understand. Also, the grapevine supplies the manager with information about subordinates and their work experiences, thereby increasing the manager's understanding and enabling him to be more effective.

A constructive approach to dealing with the grapevine begins with the effort to furnish complete and accurate information. In addition, a manager may recognize the informal communication leaders. By keeping them well-informed, he can come closer to assuring the accuracy of information entering the grapevine. Also, to the extent that he can do so, listening to the grapevine will serve to keep him in closer touch with the thinking of subordinates.

Developing Effective Communication

Aggressively Sharing Information

In the typical situation, managers transmit to subordinates those messages that seem necessary in the regular course of business operations. If subordinates need directions or information, the necessary instructions are given. There is no particular attempt to hold back the facts. Rather, the attention is simply upon those communications that are essential to the operation.

As long as an organization is small and the operation simple, this approach may work reasonably well. Through personal observation, subordinates can supplement that which they learn through formal channels. As the organization grows, however, any individual employee becomes a smaller part of a larger organization. He does not automatically learn all the facts. In fact, the organization may become so compartmentalized that the individual has a very narrow view of the overall operation.

To develop understanding in the modern complex industrial organization, then, requires a vigorous approach to communication. The manager must realize that general understanding is not achieved naturally as a byproduct of regular operations. Only positive steps involving a special effort can provide the individual with a thorough understanding of his place in the corporation.

The task of providing employees with information may be approached in various ways, however. The basic attitude of the employer may itself shape the type of information that is transmitted. Alexander R. Heron suggests the following undesirable managerial viewpoints regarding information sharing:

> The "reluctant" willingness to share information with employees has a slight flavor of castor oil.
>
> The "paternalistic" willingness has some suggestion of the *noblesse oblige* of the old feudal aristocracy.
>
> The "propagandist" willingness has some elements of high-pressure salesmanship.[18]

---

[18] Alexander R. Heron, *Sharing Information With Employees* (Stanford, California: Stanford University Press, 1942), p. 33.

In contrast, Heron suggests that an *aggressive willingness* to share information has a deeper and more practical foundation. Sharing knowledge in this latter way, he believes, treats the employee with the respect he deserves.[19]

The techniques used in communication are probably less important than the principle of actively sharing information. An executive may deliver certain announcements to employees directly, the company newspaper may be used, or first-line supervisors may carry the message to their immediate subordinates. Probably some combination of these and other media is typically used. It is important, of course, to rely strongly upon the superior-subordinate link in communicating in order to strengthen the formal chain of command.

Occasionally, a company throws the mantle of secrecy around certain information. For some data, the "confidential" label is no doubt justified. It seems clear, however, that 90 per cent of the so-called confidential information in most organizations could, if released, harm nothing more than the managerial ego. Classification of such information as confidential merely constitutes an excuse based on an unwillingness to share information with members of the organization.

Need for Sincerity

A communications program is occasionally used as a type of propaganda effort. An attempt is made to sell or convince employees of some point of view. Of course, attempts at persuasion need not involve deceit. In fact, presentation of a company point of view may be justified. It is possible, however, for an organization or supervisor to slip into the habit of using information as a technique for manipulation. Rather than being forthright and open, information is tailored or withheld to produce the desired effect — "What he doesn't know won't hurt him."

Such an attitude toward communication is insulting to subordinates, and employees are quick to detect such insincerity. Attempts to manipulate subordinates, therefore, will typically be rejected and produce a negative reaction as well. The intelligence of employees should not be underestimated.

Candor and honesty are thus prime ingredients of any effective communications program. The supervisor must be genuinely convinced of the importance of saying only what he means. Although such an admonition appears to be an unnecessary platitude, it is justified by its frequent disregard.

---

[19] *Ibid.*, p. 35.

Controlling Information Overload

Communication systems often become defective by providing or permitting a greater volume of communication than the organization can handle — a condition that is termed *information overload.* A manager is not only informed, but he is deluged with a flood of information. It is clear that any communication network is capable of carrying only so much information. Any manager has only so much time available for reading letters, studying reports, talking on the telephone, and conferring with others. Beyond some point, an attempted increase in communication volume may contribute to inefficiency rather than performing its intended function. The practical experience of many managers indicates that this point is easily reached, and they feel the "burden" of communications. They have too many meetings, too much correspondence, and too little time. Weighing or counting incoming material may disclose existence of a flood of such information. They come to feel that much communication is simply a burden they must bear rather than an aid to administration. Moreover, errors may occur as a result of the excessive volume of communication.

Reduction or control of information overload may be attempted in several ways, some of which are functional and some of which are dysfunctional. *Reduction of information input* provides one possible approach. The sender or transmitter (typically a higher level of management) may eliminate some of the written materials being forwarded to others and minimize the number (and length) of conferences and other verbal contacts. This solution requires a distinction between necessary and unnecessary communication. The solution may appear obvious, but the fact remains that many unnecessary meetings are called and many useless reports are forwarded to others.

Selective receiving is another technique for dealing with overload. On the basis of some system of priorities, the receiver disregards or fails to process certain types of information. "Junk" mail, for example, is quickly consigned to the waste basket. If priorities are properly established, the method may be useful. *Queuing* involves the delaying of information processing during periods of peak activity in anticipation of lulls. Its effectiveness depends upon the cyclical nature of the activity and the degree of realism involved in postponement.

There are still other possibilities for combatting information overload. The most practical alternative in any given case depends upon the administrative situation and the type of communication network.

Other Essentials of Effective Communication

The attitude and interest of top management in communication, as in other matters, provides an example for the rest of the organization. It is possible that a chief executive may conceive of communication as a one-way process — largely order giving. To him, explanations, listening, and meetings may all sound like a waste of time. He may visualize himself as a man of action rather than a man of words. His example and point of view set the tone for communication by the next layer of management. In addition to setting a good example, a chief executive may also directly explain to subordinates the importance that he attaches to communication. In evaluation of managerial performance, for example, some weight may be given to the manager's effectiveness in communication.

Communication ability can also be improved through training, and the subject may properly be included as a part of training programs. Development of communication ability is, of course, more difficult than many types of training. To accomplish a great deal, a strong effort by the trainee toward self-development is essential. On-the-job experience is particularly important in developing managerial skill of this type.

Communication should be a regular, continuing part of management and not a special "one-shot" program. Occasionally, an executive becomes interested in communication as a result of a conference or other event that calls it to his attention. As a result, he proceeds to launch some sort of a communications program. It is important that this be more than a temporary effort. To achieve the desired relationships among members of the organization and to maximize efficiency, communication must constitute a continuing phase of each manager's activities.

Summary

Communication is an integral and necessary aspect of management. Through the process of communication, information, facts, feelings, and ideas are transmitted from one person to another. The communications network, including the formal organizational structure and also supplementary informal channels, may be visualized as an informational system used to direct and coordinate the activities of the various parts (subsystems) of the firm. Communication is accomplished not only through language, but also through physical expression and gestures, silence, and behavior. *Distortion* often occurs in communication as a result of emotions, differing points of view of the communicators, and semantics. The *listening* side of communication is an important part of the process. Through *feedback,* a communicator can determine the extent to which a message has been understood, believed, and accepted.

The role or position occupied by an individual affects the way he communicates, because each person speaks and understands in the context of his own private world. The roles of superior and subordinate are a special case of this phenomenon. A subordinate's dependency upon his superior makes the relationship between them unusually sensitive — a fact that tends to interfere with the process of communication. The subordinate is constantly concerned with the impression that he creates and tends to color information transmitted to his superior. Furthermore, the rush that characterizes the activities of many managers is not conducive to *upward communication.* A research study has shown that the net effect is a rather serious gap in communication between management levels. In overcoming barriers to communication, the superior can de-emphasize status distinctions, remove physical and time barriers, and strive to create an atmosphere which tolerates freedom of expression by subordinates.

The informal network of communication in an organization is known as its *grapevine.* The grapevine is a natural outgrowth of interpersonal contacts and circulates some combination of truth and error. In dealing with errors or unfounded rumors, management may be able to make corrections by supplying factual information. Although the grapevine may contain errors, it performs a useful function in transmitting information that cannot be easily conveyed in other ways.

An effective communication program demands an attempt to *share information aggressively.* Adequate communication does not develop naturally without some such effort. In view of the employee's ability to detect insincerity, *candor* and *honesty* are also prime features of any effective communication. Control of *information overload* is also essential if important messages are to be transmitted promptly and clearly.

Discussion Questions

1. In view of the close relationship between communication and the management process, what communication skills seem

necessary for managers? Is extensive training in writing and in public speaking desirable?

2. Communication includes more than the transmission of facts. What are the other aspects of communication? Of these, which is most difficult to transmit in writing?

3. Suppose a state governor or the President of the U.S. personally inspects a flood-stricken area. Explain the significance of such a visit from the standpoint of communication.

4. Explain the factors leading to *distortion* in communication.

5. How does one make himself a more effective listener?

6. Why is *upward communication* often less effective than *downward communication*? How can a manager improve upward communication from subordinates to himself?

7. What should a manager do about erroneous stories that are circulated on the *grapevine*?

8. What philosophy of management is implied by the phrase *aggressive sharing of information*?

Supplementary Reading

Ackoff, Russell L., "Management Misinformation Systems," *Management Science,* Vol. 14, No. 4, December 1967, pp. B-147 — B-156.

Albaum, Gerald, "Horizontal Information Flow: An Exploratory Study," *Academy of Management Journal,* Vol. 7, No. 1, March 1964, pp. 21-33.

Anderson, John, "What's Blocking Upward Communications?" *Personnel Administration,* Vol. 31, No. 1, January-February 1968, pp. 5-7, 19-20.

Applewhite, Philip B., *Organizational Behavior,* Chapter 5. Englewood Cliffs: Prentice-Hall, Inc., 1965.

Brown, Warren S., "Systems, Boundaries, and Information Flow," *Academy of Management Journal,* Vol. 9, No. 4, December 1966, pp. 318-327.

Buchanan, Paul C., "How Can We Gain Their Commitment?" *Personnel,* Vol. 42, No. 1, January-February 1965, pp. 21-26.

Davis, Keith, *Human Relations at Work,* Third Edition, Chapters 19 and 20. New York: McGraw-Hill Book Company, 1967.

Fenn, Margaret and George Head, "Upward Communication: The Subordinate's Viewpoint," *California Management Review,* Vol. 7, No. 4, Summer 1965, pp. 75-80.

Gellerman, Saul W., *The Management of Human Relations,* Chapter 5. New York: Holt, Rinehart & Winston, Inc., 1966.

Goetzinger, Charles and Milton Valentine, "Problems in Executive Interpersonal Communication," *Personnel Administration,* Vol. 27, No. 2, March-April 1964, pp. 24-29.

Haney, William V., "A Comparative Study of Unilateral and Bilateral Communication," *Academy of Management Journal,* Vol. 7, No. 2, June 1964, pp. 128-136.

Hershey, Robert, "The Grapevine — Here to Stay But Not Beyond Control," *Personnel,* Vol. 43, No. 1, January-February 1966, pp. 62-66.

Hicks, Herbert G., *The Management of Organizations,* Chapters 21-23. New York: McGraw-Hill Book Company, 1967.

Katz, Daniel and Robert L. Kahn, *The Social Psychology of Organizations,* Chapter 9. New York: John Wiley & Sons, Inc., 1966.

McMurry, Robert N., "Clear Communications for Chief Executives," *Harvard Business Review,* Vol. 43, No. 2, March-April 1965, pp. 131-147.

Melcher, Arlyn J. and Ronald Beller, "Toward a Theory of Organization Communication: Consideration in Channel Selection," *Academy of Management Journal,* Vol. 10, No. 1, March 1967, pp. 39-52.

Nathan, Ernest D., "The Art of Asking Questions," *Personnel,* Vol. 43, No. 4, July-August 1966, pp. 63-71.

Read, William H., "Upward Communication in Industrial Hierarchies," *Human Relations,* Vol. 15, No. 1, February 1962, pp. 3-15.

Sayles, Leonard R. and George Strauss, *Human Behavior in Organizations,* Chapter 10. Englewood Cliffs: Prentice-Hall, Inc., 1966.

Thurston, Philip H., "Who Should Control Information Systems?" *Harvard Business Review,* Vol. 40, No. 6, November-December 1962, pp. 135-139.

23

Employee Attitudes

Employee attitudes are of prime concern to any administrator, and his work is greatly simplified if subordinates have favorable attitudes. It is the purpose of this chapter to examine the nature of employee attitudes and their significance in the administrative process.

Nature of Employee Attitudes

The Concept of Morale

Morale is more easily illustrated than defined. A military commander, for example, can easily distinguish between units in which there is pride and *esprit de corps* and units in which the members are merely putting in their time. In athletics, a coach appreciates a team with the confidence that it can beat the No. 1 team in the conference. In the classroom, a teacher sometimes discovers a student or class that forgets about grades and eagerly responds to the challenge of learning and discovery. In the business world, the manager values employees who "can't wait to get to work."

Features that stand out in these examples, and in others that come to mind, include pride, confidence, eagerness, and enthusiasm. This is the stuff of which morale is made. These are qualities of the mind, and morale can be viewed, therefore, as a mental condition. In the employee's mind, there are feelings and attitudes with reference to many different kinds of subjects. In discussing morale in the business organization, we are concerned with employee attitudes toward the job situation. These include feelings about the employing concern, the supervisor, fellow employees, and other aspects of the job.

Formal definitions of morale conflict so greatly that one must be a courageous soul to venture into a discussion of this subject! There is some value, however, in examining two recent statements that have much in common.

One writer has defined morale as "*the extent to which an individual's needs are satisfied and the extent to which the individual perceives that satisfaction as stemming from his total job situation.*"[1] Another suggests it is "an index of the extent to which the individual perceives a probability of satisfying his own motives through cooperation with the group."[2] Both of these are concerned with individual satisfaction as it is related to the group or organization. The individual or group having high morale would undoubtedly possess many of the characteristics specified in other definitions of morale — ego involvement, equilibrium or personal adjustment, happiness, "we-feeling," and acceptance of group goals.

Although the term "morale" frequently carries the connotation of good morale, it is not difficult to see that morale may also have a negative side. Some groups may be enthusiastic, but others may be bitter. Morale levels might be described by a continuum ranging from low to neutral to high. The extremes of very high or very low morale may be rare, but they are known.

Morale in a business organization involves the relationship of the individual to the work group. Morale concerns the individual; it is not some ethereal substance that exists apart from the group members. It may be contagious, but individual attitudes add up in some way to group morale. In view of this, the attitude of any particular individual may differ somewhat from generally accepted attitudes of the group.

Specific Employee Attitudes

In view of the somewhat slippery nature of the concept of morale and the general confusion in its definition, our discussion may pro-

---

[1]Robert M. Guion, "The Problem of Terminology," *Personnel Psychology,* Vol. 11, No. 1, Spring 1958, p. 62. See also Gene F. Summers, "Morale Research in Industry: A Critical Summary," *Personnel Administration,* Vol. 28, No. 3, May-June 1965, pp. 39-44.

[2]Ross Stagner, "Motivational Aspects of Industrial Morale," *Personnel Psychology,* Vol. 11, No. 1, Spring 1958, p. 64.

ceed directly to the subject of job attitudes. These are closely related to, if not the substance of, morale.

The definition of attitude entails much less controversy than is the case with morale. In the language of the layman, we may describe an attitude as the way we feel about something. This may be a feeling toward school, football team, church, parents, democracy, capitalism, or supervisor. The object (which every attitude must have) may be anything — people, things, ideas, policies, and so on. Attitudes vary in direction (favorable-unfavorable), intensity (how strongly they are held), and extent of consciousness (awareness of individual concerning his attitudes).

In the business organization, it seems likely that some attitudes have unusual significance in describing the individual's relationship to his total job situation. The factors listed below appear to constitute important objects of employee feelings. (They might also be described as components or dimensions of employee morale.)

1. The organization (for example, pride in the employing corporation).
2. Immediate supervision.
3. Financial rewards.
4. Fellow employees.
5. The job (intrinsic satisfaction in doing the job).

Employees also have attitudes related to the work environment, job security or uncertainty, prestige of the product or department, and plant location. The individual's attitudes toward these factors are indicative of his apathy or enthusiasm toward the activities and objectives of the organization.

Of course, there are other factors that might be noted, and those above might be subdivided. In a sense, an employee has a cluster of feelings in each area. Specific attitudes, moreover, need not be uniformly favorable or unfavorable. An employee, for example, may feel proud of the company and its contribution to society. At the same time, he may dislike the monotony of his work.

Attitudes and the Systems Viewpoint

In examining employee attitudes, we are concerned with the individual as a component or subsystem of the larger organizational system. Satisfaction (or dissatisfaction) is one output of the system. The organization member, in other words, receives satisfaction as well as dollars. The system—that is, the department, unit, or company—may function in such a way as to produce an output of great satisfaction to individual participants, or it may create dissatisfaction and low morale.

Conversely, attitudes may also affect individual performance and thus regulate system input in some way. The individual contributes his services to the system, and the services of a satisfied employee may differ from the services of a disgruntled employee. To analyze the nature of attitudes as an input, it is necessary to examine their relationship to such factors as productivity and absenteeism. (This relationship is considered later in this chapter.) To the extent that attitudes influence employee attendance or effort in any way, they affect system input accordingly.

In a more general sense, the morale level of a group reflects the strength of ties among all components of the system. Morale is often treated as a group concept. We speak of high-morale units or low-morale units. Groups whose members have a strong attraction to their groups and want to stay in the groups may be described as highly cohesive. Such groups constitute systems with an internal strength that facilitates accomplishment of group purposes.

Attitudes and Productivity

One of the perplexing questions concerning employee attitudes is the extent of their relationship with employee efficiency or productivity. Intuitively, we are inclined to expect a strong positive correlation. Yet, a moment's reflection reminds us that a happy, sociable employee may spend his time in socializing rather than working. For that matter, most of us can think of dissatisfied individuals with numerous complaints who are pretty good producers. A number of studies have attempted to analyze the relationship, but to date no close correlation has been established. At best, the results are inconclusive. In this section, attention will be given to several of these studies.

Attitude Toward Employer and Operating Efficiency

What is the relationship between the productivity of employees and their attitude toward the company that employs them? Research on this subject has been conducted by the Institute for Social Research of the University of Michigan. In one study of a large company, employees in high-productivity sections were found to have no more favorable attitudes toward the company than those in low-productivity sections engaged in the same kind of work. In fact, the distribution of employees into the various attitude groups was reported as follows:[3]

	Percentage of Employees Whose Satisfaction with Company Is:		
	High	*Average*	*Low*
High-producing sections	37%	39%	24%
Low-producing sections	40	40	20

It is apparent from these figures that no correlation existed between this general attitude and productivity.

This study was repeated in other situations with similar results. In other studies, the productivity of individuals was found to have a low positive relationship with the attitude toward the company.[4] The degree of correlation was so low, however, as to be considered negligible. The effect of these particular studies, then, is to suggest that employees with favorable attitudes toward the employer are unlikely to be more productive employees than are those with unfavorable attitudes.

On the basis of this analysis, it appears doubtful that a simple relationship exists between the general morale level — that is, the attitude toward the company as a whole — and the level of efficiency. The nature of the work being performed, however, seems to affect this relationship. Many research studies have considered only *repetitive* jobs. In other types of work — which Likert calls *varied* work — a positive correlation exists between productivity and attitudes.[5] (*Varied* work is the type of work involved in research, engineering, and selling ordinary life insurance.) It is apparent that the relationship between attitudes and productivity is more complex than is commonly assumed.

Productivity and Specific Job Attitudes

As a result of the research cited above, the assumption that a happy employee is a productive employee appears questionable. Is it possible, however, that more specific attitudes might have a direct relationship with employee performance? The research conducted

---

[3]Rensis Likert, *New Patterns of Management* (New York: McGraw-Hill Book Company, 1961), p. 14.

[4]*Ibid.*

[5]*Ibid.*, pp. 16, 77-78.

by the Institute for Social Research of the University of Michigan included an analysis of the relationship between specific attitudes and productivity. The results of this research were summarized in 1960 by Robert L. Kahn.[6]

The earliest project in this research program was conducted in a life insurance company and involved a comparison of work groups differing significantly in their productivity as measured by accounting procedures of the company. The attitudes of members of the different groups were analyzed in an attempt to discover significant differences between those in low-production groups and those in high-production groups. The analysis checked employee satisfaction with the job itself and with the financial and job status of the employee. The researchers discovered no positive correlation between the productivity of the clerical workers and any of these types of satisfaction.

> In other words, employees in highly productive work groups were no more likely than employees in low-producing groups to be satisfied with their jobs with the company, or with their financial and status rewards.[7]

A second study made a somewhat similar type of analysis of maintenance-of-way workers of a railroad. About 300 laborers and 72 foremen were involved. Although the research was similar in design to the study of clerical workers in the insurance company, there were obvious, drastic differences in the research setting in terms of age, sex, type of work, and so on. Once again, however, the analysis revealed a lack of correlation between employee satisfaction and productivity.

> In the matter of productivity and satisfaction, the results of the railroad study were identical with those of the work in the insurance company. There was no systematic relationship between productivity and such morale variables as intrinsic job satisfaction, financial and job status satisfaction, and satisfaction with the company.[8]

A subsequent major study produced an all-out effort to eliminate all reasons for failure to establish the connection between job satisfaction and productivity. A midwestern cluster of factories manufac-

---

[6]The research cited in this section is summarized in Robert L. Kahn, "Productivity and Job Satisfaction," *Personnel Psychology*, Vol. 13, No. 3, Autumn 1960, pp. 275-287.

[7]*Ibid.*, p. 277.

[8]*Ibid.*, p. 279.

turing agricultural equipment and tractors was selected for the study. All of 20,000 employees were included, including 6,000 employees on jobs providing individual daily productivity data. By examining the individual records, it was thought that it might be possible to locate relationships that were obscured by the group nature of previous research.

> A factor analysis was done to identify the components of satisfaction among the approximately 6,000 workers for whom individual productivity scores were available. Four identifiable factors resulted from this analysis and were labeled: Intrinsic job satisfaction, satisfaction with the company, satisfaction with supervision, and satisfaction with rewards and mobility opportunities. None of these factors was significantly related to the actual productivity of employees in the tractor factories.[9]

The effect of this series of studies is, once again, to indicate an apparent absence of any positive relationship between productivity and these specific job attitudes. This is true even though the attitudes concern the job, supervision, rewards, or the company as a whole. It is possible, of course, that these studies might have discovered a positive relationship if they had concentrated upon nonroutine jobs.

Other Studies of Attitudes and Performance

The general results reported in the preceding sections have also been confirmed by other studies. One summary in 1955 of the research in this area is particularly interesting.[10] Several of the studies examined by Brayfield and Crockett were based on a comparison of individual performance with job attitudes. As one example of these studies, over 9,000 insurance agents were asked, "How do you feel about your job as a life underwriter?" (Seventy-five per cent of the questionnaires were returned, of which more than 90 per cent were usable.)

> The performance rating was in the form of a self-report since each agent was asked to check whether his previous year's production was "under $200,000" of insurance or "$200,000 or over." Agents producing under $200,000 scored 4.15 on what

[9] *Ibid.*, p. 285.

[10] Arthur H. Brayfield and Walter H. Crockett, "Employee Attitudes and Employee Performance," *Psychological Bulletin*, Vol. 52, No. 5, September 1955, pp. 396-424.

> evidently was the single general satisfaction item as compared to 4.11 for the high producers. The "Extremely Satisfied" score is 5.00. The relationship is insignificant or slightly in favor of the lower producers.[11]

In summarizing studies of fourteen homogeneous occupational groups and one large sample of assorted hourly factory workers, Brayfield and Crockett reported that "statistically significant low positive relationships between job satisfaction and job performance were found in two of the 15 comparisons."[12]

A review of further studies that related group performance (in contrast to individual performance) to employee attitudes produced similar conclusions.

> The results . . . are substantially in agreement with the previous findings of minimal or no relationship between employee attitudes and performance. They do supply the hint that morale, as a group phenomenon, may bear a positive relationship to performance on the job.[13]

The general impact of this review of research is to reveal at best a tenuous relationship between attitudes and performance. It may be going too far to say that no relationship exists. More recently, Herzberg, Mausner, and Snyderman have concluded that there "probably is some relationship between job attitudes and output or productivity."[14] In reconciling this opinion with the conclusion of Brayfield and Crockett, they commented as follows:

> The difference between their conclusion and ours was due to their greater scepticism of studies in which low, but positive, correlations were reported and to our citation of a number of studies with such low positive findings not included by them. Certainly there is no basic disagreement as to the tenuous nature of the relationship as it has been so far demonstrated.[15]

A Final Note on Attitudes and Performance

The difficulties in clearly establishing or disproving the relationship between attitudes and performance is not surprising in view of

---

[11] *Ibid.*, pp. 399-400.
[12] *Ibid.*, p. 402.
[13] *Ibid.*, p. 405.
[14] Frederick Herzberg, Bernard Mausner, and Barbara Bloch Snyderman, *The Motivation to Work* (New York: John Wiley & Sons, Inc., 1959), p. 8.
[15] *Ibid.*

the complexities in work situations and the difficulties in measuring either attitudes or performance. For example, a work group may agree informally upon output quotas that apply to all members of the group. Or, the device for measuring employee performance may be faulty. Either condition would interfere with the detection of a relationship that might otherwise be found to exist. Some apparent contradictions may be resolved, therefore, as further research occurs. Even if established, of course, a relationship between performance and morale would not necessarily be causal. And even if the relationship were causal, the causative factor might be either the attitude or the performance level.

In summary, the relationship between job satisfaction and job performance is not a simple one. Much work is highly standardized so that individual employees have little opportunity to distinguish themselves other than by performing satisfactorily their assigned duties. It may be that, given certain conditions, performance and attitudes are more closely related than would appear otherwise. Likert's findings noted earlier seem to point in this direction.

Other Beneficial Morale Effects

Even though it appears that favorable attitudes may not inspire high productivity, there are other beneficial effects. Favorable employee attitudes, according to different studies, are associated with a lower rate of personnel turnover and less absenteeism.[16] In view of this fact, favorable attitudes could significantly affect company profits. A high rate of turnover, for example, has a tendency to increase recruitment and training costs.

It seems likely that a high morale level also represents a "plus" in terms of public relations. In addition to general benefits accruing from a favorable public relations image, there is probably an advantage in recruitment. A favorable public attitude encourages the best applicants to apply and this is particularly significant in times of short labor supply.

Union relationships may also be helped or hindered by the general attitudes of personnel. Grievances, and work stoppages as well, can result from negative attitudes. No doubt the task of supervision is

---

[16]See Bernard M. Bass, *Organizational Psychology* (Boston: Allyn & Bacon, Inc., 1965), pp. 36-38; and Daniel Katz and Robert L. Kahn, *The Social Psychology of Organizations* (New York: John Wiley & Sons, Inc., 1966), pp. 375-377.

also less burdensome if morale is high. A manager, therefore, has a number of reasons for seeking positive attitudes in his work group.

Analyzing Employee Attitudes

Management Observation

A manager acquires some idea of employee attitudes in his day-to-day contacts with subordinates. Indeed, most of management's knowledge of attitudes is acquired through communication with subordinates and by observation of their behavior. The understanding of employee attitudes developed in this way may be accurate or completely false. Much depends upon the manager's sensitivity and objectivity in observation and also upon the degree of rapport he has established with subordinates.

A general weakness of supervisory observation as a technique for analyzing attitudes is the customary absence of any systematic approach. The supervisor becomes aware of attitudes only as they become sufficiently strong to come to his attention. Negative attitudes may not be detected before they reach a troublesome stage. Moreover, certain dissatisfactions may never be expressed in the absence of a direct query. Such dissatisfactions may lead, however, to undesirable behavior or to other types of complaints.

One advantage of managerial observation is the possibility of a more penetrating analysis than that possible in a formal survey. The manager may be able to probe behind employee behavior or statements to discover the real nature of the difficulty or attitude. This approach is constructive, then, in spite of its limitations. It may be supplemented with other measurements in maximizing knowledge of employee attitudes.

Objective Indicators of Morale

The relationship between attitudes and such other factors as absenteeism and turnover was noted above. This suggests the possibility that measures of these factors might reveal morale levels. That is, the rate of turnover or absenteeism might constitute a sort of morale barometer.

One major difficulty in accurate attitude appraisal in this way is the probable existence of other significant variables in connection with each of these measures. Attitude is not the only factor that influences them. Grievances, for example, may reflect the extent of dissatisfaction, but they may also reflect the strategy of the union. High turnover may indicate low morale, but it may also indicate a tight labor market. While objective data of this kind may be worth checking, they do not provide a simple scale by which to measure attitudes. Nor do they reveal specific attitudes that deserve attention.

Systematic Surveys of Job Attitudes

If we wish to know how employees feel about the company or some aspect of it, why not ask them? It would seem that this direct approach should avoid some of the difficulties involved in other attempts to appraise attitudes. Although an *attitude survey* appears simple, there are more complexities than appear on the surface.

Systematic investigation of employee attitudes may be attempted by either interviews or questionnaires. As a technique for surveying the attitudes of a large group, the interview tends to be time consuming and costly. For this reason, questionnaires are customarily used although they may be supplemented with interviews. The printed questionnaire usually contains a series of questions on a wide variety of subjects such as the company itself, working conditions, supervision, and chances for advancement. The employee is given some simple method of checking to show his attitudes on the various questions.

If a survey is to be effective, an employee must be able to respond freely. If he fears that his comments may be held against him, he is unwilling to reveal his true feelings. This means that his reply must be treated anonymously and that the employee must be convinced of that fact. Management must accordingly take every precaution to guarantee this confidence. Supervisors, of course, should never receive completed questionnaires directly from their subordinates. Some companies arrange for employees to mail questionnaires to the personnel department or even to an outside consultant.

The employee must also be convinced of the sincerity of management in wishing to discover and act on the basis of employee attitudes. Typically, management agrees to publish the survey results in a company publication or to make them available in other ways. Management also has the responsibility of following up a survey and correcting any conditions revealed as needing attention. Otherwise, the employee may conclude that management has little genuine concern for human relations. One possible difficulty is that employees may be allowed to expect impossible changes as a result of an attitude survey — for example, a drastic immediate change in supervisory behavior. This suggests the need for acquainting them with the practical limitations of the survey in order to establish a boundary for their expectations.[17]

Questionnaires may locate areas of difficulty by identifying general negative attitudes. The reasons behind the negative attitudes, however, are not always immediately apparent. Consultants or company representatives from outside the department may conduct interviews to delve more deeply into the troublesome issues. If skilled, experienced interviewers are used in an atmosphere that respects confidences, employees are typically quite open in expressing their views about the job, supervision, and working relationships.

Building Positive Employee Attitudes

There are undoubtedly many factors influencing job attitudes. In a particular situation — that is, a particular shop or office or other administrative unit — the relative importance of these factors would be likely to differ. In other words, each organization is to some extent unique in the configuration of factors affecting morale. Attitudes must be interpreted, therefore, in the light of the specific structure of administrative relationships. While recognizing this complicating fact, it is still useful to note some of the factors that typically have a bearing on employee attitudes.

The Crucial Role of Leadership

To attain high morale, employees must come to see an identity of personal and organizational objectives. If the two types of objectives or goals are conceived as existing independently, there is no basis for favorable attitudes. It is the task of leadership to secure this integration of goals.

Research studies have demonstrated the significance of leadership style in shaping employee attitudes. Measures of supervisory behavior have been correlated in these studies with job satisfaction of subordinates. They show a marked relationship between job satisfaction and the degree to which subordinates perceive their superiors

---

[17] See G. M. Worbois, "Following Through on Morale Studies," *Personnel Psychology,* Vol. 11, No. 1, Spring 1958, pp. 92 and 94.

as being considerate and supportive.[18] Subordinates who have an opportunity to make or influence decisions affecting them also tend to be more satisfied. This latter relationship — influence of the superior's decision making— is apparently true for managerial as well as nonmanagerial personnel.

The following comments illustrate the nature of a subordinate's feelings about a manager:

> My present foreman is the nicest guy I ever worked for. The other foremen respect him also. I saw him stick his neck out with the general foreman over work loads. You won't find a lot of other foremen doing that. He'll argue a point with the general foreman if he thinks he's right.[19]

This provides an example of the type of supervisory behavior that is perceived favorably by subordinates. In general, the positive or democratic leadership qualities stressed in Chapter 21 are those most essential in developing high morale.

Technology and Job Satisfaction

Technology imposes its requirements on the nature of work. The technology of production, for example, may call for assembly line operations, for various degrees of skill, for teamwork in production, or for isolated labor. As noted in Chapter 8, management may design jobs with varying degrees of variety and skill, depending upon the type of industry and management philosophy. In view of these considerations, the technology and technological change may make work more or less attractive and satisfying to employees.

As an example of the relationship between technology and satisfaction, one company experienced a sharp drop in morale during a period of technological change.[20] This company was a large baking firm that built a new plant and changed its production processes in the direction of automation. The sag in attitudes occurred in spite of the improvement in physical facilities. Moreover, subsequent improvement in the months after the morale plunge was extremely

---

[18] Victor H. Vroom, *Motivation in Management* (New York: American Foundation for Management Research, 1965), pp. 54-55.

[19] Charles R. Walker, Robert H. Guest, and Arthur N. Turner, *The Foreman on the Assembly Line* (Cambridge: Harvard University Press, 1956), p. 27.

[20] Otis Lipstreu, "Automation and Morale." Reprinted from the *California Management Review,* Vol. 6, No. 4, Summer 1964, pp. 81-89. Copyright 1964 by the Regents of the University of California.

sticky, and morale was far below its original level even after several months.

The relationship between technology and employee attitudes has been clearly established by a research study of Turner and Lawrence.[21] The forty-seven production jobs included in their study were taken from eleven companies in a variety of industries. The jobs were analyzed in terms of their prescribed and discretionary activities, requirement for knowledge and skill, and degree of responsibility. The nature of the jobs, evaluated in this way, was found to have a significant relationship to employee attendance. In particular, the factors of authority and responsibility were found to be closely related. Absenteeism, which is often considered indicative of satisfaction, was thus discovered to be dependent upon the technological characteristics of work.

This research also examined the relationship between expressions of job satisfaction and type of work. Although workers' expressed attitudes were not correlated in a simple, direct way with the nature of the work, some relationships were discovered. A significant positive relationship was found between job satisfaction and a number of specific characteristics — namely, optional interaction off-the-job, learning time, and time span of discretion.

Another study pertinent to the present discussion is Blauner's investigation of worker *alienation* in four different industries — printing industry (*craft* technology), textile industry (*machine-tending* technology), automobile industry (*assembly-line* technology), and chemical industry (*continuous-process* technology).[22] Alienation includes such dimensions as powerlessness, meaninglessness, isolation, and self-estrangement. The intensity of alienation was found to vary according to the industrial setting.

> Inherent in the techniques of modern manufacturing and the principles of bureaucratic industrial organization are general alienating tendencies. But in some cases the distinctive technology, division of labor, economic structure, and social organization — in other words, the factors that differentiate individual industries — intensify these general tendencies, producing a high degree of alienation; in other cases they minimize and

---

[21]Arthur N. Turner and Paul R. Lawrence, *Industrial Jobs and the Worker: An Investigation of Response to Task Attributes* (Boston: Harvard University Graduate School of Business Administration, 1965).

[22]Robert Blauner, *Alienation and Freedom: The Factory Worker and His Industry* (Chicago: The University of Chicago Press, 1964).

> counteract them, resulting instead in control, meaning, and integration.[23]

To a considerable extent, then, management's morale building is limited by technological constraints. In most cases, the technology is not easily changed. However, efforts in the direction of job enlargement and job rotation among very simple jobs may serve to minimize the impact of technology on employee attitudes. Proper selection of employees is likewise desirable — for example, staffing routine jobs with personnel who do not object to this type of work. As a practical matter, solution of such problems is not easy, and these comments merely suggest the direction that improvement might take.

Importance of Personnel Policies

A company's personnel policies and practices are of major importance in building favorable attitudes. Through personnel policies, management indicates its attitudes and philosophy with regard to personnel. If the employee respects the employer's point of view as expressed in this way, he may respond favorably. Although sound policies in themselves may not guarantee favorable attitudes, their absence would make it virtually impossible to develop such attitudes.

Policies and administrative actions affecting advancement might be cited as an example. The individual's response to questions about favoritism, ability to get ahead in the company, need for "pull" in getting promotions, and the possibility of being lost in the company are based upon his observation of personnel policies in action. It is not only the written policy but also the implementation of that policy that affects employee attitudes. Similarly, policies affecting recruitment, placement, compensation, discipline, safety, and many other subjects are significant in shaping employee attitudes.

Wages, Hours, and Working Conditions

It would be a mistake to assume that these factors — which are invariably stressed in formal negotiations between labor and management — are always of most critical importance in shaping attitudes. It seems likely, in fact, that adequate wages, hours, and working conditions would not guarantee a positive response from

---

[23] *Ibid.*, pp. 166-167.

employees. In attitude polls, factors of this type are often played down in the responses of employees. It is wrong, however, to dismiss them as insignificant.

The absence of "adequate" or "fair" wages, hours, and working conditions may be more significant than their presence. While they may not assure favorable attitudes, it is difficult to achieve high morale without them. Even this statement may deserve qualification. Factors such as wages and hours appear significant in what they reveal to be the attitude of management. If management declines to compensate employees adequately or to provide reasonably adequate working conditions, the employee is left to question the basic outlook or attitude of management. If, on the other hand, improvement in these factors is out of the question for some reason, the employee may accept the situation and react favorably in spite of such limitations.

In their attitudes concerning compensation, individuals are often more concerned with their relative standing than with their absolute level. It seems the worker is more concerned about his pay and benefits relative to fellow employees. This is true, of course, not only for operative employees but also for executives and professional personnel. The influence of wages, hours, and working conditions upon job attitudes is, therefore, significant, but it is more subtle than appears on the surface.

Size of Organization

There appears to be a relationship between organization size and job attitudes. In general, this seems to favor the small organization. This does not necessarily mean the size of the company as a whole. Branch plants or branch offices may have many of the same natural morale advantages as those of small firms. Studies of attitudes in Sears, Roebuck and Company showed a clear tendency for morale to decline sharply with increasing size even though the same management and personnel policies were followed.[24]

Other studies have discovered a similar inverse relationship between job satisfaction and organization size.[25] One investigation

---

[24]James C. Worthy, "Factors Influencing Employee Morale," *Harvard Business Review,* Vol. 28, No. 1, January 1950, p. 68.

[25]For a summary of such studies, see Michael Beer, "Organizational Size and Job Satisfaction," *Academy of Management Journal,* Vol. 7, No. 1, March 1964, pp. 34-44.

of this type studied the relationship of employee satisfaction to size of organization in each of ninety-three industrial organizations.[26] A significant negative relationship was discovered. That is, employees in larger organizations expressed lower satisfaction than those in smaller organizations.

The evidence showing higher satisfaction in smaller organizations is not entirely consistent, however. For example, Porter's study of job satisfaction among managers at several levels showed no clear-cut superiority of small organizations over large organizations.[27] At the two lowest management levels (and perhaps at the president level), small organization size did seem to be related to perceived deficiencies in need fulfillment. However, the picture was reversed at upper-middle and vice president levels. In spite of such findings that limit the scope of generalization, an inverse relationship between size and satisfaction apparently exists in at least some settings.

Differences in satisfaction among employees of various size firms may result from differences in organizational characteristics. In other words, growth in size of organizations may produce intervening variables that interfere with management's efforts to build morale. For example, large organizations typically involve more organizational levels, longer lines of communication, and greater work specialization. These intervening variables may serve to lower morale. In the small unit, it is often possible for the individual to recognize the significance of his own contribution more clearly. The total activity or function is also more easily comprehended. He is closer to management and often subject to more flexible regulations and administration than is common in most large organizations.

To some extent, organization size is "given" and thus beyond administrative control. Even in large corporations, however, component units may be large or small. Many of the studies, in fact, stress satisfaction differences among different size units of the same organization. By limiting unit size, therefore, some contribution may be made to job satisfaction. In addition, management may deal with such intervening variables as communication. An aggressive approach by a manager to sharing information with subordinates may offset the otherwise negative effects of large size. In this way,

---

[26]Sergio Talacchi, "Organization Size, Individual Attitudes and Behavior: An Empirical Study," *Administrative Science Quarterly,* Vol. 5, No. 3, December 1960, pp. 398-420.

[27]Lyman W. Porter, "Job Attitudes in Management: Perceived Deficiencies in Need Fulfillment as a Function of Size of Company," *Journal of Applied Psychology,* Vol. 47, No. 6, December 1963, p. 395.

the manager may attempt to regain the morale benefits associated with smallness.

Organization Practices

A number of organization practices discussed in other chapters have a direct bearing on organization morale. One of these, noted in Chapter 12, is that of decentralization. When this concept is not only accepted in theory but followed in practice, subordinate units possess greater freedom in operation. In effect, it reduces the negative morale effects of large-scale organization. The majority of personnel apparently respond favorably to administrative decentralization.

Extreme specialization of work has also been noted as a frequent cause of dissatisfaction. There is a definite tendency to minimize job satisfaction by reducing interest and pride in the job and creating monotony and boredom. Some specialization, of course, may increase satisfaction by providing a function that is manageable. This may seem better than being a "Jack-of-all-trades." The ideal job content, from the morale standpoint, probably falls somewhere between these extremes.

These organizational features merely illustrate the nature and influence of such factors. Other organization practices similarly affect the morale level of organization members. Effective line-staff relationships, a reasonable span of control, and unity in supervision, for example, likewise contribute to favorable job attitudes.

Personal Factors and Attitude Formation

It is a mistake to conclude that the environmental factors discussed in this section are the sole determinants of employee attitudes. Attitudes emerge from the interaction of employees with their environments; individual characteristics are significant, therefore, in attitude formation. As noted in Chapter 20, individuals differ greatly in emotional adjustment, perception, and need priority. Some are able to meet the demands of life and to have personal relationships that are satisfying and lasting. Some are unrealistic in the goals that they set for themselves or have feelings of inferiority with respect to their own abilities. Employees also differ in the needs that are dominant in their thinking at any one time. It is unrealistic, therefore, to assume that any given type of leadership, technology, or personnel policies will produce identical attitudes in all individuals.

In attempting to understand attitudes, therefore, one must recognize the significance of personal as well as environmental factors.

One could not predict job satisfaction, for example, without knowing something about individual abilities on one hand and job requirements on the other. Numerous studies, in fact, have examined the significance of differences in age, education, intelligence, and sex upon job satisfaction.[28] Some studies have found apparent relationships between personal factors and job satisfaction, even though the evidence is not completely uniform.

Management is limited, therefore, by individual differences in its attempt to build favorable attitudes in the work organization. Of course, management may through proper selection, counseling, and attention to individual characteristics recognize the significance of individual differences in attempting to build high morale.

Satisfiers and Dissatisfiers

It is easy to assume that various factors have equal significance in contributing to job satisfaction or dissatisfaction. A favorable attitude toward the supervisor, for example, might cancel out an unfavorable attitude toward salary. This assumption is questionable on two counts. First, there is no reason to believe that all factors and attitudes, whether favorable or unfavorable, have equal weight in the mind of an employee. A particular objectionable feature may be more onerous than others. One proposal for measuring attitudes asks the respondent not only for an indication of favorable or unfavorable attitude but also for an assessment of the importance of the item in his thinking.[29]

A second possibility is that certain factors have more strength as *satisfiers* while others are more potent as *dissatisfiers*. A series of studies, in fact, seems to show just this. One noted study indicated that five factors in particular seemed to play an important role in increasing job satisfaction.[30] These factors were as follows:

1. Achievement.
2. Recognition.
3. Work itself.
4. Responsibility.
5. Advancement.

[28]For a review of such studies see Glenn P. Fournet, M. K. Distefano, Jr., and Margaret W. Pryer, "Job Satisfaction: Issues and Problems," *Personnel Psychology,* Vol. 19, No. 2, Summer 1966, pp. 165-183.

[29]J. R. Glennon, W. A. Owens, W. J. Smith, and L. E. Albright, "New Dimension in Measuring Morale," *Harvard Business Review,* Vol. 38, No. 1, January-February 1960, pp. 106-107.

[30]Herzberg, *et al., op. cit.,* pp. 59-63.

These factors have in common a focus on the job being performed. They are concerned with doing the job, liking it, experiencing success in it, receiving recognition for it, and moving upward as an indication of professional growth.

In contrast to these factors, a number of dissatisfiers were identified. These included the following:[31]

1. Company policy and administration.
2. Weak technical supervision.
3. Salary.

Of course, other factors, including the absence of some satisfiers, were cited, but the noteworthy fact is that the top satisfiers and dissatisfiers differed.

These findings have been confirmed by other studies. Researchers at Texas Instruments Incorporated, for example, investigated the satisfiers and dissatisfiers of scientists, engineers, manufacturing supervisors, technicians, and assemblers.[32] They discovered that positive motivation typically stemmed from the challenge of the job through such factors as achievement, responsibility, growth, advancement, work itself, and earned recognition. Dissatisfiers, on the other hand, were peripheral factors such as compensation, physical facilities, noise, work rules, social relationships, and security.

Another study based on interviews with eighty-two scientists and engineers in a research and development laboratory sought to compare the factors operating to keep them in the organization with the factors that might cause them to leave.[33] The study revealed that the two sets of reasons were quite different in nature and not merely opposites. Prime satisfiers that attracted and held scientists were central to the work process, such as interest in work, importance of work, challenging projects, and so on. Negative motivations that encouraged personnel to leave were peripheral to the work process and concerned with the work context — for example, promotion, pay, supervisory opinions, leadership and management, and the like. In summary, satisfaction depended upon the intrinsic content and process of the work itself, whereas dissatisfaction depended upon the contextual and environmental setting of the job.

---

[31] *Ibid.*, pp. 70-74.

[32] M. Scott Myers, "Who Are Your Motivated Workers?" *Harvard Business Review*, Vol. 42, No. 1, January-February 1964, pp. 73-88.

[33] Frank Friedlander and Eugene Walton, "Positive and Negative Motivations Toward Work," *Administrative Science Quarterly*, Vol. 9, No. 2, September 1964, pp. 194-207.

Herzberg has reviewed a number of studies, including the two just described, which deal with the satisfier-dissatisfier concept.[34] The studies provide strong support for the idea by verifying its existence in a wide variety of environmental contexts.

These findings should not be taken to mean that dissatisfiers — which are also called *maintenance* or *hygiene* factors — are unimportant. Even though these factors are environmental in nature, management must meet employee expectations to avoid dissatisfaction. Although these needs are not static, management undoubtedly does a better job of satisfying them than in meeting positive motivational needs. Meeting hygiene requirements may minimize dissatisfaction, but it does not assure high morale. Management action that emphasizes the intrinsic rewards and challenges associated with work is necessary. Leadership appealing to the higher level needs discussed in Chapter 20 — that permits pride in work and a sense of accomplishment — is essential for providing the satisfiers in industrial work.

Summary

The concept of *morale* is concerned with satisfaction of individual needs through the job and the working relationships with the employer. In addition to a general attitude toward the employing organization, the individual also has specific *attitudes* toward the job, supervision, fellow employees, financial rewards, and other aspects of employment. In the systems context, attitudes may be visualized as output, as input, or in a more general sense, as the cement which binds together components of the organizational system.

On the basis of research studies to date, there is little empirical evidence for a simple relationship between productivity and employee attitudes. The nature of the work being performed apparently affects this relationship, however, with a closer correlation appearing in the case of *varied* work than in *repetitive* work. Other beneficial effects resulting from favorable attitudes include reduction in the rates of personnel turnover and absenteeism, improvement in public relations and recruitment, better union relationships, fewer grievances, and easier supervision.

---

[34]Frederick Herzberg, *Work and the Nature of Man* (Cleveland: The World Publishing Company, 1966).

To discover attitudes of employees, management may proceed along several paths. Through communication and *observation,* the supervisor may gain some impression of employee attitudes. Although this lacks a systematic approach, it provides most of management's knowledge of employee attitudes. Certain *attitude indicators,* such as the rate of absenteeism or turnover, may also be used, but these are difficult to evaluate because other variables are often involved. *Attitude surveys* by interview or questionnaire are used for the systematic analysis of employee attitudes. In securing a sound appraisal of employee attitudes, it is important that such surveys be conducted with the full confidence of participating personnel.

In building positive employee attitudes, it is important that supervisory management be of top quality. Many studies show that a considerate, supportive style of leadership, one that gives subordinates the opportunity to make or influence decisions concerning them, is associated with job satisfaction. Production technology — for example, craft technology, assembly-line technology, and so on — also affects the employee's degree of job satisfaction. In addition, the company's personnel program and policies are basic in importance. Other factors having a direct or indirect bearing on attitudes include wages, hours, and working conditions; size of organization; and organization practices. These environmental factors interact with the individual employee's interests, perceptions, needs, and other personal factors in shaping his attitudes. It has been discovered, furthermore, that some factors have a more profound effect as *satisfiers* while others have a primary impact as *dissatisfiers.*

Discussion Questions

1. Describe the general point of view and behavior that one would expect in a high-morale employee.

2. What is an *attitude*? What is meant by an attitude's *object, direction,* and *intensity*?

3. What seems to be the relationship between productivity and attitudes toward the company and the job?

4. What types of benefits, apart from any possible direct effect upon productivity, may result from favorable employee attitudes?

5. Employee attitudes may be analyzed in various ways. Compare the effectiveness of supervisory *observation* of attitudes with formal *attitude surveys.*

6. If a company president wishes to improve employee attitudes, where should he begin?

7. How significant is the paycheck in developing favorable employee attitudes?

8. What is the difference between a *satisfier* and *dissatisfier*? How is this related to the managerial objective of building morale?

Supplementary Reading

Applewhite, Philip B., *Organizational Behavior,* Chapter 2. Englewood Cliffs: Prentice-Hall, Inc., 1965.

Bass, Bernard M., *Organizational Psychology,* Chapter 2. Boston: Allyn & Bacon, Inc., 1965.

Behling, Orlando, George Labovitz, and Richard Kosmo, "The Hertzberg Controversy: A Critical Reappraisal," *Academy of Management Journal,* Vol. 11, No. 1, March 1968, pp. 99-108.

Blauner, Robert, *Alienation and Freedom: The Factory Worker and His Industry*. Chicago: The University of Chicago Press, 1964.

Brayfield, Arthur H. and Walter H. Crockett, "Employee Attitudes and Employee Performance," *Psychological Bulletin,* Vol. 52, No. 5, September 1955, pp. 396-424.

Fournet, Glenn P., M. K. Distefano, Jr., and Margaret W. Pryer, "Job Satisfaction: Issues and Problems," *Personnel Psychology,* Vol. 19, No. 2, Summer 1966, pp. 165-183.

Friedlander, Frank and Eugene Walton, "Positive and Negative Motivations Toward Work," *Administrative Science Quarterly,* Vol. 9, No. 2, September 1964, pp. 194-207.

Gellerman, Saul W., *The Management of Human Relations,* Chapter 10. New York: Holt, Rinehart & Winston, Inc., 1966.

Herzberg, Frederick, "One More Time: How Do You Motivate Employees?" *Harvard Business Review,* Vol. 46, No. 1, January-February 1968, pp. 53-62.

____________, *Work and the Nature of Man.* Cleveland: The World Publishing Company, 1966.

Kahn, Robert L., "Productivity and Job Satisfaction," *Personnel Psychology,* Vol. 13, No. 3, Autumn 1960, pp. 275-287.

Lipstreu, Otis, "Automation and Morale," *California Management Review,* Vol. 6, No. 4, Summer 1964, pp. 81-89.

Porter, Lyman W. and Edward E. Lawler, III, "What Job Attitudes Tell About Motivation," *Harvard Business Review,* Vol. 46, No. 1, January-February 1968, pp. 118-126.

Purcell, Theodore V., "Work Psychology and Business Values: A Triad Theory of Work Motivation," *Personnel Psychology,* Vol. 20, No. 3, Autumn 1967, pp. 231-257.

Summers, Gene F., "Morale Research in Industry," *Personnel Administration,* Vol. 28, No. 3, May-June 1965, pp. 39-44.

Turner, Arthur N. and Paul R. Lawrence, *Industrial Jobs and the Worker: An Investigation of Response to Task Attributes.* Boston: Harvard University Graduate School of Business Administration, 1965.

Vroom, Victor H., *Work and Motivation.* New York: John Wiley & Sons, Inc., 1964.

Whitsett, David A. and Erik K. Winslow, "An Analysis of Studies Critical of the Motivator-Hygiene Theory," *Personnel Psychology,* Vol. 20, No. 4, Winter 1967, pp. 391-415.

Controlling Organizational Performance

24

Fundamentals of Control

The administrator must keep in touch with operations occurring under his direction. It is seldom possible for him to formulate plans and pass them on to subordinates with the assurance that they will be completed without further concern or checking. Instead, he must regulate work assignments and review work progress. In some cases, this control function is accomplished through face-to-face contacts, and in other cases intricate work scheduling and voluminous reports are required.

Basic Factors in Control

The Concept of Control

The concept of control includes the regulation of many different aspects of business activity. At the top corporate level, for example, it involves the appraisal of a firm's operating results and the institution of any necessary corrective action. At a much lower level, it entails the supervisory activities of a shop foreman in checking the work progress of employees subject to his control. In every unit of the organization, management must regulate in some way the contributions of the organization members.

Formal, detailed reports are often associated with the control process. The accounting department prepares periodic analyses of operating results. These reports typically break down overall operating results by the use of department-by-department and product-by-product analyses. In themselves, however, these reports are of only historical value. They do not constitute control, although they provide a basis for control. Control is concerned with the present— a regulation of what is happening. In controlling, the manager regulates the way in which members of the organization apply their efforts. Controlling is particularly concerned with locating operational weaknesses and taking corrective action. The project that is getting behind schedule or the quality that is slipping below standard is detected and corrected. The controlling function results in many different types of controls. The following classification suggests the variety of controls involved in a control system.[1]

1. *Controls used to standardize performance* in order to increase efficiency and to lower costs. Included might be time and motion studies, inspections, written procedures, or production schedules.
2. *Controls used to safeguard company assets* from theft, wastage, or misuse. Such controls typically would emphasize division of responsibilities, separation of operational, custodial, and accounting activities, and an adequate system of authorization and record keeping.
3. *Controls used to standardize quality* in order to meet the specifications of either customers or company engineers. Blueprints, inspection, and statistical quality controls would typify the measures employed to preserve the integrity of the product (or service) marketed by the company.
4. *Controls designed to set limits within which delegated authority can be exercised without further top management approval.* Organization and procedure manuals, policy directives, and internal audits would help to spell out the limits within which subordinates have a free hand.
5. *Controls used to measure on-the-job performance.* Typical of such controls would be special reports, output per hour or per employee, internal audits, and perhaps budgets or standard costs.
6. *Controls used for planning and programming operations.* Such controls would include sales and production forecasts, budgets, various cost standards, and standards of work measurement.

---

[1]William Travers Jerome III, *Executive Control—The Catalyst* (New York: John Wiley & Sons, Inc., 1961), pp. 32-33.

7. *Controls necessary to allow top management to keep the firm's various plans and programs in balance.* Typical of such controls would be a master budget, policy manuals, organization manuals, and such organization techniques as committees and the use of outside consultants. The overriding need for such controls would be to provide the necessary capital for current and long-run operations and to maximize profits.
8. *Controls designed to motivate individuals within* a firm to contribute their best efforts. Such controls necessarily would involve ways of recognizing achievement through such things as promotions, awards for suggestions, or some form of profit sharing.

Predetermined Standards or Objectives

The function of controlling assumes the existence of some type of target or objective. A firm has certain overall objectives as well as more specific goals applying to its individual departments and members. Individual and organizational performance are directed toward the accomplishment of these goals, and performance may be evaluated in terms of such objectives. These goals, which are determined through planning, constitute the standards employed in the controlling process.

Some examples may clarify the nature of such standards. For the enterprise as a whole, the projected profit provides a checkpoint for measuring overall performance. Such broad control standards are essential tools of the administrator in his control of an organization. These general control standards are supplemented, however, by a vast number of more specific controls. In manufacturing, for example, product specifications provide predetermined standards that regulate the manufacturing process. A given dimension may be specified as fifteen inches with a tolerance of plus or minus one-fourth inch. A monthly sales quota establishes an output standard for a salesman. A budgeted expense item sets a standard for expenditures. A standard operating procedure specifies a standard to regulate the order or method of performance. A work schedule provides a standard controlling time and order of work.

From the standpoint of the company as a whole, there is a wide variety of standards that may be used. Many factors may be selected to supplement the overall profit figure. The rationale for selection of performance criteria is discussed later in this chapter.

Quantification of the objective or standard is obviously difficult in the case of certain factors. Consider the goal of product leadership, for example. In evaluating its product leadership, a company compares its products with those of competitors and determines the extent to which it pioneers in the introduction of basic products and later product improvements. Such standards may exist even though they are not formally and explicitly stated. In a similar fashion, at the operative level, a supervisor may find it difficult to express in quantitative terms the exact amount of output required of a particular employee. Inability to quantify the output standard, however, does not indicate the absence of some conception as to what constitutes reasonable or standard output or performance. This conception, in effect, constitutes a standard for controlling.

Comparing Performance with Standards

In controlling, the administrator attempts to make sure that the organization is functioning properly in the accomplishment of its goals. He must periodically check on the organization's position to answer the question, "How well are we doing?" This requires a measurement of performance so that it may be compared with the predetermined standard. A company's return on investment, for example, is calculated and compared with prior results or with other figures that are accepted as standards. In the manufacturing process, an inspector measures the product to make sure it falls within tolerance limits established by the specification.

A critical stage is reached in the comparison of actual or measured performance with projected or standard performance. If the standard is explicitly expressed and performance accurately measured, the direct comparison is simple enough. Considerable interpretation may be required, however, to make sense of the figures. Some deviations from standard are justified because of inaccuracies in the standard, changes in environmental conditions, or other reasons. The data must be examined in the light of existing circumstances.

Corrective Action

Control is not confined to measurement of performance, detection of errors, and preparation of reports. Managerial action is required to correct existing weaknesses or mistakes. This means that control is never completed by the analysis and reports of a staff officer even though he may be designated as the "controller." It is the responsible manager who must act to bring performance back into line or to hold it in line. If labor cost is becoming excessive, supervisors must take steps to secure more efficient personnel utilization.

What action is appropriate to correct out-of-line performance depends upon the unique nature of each situation. Delays and excessive cost in production, for example, may result from defective equipment or from inefficiency of labor. The former would require repair or replacement of equipment. The latter—inefficiency of labor—might be corrected by any of a number of actions depending upon the cause of the inefficiency. It might result from such factors as poor personnel selection, inadequate training, poor motivation, lack of discipline, or confusion in work assignments. To be effective, corrective action must locate and deal with the real cause.

A Systems Approach to Managerial Control

The Nature of the Control System

Managerial control activities comprise an essential subsystem of the total operating system, whether the latter be visualized as the firm or one of its component departments. In brief, the purpose of managerial control is to assure the coordination and effective performance of all other subsystems — for example, production, sales, and finance—so that organizational plans are properly implemented and organizational goals achieved.

> *The objective of the system is to perform a specified function, while the objective of control is to maintain the output which will satisfy the system requirements.* The objective of control-system design, therefore, is to determine the relevant characteristics which, when controlled, maintain the function of the system within allowable variations.[2]

Based on the analysis of the control function in the preceding section, it is evident that the steps of control might be described as follows:

1. Establishment of a standard.
2. Measurement of performance.
3. Comparison of performance with the standard.

---

[2]Richard A. Johnson, Fremont E. Kast, and James E. Rosenzweig, *The Theory and Management of Systems,* Second Edition (New York: McGraw-Hill Book Company, 1967), p. 86.

4. Corrective action, when needed, to bring performance into line.

It is evident that these steps are interrelated parts of the control system (or subsystem). These interrelationships as well as the essential elements of the control system are easily discerned in the diagram in Figure 28.

Figure 28. *Essential Elements of a Control System*

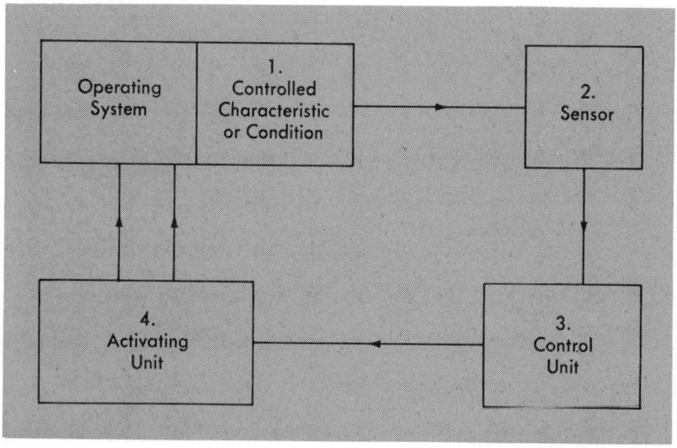

Source: Richard A. Johnson, Fremont E. Kast, and James E. Rosenzweig, *The Theory and Management of Systems,* Second Edition (New York: McGraw-Hill Book Company, 1967), p. 73.

The relationship of the control system to the operational system which it regulates is found in the characteristic or condition of the operating system which is measured. The measured element might be profit, sales, number of rejects, personnel turnover, product weight, or any of numerous other characteristics. In the control of a heating system, the selected characteristic is temperature. The controlled characteristic is measured by the second element of the control system — the sensor. The latter might be the manager's observation of performance, cost reports on a production operation, or the thermostat in a heating system.

The third element of the control system — the control unit — compares performance with a predetermined standard and releases correcting information. Checking actual expense against budgeted expense and comparing inspection results with the product specification provide business examples. In the heating system example, the thermostat compares the measured temperature with the desired standard and initiates any necessary action to restore the temperature to the prescribed level.

Taking corrective action occurs in the fourth element — the activating unit—of the control system. For example, a machine operator may adjust the machine, or a manager may train his employees. In the heating system, the furnace is turned on when the temperature drops.

The control process requires a flow of information — measurement information and correcting information. This might be described as a "feedback loop." The sensor unit procures measurement information and passes it on to the control unit which, in turn, releases any necessary correcting information. The nature and use of feedback is discussed in more detail later in the chapter.

Integration of Control Activities

The manager's control function entails the use of budgets, quality control charts, internal control procedures, and other control devices and techniques. In approaching the control function from the systems point of view, we must move beyond a view of these as isolated techniques for controlling specific variables. Rather, it is desirable to think in terms of a control system that regulates operation of the total system. The following analogy illustrates the systems view of control as an integrated set of activities:

> To use an analogy, there is a tendency to describe management control (and planning) in the same way that many professionals teach the novice the game of golf. Thus the beginner is drilled on the basic principles of the game (such as head down, firm left arm, and hips ahead of club head). Any ineptness or failure to follow directions is attributed to lack of skill, poor coordination, or indifference. Such criticisms may all be valid, but the basic cause for this ineptness actually runs deeper, namely, the failure of the professional to give the student any concept of how body and club head must be positioned to achieve maximum controlled power. The shortcomings in execution, then, are caused not so much by mechanical failure as by a conceptual lack — by the inability of the teacher and the student to visualize the swing as involving more than the sum of many separate movements. It is useful for descriptive or teaching purposes to analyze the golf swing or management control or

> planning or any other activity aspect by aspect. It is fatal, however, if we mistake an understanding of the analysis of the parts of a process for comprehension of the process itself.[3]

In keeping with this viewpoint, control arrangements should be formulated in terms of the particular system requirements. Rather than adopting standardized control devices in any area, creation of a control system properly begins with a consideration of system objectives.

Deficiencies in the control system may occur at specific points — that is, in regulating specific subsystems. Plans or standards may be poorly formulated, or flaws may develop in the flow of information that is necessary in controlling. Only a review of the total control system can correctly reveal points of difficulty.

Criteria for System Performance

It is clearly impossible to control every condition associated with system performance. Control of the system consequently requires a selection of performance criteria. The natural inclination is to assume that a simple measure such as a profit figure — for example, a stipulated rate of return on investment — constitutes an adequate criterion. The difficulty with such an approach is its tendency toward oversimplification. In some cases, the rate of return on investment may be misleading. As will be noted later in the chapter, short-run profits may be achieved at a long-run cost.

> It can be established that many companies have faced their most critical tests of survival in precisely those years when they were reporting the highest net profits in their history — mainly because these were being achieved at the price of not keeping up with competitors in research, equipment renewal, and management development.[4]

Conventional controls, furthermore, disregard the condition of the human organization. In calculating profit, the accountant allows for deterioration of the physical part of the system by charging depreciation as an expense of doing business. The human part of the system, however, is not subject to the same treatment. Rensis Likert argues that human assets of the system may also be dissipated in the process of operation.[5] Extreme pressure on the human organization

---

[3]Jerome, *op. cit.*, pp. 71-72.

[4]Seymour Tilles, "The Manager's Job: A Systems Approach," *Harvard Business Review*, Vol. 41, No. 1, January-February 1963, p. 77.

[5]Rensis Likert, *The Human Organization: Its Management and Value* (New York: McGraw-Hill Book Company, 1967), Chapters 5, 6, and 9.

is similar to prolonged usage of physical equipment without adequate maintenance. Higher production is achieved in the short run, but at the cost of wear and tear on human resources — increased hostility and reduced loyalty, skills, and confidence. Conventional measurements must be supplemented by measurement of human assets in order to detect this type of change.

> Human asset accounting refers to activity devoted to attaching dollar estimates to the value of a firm's human organization and its customer goodwill. If able, well-trained personnel leave the firm, the human organization is worth less; if they join it, the firm's human assets are increased. If bickering, distrust, and irreconcilable conflict become greater, the human enterprise is worth less; if the capacity to use differences constructively and engage in cooperative teamwork improves, the human organization is a more valuable asset.[6]

The profit criterion is principally concerned with the firm's contribution to its stockholders. Obligations to other groups also require measurement, however, if total system performance is to be controlled. To replace the simple profit criterion in evaluating overall system performance, the use of *sets of criteria* has been advocated.[7] Each of these corresponds to some wider system of which the company is a part. Figure 29 presents some suggestions concerning appropriate criteria for the company with respect to various superordinate systems.

Figure 29. *Systems Criteria for Judging Company Performance*

Superordinate System	*Criteria*
Stockholders	Price appreciation of securities
	Dividend payout
Labor force	Wage levels
	Stability of employment
	Opportunity
The market: consumers	Value given
The market: competitors	Rate of growth
	Innovation
Suppliers	Rapidity of payment
Creditors	Adherence to contract terms
Community	Contribution to community development
Nation	Public responsibility

Source: Seymour Tilles, "The Manager's Job: A Systems Approach," *Harvard Business Review,* Vol. 41, No. 1, January-February 1963, p. 78.

---

[6]*Ibid.,* pp. 148-149.
[7]Tilles, *op. cit.,* p. 77.

Behavioral Consequences of Control

In the design of control systems and the application of controls to the organization, unanticipated and undesirable effects are often realized. Instead of, or in addition to, controlling organizational activity as intended, the controls produce side effects, a sort of byproduct of the control system. Such undesired side effects result from the human reactions of members of the organization.

The Narrow Viewpoint

One such undesirable effect is the tendency of some control systems to narrow one's viewpoint unduly. The controls act as a set of blinders to limit the individual's vision or concern to his own sphere, with possible disregard for broader organizational values. A pay incentive system in manufacturing, for example, may base the reward upon output to the extent that quality suffers. Such a system may give the individual little or no encouragement to think beyond his daily production record to the broader objectives of the organization and the contributions he might make to these. There may be absolutely no incentive for improvement in the operations and methods. The incentive system has conditioned the employee to believe that only daily output is important.

At a managerial level, an example may be found in the restricted viewpoints of divisional managers in a decentralized corporation. In the eyes of a division manager, a good investment decision may depend upon the rate of return on investment expected by corporate management on the part of the particular division. And all divisions would not necessarily be expected to produce the same rate of profit. One division might be permitted to operate with little or no profit, whereas others might be expected to produce as high as 30 per cent after taxes.

The divisional manager would normally approve any investment that would tend to raise the rate of return of his division. This could lead to approval of investments promising a 5 per cent return in some divisions and rejection of proposals promising a 25 per cent return in other divisions. From the standpoint of the company as a whole, such decisions are clearly unwise.

> In a highly profitable division of a multidivisional company, the purchasing agent requested permission to increase the inventory in order to take quantity discounts; the return on investment would have been 25% on the inventory increase.

> His request was refused because the division was already earning 35% on its book investment. Therefore, a 25% investment would have averaged down the 35%. Incidentally, the company as a whole was earning less than 10%![8]

The Short Run Versus the Long Run

Another unfortunate consequence of some control systems is the premium they may unwittingly place upon the short run. The control system encourages a short-run course of action that may run counter to the long-run interests of the organization. Consider, for example, the profit control applied to the different divisions of a decentralized company. The profit goal of the division serves as a powerful incentive for the divisional manager and his associates, who are under tremendous pressure to achieve that objective. Under certain conditions, this presents a strong motivation to win in the short run, even though the long-run effects may be disastrous.

The following decisions by division managers illustrate this type of undesirable short-run reaction to a control system.

> In order to increase his rate of return, a division manager reduced his research costs by eliminating all projects that did not have an expected payout within two years. He believed that if he did not improve his rate of return, he would be replaced.
>
> A division manager scrapped some machinery that he was not currently using in order to reduce his investment. Later, when the machinery was needed, he purchased new equipment.[9]

As another example, the behavior of production supervisors is illuminating. One study of efficiency controls in large corporations has reported the reactions of department supervisors to efficiency ratings of their departments.[10] In this company, monthly efficiency ratings of each department were compiled to show the accomplishment of the department for the monthly period. The plant manager took these ratings seriously and was quick to investigate any deficiency revealed by the monthly reports. As a result, department supervisors were under considerable pressure to show up well each month.

---

[8]Bruce D. Henderson and John Dearden, "New System for Divisional Control," *Harvard Business Review,* Vol. 44, No. 5, September-October 1966, p. 149.

[9]*Ibid.,* p. 150.

[10]Frank J. Jasinski, "Use and Misuse of Efficiency Controls," *Harvard Business Review,* Vol. 34, No. 4, July-August 1956, pp. 105-112.

This led to a number of undesirable short-run expediencies. As the end of the month approached, attention was shifted to *completing* units in order to get them beyond the checkpoint into finished stores. In this way, they would show up as completed work in the department's efficiency ratings. This practice is known as *bleeding the line*, and one foreman described it as follows:

> What actually happens is that in the beginning of the month I have to put all of my men at the beginning of the line to get pieces going for the month's production. This is because we cleaned out the department in the previous month. Then, during the last two weeks I have to put all of the men at the end of the line to finish up the pieces.[11]

It is apparent that a great deal of inefficiency would result in this and other departments from such practices.

Department supervisors were similarly inclined to neglect necessary maintenance in their rush to achieve the month's production goal. They would run a machine to the breaking point in order to make the right efficiency rating. One foreman's explanation ran as follows:

> We really can't stop to have our machines repaired. In fact, one of our machines is off right now, but we'll have to gimmick something immediately and keep the machine going because at the end of the month, as it is now, we simply can't have a machine down. We've got to get those pieces out. Many times we run a machine right to the ground at the end of the month trying to get pieces out, and we have to spend extra time at the beginning of the month trying to repair the machine.[12]

Interestingly enough, a strong control system has produced strikingly similar results in a completely different culture. In Soviet Russia, factory managers also work under a monthly output plan.[13] Plant managers have tremendous pressure to achieve their output quotas. They may double their income, for example, by producing the proper amount. This has led to the practice of *storming*—that is, concentrating great effort upon production in the last part of each month. The problem has been sufficiently widespread to merit attention at the highest levels of government.

---

[11]*Ibid.*, p. 107.

[12]*Ibid.*

[13]The practice described here is reported in Joseph S. Berliner, "A Problem in Soviet Business Administration," *Administrative Science Quarterly*, Vol. 1, No. 1, June 1956, pp. 86-101.

> This practice of "storming" leads to a number of uneconomic consequences. States of emergency constantly arise; men and equipment are subject to periods of unnecessary idleness; during the days of storming the rate of spoilage increases, overtime pay mounts up, the machines suffer from speed-up, and customers' production schedules are interrupted.[14]

Evasion of Controls Through Falsification of Reporting

The individual who is subject to the control system may also be tempted to beat the system by making himself look good on paper. Various strategems may be used for this purpose. In the Jasinski study cited above, top supervisors were sometimes guilty of fudging figures.[15] In a desire to equalize efficiency ratings of departments under their direction, supervisors would go so far as to transfer personnel "on paper" from low efficiency departments to high efficiency departments. The effect, of course, was to produce a more consistent ratio of output to manpower in the various departments.

Soviet managers also practiced the *sharp pencil* technique at times to make their records appear satisfactory.[16] In effect, this amounts to tinkering with the figures so that they will show what the manager wishes them to show. One of the most common methods involves borrowing output from the next period. For example, work in process may be valued at an unreasonably high percentage of completion.

An opposite type of falsification occurs in the manager's tendency to avoid exceeding quota too much in any period. Because of the *ratchet* principle, an attained quota in one period may be established as a minimum for a later period. For this reason, it is dangerous for a manager to look too good. In fact, this may lead him to fall below quota occasionally. A Soviet informant is quoted as follows with respect to this practice:

> Sometimes the plan is deliberately underfulfilled. This may happen once or twice a year. They underfulfill it because they want to remove any suspicion that might arise if the plan is fulfilled every single month. The purpose of this is to give the assistant commissar the impression that he is really putting pressure upon the enterprise. Because if month after month the plan is fulfilled, then the commissar might crack down upon

---

[14] *Ibid.*, p. 89.

[15] Jasinski, *op. cit.*, pp. 107-108.

[16] For a discussion of this practice, see Joseph S. Berliner, *Factory and Manager in the USSR* (Cambridge: Harvard University Press, 1957), Chapter 10.

> them. But if in some months the plan is not fulfilled, then it will seem like a very hard program. They are willing to give a few months' premiums for this.[17]

Adverse Morale Effects

In view of the malfunctioning of control described above, it is hardly surprising that morale may be impaired at times. The combination of pressure and seemingly necessary but illogical behavior would hardly make one wildly enthusiastic about the organization. In fact, management personnel may easily experience a strong reaction against such a control system. Consider the faking of figures, for example. One foreman expressed the following reaction:

> They even want you to lie about production here so as to make the record look better than it is. I won't do that. O.K. if *they* want to, but I won't.[18]

If management appears unreasonable in the application of controls, the subordinate naturally becomes disturbed. A superior, for example, may refuse to accept reasonable explanations for delays. As a consequence, the subordinate must be content with an unfavorable evaluation by his superior or resort to one or more of the devious means available in combating the situation. A straightforward, honest effort may not secure the approbation of his superior. Those subject to such types of control are understandably critical.

Improving Effectiveness of Control

Minimizing Adverse Behavioral Effects

It is clear that managers, in installing and using controls, do not desire the unfortunate effects described above. Nor are these effects an inescapable consequence of all control systems. Establishing controls, however, does create pressures often leading to these undesirable effects. Managers should, therefore, be aware of this tendency and attempt to minimize the harmful effects.

---

[17]Used with permission of the publishers from Joseph S. Berliner, *Factory and Manager in the USSR,* Cambridge, Mass.: Harvard University Press, Copyright, 1957, by the President and Fellows of Harvard College, p. 165.

[18]Jasinski, *op. cit.*, p. 108.

The control system may be poorly designed. The adequacy of controls must be evaluated by examining their results. Do they produce the operational results desired? Or do they encourage undesirable short-run expediencies, narrowness of viewpoint, and distortion of reports? All controls need to be examined from this point of view in evaluating their overall effects on company operation.

To gain general acceptance, standards must be established in such a way that they are perceived as fair by those whose performance is controlled. The use of participative management, for example, tends to induce acceptance of standards as reasonable. Standards which recognize some range of acceptable performance and which appear to be established objectively, as is the case with statistical quality controls, also encourage acceptance by those whose performance is controlled.

In addition, controls must be recognized as means and not as ends in themselves. Higher-level management can assure this, however, only by a reasonable interpretation of results being controlled. The threat of being sent to Siberia, either literally or figuratively, in spite of an outstanding effort, would make one wary of the control system. If all explanations, regardless of validity, are unacceptable, the control system will almost inevitably become an end in itself.

The Extent of Control

In any situation, it is possible to vary the formality and nature of the controlling. Control may be loose and general or close and detailed. The concepts of delegation and decentralization, for example, involve a philosophy of only general control. Higher management expects certain results but permits lower levels to proceed without detailed control in accomplishing those results. The extent to which a decentralized management approach is adopted, therefore, governs the closeness of control that may be appropriately used. The arguments for decentralization were presented in Chapter 12.

It is pertinent at this point to recall the research relative to the effectiveness of different types of supervision. The studies cited in Chapter 21 indicated that successful supervisors on the average allowed considerably greater freedom to their subordinates. Rather than closely controlling subordinate behavior, the more successful supervisors allowed subordinates to determine their own work pace and to make various choices on their own initiative.

An excessive amount of control may lead to a system involving voluminous reports that somehow fails to accomplish that for which it is designed. Note the following comments of a management consultant regarding weaknesses in such burdensome systems of control:

> I have found all the shortcomings of the usual dictatorial and all-embracing regime, including the inevitably weak, insecure, or overambitious executive at the top; mountains of forms, reports, manuals, directives, and interpretive bulletins which nobody reads or which, if they are read, require special staffs to pore over them to keep executives abreast; bad morale in the second and third layers of management; and, believe it or not, usually poor planning and lack of significant management information when and where it is needed — the very things you would think *could* be accomplished by these immense, involved, and demanding systems of control.[19]

Improvement in managerial control may thus call for a paradoxical solution. By controlling less, the manager may control better. If he follows a natural bent toward overcontrol, on the other hand, the results may be destructive rather than helpful. Within limits imposed by the situation, a manager may lighten his control — delegating, avoiding close supervision, and eliminating burdensome control procedures — and still achieve greater success than he could otherwise.

Management by Objectives

One management approach that tends to minimize undesirable behavioral effects is known as *management by objectives*.[20] The principal feature of this type of management is the establishment of specific performance goals for each position, particularly for each managerial position. By stressing these objectives, overall control is achieved through self-control by individual participants. Rather than applying control from above, the emphasis is placed upon control from within. Of course, establishment of objectives and appraisal of performance is performed under the direction of a higher-level

---

[19]Arnold F. Emch, "Control Means Action," *Harvard Business Review*, Vol. 32, No. 4, July-August 1954, p. 93.

[20]This approach to management has received much attention in recent years. See, for example, Peter F. Drucker, *The Practice of Management* (New York: Harper & Row, Publishers, 1954), Chapter 11; Dale D. McConkey, *How to Manage by Results* (New York: American Management Association, 1965); and George S. Odiorne, *Management by Objectives: A System of Managerial Leadership* (New York: Pitman Publishing Corp., 1965).

manager. In each case, however, the stress is upon accomplishments and results.

A system of management by objectives may not sound appreciably different from any other method of management. Its distinction is found in its careful delineation of formal objectives for a specific time period. There is danger, of course, if this type of management is not supplemented by the use of other controls. Ignoring other aspects of performance could lead to an undesirable Machiavellian attitude among managers. There is no need for this management approach to be pushed to such extremes, however.

Figure 30. *Simplified Statement of Results Expected (Accountability) for a Plant Manager*

Within the period specified, the Plant Manager is accountable for achieving the following results. He may delegate to persons under his direction responsibility for certain of these activities, but he may not delegate his accountability for the results expected.

1. *Plant Construction:* Complete the construction and equipping of the approved addition to Plant No. 1 as follows:
   a. Engineering completed by . . . . .
   b. Construction completed by . . . . .
   c. Equipment installed by . . . . .
   d. Plant producing by . . . . .
   e. Approved capital appropriation . . . . .

2. *Production Costs:* Produce product at Plant No. 1 in accordance with the following unit costs:

Production Level (Units)	*Allowable Unit Cost*
1,000	$ .10
2,000	.09
3,000	.08
4,000	.07
5,000	.06

3. *Equipment Installation:* Install the approved XYZ packaging line in Department A and have it operational by . . . . .

4. *Operations Analysis:* Complete comprehensive operations analysis study of Departments A, B, and C and submit findings and recommendations by . . . . .
5. *Employee Relations:* Formulate service award program for recognizing employees with 25 or more years of service and submit recommendations by . . . . .

Source: Dale D. McConkey, *How to Manage by Results* (New York: American Management Association, 1965), p. 126.

If the management-by-results approach is followed throughout a company, specific objectives are established for each position at each level. Figure 30 provides an example of a statement of objectives for a plant manager.

One example of the successful use of this approach is found in the "Goals and Controls" program of the Purex Corporation.[21] This program, inaugurated in fifteen manufacturing plants in 1961, entailed goal setting by individual managers, opportunity for self-control by furnishing control reports to these managers, and periodic performance reviews. In spite of the problems inherent in such a major change, the program resulted in substantial achievement—including, for example, an increase in individual plant productivity.

Use of Strategic Control Points

The effectiveness of control is partially dependent upon the selection of the points at which control is applied. Consider a process or activity, for example, starting at point *X* and proceeding through stages *a*, *b*, and *c* to reach completion at point *Y*.

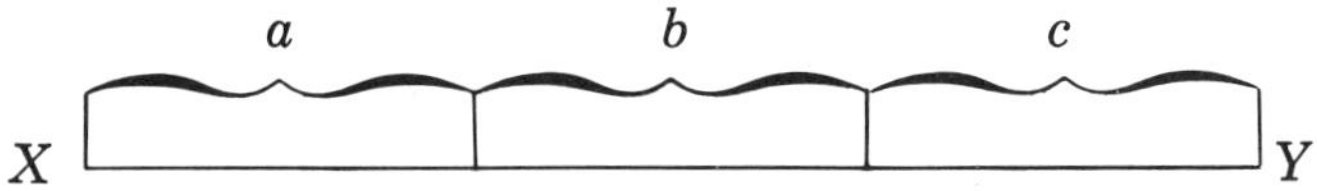

To control the process, checking may be employed at various points. The work may be checked at the end of the process, at the end of each stage, or at various points during each stage. The best combination of control points would keep the process in line with a minimum of cost and control effort.

Management by Exception

Economy of control effort utilizes the principle of *management by exception.* In using this approach, the manager devotes effort to unexpected or out-of-line performance. Some standard is assumed, and significant deviations from that standard constitute the exceptions. If performance conforms to anticipations, time spent in review-

[21]Anthony P. Raia, "A Second Look at Management Goals and Controls." Reprinted from the *California Management Review,* Vol. 8, No. 4, Summer 1966, pp. 49-58. Copyright 1964 by the Regents of the University of California.

ing this fact is largely wasted. Managing by exception permits the manager to isolate nonstandard performance and to concentrate upon it.

Suppose that six sales territories are each expected to produce $50,000 in sales. If one produces $40,000, another $60,000, and four others between $49,000 and $51,000, the manager can focus upon two territories. In the low-volume territory, he will wish to locate the cause and correct it. In the high-volume territory, he will attempt to discover the reason for the exceptional performance, taking steps to continue it and attempting to extend it into other territories.

The management-by-exception principle was recognized by the pioneers in professional management and has been followed by professional managers for many years. Frederick W. Taylor's strong support for this type of management is indicated by the following comments:

> It is not an uncommon sight, though a sad one, to see the manager of a large business fairly swamped at his desk with an ocean of letters and reports, on each of which he thinks that he should put his initial or stamp. He feels that by having this mass of detail pass over his desk he is keeping in close touch with the entire business. The exception principle is directly the reverse of this. Under it the manager should receive only condensed, summarized, and *invariably* comparative reports, covering, however, all of the elements entering into the management, and even these summaries should all be carefully gone over by an assistant before they reach the manager, and have all of the exceptions to the past averages or to the standards pointed out, both the especially good and especially bad exceptions. . . .[22]

In the customary operations and activities of business firms, some variation occurs. There are dozens of reasons for such variation, and much of it must be regarded as normal. In managing by exception, then, the manager must first distinguish that performance which varies sufficiently to constitute an exception. He often relies upon his experience in judgments of this nature. If his experience is extensive and if he is sufficiently alert, he may readily locate unusual situations that deserve his attention.

Statistical quality control provides an example of a more systematic and objective search for exceptional performance. By using the laws of probability, management is able to distinguish between

---

[22]Frederick Winslow Taylor, *Scientific Management* (New York: Harper & Row, Publishers, 1947), p. 126.

typical variation in a process and a process that is definitely "out of control."

Simplification of Control Procedures

It is a mistake to assume that elaborate controls are always best and that simplicity inevitably spells weakness in a control system.

> One of our leading company presidents tells the following story on himself. Fifteen years ago he bought for his company a small independent plant in Los Angeles. The plant had been making a profit of $250,000 a year; and it was purchased on that basis. When going through the plant with the owner — who stayed on as plant manager — the president asked: "How do you determine your pricing?" "That's easy," the former owner answered; "we just quote ten cents per thousand less than your company does." "And how do you control your costs?" was the next question. "That's easy," was the answer; "we know what we pay for raw materials and labor and what production we ought to get for the money." "And how do you control your overhead?" was the final question. "We don't bother about it."
>
> Well, thought the president, we can certainly save a lot of money here by introducing our thorough controls. But a year later the profit of the company was down to $125,000; sales had remained the same and prices had remained the same; but the introduction of complex procedures had eaten up half the profit.[23]

Some forms and procedures are desirable and indeed necessary for proper control. The forms and procedures in control systems have a way of proliferating and becoming elaborate, however. New forms are added and others made more complex. A vast amount of time may be spent in making reports, and mountains of data may be handed over to executives. It is possible that the size and complexity of such systems may burden the executive more than they assist him. Their excessive complexity prevents their serving as a sharp tool of management.

The only correction of undue complexity is through the elimination of unnecessary reports and procedures and streamlining those that are retained. Such pruning is often painful. Control systems become clothed with tradition as time goes on. Periodical review of control procedures and systems is essential, however, in making the control system completely functional.

---

[23]Drucker, *op. cit.,* pp. 134-135.

Use of Feedback in Control

The Feedback of Information to Management

In controlling an operation, management requires a system like the thermostat for measuring performance and reporting the results back to the manager. Performance information of this type that is channeled back to management is known as *feedback*. It is designed to show just what kind of job is being done. It tips off management as to deficiencies or variations from expected results. The data supplied to managers include not only accounting and financial information but also other types pertaining to such factors as product quality, customer service, productivity, and share of market. The control function must locate and report pertinent factual information if the management process is to be effective. It must also evaluate these facts, measuring performance against plans and interpreting the results.

The feedback of information contributes to planning as well as to regulation of an existing process. In contrast to more general planning information, however, the feedback on control is particularly concerned with the past and is detailed in its nature.

Techniques of Getting Feedback

Not all feedback is highly formalized in nature. Personal observation and informal discussions are used extensively in many organizations in keeping managers in touch with organizations under their direction. In fact, informal feedback systems are most appropriate for certain types of control situations. Most first-line supervisors, for example, must rely heavily upon such methods for keeping in touch with their subordinates. Formal, written reports by the subordinates are usually a poor substitute and a waste of time. At any level of any organization, it is likely that some feedback is accomplished by such informal techniques.

Informal feedback is typically inadequate for the organization as a whole, however, and must be supplemented with more formal methods. This is particularly true as organizations grow in size. In the large corporation, extensive reliance must be placed upon formal techniques. Top management comes to live in a world of financial statements, statistical analyses, and other formal reports. But even though the emphasis shifts to formal feedback, no organization dispenses completely with informal methods.

Improving Feedback of Information

In controlling, the administrator is often conscious of gaps and deficiencies in the feedback he gets from his own organization. At best, feedback seems imperfect, and at worst the manager is completely in the dark, not knowing how well the organization is performing. That such weaknesses in feedback are more than a figment of the imagination is indicated by the following examples cited in 1961 by D. Ronald Daniel, who was associated with the well-known management consulting firm of McKinsey & Company, Inc.:

> In late 1960 a large defense contractor became concerned over a major project that was slipping badly. After 15 months costs were running far above the estimate and the job was behind schedule. A top-level executive, assigned as program manager to salvage the project, found he had no way of pinpointing what parts of the system were causing the trouble, why costs were so high, and which subcontractors were not performing.
>
> Recently an American electronics company revamped its organization structure. To compete more aggressively in international markets, management appointed "area managers" with operating responsibility — e.g., in Latin America, Western Europe, and the Far East. After nine months it was apparent that the new plan was not coming up to expectations. On checking with three newly created area managers, the company president heard each say, in effect:
>
> • "In half of the countries in my area the political situation is in flux, and I can't anticipate what's going to happen next."
>
> • "I'm still trying to find out whether our operating costs in Austria are reasonable."
>
> • "I don't know where in South America we're making a profit."
>
> A small but highly successful consumer products company recently followed the lead of its larger competitors by establishing product-manager positions. Although outstanding men were placed in the new jobs, an air of general confusion soon developed, and the product managers began to show signs of frustration. After much study it became apparent that an important cause of the trouble was that no one had determined what kind of information the product managers would need in order to perform their new functions.[24]

---

[24]D. Ronald Daniel, "Management Information Crisis," *Harvard Business Review,* Vol. 39, No. 5, September-October 1961, p. 111.

These concerns were all troubled with defective information feedback systems. Although there may have been enough facts and figures, they were not tailored in such a way as to facilitate control.

Correcting such informational weaknesses requires the design or redesign of feedback systems. Although accounting information and reports may be suitable as they exist, there is no guarantee that adaptation of these is not needed. Traditional methods of presentation often fail to furnish the manager data that are easily digested and entirely pertinent to his control problems. It is necessary to determine first what information is required for control purposes. Procedures and reports must then be developed to provide this type of information.

Moreover, the information system established at one time in the life of an organization may become inadequate as time goes on. The nature of the business changes, and adaptations in the organization occur. This leads to a change in the type of information flow that is most useful. In addition, new techniques of gathering and reporting data are developed — such as electronic data processing — and these permit a type of feedback that was previously impractical.

Summary

In the exercise of his controlling function, a manager regulates the operation of his organization, holding performance in line or taking corrective action where necessary. On the basis of either implicitly or explicitly stated *standards* or objectives, he *evaluates* performance and *takes corrective action* to rectify errors or remedy deficient performance. Managerial control activities comprise an organizational subsystem whose objective is to regulate output in accordance with the requirements of the total organizational system. In view of the many variable characteristics and objectives in any organization, one important choice in designing a control system is selection of appropriate criteria for measurement.

The control process has a tendency to produce certain unwanted *behavioral consequences* in the organization that is being controlled. To some extent, these reflect weaknesses in the control system, but it is difficult to perfect the control techniques sufficiently to avoid them completely. Some of these undesirable reactions are narrowness of viewpoint, short-run expediencies with long-run disadvantages, evasion of controls through falsification of reporting, and reduced morale.

A number of possible variations or changes in control systems are available to managers who wish to improve their effectiveness. Harmful behavioral consequences may be minimized, for example, by careful development of the elements of the control system and its equitable administration. Improvement is also possible in many situations by reducing the extent of control through delegation of authority and avoidance of close supervision. *Management by objectives*, use of *strategic control points*, *management by exception*, and *simplification of control procedures* may also contribute to a workable control system.

Feedback of information about performance to management is an essential part of the control process. Some feedback occurs informally, but much of it must also be accomplished through formal reports and analyses. An examination of information feedback systems in large organizations reveals numerous weaknesses. Correction of such weaknesses involves the careful design and periodic redesign of feedback systems to provide the information that is necessary for management control.

Discussion Questions

1. The function of controlling assumes the existence of some type of *standard*. What kinds of standards are used for the following: (1) quality of product; (2) work pace of a crew of employees; (3) travel expense for company executives; and (4) inventory level?
2. Suppose that a comparison of labor expense with the budgeted figure reveals the expenditure of 10 per cent more than had been budgeted. What corrective action is called for?
3. How is closeness or looseness of control related to decentralization? To effectiveness of supervision?
4. How can controls cause undesirably narrow viewpoints in individual members or departments of an organization?
5. Evaluate the practice of *storming* in Russian factories. Is this a consequence of Communism?
6. Explain the principle of *management by exception.*
7. How is *feedback* of information related to the control function?
8. What weaknesses typically exist in information feedback systems?

9. An office manager commented as follows: "It is my responsibility to keep up with all aspects of every activity and project that are assigned to this office." Evaluate this statement in the light of managerial control theory.

Supplementary Reading

Arrow, Kenneth J., "Control in Large Organizations," *Management Science,* Vol. 10, No. 3, April 1964, pp. 397-408.

Bittel, Lester R., *Management by Exception.* New York: McGraw-Hill Book Company, 1964.

Bonini, Charles P., Robert K. Jaedicke, and Harvey M. Wagner, eds., *Management Controls: New Directions in Basic Research.* New York: McGraw-Hill Book Company, 1964.

Carzo, Rocco, Jr. and John N. Yanouzas, *Formal Organization: A Systems Approach,* Chapter 12. Homewood: Richard D. Irwin, Inc., and The Dorsey Press, 1967.

Gibbons, Charles C., "Management By Exception," *Advanced Management Journal,* Vol. 29, No. 1, January 1964, pp. 12-16.

Howell, Robert A., "A Fresh Look at Management by Objectives," *Business Horizons,* Vol. 10, No. 3, Fall 1967, pp. 51-58.

Johnson, Richard A., Fremont E. Kast, and James E. Rosenzweig, *The Theory and Management of Systems,* Second Edition, Chapter 4. New York: McGraw-Hill Book Company, 1967.

Koontz, Harold and Cyril O'Donnell, *Principles of Management,* Fourth Edition, Chapter 28. New York: McGraw-Hill Book Company, 1968.

Leathers, James O., "Applying Management by Objectives to the Sales Force," *Personnel,* Vol. 44, No. 5, September-October 1967, pp. 45-50.

Livingstone, John Leslie, "Management Controls and Organizational Performance," *Personnel Administration,* Vol. 28, No. 1, January-February 1965, pp. 37-43.

McFarland, Dalton E., *Management Principles and Practices,* Second Edition, Chapter 18. New York: The Macmillan Company, 1964.

Miles, Raymond E. and Roger C. Vergin, "Behavioral Properties of Variance Controls," *California Management Review,* Vol. 8, No. 3, Spring 1966, pp. 57-65.

Newman, William H., *Administrative Action,* Second Edition, Chapters 24 and 26. Englewood Cliffs: Prentice-Hall, Inc., 1963.

Newman, William H., Charles E. Summer, and E. Kirby Warren, *The Process of Management,* Second Edition, Chapters 27 and 29. Englewood Cliffs: Prentice-Hall, Inc., 1967.

Pickle, Hal and Frank Friedlander, "Seven Societal Criteria of Organizational Success," *Personnel Psychology,* Vol. 20, No. 2, Summer 1967, pp. 165-178.

25

Control Through Accounting Techniques

So much accounting is involved in the process of managerial control that a chapter may be appropriately devoted to this specific area. The accounting executive is, in fact, often designated as the *controller* of a firm. In our review of accounting concepts and methods, however, we shall consider them more from the viewpoint of the general manager than from that of the controller. For this reason, it is necessary to neglect some of the important but more specialized aspects of subjects that appear in the accounting literature.

The Role of Accounting in Managerial Control

Financial Information Systems

At any one time, there are numerous facts, both inside and outside a business organization, that are pertinent to its operation. Many of these facts are trivial or meaningless; only a portion of them are significant to the management. Management information systems screen these facts, selecting those that are most significant and providing the flow of information that is necessary for control.[1] The

[1]Management information systems also serve non-control purposes as well. Payroll records, for example, are used to compute wage payments as well as to control labor costs.

feedback flow described in the previous chapter is part of the information system. Information that is collected and transmitted by management information systems is as varied as the organization itself — including, for example, financial information, personnel reports, logistics data (those dealing with the physical flow of goods), and marketing statistics. All business information systems have an underlying financial structure, however, and the discussion in this chapter will deal particularly with these financial aspects of the information system.

In a systems theory of management, the management information system may be visualized as a communication network linking information sources with users or recipients of the information.[2] The elements of the system may be portrayed as follows:

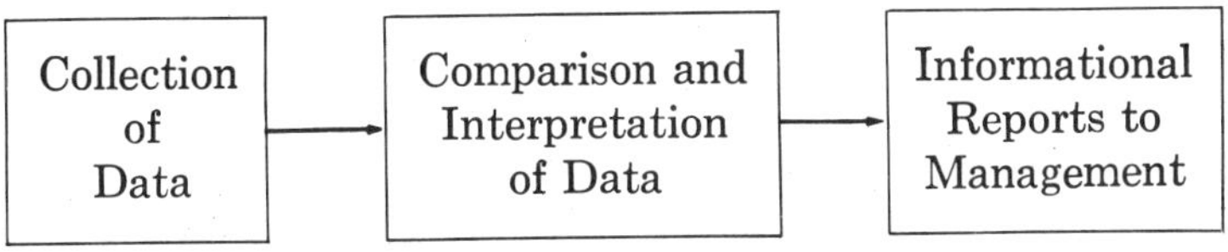

The first step, that of collecting data, may be illustrated by the act of recording wage payments. In the second stage, these payments are evaluated as labor costs and compared with standards or with previous labor costs. Reports to management may then employ the management-by-exception principle in reporting significant discrepancies between actual and expected costs.

Automation of the information flow by use of the electronic computer has revolutionized management information systems. In processing financial information, these more sophisticated systems perform essentially the same function as simple, traditional systems, but they permit a much more rapid and comprehensive review and interpretation of data. In extremely advanced systems, known as *real-time* systems, the computer receives and updates information on a transaction-by-transaction basis. As a bank depositor makes a deposit, for example, the complete accounting transaction is processed, including updating of the depositor's balance. Although the complexities inherent in designing real-time information systems have thus far prevented their general use, there is an obvious trend toward more advanced information systems.

[2]In view of its relationship to the overall organization, the information system might be more accurately labeled the *information subsystem*. However, there is little value in being overly technical on the point. The terminology of *management information systems* and *business information systems*, moreover, is well established.

The effect of developments in information technology is to make possible a control function that is detailed in nature and almost instantaneous in timing. Vast quantities of data can be processed with great speed. Managers can have on their desks information reports giving an analysis of business transactions occurring only a few hours earlier. Greater centralization of control, both organizationally and geographically, becomes possible as systems of this type are developed. (A move toward centralization cannot be considered to be inevitable, however, in view of the numerous other factors involved in decisions concerning organization structure.)

Examining the flow of financial information in the systems context permits the systems analyst to design the overall information network, rather than to devise specific reports as isolated projects. Indeed, information flow may be seen as a planned system. Information sources may be matched with information needs at each level of the organization. One weakness thus far in the use of computers has been the tendency to adapt them to existing systems, with an emphasis on immediate cost savings, rather than to study informational needs and to design the systems in these terms. The resultant system is often "electronic bookkeeping" rather than effective reporting of business information to management.

To be consistent with this view of the management information system, the informational requirements of managers should govern the collection and processing of financial data. Accounting procedures in themselves are merely a means to an end. Financial information that is supplied by the accounting system should be timely and appropriate for the control and other decision-making functions of the manager.

Control Through Profit Analysis

The profit objective is critically important to any privately owned business organization. Profits are essential for survival and are regarded as a major objective by owners and managers. As a control device, the profit figure provides an overall measure of managerial success or failure. Profits, for example, may be too low as measured by some pertinent standard and thus be indicative of unsuccessful management.

To interpret the dollar profit figure, we must relate it to other figures. One customary comparison relates profits to sales. A profit of $100,000 provides a 5 per cent return on sales of $2 million or a 10 per cent return on sales of $1 million. The percentage return for a given year can be compared with the rate of return for earlier years or for other firms in the same industry. In this way, one can evaluate the operating efficiency of the company as it has secured its sales.

Another comparison relates the amount of profit to the size of investment. This is intended to reveal the efficiency and intensity of utilization of facilities and other resources. A profit of $500,000, for example, represents a 10 per cent return on an investment of $5 million or a 20 per cent return on an investment of $2,500,000. As an example of its use, the Du Pont company has placed heavy emphasis upon this concept in controlling the operation of its industrial departments.[3] Once each month, at one of its regular weekly meetings, the executive committee spends some time in the "chart room" reviewing the progress of various departments. The charts focus attention upon this ratio and present information to permit a review of the factors involved in producing it.

The Use of Conventional Statements

One major function of an accounting system is the reporting of pertinent financial information to managers. It may be helpful to begin with a general review of conventional financial statements and their functions. The *balance sheet* reports the company's financial position at some point in time. This requires a presentation of *assets* (the things it owns), *liabilities* (what it owes), and the stockholders' *equity* (net ownership). The balance sheet balances because the owners' equity must be the difference between the total assets and the outstanding debts. The statement makes no attempt to describe what has happened over a period of time. By comparing balance sheets for different dates, of course, one might discover changes that have occurred.

In contrast to the balance sheet, an *income statement* summarizes financial results for some period of operation. It typically begins with a *gross sales* or *revenue* figure for the period and subtracts the *cost of goods sold* in arriving at a *gross profit*. From the gross profit are subtracted the *selling* and *administrative expenses* to discover the *operating profit*. Ordinarily, corporate income tax represents the principal deduction that must be made from the operating profit to determine the *net income* accruing to stockholders.

The income statement is typically supplemented with a statement of *retained earnings*. A primary purpose of the latter statement is to disclose errors made in previous accounting periods that would affect

---

[3]For an explanation of this system, see *Executive Committee Control Charts* (Wilmington: E. I. du Pont de Nemours and Company, 1959).

retained earnings and to report other extraordinary transactions which are not included in the income statement.

Another, less frequently used financial statement is known as the *statement of application of funds* or *statement of changes in working capital.* It is the function of this statement to analyze changes in a firm's working capital from one point of time to another.[4] It is sometimes described as a "where-got, where-gone" statement, showing the sources of funds (such as profits or long-term borrowing) and the applications or uses of those funds (such as purchase of fixed assets). The change in funds is ordinarily different from the net profit for the same period. A company that earned $500,000, for example, might invest $250,000 of this in new facilities, thereby cutting the potential working capital increase in half. Sources of funds include the following:

Net income.
Depreciation and depletion.[5]
Sale of fixed assets.
Sale of stock.
Increase in long-term debt.

Applications of funds include the following:

Net loss.
Expenditures for fixed assets.
Dividends paid to stockholders.
Investments in other companies.
Increase in net working capital.

The statement aids control by showing where the working capital is coming from and where it is being used. It thus indicates what is happening to the current financial position of a company and the reason for any changes.

Limitations of Conventional Statements

To use financial statements with any degree of sophistication requires some appreciation of their limitations. Only the naive man-

---

[4]For detailed explanation, see Hector R. Anton, *Accounting for the Flow of Funds* (Boston: Houghton Mifflin Company, 1962). There are numerous concepts of *funds,* only two of which are noted here.

[5]Although depreciation and depletion do not provide funds directly, they must be added to net income to reflect total funds provided by operations. These expenses, used in computing net income, do not require an outlay of funds.

ager accepts such statements as the simple truth. As a matter of fact, there are many limitations, only a few of which can be noted here. This is not a criticism of the accounting profession, of course, but merely a recognition of the difficulties involved in the analysis of financial data and the fact that accounting involves a combination of science and art.

As one example of these difficulties, the changing value of the dollar presents continuing problems. Assets are typically shown at cost or, in the case of inventory, at the lower of cost or market. But when general price levels change markedly, the worth of assets as shown on the books becomes unrealistic. Charging depreciation on the basis of cost, therefore, may be insufficient to make possible replacement of fully depreciated assets. The accountants utilize the cost basis for a good reason, of course. We would have even less confidence in the figures if the accountant were using his judgment in periodically juggling them to allow for price changes. Knowing that a discrepancy may exist between the cost value and market value, however, cautions against the acceptance of stated values as the truth, the whole truth, and nothing but the truth.

Another related difficulty is associated with the valuation of inventories. Some companies use a FIFO (first-in, first-out) method, while others use a LIFO (last-in, first-out) method. The FIFO method, for example, treats inventory costs as if items purchased first are sold or consumed first. When inventory is purchased at different prices over a period of time, asset values and profits differ according to the method of inventory valuation used. Someone's judgment regarding inventory valuation is involved, therefore, in "scientifically" determining profit results.

Many accounting figures must be approximations. Although a given obligation — a promissory note, for example — may be valued down to the exact penny, such precise calculations are not possible in all phases of the accounting process. As an example, the portion of equipment cost to be charged as an expense in a particular period must be estimated. The useful life cannot be predicted with complete accuracy. A particular machine may last well beyond its expected life or become obsolete earlier than anticipated. Either of these eventualities could cause depreciation estimates to prove inaccurate.

Accounting information, furthermore, supplies only part of the total relevant information for control purposes. Some aspects of business operations are difficult to reduce to a dollar basis for inclusion in financial statements. Suppose, for example, that two managers are being compared on the basis of the profit performance of their respective divisions. The fact that one division suffered the loss of several key executives during the year or that unexpectedly strong competition developed for one division may not be shown on the financial statements.

Accounting information, it should also be noted, supplies facts for control, but it cannot in itself provide such control. Financial statements may reveal a weakness in operation. It is incumbent upon management to act on the basis of this information in correcting the problem.

The practice of including assets on the basis of their cost may lead to misstatement of asset values. For example, patents or goodwill may come to have great value that never appears on the financial statements. However, it is possible for such facts to be noted in a footnote to the statement, thus making the statement more realistic.

The point of this discussion is not to argue against the use of accounting information. Rather, it is to urge a cautious, intelligent use of such data. The manager needs to question the data at hand and their pertinence to the problems that confront him.

Different Concepts and Data for Different Purposes

It is important that the accounting data and concepts employed in any particular situation be pertinent to the problem at hand. The same accurate information might be appropriately used in the analysis of certain problems and inappropriately used in other cases.

To illustrate, suppose that a manufacturer is considering elimination of one of six sales territories. This decision should seemingly hinge on a comparison of costs and revenue in that territory. If revenue exceeded costs in the territory in question, the territory could be regarded as profitable and retained. But how does one determine costs in such a situation? Should one-sixth of the overhead costs, for example, be assigned to this territory in computing its profitability?

Clearly, a decision based on total cost, including a portion of headquarters overhead costs prorated to this territory, might be illogical. What the manager needs in this case is the figure that will show those costs that can be eliminated by dropping the territory. These might be described as *decremental* costs. A long-term lease may bind the company to payment of rent expense that cannot be eliminated even if operations are terminated. The lease payments would be excluded, in such a case, in the computation of decremental costs.

If, on the other hand, the problem is the establishment of a price that will guarantee profitable operation in the long run, a different cost concept may be employed. In this case, it is necessary to include some portion of overhead costs. It is the purpose of the analysis that determines the type of data to be used.

The Concept and System of Internal Control

Objective of Internal Control

Internal control refers to the oganizational plan and the operating methods and procedures employed within a company to safeguard its assets, insure accuracy of accounting data, and encourage compliance with management policy. An arrangement whereby one employee checks on the work of another provides a simple example of such control. Most internal control measures involve some application of the *checks and balances* principle.

A major purpose of internal control is the prevention of errors—intentional or accidental—in the accounting records. Fraud, for example, is made difficult by designing a set of controls to regulate the use of company assets. Unintentional errors are likewise detected by systems that provide for cross checking of records and transactions.

Internal control is frequently defined in such a way as to limit it to control methods for protecting cash and other liquid assets. The control concept that is involved, however, can apply to all aspects of the accounting process. In fact, the principle of internal control may be applied to operations that are unrelated to accounting controls. A production manager, for example, might be required to secure the approval of the personnel manager before dismissing an employee. Such an arrangement, whether wise or unwise, constitutes a type of internal control. Our concern at this point, however, is with those aspects of internal control closely related to the accounting process.

Techniques of Internal Control

The organization structure may be designed in such a way as to facilitate internal control. A clear-cut organization with carefully defined responsibilities constitutes the first step in this direction. Separation of various operating and accounting departments contributes further to the same objective. The purchasing and accounting functions, for example, may be assigned to different departments. Control is achieved by requiring the work of both departments in completing a purchase transaction. With this arrangement, it is difficult for the purchasing department to conceal its errors. A discrepancy would be noted in the records, and an investigation would follow.

A suitable system of records and operating procedures is also essential for internal control. Printed forms provide for proper authorization of transactions and establish a basis for auditing. The procedural steps specify the functions, relationships, and responsibilities of various individuals and departments in completing any particular transaction. In purchasing, for example, procedures are adopted to regulate all steps from initiation of the purchase request to receipt of the materials and payment of the invoice. The basic principle in establishing these routines is that no employee should have control over an entire transaction from beginning to end.

Even good systems require qualified personnel if they are to operate properly. This calls for careful selection, training, and supervision. Only in this way can management be sure the company has employees who will make the system work. No system is so good that it can be fully effective with the wrong type of personnel.

Examples of Internal Control

A few examples will illustrate the practical application of the internal control principle. Consider, for example, control of a sales transaction. In some types of business, it is possible to separate the handling of merchandise and the receipt of cash. A manufacturer may have a shipping department separate from the department receiving payment. Under these conditions, personnel having physical custody of merchandise would find it difficult to sell merchandise and pocket the cash. In a department store, a different type of internal control is required. One technique is to use a cash register, thus permitting the customer to check upon the sales clerk. Another arrangement requires the sales ticket to be prepared by the sales clerk but cash to be received by a cashier.

In controlling purchasing activities, establishment of a purchasing department separate from accounting and operating departments provides for cross checking among these departments. The purchasing agent is inclined to buy on the basis of price and to question purchase requests based upon convenience and tradition. The purchasing agent is controlled, in turn, by the use of purchase authorizations from operating departments. Receiving documents may likewise be necessary before payment is made, and the paper work is completed by the accounting department, separate from production, purchasing, and receiving. Considerable cross checking is involved in such a system.

The nature of cash makes it the number one target for fraud. In controlling cash, it is important to require deposit of all cash in the bank as quickly as possible. This necessitates procedures to avoid loss in the process of receiving payment. Use of cash registers, as noted above, provides one approach. Separating the record keeping of cash receipts and the physical handling of cash is the generally desired practice. Regular deposit of all receipts permits a comparison of bank records and business records. Payment of all bills, other than trivial cash amounts, by check provides a control against misappropriation of cash. In view of the fact that cash requires such close control, the procedures are often more elaborate and detailed than the general measures indicated here.

The Budget as a Control Device

Nature and Importance of Budgeting

As planning becomes formalized in any business organization, budgeting typically becomes a major part of the planning process. But the budget is more than a plan; it is also a device for controlling operations. As originally formulated, the budget is a plan of operation, expressed in financial terms, and prepared to cover some month, quarter, year, or other period of time. During the period to which it applies, management may use it to regulate decision making and to check performance.

Most companies use their fiscal year as the time period for budgeting. It is common practice to prepare the budget during the quarter preceding the start of the fiscal year, with final adoption just prior to the beginning of the new year. Before the beginning of each quarter, the budget for that quarter is often prepared in greater detail. During the year, the budget tends to become outdated because of changing conditions. For this reason, it is common to revise the budget periodically during the budgetary period.

Many of the values of planning are realized through budgeting. The very process of budgeting forces scrutiny of operations and planning at all levels — steps that are beneficial in most instances. The control function also benefits from the budgetary program, because standards of performance are thereby established. If it appears desirable, certain classes of decisions may be required to conform to the budget — for example, by checking purchase orders with the budgeted amount. Or, performance may be compared with the standard — that is, with the budgeted figures — to discover and analyze out-of-control situations. Corrective action is then the final control step in bringing performance back into line. The budget may thus serve as a comprehensive control tool.

Types of Budgets

Budgets are prepared for the various activities of a business organization. The sales budget, which entails a forecast or projection of sales volume for a future period, serves as a starting point. It establishes a standard against which to judge sales performance and provides a basis for formulation of other budgets. Sales budgets are based upon a review of past performance, forecasts of business conditions, analysis of competitive conditions, anticipated changes in advertising outlays, and other such factors. Estimates are often prepared by salesmen and reviewed by sales managers as the first step in formulating a sales budget. These are reviewed by a budget officer or committee and possibly other officials in arriving at a final sales budget.

Other budgets are linked directly to the sales budget. The purchases budget, for example, estimates required buying, taking into account beginning and ending inventory levels. In a manufacturing business, production budgets are likewise required. Operating expense budgets establish standards for the various selling and administrative expenses of the business.

Still other items are involved in budgeting. Cash receipts and expenditures are planned, and capital expenditures may likewise be anticipated in the budgetary program. When the various other budgets are complete, it is possible to draw up a budgeted income statement and balance sheet for the forthcoming period. This provides an overall target for management.

Budgets may be *static* in nature — that is, based upon one particular volume level. In cases in which the sales or production volume is unpredictable, however, management sometimes employs a *flexible* (or *variable*) budget. The flexible budget provides for a range of volume levels by creating a series of budgets applicable to the different levels. When sales or production volume becomes known, the appropriate budget can be selected for expense control purposes. When volume fluctuates, such budgeting enables management to control individual production expenses more intelligently. It thus serves to sharpen the budget as a control device.

Formulation and Administration of the Budget

It is generally considered sound budgetary practice to get budget preparation into the hands of line management, even down to the lowest levels of supervision. There are several reasons for attempting to do this. For one, the support of managers for the budgetary program is dependent upon their understanding and acceptance of it as being realistic. They must consider it as reasonable if the budget is to have a good chance for success. If managers have a hand in formulating a budget, it is reasoned, there is less chance it will be viewed as something forced upon them. Furthermore, most managers are in the position of knowing more about their operations than anyone else. Their knowledge must be tapped if budgeting is to be fully realistic.

As with other types of participative management, much depends upon the organizational context in which it is used. An autocratic type of administration might be expected to experience difficulty in securing genuine participation in budgeting.[6] Most companies go through the motions of participation or at least give lip service to this concept. The extent to which they really accomplish participation in budget preparation, however, may be a different matter. One study of the human problems involved in budgeting included the following analysis of participation in the process:[7]

> The typical controller's insistence on others' participation sounded good to us when we first heard it in our interviews. But after a few minutes of discussion it began to look as if the word "participation" had a rather strange meaning for the controller. One thing in particular happened in *every* interview which led us to believe that we were not thinking of the same thing. After the controller had told us that he insisted on participation, he would then continue by describing his difficulty in getting the supervisors to speak freely. For example:
>
> > "We bring them in, we tell them that we want their frank opinion, but most of them just sit there and nod their heads. We know they're not coming out with exactly how they feel. I guess budgets scare them; some of them don't have too much education. . . . Then we request the line supervisor to sign the new budget, so he can't tell us he didn't accept it. We've found a signature helps an awful lot. If anything goes wrong, they can't come to us, as they often do, and complain. We just show

---

[6]See Selwyn Becker and David Green, Jr., "Budgeting and Employee Behavior," *The Journal of Business,* Vol. 35, No. 4, October 1962, pp. 392-402.

[7]Chris Argyris, "Human Problems with Budgets," *Harvard Business Review,* Vol. 31, No. 1, January-February 1953, p. 108.

> them their signature and remind them they were shown exactly what the budget was made up of. . . . "

> Such statements seem to indicate that only "pseudo-participation" is desired by the controller. True participation means that the people can be spontaneous and free in their discussion. Participation, in the real sense of the word, also involves a group decision which leads the group to accept or reject something new. Of course, organizations need to have their supervisors accept the new goals, not reject them; however, if the supervisors do not really accept the new changes but only say they do, then trouble is inevitable.

One might think that the practice of allowing subordinate managers a voice in establishing their own budgets would lead to distortion of budgetary standards. There is some danger in this direction, of course, but there is also danger in failing to give the affected managers some voice in the matter. Also, it is the function of higher levels of management to check their subordinates by reviewing budgetary proposals originating at lower levels. Furthermore, subordinate managers may be entirely capable of thinking in terms of company objectives.

Periodic analyses and reports of performance are required in completing the process of budgetary control. These reports show the performance of a unit in comparison with its budgeted performance. To be most effective, results must be reported in sufficient detail to enable the manager to discover the cause of any difficulties. In a department store, for example, a given department might have a budgeted labor expense of $2,400 for the quarter. The report would show the actual labor expense, highlighting any unusual variance.

Using the exception principle, management concentrates upon significant exceptions from the budgeted figures. Failure to meet a budgeted standard does not always indicate inefficiency in management, however. External conditions sometimes change. An unfavorable variance does call for analysis to determine its cause and to devise corrective action as required.

Other Accounting Concepts and Techniques

Responsibility Accounting

The concept of responsibility accounting is concerned with matching the accounting function directly with the responsibilities of the various organizational components.[8] This requires, as a beginning step, the establishment of a clear-cut organization structure that identifies the particular responsibilities of each manager. Accounting records and reports are then adapted to the different areas of responsibility. In this way, each manager can see the accounting analysis pertaining to his specific responsibilities. If the accounting system were to lump together results of two separate departments, neither department would know the precise significance of the reported results.

Budgets for individual departments normally include only those items subject to control by the department. In reporting costs, the emphasis is upon those costs over which a manager may exert control. Costs are reported to a particular supervisor only if he has some possibility of controlling those costs. Overhead costs beyond his control are not considered a part of his responsibility, and accounting reports concerning the department exclude costs of this nature or clearly label them as such. Higher organizational levels may be able to control certain of these costs, however, and they are accordingly assigned to management at those levels.

The importance of this concept to the control function is immediately apparent. Each manager is confronted with a more realistic analysis of his operations. By excluding those items beyond his control, the focus is upon the truly controllable items. From the standpoint of individual motivation, this is superior to a system that is fuzzy in its analysis. It also provides higher management with a sounder basis for appraisal and correction.

Cost Accounting Systems

As business organizations grow in size and complexity, managers can no longer control costs by merely "keeping an eye" on operations. A system must be devised to provide information and assist in control of costs. Maintaining records of manufacturing costs and other operational costs on an overall basis is a part of any accounting system. To improve control, however, it is desirable to maintain these records in such a way as to reveal the cost of producing particular products and operating particular departments. This more detailed analysis of costs is a function of the *cost accounting system.*

---

[8]For a discussion of business usage, see "Keeping Closer Tabs on Costs," *Business Week,* No. 1684, December 9, 1961, pp. 80-86; for a discussion of the theory, see Thomas R. Prince, *Information Systems for Management Planning and Control* (Homewood: Richard D. Irwin, Inc., 1966), Chapter 4.

This system constitutes an extension or refinement of general accounting and attempts to answer such questions as "How much did it cost to produce the products sold last month?" or "How much did it cost to produce the items now in inventory?" Superficially, it may appear that these are simple, straightforward questions requiring no elaborate system for their determination. As a matter of fact, cost analysis is quite complicated, requiring large amounts of clerical effort and the use of much managerial judgment.

Cost accounting systems now constitute a major element in managerial control of business organizations. At one time, these systems were concerned primarily with factory costs and used for profit determination and pricing. Although these are still important areas of cost control, the field has been broadened considerably. Directly or indirectly, most of the applications of cost accounting are concerned with operational control of the business.

Cost accounting supplies information necessary in establishing budgets. Only as data are available concerning historical costs can one proceed to project these costs into the future. Cost control, through the budget or otherwise, is also dependent upon cost accounting. In the case of budgeted items, the cost accounting system collects data on actual costs and makes the comparison with budgeted costs. Cost reduction is also approached on the basis of cost information derived through the cost accounting system.

Another use of cost accounting data is in income determination. In calculating profit for a period, it is necessary to compute the total costs associated with doing business. In the case of a manufacturing business, this requires a division of total production costs between items still in inventory and those which have been sold. Cost accounting thus facilitates control through its contribution to the formulation of accounting statements. Still other applications of cost accounting could be cited, but these are sufficient to demonstrate its close relationship to the managerial function of control.

Standard Costs

Cost accounting systems sometimes utilize what are known as *standard costs*. These are particularly important in their contribution to the control function. The standard cost differs from a historical cost in that it is determined prior to the production process and represents what is considered the proper or appropriate cost. Suppose a manufacturing department has a standard cost of eight cents for producing a ball-point pen. This amount serves as a target cost for the department and includes provision for material, labor, and overhead costs.

Although standard costs may be used in budgeting, a budgetary system is not essential for their use. From a control standpoint, the standard cost provides a basis for analysis of actual costs. Discrepancies or variances between standard and realized costs call attention to possible inefficiencies. Using the principle of management by exception, managers can investigate costs that appear to be out of control.

Direct Costing

Direct costing, a subject of controversy in accounting circles, applies only the *variable* production costs, such as labor and materials costs, to the product being manufactured.[9] *Fixed* factory overhead costs, in contrast to these variable costs, are not assigned to the product. In view of this distinction, it might also be called *variable costing.* The traditional method of costing is known as *conventional* or *absorption costing.* Although there are varied opinions about the desirability of direct costing, most accountants acknowledge some value in the general approach that emphasizes differences in cost behavior between fixed and variable costs.

In using direct costing, the total fixed factory overhead costs are written off in the period in which they occur. This is true regardless of the level of production for the period. Inventory items are valued only on the basis of the variable costs incurred in their production. Proponents of direct costing point out that this procedure is useful in eliminating income distortion created by producing for inventory rather than for sales. The following figure illustrates the nature of a direct costing report:

Direct Costing

Sales		$20,000
Variable Cost of Sales		12,000
Variable Gross Margin		$ 8,000
Less Variable Selling and Administrative Expenses		1,000
Operating Contribution Margin		$ 7,000
Less Period Costs		
Fixed manufacturing costs	$3,000	
Fixed selling and administrative expenses	1,000	
		4,000
Net Profit		$ 3,000

[9]A discussion of contemporary business use of this concept appears in "The Controversy in Costing," *Dun's Review and Modern Industry,* Vol. 80, No. 2, August 1962, pp. 36-38 ff.

The significant contribution of direct costing, as can be seen in this report, is the highlighting of differences between variable and fixed costs and the effect of volume changes upon these costs. It is the variable costs that are more directly susceptible to control by direct action of management in the short run. The fixed costs are affected more by volume of operation during the period. In controlling overall business operations, a manager may occasionally decide to take business that will provide some additional *contribution margin,* even though it will not cover its entire share of fixed costs. This can increase aggregate profits if there are no adverse effects on other operations.

It is not important to attempt a definitive answer to this question of direct costing versus conventional costing. The important element in this discussion is the distinction between types of costs and their significance for business decisions. To the extent that direct costing can better distinguish these costs for the benefit of management, it is a useful device.

Ratio Analysis

The fact that a boy named Bill threw a shotput fifty feet gives us an inadequate basis for judging his performance. We need to know something about Bill's age and whether he is throwing a twelve- or sixteen-pound shot. In addition, we need to know something about the performance of other individuals in a similar bracket. In other words, some basis for comparison is necessary.

In the same way, knowing that a given firm earned $20,000 is not very informative. It is important to know something about the size of the firm, the sales volume, and the investment. In addition, it is desirable to know something about the performance of similar firms. To aid in the interpretation of accounting data, managers resort to analysis through the use of *ratios.*

One common type of analysis relates individual expense items to the total sales figure. Selling expense, for example, may be calculated to be 14 per cent of sales. This figure, in turn, may be compared with the selling expense percentages of previous years and of other firms. Balance sheet items may similarly be related to the total asset figure. Other financial ratios may also be used to aid management by testing *liquidity* and *profitability*. The first of these objectives (testing liquidity) is illustrated by the *current ratio* and the *acid-test ratio.*

$$\text{Current ratio} = \frac{\text{Current assets}}{\text{Current liabilities}} = \frac{\$100{,}000}{\$\ 50{,}000} = 2 \text{ to } 1$$

$$\text{Acid-test ratio} = \frac{\text{Cash} + \text{Receivables} + \text{Marketable securities}}{\text{Current liabilities}}$$

$$= \frac{\$50{,}000}{\$50{,}000} = 1 \text{ to } 1$$

The use of profitability calculations was illustrated earlier in the chapter. A large number of both types of ratios may be computed. The type of analysis determines the ratios that are most helpful in a particular case.

Effective use of these ratios necessitates comparisons with other ratios. Various difficulties exist in making such comparisons, particularly those with other companies. Differences in the nature of the businesses and their accounting practices often introduce distortions into such comparisons. Nevertheless, such evaluations may be helpful in acquiring general impressions concerning the business and its performance.

Human Problems in Accounting Control

Pressure Through Budgeting

Any control device has a tendency to create problems in human relations. The importance attached to budgeting in most companies and the precise nature of this control make budgeting unusually vulnerable to human problems. Because of the budget's function in controlling the operations of divisions, departments, and units, it introduces the possibility of conflict among different layers of management. The human problems connected with budgeting, therefore, are concentrated largely at the managerial level. For this reason, such human relations problems must be viewed as unusually serious.

An excellent study of human problems in budgeting, reported in 1953, analyzed the effects of manufacturing budgets upon first-line supervisors.[10] It was a common assumption, recognized by these researchers, that a budget can be used as a pressure device for increasing efficiency. First-line supervisors realized that their ability in meeting their budget was of extreme importance in showing a good

[10]Argyris, *op. cit.*, pp. 97-110.

performance record. Higher-level officials often saw the pressure imposed by the budget as a value of the budgetary system.

> I think there is a definite need for more pressure. People have to be needled a bit. Man is inherently lazy, and if we could only increase the pressure, I think the budget system would be more effective.[11]

The passage of time has not eliminated the sense of pressure in budgetary systems. A more recent study of supervisory attitudes toward budgets revealed that one out of five first-line supervisors felt that budgets are held as a "club" over the head of the supervisor.[12]

Some pressure is to be expected in a responsible administrative position. A question may be raised, however, concerning the effects of building up a larger and larger head of pressure. It is not surprising to discover that strong pressure may lead to tension, suspicion, and hostility. The following explanation reveals the possible results of such pressure upon first-line supervisors:

> 1. *Interdepartmental strife* — Some foremen seek release from pressure by continuously trying to blame others for the troubles that exist. In the three plants observed, much time was spent by certain factory supervisors in trying to lay the blame for errors and problems on their fellow supervisors. As one foreman put it, "They are trying to throw the cat in each other's backyard."
>
> 2. *Staff versus factory strife* — Foremen also try to diminish pressure by blaming the budget people, production-control people, and salesmen for their problems.
>
> 3. *"Internalizing" pressure* — Many supervisors who do not complain about the pressure have in reality "internalized" it and, in a sense, made it a part of themselves. Such damming up of pressure can affect supervisors in at least two different ways:
>
> (a) Supervisor A is quiet, relatively nonemotional, seldom expresses his negative feelings to anyone, but at the same time he works excessively. He can be found at his desk long after the others have gone home. He often draws the comment, "That guy works himself to death."
>
> (b) Supervisor B is nervous, always running around "checking up" on all his employees. He usually talks fast, gives one the

[11] *Ibid.*, p. 98.

[12] Burnard H. Sord and Glenn A. Welsch, *Managerial Planning and Control as Viewed by Lower Levels of Supervision* (Austin: Bureau of Business Research, The University of Texas, 1964), p. 94.

impression that he is "selling" himself and his job when interviewed. He is forever picking up the phone, barking commands, and requesting prompt action.[13]

Organizational Conflicts

Another problem in human relations is created by the conflict between budget people and operating people. A budget director appears efficient if he can find fault with operating departments—their failures provide the opportunity for his successes. In displaying his own achievements, moreover, he must draw operating weaknesses to the attention of his own superiors. The seeds of conflict are apparent in such a relationship.

Correcting Human Problems

No doubt other aspects of the human relations problem might also be cited. It seems clear, however, that there are serious human problems involved in budgeting. Recognition of the existence of the problem should not lead to the conclusion that nothing can be done about it. The reason for stressing the human problems is to point out the lack of realism in viewing budget problems as problems involving only facts and figures.

Eliminating or minimizing human difficulties depends upon the management practices that are followed. In general, the democratic style of leadership discussed in Chapter 21 represents a constructive approach for dealing with many of these problems.

Summary

The management information system provides the flow of financial and other data necessary for managerial control. In keeping with the systems view of organization, the information network should be designed in terms of management's informational needs. Introduction of the electronic computer has greatly increased the capacity, speed, and potential usefulness of data-processing systems.

The profits realized on business operations provide a general performance measure useful in overall control. The basic conventional statements utilized in managerial control are the *balance sheet*,

[13]Argyris, *op. cit.*, p. 101.

income statement, *statement of retained earnings*, and *statement of application of funds*. Various limitations are associated with the use of these statements, and it is important that managerial personnel be aware of these limitations in order to use the statements intelligently. It is also important to recognize that different accounting data and concepts may be used for different purposes.

Internal control refers to the organization plan and methods utilized within a company to safeguard its assets, insure accuracy of accounting data, and encourage compliance with policy. In particular, it is concerned with the avoidance of either intentional or unintentional errors. Internal control requires an organization structure that clearly fixes responsibilities and a system of records and operating procedures that provides a correcting influence.

One of the major accounting tools for control purposes in business organizations is the *budget*. Budgets are prepared not only for sales but also for various types of expense and inventory items. In the preparation of the budget, an attempt is ordinarily made to secure the participation of the affected line management.

A number of other accounting concepts and techniques are of importance to the manager in his control function. Through *responsibility accounting*, an attempt is made to match the accounting process with the individual manager's responsibility. The *cost accounting* system, often utilizing *standard costs*, constitutes a major tool of accounting control in most business organizations. One of the more controversial accounting concepts is that of *direct costing*, which emphasizes the distinction between *variable* and *fixed* costs in the production process. The analysis of accounting data for control purposes is facilitated by the use of *ratio analysis*.

Various human problems have been encountered in the process of accounting control. There is a tendency for the budget, for example, to be used as a pressure device upon supervisors, with possible undesirable effects in terms of supervisory behavior. Budgets may also create conflict between financial and operating personnel and among operating departments.

Discussion Questions

1. Identify several limitations of conventional financial statements and explain the relevance of each limitation to managerial decision making.

2. What is the basic concept involved in *internal control*? What techniques does it use?

3. Explain the difference between a *static budget* and a *flexible* or *variable budget*. What is the significance of this distinction in controlling?

4. What difficulties may be involved in using participative management in the formulation of budgets?

5. Explain the concept of *responsibility accounting*. What changes may be required in a conventional accounting system to make this possible?

6. What basic difference exists between *variable (direct) costing* and *conventional (absorption) costing*?

7. Discuss the possible values in computing the *current ratio* and *acid-test ratio*.

8. What is wrong with the application of pressure through budgeting? Isn't pressure normal for an efficient organization?

Supplementary Reading

Anthony, Robert N., *Planning and Control Systems: A Framework for Analysis*. Boston: Graduate School of Business Administration, Harvard University, 1965.

Argyris, Chris, "Human Problems with Budgets," *Harvard Business Review*, Vol. 31, No. 1, January-February 1953, pp. 97-110.

Bierman, Harold, Jr., *Financial and Managerial Accounting: An Introduction*, Part II. New York: The Macmillan Company, 1963.

Dearden, John and F. Warren McFarlan, *Management Information Systems: Text and Cases*. Homewood: Richard D. Irwin, Inc., 1966.

Hughes, Charles L., "Why Budgets Go Wrong," *Personnel*, Vol. 42, No. 3, May-June 1965, pp. 19-26.

Likert, Rensis, *The Human Organization: Its Management and Value*, Chapter 6. New York: McGraw-Hill Book Company, 1967.

Miller, Vergil V., "Human Behavior and Budget Controls," *Advanced Management-Office Executive*, Vol. 1, No. 12, December 1962, pp. 30-34.

Moore, Francis E. and Howard F. Stettler, *Accounting Systems for Management Control*, Section 1. Homewood: Richard D. Irwin, Inc., 1963.

Newman, William H., Charles E. Summer, and E. Kirby Warren, *The Process of Management,* Second Edition, Chapter 28. Englewood Cliffs: Prentice-Hall, Inc., 1967.

Prince, Thomas R., *Information Systems for Management Planning and Control.* Homewood: Richard D. Irwin, Inc., 1966.

Savoie, Leonard M., "Accounting Improvement: How Fast, How Far?" *Harvard Business Review,* Vol. 41, No. 4, July-August 1963, pp. 144-160.

Seiler, Robert E., *Elementary Accounting: Theory, Technique, and Applications,* Part IV. Columbus: Charles E. Merrill Publishing Co., 1963.

Sord, Burnard H. and Glenn A. Welsch, *Managerial Planning and Control as Viewed by Lower Levels of Supervision.* Austin: Bureau of Business Research, The University of Texas, 1964.

26

Special Areas of Control

Specialized control concepts and techniques have been developed in various areas of manufacturing and selling. This chapter examines four of the more important specialized areas of control.

Quality Control

Meaning and Purpose of Quality Control

To many people, the term *quality* carries a connotation of *high* quality. They think of Cadillacs, Stetson hats, and sterling silver as symbolic of quality. To the manufacturer, however, quality refers to the particular quality standards he is attempting to achieve. In the eyes of customers, they are not necessarily high standards. The Chevrolet Division does not attempt to produce Cadillacs.

Product quality is directly related to the basic objectives of the firm and rests, therefore, upon fundamental policy decisions of management. A numbe- of factors are involved in these basic decisions. One manufacturer, for example, may elect to sell to a segment of the market desiring superior quality, while another may decide to sell to the mass market which accepts a lower quality product. Such decisions entail evaluation of market potential at various levels as well as an evaluation of production capacity to produce at these levels. Production cost is also pertinent. Higher quality typically entails higher production cost. Quality objectives emerge in this way from the general strategy and purposes of the enterprise.

The manufacturer's concept of quality may involve standards for a number of different characteristics such as physical dimensions, chemical composition, weight, color, strength, freedom from scratches, and so on. In the light of market and cost conditions, the manufacturer chooses a specific quality level, not necessarily the best. But, having chosen it, he attempts to meet that standard consistently.

Although inspection is an integral part of quality control, it is not fully synonymous with control of quality. Inspection provides feedback to management by measuring the product to determine the extent to which it conforms to established standards. This is one part of control activity, but control also includes those steps necessary in regulating and correcting the manufacturing process to meet the stipulated standards.

Traditional Quality Control Methods

Some type of inspection is required in the quality control process. This inspection may be limited to the finished product and occur at the end of the production process, or it may occur at different stages during the process. A key question, in fact, concerns the number of times the product should be inspected. The ideal is to minimize inspection costs without losing control of the product. Other questions relating to inspection concern the number of items to be inspected—100 per cent or some fraction of the items—and the location of the inspection—floor versus central inspection.

In one sense, inspection activities constitute wasted effort. They are necessary, but they add nothing to the product. Furthermore, inspection is not perfect and seldom catches all defects. Even 100 per cent inspection fails to produce perfect results. Inspectors are human and fail to exercise consistently good judgment.

Inspection may be accomplished by operators who check their own work or by full-time inspectors. If inspectors are used, the results must be reported to line managers or operators in order to permit corrective action. One traditional technique for this purpose consists of scrap reports that inform management of defective items discovered by inspectors. Incentive wage plans, which often militate against quality control, may also be adapted to incorporate bonus payments that encourage high-quality workmanship.

Statistical Quality Control

During recent decades, management has improved the control of quality by the introduction of statistical quality control. This applies the theory of probability to the process of inspection and quality control. Even without statistical quality control, inspection is often conducted on the basis of systematic sampling. Rather than using 100 per cent inspection, only a part of a lot is singled out for inspection. The assumption is that the quality of the entire lot will be indicated by the inspected items. Lacking statistical methodology, however, there is little knowledge of the degree of risk involved. The sample may be insufficient in size or unrepresentative in nature and thus fail to present a true picture. On the other hand, the sample may be unnecessarily large and thus involve unnecessary and wasteful inspection effort.

By the use of statistical quality control methods, management is able to make a choice as to the degree of risk that can be tolerated—that is, the proportion of below-standard items that can be accepted. The extent of risk can be specified by the statistician, and the risk (of accepting defective items) can be reduced with the expenditure of additional time and money. Statistical quality control tells the manager how likely it is that bad products will slip by with a given inspection plan. He can then weigh this problem against the increased cost required to reduce that risk.

Statistical quality control also makes it possible for management to maintain control of quality more effectively during the production process. Quality is checked periodically during the processing period. By analyzing the trend in these readings, it is possible to discover an out-of-control condition before it becomes serious. In other words, an analysis may indicate the process to be out of control even though the quality still falls within tolerance limits. A consecutive series of readings, for example, may show a quality variable to be close to the upper tolerance limit and thus outside the customary range of variation. A statistician knows this does not happen by chance, so an investigation must then be made to locate the cause of the difficulty.

Most large companies and some small companies currently use statistical quality control methods.

> The fact is that SQC methods are widely used in American industry. Small manufacturers, who predominate in numbers, do not use them nearly so much as medium-sized and large manufacturing concerns, but even small industry characteristi-

> cally uses some SQC methods, while large-scale producers, in some cases, use them almost exclusively, to an extent that they confuse the terms "quality control" and "statistical quality control."[1]

It seems likely that most quality control is still on a nonstatistical basis. To the extent that it can be profitably adopted, however, the statistical method offers improvement in the quality control process.

Production Control

Objectives and Values of Production Control

A busy manufacturing department appears to be a beehive of activity. Hundreds or thousands of employees are performing specialized functions, many of them requiring unique skills. Almost miraculously, it appears, their individual efforts blend together to complete products as scheduled. The brain or nervous system behind this bustle of activity is known as *production control.*

Production control basically involves a coordinating function. The various manufacturing activities must be regulated to achieve production in accordance with customer demands. In addition, the manufacturing operations must occur in an orderly and efficient manner to achieve economy of operation. The objectives of production control, then, are both efficiency in operation and customer satisfaction.

Production control is concerned with the orderly flow of materials and work through the production process. At just the right time, the production process begins. Products are shifted from department to department at a rate or at a time that avoids delay in work schedules and at the same time prevents bottlenecks. Subassemblies must be completed on a schedule permitting their efficient combination into finished products. Work must move through the manufacturing process on a schedule that achieves promised delivery dates. Management must keep in touch with progress on individual orders and take corrective action if unusual delays occur. Materials, tooling, and labor must be available at the right place at the right time. Idleness of equipment and of manpower must be avoided.

It is easy to see that production control may become a most complex process. In a large or involved manufacturing process, entire

---

[1]Reprinted by permission from H. N. Broom, *Production Management* (Homewood, Ill.: Richard D. Irwin, Inc., 1967), p. 160.

departments are created to maintain surveillance over production activities. This production control department typically reports to a production executive. Although smaller plants may not establish production control departments, the same control functions must be exercised. In any organization, much of the production control function is of necessity performed by first-line supervisors.

Production control has been discussed here in the context of the manufacturing plant. It is in this connection that it has been most fully developed. The idea need not be limited to manufacturing, however. We may think of activity control as applicable to office operations, selling, and so on. Many of the concepts of production control can be applied directly to nonmanufacturing activities.

Functions of Production Control

It is possible to group production control activities around a number of basic functions. Although different writers on production management differ in the functions that they recognize, the following are common to many such analyses:

1. Routing.
2. Scheduling.
3. Dispatching.
4. Followup.

Routing refers to the sequence of operations to be performed and the path to be taken by a manufacturing order. It may also include an analysis of materials required and a determination of items to be purchased. In some types of manufacturing, there is a choice in the order and location of work performance. The product may be processed through Department *A*, then to *B*, then to *C*; or it may begin with *A* and then be routed to *C*, then to *B*. Differences in the ability and experience of operators may also call for variations in routing. In assembly-line manufacturing, the routing function occurs in the original design of the assembly line.

In *scheduling*, the time of performance is determined. This includes the time for beginning work on a given order or project and may also be extended to include the time that individual operations will be performed. Schedulers must observe completion dates and work backward sufficiently to find the appropriate time for beginning operations. The objective in scheduling is to meet delivery dates and to accomplish necessary work without inefficiently overloading production equipment.

Dispatching refers to the order-giving function. The various departments and operators must be notified as to when they should begin work on particular items. Authorization is also necessary for the issuance of tools and materials, the movement of materials, and so on.

Followup includes those procedures designed to keep track of production operations. As a first step, it is necessary to keep tab on purchase orders and material requisitions. The production orders must also be checked from time to time to see whether they are falling behind schedule. If delays are discovered, action may be required to expedite the order to bring it back up to schedule.

Variation in Types of Manufacturing

Production control activities vary in form and complexity in different types of manufacturing. It is desirable to note the extreme differences that exist and the implications that these have for production control. In the *mass production* of automobiles and electrical appliances, for example, hundreds or thousands of parts must be assembled to produce the finished product. In addition to a final assembly line, there are production lines for assembly of components. Raw materials and parts enter the production process at many different stages of manufacturing.

In contrast to this type of manufacturing, there are types of large-scale production in which all or most raw materials or parts are introduced at the beginning of the manufacturing process. Processing steps are then taken to condition the product in some way. Operation of a bakery illustrates this arrangement, with the initial mixing of ingredients being followed by baking and packaging. Tire and glass manufacturing also have many of these characteristics.

Another variety of manufacturing is known as *job-order production*. Machinery and locomotives, for example, may be produced on this basis. A local machine shop and printing plant also provide examples. Rather than producing a large number of similar products, a job-order shop produces one or a few products of any one type, often to customer specifications.

These differences in production methods have implications for the production control function. In general, the difficulty of production control increases with the number of component parts. Also, introduction of parts or ingredients at many different stages places even more pressure on production control. In job-order production, control is complicated because of the impossibility of standardizing the production process.

Assembly-line production, as noted above, accomplishes routing by the original layout of the line. Job-order production, in contrast, must consider routing separately for each order.

Methods and Tools of Production Control

Schematic drawings and graphs have been used extensively in production planning and control. One of the oldest and most widely used devices of this type is the *Gantt Chart.* This tool was originated by one of the pioneers in scientific management and is used in scheduling and controlling the work of particular machines or production centers. There are numerous variations of the Gantt Chart in current use. One example is presented in Figure 31.

Figure 31. *Gantt Progress Chart*

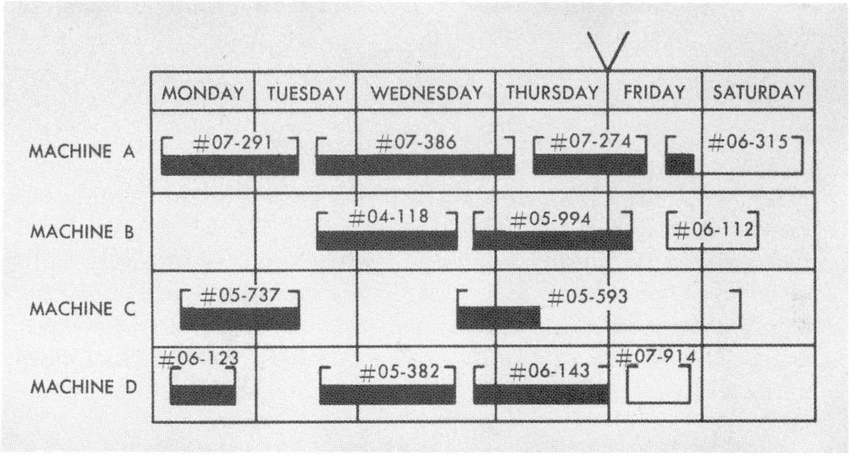

Source: Robert H. Bock and William K. Holstein, *Production Planning and Control: Text and Readings* (Columbus: Charles E. Merrill Publishing Co., 1963), p. 8.

In this chart, the light lines and the numbers above them show jobs that are scheduled. The brackets indicate the scheduled beginning and end of each job. The heavy lines show the proportions of jobs completed, and the "V" at the top of the chart indicates the present date. In examining this chart, it can be seen that work on Machine *A* is running well ahead of schedule while work on Machine *C* has fallen behind.

One limitation of the Gantt Chart for production planning is its concentration upon the single dimension of time. An important, neglected factor, however, is the relative cost of producing on one machine rather than another. The method of *linear programming* has been utilized in recent years to assign production to machines or production centers on a least-cost basis.[2] This method takes into account the relative efficiencies of the various production units — differences in maintenance, operation time, and so on.

Data processing equipment is also being applied to the clerical aspects of production control. As orders are received from customers, for example, the computer may be checked to determine availability of materials and facilities to fill the orders by the desired dates. Inventory records and prior commitment of facilities can be quickly checked in this way. Necessary requisitions and shop orders may then be printed automatically. Information as to work completed may also be entered in the computer, which can then prepare production reports. The equipment for this purpose is expensive, of course, and thus is practical only for large organizations with highly centralized production control.

Control With Network Techniques

Two analytical tools of production planning and control originated in the late 1950's are known as PERT (for Program Evaluation Review Technique) and CPM (for Critical Path Method). Both techniques are basically similar and are designed to facilitate management of complex projects.[3] PERT was first introduced in 1958 as a system for monitoring development of the Polaris Ballistic Missile, a primary weapon of United States nuclear-powered submarines, and is widely credited with saving years of time in making the Polaris operational. The Navy Special Projects Office collaborated with Lockheed Aircraft Corporation and Booz, Allen and Hamilton, a prominent management consulting firm, in developing the PERT approach. The Polaris program was large in size and extremely complex in nature. Many business and governmental organizations were involved, and the work was widely spread geographically. There was

---

[2]For an excellent summary of modern analytical methods, see Robert H. Bock and William K. Holstein, *Production Planning and Control: Text and Readings* (Columbus: Charles E. Merrill Publishing Co., 1963), pp. 9-12.

[3]Although there are some differences in PERT and CPM, the present discussion will stress features that are common to both. Numerous variations of these techniques have been developed and carry such labels as LESS, PACT, SCANS, and so on.

also much uncertainty concerning performance times. The Critical Path Method was originated by the Du Pont Company at about the same time in order to manage major construction projects more efficiently. In both cases, therefore, the tool was devised to help management control large, complicated projects.

The interrelationships among the various parts of major projects required a type of control that would regulate the system as a whole. In fact, both PERT and CPM utilize network analysis, which, as the name indicates, deals explicitly with the network of relationships among the various phases of the total program. The network shows what activities must await completion of other tasks and what activities can be performed concurrently with other tasks. PERT and CPM thus represent an application of the systems concept to managerial control. The network technique, which is illustrated in Figure 32, is used to discover what is called the *critical path.* The number of days required for each step of the illustrated production process is shown by the numbers above the arrows. It appears that the body

Figure 32. *Arrow Diagram*

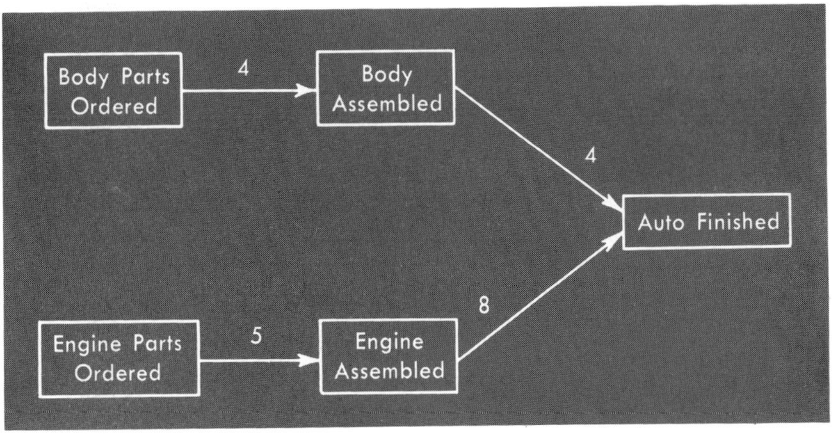

Source: **Robert H. Bock and William K. Holstein,** ***Production Planning and Control: Text and Readings*** **(Columbus: Charles E. Merrill Publishing Co., 1963), p. 11.**

can be assembled in a total of eight days, whereas the engine requires a total of thirteen days.

The bottom path (that of the engine) is therefore the critical path. Any delay here results in a delay in final production of the automobiles.

> With a knowledge of the critical path, planners can be made aware of possible delays and can expedite progress by using resources from slack paths. In our example, manpower could be transferred from body assembly to engine assembly. Engine assembly might be cut to six days, and body assembly increased to six days. In this way, two days could be cut from the final date for the finished automobile. The revised top path would be 4 + 6 or ten days. The revised bottom path, still the critical path, would be 5 + 6 or 11 days.
>
> As a control device, a PERT program focuses attention on the most important areas for management action — the steps in the critical path. Small delays on slack or non-critical paths usually are not significant enough to affect the final completion date. Delays on the critical path, however, require immediate attention and effective follow-up if the target completion date is to be met.[4]

Network techniques are particularly well adapted to control of major, complex, one-time projects. In addition to the applications cited above, they have been used in the following ways:

New product introduction
Retooling program
Revising an accounting system
Timing and placing a new stock issue
Installing a computer system
Installing a new organization structure

These techniques are concerned with time scheduling, but they are also useful in analyzing costs and improving efficiency in usage of resources. For example, the analysis may suggest the desirability of expediting critical jobs at higher cost in order to reduce total cost. Although relatively simple applications of PERT and CPM can be accomplished manually, an electronic computer is essential for network analysis of major projects. The computer may be used, for example, to locate the longest or critical path and to determine slack time on non-critical tasks.

Inventory Control

Need for Inventory Control

In many organizations, the inventory is the largest current asset. For this and other reasons, inventory control is essential for business

[4] Bock and Holstein, *op. cit.*, pp. 11-12.

success. From a cost standpoint, control of inventory quantity is necessary. If a substantial investment in inventory is required, the expense of maintaining it is considerable. These costs are of several types. The cost of capital invested in excessive or unnecessary inventory represents a waste. Interest costs on such capital may be avoided, or the money may be invested more profitably elsewhere by the use of effective inventory control. Other costs arise from increased warehouse space requirements, insurance, and taxes. In addition, inventory items may be subject to deterioration or obsolescence as well as to loss through price changes. Limitation of the inventory to the smallest practical size serves to minimize these losses.

From the standpoint of operating efficiency, it is also essential to have effective inventory control. If a production tie-up is caused by an out-of-stock condition, the resulting costs may be staggering. In a retail store, customer dissatisfaction occurs if the shelf is bare when the customer wishes to buy.

The objective of inventory control, then, is an adequate but not excessive inventory. In a marketing institution, this refers to merchandise on the shelf or in the warehouse. In a manufacturing plant, it refers to the inventory of raw materials, supplies, goods in process, and finished goods.

Inventory Turnover Calculations

One technique used by management in controlling inventory is the calculation of an *inventory turnover rate.* This computation compares inventory cost with cost of sales (or with sales) for a given period. For example, assume that the current income statement of a retail department having an inventory of $50,000 (at cost) reports the cost of goods sold for the year as $350,000. In this case, the inventory turnover rate is seven times. It means that the department sold, during the year, seven times as much inventory as it had on its shelf at one time. In a similar manner, the raw materials of a manufacturing plant may be compared with the materials put into production during the year.

By comparing the turnover rate with industry standards or with an earlier turnover rate, some idea can be gained of the effectiveness of inventory control. If the rate is low, the apparent indication is that the inventory is unnecessarily large relative to usage or sales. Of course, the difficulty may be with either sales or inventory or both. The turnover rate also constitutes an indicator of efficiency of management in the exercise of the control function. A manager whose inventory turnover rate is consistently low reveals himself to be an ineffective manager of this asset. Some caution is necessary in interpreting data of this type. It is possible, for example, to achieve a higher rate of turnover by passing up quantity discounts and purchasing only small amounts at any one time.

Determining Minimum and Maximum Inventory Size

Effective control of regularly stocked inventory items requires an accurate determination of minimum and maximum inventory levels. A number of factors must enter into decisions of this type. If the product is subject to substantial loss in value through obsolescence or physical deterioration, for example, the inventory must be held near the minimum level. If a policy of speculative buying is followed, a maximum size may be attained that is higher than would otherwise be justified. Of course, there are strong arguments against the practice of speculative buying.

In the absence of compelling considerations based upon price fluctuations, obsolescence, or deterioration, the manager has some margin of freedom in determining appropriate inventory levels. Assuming a standardized item, the minimum amount to be carried may be considered a *safety stock* or *minimum reserve stock*. Normally, this level cannot safely be zero. This would be possible, of course, if stock were always replenished by the time the last item was removed. This is not always possible, however, and the safety stock is provided as a "cushion." Lack of precision in estimates and uncertainties in procurement and deliveries explain the need for the safety stock. It allows for such contingencies as unanticipated delays in shipment and unexpected withdrawals from stock.

In calculating the size of the minimum reserve stock, it is clear that some judgment is necessary concerning the seriousness of stockouts. If stockouts are extremely dangerous — say a part whose shortage would shut down a production line — the minimum reserve stock must be higher than is otherwise necessary. The pattern of withdrawals also has a bearing on the proper level. A relatively large stock is required in the case of items in which withdrawals occur irregularly and possibly in large quantities.

Given a specified minimum stock level, the maximum is determined by the amount procured at one time. Buying in large quantities increases both the maximum and average inventory size. To determine the most economical level, the manager must calculate an amount known as the *economic order quantity*. This is the purchase quantity that minimizes total costs by properly balancing costs associated with large orders (such as cost of money tied up in inventory and warehouse space) and costs associated with small orders (such as loss of quantity discounts, costs of stockouts, and overhead clerical cost in placing purchase orders). Today many companies use complex mathematical techniques — some employing electronic computers—in deciding how much inventory to carry.

Receiving and Physical Control of Inventory

As a first step in maintaining physical control of a product, a receiving procedure is called for. Items coming into inventory from outside the business normally arrive by truck or rail. Personnel in the receiving room open the shipment, examine the material, and prepare receiving reports which are compared with ordering documents. This step assures both the proper quality, by detecting broken or defective items, and the proper quantity.

While awaiting usage, inventory items are typically kept within enclosed stockrooms. This practice and the record keeping associated with it provide physical protection and also assure availability of inventory items as needed. Restricting access to the stockroom tends to eliminate pilfering. Withdrawals are made on the basis of duly authorized requisitions.

Some types of items may be controlled adequately by keeping them in open stock, possibly near the point of usage. This reduces the amount of paper work and clerical cost. Some parts used in manufacturing, for example, may be stored at a point where they enter the manufacturing process. The extent to which this practice is possible obviously depends upon the nature of the inventory item. Close control is most important for large-investment items and for those subject to pilferage.

Some inventory items are controlled by records known as a *perpetual inventory system.* Such a system requires the entry on the records of every receipt and withdrawal of items from stock. At any time, it is possible to check the inventory level by referring to the appropriate stock card. Another method, that of the *physical inventory,* requires a periodic count of items on hand. Because inventory records customarily involve some errors, even the perpetual inventory records must be checked from time to time by taking a physical inventory. According to the principle of internal control, inventory taking and inventory records should be placed under the jurisdiction of the accounting department.

Control of Sales Operations

Controlling Sales Volume

Sales results may appear beyond control, and it is true that competitive forces and market conditions do exert great influence upon sales volume. In any competitive situation, however, the marketing program of a particular company exerts some influence upon the volume of sales. Control of selling operations begins with an evaluation of sales volume. How much sales volume did we get, or are we getting, and how does this measure up to expectations? If sales results are below standard, corrective action in terms of selling effort or expenditures may be required.

An evaluation of selling results calls for standards of performance. These standards reveal to salesmen and to sales management the results they are expected to achieve. The sales quota, on either a unit or dollar basis, prescribes a target for a given period.

Many types of volume objectives are possible. Geographically, for example, the sales quota may be broken down by sales territories. In addition, sales objectives may be established for each product or product line. Each salesman may also be assigned a goal by which his personal performance is judged. In a retail store, for example, a salesman may be expected to produce a given dollar volume each week or month. This may or may not be related to the compensation plan.

Sales volume objectives may be developed with varying degrees of sophistication. Someone may "guesstimate" the amount, or complex analytical tools may be employed. In any event, determination of the objective ordinarily entails considerable subjective judgment. Any sales objective which is soundly conceived must take into consideration market potential, the amount of sales promotion and advertising effort, past sales performance, estimates by salesmen, business forecasts, and other factors of this nature.

If a budget is used, the sales objective is incorporated in the budget. In any event, the basic control effort occurs as realized sales volume is compared with sales projections. Areas or lines in which sales volume appears low are subjected to scrutiny in an effort to locate the source of difficulty.

Controlling Sales Effort and Expense

Control of the activities of sales personnel usually goes beyond the use of sales quotas. Supervision of sales work itself involves the exercise of the control function. The sales manager trains his subordinates and observes their performance. The sales manager, for example, makes sales calls with a traveling salesman. As the manager detects opportunities for improvement, he guides the subordinate accordingly.

Direct supervisory contacts are often supplemented by various control devices. In the hope of achieving thorough coverage of sales territory, for example, standards are established for sales effort. The average number of customer calls that can reasonably be made in a day or week is determined. Calling schedules may then be set up, stipulating calls to be made on particular days and possibly at particular hours. The schedules are often arranged in such a way as to concentrate upon a given geographical territory.

Reports may be required from the salesmen to provide detailed day-by-day accounts of their activities. In these reports, salesmen record calls made, individuals contacted, extent of "missionary" work, and other information of this nature.

Expense standards may also be established for traveling salesmen. A variety of methods is used for this purpose. Most of these require the salesmen to submit reports classifying their expenses in detail. Some companies go so far as to set standards for various types of expenditures.

Expense standards are incorporated into the budget, as discussed in the preceding chapter. The selling expense budget includes not only sales salary expense estimates but also all other marketing expense items. Expenses associated with all marketing programs necessarily appear in the budget, which provides a basis for control by marketing and other executives.

Marketing Cost Analysis

Analysis and control of marketing costs are generally conceded to be more difficult than analysis and control of manufacturing costs. These difficulties are caused by the influence of external conditions and by difficulties in measuring costs of this type. Selling standards may be more difficult to achieve than manufacturing standards, for example, because of the effect of business trends and the action of competitors. It is also easier to set standards for most types of manufacturing effort than it is for sales activities. At present, the techniques of cost accounting are less developed in distribution cost accounting than they are in manufacturing. It seems likely, however, that substantial progress will continue to be made in this field.

Some selling activities are much more susceptible to standardization and control than are others. Indeed, some sales activity has many of the same characteristics of work in the manufacturing field. Routine order filling activities such as packing and shipping are illustrative. Work of this nature is being increasingly subjected to accounting control.

Allocation of costs to sales territories or product lines provides a particularly troublesome accounting problem. The allocation of overhead costs is especially difficult. The problem is minimized by treating as many costs as possible as direct charges. The discussion of direct costing in the preceding chapter is also pertinent to this problem. By making a sharp distinction between fixed and variable costs, the cost study can provide a superior basis for decision making with regard to particular territories or products.

Order-getting costs — that is, the costs of sales force salaries and advertising — are partially determined by the budgeted sales program. These costs cannot be cut to the minimum without reducing sales volume. It is possible, however, for such expenditures to be made carefully or wastefully, and this makes it desirable to control them as much as possible. Through proper cost analysis, costs may be collected in a fashion that permits their careful examination. Expenses may be tabulated salesman by salesman, for example, thus giving the individual salesman some incentive for self-control.

Summary

Quality refers to the standards applicable to various characteristics of a product; such standards do not necessarily specify high quality. It is the purpose of *quality control* to assure consistent performance in terms of the quality standards that are accepted. This requires a comparison of products with quality standards and corrective action when quality deviates from standards. During recent decades, management has improved the function of quality control by the adoption of various *statistical techniques*.

Through *production control*, a manufacturer attempts to meet delivery schedules while maximizing operational efficiency. Of the various functions of production control, those of *routing*, *scheduling*, *dispatching*, and *followup* are recognized by most writers. The production control process is most difficult in job-order manufacturing and in types of manufacturing involving complex products with many parts. Modern analytical methods used in production control include *linear programming* and *network techniques* such as *PERT* and *CPM*.

Inventory control is designed to minimize operational costs and to assure the presence of inventory items as required for sale or production use. The *inventory turnover rate* provides a measure of the efficiency of inventory management. In controlling inventory levels, managerial decisions concerning *minimum and maximum inventory size* are necessary. The minimum inventory size is determined by the size of the *minimum reserve stock*, and the maximum inventory size involves a calculation of the *economic purchase quantity*.

Control of selling entails control of sales volume and also control of sales effort and expense. Efforts to control sales volume lead to the establishment of sales estimates or standards and a comparison of sales results with those standards. The field of *distribution cost analysis*, while lagging behind manufacturing cost analysis, is of growing importance in the control of marketing programs. Some selling activities possess many of the characteristics of manufacturing operations and, for this reason, are relatively easy to control. The nature of most selling activities, however, makes the development of cost standards and the analysis of expenditures extremely difficult.

Discussion Questions

1. Distinguish between inspection and quality control.
2. Explain the concept of *statistical quality control.*
3. Why does 100 per cent inspection fail to produce perfect results?
4. What specifically do production managers wish to accomplish through *production control*?
5. Distinguish between the *routing*, *scheduling*, and *dispatching* functions of production control.
6. In what types of manufacturing is the control of production most difficult? Explain the reasons for differences in difficulty.
7. What is the purpose of a *Gantt Chart*? What is a limitation in its use?
8. What is the *critical path* in *PERT*? What is its significance?
9. In computing the rate of *inventory turnover*, should one use sales figures or cost-of-sales figures? Why?
10. How can sales volume be controlled? Isn't this subject to consumer preferences and therefore beyond managerial control?

Supplementary Reading

Avots, Ivars, "The Management Side of *Pert*," *California Management Review,* Vol. 4, No. 2, Winter 1962, pp. 16-27.

Bock, Robert H. and William K. Holstein, *Production Planning and Control: Text and Readings,* Parts I and II. Columbus: Charles E. Merrill Publishing Co., 1963.

Broom, H. N., *Production Management,* Revised Edition, Chapters 4 and 18-21. Homewood: Richard D. Irwin, Inc., 1967.

Buck, Vernon E., "Too MUCH Control, Too LITTLE Quality," *Business Horizons,* Vol. 8, No. 3, Fall 1965, pp. 34-44.

Buffa, Elwood S., *Modern Production Management,* Second Edition, Chapter 19. New York: John Wiley & Sons, Inc., 1965.

Dooley, Arch R., "Interpretations of PERT," *Harvard Business Review,* Vol. 42, No. 2, March-April 1964, pp. 160-172.

Dusenbury, Warren, "CPM for New Production Introductions," *Harvard Business Review,* Vol. 45, No. 4, July-August 1967, pp. 124-139.

Evarts, Harry F., *Introduction to PERT.* Boston: Allyn & Bacon, Inc., 1964.

Holstein, William K., "Production Planning and Control Integrated," *Harvard Business Review,* Vol. 46, No. 3, May-June 1968, pp. 121-140.

Levy, Ferdinand L., Gerald L. Thompson, and Jerome D. Wiest, "The ABCs of the Critical Path Method," *Harvard Business Review,* Vol. 41, No. 5, September-October 1963, pp. 98-108.

Miller, Robert W., *Schedule, Cost and Profit Control with PERT.* New York: McGraw-Hill Book Company, 1963.

Moore, Francis E. and Howard F. Stettler, *Accounting Systems for Management Control,* Chapters 20 and 21. Homewood: Richard D. Irwin, Inc., 1963.

Morgan, James I., "Questions for Solving the Inventory Problem," *Harvard Business Review,* Vol. 41, No. 4, July-August 1963, pp. 95-110.

Schoderbek, Peter P., "A Study of the Applications of PERT," *Academy of Management Journal,* Vol. 8, No. 3, September 1965, pp. 199-210.

Schoderbek, Peter P. and Lester A. Digman, "Third Generation, PERT/LOB," *Harvard Business Review,* Vol. 45, No. 5, September-October 1967, pp. 100-110.

Professional Management—Present and Future

27

Professional Management in a Changing World

Throughout this book, we have observed the manager in various roles. We have thought of him as a planner, organizer, leader, and controller — each in a variety of contexts. It is desirable now to blend these ideas into a composite picture of the manager and his role in a changing environment.

The Changing World of Business

Business and Environmental Change

The world in which business firms operate is anything but static. Environmental changes, moreover, affect both firms and managers. As a result, present-day business concerns will quickly become different types of organizations, and the role and responsibilities of management will likewise change.

The impact of change upon business is apparent to the casual observer. New firms are launched, many of them to die within a few months or years. Products emerge and disappear. Management methods are drastically altered. Youthful corporations climb into the list of the elite "top one hundred," while many of yesterday's leaders drop from sight.

One need not be a prophet to discern a number of environmental trends significant to business. The future is at least dimly evident in developments that are now apparent. As an open system, the firm must be concerned with its relationship with the outside world. Adaptation to changes in the external environment is vital, therefore, to the life and management of any firm. Ansoff has stressed the crucial importance of the following external forces:[1]

1. Product dynamics.
2. Market dynamics.
3. Changing role of the firm in society.

The significance of these factors will be discussed in the following section. Recognition of change in these areas, while essential for competent business leadership, is insufficient in itself. Management must both recognize and learn to cope with environmental change. This chapter views the manager in his changing role as an adapter to change and as a change seeker.

Product and Market Dynamics

Product dynamics and *market dynamics* are closely related forces. The former is concerned with changes in the products sold by a firm and the latter with changes in the marketplace in which those products are sold.

A moment's reflection makes apparent the tremendous product changes in the American economy. Products that were unknown a few generations ago — transistor radios, jet aircraft, ballpoint pens, Polaroid cameras, computers, Xerox copy machines, and many others — are important in today's economy. Established products, moreover, are constantly being adapted and modified.

In recent years, the rate of product change has rapidly accelerated. New products have always posed a competitive threat to existing products. The automobile made the buggy obsolete, and the electric shaver took part of the safety razor market. In recent years, the rate of new product introduction has been greatly increased and the profitable life of the average product drastically shortened. A key factor in the accelerating rate of change is the current emphasis upon research and development. Between 1946 and 1961, industry's investment in fixed facilities increased by 135 per cent, while research and development expenditures grew by 735 per cent.[2] In 1967, industry spokesmen estimated that 17 per cent of their 1970 sales volume would come from research then in progress or yet to be

[1]H. Igor Ansoff, "The Firm of the Future," *Harvard Business Review,* Vol. 43, No. 5, September-October 1965, pp. 162-178.

[2]*Ibid.,* p. 163.

started.[3] It appears likely that the trend toward increased product research will continue and that this will affect the market environment in which business firms operate.

The growth of international business and the rise of the multinational firm, as noted in Chapter 3, illustrate the *market dynamics* that affect managerial decision making. Foreign products compete in the domestic market, and the market areas of many firms have become worldwide in scope. American markets also change as population shifts, industrial changes occur, and levels of income rise.

An Example of Successful Adaptation: The Coca-Cola Company

To understand the practical nature of product and market dynamics, let us examine the history of a firm that has adapted to changes in both areas. The Coca-Cola Company is an American business firm with an impressive history of growth and success.[4] Coca-Cola is known throughout the world, and Communists look upon the Coke bottle as a symbol of U. S. imperialism. In the United States, Coca-Cola supplies an estimated 40 per cent of the $3.2 billion soft drink market. Its attainment of this market position and its worldwide popularity are a tribute to its ability to react successfully to dynamic changes in its environment.

Even for a company like Coca-Cola, the rate of product and market change is accelerating. For nearly half a century, the Coca-Cola Company had the cola drink market almost to itself. When it relaxed in the 1950's, however, it lost ground to rival Pepsi-Cola. One feature of Pepsi's attack was the sale of drinks in bottles of different sizes. The independent Coca-Cola bottlers were reluctant to change from the six and one-half ounce bottle that had been so successful in the past even though the Coca-Cola Company had designed ten-ounce and twelve-ounce bottles. Eventually, however, the bottlers added larger bottles, and the company began to regain lost ground. Sales increased from $309 million in 1958 to $342 million in 1959, $502 million in 1960, $536 million in 1961, and $568 million in 1962.

Another major product change involved the introduction of dietary soft drinks. In the early 1960's, the Royal Crown Cola Company jumped ahead of Coca-Cola (and also Pepsi-Cola) by introducing Diet-Rite Cola and capturing 50 per cent of the low-calorie beverage market. Coca-Cola later enjoyed spectacular success in this field by

---

[3]"R & D Looms Big in Fiscal Budgets," *Business Week,* No. 1967, May 13, 1967, p. 72.

[4]For a brief review of the history of Coca-Cola, see "The Coca-Cola Co.," *Forbes,* Vol. 100, No. 3, August 1, 1967, p. 26-34.

introducing "Fresca," a highly carbonated, low-calorie citrus drink. Following its introduction in 1966, this drink became the fastest growing drink in the United States.

Another important product trend for the Coca-Cola Company was the increasing use of disposable containers — bottles and cans. Once again, independent bottlers franchised by the Coca-Cola Company were reluctant to change to disposable containers. Because of the apparent trend in this direction, however, the Coca-Cola Company provided strong incentives for dealers to promote this type of product. Continued success in the changing world of soft drinks will require vigilance in meeting challenges of this type.

Market dynamics in the case of the Coca-Cola Company is illustrated by the drastic changes in international marketing. The company created an international division in 1926, but substantial growth in international sales did not come until World War II. During the war, Coca-Cola products were sold to Allied servicemen around the world. The company attempted to see that no American G.I., wherever he might be, would ever lack for a five-cent Coke. And the company stopped at nothing to make this promise good. For example, a dismantled Coca-Cola plant was flown over the hump from India piece by piece and reassembled in China. By the end of the war, Coca-Cola had sixty-four bottling plants in war theaters around the world. When hostilities ended, these plants simply went into production for the civilian market. Natives had learned to drink Coca-Cola through contacts with servicemen, so that the company had both production facilities and a ready market. The company was thus in excellent position to capitalize upon the expanding international market for American products.

An Example of Difficulty in Adaptation: CF & I Steel Corporation

Another example, this time of a firm victimized by product and market dynamics, is provided by CF & I Steel Corporation — known until recently as Colorado Fuel & Iron Corporation.[5] Of the nation's sixteen major steel companies, this firm for years experienced the slowest rate of growth and, with one exception, the lowest rate of profitability. In 1966, its sales and pre-tax earnings were even lower than its sales and earnings of a decade earlier.

---

[5]The following resume of the recent history of the CF & I Steel Corporation is based upon "A New Spur for Steel's 'Also-Ran,' " *Business Week,* No. 1967, May 13, 1967, pp. 188-192.

This dismal record reflected the company's unsuccessful adaptation to the forces of product and market dynamics. Two of its major problem areas were product mix and plant location. The company's main products — rails, wire, bar, pipe, and tubing — were the least profitable, most vulnerable to import competition, and least promising in growth potential of all steel products. After 1929, demand for steel rails and accessories, which then made up almost 70 per cent of sales, collapsed.

As to location, the company's principal plant at Pueblo, Colorado, was far from major steel consuming centers. In addition, the center of steel making shifted westward from Pittsburgh to Chicago, thereby bringing new and stiffer competition into the natural market area of this company.

The company's efforts to adjust to product and market changes were less than spectacularly successful. For example, construction of a $20 million tube mill to produce oil field drilling goods was followed by a subsequent recession in domestic drilling operations which wrecked the anticipated market for the mill's output. As another example, the company, over a seven-year period, stepped heavily into the steel wire products market through the purchase of eight steel mills. This provided a new trap for the company in that growing imports of foreign wire mill products quickly depressed the steel wire market.

As of 1967, the president expressed the following plans for placing the corporation on a more profitable basis:

> We aim to develop an expanded enterprise (1) which will be diversified so that all of its activities will not be concentrated solely in producing basic steel; (2) whose products within the steel industry will, in addition to run-of-the-mill carbon steel, extend into some of the more modern alloys and alloy products; (3) whose participation in international markets will not be limited to the mere export of products manufactured domestically; and (4) whose mining divisions will perform a profit-making function as well as performing the supply function of feeding coal, iron ore, and limestone to the steel mills.[6]

The logic of this strategy and the ability of the company to implement it successfully will be evident in the company's record during the next few years. An improvement is clearly necessary. One local observer made the following comments regarding the firm's management:

---

[6] *Ibid.*, p. 190.

They have never been too imaginative, and that is why they are what they are. The power moves in the old days led to a situation where they haven't attracted the kind of young, imaginative blood the aerospace companies have.[7]

It may be that the combination of past experience and new management will bring about a more successful adjustment to the product and market forces of the steel industry.

The Firm and Society

A third major external force is found in the firm's relationship to society. (The firm's proper role in this area was discussed in Chapters 3 and 4.) There is no question as to the rising expectations of society concerning business objectives. Rightly or wrongly, there is a widespread feeling that business firms should demonstrate responsibility and leadership in areas of social concern. It appears, furthermore, that this is a growing expectation on the part of our citizenry.

Many types of social concerns involve the business community. For example, industry must help solve problems of water and air pollution. Business is also considered responsible for supporting education and for contributing to the nation's goals of equality of opportunity. Unemployment and poor housing in city ghettos are likewise seen as areas of business concern. Traditionally, business firms have been expected to contribute, without profiteering, to the nation's military and defense efforts. Change in the nature of social problems calls for change in the relationship of business to society. Consequently, awareness and understanding of social change have become essential for business leadership.

An example of active business involvement in areas of social concern is found in attempts by U. S. Gypsum, National Gypsum, Westinghouse, Pittsburgh Plate Glass, and others to improve slum housing. Rehabilitation of slum housing is expected to earn profits, but it also contributes to the nation's objective of improving the blighted areas of our cities. As another example, companies such as International Telephone and Telegraph and I.B.M. have operated Job Corps training centers for the United States government. These programs involve an application of industrial skill and experience in solving the problem of inadequately trained personnel.

Another major area of social concern is the corporation's responsibilities in equal employment opportunity. If problems of employment for minority groups are to be solved, the solution must

---

[7] *Ibid.*, p. 192.

eventually include enlightened employment practices by those corporations who are the nation's major employers. To some extent, the rising expectations concerning business responsibility in this area have been spelled out in law. Some companies are going further than the law requires, however, in aggressively seeking to provide opportunities for minority groups. This has sometimes necessitated changes in traditional recruitment sources, selection methods, and training programs. Although solutions to problems of this type are not simple, it is clear that business responsibility in such areas is a matter of growing concern. Moreover, if the trend of recent years is an accurate indicator of the future, a firm's involvement in social problems can be expected to increase.

The Changing Organization

Increasing Importance of Behavioral Sciences

Organizations have always been staffed with people. Thus, they have always been social or behavioral systems. However, behavioral factors were only dimly understood in past generations. In recent years, the comprehension of the social dimensions of business organizations has been rapidly increasing.

Behavioral aspects of organizations are not only better understood, but they are also increasingly important in the functioning of the enterprise. As physiological and security needs are satisfied, higher-level social and egoistic needs become dominant. The standard of living continues to rise at a rapid rate. As a result, members of organizations now place greater value upon human relationships and the social environment of business.

The success of a manager of the future, therefore, will depend upon his ability as a manager of behavioral systems. He must possess an ability to work effectively with people. He must develop skills of communication in human relations. In short, a greater premium is being placed upon the social skills of management.

Changing Methods and Technology

Another significant area of change is that of technology and methods. Developments in production technology, for example, are constantly changing the nature of the manufacturing process. Development of the sophisticated tools of management science further illustrates the drastic changes in methods of decision making.

Entire industries are being reshaped by the dynamic forces of technological change. The field of communications is typical of those areas experiencing rapid growth and revolutionary change. The combined sales and service revenues of telephone, telegraph, broadcasting, and communications product industries have shown a phenomenal growth rate of some 10 per cent or more annually over the last twenty years. Future prospects appear even brighter. This growth involves not only a simple expansion of existing facilities and services but also many new developments such as communications satellites, laser beam transmission systems, and computer networks.

The direction that future change will take is not clear, but it is certain that major changes will occur. The banking industry, for example, faces changes so profound that they will directly affect all individuals and business firms. The possibility of "moneyless" banking and a "checkless and cashless" society is widely discussed, and it seems likely that steps in this direction will continue. Widespread use of computers will make possible an electronic payment and bookkeeping network that will minimize the use of cash and checks. Among the changes predicted for the next two decades are the following:[8]

> • A single identification card will replace cash in all but a few minor transactions.
>
> • Credit will become more readily available, changing many buying and borrowing habits. Also, hidden interest rates, now masquerading as such things as cash discounts, will emerge, and people will be encouraged to play rates much as housewives play supermarket sales.
>
> • Banking's "float" will disappear. Common tactics to get free short-term loans, such as overdrawing checking accounts for two or three days, will vanish. Similarly, corporate cash managers will have to devise new investment strategies for their surpluses when the "time value" of all money will have its price tag and idle funds become an anachronism.
>
> • Economists will devise new indicators based on daily statistics from computers. And the Federal Reserve Board will find more specific and effective methods to steer the nation's credit.
>
> • Service fees will provide the banks with an increasingly larger share of their profits, including fees for services yet undreamed of. . . .

---

[8]"Money Goes Electronic in the 1970's," *Business Week,* No. 2002, January 13, 1968, pp. 54-56.

- Banks will move into collision courses with other industries. Battles have already been joined with the insurance industry, accountants, investment bankers, mutual funds, loan companies, retailers, and service bureaus. . . .
- Public and political outcries will arise over whether computerized credit ratings and data storage encroach on individual rights.
- New concepts of banking regulation will evolve.

The magnitude of technological change and its enormous importance in management thinking are clearly evident from this one example.

Growth of the Systems View of Organization

Throughout this book, attention has been given to the systems concept of organization and management. The view of an organization as a group of isolated parts has been replaced with the concept of an integrated whole that is more than the sum of the parts. Within the organizational system, there are centrifugal forces — those that tend to cause the system to disintegrate. There are also centripetal forces that tend to bind the component parts into a functioning organism. One category of factors that can serve either to build or to destroy the system as a functioning mechanism is that of managerial policy and decision making. Effective management in the present age demands an awareness of the systems nature of organization. This requires a breadth of comprehension and understanding not always possessed by managers in the past.

The manager who grasps the principle of the systems concept will organize in terms of this concept. This will undoubtedly lead to continued deemphasis of traditional functional specialization. Increasingly, the manager must organize in terms of smoothly meshing units of the organization, and he must recognize social groupings that are involved in the system. Perhaps the most general way in which the systems approach will affect planning is by the process of integrated planning itself. The logical hierarchy of plans will be understood, and the importance of linking the plans of one unit with those of another will become evident. As relationships are determined with greater precision, tools of operations research can be applied and the electronic computer utilized more extensively in decision making.

Control in terms of the entire system is likewise possible. This differs from a control process that regulates one part at a time. Control of one part may leave another part out of control. Control action in one area may call for adjustments in other areas. The network concept of control is pertinent at this point.

> Managerial control will be improved as a result of the application of the systems concept. . . . Under the systems concept there will be improvements in the application of automatic data processing, management science, and other techniques of control and measurement. Not only will management know, through the feedback system, that the planned objective is not being met, it also will be able to determine what forces are causing deviation from the plan. Great improvement in the control function also will occur because of the advancements in communication networks and systems of information flow.[9]

The probable increasing emphasis upon systems management in the future is discernible in recent trends. Numerous concepts and tools of a systems nature have been devised and utilized. Managerial approaches employed in project management and network analysis, for example, illustrate this trend. The increasing use of automation and automated data-processing systems are likewise examples of this approach. The adoption of operations research tools is similarly consistent with the systems concept. It seems likely that these trends will continue and that management will necessarily need to adopt a philosophy and approach compatible with the systems view.

> I suppose that managers will be called on, as automation proceeds, for more of what might be described as "systems thinking." They will need, to work effectively, to understand their organizations as large and complex dynamic systems involving various sorts of man-machine and machine-machine interactions.[10]

The Managerial Role in Meeting Change

Increasing the Level of Managerial Competence

The increasing complexity and responsibilities of modern management call for greater skill and sophistication on the part of man-

---

[9]Richard A. Johnson, Fremont E. Kast, and James E. Rosenzweig, *The Theory and Management of Systems,* Second Edition (New York: McGraw-Hill Book Company, 1967), pp. 411-412.

[10]Herbert A. Simon, "The Corporation: Will It Be Managed By Machines?" *Management and Corporations 1985,* eds. Melvin Anshen and George Leland Bach (New York: McGraw-Hill Book Company, 1960), p. 52.

agerial personnel. The need for greater technical knowledge, conceptual ability, awareness of social issues, and familiarity with the methods of modern professional management necessitates higher staffing standards. To some extent, this requirement is reflected in the need for a broader educational preparation on the part of today's executives. Education and development are also coming to be viewed as a continuing process, receiving a strong emphasis throughout the working life of the manager.

Professional managers often supplement their own experience and abilities by utilizing management consultants. Surrounded by major problems, many leading executives have little reluctance in calling in specialists for research and advice in reaching decisions. The majority of America's largest corporations engage management consultants either continuously or as needed from time to time.

Change Seekers

An even greater problem than managerial competency is the managerial attitude toward change. It is well known that some members of organizations, even managerial members, resist change. It is also evident, in view of the changing world and changing organization noted above, that such managers are quickly obsolete. It would seem that the successful organization of the future must be staffed by managers who are change seekers rather than change resisters.[11]

How to identify and develop change seekers is a problem. Age is one factor, of course. Although there are exceptions, people become more conservative as they advance in age. This has led to the suggestion that men be moved into top level managerial positions at an earlier age than heretofore — for example, thirty-five to forty-five, rather than forty-five to fifty-five.[12] If this policy were to be followed consistently, it would also be necessary for managers to step down from top level positions at an earlier age than heretofore. This might require a change from past practice whereby one retires at the highest point reached on the managerial pyramid.

Age is not the only factor, however. It is important that the organization of the future be able to detect and reward innovative members of the organization. Highly creative individuals are often poor "organization men." A tolerance for nonconformity and creativity is, therefore, important for developing change seekers.

[11]Patrick H. Irwin and Frank W. Langham, Jr., "The Change Seekers," *Harvard Business Review,* Vol. 44, No. 1, January-February 1966, p. 83.

[12]*Ibid.,* p. 92.

Any manager, however, may increase or decrease his awareness of change and its implications for management. There is a common tendency to forget that change is inevitable even though one recognizes that it has consistently occurred in the past. The organization may, therefore, need to arrange for experiences that will enable managers to recognize and appreciate the nature of change in organizations and methods of management. Many university programs for business executives are designed to provide this sort of stimulus. When Paul Austin became president of Coca-Cola Company, he began to emphasize continuing education for the Coca-Cola executives. One member of management was quoted as follows:

> When I was graduated from college, I thought I had finished with my education, but since Paul has been president, I've had more education than in my whole life. He's had us runnin' up to Harvard where he set up these special bottler schools and management programs and we were the first ones to test them out.[13]

Austin himself expressed his philosophy with regard to this point as follows:

> What we do, a lot of us strive for a spirit of self-renewal in management. We have to guard against the pitfalls of size alone. You know, when companies get big and successful, they build Maginot Lines. A swift competitor goes through a Maginot Line, always does. We don't believe in Maginot Lines. We have to keep the flexibility, keep in competition.[14]

The Innovative Organization

Recruitment and encouragement of creative, innovative, change-seeking individuals are major parts of any organization's effort to achieve continuing success in this rapidly changing environment. It is impossible to have a forward-looking organization with backward-looking management. In fact, the organization as a whole may be either vigorous and alert or decadent and dying.

The following comments by John W. Gardner are particularly pertinent to vitality of business organizations:

> Like people and plants, organizations have a life cycle. They have a green and supple youth, a time of flourishing strength, and a gnarled old age. We have all seen organizations that are still going through the diseases of childhood, and others so far

[13]"The Coca-Cola Co.," *Forbes,* Vol. 100, No. 3, August 1, 1967, p. 32.
[14]*Ibid.,* p. 34.

> gone in the rigidities of age that they ought to be pensioned off and sent to Florida to live out their days.
>
> But organizations differ from people and plants in that their cycle isn't even approximately predictable. An organization may go from youth to old age in two or three decades, or it may last for centuries. More important, it may go through a period of stagnation and then revive. In short, decline is not inevitable. Organizations need not stagnate. They often do, to be sure, but that is because the arts of organizational renewal are not yet widely understood. Organizations can renew themselves continuously. That fact has far-reaching implications for our future.[15]

Let us consider some of the features that make for a viable organization in a world of change.[16] One essential feature is a built-in provision for self criticism. People and organizations tend to resist criticism. It is the organization with an eye for the future that formulates procedures for critical review of existing practices. To some extent, this is accomplished in an informal way as management tolerates criticism by organization members. More formal arrangements can also be designed to stimulate critical self-examination. Study groups, for example, may be established to review organizational policy, or a management consultant may be engaged to analyze company operations. These are merely illustrative of steps that might provide critical self-evaluation.

Closely related to the foregoing is the need for an adequate system of internal communication. Lines of communication need to be established not only internally, on both a horizontal and vertical basis, but also with the external environment in which the company operates. Adequate exchange of information among levels of management and among divisions of an organization does much to eliminate the stagnation that may otherwise occur.

The innovative organization also requires a fluidity of structure and flexibility of procedure. Tradition in either structure or procedure makes change difficult, and a vigorous approach is necessary to avoid difficulty in this area. The *status quo* is always comfortable. However, a firm may fail because of dogmatic adherence to traditional procedures or a structure designed to solve problems that no longer exist. The successful organization, therefore, must develop a

---

[15]John W. Gardner, "How to Prevent Organizational Dry Rot," *Harper's Magazine,* Vol. 231, No. 1385, October 1965, p. 20. Copyright © 1965, by Harper's Magazine, Inc. Reprinted by permission.

[16]Many of the characteristics suggested here are based upon those suggested by John W. Gardner in the article cited in note 15.

flexibility and capacity to change as conditions make such change desirable.

The successful, vigorous organization must also avoid the hazards of catering to vested interests. These exist in every organization and destroy the flexibility necessary for health and vigorous growth. Once again, the achievement of this goal requires a philosophical viewpoint of management that looks to the future of the organization as a whole and avoids the pitfalls of narrow self-interest.

Adaptation to meet the demands of a changing world is illustrated by a recent organizational innovation of Texas Instruments, Inc. In the first of what was intended to be a series of similar appointments, Texas Instruments named a former vice president as an "officer of the board." The new officer will be a salaried full-time executive but virtually free from customary job activities. It will be his function to consider the future of Texas Instruments in a changing environment. Texas Instruments board chairman Patrick E. Haggerty described his responsibilities as follows:

> Both to minimize interference with the operating executives of the company and to insure that they do have the time to study, to think quietly about, and to comprehend the impact of this rapidly changing internal and external environment, these directors will have no operating responsibilities. Their duties will relate entirely to their function as directors and advisers to the board.[17]

An Example: Managerial Adaptation to Change

One firm which has prospered more than other firms in its industry is Levitt & Sons, Incorporated — a company which gained fame in the 1940's by building thousands of low-cost houses in Long Island potato fields.[18] The first Levittown was built on Long Island, and others were built in Pennsylvania and New Jersey. The firm's management no doubt experienced the usual tendency to follow the same formula or approach that provided its initial success. The firm declined to limit itself to this type of house construction, however, and it managed thereby to hang up a better record than the

---

[17]"Texas Instruments Board Sets Up a Job Whose Sole Function Is Pondering Deeply," *Business Week,* No. 1976, July 15, 1967, p. 90.

[18]"Levitt's Secret Is Change," *Business Week,* No. 1978, July 29, 1967, pp. 46-55. Levitt & Sons, Inc., was acquired by International Telephone & Telegraph Corporation in 1967. Levitt is expected to operate independently as an autonomous subsidiary.

house construction industry generally. In 1966, while housing starts in the nation dropped 19 per cent, Levitt boosted sales 25 per cent. Levitt's secret of success has been described as "a talent for adapting to change."

During World War II, the company became acquainted with mass production techniques and low-cost housing by building 1,600 houses in a Naval housing project at Norfolk, Virginia. After the war, the assembly line approach to home building was adapted to the first Levittown on Long Island. However, this type of housing development was not adequate for perpetuating company success and growth. Housing demands tapered off, and massive tracts of cheap land near major metropolitan areas became scarce. Home buyers also rebelled against the look-alike houses. In short, the formula that spelled initial success became outmoded.

Levitt adapted to the changing environment in a number of ways. For one, the company shifted from concentration upon one massive development at a time to building widely scattered, smaller-sized projects. The company also shifted from a primitively organized, family-run business into a modern corporation with sophisticated management.

The company decentralized geographically. It moved into the Baltimore and Chicago areas. The company also established operations in Washington, D. C., Florida, Puerto Rico, and Paris, in addition to Long Island and New Jersey.

At the Willingboro, New Jersey, development, the company opened a home furnishings store. This store was the first of a chain to have outlets at all Levitt projects containing shopping centers. The store carried sixty-one lines of furniture and other household items and used model homes as built-in showrooms.

The company also opened a townhouse development, Rittenhouse Park, at Willingboro. The company planned to announce in 1967 the location of the company's first "village-centered planned community" at a site near one of its eastern projects. The development was expected to include garden and high-rise apartments, detached houses, and town houses. Focal point of the town center was to be a twelve-acre lake with a thirty-acre park.

Late in 1967, Levitt was also considering its most ambitious project to date — a new city to be built in the midwest far from any major urban center. From the opening day, the town was expected to contain all the elements of an integrated community — homes, factories, stores, offices, schools, churches, and recreational facilities. The company was planning in terms of modules of 50,000 population.

The innovative character of the firm's management is readily apparent from these unusual steps that have given it an exceptional degree of success in the construction industry. The youthfulness of the company's management may have been a significant factor in its adaptation to changes in environment. Although Bill Levitt, major stockholder and president, was sixty years old, a six-man committee, none of whose members was over forty-seven, directed company operations and was responsible for most of the new ideas that have sparked Levitt's recent growth. The next in command to Levitt in 1967 was a forty-one-year-old business school graduate.

Youthfulness is not the most essential ingredient, however, in determining the adaptability of a firm's management. Instead, it is an attitude that is pointed toward the future and a consciousness of current trends which will make the future.

Management of an Open System

Once again, it is well to recall the concept of the business firm as an open system. In the context of this view, the firm is dependent upon its external environment and subject to the forces imposed by this environment. Any living system, whether biological or social, will die if it fails to maintain a proper relationship to its environment. Management's natural preoccupation with the problems of internal management, however, tends to obscure the vital link between business and its environment.

> Thinking of the organization as a closed system, moreover, results in a failure to develop the intelligence or feedback function of obtaining adequate information about the changes in environmental forces. It is remarkable how weak many industrial companies are in their market research departments when they are so dependent upon the market. The prediction can be hazarded that organizations in our society will increasingly move toward the improvement of the facilities for research in assessing environmental forces. The reason is that we are in the process of correcting our misconception of the organization as a closed system.[19]

The openness of the system necessitates an alertness not only to the needs of customers but also to public demand for acceptable

---

[19] Daniel Katz and Robert L. Kahn, *The Social Psychology of Organizations* (New York: John Wiley & Sons, Inc., 1966), p. 27.

business behavior. Business firms have often ignored or misjudged public dissatisfaction with their practices, only to face restrictive regulation a short time later. The following perceptive comments by Golden underline past weaknesses of management in this area:

> Public relations men are at fault in good measure, for they have, with few exceptions, failed to warn their managements of the changing public attitudes. In fact, in some cases, they have closed their eyes to clear warnings of public changes of mood, for warnings can easily be interpreted by management as troublesome, and the warners as nuisances who just do not understand the problems managements face in a highly competitive, profit-oriented society. But these past few years, and the legislation now passed and in the offing, have brought an altered approach by corporate public relations directors of better-run firms. Both they and their managements now are looking for these new currents of change which can so deeply affect industry.[20]

Golden goes on to suggest that business needs "an industrial DEW line, which will alert management to new trends in public thinking, to new desires, to new demands which can affect the successful conduct of business."[21] The ultimate test of business management lies in the degree of wisdom exercised in coping with the openness of the system. Internally, the firm must adjust to meet successfully the changes in its external environment.

Summary

Business firms function in a constantly changing environment. As a result, the role and responsibilities of professional managers are likewise constantly changing. Three of the crucially important external forces are (1) product dynamics, (2) market dynamics, and (3) the changing role of the firm in society.

There are also significant internal changes in the business organization as well as changes in its external environment. Behavioral aspects of organizations, for example, are becoming better understood and increasingly important in the functioning of the enterprise. Technological change is constantly reshaping business institutions and their methods. Also, the systems concept is coming to have great value in the proper performance of managerial functions.

---

[20] L. L. Golden, "DEW Line for Business," *Saturday Review*, Vol. 50, No. 36, September 9, 1967, p. 60. Copyright 1967 Saturday Review, Inc.

[21] *Ibid.*

Successful management of the changing organization in a changing world requires increasingly competent and better educated managers who are also change seekers. A current problem concerns effective methodology for identifying and developing managers as innovators. Other factors contributing to an innovative organization are (1) a built-in provision for self-criticism, (2) an adequate system of internal communication, (3) a fluidity of structure and flexibility of procedure, and (4) a refusal to cater to vested interests. The business managers must also realize that the firm is an open system and that its management must properly analyze and regulate the firm's relationship with its external environment.

Discussion Questions

1. What is the distinction between *product dynamics* and *market dynamics*, and what is the significance of these forces to the business manager?

2. Discuss the current significance and nature of (1) product dynamics, (2) market dynamics, and (3) the changing role of the firm in society as these apply to a major automobile manufacturer.

3. Early in 1968, a leading businessman associated with a well-known retail organization said that big city retailers cannot wait for the government to solve urban problems. He pointed to the problem of ghetto unemployment and called on stores to recruit and train the hard-core unemployed even if they must "fit the job to the man." How do you explain or interpret these comments in the light of the ideas discussed in this chapter? Does this executive appear to be a "hard-headed businessman" or a "soft-headed philanthropist"?

4. In the Coca-Cola Company, the independent dealer organization seemed to act as a brake in Coca-Cola's adaptation to change. How can the company minimize the natural resistance to change on the part of its independent dealers?

5. What explains the increasing importance of behavioral science in contemporary business organizations?

6. What is meant by the greater requirement for "systems thinking" on the part of future business managers?

7. Consider the most creative, innovative, change-seeking individual whom you know. Does it appear that his creativity is an innate quality or an attitude that has been developed? Is it possible to develop an innovative attitude in managerial personnel?

8. Assuming an organization has reasonably creative and innovative individuals on its staff, what feature appears to be most essential in order for this spirit of innovation and change to be properly exercised?

9. What are the values, difficulties, and limitations involved in relieving an executive of customary managerial duties and giving him responsibility for considering the broad problem of the firm's future in a changing environment?

10. Consider the case of a company that became stagnant over years of operation. An observer described one such sick company by saying that "its name is 'lethargy.' " In speaking of the problems of correcting this weakness in the same organization, another observer asked, "How do you get an organization to move and accept change when it hasn't done it for years?" What *is* the answer to this latter question?

Supplementary Reading

Ansoff, H. Igor, "The Firm of the Future," *Harvard Business Review,* Vol. 43, No. 5, September-October 1965, pp. 162-178.

Bennis, Warren, "Organizations of the Future," *Personnel Administration,* Vol. 30, No. 5, September-October 1967, pp. 6-19.

Gardner, John W., "How to Prevent Organizational Dry Rot," *Harper's Magazine,* Vol. 231, No. 1385, October 1965, pp. 20-26.

———, *Self-Renewal: The Individual and the Innovative Society.* New York: Harper & Row, Publishers, 1964.

Harvey, Allan, "Systems Can Too Be Practical," *Business Horizons,* Vol. 7, No. 2, Summer 1964, pp. 59-69.

Irwin, Patrick H. and Frank W. Langham, Jr., "The Change Seekers," *Harvard Business Review,* Vol. 44, No. 1, January-February 1966, pp. 81-92.

Klasson, Charles R. and Kenneth W. Olm, "Managerial Implications of Integrated Business Operations," *California Management Review,* Vol. 8, No. 1, Fall 1965, pp. 21-32.

Miller, Delbert C., "Using Behavioral Science to Solve Organizational Problems," *Personnel Administration,* Vol. 31, No. 1, January-February 1968, pp. 21-29.

Peterson, William H., "The Future & the Futurists," *Harvard Business Review,* Vol. 45, No. 6, November-December 1967, pp. 168-186.

Petit, Thomas A., *The Moral Crisis in Management.* New York: McGraw-Hill Book Company, 1967.

Walton, Clarence C., *Corporate Social Responsibilities.* Belmont: Wadsworth Publishing Co., Inc., 1967.

Ways, Max, "Tomorrow's Management: A More Adventurous Life in a Free-Form Corporation," *Fortune,* Vol. 74, No. 1, July 1, 1966, pp. 84-87, 148-150.

Cases

Case 1

Stewart's Department Store*

Stewart's Department Store had been in existence 97 years when a firm of retail consultants was approached to solve the store's complex problems. Its founder, Jack Stewart, had come over from Scotland as a young man and after moving about the country, working and saving his money, he opened up a small dry goods store in a village about one hundred miles from a large city. The village was surrounded by prosperous farmers and had good road and rail connections to the city. Because it was so easy to go to town, Stewart was able to make frequent trips to wholesalers in the city and soon learned he could buy goods as he required them. In this way he was able to finance the store, first from his savings and then from his profits. Thus, although he was not aware of the value of maintaining low inventories, he reaped its benefits through fast turnover, continuous fresh stock and high markups.

When Stewart opened his business, there were two stores larger than his in the village. He soon surpassed these competitors because he was very personable, and learned to buy only those goods his customers wanted. Moreover, he adopted a number of new retailing techniques that were being introduced by the more progressive stores in the city. Some of these retailing principles were: clearly marked prices on all merchandise, money refunded if goods not satisfactory and clearing out old stock. On the other hand, his competitors continued to do business as they always had done, that is, buying what they liked, haggling over every sale, and allowing no merchandise returns or cash refunds.

Stewart also threw himself into the life of the community and became known for miles around as a good man whose store was a pleasant place to visit, and who sold good merchandise at fair prices. As he accumulated more wealth than his business required, Stewart invested it in real estate and in shares of certain industries that began to move into the area. He was as shrewd an investor as he was a merchant and when he died he left his son James with the largest store in the area and a very comfortable income from his real estate and stock holdings.

James Stewart was not only as able a business man as his father but much more ambitious. He decided to increase his father's estate and also to be a social leader in the community, and on the whole, he succeeded. Because he was so well known and thought of in the community, and because he was a good merchant, the store grew until it covered half a city block and consisted of a complete basement and five selling floors. In James Stewart's lifetime, Stewart's became the only full line department store in what had grown from a village to a town, and actually dominated the entire retail area for miles around.

---

*Case prepared by Professor Harold Shaffer of Sir George Williams University.

James had his faults. He was a complete autocrat and demanded unquestioned obedience from his employees and his family. He worked very hard because he never learned to delegate authority and so made all administrative decisions himself. But hard work seemed to agree with him for he lived until he was 81 and actively ran the store and his other possessions until the day he died.

However, during the last eight years of his life, James was a wheelchair cripple. Nevertheless, he still came to the store every day and, as he wheeled about the various departments, he greeted customers, gave orders and made both major and minor decisions.

James had only one son, Bill Stewart, who wanted to be an engineer, but his father would have none of that nonsense. After the boy finished college, he went into the store as a receiver, and slowly moved up the ladder until, at the time of his father's death, he had become an assistant buyer in the men's furnishings department. James, always an impatient and critical man, was even more so with his son. He criticized him continuously and usually within the hearing of customers or staff. The young man had no alternative but to cringe and become less and less certain of himself and his ability as a merchant.

Even though James was incapacitated during the last years of his life, he left the store in excellent condition. Moreover, his estate included a considerable fortune in real estate holdings, stocks and bonds. He left the store and a small part of his investments to Bill and the balance of his estate to his wife.

Thus, Bill became president of Stewart's. He soon discovered, however, that he was incapable of making executive decisions and that there was no one in the store who could help him. Moreover, as the staff kept comparing him to his father and grandfather, and found him wanting, they soon became openly hostile to his leadership. Soon Bill began to drink heavily, and although he put in as many hours in the store as any of his employees, he isolated himself in his office and so saw less and less of his staff or his customers. The organization rapidly fell apart, yet for one reason or another, the staff remained loyal to the store, with each employee trying to operate as he thought the old man would want him to.

As sales dropped, Bill not only drank harder, but began to stay away from the store for days on end. Under these circumstances, Miss Beach, the office manager, took it upon herself to move into the administrative vacuum. Miss Beach had idolized James Stewart and so had nothing but contempt for his son. Nevertheless, in her new role, Stewart's became her whole life. She had always worked hard, but now she spent even longer hours in the store trying to keep up with the office routine, listen to employee complaints and make whatever administrative decisions she felt were required. But although she acted as chief administrator, she always felt uncertain of her decisions and resented the fact that she, rather than Bill, was making them. This attitude increased her loyalty to the store and her animosity towards its president.

In spite of Miss Beach's efforts, Stewart's continued to lose money and Bill was forced to sell more and more of his outside investments. Occasionally he would sober up and try to run the business himself but even when he set up good administrative policies, he could never obtain the desired results. For example, he hired a capable executive, Al Smith, to be his general merchandise manager. However, he never formally announced the appointment to his staff, the people in his area or his vendors, nor would he support Smith against the open hostility of the buyers and Miss Beach.

At first Smith attempted to gain and exert control over the buyers by devious methods. For example, he persuaded Bill to install a retail inventory method. However, it was never used because the buyers simply ignored it and Smith, without Bill's authority behind him, could not force them to adhere to their open-to-buy positions or even to plan merchandise budgets. Moreover, they persisted in going to Miss Beach rather than to Smith for any major merchandise decisions.

Smith then installed a stock-age system but the buyers ignored this too. Finally, he attempted to compare each department's cumulative daily sales against their former figures, in the hope that this tactic would increase the buyers' incentive to make more sales and so turn to Smith rather than Miss Beach for advice. But the store's sales tabulating system made it impossible to obtain department sales figures soon enough for this purpose.

Because both Jack and James Stewart felt that balancing the cash was more important than knowing what merchandise was sold, the store's daily cash was totalled first, and then, in their spare time, the office staff would break down the sales slips into departments and tabulate department figures. Thus the buyers received their sales progress so late they could not use this as an active merchandise control.

Smith tried to reverse the process and use the sales slips to first report the merchandise sold by departments and then to balance the cash. Stewart agreed to the new procedure but when it was actively opposed by Miss Beach he withdrew his support and left Smith to cope with the problem alone. The new system soon became inoperable and after this experience, Smith decided not to fight the system but to accept the situation as gracefully as he could.

As sales and profits continued to fall, Bill Stewart was faced with the possibility that he would have to liquidate the last portion of the estate his father had left him. In desperation he searched for a magic formula that would relieve him of his administrative duties and decisions, yet increase sales and turn losses into profits. In this way, he would prove to the staff and to himself that he was every bit as good a merchant as his father and grandfather had been. He decided that modernizing the store was the answer and sold this idea to his mother, who said she would help to finance it.

Bill threw himself into this project with unaccustomed zeal and enthusiasm. He obtained the services of a reputable fixture house, who researched the size and locations of the store's present departments and then made a number of recommendations for improving the Stewart operation. For example, they suggested that the ladies' hosiery, blouses and skirts department should be moved from the third floor and placed on the street floor, immediately to the right of the ladies' entrance. Currently this area was taken up with ankle sox, umbrellas and handbags. They also thought that the piece goods department should be moved from the main floor to the third floor, and so on.

Again, they suggested closing up non-profitable departments such as notions, and using the area to enlarge more profitable departments, or to establish new departments or merchandise classifications.

They also pointed out that Stewart's millinery department carried the highest priced hats in town, while its dress department was unsucessfully competing with the town's chain stores and implied that a uniform buying and price-lining policy would be much in order.

Stewart agreed with the fixture people but those department heads who felt they would suffer or lose face if the plans went into effect, objected to the proposals. They were supported by Miss Beach who took the position that what was good enough for Bill Stewart's father, was good enough for his son. Thus, while Stewart's acquired linoleum covered floors, colourful walls, fluorescent light fixtures, and functional open shelving fixtures, little was done to improve the store's profit position, for the merchandising techniques remained almost as old-fashioned as when Jack Stewart first opened his store.

Actually, the interior alterations had been only phase one of Stewart's plan to renovate the store. Phase two was to modernize the store's exterior, but after the poor results of his interior project, his mother refused to throw good money after bad. Thus, the store remained with a late nineteenth century exterior, including bust forms and other fixtures of the period, while its interior was middle twentieth century modern.

About this time, Stewart was offered a handsome price for the store. He would have been happy to sell it but he had a son who was studying business administration and who showed a marked desire to go into Stewart's when he graduated. Moreover, the boy seemed to have his grandfather's flair for store leadership, and during the summer vacations when he worked in the store, Stewart's employees, including Miss Beach, were more content and happy than at any other time of the year.

Unfortunately, Stewart did not get along with his son and they quarrelled incessantly, with their bitterest fights over store policy. Aside from other considerations, then, Bill Stewart felt that if he sold the business, there might be less tension in the family. But, Bill's mother put a lot of pressure on him not to sell. She wanted to keep the business in the family, if at all possible, and felt that her grandson would be capable of making the store an even greater success than her husband had done. Therefore, she said she was quite prepared to keep financing the business until the boy graduated.

Stewart, as usual, accepted his mother's decision but felt his position of president, with whatever status it entailed, was in jeopardy. He became so obsessed with this hazard that he turned to a firm of retail consultants and asked them to suggest what could be done to make the business profitable within the next three years. In this way, he felt he would build up his reputation as a merchant and secure his position as president of Stewart's.

The consultants made surveys of the community and found that Stewart's had enormous potential. Industry was moving into the area at a rapid rate, yet there was no store within thirty miles of Stewart's that could compete with it, providing it were run properly. Moreover, a consumer survey produced a surprisingly strong loyalty to Stewart's. People wanted to shop there and were angry that the poor merchandise selections made this impossible. The consultants felt that with proper management Stewart's could rapidly increase its business and soon make a satisfactory profit.

However, after interviewing most of the personnel at Stewart's, some of the executives in the consulting firm were vehemently opposed to becoming involved with the store. They did not argue its business potential or that it could be made to run at a profit. What worried them was that Bill Stewart was the store's president and owner, and that they would have to work through him. Yet it was obvious that he was unable to exert real power. Moreover, Smith, Stewart's assistant, seemed too weak to be able to carry out orders even if they were given by Stewart. In their interviews with Miss Beach, the consultants found her both negative and frightened. Apparently she was afraid of losing her job if any changes were made and, to some extent, she was now enjoying the power she wielded in the store and would be most reluctant to give it up.

The personnel situation was further complicated by Stewart's peculiarly stubborn loyalty to his staff. He would not fire anyone. He admitted his fear of Miss Beach and his desire to get rid of her but because she was loyal to him "in her way" he must be loyal to her. Nor would he change accountants, even though the present one, "a friend of his father's" was 82, and too old and sick to even see the books. Miss Beach, for years, had drawn up the annual statements and the old man had merely signed them.

Questions

1. Name and discuss the major administrative functions and considerations that are illustrated in this case.
2. What further arguments could the consultants give for accepting the case?

3. What further arguments could the consultants give for not accepting the case?

4. Assuming the consultants agreed to accept the assignment, what steps should they take to solve Stewart's problems?

Case 2

Firestone and Trade with Rumania (A)*

As part of its policy of "building bridges to the East," the United States government in 1964 agreed to a proposal by the government of Rumania that the two countries hold talks on trade and other matters. Representatives of the nations met in Washington from May 18 to June 1, 1964, and at the end of the discussions, the governments of the United States and Rumania issued a joint communique. The communique noted that an improvement in relations had occurred between the two countries following a diplomatic understanding reached in March, 1960 (involving the reciprocal settlement of financial claims and related questions), and the two governments expressed their hope that relations would continue to improve. Toward this end, the communique noted that the following agreement, among others, had been reached:

> The U.S. Government agreed to establish a general license procedure under which most commodities may be exported to Rumania without the necessity for individual export license. In addition the U.S. Government agreed to grant licenses for a number of particular industrial facilities in which the Rumanian delegation expressed special interest.
>
> The Government of the Rumanian People's Republic agreed to authorize enterprises and institutes in Rumania to sell or license Rumanian technology to U.S. firms.
>
> The two Governments agreed that products, designs, and technology exported to Rumania from the United States would not be transshipped or re-exported without the prior consent of the U.S. Government. They agreed further that contracts between U.S. firms and Rumanian state enterprises for imports from Rumania could provide for limitations on re-export or transshipments without prior consent of the Rumanian supplier. The two Governments will mutually facilitate the exchange of information on the use and disposition of products, designs, and technology exported from one country to the other.

---

*Case prepared by Miss Frances Sheridan under the direction of Professor Richard W. Barsness, School of Business, Northwestern University.

Two weeks later, on June 16, President Johnson advised Congress that he deemed it in the national interest for the Export-Import Bank to guarantee private credits extended to Rumania for the purchase of American services and goods.[1]

The Proposed Sale of a Synthetic Rubber Plant to Rumania

During the discussions leading to the signing of the joint communique, the Rumanian delegation expressed particular interest in the purchase of a synthetic rubber plant. Indeed, for some years Rumania had sought to buy such a plant in order to provide a valuable adjunct to its important petroleum industry; however, for strategic reasons the Department of Defense had always opposed such a sale. Now, the Pentagon had altered its policy on the matter, since the technologies involved had recently become widely available in Western Europe, and because Rumania was no longer considered a close ally of Russia. The Defense Department now agreed with the U.S. Commerce Department and the State Department that the sale of a rubber plant would be in the national interest. The rationale underlying this decision was that such a sale would encourage Rumania to gain greater political and economic independence from the Soviet Union.

Soon after the communique was signed, a number of American firms, in cooperation with the State Department, discussed the possible sale of a rubber plant with a delegation of Rumanian officials. Included among these firms was Goodyear Tire & Rubber Company, the nation's largest rubber manufacturer, and Firestone Tire & Rubber Company. And in November of 1964, Firestone Tire & Rubber entered into negotiations with the Rumanian government for a contract valued at least at $40 million to design and equip a rubber plant for the production of polyisoprene, a synthetic similar to natural rubber.

In his televised State of the Union message on January 4, 1965, President Johnson told Congress:

---

[1]To encourage foreign trade, the U. S. Government originally organized the Export-Import Bank in 1934. In a normal deal, an exporter would go to his commercial bank for financing. If the bank believed there was any political risk of significance in the deal, it might insist that it be handled through the Export-Import Bank. This would mean that the latter would guarantee 85 per cent of the value of the deal against political risk, i.e., the risk of war, expropriation, and non-convertibility of currency. The exporter would pay an additional fee of about ½ of 1 per cent per annum for this guarantee and would have to pay the fee for the entire period in advance. If the deal required payments beyond a period of eighteen months, the Export-Import Bank would also guarantee the commercial risk of nonpayment of local currency in the foreign country. During the first 18 months this risk was carried by the commercial bank. The 15 per cent of the political risk not guaranteed by the Export-Import Bank would be carried by the exporter.

> In Eastern Europe restless nations are slowly beginning to assert their identity. Your Government, assisted by leaders in labor and business, is now exploring ways to increase peaceful trade with these countries and with the Soviet Union.

Following the President's message, Secretary of State Dean Rusk announced that Firestone Tire & Rubber Company and Universal Oil Products Corporation of Des Plaines, Illinois, were negotiating separate contracts with the Rumanian government to design and construct a synthetic rubber plant and a petroleum processing plant, respectively, in Rumania. The synthetic rubber plant was to adjoin the petroleum refinery and to use its by-products. These proposed projects took on special significance as possibly the first instance of American industry, with the approval of the U.S. Government, cooperating in a business venture with a Communist nation since World War II.[2]

Although it was the declared policy of the United States Government that trade with Rumania was in the national interest, the proposed contract between Firestone and the Rumanian government drew criticism from several sources.

Goodyear's View on Dealing with Rumania

On December 3, 1964, Goodyear's house organ, *The Wingfoot Clan,* carried an article entitled "An Order Goodyear Didn't Take." Excerpts from this article follow:[3]

> Even to a dedicated profitmaking organization, some things are more important than dollars. Take the best interests of the United States and the free world, for example. You can't put a price tag on freedom.
>
> And when you believe in something you may be called upon to back up your belief with action. That goes for a company such as Goodyear, just as it does an individual.
>
> Recently, Goodyear did just that — it stood firmly on the side of freedom, as a foe of aggression. Goodyear did this even though the company stood to lose financially.
>
> The company's refusal to sell a modern synthetic rubber plant to Communist Rumania has made news throughout the Nation. * * *

---

[2]*The Wall Street Journal,* April 21, 1965.

[3]The excerpts quoted here have been taken from a copy of the article which Senator J. W. Fulbright inserted in the *Congressional Record — Senate,* July 26, 1965, Vol. III, No. 135. According to the *Wall Street Journal,* July 27, 1965, a Goodyear spokesman said that the article and a private letter to dealers explaining why the company had not exercised a license to export synthetic rubber technology to Rumania "were strictly company business and weren't nor will they be disseminated to the public."

Goodyear elected not to seek the business—which could amount to some $50 million — even though the State Department had sanctioned such traffic with Rumania. * * *

At this point we'd like to take a moment to express the State Department's point of view. The Government is said to believe that the creation of greater economic ties between the United States and Rumania will encourage the Rumanians to be still more independent of the Soviet Union. This certainly is a consideration and one that is based on a sincere belief.

However, Goodyear feels that the dangers far outweigh the possible benefits in the proposed deal. For that reason Goodyear has no intention of being a party to it.

Why is Goodyear so opposed to the transaction?

Because we foresee the knowledge that Rumania seeks to purchase from the United States in the potential role of an international agitator, we don't believe that the United States should allow any Communist nation to acquire the know-how to produce a synthetic rubber which competes head-on with natural rubber. * * *

While synthetic and natural rubber are now competitively priced, Goodyear believes the Communists could — if they wished — disrupt natural rubber markets in Malaysia, Liberia and other so-called underdeveloped countries. The Communists are not governed by marketing conditions in setting their prices and in the past have, in fact, used cut-rate prices as an economic club.

The State Department, in commenting on the situation, has said that the Rumanians have assured the United States that they won't divulge the polyisoprene secrets they purchase from us to other Communist nations. With due respect for the State Department's belief in the Rumanians' promise, Goodyear would prefer not to entrust its production secrets to the Communists.

What's to keep the Rumanians from passing techniques developed in the Goodyear Research Laboratory on Goodyear Boulevard to Communist production geniuses in Moscow or Peiping? The why's and wherefore of Natsyn might make an interesting "I'll trade you" tool for the Rumanians. * * *

With voices such as that of Walter Judd and the New York *Daily News* being raised in our behalf, it's unlikely that Goodyear's dedicated stand will end up costing the company lost revenue.

As a matter of fact, there is every indication that in addition to the warmth that this decision brings, Goodyear may benefit from a sales standpoint — a benefit that could not have been further from the company's mind when the decision was made not to sell to Rumania.

The Young Americans for Freedom Campaign Against Firestone

Early in 1965, the Young Americans for Freedom, a college-age conservative organization, began picketing Firestone offices in several cities in an effort to persuade Firestone to terminate negotiations with the Rumanian government. Founded in 1960 at the Sharon, Connecticut, home of William F. Buckley, the Young Americans for Freedom claims a membership of 40,000 and has an operating budget of $25,000 a month. The statement of principles adopted by the group at its founding includes the belief that the United States "should stress victory over, rather than coexistence with" international communism.[4]

During its "informational campaign" against Firestone, the YAF contended that the proposed Firestone-Rumanian contract threatened the security of the United States. The organization distributed handbills which read:

> We are at war with the Communists. In South Vietnam, Americans are being killed daily by Communist bullets. It would be disastrous for American companies to supply the atheistic Communist governments with valuable materials, especially rubber, which the Reds must have to wage their war on free nations.
>
> In the past month, Communist Rumania shipped 500 heavy-duty trucks of military value to Red China, the principal supplier of the North Viet Communists.
>
> The Reds must have rubber to wage war. The synthetic rubber plant which Firestone plans to build in Communist Rumania parallels the steel which the United States sold to Japan prior to World War II. America got the steel back — at Pearl Harbor. No nation can wage war without large quantities of synthetic rubber.

After quoting Goodyear's house organ as to why that company had refused the Rumanian contract, the handbill continued:

> Firestone's plans to build a synthetic rubber plant in Communist Rumania can only strengthen the Communists and throw away American jobs.[5]

---

[4]For the statement of principles of the Young Americans for Freedom, see Exhibit 1.

[5]The excerpts quoted here have been taken from a copy of the handbill which Senator J. W. Fulbright inserted in the *Congressional Record — Senate,* July 26, 1965, Vol. III, No. 135.

The Philadelphia chapter of the YAF organized picketing of Firestone stores in that area, and picket signs appeared paraphrasing Firestone's slogan: "When Red wheels are rolling, the name is known as Firestone?" Following the lead of the Philadelphia group, local chapters in Los Angeles, Cleveland, and several cities on the east coast also began picketing Firestone outlets.[6] The chairman of a Brooklyn chapter was quoted in a YAF publication as saying that a petition drive to get signatures to stop the Firestone-Rumanian agreement was "an opportunity for everyone to do something positive in support of an anti-Communist policy." He further said that Goodyear deserved "the praise and encouragement of all freedom-loving Americans."[7]

Reportedly, many Firestone dealers urged the company to do something about the picketing, since they were losing business to Goodyear.[8] As a result, Firestone sent its eastern regional public relations manager, Bernard Frazier, to speak to YAF chapters in several eastern cities. Mr. Frazier argued that Firestone was acting in the national interest by "building bridges to the East," as President Johnson had urged, and Firestone representatives had been interested to note that the television program "CBS Reports" had stated that Rumanian vehicles photographed in Communist China had *Goodyear* tires on them.[9]

Following its picketing of Firestone offices in several metropolitan areas, the Young Americans for Freedom began to make some plans to set up an Indianapolis office to conduct certain activities before and during the Memorial Day 500 Mile auto race. The proposed name for this YAF group was the "Committee Against Slave Labor," and its purpose would be to "mount a massive publicity campaign urging a boycott of Firestone tires which it was hoped would ruin Firestone's normal promotional activities at that time."[10] Reportedly, the YAF was planning to hire a plane to fly over the Indianapolis speedway stadium carrying streamers denouncing Firestone and showering the stadium with leaflets criticizing the company.

Firestone officials could not be certain whether the YAF really intended to proceed with this proposed campaign, but in view of the

---

[6]The Young Americans for Freedom maintains that its campaign was not a boycott of Firestone, but a drive to "educate the consumer." See *New York Times,* July 30 and August 28, 1965.

[7]*Washington Evening Star,* May 8, 1965.

[8]*Ibid.*

[9]Firestone was spreading the word that the Rumanian vehicles included both trucks and tractors, and that Goodyear with the approval of the U.S. Commerce Department, had been selling synthetic rubber (but not plants) to Rumania. In reply, Goodyear denied it knowingly sold such tires to Red China, and said Peking might have purchased them somewhere on the black market. Goodyear also stated that in its trade overseas it requires the purchasing company to sign a statement saying that Goodyear products will not be transshipped to Communist countries. See *Ibid.*, and *Human Events,* May 8, 1965.

[10]*Washington Evening Star,* May 8, 1965.

Exhibit 1. *The Sharon Statement**

"Adopted in conference at Sharon, Conn., September 9-11, 1960."

In this time of moral and political crisis, it is the responsibility of the youth of America to affirm certain eternal truths.

We as young conservatives, believe:

That foremost among the transcendent values is the individual's use of his God-given free will, whence derives his right to be free from the restrictions of arbitrary force;

That liberty is indivisible, and that political freedom cannot long exist without economic freedom;

That the purposes of government are to protect these freedoms through the preservation of internal order, the provision of national defense, and the administration of justice;

That when government ventures beyond these rightful functions, it accumulates power which tends to diminish order and liberty;

That the Constitution of the United States is the best arrangement yet devised for empowering government to fulfill its proper role, while restraining it from the concentration and abuse of power;

That the genius of the Constitution — the division of powers — is summed up in the clause which reserves primacy to the several States; or to the people, in those spheres not specifically delegated to the Federal Government;

That the market economy, allocating resources by the free play of supply and demand, is the single economic system compatible with the requirements of personal freedom and constitutional government, and that it is at the same time the most productive supplier of human needs;

That when Government interferes with the work of the market economy, it tends to reduce the moral and physical strength of the Nation; that when it takes from one man to bestow on another, it diminishes the incentive of the first, the integrity of the second, and the moral autonomy of both;

That we will be free only so long as the national sovereignty of the United States is secure; that history shows periods of freedom are rare, and can exist only when free citizens concertedly defend their rights against all enemies;

That the forces of international communism are, at present, the greatest single threat to these liberties;

That the United States should stress victory over, rather than coexistence with, this menace; and

That American foreign policy must be judged by this criterion: Does it serve the just interests of the United States?

---

*Quoted from a copy of the Statement which Senator Strom Thurmond inserted in the *Congressional Record—Senate,* July 26, 1965, Vol. III, No. 135.

company's traditional advertising and promotional activities regarding the 500 Mile Race, the possible impact of such a harassment by the YAF could not be lightly dismissed. On the other hand, the company did not want to make the mistake of giving undue weight and consideration to a small but aggressive organization which was opposing the official foreign policy of the United States Government.

Firestone officials finally decided to review the entire matter of the Rumanian controversy in order that any additional policy decisions which might be required could be made in advance of the race. If the merits of the proposed contract indicated that Firestone should still continue with the project, then the company would have to stand ready to deal with any additional criticism and hostile publicity which might result. Conversely, if Firestone decided that it should withdraw, there was the problem of how such a withdrawal should be made, and what type of explanation should be offered.

Firestone and Trade with Rumania (B)

In the middle of April 1965, Firestone executives met with officials from the State Department to discuss the controversy which had arisen over the Rumanian venture. At this meeting, Firestone reportedly was told in effect that it was on its own and could expect no statement of support for the Firestone-Rumanian contract from the executive branch of the government.[1] Then, on April 20, Firestone issued the following announcement:

> The Firestone Tire & Rubber Company has terminated negotiations for a contract to design and equip a synthetic rubber plant in Rumania.

The Company declined to comment further on the matter. *The Wall Street Journal* reported that the president of Firestone would say only that the project "didn't work out" and that the State Department had been so advised.[2] But an article in the *Washington Evening Star* later contended:

> . . . from information on the public record and from confidential disclosures by diplomatic and rubber industry sources, it was learned that the conservative Young Americans for Freedom. almost singlehandedly caused giant Firestone, the Nation's second largest rubber manufacturer, to drop the deal.[3]

[1]This version of the Firestone-State Department meeting has been taken from Senator Fulbright's statement in the *Congressional Record — Senate,* July 26, 1965, Vol. III, No. 135.

[2]*The Wall Street Journal,* April 21, 1965.

[3]*Washington Evening Star,* May 8, 1965.

According to the *Star* article, David Jones, the national executive director of the Young Americans for Freedom, felt it was quite possible that Firestone decided to end the negotiations when it learned of the YAF's planned demonstration for the Memorial Day auto race in Indianapolis. "A top Firestone executive heard about this on April 18," Jones said. "Two days later the deal was off."[4]

The YAF itself evidently considered its anti-Firestone activities the decisive factor in Firestone's determination to cancel the Rumanian project. In a release headed "YAF Stops Aid to Reds: Setback for State Dept.," the Young Americans for Freedom printed the following letter which it received at the time Firestone announced the termination of negotiations with Rumania.

April 22, 1965

Mr. David Jones
National Executive Director
Young Americans for Freedom
514 C Street, N.E.
Washington, D.C.

Dear Mr. Jones:

We certainly hope that your organization will give as much public attention to the action of our Company described in the enclosed news release (i.e. termination of the contract) as you did to what you presumed was our action previously.

Sincerely yours,
/s/ Bernard W. Frazier
Bernard W. Frazier
Eastern Public Relations Manager

Human Events Magazine Comments on Firestone's Decision

The May 8 issue of *Human Events* carried an article entitled "Big Conservative Win," in which Firestone's withdrawal from the Rumanian project was described as a "stunning upset victory over . . . liberal elements who have been pushing America into selling its technical know-how to Communist countries." According to the article, Firestone withdrew from the negotiations because of an "avalanche" of adverse public criticism; because Firestone began to hurt financially as Goodyear, its chief competitor, started to pick up some of Firestone's longstanding customers; and finally, because Firestone ran into a "buzz-saw," the Young Americans for Freedom. The article stated that the company received thousands of letters which showed that the American people were "boiling mad" over Firestone's plan to increase trade with a com-

[4]*Ibid.*

munist country while American soldiers were dying in Vietnam. Moreover, the article declared, the American public had begun to buy from Goodyear when that company refused publicly to trade with Rumania, asserting that "even to a dedicated profit-making organization, some things are more important than dollars."

After describing the YAF's role in forcing Firestone to cancel the Rumanian project, the article concluded by warning American firms presently "dickering with Communist countries" over deals similar to the Firestone-Rumanian one to be on their guard, for the Young Americans for Freedom planned to call attention to every one of them.

Senator J. W. Fulbright's Charges

Citing the Firestone case as an example of "how the constitutional processes by which American foreign policy is made can be defeated and disrupted," Senator Fulbright, the chairman of the Senate Foreign Relations Committee, charged on July 26, 1965, that Firestone had called off its plans to build the synthetic rubber plant in Rumania because of the "nuisance activities of a minor vigilante group [Young Americans for Freedom]; second, and undoubtedly more important, the pressure of a major Firestone competitor [Goodyear]; third, the curious reluctance of the U.S. Government to give [Firestone] strong support against these pressures."

The Senator said that the Young Americans for Freedom had handed out literature containing the "familiar fulminations of the radical right along with dark hints of immorality and worse on the part of Firestone,"[5] but he said YAF members may well have been the innocent instrument of individuals more sophisticated than they, and, in any case, were quite young and "should not be taken too severely to task for their little caper."

The Senator directed his heaviest criticism against Goodyear, charging that despite the "profit-sacrificing patriotism" proclaimed in the Goodyear's *Wingfoot Clan* in December 1964, the company earlier had shown an interest in the possibility of doing business with Rumania, and had obtained an export license to export synthetic rubber to Rumania some time after the Government authorized such licenses in June 1964. "Then, for reasons which are not entirely clear, Goodyear suddenly 'got religion' and grandly refused to traffic with the Red heathen," said Senator Fulbright. He accused Goodyear of trying to profit from all the dema-

[5]In reply to Senator Fulbright's statement, Senator Strom Thurmond of South Carolina described the Young Americans for Freedom as "an oustanding and patriotic organization which is dedicated to the best interests of this nation and the free world," and he noted that thirty-nine members of Congress serve as members of the National Advisory Board of Young Americans for Freedom. See *Congressional Record—Senate,* July 26, 1965, Vol. III, No. 135.

goguery against Firestone. For example, in June 1965, almost two months after Firestone terminated the negotiations, Goodyear urged its salesmen to distribute two "right-wing" publications to commercial accounts and competitive dealers.[6] According to Senator Fulbright, these publications (the May 8, 1965, issue of *Human Events* and the May 1965 issue of the YAF's *New Guard*) contained vitriolic attacks on Firestone for its abortive Rumanian transaction.

In his speech, Senator Fulbright also scored the role of the State Department in the Firestone affair, calling it equivocal.

Having determined upon a policy of building bridges to the East, and having concluded the agreement with Rumania which made the negotiations between Firestone and the Rumanian government possible, the State Department, according to the Senator, took the "disingenuous" position that the contract negotiations were a private affair between Firestone and the Rumanian government and took no action to salvage the contract by giving Firestone vigorous backing and encouragement in the face of "irresponsible" pressures.

As for Firestone, the Senator said:

> . . . it entered the negotiations with Rumania in full awareness that complications could arise and that it had responsibilities larger than its own profits; the company was victimized by demagoguery, but it must also be said that it is more admirable to resist demagoguery than to yield to it.

Firestone continued to maintain silence about the Rumanian venture and declined to comment on Senator Fulbright's charges, while a Goodyear spokesman said that the company believed that technical know-how should not be sent behind the Iron Curtain where it might become available to Communist China. "The current situation in Viet Nam reinforces that decision," he said.[7] The spokesman further asserted that Goodyear had never exercised its license to export synthetic rubber to Rumania.

Universal Oil Completes Its Negotiations with the Rumanian Government

On July 26, 1965, Universal Oil Products Corporation of Des Plaines, Illinois, announced that it had concluded an agreement to become the prime contractor to build a $22.5 million petroleum refinery in Rumania. Universal's vice president for finance said, "the company completed the transaction despite a furor over whether 'right-wing' pressure caused Firestone Tire & Rubber Co. to withdraw last April from negotiations

---

[6]For a copy of Goodyear's Sales Department Instructions on this matter, see Exhibit 1.

[7]*The Wall Street Journal,* July 27, 1965.

with Communist Rumania." Another top executive of Universal declared the company "isn't trying to set foreign policy but is adhering to the policy of the Federal Government, which in June 1964 called for increased trade between the U.S. and Rumania."[8]

Exhibit 1. *Sales Department Instructions**

Akron, Ohio
June 11, 1965

From District Manager, No. 65-289:

I am sure that every Goodyear employee will enjoy reading the attached reprint of page 4 from the *Human Events* magazine of May 8, 1965.

Surely every Goodyear salesman will proudly show this article to commercial accounts, competitive dealers — especially Firestone and Goodyear dealers.

We are sending a small supply to your district office and I am sure if you would like additional copies to mail to some of your friends — especially those in the tire business — that you will be able to get the number you need from your district manager.

I am also attaching a photostat of page 21 from the May, 1965 issue of the *New Guard* magazine. There will not be an extra supply of these sent to your district because we have only a limited number.

C. F. Stroud
Marketing Manager, Tire Division

Questions

1. Was the U. S. public policy sufficiently clear to justify Firestone's entering into negotiations with Rumania?
2. Should Firestone consider the political and international implications of this transaction? Is the construction of the proposed synthetic rubber plant in the best interests of the United States?
3. Assuming that the proposed deal is consistent with public policy, should Firestone break off negotiations because of picketing and harassment by the young conservatives?
4. Evaluate Goodyear's actions and motives in this case.

---

[8] *Ibid.*

*The instructions as quoted here have been taken from the copy inserted by Senator Fulbright in the *Congressional Record — Senate,* July 26, 1965, Vol. III, No. 135.

Case 3

Mahrud Foods, Inc.*

The new general manager of the central kitchen of Mahrud Foods, Inc., is wondering what action, if any, he should take with respect to the problem of where the firm's large delivery trucks should be parked when not in use. Mahrud Foods owns and operates a chain of twenty-three low-priced cafeterias and four retail shops that sell prepared foods in a large midwestern city. Much of the food is prepared in a central kitchen and trucked to the cafeterias and retail shops in the firm's own ten large delivery trucks.

The problem first arose two years ago when the city passed an ordinance prohibiting the parking of trucks on the city streets during the hours from 11 p.m. to 5 a.m. in order to facilitate street cleaning. Fines of $10 per violation were established by the ordinance.

Before the ordinance was passed, Mahrud Foods had always parked its trucks overnight on the street in front of the central kitchen. At the time the ordinance became law, management had investigated the costs of buying a nearby lot for parking purposes. This lot, the only one available in the vicinity, was priced at $50,000. This high price for the lot, plus the costs of resurfacing it and the high real estate taxes (estimated at $1,500 per year), had led management to reject this solution to the problem. Leasing space in an existing parking lot would cost the company about $75 per week. Parking the trucks outside the city in a neighboring suburb without an overnight parking ordinance would involve labor costs of over $100 per week, plus additional fuel costs, as the suburb was a twenty-minute drive from the city and the workers would have to be paid for this extra driving time. Another alternative would be to continue to park the trucks on the street and pay for violations whenever the trucks were ticketed by the police.

The police precinct captain is a friend of the assistant manager of Mahrud's central kitchen. The assistant manager solved Mahrud's parking problem by providing the precinct captain with free groceries each week and free coffee to all patrolmen who stopped by the kitchen from time to time. In return for these favors, the police overlooked the daily violation of the city parking ordinance. The groceries and coffee cost Mahrud about $25 per week.

The new general manager of the central kitchen is somewhat disturbed by the present parking arrangements entered into by the assistant man-

---

*From Dan H. Fenn, Jr., Donald Grunewald and Robert N. Katz, *Business Decision Making and Government Policy: Cases in Business Government,* © 1966. Reprinted by permission of Prentice-Hall, Inc., Englewood Cliffs, New Jersey.

ager. He is uncertain, however, of what action, if any, he should take with respect to the parking problem. The empty lot is still available and the other alternatives mentioned above are also available, including a continuation of the present arrangement.

Questions

1. What alternatives are available?
2. Evaluate the desirability of continuing the existing arrangement between the assistant manager and the precinct captain.
3. What should the new general manager do about this problem?

Case 4

Tibbetts Paints*

Tibbetts Paints Limited was organized for the purpose of manufacturing paint and allied products. It was financed with Nova Scotia capital and has had Mr. R. C. Tibbetts as its President and Managing Director since its founding in 1947 to the present time.

Most of the Company's sales are within the four Atlantic Provinces, although it has sold in Quebec, and Ontario, and on the West Coast. Sales have increased every year that the Company has been in business.

Approximately half of its business is in the trade or household line which includes house paints and interior decorative paints and enamels. The other half of the business is in industrial sales which consist primarily of paints used for bridges, trucks, and railway equipment.

The following comments outline the advertising policy of Mr. R. C. Tibbetts, as told to the casewriter.

"Circumstances require that the advertising methods of Maritime manufacturers and processors, unless designed to promote sales on a national scale, must differ from the methods of national manufacturers.

The Maritime manufacturer must compete against the terrific impact of goods advertised in *Maclean's*, the Montreal *Standard*, the Toronto *Star-Weekly*. He must compete also with the immense flow of advertising in United States magazines that cross our border and which promote Canadian companies bearing names used in the United States. It is difficult to counteract this type of advertising and the approach must vary with the type of goods being manufactured or processed. It is

*Case prepared by Professor W. J. Reddin of the University of New Brunswick.

obvious that, although a Maritime manufacturer could gain prestige by advertising in national magazines, he would lose approximately eighty-five per cent of his advertising dollar. The solution lies in finding something that will appeal locally and to emphasize one or two fundamental ideas.

The fact that we advertise "Made in the Maritimes" is not enough. Many people are not aware that by buying Maritime-made goods they are helping to increase the general prosperity of the region. Some people do not care. In many cases, people resist goods known to be manufactured in the Maritimes. One reason for resistance is that there have been, and are, opportunists who use their business with no thought for the future, and do not pay attention to quality production. In consequence, all Maritime industries suffer. The Maritime manufacturer is forced to make his products even better than those of his non-Maritime competitors. Nevertheless, although the products must be better, they must sell at the same price; eventually, practice will win out for us.

Every individual industry has its own localized problems in advertising. It is obvious that a food processing industry which sells to many outlets in one town will have a policy different from that of an industry such as our own which normally has one outlet per community. The food processor must advertise his goods so that his name stands in front of everyone; the consumer, no matter what store he goes into, must be able immediately to recognize the product. This applies to other industries that sell through numerous outlets.

In the paint industry, we have a much different problem. We follow, in many respects, the method used by national advertisers of paint. We use colour cards, yardsticks, painters' caps, newspapers, radio, television, and direct mail. Our advertising is channelled in two directions: one for retail trade sales, and the other for industrial users. I shall talk mostly about retail trade sales, where seventy-five per cent of our advertising dollar is spent.

We have used many methods to refine our advertising policy. We have tried saturating one area by radio, and another by newspaper. We have tried television in two areas. The more we copied national advertising methods, however, the less the results obtained. Our newspaper mats were made from sketches drawn by artists and compared favorably with those of other paint companies, and our radio commercials were patterned after larger companies. All in all, our efforts appeared similar to campaigns promoted by others. We analyzed the results obtained over the past few years and reached the conclusion that, although our advertising story was as good as any and appeared as often as any, we were being swamped by the mass of advertising from other paint companies and by the impact of national-magazine advertising.

This year, we have made a change in our approach. We designed a small ad differing in size from what anyone else was using. We used solid black to catch the eye, advertised our name in large letters, and stated that our paint is salt air resistant and made in Trenton, Nova Scotia. This ad brought immediate results. Many people who had glanced at our previous ads did not realize that we were manufacturing in Nova Scotia. They noted for the first time that we specialize in paint made for this area, and they remembered our name. (We still have regular mats advertising our various products, for supply to our dealers when they wish inserts for local newspapers.) The over-all campaign is bringing desired results, and we plan to continue with the same scheme for another year.

We believe that advertising should emphasize dealer tie-ins; if people do not know *where* to buy a product, they will accept another in its stead. We believe that advertising should be brought to the attention of clerks in the stores in order that they can talk informatively.

In our opinion, Maritime manufacturers should avoid as far as possible the standard procedures used in national advertising. The Maritimer should create something different and bring to attention the fact that his product is made in the Maritimes, that it is better because of Maritime workmanship and know-how, and that the best way for Maritimers to gain their share of Canada's prosperity is to buy Maritime goods. If Maritimers were convinced fully of the honesty and integrity of Maritime manufacturers, they would prefer to buy Maritime goods.

Our Company's industrial advertising is entirely different from our retail advertising. For retail sales, we have standard products which do not vary except when improvements have been made or a completely new line has been developed. In contrast, each industrial paint has its own special use; and a paint that is made for one job is not suitable necessarily for the same job in another plant. This means that direct contact is the most important part of industrial advertising. We issue a catalogue of our products that includes reference to most of our industrial paints. More than stressing each individual product, we emphasize our service and the fact that we can make any paint for any purpose.

We budget our advertising in direct proportion to our sales. As our sales go up, so do our advertising dollars. This may appear to be putting the cart before the horse, for it is believed generally that the advertising dollar creates the sales. We have found, however, that this is not altogether true. When we budget our advertising, we allot two or three thousand dollars for flexible spot-emergency advertising. We consider, nevertheless, that the advertising dollar should be a fairly rigid percentage of the sales dollar. This percentage will vary, of course, from industry to industry.

Our advertising budget is worked out in the late autumn or early winter months. We check, area by area, the sales records of previous years against the sales of the immediate past year. Since we know how much we spent in each area and what type of advertising we used, we derive a fairly accurate picture of what our advertising dollar has done for us. This picture enables us to allot advertising for the coming year, to determine the type of advertising, and to decide the amount that we will spend in each area. Other industries may have a more precise way of budgeting. We have found that so many factors affect our sales (such as poor or wet painting weather) that our method of budgeting is as satisfactory as any method that we can use.

No one can guarantee a universal formula for advertising. Advertising must continue to involve a strong element of guess work. One thing must be remembered. A manufacturer may be making the best product that can be produced, but it is no good to him if he cannot sell it. Advertising alone may not sell a product, but it helps."

Questions

1. What should be Tibbetts' advertising policy with regard to emphasizing such themes as the following:
   (a) superiority of Maritime workmanship and know-how?
   (b) contribution to local prosperity by buying locally manufactured products?
   (c) honesty and integrity of the manufacturer?
2. Evaluate the policy of relating the advertising budget directly to sales volume.
3. How should the advertising policy of a local manufacturer such as Tibbetts be different from that of national firms?

Case 5

Bailey and Edwards Publishing Company, Inc.*

The Bailey and Edwards Publishing Company was established in 1938 by T. R. Bailey, an unemployed chemical engineer, and George R. Edwards, an editor with ten years experience at Harper and Brothers who was also unemployed. Their assets were six manuscripts on chemical engineering subjects and the promise of a loan of $5,000 from one of the six authors. This man was a well-to-do consultant, specializing in the new field of petrochemicals. He was convinced that there was a potentially profitable market for technical books in this field. The other manuscripts had been unearthed by Bailey while working on a W.P.A. writer's project in the Department of the Interior. There, his job had been to write a history of research in petroleum technology. In the course of his correspondence with workers in this field he had a large quantity of unpublished material called to his attention.

*Case prepared by Professor Leland L. Howell of the University of Southern California.

During the next four years the Bailey and Edwards Company published the six original manuscripts plus fourteen others. At the end of the second year, their indebtedness had reached $80,000, and they saw no alternative but bankruptcy. Their original sponsor came through once again with financial assistance, however, and the crisis was passed. In 1941, the company showed a profit of $5,000 on gross sales of $110,000. In 1942, their business began to boom as they secured contracts for the publication of technical manuals for various branches of the military service.

Following World War II, Bailey and Edwards shared in the general prosperity experienced by publishing companies resulting from the rapid growth of university and college enrollments. They did not, however, expand into the textbook field. They remained relatively small, highly specialized, and were highly esteemed in the publishing industry. In 1959 their catalog contained 95 titles and their gross sales were somewhat more than $800,000. The staff of this company consisted of Bailey, Edwards, the latter's son, and eleven other persons. In 1959, the two partners each drew salaries of $30,000. Edwards junior, who was working as the company's field editor, received $15,000, and the remaining employees received, in the form of salaries and bonuses, a total of $90,000.

This company's marketing program was one of spartan simplicity. All shipments were made from the printing plant in East Orange, New Jersey, which had handled Bailey and Edwards' work for many years on a contract basis. Orders were received by mail in the New York headquarters of the publishing company, and they were filled by mail from New Jersey. Advertising consisted of announcements of new books in technical journals, provision of free books for review purposes, and an ad in the New York Times book supplement two or three times a year. Their usual approach was to allocate about 10 per cent of the retail price of the first printing of a book for advertising that specific title. In addition, there was a general advertising budget of 1 per cent of the preceding year's sales. In 1959, the total expenditure on advertising was about $15,000.

Early in 1961, Bailey and Edwards yielded to the insistent arguments of Richard Edwards, the son, that they should explore various possibilities for expansion. There had been a running debate for several years over the wisdom of remaining out of the textbook business. Textbooks were recognized as lucrative by the two older men, but they insisted that "this simply was not their business." They argued that the company was doing well as a specialty publishing house, that they had struggled to achieve their present status, and that they were too old to undertake risky new ventures. They were sufficiently good business men, however, to recognize that it would cost them nothing, at least, to discuss new ideas.

T. R. Bailey and George R. Edwards were prepared to listen to some radical proposals from young Richard Edwards, but they were surprised at the audacious proposal that he actually laid before them. Richard

Edwards outlined a program whereby the Bailey and Edwards Publishing Company would sponsor a book club with a first year membership goal of 20,000 subscribers. He based his advocacy of mass marketing techniques on a number of developments which were already reshaping major sectors of the American publishing industry.

The 1959 peak-selling fall season had produced several cases of mass marketing of books which were without precedent. Perhaps the most extravagant example was that of Bernard Geis Associates, a new publishing house, which used an extensive television campaign. Among the "associates" were such television personalities as Art Linkletter and Groucho Marx. Linkletter had demonstrated the potency of television promotion in 1957 when he pushed his book, *Kids Say the Darndest Things,* on his two programs. During the first three months that his book was on sale in 1957, sales were 180,000 copies. Six months later the figure was 450,000, and by the fall of 1959, the paperback version was expected to reach a sales level of 2 million copies.[1]

The efficacy of television promotion had also been demonstrated by Alexander King's experience with the Jack Paar show. Before Alexander King spent several weeks as a guest on this show his book, *Mine Enemy Grows Older,* had sold only 15,000 copies. After the television promotion, the sales rose to 100,000.

These extreme examples had no direct relevance to the Bailey and Edwards Publishing Company. They were cited by Richard Edwards merely as evidence that some segments of the industry were proving that new marketing methods could be used effectively. He agreed that they represented "overt commercialism," and violated some of the finest traditions of the publishing trade. It had become established, however, that the generic product, "books," was susceptible to mass marketing.

The book business was thriving in 1960. Over the decade, 1950-60, annual sales of books, in terms of actual volumes, had nearly doubled. By category, some of the biggest increases had come in encyclopedias (up 300 per cent), juvenile books (up 210 per cent), and paperbacks (up 150 per cent). These increases far exceeded the population growth for the period, which was not quite 20 per cent.

One major category had shown a decline: the so-called "adult trade book," fiction and non-fiction in hard covers for adults. A decline of about 30 per cent, in terms of volumes, resulted almost entirely from the decline in sales of novels. From a marketing viewpoint, fiction was in trouble in 1960. The drop in sales was limited, however, to new titles published in hard covers and selling for $3.00 to $5.00 a copy. People were reading as much fiction as they ever did, but they were buying paperbacks, selling for 25 cents to $1.50, which are sold in drugstores, supermarkets and railroad and bus stations rather than bookstores.

---

[1]*The Wall Street Journal,* July 16, 1959, p. 1.

A hard cover novel selling at $5.00 retail, cost the publisher about $1.00, in 1960. Of this, 60 cents was production cost, with binding alone costing about 24 cents. By contrast, a 50 cent machine-produced paperback cost about 10 cents to produce, with binding costing less than 3 cents.

The break-even point on a hard cover novel was usually in the neighborhood of 10,000 copies, and most titles failed to sell over 5,000 copies. Thus, it was vital to a publisher to place the title with a book club which might distribute, without any special promotion, 100,000 copies. A second device for making a book profitable was the sale of reprint rights to a paperback publisher. A 50 cent paperback usually netted the author and publisher one cent each in royalties per copy. Paperback sales exceeded one million copies quite commonly.

All of this information appeared to be of only casual significance to Bailey and Edwards, which was a quality, non-fiction publishing house. Richard Edwards knew that he had aroused a genuine interest in the possibilities of some type of large scale promotion, however. The two senior men were especially interested in his description of Basic Books, Inc., a company which until now, they had only known by name. Basic Books had succeeded in combining high quality books with mass marketing methods and was a very profitable operation.

By adding a promotional verve to an academician's love for books, Arthur J. Rosenthal had developed Basic Books from a losing proposition into a business grossing about $6 million a year. The enterprise consisted of a book publishing company specializing in quality titles, a number of book clubs covering the sciences and fine literature, and a science materials center that produced kits for teaching science to children in school and in the home. Supporting all the Basic Books' activities was a promotional budget of about $1 million a year.[2]

When Rosenthal took over the company for its $10,000 in debts in 1948, Basic Books was limited to selling books to psychiatrists and other specialists in psychology, neurophysiology, and psychoanalysis. Rosenthal, a Yale graduate who spent four years in the service in World War II and had held a number of inconclusive jobs before acquiring Basic Books, immediately imposed a book club program on the operation, and sales grew rapidly. In 1960, the club had about 45,000 members whose interests covered all the behavioral sciences.

Each month, the members were given their choice of a main selection, an alternate selection, and a catalog of previous choices, plus a selection from arts and letters or general science. The members were required to buy four books a year. This program was quite successful. In an average month the membership would buy 8,000 copies of the main selection, 2,000 copies of the alternate, 6,000 copies of past selections, and 2,000

---

[2] *Printers Ink,* August 11, 1961, pp. 56-57.

copies of the general arts and science offering. Annual sales for this club were running well over 215,000 copies per year, or an average of about five books per member.

The main costs of this program were $5,000 a month for the membership mailings and about $50,000 a year for soliciting new members. New members were solicited twice a year from among the professionals in the behavioral sciences. Direct mail was used, and a list of about 200,000 names was used each time. The cost was approximately 10 cents per mailing. The returns from these solicitations ran between 2 and 2.5 per cent.

A second book club, called the Library of Science, was primarily concerned with the physical and natural sciences. This club had a membership of more than 50,000 in 1960. Like the behavioral science book club, the Library of Science relied mainly on professional mailing lists to secure new members. Unlike the former, however, the Library also used magazine and newspaper advertising.

Two more Basic Books enterprises extended the Library of Science towards younger audiences. One of these was the young adult division, a club plan designed exclusively for the very bright teen-ager. The club was organized in 1959, and a year later it had about 10,000 members. The other project was the junior division for "average" children eight to twelve years of age. This club offered a balanced series of science materials designed to encourage young people to learn the scientists' way of thinking. The materials offered were books, records, instruments, and audio-visual aids. This club had a membership of 5,000 in 1960.

The least successful of the many Basic Books enterprises was The Readers' Subscription, a book plan for readers interested in general, classical literature. This plan had 9,000 members when it was purchased by Basic Books in 1959. A year later the membership had more than doubled. The average purchases per member were considerably lower than in the other plans, however.

Basic Books was also a publisher, having brought out its first title in 1950. Ten years later, it was offering more than 40 original titles and an equal number of reprints. These books all could be characterized as specialized and high quality. Gross sales in 1960 were about $1 million. Many of these books were sold through traditional bookstore channels as well as through the book clubs.

Basic Books got good results from selective promotions. For example, a full-page ad in the New York Times Book Review, costing around $3,000, netted 456 orders for a $25 edition of the Collected Papers of Sigmund Freud. The second time the ad was run, it drew 289 responses. A special mailing to 8,000 supporters of the Boston Symphony resulted in 675 orders for a $10 book on the Boston Symphony.[3]

---

[3]*Ibid.*

Richard Edwards argued that the Basic Books case proved that high quality books could be sold through mass marketing methods which avoided the "ballyhoo" of television promotion but went beyond the old-fashioned traditions of the publishing business. Somewhat to his surprise, his book club proposal was warmly received, and he was instructed to proceed with the development of the details of the plan. It was suggested by T. R. Bailey that on the basis of a general marketing program outline and budget they hold further discussions on the strengths and weaknesses of the proposal. He suggested that they aim at the fall season of 1962 for the launching of the program if, in fact, it proved to be feasible.

Questions

1. What further research should be undertaken in the preparation of the suggested program outline?
2. What major hazards might confront a company such as Bailey and Edwards in undertaking the mass marketing of its product?
3. Does the Basic Books example provide Bailey and Edwards with a marketing formula which they can adopt more or less without modification? What modifications, if any, might be necessary?

Case 6

Hanover Electric Company*

In July of 1961, the General Manager of Division 1 summoned the Director of Purchases and the Purchasing Agent for iron products, Mr. Dorquist. (See exhibit 1.) He read a letter signed by the Manufacturing Vice-President. The letter stated that Newark foundry currently operated at 60% of rated capacity. (See exhibit 2.) The Vice-President requested that all product divisions send cast iron orders to Newark and he included fan hubs in a list of suggested possibilities. He acknowledged that some difficult decisions might have to be made.

Hanover Electric Company manufactures industrial equipment and appliances. The forty year old company operates eight decentralized divisions. A General Manager administrates each division. He is relatively independent and bears responsibility for a group of products. Administrative functions are shared with the central office in New York.

---

*Case prepared by Professor Howard T. Healy of Marquette University.

Exhibit 1. *Hanover Electric Company Organization Chart*

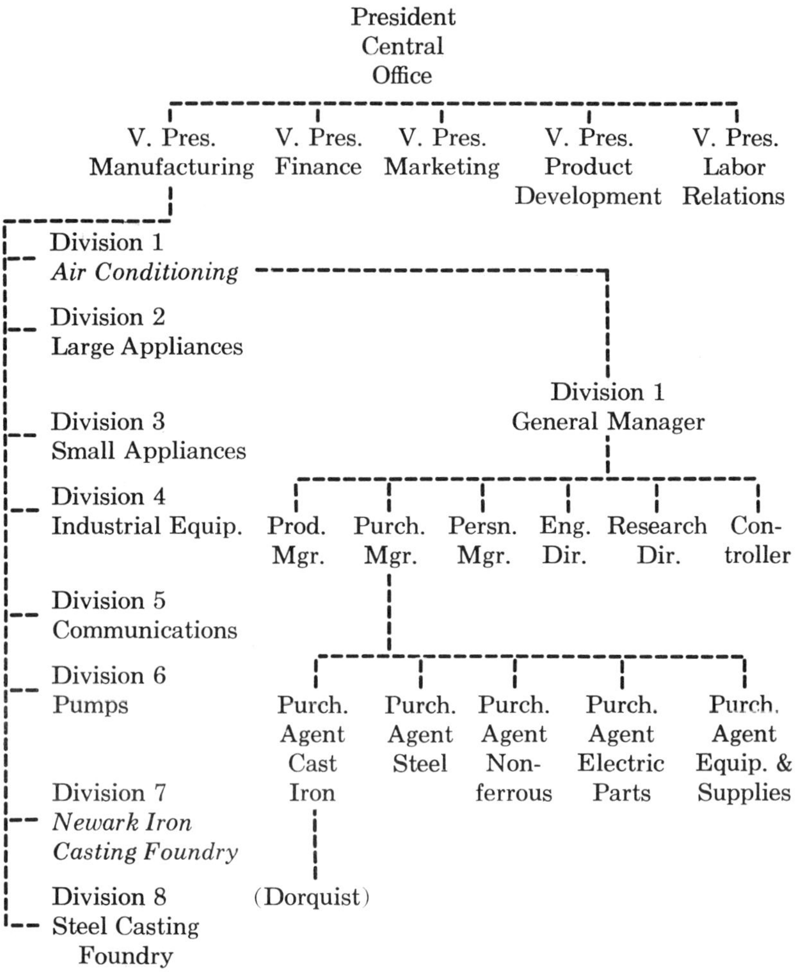

The General Managers are directly responsible to the Manufacturing Vice-President.

One of the divisions fabricates air conditioning and air exhaust systems. Most systems are engineered to individual customer specifications. There are, however, many standard parts which may be included in the planning of any system. One such part is termed a "fan hub."

Fan hub castings are made in grey iron foundries. Hanover finishes the rough castings to very close tolerances. Then, skilled assembly crews mount steel blades on the hubs to form heavy duty fans. The fans may revolve at speeds up to several thousand rpm so quality construction is essential. A defective hub becomes a potential killer.

Exhibit 2. *Hanover Electric Company*

NEWARK CAST IRON FOUNDRY — DIVISION EIGHT
SELECTED COST AND OPERATING FIGURES

Cost of operation — Production at the break even point (80% of rated capacity)

Melted metal cost	3¢ per pound
Direct labor cost	2¢ per pound
Department burden	2¢ per pound
General foundry burden	5¢ per pound
	12¢ per pound FOB Newark

Transportation cost — Newark to the Air Conditioning plant

Truck load (40,000 pounds)	$2.20 cwt.
Less than truck load (LTL)	$3.60 cwt.

Labor cost variances — Due to changes in molders' assignments

Change once per week	add 2¢ per lb. to Dir. Lab.
Change more than once per week	add 3¢ per lb. to Dir. Lab.
Change more than once per day	add 4¢ per lb. to Dir. Lab.

Burden variance — Due to changes in storage, handling, scheduling, etc.

Change more than once per week	add 2¢ per lb. to Dept. Burd.

Newark rated capacity ... 100,000 lbs. of grey iron castings per day
Newark average production per molder ... 2,000 lbs. of castings per day

Source: Company personnel

Hanover divisions ordinarily manufacture two categories of component parts: those that have a high unit cost, and those that are used in large quantities. Orders for cast iron components in these categories are forwarded by the purchasing agent to the Newark foundry (Division 7). When components have a low unit cost or are used only periodically, Mr. Dorquist purchases them locally. Cast iron fan hubs fall into the latter category. He purchases most of them from the Congress foundry.

Mr. James Warren operates the Congress foundry as a jobbing shop. He serves a variety of industrial customers. He holds most of his customers because of his success with problem castings.[1] Since problem castings generate little profit, most customers also place orders for reasonable quantities of routine castings. Mr. Warren had always considered the fan hub a routine job and a profitable one.

Hanover uses 16 sizes of hubs. They range in weight from 10 to 2500 pounds. Congress charges an average price of 20¢ per pound for all castings, FOB Hanover. Congress adjusts its own production schedule to Hanover's needs, gives priority to Hanover rush orders, and, if necessary, makes delivery on one day's notice.

[1]Problem castings. Those which possess awkward contours or unusual metallurgical specifications.

Exhibit 3. *Hanover Electric Company*

ESTIMATE OF FAN REQUIREMENTS
FROM AUGUST 1961 THROUGH 1962

Weight	*Amount*	*Total Weight*	*Prod. Hours Per Unit Congress*	*Prod. Hours Per Unit Newark*	*New Pattern Cost*
10	1,600	16,000	.20	.10	$ 150
15	1,400	21,000	.20	.10	150
20	1,000	20,000	.20	.15	150
30	600	18,000	.25	.15	175
45	500	22,500	.50	.25	175
70	400	28,000	.80	.35	175
100	200	20,000	1.00	.40	200
140	150	21,000	1.30	.50	250
200	80	16,000	1.80	.70	300
300	80	14,000	2.10	.80	350
450	70	31,000	2.80	1.20	400
650	60	39,000	4.00	1.70	450
900	50	45,000	4.60	2.00	500
1300	40	52,000	6.20	3.00	600
1800	20	36,000	10.50	3.35	800
2500	20	50,000	11.60	4.00	1,000

Source: Company records and personnel

Mr. Dorquist projected Hanover's cast iron requirements for the next six months. (See exhibit 3.) Congress had already bid its standard price on approximately one-fourth of the items. Under normal circumstances Mr. Dorquist would automatically issue purchase orders for these castings.

In addition to the hubs, Congress also held the patterns for 300 other Hanover components. One-third of these were "Problem" parts. Hanover owned all of its patterns, and whenever Mr. Dorquist decided to change his source of supply on a component, he recalled the pattern.

During the past ten years, Dorquist had increasingly concentrated his fan hub orders at Congress foundry. On three occasions Mr. Warren expanded capacity. In 1958 he installed a $35,000.00 sandslinger molding unit to increase production and reduce cost.

Mr. Dorquist realized that his superiors wished him to transfer castings from his local suppliers to the Newark Foundry on a temporary basis. He arranged a conference with Mr. Warren and acquired the information in exhibit 4.

Mr. Dorquist knew that top management evaluated executive personnel for their ability to make effective decisions. When management gave a man responsibility, it rarely interfered with his exercise of authority. The good of the company as a whole held precedence over divisional advantages. Where a conflict seemed apparent, the executive involved usually submitted a report clarifying his actions. A man's continued advancement depended upon his "batting average."

Exhibit 4. *Hanover Electric Company*

ANNUAL CAPACITY FIGURES OF THE CONGRESS FOUNDRY IN POUNDS AND ITS CASTINGS SALES IN POUNDS TO THE HANOVER ELECTRIC COMPANY, WITH PERCENTAGE RELATIONSHIPS

Year	*Fan Hub Sales to Hanover*	*Other Sales to Hanover*	*Total Sales to Hanover*	*Total Congress Capacity*	*Hubs as a % of Sales to Hanover*	*Other sales as a % of Sales to Hanover*	*Hanover as a % of Sales to Congress Capacity*
1952	4,200	7,800	12,000	200,000	35.0	65.0	6.00
1953	8,000	11,000	19,000	200,000	42.1	57.9	9.50
1954	23,000	19,000	42,000	400,000	54.8	45.2	10.50
1955	66,000	35,000	101,000	400,000	59.5	40.5	25.25
1956	85,000	40,000	125,000	600,000	68.0	32.0	20.83
1957	99,000	45,000	144,000	600,000	68.8	31.2	23.99
1958	265,000	170,000	435,000	2,300,000	60.9	39.1	18.91
1959	261,000	180,000	441,000	2,300,000	59.2	40.8	19.17
1960	333,000	180,000	513,000	2,300,000	64.9	35.1	21.87
1961 (6 mos.)	230,000	98,000	328,000	1,150,000	70.1	29.9	28.52

Source: Company Records & Personnel

Questions

1. What should be Mr. Dorquist's decision regarding procurement of fan hubs? Support your conclusions.

Case 7

Houston Wire Rope Company*

As president and major stockholder of the Houston Wire Rope Company, a relatively young organization, Mr. Paul H. Rogers was attempting to develop an organizational arrangement and operating methods

---

*From H. N. Broom and Justin G. Longenecker, *Small Business Management*, Second Edition (Cincinnati: South-Western Publishing Company, 1966).

which would maintain and improve the efficiency and profitability of the business.

Background of the Company

In 1951, Mr. Rogers, then a sales representative for a major producer of wire rope, conceived the idea of a business which would specialize in the purchase and resale of used wire rope. Acting upon the idea, he established his business in Houston, Texas, purchasing used wire rope from the oil fields and selling it to mining, logging, and marine companies. In addition to purchasing and selling, some processing of the used rope was required. This involved rewinding on to new reels, inspection and grading of the rope, cutting out seriously defective pieces, and lubrication. The company quickly gained market acceptance and increased its sales volume each year.

By 1960, the Houston Wire Rope Company was approaching an annual sales volume of $600,000. It had added new wire rope imported from Holland, Belgium, Germany, and Japan to supplement its lines of used rope. Sales were divided roughly equally between used and new rope. Approximately 50 per cent of used rope sales were made to the marine industry (including substantial sales to large dredging companies), 30 per cent to the logging industry, and 20 per cent to the mining industry. Of the imported new rope sales, about 60 per cent went to industrial customers, 25 per cent to marine customers, and 15 per cent to oil producers.

Sales were made to a nation-wide market and even to a few accounts in Canada. Branch warehouses had also been established in Jeanerette, Louisiana; Odessa, Texas; and Norman, Oklahoma. Although the major purpose of the branches was to purchase used rope from the oil industry in their respective areas, they also made sales in the same areas.

Home Office Personnel and Organization

Both Mr. Rogers, the president, and the sales manager maintained offices at the Houston headquarters of the company. Their activities were devoted to the company as a whole. In addition, the following positions comprised what might be thought of as the Houston branch:

- 1 branch manager & inside salesman
- 1 outside salesman
- 1 bookkeeper & secretary
- 2 warehouse employees
- 1 truck driver

All employees had a close personal relationship to Mr. Rogers who had hired each of them. The employee who had been with the company almost from its beginning was designated as manager of the Houston branch. His major responsibility was that of maintaining customer contacts and selling by telephone, although he did exercise some supervision over the warehouse employees and truck driver. The outside salesman reported both to the sales manager and to Mr. Rogers. The bookkeeper-secretary, whose work also applied to the entire company, was personally responsible to Mr. Rogers, although the sales manager directed some of her activities.

Position of Sales Manager

Two years earlier, Mr. Rogers had employed as sales manager an individual with extensive experience in the sale of wire rope. The sales manager had assumed a variety of sales and administrative activities. He had engaged in direct selling, worked out adjustments with dissatisfied customers, participated in the purchase of new imported wire rope, surveyed prospective locations for new branches, and exercised some supervision over branch managers.

There was some tendency for overlapping in the duties of Mr. Rogers and the sales manager. There had been no careful division of responsibilities between the positions. They both had contacts with the same customers and the same employees of the company. Their trips to branch offices were typically made at different times.

One effect of the somewhat nebulous division of responsibilities between these two top positions was a certain amount of confusion and uncertainty in the minds of other employees. All employees, including those in branch offices, had enjoyed a warm personal relationship and friendship with Mr. Rogers. His complete candor, personal interest and generosity in the past had developed a strong sense of personal loyalty to him. It required time for them to accept and understand the new position of sales manager and its relationship to them. For example, branch managers would not hesitate to check back with Mr. Rogers concerning some policy or instruction they had received from the sales manager.

Branch Office Organization

Each of the three branch offices (Jeanerette, Odessa and Norman) was expected to contain a total of three employees. The branch manager was directly responsible for overall supervision of the branch. In addition, he purchased used wire rope and made sales calls in his area. Purchasers of wire rope tended to be few in number and to purchase in large quantities. However, considerable time was required in cultivating customer goodwill and in seeking out new customers. The firm was interested in developing new markets and discovering new uses for wire rope.

Backing up the office manager were a warehouseman and a truck driver. As noted above, some processing of newly purchased used rope was required in addition to transporting and storing it. Of course, some stock of new rope was also maintained in branch warehouses as required by customer demand in each area.

Relationships Between Home Office and Branch Offices

One of the policies Mr. Rogers attempted to follow closely in dealing with branch managers was that of decentralization and delegation of authority. As he visualized it, each branch manager should operate like an independent businessman, making the decisions pertinent to the business in his own area. In fact, Mr. Rogers took considerable pride in the development of branch managers in his organization.

Each of the branch managers had started with inadequate experience but had proceeded to grow in his managerial position. For example, the manager of the Jeanerette branch had previously worked as a warehouse and office employee with a wire rope company but lacked selling experience prior to joining the Houston Wire Rope Company. He had assumed the responsibility placed upon him and developed an outstanding business record in his branch. The manager of the Odessa branch had non-selling experience as a refinery worker before joining the Houston Wire Rope Company. The Odessa branch had been successful, although it was conceded that the manager's selling abilities needed further development. The manager of thc Norman branch had some previous experience as a salesman of office equipment and insurance, although he had no prior contact with the wire rope business. The branch had not been established a sufficient length of time to permit a full evaluation of his efforts, but he seemed to be making good. Each of these managers had some training in selling and in company operations — from three to six months — before being placed in charge of a branch.

Each branch manager was made responsible for an account in a local bank and paid all bills locally. The sum of $1,000 was deposited in the account initially, and the amount fluctuated from time to time with the needs of the branch. When the cash balance was low and funds were needed, the branch manager requested additional funds from the home office, usually by telephone. Although a shortage of working capital in the business was partially responsible for this arrangement, it also provided a close control over most financial commitments by branch offices. The branch manager, for example, would often request funds to raise the bank balance sufficiently to permit a particular purchase of wire rope. Individual purchases were typically for amounts less than $300.

Personal visits were made to branch offices by either Mr. Rogers or the sales manager on the average of once a month. These visits were used to discuss branch problems, review sales contacts and make sales calls with the branch manager.

Because of the diversity in their background and experience, the branch managers differed in the progress they had made in developing a strong branch organization. The Odessa manager had experienced some difficulty in fully delegating authority and responsibility to his subordinates. He tended to supervise those working for him closely and to be exacting in his demands upon them. At the same time, he had indicated a desire for greater guidance and help from the home office.

Formal Planning and Control

The company had never used a budget for overall operations or for activities of branch offices. As a result, there were no predetermined expense or sales standards that a branch manager was expected to achieve. The operating results of each branch were shown separately and thus provided a summary report of branch operations.

Similarly, the company had not yet grown to the point that written policies had been developed. For example, major personnel decisions were made through agreement between the branch manager and Mr. Rogers on the basis of the individual circumstances. One employee of a branch office who was ill for several weeks was continued on the payroll for an extended period. No decision had ever been made concerning overall company policy in such cases.

The Houston Wire Rope Company had expanded rapidly and gave every indication of continuing its expansion. Several possible expansion moves had been under consideration for some time. Enthusiasm for various of these possibilities had a tendency to rise and fall with changes in competition, fluctuation of sales to existing customers, progress of existing branches, and development of new information concerning proposed locations. It was possible that a decision might be made rather suddenly concerning establishment of a new branch. There was no plan which specified expectations concerning additional branches for the following six months, one year, or five years. As new branch offices were opened, some managers would no doubt be shifted into new locations. While this provided an opportunity for advancement, it also introduced some uncertainty and insecurity into their thinking.

Organization Planning

Mr. Rogers realized the importance of loyal, enthusiastic personnel and the value of present employees to the company. As the business continued to expand, however, it would be desirable and necessary to adapt the company's organization and operating methods to the changing needs of the business. The question was whether the most desirable organizational arrangements and procedures, considering the size and status of the business, had yet been developed.

Questions

1. Evaluate the position of the sales manager and his placement in the organization structure. Can Mr. Rogers make this position any more effective? If so, how?
2. What weaknesses are apparent in the home office organization?
3. What is Mr. Rogers' organizational philosophy in dealing with branch offices? Does he operate consistently with this philosophy?
4. What connection is there between planning and control on the one hand and organizational arrangements on the other hand?

Case 8

Too Many Bosses*

In February, 1953, the Major Jig and Fixtures Department opened a group of jigs to production. Some of these tools had been built by outsiders and shipped in presumably ready for use in building parts, but this was only the ideal. In practice many bugs had to be ironed out, and in some instances it was even discovered that sub-contracted tools had been built to obsolete tool design. This meant that major reworking would be required — occasionally even rebuilding the tool involved.

Where this was necessary production was delayed until the tools could be made ready to build the production assemblies which were needed to turn out parts in quantity. This might require as little as three days or as long as four weeks, depending upon the amount of rework required. It is not to be wondered at that this condition generated a great deal of pressure on the tooling organization from some of the upper echelons of management.

During the peak of this confusion Fred Larson, a supervisor, found his operation to be one of the hottest spots. Jess Bradley, his division superintendent, inaugurated the practice of walking through the shop a couple of times a day to see how things were moving along. At first he always came with Phil Hawthorne, Fred's foreman, and discussed the job chiefly with the supervisor in charge. Pretty soon, however, he was coming by

*Case prepared by Professor Howard R. Smith of The University of Georgia.

himself and if the supervisor wasn't around he might talk at length with a lead man or even one or two of the workers. Then as time went on, he went a step beyond talking and asking questions, requesting job builders to tear down a set-up in order to incorporate some of his ideas.

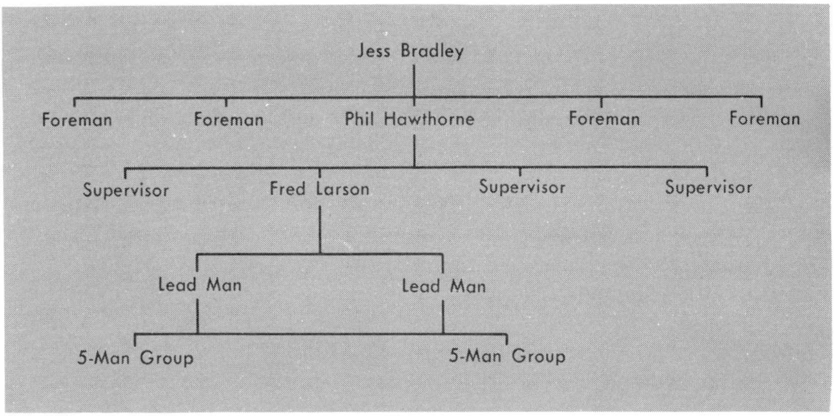

Fred's was not the only work station in the tooling organization to receive this treatment. All of the operations reporting to Phil were also on Jess' itinerary, as were a number of those for which other foremen were responsible, and Phil and his foreman colleagues well knew what was going on. It was just that the straw which broke the camel's back, so to speak, was an incident that occurred in Fred's area about 10 days after all of this started. Already the morale of his men was at low ebb, they not knowing any more whether to go ahead with a given set-up as planned or wait for Jess Bradley to tell them how to proceed. Then one day Fred returned to his station after a brief absence to learn that scheduled operations on a large job had just been changed, and that two days' set-up time for seven men had thereby gone down the drain.

Profoundly disturbed and thoroughly angry, Fred decided that things could not go on this way any longer.

Questions

1. What is responsible for Jess Bradley's behavior? Is it justified? Is it effective?
2. What problems have been created?
3. Could Jess Bradley have avoided the difficulty? How?
4. Is Fred Larson justified in complaining about the two days' set-up time that have gone down the drain?
5. What action should be taken by Fred Larson? By Phil Hawthorne?

Case 9

Jordan Company*

The Jordan Company manufactures automobile piston rings, pistons, valves, and related products. The plant is located near South Bend, Indiana. The company is relatively small, employing 350 production workers, in addition to 125 office and sales employees and executives. Growth has been rather rapid, having expanded from 12 employees in 1946 to its present size in 1957.

The founder and President, Thomas Jordan, also holds the title of Sales Manager in his company. Before organizing the Jordan Company he had been the sales manager of a large automobile parts manufacturer. Believing that his extensive contacts in the automobile industry and his proven sales ability would enable him to own his own company, he went into business for himself in 1946, after obtaining additional capital from two friends who each own 20 per cent interest in the firm.

Jordan had never given much attention to the production aspects of business. In fact, he devotes about 25 per cent of his time contacting important customers and the twenty manufacturers' agents which represent the Company in the southern and western states. Frank Elliott, his Plant Manager, started with the company at the time of its organization. He laid out the plant, established production and quality standards, and hired all the production executives under him as well as several of the first production workers who went to work with the Jordan Company.

It has been the practice of the company to allow each foreman and office supervisor to hire, discipline, transfer, promote, and otherwise make his own decisions about personnel matters within his department.

Mr. Jordan observed that as the company grew in number of employees, morale appeared to degenerate. He once commented to Elliott that "the one-big-happy-family spirit which pervaded our people during the first few years of the company disappeared during the past two years."

In 1956 Mr. Jordan decided that the Company should employ a personnel manager.

John Graham, Chief Cost Accountant, learned of Jordan's plans through one of the secretaries with whom he had lunch in the plant cafeteria one day. John had wanted to get into personnel work for some time. As he put it, "I always did prefer working with people to working with numbers."

John Graham has worked with the Jordan Company for seven years. He joined the company in the bookkeeping department immediately after graduating from college. Since the company is small and work is not highly departmentalized John has had many contacts with people

---

*Case prepared by Professor Sterling H. Schoen of Washington University.

in both production and sales. Elliott and Jordan both believe that he is an alert, conscientious employee who is "generally well liked by all."

Graham applied for the position of Personnel Manager, and he was selected for the job.

After much debate, it was decided to make the Personnel Manager a part of the production management section, the manager of which reported to the Plant Manager.

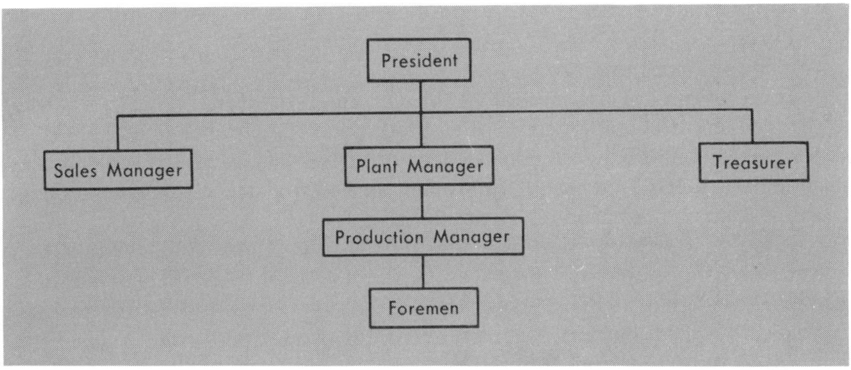

John was given an office near the entrance of the plant and a secretary was assigned to him. The President told him at the time of his appointment that "the scope and success of the personnel department's activities will be pretty much what you make them."

John immediately sent a memorandum to all foremen, over the signature of the Production Manager, advising them that "the Personnel Manager will hire all new employees in the future." In addition, the memorandum stated that the Personnel Manager would henceforth initiate all transfers and changes in pay, and that all disciplinary action and other personnel decisions must be approved by the Personnel Manager before being acted upon.

Upon receiving the memorandum several of the foremen expressed considerable resentment against this organizational change. They agreed that John had the "big-head."

After a short time, the Production Manager began to receive complaints from foremen to the effect that "new employees aren't what they were when we hired them." On one occasion when he questioned a foreman about a drop in production, the foreman said that his hands were tied; he could not hire, discipline or otherwise control his men. And, if he could not control his men, how could he be expected to get out production?

One day an employee came into John's office and protested that his foreman had just discharged him "for no reason at all." John telephoned the foreman and the following conversation took place:

John: Hello, Jim. This is John Graham. What's the story of Joe Ralfing?

Foreman: I fired him.

John: Yes, I know, but why?

Foreman: I don't like him.

John: But that's no reason. You know that you can't fire him without an O.K. from my office.

Foreman: Well, I did it.

John: But you can't, Jim. There has to be a good reason, and . . . .

Foreman: I don't like him — that's reason enough.

The foreman hung up.

John presented the matter to the Production Manager who finally insisted that the employee be reinstated. Soon the number of complaints concerning the hiring of poor workers and the lack of control over personnel began to increase. The foremen agreed to "stay clear" of the personnel department as much as possible.

Finally, the Production Manager advised the Plant Manager that he did not believe that the firm was large enough to warrant a personnel department. He further recommended that the Company return to the former plan of having foremen make their own personnel decisions. Finally, he urged that John be returned to his former job.

The Plant Manager thought about the Production Manager's recommendations for a few days and then passed them on to the President, recommending that they be accepted.

Questions

1. What went wrong in this organizational change?
2. What errors, if any, were made in organizing the personnel "department"?
3. What difficulties were experienced in Graham's use of his authority?
4. How do you interpret the firing incident?

Case 10

Self-Serve Shoe Stores

Description and History of Self-Serve Shoe Stores

The Self-Serve Shoe Stores of Portland, Oregon, were opened during 1961 and operated as an outlet for both "distress" and popular priced shoes for the entire family. Store No. 1, which was located on a heavily traveled highway just outside the city, was opened in April, 1961. Store No. 2, located on an artery in the city, occupied a part of the same building with a self-service laundry and was situated across the street from an elementary school. It was opened in May, 1961. Store No. 3, also located on an artery, but occupying an entire building adjacent to a self-service laundry, was opened in December, 1961.

Each of the locations displayed shoes in open individual boxes placed upon plain wooden racks. Sizes were plainly penciled on the boxes, and children's, men's, and women's shoes were located in different sections of the store. There was a small amount of warehouse space in each store, but most of the storage room was located in Store No. 1, which also served as the headquarters for the general manager.

The stores were organized as a corporation and owned by six stockholders, but the organization was primarily the brain child of Mr. Wesley Baldwin, who operated two "legitimate" or full-service men's shoe stores in the same city. Mr. Baldwin had opened his first shoe store some five years earlier and three years later opened a second store in a suburban shopping center. The trend toward self-service merchandising of shoes and the possibilities for profits in this type of operation provided the motivation for the organization of the new business. Although the business was that of shoe retailing, the same as Baldwin's previous business, the two ventures were for the most part non-competitive in that their appeals were to different groups of customers.

Although Wesley Baldwin was the instigator of the new self-service shoe stores, he owned less than half of the stock in the corporation. The ownership was divided as follows:

Wesley Baldwin	26.5%
Ronald Brown	22.5
David Ware	22.5
Larry Kliever	13.5
Ned Casey	10.0
Harry Stagg	5.0
	100.0%

The Board of Directors

Each of the stockholders also served as a member of its board of directors and participated actively in decisions pertaining to the operation of Self-Serve Shoe Stores. Most of the stockholders also had other business interests. As noted earlier, Wesley Baldwin was the owner and manager of two full-service men's shoe stores. He also served as president of the Self-Serve Shoe Stores but did not serve as its full-time executive in day-to-day administration. The responsibilities or other connections of the remaining members of the board were as follows:

Ronald Brown — employed as a shoe salesman for a major shoe manufacturer, traveling over most of Oregon and part of Washington.

David Ware — employed by a Portland industrial concern as a millwright.

Larry Kliever — employed as a shoe salesman for a manufacturer and also traveling over most of Oregon.

Ned Casey — employed as general manager of Self-Serve Shoe Stores on a full-time basis.

Harry Stagg — employed as shoe manager of Wesley Baldwin's second full-service shoe store.

The board was no "rubber-stamp" board. Each of the directors took a personal interest in the business, and a number of them made personal contributions of their own services to the new stores. For example, Ronald Brown and Larry Kliever located lots of distress merchandise as they called on different shoe stores and were able to arrange favorable purchases for resale in Self-Serve Shoe Stores. David Ware, having a good background in maintenance, performed all maintenance and minor construction work in adapting and keeping the store buildings in good operating condition.

Store Management by Ned Casey

The salary agreement with Ned Casey, the general manager, provided for a base salary of $500 per month with two stores in operation. Starting with Store No. 3 in December, 1961, the contract provided for $90 additional salary per month for each additional store. In addition, he was to receive one-half of one per cent of total gross volume as a bonus, payable every six months. Stores were required to do $50,000 sales volume before this bonus was paid.

The general manager was responsible for directing all store personnel. Each of the three stores had two employees, one of whom was designated as store manager. The store manager received about $80 per week, and the other employee received about $45 per week. The stores stayed open from 9 A.M. to 9 P.M., and the shifts of these two employees were overlapped so that both would be present during rush hours. Shifts were alternated so that one employee did not constantly have the late shift. Ned visited each of the stores as frequently as possible. He was in Store No. 1 daily, but he did not always visit the other two stores each day.

One of Ned's primary functions was buying shoes for sale in all three stores. It was in this particular area that he was recognized as being most skilled. In fact, one of the other stockholders described him as a "walking encyclopedia" of the shoe business. Ned had worked in the sale of shoes for many years and was thoroughly conversant with shoe styles and trends. He was also recognized as being a sharp bargainer in negotiating for the sale of distress merchandise. A jobber might call on Ned to show him some shoes that he had purchased from a bankrupt shoe store. Ned could quickly look at a few of the samples, size them up, and ask concerning the offering price. At once, drawing on his knowledge of shoes, he could reject the purchase, accept it, or make a counter offer that would secure for him the more attractive items in the lot or that would secure a type of shoe that was in short supply in his own stores.

In the use of systematic management and controls, Ned had little experience and seemingly little interest. He kept his greatest supply of information on shoe supplies, requirements, and orders in his own head. He supplemented this knowledge with a rather haphazard record system, involving notes to himself, copies of invoices, and other miscellaneous items of information. These were completely unorganized and unfiled, but, surprisingly enough, Ned could usually come up with necessary figures at the time they were needed. In fact, it was a source of amazement to his colleagues that he could keep the situation under control as well as he could with what appeared to be such a completely inadequate set of records.

Ned was criticized in particular for his lack of ability in personnel relations. He had several incidents in which employees became somewhat unhappy because of his brusque manner of dealing with them. Although he did not use a great amount of tact in dealing with these employees, he was basically big-hearted and never dismissed any of the employees in spite of his rather gruff exterior. Seemingly, some of the employees were able to adjust to Ned and his techniques once they discovered that his "bark was worse than his bite."

Relationship of the Board to the General Manager

The close personal interest of the board members in the business and their individual responsibilities in store management meant that they would inevitably be thrown into close contact, and possible conflict, with the general manager. The stockholders and directors did not always consider their services and judgment to be limited to their participation in board meetings; they also liked to discuss store administration and store policies with Ned between board meetings.

Some of the directors felt that Ned was somewhat slow in considering their suggestions and unwilling to give their ideas a full and fair trial. As one expressed it, "Ned is bull-headed and will not consider an idea from one of us fairly. He is brilliant in his knowledge of shoes, but he can't stand to listen to or to discuss a suggestion from one of us. It is a matter of pride with him." Among the types of suggestions, practices, and policies that these directors liked to discuss with Ned were his record and control system, store layout, merchandise purchases, and transfer of certain lots of merchandise from one store to another.

Ned viewed many of the suggestions coming from his associates as an intrusion into an area of management in which they had little knowledge or experience. (The possible exception as far as his own willingness to listen was concerned was the president, Wesley Baldwin, who also was an experienced shoe man.) As Ned expressed it, "I think the fellows sincerely mean to help me, but they simply don't see the entire picture. For example, they want me to buy ahead for a possible, tentative opening of a new store. But I can't build up an inventory for a store that may never materialize. They are free to criticize me when a purchase looks questionable, but they change to smiles and become very quiet when the shoes start selling and bringing in the profits."

The conflicts of ideas and close personal interest of all members in store administration resulted, then, in considerable friction among the members of the organization. In spite of the conflict, each member of the group held considerable respect for the other members and recognized the importance of the contribution that each was making to the success of the business as a whole.

Some of the individual responsibilities of different directors had grown out of this early period of development in which the organization was feeling its way along in its attempt to provide a proper organization that would assume all necessary responsibilities. The advertising function and the maintenance function would normally come under the direction of the general manager, but they had been turned over to the particular directors who had special experience and were expected to work in cooperation with the general manager. He was not in a position, however, to issue orders and instructions to them as he might be able to do in the case of a subordinate. The general manager did manage to obtain final authority over all purchases. Even though the two salesmen-stockholders would locate prospective purchases, they were never given the authority to make purchase commitments. Each of these was referred to Ned, often by telephone, and it was his decision as to whether a particular lot should be purchased or refused.

One of the plans being contemplated by the president of the corporation was an arrangement whereby the purchasing function would be split from the store administration function. As general manager, Ned had the responsibility for both areas. If the functions were split, however, Ned would limit his activities to the purchasing and warehousing of shoes. If an organizational pattern of this type were adopted, the store managers would report to the president, board of directors, or some other chief executive.

There was also a question as to the precise status of the store manager. In particular, a question existed as to whether he might be given responsibility similar to that of a store manager in a full-service shoe store. At the time, he served as a working leader with only minor authority in running his particular store.

Questions

1. What are the strong points, if any, of this board of directors?
2. What appear to be the basic organizational weaknesses in this case?
3. What changes should be made in the existing organization?
4. What should Ned Casey do about the existing situation?

Case 11

Atlas Publishing Company*

For years, expenditures for changes in the business publications of the Atlas Publishing Company had been made at the direction of Mr. Arthur Dalton, the Business Manager. It was Dalton's practice to make most of the decisions personally on problems which arose during the day's work. Some of his associates said that they often suggested planned changes and improvements in the various magazines but, they felt, Dalton rarely listened. One of the department heads said, "Arthur feels because of his experience in directing the business, that he knows what should be done, what shouldn't, and when."

When Dalton wanted any change made, he simply requested that it be done (and usually done fast). He often went on to explain in some detail how it could be done expeditiously and effectively. As a rule these changes were accomplished with a minimum of discussion with the people immediately affected by them. Some executives felt the timing of the changes was unpredictable at times.

Several Atlas business publications had doubled their advertising volumes in the last ten years. However, Atlas was beginning to encounter rougher sledding. For the last two years, the company's net profit had been below the industry's figures.

In March, 1960, the Atlas Publishing Company had been in existence for 59 years. It had consistently shown a profit, but the per cent of net to both sales and investment had gradually decreased. Competitors had "stolen" several of their large advertising accounts. Some junior executives thought that certain Atlas publications had not kept up to date with

*Case prepared by Professor Garret L. Bergen of Northwestern University. The case appears in Garret L. Bergen and William V. Haney, *Organizational Relations and Management Action* (New York: McGraw-Hill Book Company, 1966).

changes in the interests, habits, and attitudes of their readers. They felt that competitors had recognized these changes earlier and had revised their periodicals to meet readers' needs.

The record showed that Mr. Dalton was by no means opposed to change. He had initiated many changes in editorial policy. Several staff people, however, told Arthur Dalton's son, Ben, that the reasons for these changes were not always clear to them.

Apart from the Controller and members of the Board of Directors, Arthur Dalton was the only official who had consolidated figures of income, expenses, and profits of the Atlas Publishing business. He knew, he told his management group, when the expenditure of money was justified and when it was not. Since he had a substantial personal investment in the business, he felt that frills, as he called them, should be kept to a minimum. For example — advertisements occupied a substantial portion of the front covers of several Atlas publications with a relatively insignificant amount of space devoted to the title and contents of the publication. In the opinion of many in the trade, these ads were often unsightly and gave a negative impression to readers. Most competitors had long ago abandoned this practice in favor of attractive four-color illustrations relevant to the contents. Their covers were designed to create a favorable "publication image," a term that had become increasingly significant in the trade. Dalton, on the other hand, felt that his competitors were wasting space and money on "window dressing" and losing potential advertising revenue. No amount of discussion and documentation by other executives had succeeded in convincing Dalton that Atlas should at least give the prevalent trade practice a try.

Mr. Dalton often said that he maintained an "Open Door" policy. His executives could come to see him on problems whenever necessary. He didn't have to agree with them, he said, but they certainly could come to see him to secure his opinion on any subject.

Several executives, who had graduated from college before joining Atlas, often met at luncheon to discuss privately their feelings about Dalton's arbitrary manner. It seemed to them that substantive changes in the magazines might be accomplished more effectively through long-range planning than on a sporadic, crisis basis. As things were usually handled, many areas went without attention, others were treated almost as "pet projects."

Arthur Dalton had often said, "When we have the money, we'll spend it on things that are necessary. When we haven't the money, even important projects will just have to wait." One of the younger executives who had studied modern magazine business methods thought that many improvements could be considered capital items, to be depreciated over a period of years, rather than charged wholly against current income. He also felt that, in some instances, it might be wise for the publications to borrow money to make improvements, rather than to postpone them indefinitely because working capital was needed for day-to-day operations.

One of the college graduates who had been coming up through the organization was Dalton's son, Ben. On the eighth anniversary of his employment with the organization, Ben was named business manager and his father became President. Ben was told that from then on, operating responsibility of the publishing company was his job; henceforth Arthur Dalton was going to concern himself with broad matters of policy and community affairs.

Ben realized that he had moved up swiftly through the organization—that he was only superficially familiar with many of the magazines' operating problems. He decided that it would be foolish to start making major decisions solely on the basis of his own limited experience. He decided not to copy his father's methods in this regard. He said to one of his friends that many other executives in the company had gained valuable experience through their long service in the company and that he intended to make use of their know-how.

Ben also remembered the feelings and opinions he had heard younger executives express from time to time. He decided he would encourage his staff to participate in decision making. He began to consult frequently with his associates and in turn to encourage them to consult with him. To give this idea more than lip service, he appointed a Management Committee, consisting of department heads including editorial, circulation, production, advertising, and sales promotion.

After several meetings of this committee, Ben proposed that a program for improving the business be planned on a long-range basis. He asked each committee member to develop a list of projects which, in his judgment, should be initiated within the coming twelve months, plus other projects which they thought were desirable, but which could be deferred until the following year.

Within a month, the Management Committee agreed on a consolidated list of improvements which they felt were important enough to be given "top priority." The estimated cost of these improvements for fiscal 1961 was in excess of $500,000. The program included:

1. Changing magazine formats to more modern appearance
2. Hiring additional writers and upgrading salary scales
3. Maintaining a Washington sales office and editorial correspondent
4. Using more pictures, which would require additional and more up-to-date photographic equipment
5. Using four-color pictures as well as selling four-color advertising
6. Offering more merchandising services as means of selling advertising
7. Doing research on readership, magazine image and buyer motivation
8. Creating a new magazine to meet growing needs in a related industry.

When Ben received this report he was shocked. He was sure that not more than $300,000 could be appropriated for such work in the coming twelve months, and that it would be difficult to persuade his father and the Board of Directors that he could or should personally decide which items should be deferred for another year or two. All of the items had been marked by the Management Committee as "high priority"; as he looked over the list he himself felt all of them were important.

Ben finally decided against launching a new magazine at this time; this alone would require an outlay of $250,000 in 1961. If this project were put into effect now, other urgent improvements would have to wait.

Ben explained to the Committee that he felt they had set their sights too high. He asked them to review the list again to determine which items should be given "special priority" so that a final decision could be made at the next meeting, one week later.

At the next meeting, the Committee showed they had accepted this as an important problem; they had arrived at a "special priority" list of projects totaling $200,000. This list was then discussed at some length. It was concluded that while all of the work could not be included in the allocation for the next twelve months, a start could be made. If $100,000 were authorized for the coming year and the remaining $100,000 for 1962, most of the needed improvements could be initiated. This plan met with unanimous approval. The business manager decided he was ready to discuss it with his father.

The following day Ben told his father he felt he had worked out a recommended program of improvements over the next two years which would call for a total expenditure of $200,000. Arthur Dalton exploded!

"We simply can't afford it, Ben. Why is this necessary now? Some of these things may need attention, but we just can't tackle them with our working capital situation as it is. What else have you been dreaming up, son?"

Ben explained that he was not alone in feeling that these improvements were necessary. He told his father about the Management Committee he had set up to work with him in planning the needs of the business. Mr. Dalton said, "How long has this Management Committee been going on? Why take the valuable time of all these people? How long did it take the group to arrive at these recommendations? If you had come to me in the first place, it could have been all decided in less than an hour, and decided at a lower cost than $200,000."

After studying the complete list more carefully, Arthur Dalton concluded that it might be reasonable to propose to the Board spending $100,000 for several items which he agreed were urgently needed; he blue-penciled the remaining items. He said, "Some of the other directors may be more liberal, but I personally can't justify spending more than $100,000 for improvements."

Ben went back to his office. He looked out the window and pondered the future usefulness of his Management Committee and of himself.

Questions

1. Contrast and evaluate the leadership styles of Ben and his father.
2. What potential values and difficulties do you see in the committee that has been created?
3. How effective has the committee been up to now?
4. Should Ben have told his father about the committee before he started it?
5. What should be Ben's next move?

Case 12

E. G. Lomax Company*

The purchasing agent, production manager, production control manager, and plant manager at the Scott branch plant of the E. G. Lomax Company were all astounded upon coming to work one morning to find waiting on their desks identical copies of a memorandum from the general manager, blistering them for acting without proper authority in jointly making the previous day what they had all regarded at the time as a purely routine decision to drop a vendor, the Castle Stamping Company. The memorandum informed them that the general manager was reversing their decision and that in the future no final actions on such "important policy matters" were to be taken without his specific approval.

The reprimanded executives immediately got together to talk the matter over. None of them had spoken to the general manager since the meeting at which the decision had been made. They concluded, therefore, that the only other man present the day before must have been the one to bring it to the general manager's attention. This man, chief tool engineer at the company's parent plant 200 miles distant, had formerly worked for the Castle Stamping Company. He had been instrumental in having Castle selected as the second source for a new stamping to be used in large quantities at the Scott branch.

Castle had been a source of supply, for some years previously, for other parts used in both Lomax plants. During the early part of this association, while business was generally slack, Castle had been reasonably satisfactory as to delivery and price, although never as reliable as one other stamping source used by Lomax. In the previous year, however, business had been brisk and stampings procurement had become difficult. The

*From Austin Grimshaw and John W. Hennessey, Jr., *Organizational Behavior* (New York: McGraw-Hill Book Company, 1960).

attitude of Castle executives remained on the surface as cordial as ever, but deliveries were consistently late, sometimes by as much as six months, and prices were high. Extra charges were billed for short runs made by Castle at Lomax's urgent request in order to keep its lines from shutting down, in spite of the fact that it was Castle's lateness in delivery which caused the emergencies.

Feeling that the amount of business currently being placed was not enough to make Lomax a preferred customer, the latter had offered Castle a share of the business on a new large volume part. This offer had been enthusiastically received, Castle had made dies at a cost to Lomax of $6,500, and accepted an initial order for 50,000 stampings.

The decision to drop Castle and to call all dies in from its plant had been reached the previous day because, in spite of repeated promises, no stampings had been received in the six months since completion of the dies. Also, deliveries on other parts purchased from Castle were most unsatisfactory. The consensus of the meeting, with the exception of one dissenter, the chief tool engineer from the parent plant who happened to be in town and was consulted as a matter of courtesy, was that Castle would never be a trustworthy source of supply and would continue to get the Scott branch into trouble, as long as the supply situation remained tight. The dissenter's point of view was: (1), that the difficulties could be straightened out; (2), that Castle made good parts and could be brought into line on prices; and (3) that the parent plant would be embarrassed by calling in of the dies, since it was currently getting some parts from Castle and might itself be dropped as a customer as a direct result of such hostile action.

The parent plant chief tool engineer requested that Scott's general manager be called in before the decision was made final. The others present at the meeting refused, saying that the general manager knew all about the troubles with the Castle Stamping Company and on several occasions had indicated that he favored dropping it as a vendor just as soon as this could be done without endangering shipment to Lomax customers.

The production manager said that it was a routine problem with which the general manager should not be bothered, that he customarily left such decisions to the men present at the meeting, that he spent very little time on plant matters, visited the shop only occasionally and concentrated mostly on sales and product engineering problems.

The group also indicated a belief that each of the company's two plants should make its own independent decisions on purchasing. The parent company plant was free, they said, to keep or drop Castle, as it thought most advisable, regardless of the branch plant's action. Finally, the group argued, the general manager was out of town on a sales trip and the time of his return was indefinite.

The group then discussed what should be done about several dies that had been built for the branch plant's own presses at the parent plant, under the supervision of the parent plant chief tool engineer. These dies had been tried out at Scott and had not fitted its presses exactly, according to the production manager. Nor had they incorporated several features of design which the branch plant tool engineer had requested prior to their construction. The meeting broke up in order to permit all interested parties to visit the punch press department where the dies had been specially set up for retrial and for observation of the disputed points about their operation.

After rehashing the previous day's discussion with the others present, the plant manager, with a copy of the memo in his hand, went in to see the general manager. The general manager, without any preliminaries, immediately said: "I got home hot and tired after a long trip, late last night, and found Tom Norcross (the parent company chief tool engineer) waiting for me. What do you mean telling Tom that I never get into the shop any more and that I leave all production decisions to the plant executives? Maybe I don't get into the shop during working hours much now, but I often go in there evenings, when I come back to clear my desk, and on weekends. You know very well that I've had trouble more than once with the president because people at the main plant have distorted things we have said and done down here. Try to be more careful what you say to all of them in the future."

Three months later, following a series of completely unsatisfactory further dealings with the Castle Stamping Company, it was dropped as a vendor, at the general manager's express instructions, and dies were called in.

Questions

1. Was the decision to drop Castle Stamping Company a routine decision or a basic policy matter? Was it a "good" decision?
2. How do you explain Norcross' disagreement? Did the committee exercise good judgment in dealing with him?
3. Evaluate the action taken by Norcross in calling on the general manager.
4. What will be the probable effect of this incident upon delegation of authority in the future?

Case 13

Boston Edison Company

A Problem in Decentralization

In the spring of 1957, the Boston Edison Company was considering the possibility of decentralizing certain engineering functions which were then concentrated in the Dorchester Operations Center. The contemplated decentralization would be accomplished by establishing a number of district engineering offices within a twenty-five mile radius of the Operations Center.

Company Background

The Boston Edison Company produced and distributed electricity to almost one-half million customers located in the Boston metropolitan area. Although the territory served by Boston Edison was less than fifty miles across in any direction, growth of population and industry in the area had permitted rapid expansion since establishment of the company in 1886. As of 1957, approximately one-third of its sales were to residential customers and one-third to commercial users. The remaining one-third was divided largely among industrial customers, other utilities, and municipalities. In 1956, Boston Edison received $94,650,856 as revenue for 3,784,781,841 kilowatt hours of electricity. At the beginning of 1957, there were 4,105 employees on the payroll.

The idea of decentralization was not new to Boston Edison. For years, the Transmission and Distribution Department had operated through a group of service centers scattered throughout the Boston metropolitan area. Installation or repair of electric lines in any specific part of the territory was the responsibility of the service center located in that section. Growth in the number of customers, good experience with service centers, and the experience of other companies suggested in 1957 a general decentralization study to discover the practicality of more extensive decentralization.

Boston Edison's Distribution Division

One proposal for decentralization focused upon the Electrical Engineering Section and particularly the Distribution Division within that section. (See Exhibit 1 for organization chart of the Engineering and Construction Organization, including Electrical Engineering Section.) The Electrical Engineering Section designed generating stations, substations, and distribution systems. The Distribution Division, key component in the decentralization proposal, engineered distribution systems between distribution substations and customers.

The entire Electrical Engineering Section was physically located in the Dorchester Operations Center within the city of Boston. This center was some two miles from the headquarters executive offices of the Boston Edison Company, which were located in the Edison Building in downtown Boston. The Dorchester Operations Center housed not only centralized engineering offices but other administrative offices as well.[1]

[1]One of the Transmission and Distribution Service Centers was also situated on the same Dorchester property. The six other Service Centers were scattered over the Boston territory. (See Exhibit 2.)

Exhibit 1. *Boston Edison Company Engineering and Construction Organization**

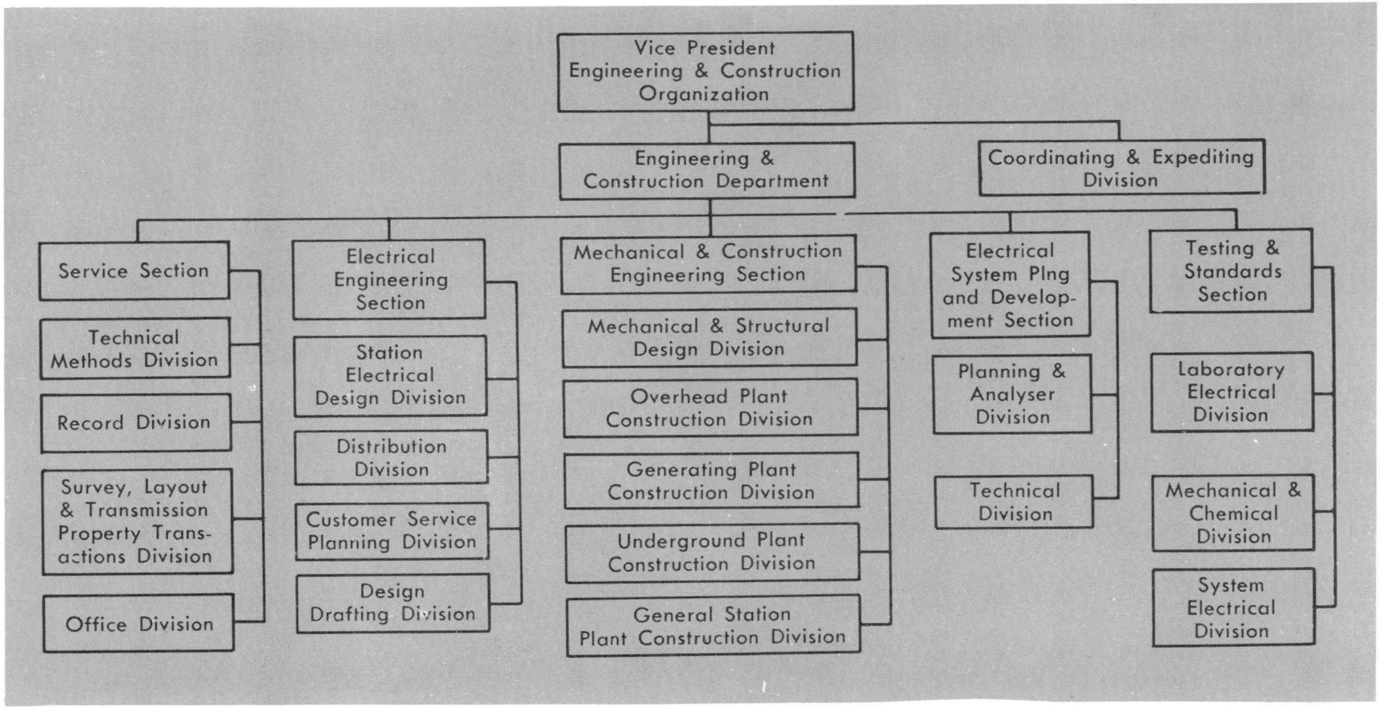

*The term "organization" is not used in its generic sense by Boston Edison. The term refers, instead, to a major component above the departmental level and headed by a vice president.

Exhibit 2 shows approximate distances from Dorchester to the Edison Building in downtown Boston and to the Transmission and Distribution Centers.

Exhibit 2. *Boston Edison Company*

HEADQUARTERS AND SERVICE CENTER LOCATIONS OF BOSTON EDISON COMPANY
(NUMBERS INDICATE APPROXIMATE MILES FROM DORCHESTOR OPERATIONS CENTER)

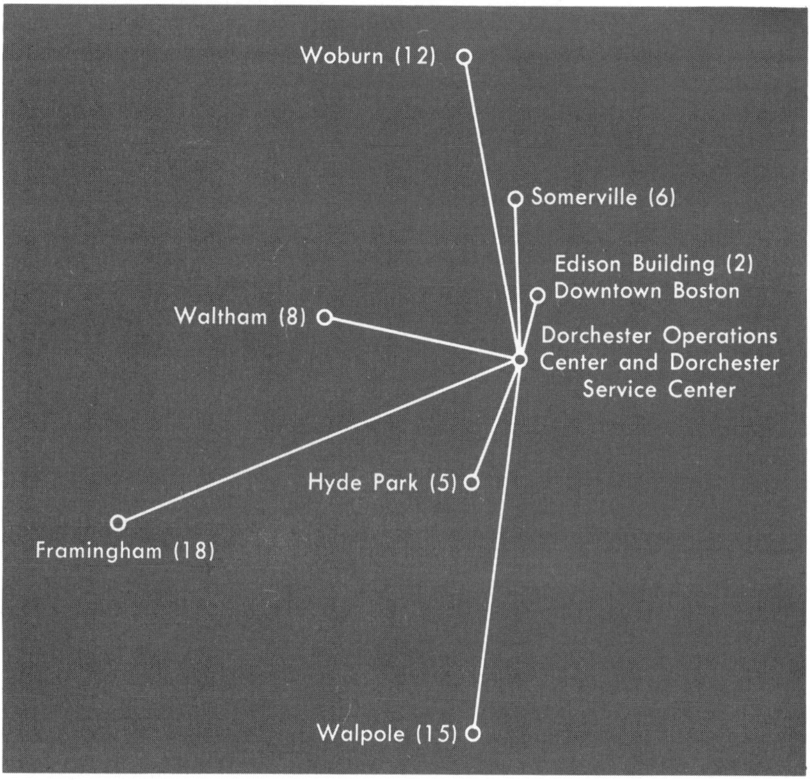

In performing its function, the Distribution Division worked closely with other components of the Boston Edison Company. Decentralization of engineering functions would necessarily involve some decentralization of activities performed by these other components. On the basis of their organizational "distance" from the Distribution Division, these other components might be classified as follows:

1. *Those Within Electrical Engineering Section.* The Customer Service Planning Division, for example, performed a technical clerical function, preparing work orders on the basis of Distribution Division instructions, obtaining data for the Distribution Division, and making cost estimates. (See Exhibit 1.)
2. *Those Outside Electrical Engineering Section but Within Engineering and Construction Organization.* All four divisions of the Service Section performed services of significance to the Distribution Division. For example, the Record Division maintained the record of electrical distribution systems, recording system changes on the basis of construction orders. (See Exhibit 1.)
3. *Those Outside Engineering and Construction Organization.* These components reported to other vice presidents of the Boston Edison Company. They included (a) Customer Work Order Control Department of the Financial and Accounting Organization; (b) Sales Departments of the Commercial Organization; (c) Transmission and Distribution Service Centers of the Steam and Electrical Operations Organization. (These components do not appear in Exhibit 1 because they were outside the Engineering and Construction Organization.)

Functions of the Distribution Division

Activities of the Distribution Division might be divided into two broad categories as follows:

1. Engineering in connection with new business of all kinds. This work was oriented toward specific customers and based upon their demands for new and additional services.
2. Engineering for system development. This work was concerned with provision of adequate electrical service in a given geographical area, including design of primary and secondary distribution systems.

The first of these functions — engineering for new business — was of particular importance in considerations of decentralization. On projects of this nature, the Distribution Division worked with many of the other components noted above. For example, a new supermarket might be planned for the Waltham area. The request for new electrical service would come from the customer to the downtown sales office (Commercial Organization) of Boston Edison. The request would then clear through the Customer Work Order Control Department (Financial and Accounting Organization) for record purposes. The engineering divisions at Dorchester would then complete the necessary engineering, consulting with the Waltham Transmission and Distribution Service Center at one stage of the process. Exhibit 3 portrays in greater detail a somewhat simplified course of a customer's request for service.

Exhibit 3. *Boston Edison Company*

PATH OF CUSTOMER REQUEST FOR SERVICE

Location	*Component*	*Function Performed*
Boston	Commercial Organization	Receipt of order from customer for new or additional service
Boston	Customer Work Order Control Department	Preparation of work order forms and establishment of record to facilitate tracing the order
Dorchester	Customer Service Planning Division	Technical clerical examination — e.g., to determine need for analysis by Distribution Division
Dorchester	Distribution Division	Engineering planning and design
Dorchester	Customer Service Planning Division	Preparation of engineering order specifying required construction
Any Service Center	Transmission and Distribution Service Center	Field "look-up" to determine details of construction—e.g., number of poles required
Boston	Customer Work Order Control Department	Review of order and preparation of requests for any necessary action by Rights and Permits Division in securing local governmental approval
Dorchester	Customer Service Planning Division	Preparation of cost estimate or request for cost estimate
Dorchester	Technical Methods Division	Preparation of cost estimate
Dorchester	Customer Service Planning Division	Preparation of forms specifying special engineering requirements
Dorchester	Electrical Engineering Section Chief	Review and approval

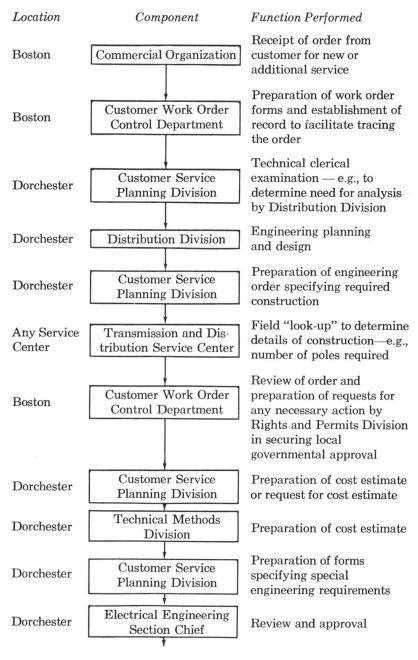

Exhibit 3. *(Cont.)*

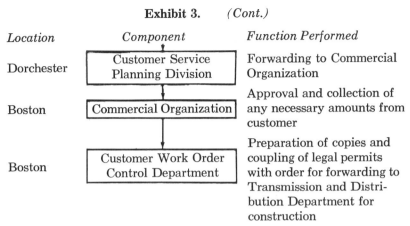

Location	*Component*	*Function Performed*
Dorchester	Customer Service Planning Division	Forwarding to Commercial Organization
Boston	Commercial Organization	Approval and collection of any necessary amounts from customer
Boston	Customer Work Order Control Department	Preparation of copies and coupling of legal permits with order for forwarding to Transmission and Distribution Department for construction

Explanatory Note

There is considerable variation in the specific routing of particular requests. It is the purpose of this exhibit to portray the somewhat circuitous path of a request as it goes from one component of Boston Edison Company to another and from one geographical location to another. By minor adjustment of functions (e.g., authorizing the District Engineer to sign for the Chief, Electrical Engineering Section), the above activities, with the exception of sales activities performed by the Commercial Organization, would occur at one geographical location — the decentralized engineering office and service center.

Proposed District Engineering Offices

Decentralization, if it occurred, would involve the establishment of district engineering offices at some or all of the Transmission and Distribution Service Centers. These service centers, carrying the names of the sections in which located, were as follows:

Center	*Number of Service Center Employees*
Waltham	153
Framingham	95
Walpole	33
Woburn	71
Somerville	57
Dorchester[2]	350
Hyde Park	93

Each district engineering office and service center would be separately administered even though located under the same roof and working together closely. The district engineering office would be staffed with

[2] The exceptionally large number of employees in the Dorchester Service Center is explained by the large proportion of underground lines in that section of the territory. This figure did not include personnel in the Engineering and Construction Organization.

representatives of the various interested components of Boston Edison. The key members of this "crew" would be the representatives of Distribution Division, one of whom would serve as supervisor and be known as the "District Engineer." It was estimated that a balanced crew for the Waltham District Engineering Office, for example, would contain the following members:

Number of Employees	*Activity Represented*
3	Distribution Division (including District Engineer)
2	Customer Service Planning Division
4	Record Division
2	Survey, Layout and Transmission Property Transactions Division
1	Office Division
2	Customer Work Order Control Department (Financial and Accounting Organization)
14	

Possible Advantages of Decentralization

One of the major reasons for seriously considering this move was the desire to speed up the process of supplying new or extended service and thus to improve customer relations. The procedures required in coordinating and completing a typical engineering project required weeks and often months. Although much of this work was not required by customers on a "rush" basis, there would unquestionably be a public relations advantage in accelerating the work. Decentralization offered the possibility of combining many of these steps within the same district office. By minor adjustment of functions, the activities indicated in Exhibit 3, with the exception of sales activities performed by the Commercial Organization, would occur at the decentralized district engineering office and service center.

In addition to reducing the time lag and customer dissatisfaction, decentralization offered a number of other possible advantages. One of these was an improvement in the quality of engineering work. The engineer would be located "in the field" sufficiently close to the problem so that he could personally visit a given site in only a few minutes. While the central engineering office at Dorchester Operations Center was only fifteen or twenty miles from many jobs, traffic congestion discouraged any substantial amount of field work. In addition, engineers would "rub shoulders" with the operating personnel of the Transmission and Distribution Service Center, thus providing a practical influence on their work.

The Boston Edison Company also recognized a possible benefit to employee morale. Instead of functioning as a part of a large engineering group, the engineer would become a member of a small work group.[3] The

[3]There were 330 employees in the Engineering and Construction Organization, of whom 60 were managerial and 270 nonmanagerial.

smaller size of the engineering group would force a greater variety of work into the engineering positions. An engineer simply could not be a specialist on transformers, for example, as might happen in the central engineering group. The new positions of District Engineer would open up new promotional possibilities and allow incumbents the prestige of being supervising engineers in these offices. In view of the popularity of decentralization programs in industry, Boston Edison would also appear progressive in its management. Even nonprofessional employees in the district office would be able to appreciate more easily the overall significance of the operations which they performed.

Difficulties in Decentralization

One problem associated with decentralization was the difficulty of evenly balancing work teams in district offices. The work load in some areas, for example, would require the services of one-half estimator or one and one-half engineers. To meet the minimum requirement, overstaffing might be required. Fluctuating work load would likewise constitute more of a problem in the smaller unit. Absences of individual employees from district offices could easily create emergencies. Some district offices would have only one engineer. His absence for vacation, sickness or other reasons would leave the position completely uncovered. Other jobs with only two or three incumbents were somewhat similarly vulnerable. To replace a particular specialist on a temporary basis, it would be necessary to pay travel time and travel pay in order to bring a replacement from the central office or from another district office. All employees, with the exception of the District Engineer, would be union members. The union contracts (Utility Workers Union of America, A.F.L.-C.I.O.) specified one hour travel each way for both engineers and clerical personnel. In effect, this would mean six hours work in an eight-hour day or eight hours work for a paid ten-hour day (allowing two hours for travel to and from regular work locations), plus transportation cost. In many cases, the replacement would lack previous experience in the particular district office. Overtime pay, of course, could provide another solution. Although it was difficult to introduce precision into estimates of increased personnel costs, predictions ran as high as a twenty per cent increase. This might amount to as many as twenty or twenty-five additional employees when decentralization was completed.

There was also some concern with the possibility that the professional interest and knowledge of engineers might suffer when they were split up and separated geographically. Engineers in the central office were "in" on new ideas somewhat automatically. When a supplier, for example, came in with a new idea, it was discussed by all concerned in the office and thus became a matter of common knowledge. Likewise, representatives of Production Department, Transmission and Distribution Department, Commercial Organization, Employee Relations Organization, and other staff offices were in close contact with the central engineering office. Although an attempt would be made to pass on important information, it seemed unrealistic to expect perfect communication. In the central office, there was also a stimulation toward participation in professional engineering organizations and activities. Committee meetings involved little travel, and contact with other committee chairmen was simple. Personal contact and encouragement from other engineers, particularly respected members of the company, helped maintain attendance and participation in professional meetings.

It seemed clear that it would be necessary to continue making certain engineering studies at headquarters; e.g., the installation of a substation affecting more than one area. This led to another weakness because of the need for duplicate engineering records in district offices and the central office. The most serious aspect of this concerned manhole cards which showed the ducts coming into each manhole. There were typically four cards showing the four sides of the manhole, but only one set of the cards was maintained. They could be microfilmed, but this would involve an expenditure of thousands of dollars. It might also be possible to solve this problem without immediate outlay by distributing records to the district offices and borrowing them occasionally as needed by headquarters.

Still another problem was involved in the establishment of authority relationships in the district office. The thinking of the company was that "administrative" supervision over all district engineering office employees should be given to the District Engineer but that "technical" supervision should come from the various activities represented. In other words, the District Engineer would be empowered to tell his employees WHAT to do, but the appropriate division would tell them HOW to do it. The District Engineer would insure that these employees performed work as assigned. He could recommend promotions, disciplinary measures, or other action to the proper division chief.

Question Facing Management

Management wished to select the arrangement that would be most logical and appropriate for Boston Edison. As a public utility, the company attached major importance to customer service in any decision of this type. As a privately owned concern, however, the company was also required to weigh carefully the profit implications of the proposed change.

Questions

1. What bearing should the factor of public relations have upon the decision to decentralize?
2. Evaluate the proposed change from the standpoint of employee morale.
3. What administrative difficulties may be involved in the organization of the district offices?
4. Should the company adopt the proposed decentralization plan?

Case 14

Promotion*

Alan Grafton is finally leaving the Oakwood Bank and Trust Company thereby creating an opening for a supervisor in the Accounting Division.

John Jones, the Department Manager, has asked his assistant, Bob Berg, to come up with a competent replacement. Jones also reminded Berg that the new Punch Card System for accounting would be installed in a few months.

Berg has screened the presently employed members of the Accounting Division and has narrowed down his choice to Betty Brown, Bill Welsh, and Paul Wilson. (Paul Wilson is currently employed by Allen, Edison, and Roberts, Certified Public Accountants.)

After considerable thought Berg picked Paul Wilson.

Betty Brown and Bill Welsh resent Berg's choosing an outsider rather than promoting from within and take their complaint to Mr. Jones. Jones asked for an explanation from Berg that would satisfy Miss Brown and Mr. Welsh.

Once again, Berg reviewed the three candidates and summarized them in the following way:

Betty Brown is a high school graduate, 24 years old, and has been with the bank in the same department for seven years. She is very accurate and fast in her work. She has a thorough knowledge of various phases of the work in the department. Employees always come to her for help when confronted with a problem. She likes her job and gets along well with the other employees. However, Miss Brown has a marked resistance to changes made in current methods. She has never made any suggestions for the improvement of working methods and procedures. Betty is getting married in a few months and is in line for a raise next month.

Bill Welsh is a college graduate, 29 years old, and has been recently married. Welsh began his employment with the bank after college. He is ambitious, gets along well with the other employees, and is cooperative. Bill has offered many good suggestions on work improvement and cost reductions. Several of his suggestions have been put into practice. He is not as accurate as Betty nor as familiar with all the procedures as she is. He is not interested in his present work and has often expressed his preference for something in selling.

Paul Wilson is 26 years old, married, and working for a Bachelor's Degree in Business Administration in night school. He is highly recommended by Allen, Edison, and Roberts. Paul has had some experience in supervision and has worked with punch card systems and their installation on his present job. Berg is favorably impressed with Wilson after several interviews and has chosen him for the job.

---

*Case prepared by Professor Samuel G. Trull of Berkeley, California.

Conclusion:

Berg decides to have separate discussions with Miss Brown and Mr. Welsh, after explaining to Jones what he intends to say.

With Miss Brown, Berg is very courteous. They even discuss her forthcoming marriage. Then, Berg brings out Wilson's attributes regarding the punch card systems and how well he will fit into the new systems to be installed in the bank. He then tactfully tells her of her resistance to change and points up several times when she resisted a proposed change. He also mentions the fact that all the problems and snags in connection with the new system will arise at the time of her marriage. He praises her on her present work, asks her to try to show more initiative, tells her not to get discouraged, that she is still in line for a supervisory job, and tells her that her raise will be forthcoming next month.

With Bill Welsh, Berg, who is aware of Bill's desire to sell, takes the offensive immediately. He tells Bill of an opening coming up in the Busi-

Exhibit 1. *Partial Organization Chart Oakwood Bank & Trust Co. Accounting Department*

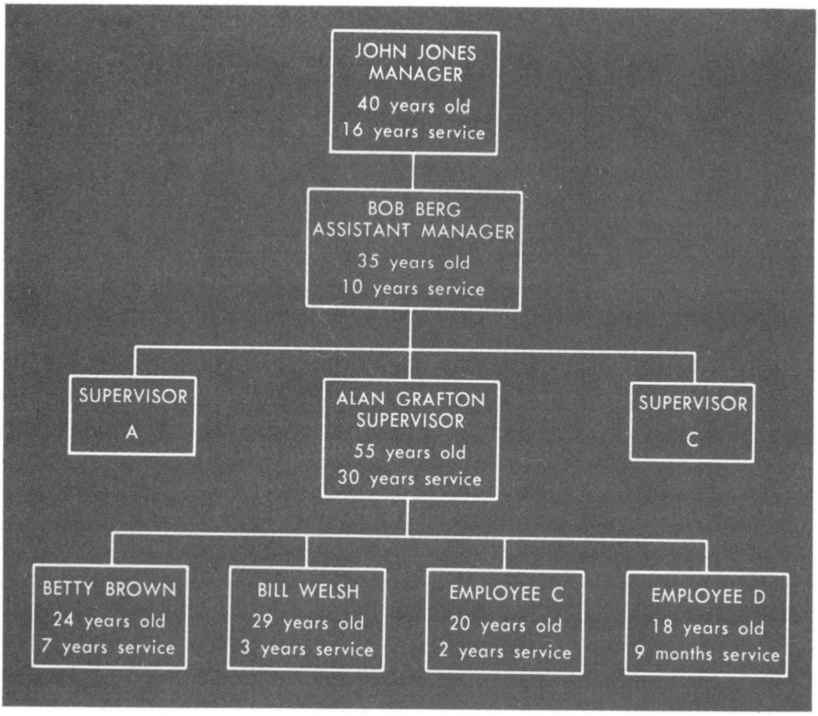

ness Development Department. Berg tells Bill he has been recommended for the position. As with Miss Brown, Berg tells Bill of Wilson's experience with punch card systems. Bill is then complimented on his work and told how much happier he will be in his new position.

Questions

1. How could Berg justify his selection to Jones and satisfy Miss Brown and Mr. Welsh? How about Employee C and Employee D?
2. Should Paul Wilson have been brought in from the outside? What are some typical obstacles to overcome in such a move?
3. Was there an alternative solution to the promotion problem?
4. It appears that Berg made the introduction of a new system his principal cause for the selection of an outsider. Do you agree with this approach?
5. Do you think Miss Brown and Mr. Welsh will be satisfied after their conference with Berg?
6. Can Berg be "sure" that Bill Welsh *will* be much happier in his new position?
7. What will happen if Bill Welsh somehow doesn't get the new position?
8. Discuss areas to be sensitive to when being promoted into a job previously held by a person similar to Alan Grafton.
9. Were you Paul Wilson, how would you proceed?

Case 15

Peoples Trust Company*

The Peoples Trust Company first opened its doors to the public on June 1, 1875, with a total salaried staff of eight members: a treasurer; a secretary; and six assistants (three of whom held the positions of day watchman, night watchman, and messenger). Located in a large, midwestern city, the original company had occupied the basement floor of a new five-story office building with an electric-bell system, steam heat, and steam-driven elevator.

---

*Case prepared by Professor Hrach Bedrosian of New York University.

During its early years, the Trust Company had concentrated its activities on providing vault services to its customers for the safekeeping of tangible items and securities. Management had been able to develop the reputation of being a highly conservative trust company that concentrated on a relatively small and select market of wealthy individuals from the local area. In the years following, the vault service had been retained as an accommodation to its customers, but the company's emphasis had slowly shifted from vault service to a wider range of banking and trust services.

Until the early 1900's, banking services had overshadowed trust services in terms of asset volume. Following the turn of the century, trust assets had begun to grow at an increasing rate. Over the years, the company had been able to achieve an impressive record of sound and steady growth. According to a story often told in banking circles: "Peoples Trust was so conservative that they prospered even during the Depression!"

In 1943, with the appointment of a new president, a new era began for Peoples Trust Company. Between 1943 and 1958, trust assets under supervision rose by $145 million, while deposits increased by more than $20 million. The company entered 1965 with about $2 billion in trust assets and $90 million in savings deposits.

Accompanying this recent growth has been the company's desire to fashion a new image for itself. In 1959, Mr. Robert Toller assumed the presidency of Peoples Trust. In 1962, he remarked: ". . . it should be said that the old concept of a trust involving merely the regular payment of income and preservation of capital is largely obsolete." Accordingly, the Investment Division of the company had been expanded and strengthened. Similar changes had been effected in the Trust and Estate Administrative Group and other customer services. Among these were the improvement of accounting methods and procedures, the installation of electronic data processing systems, and complete renovation of the company's eight-floor building and facilities. Most recently, the company has extended its services into the field of management consulting. This had been acknowledged as a "pioneer" step for a banking institution. The president recently characterized the company as "an organization in the fiduciary business."

At the time these data were gathered, the company had a total of 602 employees. Of this number, 109 were in what is considered the "officer-group"[1] positions of the company. The company's relations with its employees over the years have been satisfactory, and Peoples Trust is generally recognized by city residents and those in suburban areas as a good place to work. The company hires most of its employees from the local area.

In the period before 1960, Peoples Trust had provided satisfactory advancement opportunities for its employees, and it had been possible

---

[1]Membership in the officer group is determined by an employee's being legally empowered to represent the company in a transaction.

for a young, high-school graduate who showed promise on the job to work his way up gradually to officer status. Graduates of banking institutions were also sought for employment with the company. Ordinarily a man was considered eligible for promotion to the job above him after he had thoroughly mastered the details of his present position.

Prior to 1960, the total staff of the company was small enough so that there was no need to prepare official organization charts or job descriptions. Virtually all of the employees knew each other on a first-name basis, and they were generally familiar with each other's area of job responsibility. New employees were rapidly able to learn "whom you had to go to for what."

In 1960, the company management called in an outside consultant to appraise its organizational structure and operations and to confer on the rapid expansion and diversification of banking services that the company had planned. The presence of the consultants and the subsequent preparation of organization charts and job descriptions reportedly "shook up a lot of people" — many feared loss of their jobs or, at least, substantial changes in the nature of work and assignments. However, there was little overt reaction among the officer-level employees in terms of turnover and/or other indices of unrest.

Over the years it had been the policy of the company to pay wages that were at least average or a little above the average paid by comparable banking organizations in the area. This, combined with favorable employee relations and the stable and prestigious nature of the work, resulted in a low turnover of personnel. The bulk of employee turnover occurred among the young, female employees who filled clerical positions throughout the company's various departments.

Since 1960, the personnel picture at Peoples Trust has been shifting. Several changes have taken place in the top management of the company. By adding several new customer services, the company has altered the very nature of its business. This has resulted in a trend toward "professionalization" of many of the officer-level positions in that these positions now require individuals with higher levels of education and broader abilities. The impact of these changes on current employees has been a matter of concern to several executives in the company, particularly to Mr. John Moore, Manager of the Organization Planning and Personnel Department. Mr. Moore described his picture of the situation to the researcher as follows:

Interview with John Moore, V.P., Organization Planning and Personnel

> Our problem here is one of a changing image and along with it the changing of people. As a trust company, we had no other ties with a man's financial needs . . . we could only talk in terms of death. We wanted to be able to talk in terms of life, so we got active in the investment-advisory business.
>
> The old wealth around here is pretty well locked up, so we wanted to provide services to new and growing organizations

and to individuals who are accumulating wealth. Our problem is one of reorientation. We used to provide one service for one customer. We now want to enter new ventures, offer new services, attract new customers. The problem has become one of how to make the change . . . do we have the talent and the people to make the change?

We have a "band" of people [see Exhibit 1 and note below] in our organization . . . in the 35-50 age group who came in under the old hiring practices and ground rules. Given the new directions in which our company is moving and the changing job requirements, it's clear that, considering their current qualifications and capabilities, these individuals have nowhere to go. Some have been able to accept this; and this acceptance includes watching others move past them. Others have difficulty accepting it . . . a few have left . . . and we haven't discouraged anyone from leaving. For those who can't accept it, there is the problem of integrating their career strategy with ours. We've articulated our objectives clearly; now the individual needs clarification of his own strategy.

As I see it, change caught up with these individuals. They had on-the-job training in their own areas, but that doesn't help them much to cope with the new demands. New functional areas are being melded on top of old ones. For example, marketing is new; so is electronic data processing. They both require qualities that our existing employee staff didn't have.

To date, we have not approached any of these people in an individual way to discuss their problems with them. Our objectives are to further develop these people, but we'll first have to get the support of the department managers who supervise them.

We want to find ways to further develop personnel of the kind represented by this group through a variety of approaches. I am thinking here not only of formal job training in management development, but also of management techniques that would help individuals identify new kinds of qualifications or possible new standards of performance they must take into consideration in planning their own personal growth.

We have to change the conditioning of old times throughout the company. A recently hired MBA is now an officer. Years ago that couldn't have happened so rapidly. And not everyone here is in agreement that the appointment I just mentioned *should* have happened the way it did. We have to develop support in our company for the new recruiting image.

Note: Mr. Moore drew from his files a list of ten individuals who he felt were representative of the group whose lack of appropriate experience or qualifications created a road block to their future development and advancement with the company. These men are described in Exhibit 1.

There are two things which really concern me most about this whole problem:

1. We have a problem in under-utilization of resources.
2. There is a problem which is presented to the growth and development of the company in having some of the individuals I have been discussing settled into key spots.

The company really bears the responsibility for the current situation as I described it.

In addition, what this all means to me is that our personnel function may change considerably over the coming year.

After this interview with Mr. Moore, the researcher talked with other company executives to learn their views of the problems outlined by Mr. Moore. The findings from these interviews are presented in the following sections.

Interview with Fred Bellows — Manpower Planning

Historically we have been conservatively managed . . . you might say "ultra-conservatively." But now we want to change that image. Several years ago there was a revolution in top management. In 1959, Mr. Toller took over and brought in young people, many not from the banking field but from other types of business and consulting organizations. Our employment philosophy may be stated as follows: "We want above-average people . . . for above average pay . . . and we want to give them a chance to learn and grow and move with the organization." This applies mainly to those in whom we see management-level potential.

They are told in their employment interview that if they don't see opportunity with us, then they should leave. This is in contrast to the old philosophy that this is a secure place to work, that you can stay here by keeping your nose clean, and that you can sit and wait for pot luck to become a trust officer.

Many people are caught in this changing philosophy. A case in the Trust Administration Division is a good example. There we have a man in a Grade 10 job who has been with the bank eight years. We just hired a new man out of college and put him in that same Grade 10. Now they're both at the same level, but they're entirely different people in terms of education, social background, etc.

Now the head of our Trust Division bucks this sort of thing. He argues that we don't need all "stars" in the company. Yet, the president wants young, dynamic men who can develop and be developed. So I'm trying to get the Trust Division to define: what does the job really require?

We have a number of people with two years of accounting training who have been with the company anywhere from six to nine years. Under our old system they'd be okay, but under the new system they're not. They're not realistic about their future. Our problem is that we're being honest, but few are getting the message.

We bring in a new man . . . ask others to train him . . . and then promote him over their heads. We have people whose jobs we could get done for a lot less money. When, if ever, do we tell them to go elsewhere?

Interview with Larry Andrews — Controller

There is no question but that there has been a complete revolution around here. In the past, we were in business to serve the community; to handle small accounts; to help the little old lady who needed investment service. Our motto was "help anyone who needs help." Our employees were geared to this kind of work orientation and felt at home with it. They could easily identify themselves with this sort of approach to doing business. Most people were quite comfortable; their personal goals coincided with the company goal.

But we found that we couldn't make any money conducting this kind of business. So, we've had to extend our services to attract people who have money and can afford our service. Now the company goal has changed. For example, the Trust Department is now concerned with the management of property in general. The "dead man's bank" has become the "live people's service organization." So we've had to create a kind of snob appeal that too many of our people can't identify with or don't believe in.

Many problems have emerged from these changes. Before, a man's knowledge of the detail of his job was his greatest asset. He worked to develop that knowledge and protected it. Now — and I'm speaking of supervisory jobs — the important factor is to have some familiarity with the work but to be able to work with people; to get others to do the detail. Too many of our people still don't understand this . . .

The route to the top is no longer clear. Over a five-year period this organization has changed. There have been reorganizations, new functions created, and some realignment of existing functions. Many who felt they had a clear line to something higher in the organization now find that that "something" isn't there anymore.

We've had lots of hiring-in at higher levels. Many old-timers have been bypassed. In some cases, the new, outside hirees came into jobs that never existed before, or were hired into a job that had previously existed, but which is now a "cut" above what it was before. What used to be a top job is now a second or third spot.

What we need now are people who are "professional managers" — by that I mean a supervisor versus a technical specialist. Years ago supervision could be concentrated in a few key men . . . but in the past five years we've grown 20 to 30 per cent and have a management hierarchy. A man used to be able to grow up as a technical specialist and develop his managerial skills secondarily.

To a small extent it's a matter of personality too. We have a new president, and what is acceptable to him differs from what was acceptable to his predecessor. There's a new mix of personal favoritism that goes along with the new vogue. Technical specialists are "low need" as far as the company is concerned. I estimate we now have about thirty people in this category in officer-level jobs.

Interview with Tom Martin — Marketing Division Head

There have been many changes over the past six years. Mr. Toller took a look at the entire organization . . . and then hired a consultant to do an organizational study. It was sort of an outside stamp of approval.

His hope was to move some of the dead wood . . . the senior people who were past their peak and didn't represent what the company wanted anymore in its managerial and officer staff. Few of these individuals have the capacity to change, and for others it may already be too late to change. Many had leveled off in their development long before these changes came about, and the changes just made it more apparent. Early retirement has been given to some of those over sixty. Others remained as titular head of their departments, but in essence report to a younger man who is really running the department.

Banking used to be a soft industry . . . you were hired and never fired. If you were a poor performer, you were given a lousy job that you could stay at. No one was ever called in and told to shape up. The pay was so poor it attracted people who wanted to work in a sheltered area, and they were satisfied to try and build a career in that area. So it was a job with low pay, high prestige, and some opportunity.

Our biggest problem is to convince people that they are not technicians anymore, that they are to *supervise* their subordinates and work to develop them. Apparently for many older individuals . . . , and younger ones too, this is an impossible assignment. They can do the jobs themselves, but having anyone else do it in any other way runs against their grain.

If our rate of personnel growth over the next ten years is as fast as the previous ten years, I'm afraid we can only absorb about 50 per cent of our most promising people.

Interview with James Farren, Trust Administration Division Head

We have several people for whom there is very little opportunity anymore. We just don't see any potential in these people. There are about fifteen of them who are in their forties and are really not capable of making any independent decisions. We're trying to get them to see other opportunities . . . both inside and outside the company. For example, our Real Estate group was big in the 1940's and 1950's. We're trying to make it important again, and there may be some opportunities in that area.

To give you an idea of the problem we're faced with: One man is really a personality problem. He's an attorney but he can't get along with others. He wants people to come to him; he focuses on detail too much; and he has great difficulty in telling others what to do and how to do it. He has to do the job all by himself.

Another man: We gave him a section to supervise but he really hasn't measured up. But, he was the president's pet. I suppose we'll let him continue on . . . he's 57 . . . and then retire him early.

Another case: A female; she really has ability, and continually asks where she can go in the organization. I had to tell her that we're just not at the point where we can take a female into a higher job, and honestly suggested that she might explore opportunities outside the company. Well, she did, and apparently came to the conclusion that she's not so bad off here after all. She's got so much invested time here that it's difficult to make the break.

Interview with Mr. L. Henry, General Administration Division

The company has been undergoing basic change. In the past, if a man demonstrated technical competence he was promoted, and that was fine while the company was a small, stable group, and everyone knew what the other was thinking. But then, many in the senior group began to retire. With this "changing of the guard" and the growth of the company, many of us have lost communication with our counterparts. Many of us are new in this field, new to this company, and, of course, new to each other. But we recognize this, so half the communication problem is solved. In a sense, we're not constrained by "how it was done before."

My people have reacted to all this change by sitting back and waiting, seeing which way things are going to go, then I guess deciding whether they are going to join you or not. Most of my people are relatively recent employees — as a matter of fact, of the 278 people in my division, only 11 have been with the company more than ten years. Conversion to EDP will really create a lot of changes in my area. Out of my officer group, there is only one man — he's fifty-eight — who is a problem to me in terms of his current and future usefulness. I'm concerned about him but haven't come to any conclusions about what to do. He doesn't report to me directly, he reports to one of my immediate subordinates, which maybe lessens the irritation. I don't think it was the company's policy at any time in the past to retain a man they felt they could do without. I don't think that policy is any different today, and I certainly hope it doesn't change in the future.

Exhibit 1. *Peoples Trust Company*

Name	*Age*	*Education*	*Date of Hire*	*Positions Held*
Gerald Horn	37	2-year technical institute of business administration	1955	Messenger Clearance Clerk Accounting Clerk Unit Head (working supervisor) Section Head (supervisor)
Richard Gaul*	30	2-year junior college program in business administration	1957	Business Machines Operator Section Head (supervisor) Operations Officer
Fred James	35	B.A. Degree local university American Institute of Banking	1956	Loan Clerk Teller Accounting Unit Head (working supervisor) Section Head (supervisor)
Harold Wilson*	35	1 year at local university	1961	Methods Analyst Operations Unit Head (working supervisor) Systems Programmer Property Accounting Dept. Head

Exhibit 1. *(Cont.)*

Martin Pfieffer*	32	Prep School	1957	Messenger Accounting Clerk Section Head (supervisor) Department Head
James Klinger	38	B.A. Degree from local university	1952	Messenger Accounting Clerk Records Clerk Unit Head (working supervisor) Administrative Specialist
Ralph Kissler*	35	B.A. Degree from local university co-op program	1954	Messenger Real Property Specialist Assistant Estate Officer
Charles Ferris	42	2-year jr. college program in business administration American Institute Banking	1942	Messenger Deposit accounting Section Head (supervisor) Unit Head (working supervisor)
William Jagger	54	High School	1929	Messenger Trust Liaison Clerk Accounting Clerk Bookkeeping Section Head
Thomas Geoghigan*	42	2-year jr. college program in business administration	1949	Messenger Securities accountant Property custodian Office Manager Assistant Operations Officer

*Officer

Questions

1. What is the nature of Peoples Trust Company's staffing problem?
2. What approach has been used by management to solve the problem? Evaluate management's apparent philosophy and approach.
3. What staffing policy or program would you recommend — particularly with respect to the 35-50 age group?

Exhibit 2. *Peoples Trust Company Organization Chart (June 1965)*

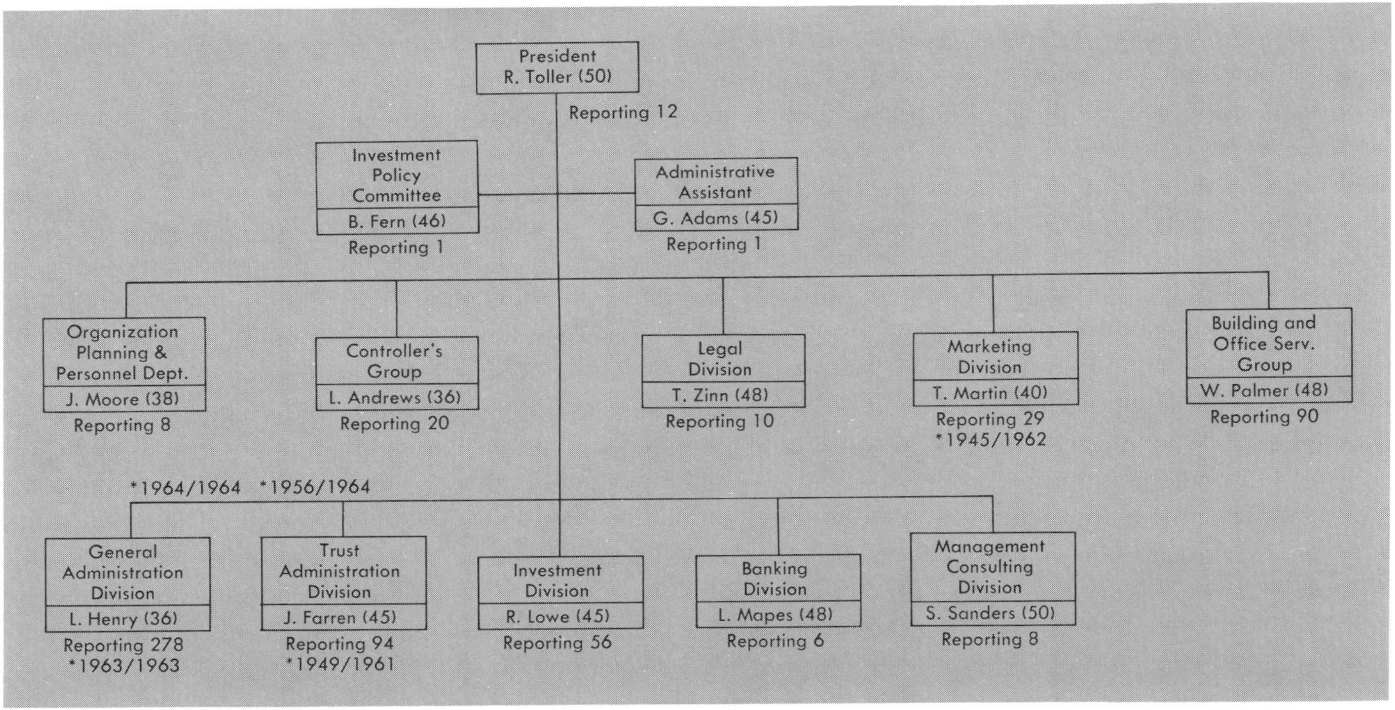

Note: Numbers in parentheses indicate manager's age. Numbers below each position indicate number of subordinates.
*Indicates year in which manager joined the Company and year in which he assumed current position. For example, Mr. Larry Andrews joined Peoples Trust Company in 1956, and became Controller in 1964.

Case 16

The Dissension Problem*

Robert Weiss, who had worked for the bank four years as the Supervisor of the International Banking Department, was being promoted and transferred. The Operations Officer of the department selected Frank Murray to succeed him. Frank was a married man with two children. He was 30 years old and had eight years of service with the bank.

When the people who worked under Weiss were notified by the Operations Officer of this change in supervisors, their reactions were mixed. Some of the people were surprised that Albert Ross, the assistant supervisor, had not been chosen. Ross was a good worker, intelligent, neat and dependable. However, he was a very gentle person and usually relied on the supervisor for decisions in matters which could have been decided and settled by himself. The Operations Officer had decided that he simply did not have the experience necessary to supervise and manage a section.

The section handles the transfer of miscellaneous currencies. Some of these transfers require the prompt sending of cables in order to avoid any delay in overdrafts of foreign accounts, kept by the bank. The section consisted of one typist-secretary and two tellers who handled the purchases and sales of foreign currencies over the counter to tourists or collectors.

One of the tellers was a male and the other female. In addition, there were three women typists who had the job of typing the necessary remittances and transfers. Two of the women had been working with the bank for almost three years. The third typist, Miss Thompson, had just joined the bank. Miss Rogers and Mrs. Haywood had worked together in the same section since they had joined the bank and they worked well. Miss Thompson was a woman of 28, intelligent and very independent in her attitude toward the other two women.

In his first few days as a supervisor, Frank sensed a tension among the three typists. Since no complaint was made to him by any of the three, he decided to wait before making a formal move. Instead he informally asked Miss Thompson if anything were wrong.

Miss Thompson reported that the two other women were always making things difficult for her. Whenever she asked either of them for some information concerning the work, they told her to look up past files. Murray decided to talk it over with Miss Rogers and Mrs. Haywood. He invited both of them for lunch. From the luncheon conversation Murray concluded that the source of the trouble was Mrs. Haywood. She, in turn, influenced Miss Rogers.

When Murray cautioned Mrs. Haywood about the dissension she was creating in the section, she became furious! She told Murray that he was trying to use his newly acquired authority to protect the newcomer with

*Case prepared by Professor Samuel G. Trull of Berkeley, California.

no regard to the past services that the other typists had given to the bank. She also added that he was new on the job and how did he know what was really going on. Mrs. Haywood finally demanded that either she or Miss Thompson be transferred.

Murray then went to the Operations Officer with the problem and they decided to dismiss Mrs. Haywood in order to prevent further dissension in the department.

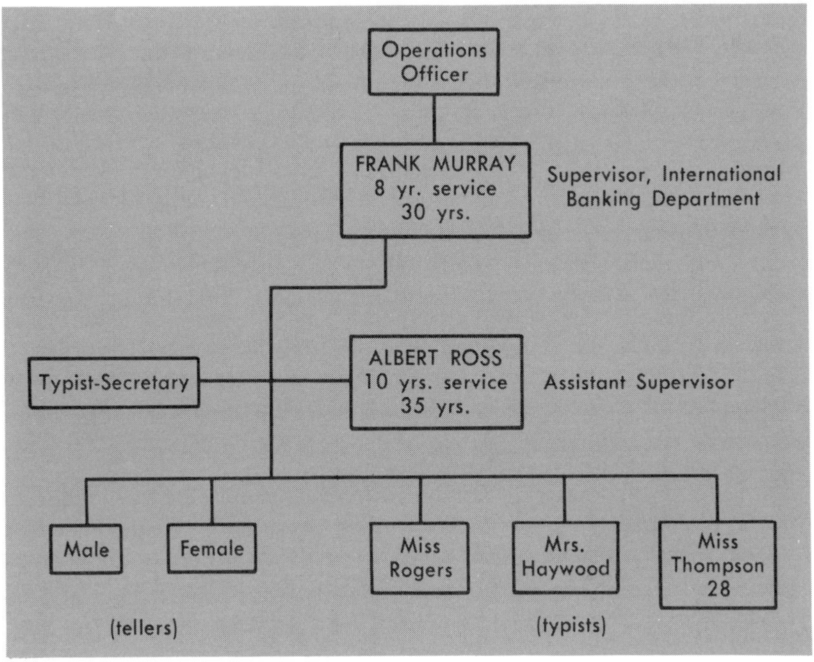

Questions

1. The problem of the three typists is connected with Murray's appointment. Comment.
2. Explain Mrs. Haywood's action.
3. Do you agree with the solution?
4. As supervisor, how would you have handled the problem?
5. When should you take decisions to your boss?
   (a) As Albert Ross
   (b) As Frank Murray
6. Suppose — for a minute — Mrs. Haywood was in the right. How would this affect the actions taken?

Case 17

The Jamison Furniture Company*

"Let me tell you about a situation I got involved in several years ago that I still can't get completely out of my mind.

"Shortly after I finished college I took a job with The Jamison Furniture Company. I had really never thought of a career in the furniture industry but when I graduated, jobs were pretty hard to get. I'd finished my education on the G.I. Bill and I was quite low on money. Consequently, when the Jamison people made me an offer at a pretty attractive salary for those times, I took it. Formally I was the assistant to Bill Blackwell, the plant manager, but actually I was a jack-of-all-trades who did just about anything that needed to be done. I worked on the books, helped with the production scheduling and shipping, and was responsible for what we vaguely called 'personnel relations.'

"As you may know, The Jamison Furniture Company is located in a small town in Ohio. It manufactures a high-quality line of occasional furniture, dinette pieces, desks, and occasional tables and chairs. When I was with them they employed about 150-160 people and had sales of about $40,000 per week. Finished furniture was sold to a large number of independent furniture stores throughout the country. The company has been quite successful and I'd guess that at the present time their sales are four or five times what they were then.

"Most of the people who worked at Jamison were relatively long-time employees. Most of the jobs didn't really require skilled labor and almost anyone with the proper attitude and a reasonable degree of intelligence and physical dexterity could be trained in time to do what had to be done. Nevertheless, as the company did produce a high-quality line of furniture, it was very important that the employees do their work well, especially in the staining and finishing operations. If a table or desk was improperly finished, for example, it had to be sold as a 'second' and the company took a terrific beating on profit.

"Well, the particular situation I referred to took place in the department which manufactured and finished occasional tables. The people involved were Bill Blackwell, the plant manager, Stu Thurston, foreman of the department, and Betty and Alice Sawyer, mother and daughter who worked for Stu. Betty, the mother, had worked for the company about twelve years before Stu came with the company. Alice Sawyer had worked for the company for about two years and had been in Stu's department since she had been initially hired. Before I go any further, let me tell you that Stu had a reputation as being quite a lady's man.

*From *Human Elements of Administration* by Harry R. Knudson, Jr. Copyright © 1963 by Holt, Rinehart & Winston, Inc. Reprinted by permission of Holt, Rinehart & Winston, Inc.

Whether he was or not I never knew, but I do know that he did take a lot of good natured kidding about 'liking the girls.' The sixteen girls who worked for Stu liked to kid him a lot about this and often told him that if they didn't need the money so badly they wouldn't take the risk of working for such a lady's man.

"When I went to work for Jamison everything seemed to be fine in Stu Thurston's department. Production was high, the girls were meeting their quotas, and everyone seemed to be happy. Stu kidded the girls a lot and they kidded him right back. In retrospect, I'd say at that time that Stu's department was one of the best I had ever seen.

"After I'd been with Jamison about four or five months it became pretty obvious that Stu Thurston and Alice Sawyer were getting pretty serious romantically and about two months later they announced their engagement to the apparent joy of the other girls in the department. I remember particularly well that Stu and Betty Sawyer did an awful lot of kidding about their forthcoming relationship as son-in-law and mother-in-law.

"When Stu and Alice got married all the girls chipped in and bought them a real nice wedding gift and everyone went to the wedding in a group. I remember one girl saying that 'This was the biggest thing that ever happened at The Jamison Furniture Company.' It was obvious that everyone was pretty much excited and enthusiastic about the wedding.

"After their honeymoon both Stu and Alice returned to work and things pretty much returned to normal. Stu was his own genial self, kidding the girls all the time and they in return continued to kid him right back. They had a big thing going about his being able to boss his wife and mother-in-law on the job but 'oh, how different it was when he was at home.' As I said, things went along swell for a while, but after about four or five months there were some inklings that the newly married couple weren't getting along as well as they might. Six months from the day on which they were married Stu started divorce proceedings against Alice on the grounds of mental cruelty. Then things really started to happen.

"At first, reaction was pretty well mixed concerning this sudden change of events. No one really knew what happened, but some of the girls felt that Stu must have had sufficient reasons for his action and attempted to keep things going as they had in the 'good old days.' The rest of the gals, headed by Alice and Betty, wouldn't have anything at all to do with Stu unless they absolutely had to. For example, the day that it became known that Stu had started divorce proceedings they stopped speaking to him unless it was in direct reply to a question or comment that he made. When they did speak they merely answered, 'yes, sir,' or 'no, sir,' as the occasion demanded, and not in a very friendly tone of voice.

"As the date for the final divorce decree got closer, Betty Sawyer, in particular, got more and more railed up. She started saying some pretty nasty things about Stu and it wasn't too long before she had all the sixteen girls so incensed that they weren't speaking to him either. It even got to the point where Betty led a delegation of the girls to see Bill Blackwell and demanded that Stu be fired for 'things that were going on in the department.' They maintained that Stu 'just wasn't a good foreman' and should be fired immediately. Bill handled the thing as well as he could, I guess. He tried to press the girls for specifics, but when it became apparent that the girls were so emotionally wrought up that they weren't making any sense, he just tried to get them quieted down and out of his office and back to work. I remember his talking to me about the girls' visit later. He said something like 'I sure don't know what to do, but we've got a real one on our hands.'

"Stu Thurston talked with me at length about the situation one day. I can't remember all of our conversation but I do recall him saying that what he did in his personal life was his own affair and that what happened on the job was business. He didn't see any reason for the girls to care about what he did on his own time. I do remember very distinctly how our conversation ended, however. Stu wanted me to fire both of the girls. He said, 'I don't care what you do — fire them — no matter what the reason, get rid of them.' His face was very flushed and he was quivering as he spoke. There was no doubt in my mind that if he had had any kind of weapon with him at the time he would have used it on either or both of the two women.

"Well, as you can see, we had a pretty bad situation on our hands. It got really bad for me personally the next day when Bill Blackwell came back from a visit to Stu's department and shouted at me, 'You're in charge of personnel relations. Do whatever you have to do to get that mess cleaned up!' "

Questions

1. What is the nature and origin of the problem in this case?
2. What action should be taken by the personnel manager?

Case 18

Militant Milly*

Milly Fulton is the private secretary of Ralph Daniels, the president of City Federal Savings and Loan Association. She is thirty-seven, single,

---

*From Edgar G. Williams, *People Problems* (Indiana University, Graduate School of Business, Bureau of Business Research, 1962).

and lives with her elderly parents whom she helps to support. Following high school, Milly completed a secretarial course at a local business college and went to work as a clerk-cashier in a branch store for a large dry goods firm. After several years with this store, she resigned in 1947 to accept a production job with a local manufacturer at substantially higher pay. She was in need of additional finances because of her parents' illnesses. In 1949, after approximately one year in production work, Milly resigned from the manufacturing firm to accept employment at City Federal, then a relatively new organization.

When Milly joined the association, the staff consisted of only four other employees, including Ralph Daniels, the manager. Her first job, operating a teller's window, required not only considerable customer contact, but also the preparation of basic accounting records for the money she handled. Carl Jones, the assistant secretary and teller supervisor, was very complimentary about Milly's early performance; she was pleasant with customers and extremely accurate in her bookkeeping work. In fact, Carl told Daniels that the young lady might even be overly precise in her record keeping. She maintained this performance record until 1950 when she left the teller's window to become Daniels' secretary. As expected, she performed well in her new job.

The continued growth of the association's assets and loans necessitated two significant changes in the organization in the short space of three years: (1) the addition of several new clerical and supervisory employees; and (2) the opening of the first City Federal branch office. The need for additional employees became acute during the 1950-51 boom in the economy and several new people joined the association.

Daniels figured that, after several months as his secretary, Milly was now familiar enough with her new job to train one of the new girls as her replacement in case she should become ill or take a vacation. At his request, Milly began to explain her job to Miss Fyfe, a new secretary in the loan department. It was not long before several of the employees told Carl that Milly seemed to resent the training in fear of anyone's encroaching on her job. It was obvious to them that Milly was teaching Miss Fyfe only the minor details of her job, not the important duties. Carl learned from the same sources that Miss Fyfe was receiving only about one hour's "instruction" every two weeks. These comments went no further; Carl knew Milly as an excellent employee who, until now, had never had a complaint of any kind lodged against her. He felt that he should personally observe her a little longer before talking to her or to the manager.

The grooming of Milly's understudy continued for a period of some four months. Milly then informed Daniels that Miss Fyfe could "pinch-hit" for her if it "ever became necessary." At this time, Daniels said, "Milly, I want you to know that I'm grateful for your excellent help. You've taken a lot of detail work off my shoulders; you've been a fine secretary, just as you were a good teller. Because I know I can count on you, I want to ask you to take on another additional job, temporarily." "Of course," replied Milly, "how can I help?" Daniels then proceeded to outline a situation that called for extra help from his secretary.

"At the last directors' meeting, plans were finalized for the opening of our first branch office. We are shooting for a target date about fifteen months away. This means that the pressure is on us to hire and train a staff to operate the branch. We have decided that the best way to solve this problem is to gradually hire the people we want as branch personnel or as replacements for a few of the people in our present office who will be assigned to the new location. As we recruit these people, we will train them for ten to twenty months here in the main office.

"This will give us an experienced staff to start off with, and it will also help us with the increasing work load we expect over the next six to twelve months.

"Now here is where we need your help. Normally, Carl Jones would handle all the training in the savings department because he is the supervisor. However, Carl has just been promoted to secretary-treasurer and must assume some additional responsibilities. The result is this: we need you to help Carl train three new tellers."

"I'll do the best I can," replied the secretary, as she turned to leave. Daniels stopped her and said, "By the way, from now on sign my correspondence 'president' instead of 'manager,' will you?" Milly congratulated him and returned to her desk.

She was considerably impressed. She was now the president's private secretary and, furthermore, she had been taken into his confidence on matters known only to the directors and officers. During the next two or three weeks, several employees were overheard mentioning Milly's new "air of importance." Some of them became miffed because she remained aloof and hardly condescended to visit with them any longer.

A short time later the three new teller trainees were hired and reported for work. Jones had already outlined what he wanted Milly to do and had given her a rather detailed training plan to follow. As she began orienting the new employees to the association and their work, her feeling of importance, which had really developed only in the last two months, increased. At last, she now had several employees under her direction, in addition to holding the very responsible and powerful position of "secretary to the president." In her own mind, her prestige and status had soared to unprecedented heights and she was intent on living up to her new responsibilities.

For the first couple of months, the teller training activities moved smoothly. Milly appeared to be handling all her responsibilities adequately. One afternoon, however, two of the new tellers went to Carl to clarify one of the operating procedures they did not understand. They told him that they would have gone to Miss Fulton, but she always seemed to be reluctant to talk to them except during their formal training sessions. The nature of the questions that they presented to Jones made it apparent to him that a part of their training had been neglected. Carl immediately called Milly into his office to check the progress and details of the training program. He asked her what topics she had covered with the new tellers and which ones were coming up in the next few weeks. She told him that she had covered everything according to his schedule and would be starting the instruction on basic bookkeeping in two or three weeks. (The new tellers were also going to perform as part-time bookkeepers in the new branch.)

After this discussion, Carl called in the new tellers to go over his copy of the training schedule with them. They pointed out several items that they said Miss Fulton had said could be omitted as they were unimportant. This incident struck a familiar note with Carl; he recalled the episode about a year ago when Milly was "training" Miss Fyfe. Carl decided that the problem could best be handled by saying nothing to the trainees or to the president. He resolved to devote more personal time to training follow-up.

Less than one month later, Carl was again advised of the same laxity in Milly's training — this time in bookkeeping work. He did not hesitate to go to Ralph on this occasion because he was "getting fed up with Milly's almighty attitude," as he put it.

After explaining the incidents of the last year to the president, he asked Daniels what he would suggest. The latter said, "Carl, I'll get you some extra help from another department and you take over the training of *all* the new people — accountants, tellers, and machine operators, too. You know we have three new people in three lines reporting to work Monday. I think that Milly has just been away from teller work too long and can't get the hang of it quickly enough to handle the training." Carl agreed to take over the training but did not comment at the time on his supervisor's appraisal of the situation.

Daniels informed Milly that afternoon that he would have to relieve her of the training job because his own work was piling up. His correspondence and clerical work were becoming an increasing burden due to all the arrangements being made for the new branch, to say nothing of the continuous growth of the association's business. Milly was noncommital concerning this development.

In addition to keeping Milly constantly busy, Daniels began to channel work to Miss Fyfe in the loan department. Late one Friday afternoon, Miss Fyfe approached the president's office when Milly stopped her saying, "Mr. Daniels is not in. I can answer whatever question you have."

Miss Fyfe replied, "I'm sorry, but the work I'm doing for Mr. Daniels is confidential. He said to see him if I had any questions."

With this, Milly became furious and said, "What do you mean — you brazen hussy — you're doing confidential work for the president? I am the secretary to the president and no one else handles his work. Give me those papers."

As she reached for the papers, she saw Daniels standing in his office doorway.

Questions

1. In what way was the status of Milly evident to others in the organization?
2. Why did Milly's advancement in status result in an uncooperative attitude on her part?
3. Could Daniels have avoided the undesirable effects in Milly's performance? How?
4. What should Daniels do about Milly's conflict with Miss Fyfe?

Case 19

Missiles Inc.*

Rodney Daniels was employed in the purchasing department of Missiles Inc., a large manufacturing company engaged in producing air defense systems for the United States Government. He had worked for Missiles Inc. for four years, was twenty-five years old, and single. When he was hired, he had had only a high school education. However, by working part time and on the swing shift he had put himself through the local university and at the time of the case had a BA degree in Business Administration. Rodney Daniels was a veteran and a member of the Army Reserve. As a part of his Army Reserve training program he was required to attend military training sessions for a period of two weeks each year. In accordance with Missiles Inc. routine policy, he was excused from his work to participate in such sessions.

About two weeks before Rodney Daniels was scheduled to leave for his current tour of reserve duty, the buying group in which he worked, along with several other buying groups of the purchasing department, was moved across town to new quarters. The security and control of classified material involved in the operations of these groups was a measure of concern in the new quarters, as the offices to which the groups had been moved had not been constructed with security considerations in mind. Because of the special circumstances involved, each

---

*From *Human Elements of Administration* by Harry R. Knudson, Jr. Copyright © 1963 by Holt, Rinehart & Winston, Inc. Reprinted by permission of Holt, Rinehart & Winston, Inc.

group was responsible for establishing and maintaining its own security program.

As in many organizations involved in defense work, each employee of Missiles Inc. was required to wear an identification badge at all times while on the job. This badge identified an employee by name and payroll number and also told by a code of colors and numbers an individual's division, whether he was a supervisor or an hourly employee, and his work group. Consequently it was fairly easy by examination of the badges of individual employees to determine which employees should or should not have access to restricted areas.

In determining the security system to be used in the new quarters, the management of Rodney Daniels' buying group established a physical arrangement of the work area as noted in Exhibit 1.

As each individual entered the area of the building in which the buying group was located he would have to walk past a security guard who would check his badge to determine if he should have access to the area. Each group was required to provide their own guards at the entrances to their area. Since Rodney Daniels' group had moved into the new offices, one of the secretaries located in front of the executives' offices handled the security function at guard post A. However, this particular girl was due to be transferred to a new assignment in the near future.

While away on his tour of army reserve duty Rodney Daniels injured his hand, with the result that his ability to write was temporarily impaired. When he returned from his military tour and made his injury known, his supervisor decided that until such time as his hand was better, it would be logical for Mr. Daniels to serve as the security guard at post A to replace the girl who was leaving. When he was informed of this decision Mr. Daniels was quite indignant. He viewed the proposed assignment as a definite downgrade, and made his view known to his supervisor. He felt that although he had injured his hand, he could still write well enough to satisfactorily perform his regular duties. He stated that all he really had to do was make adequate rough notes which could then be given to a typist for final preparation. This practice was routine, and followed by all of his co-workers.

After discussing the situation with his immediate superior to no avail Mr. Daniels stated that he would seek the advice of Pat Morgan, assistant in charge of personnel for the Chief Purchasing Agent. His supervisor encouraged him to do so. In subsequent conversations with Mr. Morgan, Mr. Daniels was again emphatic that he did not want the new position. He even suggested that as his injury had been sustained while on military duty, Missiles Inc. could, if it wished to do so, extend his two-week leave of absence so he could return to the military base where his injury had occurred and take advantage of government medical facilities until such time as his hand had healed satisfactorily. Mr. Morgan would not accept this suggestion, however, as he felt that Mr. Daniels' injury was not serious enough to warrant this type of action.

After several discussions with Mr. Daniels, Mr. Morgan noted from comments that he had made that Mr. Daniels' apprehensions about accepting the temporary position as security guard seemed to be based on the following factors:

1. If he was assigned to guard post A, even though continuing to do some of his regular buying duties, he would be the only man in a row of women employees who functioned as executive secretaries. Check diagram 1.

Exhibit 1. *Missiles Inc.*

PHYSICAL LAYOUT OF NEW OFFICE

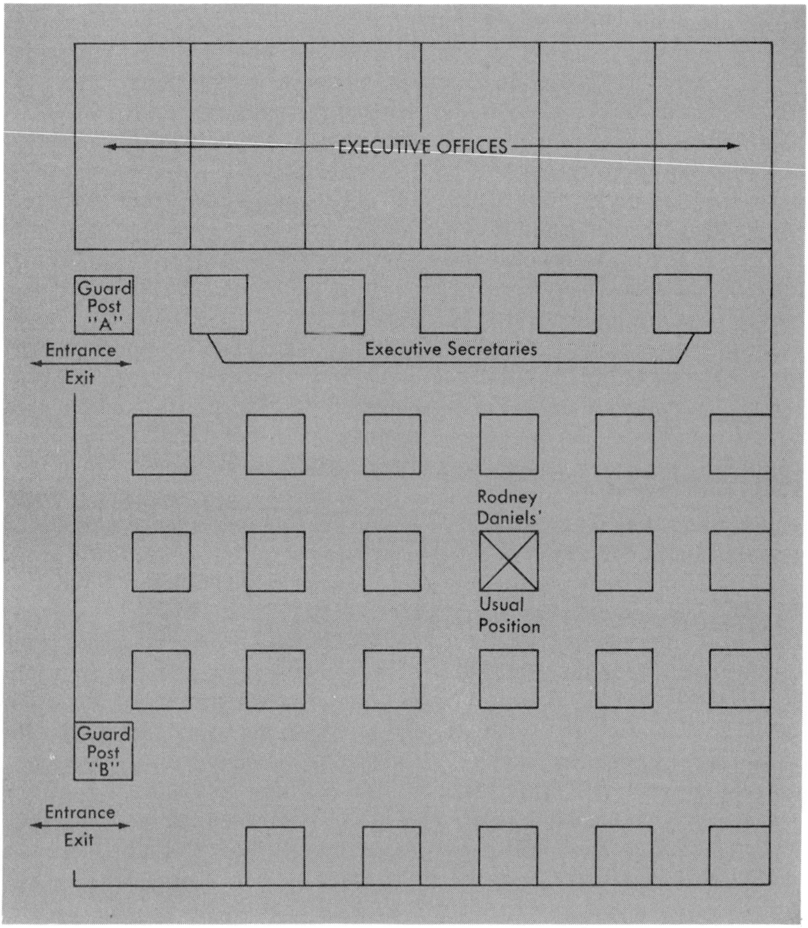

2. During his normal duties, Mr. Daniels customarily came into contact with individuals representing outside concerns which supplied various materials to Missiles Inc. Many of these individuals were of high position in their respective organizations and Mr. Morgan noticed a definite apprehension on Mr. Daniels' part that these people, seeing Mr. Daniels in his new location, would naturally assume that he had been demoted.
3. Mr. Morgan also learned from the interviews with Mr. Daniels that his family had a history of strong union membership and support and he felt that this played a factor in Mr. Daniels' reluctance to accept what seemed to be a logical, reasonable, temporary assignment.

After having had three interviews with Mr. Daniels in two days, Mr. Morgan had not yet determined what action, if any, he should take.

Questions

1. Evaluate the supervisor's decision to use Daniels as a temporary security guard.
2. What action should be taken about Daniels' complaint?
3. What are the respective responsibilities of Pat Morgan and the supervisor in resolving this problem?
4. What does this incident teach about the nature of status in business organizations?

Case 20

The Daily Press*

As Stuart Smith, circulation manager, leaned back in his chair, his mind once again turned to the turmoil that centered around Herbert Burns, one of his district managers.

The Company and Its Top Management

The Daily Press, a newspaper serving Des Moines, Iowa, had a circulation of approximately 100,000. This included out-of-town deliveries as well as sales in the central metropolitan area. It published a morning, evening, and Sunday paper.

---

*Case prepared with the assistance of Gary McAllister.

The president of *The Daily Press,* Robert Skinner, was recognized as a hard working and capable executive. Skinner did not participate actively in the operations of lower levels of the company but delegated broad authority to the vice-presidents reporting to him. One of these vice-presidents, Kenneth Miller, served as business manager, directing the Circulation, Accounting, and Credit Departments. Other vice-presidents directed the functions of editing, publishing, advertising, and composing and printing. Miller was 62 years of age and had been associated with the company for 40 years.

Organization of the Circulation Department

Stuart Smith, the circulation manager, had been appointed to the position two years earlier at the death of the previous manager, Charles Hill. Although Smith supervised city circulation, road circulation, and a group of secretaries, he devoted the majority of his time to working with the city circulation manager, Thomas Jones, and the nine district managers reporting to Jones.

Each district manager was in charge of circulation in a certain district of the city. As district manager, he was responsible for hiring, firing, and coordinating the work of a group of 30 to 40 paper boys. The district manager was also responsible for processing all "stops," "starts," and complaints originating in his district. He delivered the papers to the boys who, in turn, made home deliveries by bicycle, motor scooter, or car.

Before becoming circulation manager of *The Daily Press,* Stuart Smith served as circulation manager of another newspaper in a smaller city. In the two years with *The Daily Press,* he had earned a reputation as an efficient and well-liked manager. In particular, he had the complete loyalty of practically all subordinates as well as the respect of higher management.

One of the key district managers was Bill Roland, an intelligent and personable man who was thoroughly experienced in the newspaper business. Because of this fact, he had developed into an informal leader with the respect of his fellow district managers. Bill had been associated with the company for 17 years.

Re-employment of Herbert Burns as District Manager

Another district manager, Herbert Burns, had worked for the company from 1945 to 1952. In 1952, he became unhappy with the management and resigned to go into business for himself. Seven years later, his business failed and he returned to work at *The Daily Press* as a district manager.

Before Herb's return, the district managers were a harmonious group with excellent teamwork. They got along well together and enjoyed frequent social gatherings at their homes.

Immediately after Herb Burns returned, he attempted to develop a friendship with Bill Roland. He took Bill fishing, worked on his car, and dropped over to Bill's house almost every day. This resulted in a temporary close friendship between Herb and Bill. (As a result of later events, a definite coolness developed between them.)

After this continued for a few months, Herb shifted his attention to Tom Jones and succeeded in forming a friendship with him. Later, Herb began to build a friendship with the then circulation manager, Charles Hill. He gave Hill's two sons choice paper routes, took them fishing, and thus became a close friend of the family.

When Hill died and Smith was appointed circulation manager, Herb immediately started his program of cultivating the friendship of the boss. Smith was considerate of Herb but refrained from developing close ties, feeling that he should treat all district managers similarly. As soon as Herb recognized Smith's attitude, he turned his attention to the two sons of Vice-President Miller. He took the boys fishing, camping, water-skiing, and worked on their cars. In this way Herb built a friendship with Miller. All of these efforts by Herb appeared to be unjustified self-promotion and "politics" in the eyes of the other district managers. This led to a deterioration of the teamwork and friendship that had characterized the group. They all disliked Herb, and, as they saw Herb's "stock" with the top brass go up, morale dropped to a low level. In spite of the general dissatisfaction, however, the district managers remained loyal to Smith personally.

Exploits of Herbert Burns

A series of events during the preceding year had led to a deterioration of the situation. One incident occurred when Herb Burns intimated to Miller that Bill Roland had reported to work while intoxicated. Miller immediately approached Smith and suggested that he dismiss Bill. Smith refused to do this because of inaccuracies in the story. Although Bill had been drinking, it was after working hours for the day and thus occurred on his own time.

Another incident occurred when Smith, recognizing Herb's political activities, decided to dismiss him. He gave Herb his two-weeks' notice. Herb immediately called on Miller, and Miller called Smith to tell him Herb should not be discharged. So, Smith had no choice but to let matters ride as they were.

On another occasion, Herb went to Miller, instead of Smith, and asked him to eliminate three *weekly* routes from his district. The entire district would then consist of *monthly* routes and be much easier for Herb to handle. So Miller, hearing Herb's "logic," strongly suggested to Smith that this should be arranged.

Still other events took place that made matters worse. Herb tended to get the other district managers into trouble by telling Miller about their

Organization Chart
The Daily Press Publishing Company

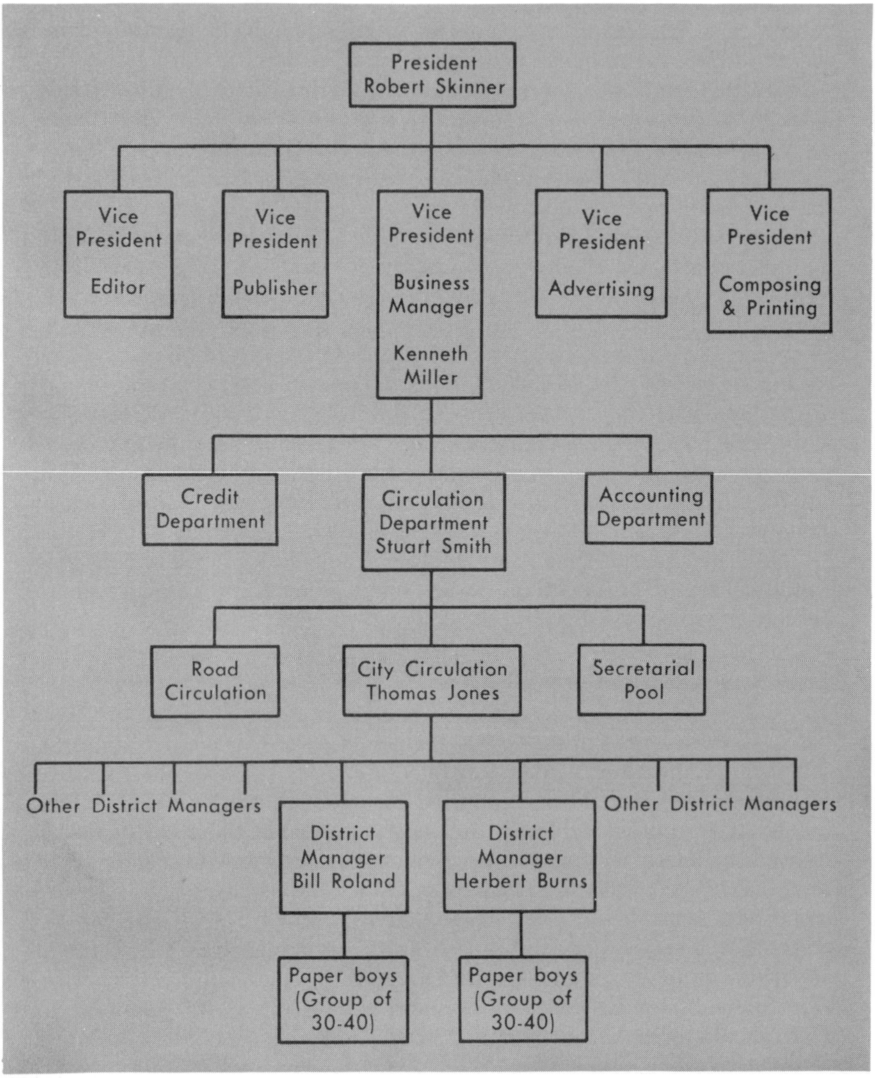

activities. Occasionally these reports concerned items of importance, but most of the time they involved matters of only minor significance.

Other district managers felt that Herb was not above falsehood. Herb had been seen several times in the recent weeks at the home of Robert Skinner, the president. Smith decided that this series of events could not continue and that something must be done.

Questions

1. How effective were the political techniques used by Herb Burns? Do you consider their effectiveness similar both for the short run and the long run?
2. What negative consequences resulted from Herb's activities?
3. What can Smith do about the unsatisfactory situation?

Case 21

Tom White Talks Back*

In early 1958 Tom White was a salesman with a real estate firm in Long City. The real estate market was depressed at that time and he told the loan officer of the Long City Federal Savings and Loan Association that he would like to make a change in employment.

Tom had, before his present realty selling job, worked part time with another realty firm in a university town some twenty miles from Long City. He lacked only two hours' academic credit in order to obtain his degree in business administration when he moved to Long City three years ago. He always gave as his reason for not obtaining his degree that he was married with one child and had to work part time in order to support his family.

In addition to his other activities Tom was also doing quite a bit of flying on weekends under the air force reserve program. He had been honorably discharged after two years of service as a combat pilot during the Korean War.

Only three months before Tom had quit college and moved to Long City, his wife gave birth to an afflicted child. With the demands of his college work, the necessity of supporting his family, and the weekend flying, the burden had proved to be a very difficult one for Tom to bear. It finally resulted in his seeking a complete change of environment and moving to Long City.

He was only moderately successful in selling real estate, but weekend flying and the concern over the afflicted child had held him back and undoubtedly accounted for part of his inability to become an outstanding real estate agent. The child died late in 1957. This brief history of Tom's background brings us up to 1958 at which time he sought the job with Long City Federal.

Alex Smith, president of the Long City Federal Savings and Loan

*From Edgar G. Williams, *People Problems* (Indiana University, Graduate School of Business, Bureau of Business Research, 1962).

Association, in checking with Tom's former employer, was told that if Tom could get his mind off flying long enough he would make a good employee as a trainee in the mortgage loan department. The mortgage loan officer and Smith both made this point to Tom in his final job interview with them. They told him that if it came to his flying or Long Federal business, his job would have to come first. He readily agreed that it probably had taken an overly prominent place in his mind in the past but that he did not feel that he would be troubled in this way any longer.

Tom was hired as a trainee in the mortgage loan department, which at that time did not have a formal training program. He was told that it would not be necessary for him to resign his reserve flying status but just to keep in mind the point that the business of the association had to come first.

The loan officer under whom Tom was to train was very busy and could not give him all the training he needed except by working after hours and on Saturday mornings. It seemed to the officer that Tom assumed a greater knowledge of the mortgage loan business than he really had, apparently on the basis of his experience in the real estate field. The loan officer and Smith discussed with Tom the problem of getting into the proper work groove, and both counseled the young man on two or three occasions concerning his availability for training. Tom explained again that he had to fly on the weekends and, in order to make up for these absences, he felt that he should get home to his family as early as possible throughout the week. The result of this was that it was most difficult for Tom and his immediate superior to find adequate mutual times for training purposes.

Meanwhile, Tom made various imprudent assumptions and decisions concerning his work, and a few of the older employees in the mortgage loan department began to develop some resentment toward him. They felt that he showed an uncommon amount of ambition for position and status and the power to make decisions, but that he took little concrete action to school himself or to get down to the details in order to validate his decisions before he acted on them.

When the collections manager was called to active duty by the marine corps, the managing officer, Smith, arranged with the loan officer to have Tom help out in collections for a short while until a replacement arrived to fill the collection manager's position.

Smith told Tom that this was an excellent opportunity for him to learn all he could about the collections end of the business before the other individual left and in this way he would be able to help brief the new collections manager when he arrived.

Tom agreed to help but made it known at the time that he did not want to be permanently placed in such a job. It was soon apparent to the departing collections manager that he could not get together with Tom because their personal schedules conflicted so badly. It is interesting to note, in retrospect, that neither Smith nor the loan officer discussed this problem with Tom anymore. Apparently other considerations of the business had higher priority.

Delinquent loans increased noticeably when the collections manager left, but the new man was soon on the job doing his best to get things under control with the help of the managing officer, the loan officer, and a clerk in the collections department. Tom contributed very little in the way of positive assistance — and none at all outside the regular work periods.

About this time it came to light that Tom had allowed a student summer employee to make a home improvement loan on his father's house in order to buy a car. On learning of this departure from established practice, Smith expressed his dissatisfaction to the loan officer with things in general concerning Tom and asked him for his advice as to what should be done. The loan officer said that because he had talked with Tom several times he could do no more, but he suggested that the president talk "straight from the shoulder" with Tom concerning his unavailability and lack of real interest in his work.

Tom was asked to report to Smith's office. When he did, he appeared shocked to learn that his performance on the job was inadequate. When Smith asked him to relate any instances where he felt he had shown any small inclination to do a little more than was asked of him, he was at a loss to answer in any way. The president then asked him to analyze his inability to work more closely with the mortgage loan officer. Tom admitted again that his weekend flying activities and his desire to give his family as much of his time as possible during the week had made it impossible for the two men to get together at mutually agreeable times. Tom also stated that he had never considered giving up flying and was unwilling to do so even now; his wife was pregnant again and she needed him as much as possible. In short, his attitude was not one of flexibility, and he gave the president the impression that the association would have to keep him pretty much as he was or let him go.

The president thought about the situation over the weekend and decided to ask for Tom's resignation the following Monday. He intended to allow Tom to stay on as long as two weeks more to help him find another job.

When the proposition was put to Tom he refused to resign. This angered the president, and he told Tom that he should consider himself discharged effective immediately.

When the discussion reached this point Tom backtracked rapidly and told the president that he would be willing to submit a letter of resignation, and he did so later that afternoon. His next step was to contact several of the board members to complain that he had been treated unfairly since he had worked for Long City Federal Savings and Loan for six months and that in his mind he was entitled to the usual two weeks' separation arrangement.

President Smith informed the members of his executive committee of the situation and they agreed with his action. The board chairman felt that a person should be discharged on the spot and not be allowed to remain on the job, thereby affecting other members of the staff or any of the customers with whom he might come in contact. It was his impression that Smith was too lenient and that Tom was not really entitled to any further consideration. He suggested that Smith draft a written separation policy to be submitted to the board for its approval at the next regularly scheduled meeting the following week.

Questions

1. What mistakes, if any, were made by the management in their relationships with Tom White?
2. Did Tom's assignment of top priority to his family and his flying disqualify him for serious consideration for a management career?
3. Did the firm have any obligation to tolerate Tom's flying as a contribution to military preparedness?
4. Did President Smith act wisely in releasing Tom?

Case 22

The Reluctant Foreman*

"How far can I push this foreman without hurting him? If I insist on the change, will it cause some type of psychological damage? On the other hand, do I have a choice? Doesn't fairness require the change regardless of the effect on one foreman?" These were the questions bothering Steve Olson as he considered a staffing decision in the pineapple cannery.

The Alcohol Plant in the Cannery Organization

The Portia Pineapple Cannery, located in Puerto Rico, is a major processor of pineapple for distribution throughout the U.S. — both under its own label and under private labels. Steve Olson served as superintendent of laboratories (the organizational title for the cannery's quality control manager) and also as superintendent of the alcohol plant. He had "inherited" the responsibility for managing the alcohol plant because of his professional knowledge and background in the field of chemistry. Alcohol is produced as a by-product of pineapple processing and is subsequently used for production of vinegar.

At the time this problem came to a head, there were nine employees assigned to the alcohol plant — two alcohol plant operators (first class);

---

*Case prepared with the assistance of Gordon L. Pickering.

one alcohol plant operator (second class); three alcohol plant operators (third class); and three general laborers. The broadest range of skills was required of an alcohol plant operator (first class). An employee in this classification was able to perform the various types of tasks involved in alcohol plant operation—including fermentation, distilling, denaturation, shipping, and general maintenance of equipment. Lower class operators required closer supervision or were more specialized in their abilities and assignments. The foreman was responsible for supervising these employees and directing the overall operation of the alcohol plant.

The Alcohol Plant Foreman

Carlos Cepeda had been promoted to the position of foreman of the alcohol plant some six years earlier. He was a native of Puerto Rico, fifty-four years of age, a high school graduate, and the father of several college-educated children. Practically all of his working career (almost thirty-six years) had been spent as an employee of the Portia Cannery. Much of his experience before assignment as alcohol plant foreman had been in warehouse work (can stacking, shipping, casing, and so on), including work as leadman and as assistant foreman.

Adapting to the Foreman Role

Cepeda's assignment to the alcohol plant was made effective a year prior to retirement of the preceding foreman. The overlap of his service with that of the other foreman was designed for training purposes. The orientation period was intended to provide a thorough acquaintance with all operating methods and procedures. Cepeda's superiors expected him to learn each operating job sufficiently well that he could step in, if necessary, and perform it. Of course, work as an operator would be required only in case of emergency. In accordance with this plan, Cepeda learned the administrative and clerical duties required of the foreman, such as the preparation of government reports and records. He was also instructed in the work duties of all employees assigned to the alcohol plant. Cepeda accepted the instructions and developed a general familiarity with the various job assignments.

Thus it appeared that Cepeda was making progress in acquiring a knowledge of the responsibilities of foreman and learning the overall operations of the alcohol plant. He was slow to accept responsibility for personally performing work operations, however, tending to rely instead upon the technical knowledge and experience of the operators. An example of this difficulty in making operating decisions on his own was revealed by his reluctance to operate the stills without assistance. He managed to avoid situations in which he operated the stills without an experienced man in the background. Thus, there was always someone to whom he could turn if he encountered problems.

Cepeda's knowledge of the operations became adequate, however, to make possible satisfactory supervision under normal operating conditions. The following events eventually focused attention upon Cepeda's limitations as alcohol plant foreman, and it became clear that he was unable or afraid to operate the stills without the assistance of an experienced operator. When it became known, at this later date, that he did not feel he could run the stills alone, he was directed to learn to do so, first by the superintendent of the alcohol plant, Steve Olson, and later, by the division general superintendent — a higher level of management. He was even denied a normal blanket pay increase because of his slowness in developing this capability.

Shift Rotation of Key Operators

The two key positions in the alcohol plant, other than that of foreman, were those of the two alcohol plant operators (first class). The incumbents of these positions, Pedro and Juan, were both veteran employees with the necessary ability to perform the most difficult and responsible work in the plant. In fact, Pedro was a twenty-five-year employee and Juan a thirty-five-year employee of the Portia Pineapple Company. Both had been assigned to the alcohol plant throughout their working careers. Pedro, however, worked only the day shift, whereas Juan was always assigned to the night shift during the twelve to fifteen weeks of the year during which two-shift operations were required.

The key fermentation duties were performed or supervised by Pedro on the day shift, and he had come to consider himself as the "fermentation man." The fermentation process was carried on by other operators after it was "set up" by Pedro. Pedro's exclusively day-shift service resulted somewhat as a matter of coincidence from the pattern of job development and training that had occurred in previous years. Even though Pedro was not the senior employee, he had been "at the right place at the right time." Thus, he had landed the daytime fermentation job for a time and adopted a proprietary attitude toward it. The attitude had been encouraged by an earlier job classification scheme that distinguished in job title between "fermentation man" and "distiller."

Juan was completely capable, however, of operating the stills and performing all of the fermentation work that was performed by Pedro. As noted above, the job titles of both men were identical. From the standpoint of length of service, however, the senior employee was penalized by regular assignment to the night shift.

It appeared to Olson, the superintendent, that the two positions should be made completely interchangeable and that Pedro and Juan should be rotated from one position to the other. This would equalize the opportunity for day work and thus provide a more equitable arrangement.

With the exception of "key men" needed on a certain shift, all laboratory workers rotated each week during the two-shift operations. It was Olson's responsibility to decide which jobs were too critical to permit regular rotation. Olson had the authority, then, to place both employees in the "rotating" category.

Initiating the Change

After deliberating on the desirability of change for some time, Olson instructed the foreman to rotate the incumbents between the two positions. Cepeda accepted the decision without protest and presumably started to implement it.

After some time had elapsed, it became apparent to the superintendent that the change had not been made. Some minor adjustments in work assignments were made, but Pedro never worked at night and Juan never worked during the day. Cepeda avoided compliance with Olson's order, in part at least, by his ability to talk Juan, who wanted relief, out of it. Juan gave in temporarily to "keep peace," knowing Pedro's resistance to change.

In discussing the problem with Olson, Cepeda insisted he was trying to make the change but finding it impossible. It appeared to the superintendent, however, that Cepeda was simply afraid to insist that Pedro comply with the order. On one occasion, Pedro had told Cepeda he wouldn't change, stating that he would quit before changing to a night shift job. In the words of Olson, "The men had Cepeda buffaloed." Cepeda appeared to feel insecure in his position. The possibility that he might need to step in and pinch hit for Pedro, if Pedro resigned, was obviously disturbing to him. As noted above, Cepeda had never acquired a thorough working knowledge of the job. In addition, Cepeda had used Pedro to perform the calculations required in his own position, and he apparently lacked the confidence that he could do the necessary "figuring" without assistance. Although Cepeda had never verbalized these difficulties, his behavior made them painfully clear.

Emotional Upset

The discussion and tentative steps to implement the decision continued over a period of several weeks. Although some changes in work assignments occurred, Pedro and Juan were never rotated. Olson remained firm in his insistence that the two operators be rotated. When Olson failed to back down or "forget" about the rotation plan, Cepeda began to show symptoms of an emotional upset. He became nervous and experienced difficulty in sleeping at night. During the day, he often appeared extremely tired and, on occasion, would almost fall asleep at his desk. This was clearly the result of his sleeplessness at night and differed from his customary behavior when he was experiencing less pressure.

Forcing the Issue

Procrastination did not solve the problem. In fact, pressure seemed to increase. Juan was suffering from a chronic cold and needed a period of daytime work to aid his recuperation. Cepeda experienced more and more conflict as he tried to walk the tightrope between the expectations of his superintendent and his subordinates. Olson grew increasingly dissatisfied as the problem was prolonged and the solution delayed.

Finally, Olson decided to take action. He called in Cepeda and told him the change was to be effected without further delay at the beginning of the following week. Pedro was to be assigned to the night shift beginning on that date. No excuses could be accepted.

Following this action, Cepeda reported off on sick leave. Olson contacted the nurse in the cannery's first-aid dispensary, who, in turn, contacted Cepeda's physician. The doctor recommended two weeks' sick leave to enable Cepeda to get back to normal. The basic problem was that of "nerves." Also, the nurse passed on to Olson the doctor's comments: "You can force Cepeda to make this change, but you may also have a psychopathic case on your hands if you do."

Questions

1. In view of Pedro's blue-collar status and his fewer years of service, how can you explain his refusal to recognize the principle of seniority in this situation?
2. What factors appear to be responsible for Cepeda's emotional upset? Does this disturbance indicate he is not "foreman material"?
3. What action should be taken by Olson?

Case 23

Martha Smith*

Martha Smith was hired by the Metropolitan Federal Savings and Loan Association as a teller trainee. Although she had had no previous

---

*From Edgar G. Williams, *People Problems* (Indiana University, Graduate School of Business, Bureau of Business Research, 1962).

experience in a savings and loan association, she showed a remarkable aptitude for the work. She had an inquisitive mind, a real desire to learn, and was well liked by both the public and her fellow employees.

After her initial training period, Martha was given cash, and assigned as a savings teller. In order to have a more flexible work force, the tellers at Metropolitan were rotated periodically from one teller window to another. Martha learned the duties of construction teller and journal teller very rapidly. The cashier of the association soon developed a high regard for Martha, and, approximately a year after she was first employed, she was promoted to chief teller when the girl who had occupied that position left her job due to pregnancy.

Martha was a very conscientious chief teller and did much to maintain high-quality work among the tellers. She was an emotionally stable individual who kept calm under the many pressures of her job.

About one and a half years after she became chief teller, Martha and another girl from the association were involved in an automobile accident while out on a double date; the automobile they were riding in was struck head on. Martha was in the front seat of the automobile, and her head went through the windshield at the impact. She received severe internal injuries and a badly lacerated face, and later lost the sight of her right eye. The other girl, who was in the back seat, also suffered internal injuries and sustained considerable damage to her spine. The two men with whom they were riding were badly injured but both ultimately recovered.

The girls were off work for several months due to their injuries. The association paid them their full salaries for a period of three months and then changed their status to a leave of absence. They were kept on the association employee insurance records so they could receive full medical benefits. Moreover, each girl was given the assurance that she would be re-employed when she had fully recuperated.

Six months after Martha was involved in the accident, it became apparent that she would be unable to return to work for an extended period of time because of the amount of plastic surgery that was required on her face. The cashier visited her at her home and discussed her future with the association. He told her that, although he had preferred not to replace her with a new chief teller, it had become necessary because of the volume of work. Martha understood the situation and said that she thought the association had been most fair in its treatment of her since the accident.

A few months after her visit with the cashier, Martha called the personnel director at Metropolitan Federal Savings and asked if there were any openings in the accounting department. At the time she called, none was available, but she was told by the personnel manager that the internal auditor needed additional help. Martha indicated her interest to him and returned to work the following week as an assistant internal auditor at her former salary.

As a result of the automobile accident, Martha still had a number of scars on her face and wore an eye patch over her right eye. As she had always been an attractive girl, she was most conscious of her change in appearance. The fact that she was exposed to the public in her new job undoubtedly contributed to a psychological change in her. Martha asked for a transfer to the bookkeeping section of the accounting department, which was located in the basement of the building. The controller and personnel director both thought that the transfer might aid her in readjusting to the work situation, and also felt that her training made her well qualified for the position; consequently, they promised to give her what consideration they could.

In a few weeks, the association's bookkeeper left and Martha was assigned to the bookkeeping section as bookkeeper. For the first two or three months after her transfer, she seemed happy in her new surroundings. Soon, however, she became bitter toward the association and resentful of the fact that she had not been reinstated in her former position as chief teller. The senior accountant, who was Martha's immediate supervisor, discussed her change in attitude with the personnel director. Both realized that Martha was going through a period of psychological adjustment and decided to take no immediate action hoping that everything would work out all right.

Time did not solve the problem, however, and matters became worse. Martha, who had always been well liked by her fellow employees, became very sharp tongued with others in the department as well as with her immediate supervisor. The people working with her became upset with her change in attitude, and the quality of her own work began to deteriorate. The senior accountant realized that some action had to be taken on his part if Martha were to be retained and if the morale of his entire group were to be restored. To that end, he asked Martha to come into his office for the purpose of discussing her job and the attitude that she had toward it and that maybe the two of them could work out something that would be more satisfactory for everyone concerned.

Martha told him that she was being discriminated against because of her misfortune and that she doubted if he could do very much to change the situation.

Questions

1. Can a firm tolerate an employee with a bitter attitude such as that of Martha Smith?
2. Why did Martha seem happy at first in the bookkeeping section but then become resentful after a few months?
3. Are Martha's emotional problems sufficiently serious as to require professional counseling? If so, how should this be arranged?
4. How should the senior accountant deal with this problem?

Case 24

Handy Hardware Company*

Handy Hardware Co. is a national manufacturer, wholesaler, and distributor of many well-known appliances and tools. In their sales department, a set, but flexible, pattern of promotion had been established.

When a man starts with the company, he spends his first six months in the warehouse as an assembler. This job provides the individual with a knowledge of all the parts that are in the warehouse and where they are located. If he proves satisfactory, his next step is to the position of counterman. In this position the individual writes up small orders and handles small cash accounts with transient salesmen who use Handy Hardware products.

After another six months, his next step will be to that of Junior Order Clerk or Stock Records Clerk, whichever one is open at the time. Here, he deals with larger accounts and meets the public on a higher level. If he proves satisfactory in these positions, the man may next be transferred to Senior Order Clerk or "Quotations" Clerk.

This latter position requires a complete knowledge of the items sold by Handy, and also an ability to read blueprints so that he may give accurate quotations of prices on large-scale operations. The next step is the most difficult.

After each six-month interval between steps, the man may be kept at his present position or advanced to salesman status. If he does not show salesman qualities, he may be given a permanent, office supervisory position. These six-month intervals are not always exactly six months, but due to the present rapid growth of the business they are usually very close to this period.

Tom Sexton came to Handy Hardware after World War II and was hired as a janitor in the Regina office. His war record was exceptional. He had enlisted as a private and advanced through the ranks to a captaincy. When he started with Handy, he was married and had one child. It was later discovered that Sexton had married, at the age of sixteen, a woman several years his senior. While cleaning up the warehouse in the evening, Sexton got to know where everything was kept and subsequently he applied for the position of warehouse receiver, when it became open. He obtained the job and performed his duties excellently.

Although promotions were not as rapid at that time, within eighteen months from starting with the company, Sexton was on the order desk where, after three or four weeks, he was handling everything very capably. He regularly received his semi-annual pay increases, but after a year on the order desk he asked for a sales job. He was turned down at

*Case prepared by Professor William A. Preshing of The University of Calgary, Calgary, Alberta.

that for three reasons: The first was that there were no openings; the second that his wardrobe was not fit for a respectable-looking salesman; and thirdly, he had a belligerent tone in his voice.

Although the management had hoped that Sexton would spend some of his pay increases on improving his appearance, he had spent it on joining an exclusive golf club. Although Sexton never missed a day of work because of drink, or was known to drink during office hours, it became known that he was drinking regularly in the evenings. At staff meetings or parties it was noticed that he was becoming very inebriated.

Though handling large accounts, Sexton did not get on the sales staff. This apparently annoyed him immensely and on certain occasions, when he had been drinking too much, Sexton would phone up the office manager in the small hours of the morning and talk wildly about the fact that he was not being promoted.

The situation continued for a period of eighteen months. Finally, Sexton quit and took a sales job with a small competitive firm. When he left Handy the firm was required to split Sexton's work, since it took one and one-half men to do the work he had been doing. In his new position, Sexton set up many major accounts which the company had been unable to place before. However, he did not receive credit for his work and soon found that he was not making enough to make ends meet. Sexton, therefore, returned to Handy.

Handy did not have any openings in Regina at that time, but a shipper was required in Calgary. Sexton told management that he had learned his lesson and would settle down and behave. He took the shipping job in Calgary and, paying his own expenses, moved his family to Calgary. In his first two months in Calgary, Sexton instituted changes in the warehouse routine which saved the company $5,000.00. He soon received the maximum salary for his job and was transferred to the office in the "quotation" department at a higher salary than usual.

He worked at this new job very efficiently but when he did not get advanced to salesman, it was noticed that he began to come in looking extremely tired each morning. Management became aware of Sexton's after-hours drinking and felt that if he were made a salesman he might start drinking with a client after hours. Sexton felt all the more disappointed when two or three men in the "quotations" department were promoted to salesmen over him. His drinking became excessive and management was at a loss as to what they should do with him.

Questions

1. What action should be taken by management in dealing with Tom Sexton?

Case 25

Carl Larson: Foreman*

Carl Larson was 26 years old, a graduate in accounting from the University of Colorado, an ex-marine lieutenant, and had been first-shift foreman for the past five months of the Corn Starch Shipping Department of the Kerton City Plant, one of five plants owned by Beacon Refining, Inc. His department, shipping, was concerned with receiving finished corn starch packaged in 100 lb. bags from the Milling Department, and either loading them in railroad cars for immediate shipment or storing them on pallets in various locations within the department. To assist him in performing his job, Larson had a clerk, Steve Jackson, to handle most of the clerical work, and a chief checker, Max Randall. Randall's job was to supervise the twenty-five men in the department as they loaded boxcars or stacked bags for inventory, to check the amount and type of bags loaded, and in general, to be Larson's "Man Friday" along with Jackson. Jackson had formerly been chief shipper before the present shipping department had been separated from the Milling Department and organized as a separate function. However, when Larson was brought in as foreman of the new department the plant manager felt it best to give him some kind of a clerk to relieve him of clerical routine, thus leaving him more floor time to learn the job. Randall had been with the company for twenty-five years, was considered extremely competent, and it was generally conceded that if he were not colored he would have been made a shipping foreman several years ago. Jackson was a seven-year man, with little education, but better than average ability.

Beacon Refining, Inc. was concerned primarily with the refining of corn, which, in many forms, was shipped to various companies throughout the country for a multiplicity of uses. It also processed many extracted products. The Kerton City Plant was its largest, spreading over three city blocks. At peak production it alone employed over 3,000 workers, many of whom were laid off during annual seasonal slumps. A good majority of the workers were Negro. The Kerton Plant was managed by Johnny Irvin, the "wonder boy" of the company. He was thirty years old, and in only ten years with the company had risen through the ranks to his present $35,000 a year job. He was known as a real production man, and was often heard to say, "No matter what, I'll always get out our plant production quotas. Nothing holds back production." Much of Irvin's time was now spent commuting back and

---

*Case prepared by Professor S. G. Huneryager of the University of Illinois.

forth from the Kerton Plant to national headquarters in New York City, a distance of 1,000 miles.

In addition to the Kerton Plant, Beacon Inc. had four other large plants located throughout the country, and plants in Belgium, England, and Korea. The one in Korea had recently been taken over by the Chinese Reds. Presently, the company was the second largest in the industry but was laying plans to launch a drive which in four years would make it number one. Total sales last year approximated $100 million. But even for its size it was for the most part family owned and controlled.

The parent company had instituted a new policy two years ago, stating that only college graduates would be employed as departmental foremen. This applied to all plants. The Kerton Plant was no exception. As these jobs were hard to come by and extremely well paid, they were highly coveted by many new graduates and each plant could well afford to be highly selective. As a general rule they preferred graduates trained in chemical engineering. Exceptions were made, of course, as was the case of Carl Larson. New men in the Kerton Plant were usually put through a short, on-the-job training course as Irvin felt the best training came from being thrust into the job and learning from one's mistakes. However, practice was not uniform throughout the company as the individual plant managers had various ideas on the subject. In the Kerton Plant they now had seven young college foremen and eighteen "old timers" who had come up the "hard way" (or so they claimed).

Carl Larson had been discharged as a second lieutenant only a year and a half ago. He had been inducted into the marines immediately upon graduation from college as he was a participant in the National R.O.T.C. program. Larson was extremely proud of his marine training and often said to Jackson, "Yes sir, Steve, the marines really make a man out of you. An officer's an officer and a private's a private. *Discipline!* That's what you learn — *discipline!* When I gave an order, I was obeyed. My men knew the meaning of the word 'obey,' or I knew the reason why. Yes sir, the marines really taught me leadership."

Larson had served his first 16 months with the company as a night-shift foreman in one of the processing departments. His fellow foremen and other workers that he supervised did not seem to like him. Many of the following comments were made:

"Boy, he sure is a hard-headed individual."

"Seems to me I'd rather be working for the Kremlin — at least then I'd be able to do my job the way I wanted to. After all, until he popped up, my job hadn't changed for six years. Now he's changed it six times in six months."

"I never saw a foreman who knew less about his job and of how to get along with people. Can't wait until he gets out of here and we can get the department running smoothly again."

"That guy's got a tremendous desire to get ahead—and nothing to do it with."

"Why is it that you just cannot like that guy? Some people are born to be disliked!"

In the spring of 1956, Irvin, in conjunction with Joe Ricos, the superintendent in charge of plant shipping, decided that a separate department for shipping was needed for the corn starch operation in the plant. Previous to this, production milling and shipping of corn starch had been combined in one department under Larry Brown. Brown, for 17 years a foreman of this department, was extremely competent, yet had come up through the school of hard knocks. He was an aggressive, hard-talking, driving type of foreman, both respected and feared by those coming in contact with him. His workers respected his ability to meet and exceed production quotas, thus enabling them to earn high bonuses on the incentive payment plan.

It was decided to leave Brown in charge of the now separate Production or Milling Department and to bring in Larson as the new foreman for the Shipping Department. Two months after the new arrangements had been put into effect, it became apparent to Ricos that much friction had developed between Brown and Larson—not only was this noticed, but in addition, the number of grievances stemming from Shipping was double what they had been when the two departments were combined. Larson was filling the personnel office with written reports reprimanding many of his men. Any person getting two of these reports in one month was subject to penalty. Eight of his men had received two in the last month as compared plantwide with the next highest department total of three. Ricos decided to have a talk with Larson and Brown. Larson claimed that with the type of people in the department—manual, colored labor—he was forced to "crack the whip" so as to meet shipping quotas. Also, the heavy amount of paperwork on the job kept him at his desk most of the working day. Brown was vehement in denouncing Larson. He called him an ignorant "gyrene" and said that "if he hadn't had a friend in the Personnel Department he would never have gotten the job." He went even further, claiming that if it were not for Max Randall and Steve Jackson, no corn starch would ever get shipped out of the plant. Both men spent most of the day on the floor supervising the loading of boxcars. Randall and Jackson declined any comment except that they were doing their jobs to the best of their abilities.

After hearing these comments, Ricos decided that the primary problem was Larson's inexperience, coupled with Brown's temperament, and that only time would remedy the situation. He thus let the matter temporarily alone.

About one month after this, two consultants were brought into Larson's department to try and solve a serious problem common to all the company's plants. None of the shipping and inventory figures of corn starch ever balanced out with the production records reported. These figures were compiled by the home office in New York and for the past several years a significant difference had been noted. As the Kerton Plant had the newest shipping department, and their figures for the last three months were also out of balance, it was thought that here would be the easiest place to trace the causes of the problem.

The two inventory men were told to work out of Larson's office and given complete freedom in their job. They were allotted two months in which to study the problem and prepare a detailed report for Ricos and Irvin as to its solution.

From the very beginning, Larson seemed to resent these men. He did not openly resist them, but when they sought his cooperation regarding certain things, he usually claimed he was too busy to help. The few times the trio lunched together, he was constantly prodding them concerning their final report. He seemed to be very worried about this report and finally secured their agreement to let him read it before it was submitted to Ricos and Irvin.

The consultants were concerned that part of the inventory problem was man-oriented. Workers didn't seem to particularly care about their jobs, bags were repeatedly broken and thrown away, bags of starch were placed in the wrong inventory piles, checkers weren't keeping accurate records of carloadings and of total bags received from the production department. The inventory storing space of the department was in overall poor condition. It was almost impossible to take an accurate inventory of present stock. The only people who knew where stock was stored were Randall and Jackson. The consultants also noticed that the department seemed to revolve around these two men — workers took orders from Larson but didn't seem to like it too much and had little confidence in him. But they did listen to and respect both Randall and Jackson — the former because he had the experience, and the latter because of his personality and experience.

All of these causes, plus many others, with the exception of the latter statement, were included in the report. When Larson read it he became very upset and angry. He told the consultants they were deliberately trying to make him look bad and to hold him back from advancing in the company. He rushed the report to Ricos, claiming that although truthful, most of the causes were beyond his control and impossible to remedy. He was so upset over the situation that Ricos realized he now faced a very serious problem.

Questions

1. What is the underlying problem in this case?
2. What were some of the causes leading to this problem?

3. What are some solutions Irvin and Ricos could avail themselves of?

4. Could something have been done earlier about this situation? If so, what?

Case 26

Southern Bank*

History and Organization

Southern Bank, established shortly after the Civil War, had developed over the years a distinguished record for prudent, conservative financial service. An independent, single-location bank located in a medium-sized city, it now (1965) employs some 550 persons and is one of the largest institutions of its kind in the area.

The bank is organized into eight divisions: General Administrative, Banking, Investment, Trust Administration, Business Development, Management Consulting, Marketing, and Legal. (See Exhibit 1.) In addition, there are three service groups: Planning and Personnel, Building and Office Services, and the Controller's Group. There are six levels of management in the bank: president, division, group, department, section, and unit.

About 100 of the bank's employees are officers, of whom six are women; another 100 employees are men in various stages of professional banking careers. The remaining 350 employees are women, about 50 of whom are highly trained career specialists. Approximately one-half of the female employees are young, unmarried high school graduates. These girls typically remain with the bank for two or three years before leaving to be married or for other reasons.

Since the inauguration of a new president in 1959 and the subsequent employment of a number of "bright young men," the bank has aggressively been exploring new ways of rendering financial services to its customers. This combination of aggressiveness and innovation has proved to be highly successful in promoting the growth and profitability of the bank. The Management Consulting Division, for example, was established to meet a perceived need and has not only become a profitable new service in its own right, but also has served, through its activities, to bring valued new accounts to the bank.

The top management people in Southern Bank believe that if the institution is to continue to grow through aggressiveness and innovation,

---

*Case prepared by Professor Jack L. Rettig of Oregon State University.

the ideas and cooperation of all employees at all levels should be solicited and encouraged. In other words, excellent communication is considered by top management to be vital to the successful operation of this dynamic organization. To this end, Mr. Harold Walsh of the personnel office was designated in 1963 as the coordinator of communications and training. Also to this end, a variety of communication techniques, channels, and devices, described on the following pages, have been adopted.

Officers' Meetings

The president meets formally with the board of directors once each month. A day or two after this meeting, the president holds his regular monthly meeting for the bank's officers. In this meeting, the president reports on selected topics from the board meeting and reviews the monthly financial statements. At the end of this presentation, which usually lasts about fifteen minutes, the president asks for and responds to questions from the officers in attendance.[1]

As the conference room is not large enough to accommodate all of the bank's 100 officers at one time, the monthly officers' meetings are held in two sections on successive days, with approximately one-half of the officers attending each session.

Each officer is free to decide for himself which of the nonconfidential topics covered in the officers' meetings, if any, will be reported back to his subordinates. Officers typically do not hold group meetings for this purpose.

The officers' meetings are the only regularly scheduled meetings in the bank designed for the purpose of routinely disseminating information.

"COMCOM"

"COMCOM" (popular abbreviation for "Communications Committee") was the brainchild of Alice Davey, an officer in the bank, who suggested her idea to President Libbert at a cocktail party one evening in 1963. Mrs. Davey had been concerned about the discontinuation of the bank's house organ, *Southern Messenger,* earlier that year, and felt that something was needed to bolster communication to and from the lower levels of the organization. The stated objective of "COMCOM" was to "promote internal understanding of all matters of common concern at all levels throughout the organization."

President Libbert accepted Mrs. Davey's suggestion and announced the establishment of "COMCOM" in White Paper No. 81, dated October 2, 1963. (See Exhibit 2.) The functions of "COMCOM" were described by the president in White Paper No. 86, dated November 25, 1963. (See Exhibit 3.)

---

[1]More will be said later about the sources of these questions.

Each of the eleven members of "COMCOM" is an officer in the bank; all eight divisions are represented on the committee. George Storm and Alice Davey are the co-chairmen. Each "COMCOM" member is expected to solicit questions from employees at all levels in his division for submission to President Libbert for discussion at the monthly officers' meetings. Questions on any topic except grievances and personalities are welcomed.

"COMCOM" members report that they devote perhaps two hours each month to the task of gathering questions. These questions are reviewed at a regular monthly "COMCOM" meeting held one week prior to the officers' meeting. Suitable questions are agreed upon and then forwarded to the president well in advance of the officers' meeting. Typically about five members attend "COMCOM" meetings.

"COMCOM" presents to the president an average of four questions per month. Most of these questions originate with the "COMCOM" members themselves or from persons in the top three levels of the organization. One of the "COMCOM" co-chairmen stated that perhaps twenty questions per month could be submitted to the president if the members had more time to devote to the task and if "people thought in terms of communications problems."

The president feels that "COMCOM" is working well; the "COMCOM" co-chairmen feel that the committee is reasonably successful in reaching its objectives; the personnel manager feels that "COMCOM" is failing to attain its objectives and wonders how it might be made more effective.

Southern Messenger

The *Southern Messenger,* the bank's unusual house organ, originated in 1946 through spontaneous employee interest. A few employees volunteered to produce the publication on their own time if the bank would provide the necessary supplies and equipment. The paper was started on this basis.

Typewritten, then reproduced by the mimeograph process, the *Southern Messenger* was primarily a "gossip sheet" published approximately quarterly. Over the years the paper grew until, by early 1963, an issue might consist of as many as 100 single-spaced, typewritten pages.

By this time, however, employee interest in the paper apparently had declined and when the volunteer editor left the bank for other employment in 1963 *Southern Messenger* collapsed from the lack of volunteer workers.

Largely through the efforts of Alice Davey and "COMCOM," *Southern Messenger* was reactivated in September 1964 as an official house organ.

Southern Messenger is now published bi-monthly, entirely on company time and entirely at company expense. The present editor spends about

40 per cent of her time at the editor's job; the remainder of her time is spent at a clerical job in the bank. The paper now runs six $8\frac{1}{2}'' \times 11''$ pages in length; the bank allocates $500 per issue to cover printing, photographic, and other costs. Seven hundred fifty copies of each issue are printed.

The editor has twenty people (including three officers), scattered throughout the bank, who serve as informal reporters. These reporters serve on a voluntary basis and tend to obtain and report news items on an opportunistic, rather than a systematic, basis.

According to the editor, *Southern Messenger* space allocations run about as follows:

1/3	News about company plans and activities
1/6	Information regarding company policy
1/6	"Profiles of New Employees"
1/12	Gossip and personal items
rest	Crossword and scientific puzzles

The puzzles have proved to be highly popular with the employees, partly because of their intrinsic appeal and partly because of the prizes offered for the best solutions. The winner for each puzzle receives a pair of theater tickets. The crossword puzzles often contain words related to business and banking.

Although *Southern Messenger* is mailed to each employee at his home, the paper often finds its way back to the bank, where stimulating discussions regarding the puzzles sometimes occur.

Task Force

The Communications Task Force was established in February 1965 at the suggestion of John Templeton, vice president and personnel manager for the bank. Templeton felt that the Task Force might be more successful than "COMCOM" had been in improving communication to and from personnel in the lower echelons of the bank. The Task Force consists of five nonofficer employees nominated for the part-time assignment by their respective division heads. Task Force members were notified of their appointments by inter-office memorandum from Mr. Templeton. (See Exhibit 4.)

The Task Force's basic assignment, as seen by the chairman, Stuart Seaton, is to circulate among and talk with lower level employees to discover questions, problems, and suggestions from the ranks. These items are then cleared by "COMCOM" which may modify but not block them, after which they are passed on to the Management Committee.[2] John Templeton's concept of the Task Force's assignment is presented in Exhibit 4.

---

[2]The Management Committee consists of the president and four key vice presidents.

The Task Force, which has now been in existence for five months, had a flurry of meetings immediately following its establishment but has had only one meeting during the past two months because of vacations and the demands of other work. To date, the Task Force has made six suggestions to the Management Committee via "COMCOM."

The Communications Task Force is only one of several task forces presently operating in the bank. Others include the Training, New Services (Marketing), and Trust Administration task forces. Conceptually, each task force is assembled to accomplish a particular, well-defined job and upon completion of that job, or task, it is to be disbanded.

Chairman Seaton indicated that Communications Task Force members spend perhaps one hour per week on this assignment, and that most of the group's suggestions to date have originated from among its members.

When asked what caused him to believe there was a need for a Communications Task Force, the personnel manager replied, "There's no feedback around here, particularly from the lower levels. An order, report, or policy change is sent down the line and we wait for questions, or complaints, or some kind of response. What we get back is silence. Absolutely nothing. We find it very difficult to measure the impact of, say, a policy change. It's like shouting down a well and getting no echo. It's eerie."

Asked whether employees complain about poor communication in the bank, the personnel manager replied, "No. Oh, there is an occasional comment in the lunch room, but these are not specific and are mentioned in a very casual way. No one appears to be disturbed about it."

The chairman of the Communications Task Force, when asked about the condition of the bank's grapevine, replied, "Healthy."

Suggestion System

Southern Bank's suggestion system has been in continuous operation since its installation in 1952. Suggestion boxes are conveniently located on all floors, with a rack of blank suggestion forms attached to each box.

Suggestion forms are collected monthly. Over the years the input of employee suggestions has consistently averaged about ten per month. Most of the suggestions come from the Operations Group of the General Administration Division and deal with improving the heavy flow of paper processed by that group.

The suggestions are reviewed and evaluated by a six-man Suggestion Committee, presently comprised of both officers and nonofficers, representing the Trust Division (three members), the General Administration Division (two members), and the Investment Division (one member). An effort has been made to staff the committee with younger people from the lower echelons of the bank in the hope that this might stimulate employee interest in the suggestion system.

Committee members serve staggered two-year terms. When a replacement is needed, the committee meets to discuss individuals who may be interested in and suitable for a Suggestion Committee assignment. The most promising prospect is then contacted, and if he is willing to serve he is added to the committee after the approval of his supervisor is obtained.

When a suggestion is to be evaluated, it is given to the committee member most familiar with the operations of the department from which the suggestion came. This member then discusses the suggestion with the person who made it and with the head of the affected department(s). The member then reports back to the full committee, making a recommendation as to the disposition of the suggestion. The committee ordinarily accepts these recommendations.

If a suggestion is deemed to be practical and useful, the committee's next task is to determine the amount of money appropriate as the suggestion award. The usual award range is from $10 to $50. The criteria used to determine the amount of the award are the estimated amounts of time and/or money saved by the suggestion. The committee often finds it difficult to arrive at the amount of this saving.

Every two months the committee issues a report listing all the suggestions made and the awards given during the preceding period. A copy of this report is placed on each bulletin board in the hope that it will stimulate further suggestions. When an award is given, the report indicates the suggestor's name; suggestions receiving no award are listed by number.

The committee's decisions as to whether or not a suggestion is deserving of an award, and the amount of the award, are final. Approximately one-third of the suggestions submitted are considered worthy of awards.

Performance Review

Top management at Southern Bank believes that the bank's system of regular performance review provides an excellent opportunity to foster communication between each supervisor, at whatever level he might be, and his subordinates. The private performance review sessions, which deal primarily with the employee's job performance, also provide an opportunity for the employee to talk with his boss about his problems and for superior and subordinate to plan together the employee's future growth and progress.

Performance reviews are held after ninety days for new employees, then annually on the employee's anniversary date.[3] The reviews, which are keyed to the employee's job description, average perhaps thiry minutes in length. The same basic system is used for all employees — from clerks to vice presidents.

A few days before his anniversary date, the employee receives from his supervisor a form notifying him when the review will occur, and

[3]Reviews may be held more frequently if the supervisor considers this desirable. The personnel officer encourages more frequent reviews to facilitate communications.

inviting him to write on the form any questions that he would like his boss to answer during the review. This form is then returned to the supervisor. It is not uncommon for employees to write questions on these forms which the supervisor considers sensitive and/or difficult to answer. Nevertheless, the supervisor is expected to answer the questions. The form is destroyed after the review session.

Supervisors use a checklist form in rating their subordinates and use this form as a basis for the performance review discussion. Items on the checklist include such things as job knowledge, quality of work, effort, dependability, teamwork, communication, and profit-mindedness. The applicability of each item on the form with respect to the employee's particular job is recorded. The supervisor then checks whether the employee's performance "exceeds," "meets," or "falls short" of standard on each item. The resulting profile provides the core of the review discussion.

The supervisor retains the checklist rating form and notifies the personnel office regarding the result of the review in a separate summary report. Most employees receive a pay increase following their annual performance review. The amount of this increase, which usually ranges between 5 and 10 per cent of present rate, depends upon the supervisor's evaluation of the employee's performance. The typical supervisor in the bank has from eight to ten subordinates to review during the course of a year.[4]

The personnel manager believes that many of the performance reviews are too superficial, but wonders how much time and effort a supervisor should spend in reviewing a young, female clerk who may marry and leave the bank next month. He also is concerned about what he believes to be inadequate training in interviewing techniques on the part of some supervisors in the bank. (Supervisors receive nine hours of in-bank training on the performance review system, of which one hour is devoted to interviewing techniques).

When asked how the nonmanagement people feel about the performance review system, the personnel manager said, "We really don't know. There is very little feedback. Occasionally, in an exit interview, a terminating employee will say that his supervisor had not kept him informed as to the adequacy of his performance or about his future potential with the bank."

White Paper

When information on matters of bank-wide interest is to be disseminated, a "White Paper" is used. Each employee receives a personal copy. An average of two White Papers per month are issued. Examples are White Papers No. 81 and 86 (Exhibits 2 and 3), dealing with the

---

[4]It should be noted that not all officers are supervisors, nor are all supervisors officers.

Exhibit 1. *Southern Bank*

ORGANIZATION CHART

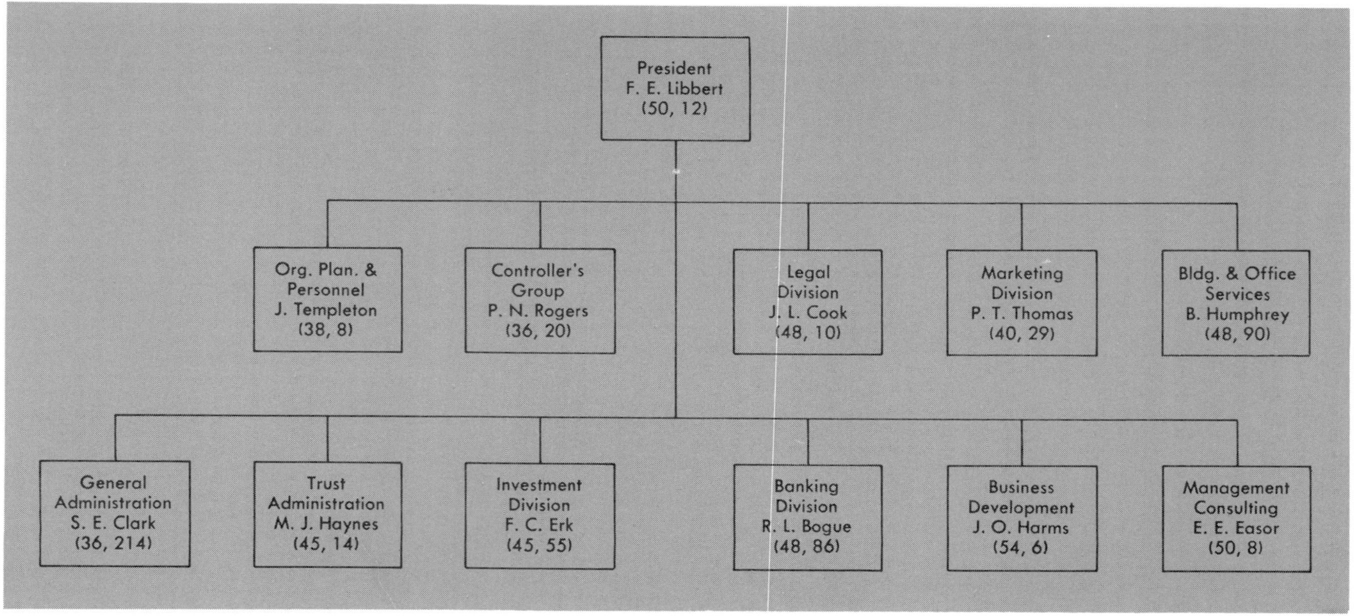

Note: Numbers in parentheses indicate manager's age and number of subordinates. For example, Mr. Cook, Head of the Legal Division, is 48 years old and has 10 people in his division.

formation of "COMCOM." Other White Papers may deal with such matters as holiday announcements, changing hours of work, etc.

Occasionally a White Paper deals with a policy change. In such cases, supervisors sometimes call their subordinates together to discuss the change and to answer pertinent questions.

Exhibit 2. *Southern Bank*

WHITE PAPER

No. 81 October 2, 1963

COMMUNICATIONS COMMITTEE

For an extended period of time, I have personally felt that a committee should be established to serve as an organized pipeline for the flow of information throughout the organization. We all like to know "what's going on when it's going on," and I believe that the *Communications Committee* can provide this type of information for all of us. I have appointed the following to serve on this committee:

George Storm — Co-Chairman
Alice Davey — Co-Chairman
Ronald Brooks
John Cassidy
Norman Euler
Ruth Hobgood
Roy Munford
Elmer Nagel
Jack Phillips
Ed Ralston
George Robinson

The committee is currently in the organizational stage, and when its program for effective internal communications has been established, it will be announced.

(signed)

Frederick E. Libbert

Exhibit 3. *Southern Bank*

WHITE PAPER

No. 86 November 25, 1963

COMMUNICATIONS COMMITTEE

Our Communications Committee, which I appointed last month, has recommended several steps to improve our communications program.

The Committee feels strongly, and I agree, that all employees should be informed promptly of what we're doing, why, and how it affects them; and that they should be able to communicate their ideas to top management and get timely answers to their questions and requests.

If you have any questions or ideas you want to pass along, see your supervisor or a bank officer, or use our Suggestion System if it is a formal suggestion you wish to make. And during the formative stages of the new program, members of the Committee will welcome your suggestions, recommendations, and questions.

Members of the Committee are

George Storm — Co-Chairman
Alice Davey — Co-Chairman
Ronald Brooks
John Cassidy
Norman Euler
Ruth Hobgood
Roy Munford
Elmer Nagel
Jack Phillips
Ed Ralston
George Robinson

(signed)

Frederick E. Libbert

Exhibit 4. *Southern Bank*

INTEROFFICE MEMO

To: Stuart Seaton

cc: June Hugger — Louis Newton
Benjamin Allen — Byron Edwards

The Management Committee of Southern Bank is interested in the effectiveness of communications within the Company, especially as it affects the ability of supervisors and officers to apply and to interpret to others the policies and procedures of the Company, and to supply information about new developments that should be of interest to all employees.

The Committee requested nominations from division heads and selected you to organize and direct the project. You will be assisted in this task force study by the persons listed above as recipients of copies of this memo.

For purposes of this project, "communications" refers to formal and informal exchange or diffusion of information about such matters as:

a. Responsibilities and authorities
b. Policies governing personnel administration
c. Applications of various procedures, such as performance review, purchase requisitions, expense approvals, etc.
d. Information about significant new developments, new personnel, changes in benefit programs
e. Problems in supervision and administration which require the attention of higher levels of management.

To carry out this project, the task force will be expected to:

a. Determine the best way to assess communications; e.g., by interviews, questionnaires to supervisors, etc.
b. Consult with the Chairmen of the Communications Committee, with personnel officers, and with the Supervisory Development Groups, to establish the kinds of possible communications problems that may exist.
c. With the Chairmen of the Communications Committee, meet with the Management Committee to discuss findings.

I shall be available to assist in whatever way seems appropriate to the task force.

(signed)
John Templeton
February 1, 1965

Questions

1. What is the nature of Southern Bank's communication problem?
2. Evaluate the effectiveness of each of the techniques, channels, and devices described in the case. What does each contribute to the total communication flow of the bank? How could it be improved?

Case 27

Atlantic General Insurance Company*

In July, 1960, Mr. R. Taylor, the fire insurance manager of the Atlantic General Insurance Company of Montreal, was killed in an automobile accident. The employees of Taylor's department were deeply shocked by this mishap, for the manager had been very well liked.

Mr. Taylor, a man in his late fifties, had been with the company since its founding in 1938. Under his guidance, the fire insurance department had grown from two people to over twenty-eight inspectors, underwriters, stenographers and clerks. As the years passed, Taylor found it possible to delegate more and more authority to his well trained staff who always seemed willing to take on additional responsibility. Taylor, an employee recalled, encouraged the office to run with as little direction from him as possible. In reply to almost any question he would reply, "Well, what do you think?" and would frequently allow suggestions that he did not entirely agree with to be implemented. He took a keen interest in his staff and always had a jaunty word for everyone. No office get-together was complete without his presence, and at Christmas and on his birthday his staff always presented him with a small gift financed through a staff collection. While salaries in his department were by no means competitive with other departments in the company, or other companies, Taylor always had on file a great number of applicants for the positions that became available. Such vacancies were quite rare and most of his staff had above five years' service in his department.

Taylor's two assistants were Ellen Robichaud, a married woman in her early forties, and Jack Carr, whose son, now at university, was considering joining the company. Mrs. Robichaud was in charge of the stenographers and clerks in the department, while Carr supervised the activities of the underwriters. The three inspectors reported directly to Taylor.

Mr. Fisher, the general manager, chose as Taylor's successor Mr. Harold Weston, a man of twenty years seniority with the company, and who for the past ten years had managed a small branch office in Toronto.

---

*Case prepared by Professor W. J. Reddin of the University of New Brunswick.

Weston was somewhat out-of-touch with the situation in head office and lacked any broad administrative experience. The general manager felt that these shortcomings could be quickly remedied and that Weston was due for a promotion as he had performed so well in Toronto. During his ten-year stay there, he had increased premium income in that area from practically nothing to nearly $500,000 per year. Fisher attributed this success to the fact that, unlike many branch managers, Weston had made a point of visiting regularly all the company agents and successfully cultivating their confidence and friendship.

Soon after this new appointment was made, the company moved its headquarters from the City Building, a large and imposing structure in midtown Montreal, to a newly constructed building located in a rapidly developing commercial area about two miles away. The third floor of this new building was occupied by the Atlantic General. Unlike the previous building, where the company was spread over four floors, the new building was large enough that one floor could hold all departments of the company: fire, automobile, casualty and claims, totaling over two hundred and fifty people. A striking design feature was an almost complete absence of partitions or pillars of any kind, thus allowing a relatively unobstructed view of the whole office. Some small offices had been constructed around the perimeter of the floor for the department managers and other executives. All employees knew of the move well in advance and most seemed well pleased with the building although some said they missed the convenience of proximity to the big downtown department stores.

In due course Weston settled into the fire manager's job. The staff, although somewhat apprehensive at first, were soon reassured by their new manager's easygoing manner. He was a friendly, soft-spoken, approachable man who always did his best to put his employees at their ease when they were talking to him. Soon after the move Weston made it apparent to his department that he wanted to introduce an open door policy and staff members began to consult him with increasing frequency, particularly on personal matters such as pay, holidays and promotions. Most of these matters had previously been taken up with Robichaud and Carr although, a staff member said, "Taylor would have been pleased to listen if we had ever wanted to go to him."

Many of the department employees usually found in the course of a day some problem which required the attention of the manager. Consequently, Weston had an almost constant stream of people moving to and from his office. In order to get time to do his own work Weston started to stay late at night and even come in early in the morning. Nonetheless, he took no action to discourage these practices, believing that things would settle down after a few months.

Carr was not displeased by this new development because he had recently been appointed to a newly created position of assistant fire insurance manager. This job took him away from the office about half the time and sometimes for a week at a time. His new job involved acting as liaison between the head office and the many company branches and agents. He did, however, express the opinion that he was surprised that Weston allowed the continual parade of staff in and out of his office all day.

Mrs. Robichaud, however, reacted somewhat differently. After moving to the new building she found it increasingly necessary to visit other departments, she occasionally came in late, which she had never done before, and she started to experience sickness which often necessitated her staying at home for a day.

While things settled quickly to normal in most departments in the new location, a somewhat different spirit seemed to prevail in the fire department. Several of the staff habitually reported late for work and extended both their coffee breaks and lunch hours. Both Robichaud and Carr, at Weston's request, tried to do something about this development, but met with little success. Less work seemed to be accomplished in the department and many employees became several days behind in their work, although many worked voluntarily through their lunch hours to try and bring their work up-to-date. More ominous as far as Weston was concerned was the fact that several of his agents complained that they were receiving policies that were incorrectly typed.

About four months after being made manager, Weston was called into the general manager's office and asked why several employees of his department had been coming to work with the executives of the company about fifteen minutes after the normal starting time. Immediately after this meeting, Weston called a meeting of his staff, read the following notice, explained that he wanted more cooperation and then posted the notice on the department bulletin board.

TO THE FIRE INSURANCE DEPARTMENT

This office opens for business at 8:30 a.m. All staff will be present at this time or will see me when they arrive.

H. Weston
Fire Manager

The notice had an immediate effect. For several weeks no lateness occurred. The situation soon began to deteriorate, however, and after two more months lateness had again developed. Weston was very disturbed by this state of affairs and realized that some action would have to be taken but was uncertain as to just how he should proceed.

Questions

1. To what extent does the deteriorating attitude of employees appear to hamper the work of the office?
2. Are Jack Carr and Mrs. Robichaud helping Weston, or are they contributing to the negative attitude of employees?

3. What mistakes, if any, has Weston made?

4. What action should Weston take to improve the situation?

Case 28

Thompson Metal Works Company*

Thompson Metal Works Company was founded in 1947 by Mr. Lee Thompson. From its beginning the company has been in the business of fabricating and selling tin and aluminum products. Among the items made and sold by the company are duct work for home and industrial heating and air conditioning, ventilation louvers for various types of buildings, and paneling for any need whatever. In addition the company has followed the practice of taking orders for any special items a customer may request, provided the company is capable of filling the order. Most work is done on a job-lot basis, and inventories of finished goods have been practically nil.

The company showed a rapid and steady growth and until 1958 was very profitable. From 1959 to 1961 profits declined and in 1962 there was a small operating loss, even though the volume of business in each of these years had shown a slight increase. Mr. Thompson felt certain that the reason for this trend was because of higher-priced materials and wage increases while at the same time the selling prices of most products, because of increasing competition, had gone up very little or, in some instances, not at all over the past several years. By 1962 sales amounted to some $750,000 annually.

At the end of 1962 the company had six employees in sales, thirty employees in the fabrication department, and two installation crews, each consisting of an in-charge man and two helpers. Because of the diversity of jobs undertaken, the investment in tools and equipment had become quite sizeable. Mr. Thompson, after talking the situation over with his key employees, decided that the problem was poor cost control. He hired Mr. Bruce Keys, CPA, as controller and office manager and it was agreed a budgetary system was needed. Mr. Keys went to work on the problem and by the end of 1963 had installed a profit-planning-and-reporting system which he deemed adequate.

With the aid of Mr. Keys, Jake Brown, shop foreman, was able to cut out some waste in the shop. The men were given written assignments and schedules and the work stations of the shop were rearranged to provide for a better flow o goods through the processes. In addition,

*Case prepared by Professor Wilbur R. Ross of the Oklahoma State University.

punctuality rules were strictly enforced and coffee breaks or rest periods were permitted only at scheduled times. By the end of 1964 some improvement in cost control was evident and the company was out of the red, but Mr. Thompson felt the results should be better and decided to get his key employees together and see if anything more could be done to improve the profits of the company. Those present at the meeting besides Mr. Thompson and Mr. Keys were

Jake Brown — shop foreman
Tim Wilde — commercial and industrial salesman
Wade Smith — residential salesman
Bob Hearn — in charge of incidental orders taken at the plant
Keith Allen and Ray Boales — installation crew supervisors

Mr. Thompson (owner and president of the company):

Gentlemen, as you probably know I have been concerned about the low profit margin the company has shown over the past few years. I am not blaming you for the unfavorable profit margins, but it is certain we are going to have to work together in order to remedy the situation or possibly go out of business before long. Jake, since you are in charge of the shop, what do you think we could do to further lower our costs?

Jake Brown (shop foreman):

Well, as far as I'm concerned the real problem is that we make too many different products and in too small quantities. I believe Mr. Keys will agree that this is a costly way to manufacture anything. We lose entirely too much time in setting up for the various jobs, and also we usually have a lot of idle equipment since some of the equipment is required only for special jobs or for a small amount of time.

Tim Wilde (commercial and industrial salesman):

I can certainly appreciate Jake's situation, but Wade, Bob, and I and the other salesmen have got to make sales when we can or there won't be any business. You all know that this is a competitive market and individual jobs call for small quantities. Mr. Keys will agree that we've got to make sales. I know our actual sales don't necessarily agree with our forecast, especially by types of products, but I'm sure all will agree that we face a peculiar situation. We have discussed this with Mr. Keys and he understands our problem and, I believe, is convinced we are doing our best to meet our quotas.

Mr. Keys (controller):

I think we have hit on some important problems here. I'm not sure of how to solve them. One way somctimes available to a company is to manufacture for inventory. However in our case I feel this is out because most of our work is of a custom nature. Do you installation men have any comments?

Keith Allen (installation crew supervisor):

We review each job with Mr. Keys prior to doing it and he approves our estimates of installation costs. So far, we've been doing the work within these approved budgets. I don't know what else we could do.

Mr. Thompson:

Gentlemen, I believe I have discovered our primary problem. Right now you salesmen are estimating sales; Brown is estimating and planning the shop work; and the installation men plan their work. Each of you has indicated that Mr. Keys helps you considerably in your planning. Since Mr. Keys is so familiar with all aspects of the business and understands the problems completely, it appears to me that he should be responsible for all forecasting and planning. This would give us better coordination and, after all, what's a budget director for if he doesn't provide a budget from which the rest of us can get our quotas and work schedules?

Questions

1. If you were Mr. Keys, what would be your reply to Mr. Thompson's last comment?
2. What impression do you get as to the adequacy of the budgetary system installed by Mr. Keys?
3. Do you feel that the company might need to change some of its operating policies? If so, in what way and why?
4. Is there a possibility that this company is too small or that production is too unstable to require a formal system of profit planning and control? Explain.

Case 29

Big Pine Paper Company*

The expanding market for paper products in the South, and the technological developments which made it possible to utilize southern yellow-pine as pulpwood for the manufacture of newsprint and of enameled

*Case prepared by Professor Kenneth W. Olm of The University of Texas.

white paper for mass-media magazine stock, led to the establishment of the Southern Division of the Big Pine Paper Company in 1936.

Big Pine's Southern Division was located in a rapidly growing industrial area which afforded an adequate supply of water and of pine pulpwood, and which afforded transportation by rail, highway, or inland waterway. Only white sulfite paper pulp was produced initially. This pulp, produced in large felt-like sheets, and shipped in bales or rolls, served as a raw material to be mixed with water and other ingredients for the paper machines of other mills, and thus was an intermediate product in the manufacture of finished paper stock. Shortly afterward, in 1940, following a rapid increase in the local demand for finished paper, additional paper-making machinery was installed, and manufacture of enameled white paper was begun. Until the Finishing Section was set up in 1947, the paper was sold in rolls.

Substantial growth in capacity, output, and employment took place in the Southern Division. In 1958 there were approximately 1,500 employees in the mill, and production of a wide variety of grades of white paper and of the single grade of pulp had reached a total of more than 500 tons per day. This growth was expected to continue as the population of the trade territory increased, and as a rising standard of living might require an accompanying increase in the use of paper.

Owing to the strong reliance upon management decentralization practiced by the home office of Big Pine Paper Company, the Southern Division enjoyed a high degree of autonomy in its operation. The managerial philosophy of Big Pine Paper Company was characterized in a company publication as "decentralized operation with centralized coordination and control." Late in 1957 a slow-moving trend toward more centralized control began to take shape with a minor reorganization in the General Office. At this time, the Vice President of Manufacturing at the General Office was changed from a strictly staff to a line position.

Certain policies were set down to guide the operating management of the company's divisions, especially in dealing with the work force. The top-management of the Big Pine Paper Company had striven to develop a human relations program which would be a model for the industry. One example of action taken to implement this policy was an annual guaranteed work plan which was designed to offer a high degree of economic security to the employees of the company.

Labor relations in the Southern Division were stable from the beginning. The workers in the Southern Division had organized themselves in an independent union in 1938, and had vigorously and effectively resisted several organization drives designed to bring them into unions affiliated with the internationals of nationally organized trade unions.

Betterment of the community was a basic objective of the company. The management sought to realize this goal by maintaining a prosperous and growing enterprise which offered stable and well-paid employment, and which, in addition, was a substantial taxpaying and participating "citizen" itself in its community.

The organization structure of the Southern Division is outlined in Exhibit 1.

Exhibit 1. *Partial Organization Chart—Big Pine Paper Company Southern Division*

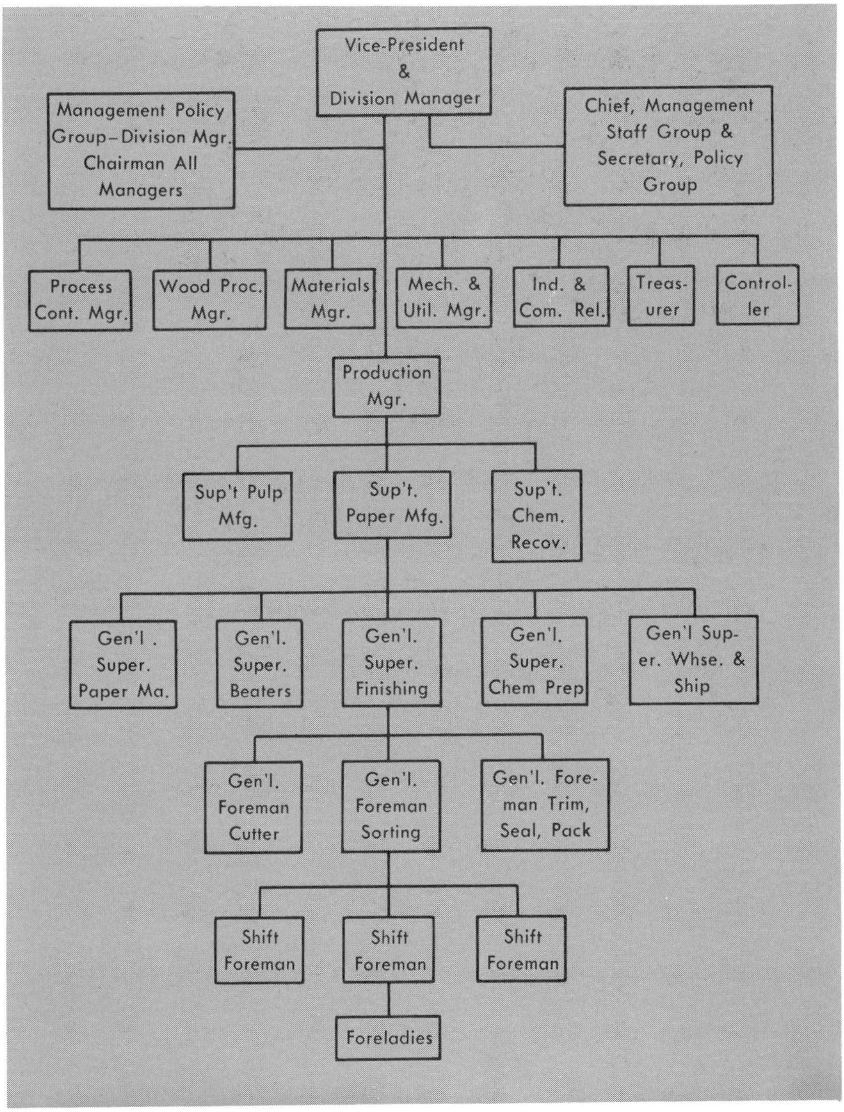

The mill produced mainly to order, although there was some production to stock. All sales were made by a centralized sales organization, located at the home office. For communication, a direct-wire system connected all regional offices and producing plants with the home office. Production at the mill was initiated upon receipt from the home office of a request to fill an individual sales order or to meet periodic delivery requirements under a long-term contract. See Exhibit 2 for a description of the production cycle.

Exhibit 2. *Production Cycle — Big Pine Paper Company*

The length of the production cycle for paper depends largely upon where one chooses to begin. Assuming that the pulpwood trees are already grown, the cycle would then consist of the following steps:

1. Cut and transport wood to pulp mill.
2. Debark, chip, and convert chemically into pulp.
3. Prepare pulp and process it into paper stock.
4. Prepare for delivery according to finishing specifications.
5. Deliver to customer.

Up to the finishing stage, paper production is a highly automatic continuous-process, requiring massive machinery and great quantities of water and chemicals. Investment in fixed capital is high, averaging about $13,000 per employee in 1957.

Only in the finishing operation is there a large proportion of handwork. In the finishing operation the work is routine, largely worker-paced, and occasionally involves considerable muscular effort. Certain operations require a high degree of manual dexterity. Inspection operations require considerable visual acuity.

Generally speaking, most paper manufacturers preferred to sell their paper in large lots to outside wholesalers and finishers, especially prior to 1950. Thereafter, the possibility of obtaining higher margins from sales, and the prospect of partial mechanization in finishing, encouraged many manufacturers to expand finishing operations within their existing plant.

The Finishing Section (see Exhibit 1) was organized in 1947 with an initial work force of fifty men and women. This group was afterward expanded to include over 350 employees, about two-thirds of them female. Because so much of the work performed was handwork and largely worker-paced (see Exhibit 2), it was decided to install a system of work measurement in the finishing section about 1951.

Dick Grant, then a member of the Management Staff Group, conducted a number of stop-watch time studies of finishing operations for the purpose of developing "standard minutes of work" for each operation being performed. No attempt was made to install an individual incentive pay plan, although the company had installed an individual incentive bonus plan in the finishing section of another division. Work standards were intended to be used for the following purposes:

1. To provide a specific production goal for each foreman and worker.
2. To provide the supervision of the finishing section a basis for planning production and for scheduling within the section.
3. To provide a basis for estimating manpower requirements used in preparation of the budget.
4. To provide a basis for the projection of operating costs.

The time study procedure used was designed only to develop standards of work performance for the jobs as they were then being performed. As a result, a general job description was developed for each job, but no statement of method was established. No attempt was made to improve existing methods before the time studies were conducted.

Initially, standards were set only on female-staffed sorting operations. Later, standards were set on all productive jobs in the Sorting and Trim and Pack groups. Standards were put into effect on a job as soon as they were developed, without waiting for completion of the whole standards program. Workers readily accepted the standards, and no serious obstacles were encountered in setting the standards. Within eighteen months, most of the standards had been set and were in use, as intended, for the purposes listed above.

The work measurement program was well-accepted, not only by the workers, but also by the supervisors, and by the management generally. This success was attributed to the following: (1) the improvement in the method of work measurement, compared with the previous "rule of thumb" method; (2) the acceptability of the new methods of work measurement as being fair and above-board; (3) an elaborate program to explain standards and uses of standards to the workers; and (4) daily and cumulative monthly reporting of performance to the workers.

Although the program was well-received at the start and was immediately useful, there was no provision for keeping the standards up to date. In the years that followed, changes in sizes and types of product, and gradual changes in job methods led to numerous inconsistencies in job standards. By 1957 many of the standards were so far out of line that they could no longer be applied to individual workers.

While no provision had been made to bring old standards up to date, there had been some setting of new standards. For example, whenever a new size of paper was introduced which had not previously been studied, it was necessary to set a new standard. The procedure adopted was as follows: If the new size was within the limits of the standard-data curves previously established, the new standard was obtained by interpolation.

But if the new size was outside the limits, extrapolation was not used. Rather, "allowed" work units of performance, based on the average performance report of the previous month, were applied. No changes were made in the standards to recognize changes in equipment, changes in the methods of handling or sorting rejected product, or operations added to the finishing process, such as the palletization program for paper handling, or changes in packaging specifications. Thus, although the standards were still being used in 1958, there were many discrepancies which impaired their usefulness.

Inasmuch as no formal procedure had ever been established to keep the standards up to date, it was clear that the situation would become more critical with the passage of time. The need to modernize the work standards was first recognized by the supervisors. The situation was brought to the attention of the General Supervisor of the Finishing Section, and in turn to the Superintendent of Paper Manufacturing. In addition, numerous employees requested that the standards be brought up to date so that they would know exactly what was expected of them in their work.

The Superintendent of Paper Manufacturing, with the help of the General Supervisor of Finishing, made a presentation dealing with the problem of standards revision to a meeting of the Policy Group. In this presentation were included the Superintendent's recommendations; the Superintendent was not a member of the Policy Group. During the preliminary discussion, a number of questions were raised concerning the desirability of making any changes in the standards. The Industrial Relations Manager wondered what implications might be involved if no attention at all were given to the question by the management, thus letting the situation lie dormant. This sentiment was echoed by others in the group. The Controller wondered whether the standards were of any real importance to him in his cost-analysis activities. He suggested that his office could perform effectively without labor standards. An opposite viewpoint was pressed strongly by the Superintendent of Paper Manufacturing and by the General Supervisor of Finishing, both of whom pointedly requested a revision of the standards, maintaining that this would provide them with a needed control device which was effective in the operation of the Finishing Section.

The Chief of the Management Staff Group, Dick Grant (see Exhibit 1), was inclined to agree with the request for standards revision, but he asked who was to do the revising. He stated that his office no longer had manpower sufficient to conduct the required studies. After some deliberation, the Policy Group agreed that, while they were generally in favor of revision, the matter should be turned over to the Management Staff Group for further study and for recommendations for action.

Dick Grant had been General Supervisor of Finishing immediately prior to being installed as Chief of Management Planning. The previous Chief had been transferred to a newly established division. Prior to becoming Chief he had served as Division Controller. In 1958, the men serving as Division Manager, Production Manager, and Industrial Relations Manager had occupied their present positions less than two years.

Any questions submitted to the Management Policy Group which required further study, additional data, or so forth, would usually be assigned to the manager most concerned with the problem. A technical problem of concern to more than one manager was usually turned over to Process Controls Research. The Management Planning Group was designed to perform services for the Division Manager and indirectly for the Management Policy Group. Their regular staff was very small; when additional staff members were needed they would borrow men to form a sort of "task force" for a specific problem. Their efforts were largely devoted to management engineering studies, such as return on investment, manpower controls, and systems and procedures.

Shortly following the meeting described above, the Chief of the Management Staff Group sent a letter in June 1958 to each member of the Policy Group setting forth his findings and recommendations on standards revision. Four possible courses of action were listed: (1) Do not attempt any revision. (2) Hire an outside consultant to make the revision. (3) Train employees to make the revision with the assistance of a qualified technician. (4) Employ a group of college students during the summer months to conduct the necessary time studies under the supervision of Management Planning Staff. The letter recommended that the revision be undertaken and that alternative three (3), above, be employed, plus, if necessary, alternative four (4).

A year passed with no action by the Policy Group on the letter described above. The General Supervisor of the Finishing Section was still strongly of the opinion that standards revision should be undertaken in order to provide him with an effective device for controlling his section.

Questions

1. Evaluate the initial development and installation of standards.
2. What deficiencies existed in the program of updating standards? How serious were these?
3. In view of the varied reactions by members of the Policy Group, how urgent is it that standards be brought up to date?
4. What action should be taken by the General Supervisor of the Finishing Section? By the Policy Group?

Index